P9-DFU-522

INTRODUCING
philosophy
PROBLEMS AND PERSPECTIVES

for
Vita P. Solomon
who brought me into life
and taught me it was art.

INTRODUCING

philosophy

PROBLEMS AND PERSPECTIVES

ROBERT C. SOLOMON

University of Texas at Austin

HARCOURT BRACE JOVANOVICH, INC.

New York   Chicago   San Francisco   Atlanta

© 1977 by Harcourt Brace Jovanovich, Inc.

All rights reserved. No part of this publication may be reproduced
or transmitted in any form or by any means, electronic or mechanical,
including photocopy, recording, or any information storage and retrieval system,
without permission in writing from the publisher.

ISBN: 0-15-541558-1

Library of Congress Catalog Card Number: 76-39657

Printed in the United States of America

COVER:
Pierre Soulages, *Composition IV*, 1957. Etching, 21⅝ x 15¼". Collection, The Museum of
Modern Art, New York. Gift of Mr. and Mrs. Armand P. Bartos.

COPYRIGHTS AND ACKNOWLEDGMENTS

AIRMONT PUBLISHING COMPANY For the excerpt from *The Prince* by Niccolo
Machiavelli, translated by Christian E. Detmold. Reprinted by permission.

GEORGE ALLEN & UNWIN LTD. For the excerpt from *The Nature of Thought* by
Brand Blandshard. For the excerpt from *The Phenomenology of Mind* by G. W. F. Hegel,
translated by J. B. Baillie. For the excerpt from *Ideas* by Edmund Husserl, translated by
W. R. Boyce-Gibson. For the excerpts from *Beyond Good and Evil* by Friedrich Nietzsche,
translated by Helen Zimmern. For the excerpts from *The Joyful Wisdom* by Friedrich
Nietzsche, translated by T. Common. All reprinted by permission of the publisher,
George Allen & Unwin Ltd.

THE ARISTOTELIAN SOCIETY For the excerpt from "Gods" by J. Y. T. Wisdom
(*Proceedings of the Aristotelian Society,* XLV [1944–45]). Reprinted by courtesy of the
Editor of The Aristotelian Society, © 1945 The Aristotelian Society.

ASSOCIATED BOOK PUBLISHERS LTD. For the excerpt from *The Divided Self* by
R. D. Laing. Reprinted by permission of the publisher, Tavistock Publications Ltd. For
the excerpt from *The Dwarfs* in *A Slight Ache and Other Plays* by Harold Pinter. Reprinted by permission of the publisher in the British market, Eyre Methuen & Co.

BANTAM BOOKS, INC. For the excerpt from "Clouds" by Aristophanes, translated
by Moses Hadas, as it appears in *The Complete Plays of Aristophanes,* edited by Moses
Hadas; copyright © 1962 by Bantam Books, Inc. For the excerpt from *The Brothers
Karamazov* by Fyodor Dostoevsky, translated by Andrew R. MacAndrew. English
language translation copyright © 1970 by Bantam Books, Inc. Both reprinted by
permission of Bantam Books, Inc.

BEACON PRESS For the excerpts from *The Structure of Behavior* by Maurice
Merleau-Ponty. Copyright © 1963 by Beacon Press; originally published in French under
the title *La Structure du Comportement,* copyright © 1942 by Presses Universitaires de
France.

Acknowledgments continue on pages 606–09, which constitute a continuation of the
copyright page.

PREFACE

Introducing Philosophy: Problems and Perspectives presupposes no background in the subject and no special abilities. Intended primarily as a textbook for a one- or two-semester introductory course, the book provides not so much a course in itself as the materials for a course from which instructors and students can focus on a variety of problems and perspectives. The point of this book is to present students with alternatives on every issue and let them arrive at their own individual conclusions. These conclusions should be based on arguments in class and with friends or classmates, as well as on the discussions in the book. The assumption here is that the purpose of philosophy is to encourage everyone to think for himself or herself and that no single source of arguments or information can take the place of personal dialogues and discussions. A textbook is ultimately a sourcebook; everything in it is to be taken as a cause for further argument, not as a final statement of results. This text does not attempt to sway students toward any particular philosophical positions but rather presents basic philosophical problems and powerful philosophical arguments to enable students to think for themselves. That is what philosophy is about—thinking for oneself on basic issues.

This book derives from ten years of teaching in very different schools in various states and cities. It is based on the belief that philosophy is a genuinely exciting subject, accessible not only to specialists and a few gifted undergraduate majors but to everyone. Everyone is a philosopher, whether enrolled in a philosophy course or not, for everyone is concerned with the same basic problems and uses the same essential arguments. The difference is that someone who has studied philosophy has the advantage of having encountered stronger and more varied arguments than might have been available otherwise. In this book, the views of the major philosophers of the past 2,500 years are used to give students these various arguments. This has the advantage of offering introductory students the opportunity of having direct contact with significant works in the history of philosophy, but without the unreasonable demand that they confront these often difficult works without commentary or editing, as they would in the originals or in most anthologies. This is not, however, a historical introduction as such but rather an introduction to the various problems of philosophy and the various perspectives from which they have been answered. The history of philosophy thus serves to illuminate these problems and perspectives, not the other way around.

Although the language of philosophy is often specialized and sometimes difficult, this book is as free of jargon and special terminology as is possible.

Where necessary, the most important and widely used philosophical terms are carefully introduced within the text and also summarized in glossaries at the end of each chapter. At the end of the book there are biographies of the philosophers discussed in the text. Although the book deals principally with their ideas, rather than with their lives, it is nevertheless valuable to have the student learn their place in history.

How to use this book

Introducing Philosophy is written for a complete course, and the chapters build on one another in a logical sequence. But the book is also flexible, and each chapter has been written as an independent unit so that it is possible to use the text in a variety of ways and for a variety of courses. Within each chapter, too, various sections can be selected for shorter discussions. For example, some teachers may want to use only the first sections of Chapter 7 ("Religion"), or only a few key sections from Chapters 8 ("Self-Identity") and 10 ("Freedom").

A full course might include the Introduction and all thirteen chapters, but this may be a heavy load for an average one-term course. At the other extreme, a short course (for example, a summer term or a class that meets only once a week, a quarter system, or a class that prefers to treat a few central issues in more detail) might use only half the chapters. The following outlines are suggestions for a variety of uses of the book adapted to different lengths and kinds of classes:

> Maximum course (one very full term) :
> Introduction, Chapters 1–13.
> Minimum course (summer, part-time, quarter) :
> Introduction, Chapters 1, 3, 7, 10, and either 8 or 9; possibly 11.
> Two-term course:
> First term: Introduction, Chapters 1–7;
> Second term: Introduction, Chapters 8–13.
> Average course (14–16 week term; chapters in parentheses are optional) :
> Introduction, Chapters 1, (2), 3, 7, 8, 9, 10, 11, (12), (13).
> Ethics and Religion course:
> Introduction, Chapters 7, 8, 10, 11, 12, (13).
> Metaphysics and Epistemology course:
> Introduction, Chapters 1, 2, 3, (4), (5), (6), (7), 8, 9, 10.

Chapters 4–5 are the most difficult and thus may be the first dropped by some classes. Other classes may prefer to begin with either Chapter 7 ("Religion") or Chapter 11 ("Morality and the Good Life") and reorder the sequence of chapters. Chapter 2 (which discusses Spinoza's and Leibniz's metaphysics) also may be skipped for many shorter courses. Chapter 12 is a somewhat detailed discussion of various moral theories, and many classes may prefer to use only Chapter 11. The basic course, therefore, tailored to the average one-term, 14–16 week class, meeting three times a week, would be:

Introduction, Chapters 1, 3, 7, 8, 9, 10, 11.

The remaining chapters can be added as time and interest permit.

For the student

Your attempt to develop your own thoughts—to "do" philosophy as well as to read what others have done—is central to any study of philosophy. Philosophy, more than any other "field," is not so much a "subject" as it is a way of thinking, one that can be fully appreciated only by joining in. While reading each section, therefore, do not hesitate to put the book down at any time and do your own thinking and writing. When reading about metaphysics, for example, think about how you would develop your own view of reality and how you would answer the questions raised by the first philosophers of ancient Greece. When confronted by an argument, consider how you might argue for—or against— the same position. And when facing a problem, always be certain that you make the attempt to answer it in your own terms, as well as read through the answers offered by earlier thinkers. In philosophy, unlike in physics or biology, your own answer may be just as legitimate as those given by the philosophers of the past. That is what makes philosophy so difficult to learn at first, but it is also what makes it so personally valuable and enjoyable.

Acknowledgments

This book has been made possible through the encouragement and help of many people, most importantly the several thousand introductory students I have had the pleasure of meeting and teaching over the past decade. More immediately, I want to thank Susan Zaleski, Boston College, for her very special insights and criticism of the manuscript in its early stages; Robert Fogelin, Yale University, John McDermott, Queens College of the City University of New York, and George Cronk, Bergen Community College, for their encouragement and helpful suggestions; and Terry Boswell, Lisa Erlich, David Blumenfeld, Paul Woodruff, Harry O'Hara, all of University of Texas at Austin, Stephanie Lewis, Trenton State College, and Barbara Barratt for their time and good advice. Richard Wilson was of considerable help with the index. Robert Hanson started the ideas in motion many years ago; Doris Yokum, Elizabeth Flower, and James Ross, all of University of Pennsylvania, gave me my first lessons in teaching philosophy; C. G. Hempel, Princeton University, provided the model for the ideal introductory course. Rick Kennedy initiated the idea of writing a textbook, and Bill Pullin convinced me that Harcourt Brace Jovanovich was the proper home for it. Special thanks to John Holland, Sid Zimmerman, Laurel Miller, and Anne Boynton; their efforts in getting the book through the editorial process were sometimes superhuman. But mainly, thanks to the many students who continue to make the teaching of philosophy one of the most satisfying professions in a not easily satisfying world.

R. C. S.

CONTENTS

3

KNOWLEDGE 81

4

NECESSITY 130

5

TRUTH AND RATIONALITY 167

6

IS IT ALL RELATIVE? 190

7

RELIGION 209

PART TWO

perspectives and values 263

SELF-IDENTITY 265

9

MIND AND BODY 308

10

FREEDOM 356

11

MORALITY AND THE GOOD LIFE 405

12

PERSPECTIVES ON MORALITY 437

13

POLITICS 495

INTRODUCTION: PHILOSOPHY

The unexamined life is not worth living.

Socrates

He was not the first philosopher, but he was, and is still, the ideal of philosophers. Once assured by the oracle at Delphi that he was the wisest man in Athens, Socrates (470–399 B.C.) borrowed his view of life from the inscription at Delphi, "Know Thyself." Mixing humility with arrogance, he boasted that his superiority lay in his awareness of his own ignorance, and he spent the rest of his life making fools of the self-proclaimed "wise men" of Athens.

In the opinion of Socrates and other critics of the time, the government of Athens was corrupt and notoriously bumbling, in marked contrast to the "Golden Age" of Pericles a few years before. Philosophical arguments had become all cleverness and demagoguery, rhetorical tricks to win arguments and legal cases; political ambition replaced justice and the search for the good life. Socrates believed that the people of Athens held their principles glibly, like banners at a football game, but rarely lived up to them and even more rarely examined them. Against this, he developed a technique of asking seemingly innocent questions, trapping his audience in their own confusions and hypocrisies, exploding the pretentions of his times. And against their easy certainties, he taught that "the unexamined life is not worth living." He referred to himself as a "gadfly" (an obnoxious insect with a painful bite), keeping his fellow citizens from ever becoming as smug and self-righteous as they would like to have been. Accordingly, he made many enemies and was satirized by Aristophanes in his play the *Clouds*.

1

STUDENT OF SOCRATES: Socrates asked Chaerephon how many of its own feet
a flea could jump—one had bitten Chaerephon's brow and then jumped
to Socrates' head.

STREPSIADES: And how did he measure the jump?

STUDENT: Most ingeniously. He melted wax, caught the flea, dipped its feet,
and the hardened wax made Persian slippers.
Unfastening these, he found their size.

STREPSIADES: Royal Zeus! What an acute intellect!

STUDENT: But yesterday a high thought was lost through a lizard.

STREPSIADES: How so? Tell me.

STUDENT: As he gaped up at the moon, investigating her paths and turnings,
from off the roof a lizard befouled him.[1]

In the play, Aristophanes made Socrates and his students look utterly
ridiculous, and the Athenian public enjoyed Aristophanes' sarcasm as a mild
form of vengeance for Socrates' constant criticisms. Aristophanes' "clouds" of
course, are what we mean when we talk of someone "having his head in the
clouds." Aristophanes probably expressed the general public opinion when he
described Socrates as "shiftless" and merely a master at verbal trickery.

Socrates' students, however, virtually worshipped him. They described him
as "the bravest, most wise and most upright man of our times" and perceived
him as a martyr for the truth in a corrupted society. The price of his criticism
was not merely the satire of the playwrights. Because he had been such a
continual nuisance, the government arranged to have Socrates brought to trial
for "corrupting the youth of Athens" and being an "atheist." And for these
trumped up "crimes," Socrates was condemned to death. But at his trial, not
only did he refuse to defend himself against these absurd charges, he used the
trial, once again, to act as a "gadfly" to those who condemned him.

There are many reasons why I am not grieved, O men of Athens, at the
vote of condemnation. I expected it, and am only surprised that the votes are
so nearly equal; for I had thought that the majority against me would have
been far larger. . . .

And so death is proposed as the penalty. And what shall I propose on my
part, O men of Athens? Clearly that which is my due. And what is my due?
What ought I to have done to me, or to pay—a man who has never had the
wit to keep quiet during his whole life; but has been careless of what the
many care for—wealth, and family interests, and military offices, and speaking
in the assembly, and magistracies, and plots and parties. Reflecting that I was
really too honest a man to be a politician and live, I did not go where I could
do no good to you or to myself; but where I could do privately the greatest
good (as I affirm it to be) to everyone of you, thither I went, and sought to
persuade every man among you that he must look to himself, and seek virtue
and wisdom before he looks to his private interests, and look to the state
before he looks to the interests of the state; and that this should be the order

---

[1] Aristophanes, Clouds, in The Complete Plays of Aristophanes, trans. Moses Hadas (New
York: Bantam, 1962).

which he observes in all his actions. What shall be done to such an one? Doubtless some good thing, O men of Athens, if he has his reward; and the good should be of a kind suitable to him.

Socrates here suggests that the state should give him a pension rather than a punishment, for being so virtuous.

Not much time will be gained, O Athenians, in return for the evil name which you will get from the detractors of the city, who will say that you killed Socrates, a wise man; for they will call me wise, even although I am not wise, when they want to reproach you. If you had waited a little while, your desire would have been fulfilled in the course of nature. For I am far advanced in years, as you may perceive, and not far from death. [He was in his 70s.] I am speaking now not to all of you, but only to those who have condemned me to death. And I have another thing to say to them: You think that I was convicted because I had no words of the sort which would have procured my acquittal—I mean, if I had thought fit to leave nothing undone or unsaid. Not so; the deficiency which led to my conviction was not of words—certainly not. But I had not the boldness nor impudence nor inclination to address you as you would have liked me to do, weeping and wailing and lamenting, and saying and doing many things, such indeed as you have been accustomed to hear from others, but I maintain to be unworthy of myself. I thought at the time that I ought not to do anything common or mean when in danger: nor do I now repent of the style of my defence; I would rather die having spoken after my manner, than speak in your manner and live. For neither in war nor yet at law ought I or any man to use every way of escaping death. Often in battle there can be no doubt that if a man will throw away his arms, and fall on his knees before his pursuers, he may escape death; and in other dangers there are other ways of escaping death, if a man has the hardihood to say and do anything. The difficulty, my friends, is not to avoid death, but to avoid unrighteousness; for that runs faster than death. I am old and move slowly, and the slower runner has overtaken me; my accusers are keen and quick, and the faster runner, who is wickedness, has overtaken them. And now I depart hence condemned by you to suffer the penalty of death,—they too go their ways condemned by the truth to suffer the penalty of villainy and wrong; and I must abide by my award—let them abide by theirs. I suppose that these things may be regarded as fated,—and I think that they are well.

And now, O men who have condemned me, I would fain prophesy to you; for I am about to die, and in the hour of death men are gifted with prophetic power. And I prophesy to you who are my murderers, that immediately after my departure punishment far heavier than you have inflicted on me surely awaits you. Me you have killed because you wanted to escape the accuser, and not to give an account of your lives. But that will not be as you suppose: far otherwise. For I say that there will be more accusers of you than there are now; accusers whom hitherto I have restrained: and as they are younger they will be more severe with you, and you will be more offended at them. If you think that by killing men you will stop all censure of your evil lives, you are mistaken; that is not a way of escape which is either very possible, or honourable; the easiest and the noblest way is not to be disabling others, but to be improving yourselves. This is the prophecy which I utter before my departure to the judges who have condemned me.[2]

In prison, he was given the opportunity to escape. He refused it. He had always taught that "the really important thing is not to live, but to live well." And to "live well" meant, along with the more enjoyable things in life, to live according to your principles. When his friend Crito tried to persuade him otherwise, Socrates responded:

SOCRATES. But my dear Crito, why should we pay so much attention to what 'most people' think? The really reasonable people, who have more claim to be considered, will believe that the facts are exactly as they are.

CRITO. You can see for yourself, Socrates, that one has to think of popular opinion as well. Your present position is quite enough to show that the capacity of ordinary people for causing trouble is not confined to petty annoyances, but has hardly any limits if you once get a bad name with them.

SOCRATES. I only wish that ordinary people *had* an unlimited capacity for doing harm; then they might have an unlimited power for doing good; which would be a splendid thing, if it were so. Actually they have neither. They cannot make a man wise or stupid; they simply act at random. . . .

CRITO. Very well, then. . . . I know some people who are willing to rescue you from here and get you out of the country for quite a moderate sum. . . . Besides, Socrates, I don't even feel that it is right for you to try to do what you are doing, throwing away your life when you might save it. You are doing your best to treat yourself in exactly the same way as your enemies would, or rather did, when they wanted to ruin you. . . .

SOCRATES. My dear Crito, I appreciate your warm feelings very much—that is, assuming that they have some justification; if not, the stronger they are, the harder they will be to deal with. Very well, then; we must consider whether we ought to follow your advice or not. . . . At the same time I should like you to consider whether we are still satisfied on this point: that the really important thing is not to live, but to live well.

CRITO. Why, yes.

SOCRATES. And that to live well means the same thing as to live honourably or rightly?

CRITO. Yes.

SOCRATES. Then in the light of this agreement we must consider whether or not it is right for me to try to get away without an official discharge. If it turns out to be right, we must make the attempt; if not, we must let it drop. If it becomes clear that such conduct is wrong, I cannot help thinking that the question whether we are sure to die, or to suffer any other ill effect for that matter, if we stand our ground and take no action, ought not to weigh with us at all in comparison with the risk of doing what is wrong. . . . Ought one to fulfil all one's agreements, provided that they are right, or break them?

[2] Plato, *Apology*, in *The Dialogues of Plato*, 4th rev. ed., trans. Benjamin Jowett, ed. D. J. Allan and H. E. Dale (Oxford: Oxford University Press, 1953).

CRITO. One ought to fulfil them.

SOCRATES. Then consider the logical consequence. If we leave this place without first persuading the State to let us go, are we or are we not doing an injury, and doing it in a quarter where it is least justifiable? Are we or are we not abiding by our just agreements?

CRITO. I can't answer your question, Socrates; I am not clear in my mind.

SOCRATES. Look at it in this way. Suppose that while we were preparing to run away from here (or however one should describe it) the Laws and Constitution of Athens were to come and confront us and ask this question: 'Now, Socrates, what are you proposing to do? Can you deny that by this act which you are contemplating you intend, so far as you have the power, to destroy us, the Laws, and the whole State as well? Do you imagine that a city can continue to exist and not be turned upside down, if the legal judgments which are pronounced in it have no force but are nullified and destroyed by private persons?'—how shall we answer this question, Crito, and others of the same kind? There is much that could be said, especially by a professional advocate, to protest against the invalidation of this law which enacts that judgements once pronounced shall be binding. Shall we say 'Yes, I do intend to destroy the laws, because the State wronged me by passing a faulty judgement at my trial?' Is this to be our answer, or what?

CRITO. What you have just said, by all means, Socrates.

SOCRATES. Then what supposing the Laws say 'Was there provision for this in the agreement between you and us, Socrates? Or did you undertake to abide by whatever judgements the State pronounced?' [Notice that here and in what follows it is "the Laws" talking to Socrates.] 'Now first answer this question: Are we or are we not speaking the truth when we say that you have undertaken, in deed if not in word, to live your life as a citizen in obedience to us?' What are we to say to that, Crito? Are we not bound to admit it?

CRITO. We cannot help it, Socrates.

SOCRATES. 'It is a fact, then,' they would say, 'that you are breaking covenants and undertakings made with us, although you made them under no compulsion or misunderstanding, and were not compelled to decide in a limited time; you had seventy years in which you could have left the country, if you were not satisfied with us or felt that the agreements were unfair. You did not choose Sparta or Crete—your favourite models of good government—or any other Greek or foreign state; you could not have absented yourself from the city less if you had been lame or blind or decrepit in some other way. It is quite obvious that you stand by yourself above all other Athenians in your affection for this city and for us its Laws;—who would care for a city without laws? And now, after all this, are you going to stand by your agreement? Yes, you are, Socrates, if you will take our advice; and then you will at least escape being laughed at for leaving the city. . . . Do not take Crito's advice, but follow ours.'

That, my dear friend Crito, I do assure you, is what I seem to hear them saying, just as a mystic seems to hear the strains of music; and the sound of their arguments rings so loudly in my head that I cannot hear the other side. I warn you that, as my opinion stands at present, it will

> be useless to urge a different view. However, if you think that you will do
> any good by it, say what you like.
> CRITO. No, Socrates, I have nothing to say.
> SOCRATES. Then give it up, Crito, and let us follow this course, since God
> points out the way.[3]

Socrates preferred to die for his ideas than live as a hypocrite. An idea worth
living for may be an idea worth dying for as well.

> . . . quite calmly and with no sign of distaste, he drained the poison cup in
> one breath.
> Up until this time most of us had been fairly successful in keeping back
> our tears, but when we saw that he had drunk the poison, we could do so no
> longer. Everyone in the room broke down, except Socrates himself, who said,
> 'Really my friends, what a way to behave!'
> Such was the end of our comrade, who was, we may fairly say, the
> bravest, most wise and most upright man of our time.[4]

Is there anything that you believe so passionately that you would die for
it? Is there anything that you believe so passionately that it really makes your
life worth living? For most people, now as always, life is rather a matter of
"getting by." If you look closely at your life, not only at your proclaimed ideals
and principles but your desires and ambitions as well, do the facts of your life
add up to its best intentions? Or are you too just drifting with the times, dissatisfied with ultimately meaningless jobs and mindless joyless entertainments,
concerned with the price of gasoline and some stupidity of the government, the
petty competitions of school and society, the hassles of chores and assignments,
car troubles and occasional social embarrassments, interrupted only by all too
rare and too quickly passing pleasures and distractions? What we learn from
Socrates is how to rise above all of this. Not that we should give up worldly
pleasures—good food and fun, sex, sports, and entertainment—and put our
heads in the "clouds"; but we should see them in perspective, and examine for
ourselves that jungle of confused reactions and conditioned responses that we
have unthinkingly inherited from our parents and borrowed from our peers.
The point is not necessarily to give up what we have learned or to turn against
our "culture." Rather, the lesson to be learned from Socrates is that thinking
about our lives and clarifying our ideals can turn it from a dreary series of
tasks and distractions into a self-conscious adventure, one even worth dying for
and certainly worth living for. It is a special kind of abstract thinking, rising
above petty concerns and transforming our existence into a bold experiment in
living. This special kind of thinking is called philosophy.

> So the philosopher, with his passion for wisdom, will be one who desires all
> wisdom, not only some part of it. . . . Only the man who has a taste for

[3] Plato, *Crito,* in *The Last Days of Socrates,* trans. Hugh Tredennick (Harmondsworth,
Middlesex: Penguin, 1964).
[4] Plato, *Phaedo,* trans. R. Hackforth (Cambridge: Cambridge University Press, 1935).

every sort of knowledge and throws himself into acquiring it with an insatiable curiosity will deserve to be called a philosopher. Am I not right?[5]

WHAT IS PHILOSOPHY?

Philosophy is not like any other academic subject; rather it is a critical approach to all subjects. Philosophy is a style of life, a life of ideas or the life of reason, which a person like Socrates lives all his life, which many of us live only a few hours a week. It is thinking, about everything and anything. But mainly, it is living thoughtfully. Aristotle, the student of Plato, who was the student of Socrates, called this "contemplative" or philosophical life the ideal life for man. He did not mean, however, that one should sit and think all of the time without doing anything. Aristotle, like the other Greek philosophers, was not one to abstain from pleasures of all kinds or from political and social involvement for the sake of isolated thinking. Philosophy need not, as commonly believed, put our heads in the clouds, out of touch with everyday reality. Quite to the contrary, philosophy takes our heads out of the clouds, enlarging our view of ourselves and our knowledge of the world, allowing us to break out of prejudices and harmful habits which we have held since we were too young or too naive to know better. Philosophy puts our lives and our beliefs in perspective, by enabling us to see afresh the ways in which we view the world, to see what we assume, what we infer, and what we know for certain. It allows us to see the consequences of our views and sometimes their hopeless inconsistencies. It allows us to see the justification (or lack of it) for our most treasured beliefs, and to separate that which we will continue to believe with confidence from that which we should consider doubtful or reject. Philosophy gives us the intellectual strength to defend what we do and what we believe to others and to ourselves. It forces us to be clear about the limits as well as the warrants for our acts and beliefs. And, consequently, it gives us the intellectual strength to understand, tolerate, and even sympathize with views very different from our own.

Suppose you have been brought up in a deeply religious home; you have been taught respect for God and Church, and you have learned that, although there are people who would disagree with you, your belief is a righteous and necessary one. But now you enter college and immediately you are confronted by fellow students, some of whom you consider close friends and admire in many ways, who are virulently anti-religious. Your first reactions will be almost like physical illness; you feel weak, nauseous, flushed and anxious. You refuse to listen, and if you respond at all, it is with a tinge of hysteria. You may get into fights as well as arguments. You feel as if some foundation of your life, one of its main supports, is slipping away. But slowly you gain some confidence; you begin to listen. You give yourself enough distance so that you will consider arguments about religion in just the same way you would consider arguments

[5] Socrates' speech in Plato, *The Republic*, BK. V, trans. Francis M. Cornford (Oxford: Oxford University Press, 1941).

about some scientific or political dispute. You begin asking yourself how you came to believe in your religion in the first place, and you may well come up with the answer (many freshmen do) that you were "conditioned" by your parents and by society in general. Consequently, you may, perhaps for a time, perhaps for a lifetime, reject the ideas you had once "naturally" accepted and join the ranks of the atheists. Or, you may reaffirm your faith with new commitment, determined that, whatever the source, your beliefs are right. But after further consideration and argument, perhaps with some new religious experience, you now see both sides of the arguments. For the first time, you can weigh their merits and demerits against each other without defensively holding onto one and attacking the other. You may remain an atheist; you may remain a believer; or you may adopt a position in which you give all religions (and non-religion) equal weight, continuing to believe but not insisting that your belief is the only correct one or that you are necessarily a superior person because of it. But whatever you decide, your position will no longer be naive and unthinking. You know the arguments, both for and against. You know how to defend yourself. And, most importantly, you have confidence that your position is secure, that you have considered its objections and that you have mastered its strengths. So it is with all philosophical problems and positions. Philosophy does not pull us away from our lives; it clarifies them. It secures them on intellectual ground in place of the fragile supports provided by inherited prejudices, fragments of parental advice, and mindless slogans borrowed from television commercials and televised demagogues.

"Philosophy" sounds like a new and mysterious discipline, unlike anything you have ever encountered. But the basic ideas of philosophy are familiar to all of us, even if we have not yet formally confronted the problems. In this sense, we are all philosophers already. Watch yourself in a crisis, or listen to yourself in an argument with a friend. Notice how quickly abstract concepts like "freedom," "mankind," "self-identity," "nature" and "natural," "relative," "reality," "illusion," and "truth" enter our thoughts and our conversations. Notice how certain basic philosophical principles—whether conservative or radical, selfish or idealistic, confident or skeptical, pedestrian or heroic,—enter into our arguments and our thinking as well as our actions. We all have some opinions about God, about morality and its principles, about the nature of man and the nature of the universe. But because we haven't questioned them, they are merely the *assumptions* of our thinking. We believe many things without having thought about them, merely assuming them, sometimes without evidence or good reasons. What the study of philosophy does for us is to make our ideas explicit, to give us the means of defending our presuppositions, and to make alternative suppositions available to us as well. Where once we merely assumed a point of view, passively and for lack of alternatives, we now can argue for it with confidence, knowing that our acceptance is active and critical, systematic rather than merely a collection of borrowed beliefs (who knows from where). To be *critical* means to examine carefully and cautiously, willing, if necessary, to change one's own beliefs. It does not need to be nasty or destructive. There is "constructive criticism" as well. And to "argue" does not mean "to have a fight": an *argument* may simply be the justification of our beliefs.

So what is philosophy? Literally, from the Greek, (*philein, sophia*) it is "the love of wisdom."[6] It is an attitude of critical and systematic thoughtfulness rather than a particular subject matter. This makes matters very difficult for the beginner, who would like a definition of philosophy of the same kind received when he or she began biology, as "the study of living organisms." But the nature of philosophy is itself among the most bitter disputes in philosophy. Many philosophers say that it is a science, in fact, the "Queen of the Sciences," the womb in which physics, chemistry, mathematics, astronomy, biology, and psychology began their development before being born into their own distinguished worlds and separate university departments. And insofar as one says that philosophy is the road to reality and that the goal of philosophy is truth, that would seem to make it the ultimate science as well. But it has also been argued, as far back as Socrates, that the main business of philosophy is a matter of definitions—finding clear meanings for such important ideas as truth, justice, wisdom, knowledge and happiness. Accordingly, many philosophers have taken advantage of the sophisticated tools of modern logic and linguistics in their attempt to find such definitions. Other philosophers, however, would insist that philosophy is rather closer to morality and religion, its purpose to give meaning to our lives and lead us down "the right path" to "the good life." Still others insist that philosophy is an art, the art of criticism and argument as well as the art of conceptual system building. There are philosophers who place strong emphasis upon proof and argument; there are others who place their trust in intuition and insight. There are philosophers who reduce all philosophizing to the study of experience; there are philosophers who take it as a matter of principle not to trust experience. There are philosophers who insist on being practical, in fact, who insist that there are no other considerations but practicality; and then there are philosophers who insist on the purity of the life of ideas, divorced from any practical considerations. But philosophy cannot, without distortion, be reduced to any one of these preferences. All enter into that constantly re-defined critical and creative life of ideas that Socrates was willing to die for.

THE LOGIC OF MODERN PHILOSOPHY

The approach to philosophy in this book is essentially a modern approach. This means not only that it is the approach (or set of approaches) that has dominated the last three hundred years of philosophy but also that it has an identifiable character that distinguishes it from most previous philosophies and

[6] The word was invented by Pythagoras (whom we shall meet in the next chapter). When he was asked if he was already a wise man, he answered "No, I am not wise, but I am a *lover* of wisdom."

makes it extremely close to our own ideas. Its central concern is the autonomy of the individual person. This means that each of us must be credited with the ability to ascertain what is true and what is right, through our own thinking and experience, without the usual appeal to outside authority: parents, teachers, popes, kings or a majority of peers. Whether you believe in God or not must be decided by you, by appeal to your own reason and arguments which you can formulate and examine by yourself. Whether you accept a scientific theory, a doctor's diagnosis, a newspaper's version of the news, or the legitimacy of a new law are also matters to be decided by you on the basis of evidence, principles which you can accept, and arguments which you acknowledge as valid. This stress on individual autonomy stands at the very foundation of contemporary Western thought. We might say that it is our most basic assumption. (Accordingly, we shall have to examine it as well; but the obvious place to begin is to assume that we are—each of us—capable of carrying out the reflection and criticism that philosophy demands of us.)

Historically, the position of individual autonomy can be found in Socrates, most famously, who sacrificed his life for the "Laws" and principles he believed to be right. It also appears in several medieval philosophers, some of whom also faced grave danger in their partial rejection or questioning of the "authority" of the Church. The stress on individual autonomy comes to dominate Western thinking in that intellectually brilliant period of history called "the Enlightenment," sometimes called "the Age of Reason." It began in the seventeenth century and continued through the French Revolution (1789). It appeared in different countries with varying speed and intensity, but ultimately, it influenced the thinking of Europe, from England and France to Spain and Russia, and it became the ideology of young America, which used Enlightenment doctrines in the formulation of a "Declaration of Independence," a war for its own autonomy, and a new government established solely on Enlightenment principles. And those principles were, whatever the variations from one country or party to another, the autonomy of the individual and each person's right to choose and to speak his[7] own religious, political, moral, and philosophical beliefs, to "pursue happiness" in his own way and to lead the life that he, as a reasonable person, sees as right. And if these principles have often been abused, creating confusion and sometimes anarchy, encouraging ruthlessness in politics and strife in a mixed society, they are principles which we are capable of challenging only with great difficulty and a sense of imminent danger. Once we deny the individual the right or the ability to decide such matters for him or herself, who shall decide? We no longer agree on any single unambiguous set of instructions from the Scriptures. We no longer trust everyone in power. And we are rightfully suspicious of those who attack the individual, because we always wonder what else they have in mind. Whatever the abuses, and whatever political, social or economic systems might be required to support it, philosophical autonomy is our starting point.

[7] Not, at that point in history, *hers* as well.

The metaphor of enlightenment is common to many cultures. The comparison of clear thinking with illumination is to be found in ancient, Christian and Eastern thought as well as in comic book symbolism and modern philosophy. The most important employer of that metaphor, for our purposes, is a French philosopher of the seventeenth century, René Descartes. Descartes was one of the founders of the Enlightenment, and he is generally recognized as the father of modern philosophy. Like Socrates 2000 years before, Descartes believed that each of us was capable of ascertaining what beliefs were true and what actions were right. But where Socrates searched through dialogue and discussion, Descartes searched for the truth in the solitude of his own thinking. With considerable risk to his safety, he challenged the authority of the French government and the Catholic Church. He insisted that he would accept as true only those ideas which were demonstrably true to him. Against the obscure teachings of the Church and the often opaque commands of his government, Descartes insisted upon "clear and distinct ideas" and arguments based upon "the light of reason." The modern philosophy of individual autonomy begins with Descartes. As a matter of fact, his results were quite conservative; he retained much of his medieval teachings; he continued to believe in God and the Church; and he made it his first "moral maxim" to "obey the laws and customs of my country." His challenge to authority was rather his method, which signified one of the greatest revolutions in Western thought. From Descartes on, the ultimate authority was to be found in our own thinking and experience, nowhere else.

None of this is meant to deny authority as such. We still make appeals to authority, but authorities are never to be taken as absolutes. For example, none of us would particularly like to go out and establish on our own the figures of the 1970 census of the American population. But it is up to us whether or not to accept the official "authoritative" figures, to question, if necessary, the integrity or motivation of the authorities, and to appeal, if necessary, to alternative sources of information.

For anyone beginning to study philosophy today, Descartes is the ideal starting point. His method is both easy to follow and very much in accord with our own independent temperaments. Descartes procceded by means of logical arguments, giving us a long monologue of presentations and proofs of his philosophical doubts and beliefs. Like Socrates before him, Descartes used his philosophy to cut through the clouds of prejudice and unreliable opinions. He was concerned with their truth, no matter how many people already believed them, and no matter how few. Descartes' arguments were his tools for finding this truth, and distinguishing it from falsehood and mere opinion.

Philosophy has always been concerned with truth and our knowledge of reality. The truth, however, is not always what most people believe at any given time. (Most people once believed that the earth was flat, for example.) But, at the same time that they refuse to simply accept "common sense," philosophers try not to say things that common sense finds absurd. For example, a philosopher who denied that anyone existed besides himself would clearly be absurd.

So too, the philosopher who argued that he knew that nobody ever knows anything is caught in an obvious absurdity. Accordingly, two of the most important obstacles to the philosophers' search for truth are (1) skepticism and (2) paradox. In *skepticism,* the philosopher finds him or herself unable to justify what every sane person knows to be the case; for example, that we are not merely dreaming all of the time. In a *paradox,* an absurd conclusion seems to result from perfectly acceptable ways of thinking. For example, there is the familiar paradox of Epimenides the Cretan, who claimed that "all Cretans are liars." (That sounds reasonable enough.) But . . . if what he said was true, then he was lying and what he said, accordingly, was false. But how can the same statement be both true and false? What Epimenides said was true only if it was false at the same time. That is a paradox. And whenever a philosophical argument ends in paradox, we can be sure that something has gone wrong.

Skepticism begins with *doubt.* The philosopher considers the possibility that something that everyone believes is possibly mistaken. Some doubt is a healthy sign of intellectual autonomy; but excessive doubting becomes skepticism, which is no longer healthy. It has its obvious dangers: if you doubt whether you are ever awake or not, you might well do things that wouldn't have serious consequences in a dream but would be fatal in real life (jumping out of a plane, for example). Philosophers who have doubts about the most ordinary and seemingly unquestionable beliefs are called *skeptics.* But however challenging skeptics may be as philosophers, in practice their skepticism is impossible. Accordingly, one of the main drives in philosophy has been to refute the skeptic and return philosophy to common sense (to prove, for example, that we are *not* dreaming all of the time). Opposed to skepticism is an ancient philosophical ideal, the ideal of *certainty,* the ability to prove beyond a doubt that what we believe is true. Socrates and Descartes, in their very different ways, tried to provide precisely this certainty in our most important beliefs, and thus refute the skeptics of their own times.

For Descartes, certainty is the *criterion,* that is, the test, according to which our beliefs are to be evaluated. But do we ever find such certainty? It seems that we do, at least in one discipline Descartes suggests—in mathematics. Who can doubt that two plus two equals four? or that the interior angles of a triangle total 180°? Using mathematics as his ideal, Descartes (and many generations of philosophers following him) attempted to apply a similar method in philosophy. First, he must find, as in Euclidean geometry, a small set of "first principles" or *axioms* which are obvious or *self-evident.* They may be assumed without proof or are so fundamental that they seem not to allow any proof. These will serve as *premises* or starting points for the *arguments* which will take us from the self-evident axioms to other principles which may not be self-evident at all. But if they can be *deduced* from other principles which are already certain, like the theorems of geometry, then they share the certainty of the principles from which they have been derived. (We will discuss "deduction" on page 17.)

In his *Discourse on Method,* Descartes set out four basic rules which would define philosophy for many years:

The first of these was to accept nothing as true which I did not clearly recognise to be so: that is to say, carefully to avoid precipitation and prejudice in judgments, and to accept in them nothing more than what was presented to my mind so clearly and distinctly that I could have no occasion to doubt it.

The second was to divide up each of the difficulties which I examined into as many parts as possible, and as seemed requisite in order that it might be resolved in the best manner possible.

The third was to carry on my reflections in due order, commencing with objects that were the most simple and easy to understand, in order to rise little by little, or by degrees, to knowledge of the most complex, assuming an order, even if a fictitious one, among those which do not follow a natural sequence relatively to one another.

The last was in all cases to make enumerations so complete and reviews so general that I should be certain of having omitted nothing.[8]

One might say that the essence of these rules is to be cautious and to think for oneself. The premises, upon which all else depends, must be utterly beyond doubt, "perfectly certain," otherwise all else is futile. The test or criterion of such a premise is that it be "a clear and distinct idea," self-evident, and "springing from the light of reason alone."

To assure the certainty of his premises, Descartes developed a method which is often called the *method of doubt* (or *methodological doubt*). In order to make sure that he did not accept any principle too quickly ("precipitously") and without thoroughly being convinced of its "perfect certainty," he resolved to begin by doubting everything. The idea behind this procedure is to find those beliefs which are so absolutely certain that they cannot be doubted, that their very doubting leads to paradox. The point is not, we must emphasize, to become a skeptic; quite the contrary, the point is to find those beliefs which even the skeptic cannot doubt. And so Descartes begins; he doubts that his senses are trustworthy. Could they not be fooling him, as in an optical illusion or a hallucination? He examines his belief in God, and all else in theology and morals that had been taught by his Jesuit teachers. He even doubts the existence of the world. Is it not conceivable that he is merely dreaming? The method is extreme, but so are its ambitions. Descartes explains them to us in the first of his six famous "Meditations":

MEDITATION I
Of the Things Which May Be Brought Within the Sphere of the Doubtful

It is now some years since I detected how many were the false beliefs that I had from my earliest youth admitted as true, and how doubtful was everything I had since constructed on this basis; and from that time I was convinced that I must once for all seriously undertake to rid myself of all the opinions which I had formerly accepted, and commence to build anew from the foundation, if I wanted to establish any firm and permanent structure in the sciences. But as this enterprise appeared to be a very great one, I waited

[8] René Descartes, *Discourse on Method,* in *The Philosophical Works of Descartes,* trans. Elizabeth S. Haldane and G. R. T. Ross (Cambridge: Cambridge University Press, 1911).

until I had attained an age so mature that I could not hope that at any later date I should be better fitted to execute my design. This reason caused me to delay so long that I should feel that I was doing wrong were I to occupy in deliberation the time that yet remains to me for action. To-day, then, since very opportunely for the plan I have in view I have delivered my mind from every care [and am happily agitated by no passions] and since I have procured for myself an assured leisure in a peaceable retirement, I shall at last seriously and freely address myself to the general upheaval of all my former opinions.

Now for this object it is not necessary that I should show that all of these are false—I shall perhaps never arrive at this end. But inasmuch as reason already persuades me that I ought no less carefully to withhold my assent from matters which are not entirely certain and indubitable than from those which appear to me manifestly to be false, if I am able to find in each one some reason to doubt, this will suffice to justify my rejecting the whole. And for that end it will not be requisite that I should examine each in particular, which would be an endless undertaking; for owing to the fact that the destruction of the foundations of necessity brings with it the downfall of the rest of the edifice, I shall only in the first place attack those principles upon which all my former opinions rested.

All that up to the present time I have accepted as most true and certain I have learned either from the senses or through the senses; but it is sometimes proved to me that these senses are deceptive, and it is wiser not to trust entirely to any thing by which we have once been deceived.

But it may be that although the senses sometimes deceive us concerning things which are hardly perceptible, or very far away, there are yet many others to be met with as to which we cannot reasonably have any doubt, although we recognise them by their means. For example, there is the fact that I am here, seated by the fire, attired in a dressing gown, having this paper in my hands and other similar matters. And how could I deny that these hands and this body are mine, were it not perhaps that I compare myself to certain persons, devoid of sense, whose cerebella are so troubled and clouded by the violent vapours of black bile, that they constantly assure us that they think they are kings when they are really quite poor, or that they are clothed in purple when they are really without covering, or who imagine that they have an earthenware head or are nothing but pumpkins or are made of glass. But they are mad, and I should not be any the less insane were I to follow examples so extravagant.

At the same time I must remember that I am a man, and that consequently I am in the habit of sleeping, and in my dreams representing to myself the same things or sometimes even less probable things, than do those who are insane in their waking moments. How often has it happened to me that in the night I dreamt that I found myself in this particular place, that I was dressed and seated near the fire, whilst in reality I was lying undressed in bed! At this moment it does indeed seem to me that it is with eyes awake that I am looking at this paper; that this head which I move is not asleep, that it is deliberately and of set purpose that I extend my hand and perceive it; what happens in sleep does not appear so clear nor so distinct as does all this. But in thinking over this I remind myself that on many occasions I have in sleep been deceived by similar illusions, and in dwelling carefully on this reflection I see so manifestly that there are no certain indications by which we may clearly distinguish wakefulness from sleep that I am lost in astonishment. And my astonishment is such that it is almost capable of persuading me that I now dream.

Now let us assume that we are asleep and that all these particulars, e.g. that we open our eyes, shake our head, extend our hands, and so on, are but false delusions; and let us reflect that possibly neither our hands nor our whole body are such as they appear to us to be. At the same time we must at least confess that the things which are represented to us in sleep are like painted representations which can only have been formed as the counterparts of something real and true, and that in this way those general things at least, i.e. eyes, a head, hands, and a whole body, are not imaginary things, but things really existent. For, as a matter of fact, painters, even when they study with the greatest skill to represent sirens and satyrs by forms the most strange and extraordinary, cannot give them natures which are entirely new, but merely make a certain medley of the members of different animals; or if their imagination is extravagant enough to invent something so novel that nothing similar has ever before been seen, and that then their work represents a thing purely fictitious and absolutely false, it is certain all the same that the colours of which this is composed are necessarily real. And for the same reason, although these general things, to wit, [a body], eyes, a head, hands, and such like, may be imaginary, we are bound at the same time to confess that there are at least some other objects yet more simple and more universal, which are real and true; and of these just in the same way as with certain real colours, all these images of things which dwell in our thoughts, whether true and real or false and fantastic, are formed.

To such a class of things pertains corporeal nature in general, and its extension, the figure of extended things, their quantity or magnitude and number, as also the place in which they are, the time which measures their duration, and so on.

That is possibly why our reasoning is not unjust when we conclude from this that Physics, Astronomy, Medicine and all other sciences which have as their end the consideration of composite things, are very dubious and uncertain; but that Arithmetic, Geometry and other sciences of that kind which only treat of things that are very simple and very general, without taking great trouble to ascertain whether they are actually existent or not, contain some measure of certainty and an element of the indubitable. For whether I am awake or asleep, two and three together always form five, and the square can never have more than four sides, and it does not seem possible that truths so clear and apparent can be suspected of any falsity [or uncertainty].

Nevertheless I have long had fixed in my mind the belief that an all-powerful God existed by whom I have been created such as I am. But how do I know that He has not brought it to pass that there is no earth, no heaven, no extended body, no magnitude, no place, and that nevertheless [I possess the perceptions of all these things and that] they seem to me to exist just exactly as I now see them? And, besides, as I sometimes imagine that others deceive themselves in the things which they think they know best, how do I know that I am not deceived every time that I add two and three, or count the sides of a square, or judge of things yet simpler, if anything simpler can be imagined? But possibly God has not desired that I should be thus deceived, for He is said to be supremely good. If, however, it is contrary to His goodness to have made me such that I constantly deceive myself, it would also appear to be contrary to His goodness to permit me to be sometimes deceived, and nevertheless I cannot doubt that He does permit this.

There may indeed be those who would prefer to deny the existence of a God so powerful, rather than believe that all other things are uncertain. But let us not oppose them for the present, and grant that all that is here said of a God is a fable; nevertheless in whatever way they suppose that I have arrived at the state of being that I have reached—whether they attribute it to fate or to accident, or make out that it is by a continual succession of antecedents, or by some other method—since to err and deceive oneself is a defect, it is clear that the greater will be the probability of my being so imperfect as to deceive myself ever, as is the Author to whom they assign my origin the less powerful. To these reasons I have certainly nothing to reply, but at the end I feel constrained to confess that there is nothing in all that I formerly believed to be true, of which I cannot in some measure doubt, and that not merely through want of thought or through levity, but for reasons which are very powerful and maturely considered; so that henceforth I ought not the less carefully to refrain from giving credence to these opinions than to that which is manifestly false, if I desire to arrive at any certainty [in the sciences].

But it is not sufficient to have made these remarks, we must also be careful to keep them in mind. For these ancient and commonly held opinions still revert frequently to my mind, long and familiar custom having given them the right to occupy my mind against my inclination and rendered them almost masters of my belief; nor will I ever lose the habit of deferring to them or of placing my confidence in them, so long as I consider them as they really are, i.e. opinions in some measure doubtful, as I have just shown, and at the same time highly probable, so that there is much more reason to believe in than to deny them. That is why I consider that I shall not be acting amiss, if, taking of set purpose a contrary belief, I allow myself to be deceived, and for a certain time pretend that all these opinions are entirely false and imaginary, until at last, having thus balanced my former prejudices with my latter [so that they cannot divert my opinions more to one side than to the other], my judgment will no longer be dominated by bad usage or turned away from the right knowledge of the truth. For I am assured that there can be neither peril nor error in this course, and that I cannot at present yield too much to distrust, since I am not considering the question of action, but only of knowledge.

I shall then suppose, not that God who is supremely good and the fountain of truth, but some evil genius not less powerful than deceitful, has employed his whole energies in deceiving me; I shall consider that the heavens, the earth, colours, figures, sound, and all other external things are nought but the illusions and dreams of which this genius has availed himself in order to lay traps for my credulity; I shall consider myself as having no hands, no eyes, no flesh, no blood, nor any senses, yet falsely believing myself to possess all these things; I shall remain obstinately attached to this idea, and if by this means it is not in my power to arrive at the knowledge of any truth, I may at least do what is in my power [i.e. suspend my judgment], and with firm purpose avoid giving credence to any false thing, or being imposed upon by this arch deceiver, however powerful and deceptive he may be. But this task is a laborious one, and insensibly a certain lassitude leads me into the course of my ordinary life. And just as a captive who in sleep enjoys an imaginary liberty, when he begins to suspect that his liberty is but a dream, fears to awaken, and conspires with these agreeable illusions that the deception may be prolonged, so insensibly of my own accord I fall back into my former opinions, and I dread awakening from this slumber, lest the laborious wakefulness which would follow the tranquility of this repose should have to be spent not in daylight, but in the excessive darkness of the difficulties which have just been discussed.[9]

In Chapter 3, we shall find out the principle that Descartes claims is perfectly certain and undoubtable. (It is, we can anticipate, the fact of his own existence.) For the moment, however, we are concerned with his method and its logic, that is, the kinds of arguments by which he moves from one belief to another. An *argument* in this important sense is a manner of supporting a belief with reasons. It need not involve a quarrel with anyone; philosophy often requires "arguments" even when everyone already agrees with the belief in question. We have already seen that Descartes' method is modeled after the forms of proof that you learned in high school geometry. The starting point of these proofs are premises. From them, Descartes can deduce further principles with as much certainty as the premises. In a *deductive* argument, the conclusion follows necessarily from the premises according to certain *rules of inference,* that is, the laws of thinking such as "never believe that a statement is both true and false at the same time" or "if *p* is false, then *not-p* is true."

The best-known deductive arguments are called *syllogisms.* (The development of this form of logic is mainly due to Aristotle, two thousand years before Descartes.) An example of a syllogism is:

> All philosophers are wise.
> Socrates is a philosopher
> _____
> Therefore, Socrates is wise.

What is important in such arguments is the form of the component statements:

> All P's are Q's.
> S is a P.
> _____
> Therefore, S is a Q.

When a deductive argument proceeds correctly according to this form, we say that it is *deductively valid* or simply *valid.* When it does not proceed correctly,

[9] Descartes, *Meditations on First Philosophy,* in *The Philosophical Works of Descartes.*

we say that it is *invalid*. Deduction guarantees that our conclusions will be as certain as the premises. If the premises are certainly true, then the conclusions will certainly be true as well. But it is important to emphasize that an argument can be valid even if its premises and conclusion are false. For example, the following syllogism correctly follows the above form and is therefore valid:

> All cows are purple.
> Socrates is a cow.
> _____
> Therefore, Socrates is purple.

This is a valid argument even though both the premises and the conclusion are false. But without true premises, even a valid argument cannot guarantee true conclusions. This is why it is so absolutely necessary for Descartes to find premises which are beyond doubt and certainly true. Without them, his mathematical method is nothing but an intellectual exercise. Notice that, contrary to common usage, philosophers restrict their use of the words "valid" and "invalid" to talking about correct and incorrect arguments; the words *true* and *false* apply to the various claims that one makes in an argument—its premises and its conclusion. Thus, the claim that "three plus two equals eight" is false, not invalid; and the argument, "If Socrates is a man and all goats eat cabbage then Socrates is a goat" is invalid, not false (whether or not its premises or conclusion are false). When an argument is both valid and has true premises, it is called a *sound* argument. An argument is *unsound* if its premises are false, or if it is invalid.

These basic logical points are but one aspect of the most crucial test of a philosophy: its starting point must be generally acceptable, or we cannot even begin. And its arguments must be sound, or else there is no reason to have any confidence at all in the conclusions. But the reason for this transcends the particular and peculiar mathematical method defended by Descartes; it is the central characteristic of all good (as well as great) philosophy that it not be a random assortment of thoughts and suggestions but instead be systematic. In *systematic* thought the various principles are tied to each other by logical bonds, sometimes by straightforward deductive arguments, but also by many other forms of *inference* (the general term for moving from one principle or belief to another, whether deductively or not). A good philosophy is systematic, which is to say only that the philosopher always has his or her eyes open for the possible implications and applications of ideas, the possible objections and problems and how to get around them. (Even those philosophers who are famous for their "aphoristic" styles depend upon systematic thinking to hold their ideas together.)

One way to criticize any philosophy is to show that it consists of unsound arguments, that the principles from which it begins are false or that its deductions are invalid. More seriously still, one can show that a philosophy is *inconsistent,* that one of its claims contradicts another. In the same way, one can show that a philosophy results in paradox, and consequently, must be thoroughly reexamined. (Philosophers have a special name for this sort of refutation; they call it a *reductio ad absurdum* argument, a "reduction to absurdity," in which a position is rejected because it results in a paradox.) And even when a philosophy does not contain outright inconsistencies or lead to paradoxes, it may be *incoherent*, such that the various claims have virtually nothing to do with each other, or mean very little, or can be interpreted only in an absurd way. A philosophy can be accused of *begging the question*, repeating as a supposed solution the very problem that it is attempting to resolve. An example of begging the question is the argument "Other people exist. I know because I've talked to them." And, worst of all, a philosophy can be accused of being silly or trivial, which is just about the most offensive thing that you can say, indicating that it is not even worth your time to investigate it further. It is much better to say something false but interesting rather than silly or trivial.

As you proceed with your course, you will have the opportunity to use most of these forms of criticism, not only on the great philosophers of the past but on your own thinking as well. You will find that philosophical criticism is a powerful tool in the arguments you have with your friends and the debates you carry on, whatever the topic. Most importantly, philosophy is a valuable aid to getting together your own thoughts about things, about the problems of philosophy which you will encounter in this book, and "life in general." For that is what philosophy is ultimately about.

GLOSSARY

abstract: a general consideration, independent of particular concerns or objects. For example, a philosopher may attempt to ascertain the nature of justice without particular reference to any concrete practical case.

argument: process of reasoning from one claim to another. An argument may, but need not be, directed against an explicit alternative. A philosophical argument does not require an opponent or a disagreement.

assumption: a principle taken for granted, without argument or proof.

autonomy: intellectual independence and freedom from authority; the presumed ability to determine the acceptability of one's own beliefs and actions.

axiom: a principle that is generally accepted from the beginning and so may be used without further debate as a starting point of argument.

begging the question: to put forth as the solution to a problem merely a restatement of the problem itself. For example, "Why do oysters cause me indigestion? Because they upset my stomach."

Cartesianism: concerning Descartes. In particular, concerning his philosophical method. (Descartes' followers are generally called "Cartesians" and their method "Cartesianism.") The Cartesian method is essentially a deductive method, as in geometry, starting with self-evident axioms and deducing the rest.

certainty: beyond doubt. But it is important to insist that certainty in the philosophical sense is more than the common psychological use of certain ("feeling certain"). One can feel certain and yet be wrong or foolish. One can be certain, in this philosophical sense, only if one can prove that the matter is beyond doubt, that no reasons for doubt could be raised.

coherence: logical connection. A statement by a witness in a courtroom coheres with other testimony and evidence when it fits in and follows from that other testimony and evidence. To say that a philosophy must be coherent is to say that its various principles must fit together in an orderly and logically agreeable fashion.

consistent: fitting together in an orderly logical way. Two principles are consistent if they do not contradict each other. A philosophy is consistent if none of its principles contradict each other.

contradiction: logical relation of two principles in which the truth of one requires the falsity of the other. A witness's statement in court contradicts other testimony if both statements cannot be true.

criterion: the test or standard according to which a judgment or an evaluation can be made. For example, a test for a substance being an acid is that it turns litmus paper red.

critical: thinking carefully; not necessarily nasty.

deduce: to reason from one principle to another in accord with accepted rules of inference. What is crucial to deduction or deductive argument is that the conclusion is guaranteed as much certainty as the premises. Deduction is sometimes defined more narrowly as the inference from a general premise to a particular conclusion by means of a syllogism: for example, from "All men are mammals" and "Socrates is a man" to "Socrates is a mammal." This is not what is meant by deduction in general, however, and it is not what Descartes intends by that term.

dialectic: argument through dialogue, disagreement, and successive revisions, out of which comes agreement.

doubt: lack of certainty; lack of reasons to believe and perhaps having reasons not to believe. It is important to distinguish doubt in this philosophical sense from doubt in the ordinary psychological sense. Mere personal uncertainty or distrust is not sufficient; there must be a demonstrable reason for doubt, that is, reasons for not accepting the beliefs in question.

Enlightenment: an important cultural and philosophical movement in the seventeenth and eighteenth centuries in Europe defined by a new confidence in human reason and individual autonomy. Some of the major figures of this movement were René Descartes, the metaphysician Baron Henri d'Holbach, the political philosopher Jean-Jacques Rousseau, and the political reformer-writer Voltaire in France. In Great Britain, Enlightment philosophers were John Locke and David Hume; in Germany Immanuel Kant.

first principles: those axioms and assumptions from which a philosophy begins. These must be solid and indisputable principles; they need not be those principles which one happens to first believe.

implication: one statement logically follows from another. Statements imply one another: we infer one from the other.

incoherent: lacking coherence; not fitting together in an orderly or logically agreeable fashion. Using fancy jargon which has no precise meaning may be a source of incoherence. So is a mere list of random beliefs, without any order or logic to hold them together. (They may even contradict each other as well.) An incoherent philosophy may be insightful and true in parts, but because it never coheres into a single system, it may well appear to be nonsense, or simply a jumble of words and phrases. In other cases, an incoherent philosophy may be one that makes no sense, whose terms are utter gibberish or whose principles are mere ramblings without intelligible connection or interpretation.

inconsistent: not compatible; contradictory. One might also say that a person's actions are inconsistent with his or her principles. People as well as other principles can be inconsistent with a principle.

inference: reasoning from one set of principles to another, as in an argument. Deductive inference is but a single kind of inference.

invalid: not valid; not correctly following agreed upon rules of inference in an argument. Always applied to arguments, not to statements.

logic: the study of the rules of valid inference and "rational argument." In general, a sense of order.

method: (sometimes, **methodology**) approach and strategy for resolving philosophical problems. For example, the appeal to experience, the appeal to divine revelation, the insistence upon mathematical logic, confidence in reason or trust in authority: all of these are aspects of philosophical methodology.

method of doubt: (or **methodological doubt**) Descartes' technique for discovering those principles of which we can be "perfectly certain"; namely, doubt everything, until you discover those principles which cannot be doubted.

modern philosophy: usually dated from Descartes, characterized by emphasis on individual autonomy and confidence in human reason and experience to ascertain what is true, what is good, and what is right.

paradox: an absurd conclusion drawn from seemingly acceptable premises. A self-contradiction that nevertheless seems impossible to reject. For example, suppose you try to help all and only those people who do not help themselves. That sounds reasonable enough. But then, do you help yourself? If you do help everyone, then you would also help yourself. But if you are helping only those people who don't help themselves, then you can't help yourself. But if you don't help yourself, then you aren't helping everyone who doesn't help themselves. That is a paradox.

premise: the principle or one of those principles upon which an argument is based. The starting point of an argument.

presupposition: a principle which is assumed as a precondition for whatever else one believes, which itself may remain unexamined and uncriticized throughout the argument. For example, a lawyer presupposes that the court aims at justice and has some idea what is just. It is the philosopher, not the lawyer, who challenges those claims.

proof: in a deductive argument, a proof is a sequence of steps, each according to an acceptable rule of inference, to the conclusion to be proved.

reason: the ability to think abstractly, to form arguments and make inferences. Sometimes referred to as a "faculty" of the human mind (a leftover from eighteenth century psychology). More specialized meanings will be discussed in later chapters.

reductio ad absurdum: a form of argument in which one refutes a statement by showing that it leads to absurdity.

reflection: to think about something, to "put it in perspective." We often do this with our beliefs and our emotions. For example, "This morning I was furious at you, but after reflecting on it at lunch, I decided that it was nothing to be angry about." One might say that philosophy is reflection about life and knowledge in general.

rule of inference: a generally accepted principle according to which one may infer one statement from another. (We have not yet said anything about the nature of these "generally acceptable" rules; for now, we have simply presupposed that some such rules are acceptable to everyone; for example, "if *either* A is true *or* B is true, but we know that B is false, then we can conclude that A is true.")

self-contradictory: a contradiction within one and the same statement or set of statements. What I say may contradict what you say; but what I say might also contradict something else that I said, in which case I am being self-contradictory. Moreover, in a few strange cases, my own statement may be self-contradictory; for example, "I do not exist."

self-evident: obvious without proof or argument. For Descartes, a "clear and distinct idea," one about which there could be no doubt and it is obvious that there could be no doubt.

skepticism: the philosophical belief that knowledge is not possible, that doubt will not be overcome by any valid arguments. A philosopher who holds this belief is called a skeptic. Again, skepticism is not mere personal doubt; it requires systematic doubt with reasons for that doubt.

sound: an argument whose premises are true and which is valid.

syllogism: a kind of deductive reasoning; the best known examples are those arguments of the form,

> All P's are Q's. (Major premise)
> S is a P. (Minor premise)
>
> ---
>
> *Therefore,* S is a Q. (Conclusion)

The major premise is a general claim, the minor premise is a specific statement.

system: an orderly formulation of principles (together with reasons, implications, evidence, methods, and presuppositions) which is comprehensive, consistent, and coherent and in which the various principles are interconnected as tightly as possible by logical implications.

trivial: obvious and not worth saying.

unsound: an argument whose premises are false, or which is invalid.

valid: an argument that correctly follows agreed upon rules of inference. Always applies to arguments, not statements.

PART ONE

some basic problems

1

REALITY:
ANCIENT VIEWS

Facts are only the shadows of truth.

Muhammad Ali

"THE WAY THE WORLD REALLY IS":
THE PRE-SOCRATICS

The beginning of philosophy, and a major step in the intellectual development of the Western world, was a seemingly odd claim made by the Greek philosopher Thales on the coast of Turkey sometime around 580 B.C. He said, quite simply, that the source of everything was water. The earth floats upon water, and it and all things on it are made of water. Aristotle later called his theory "childish." But it is one of the remarkable claims of the ancient world, not because it is so implausible (as his own students pointed out to him) but because it was the first recorded attempt to describe "the way the world really is," beyond all appearances and day-to-day opinions. Accordingly, Thales' theory marks the beginning of Western science as well as philosophy. He was the first thinker to break with common sense and offer a general theory about the ultimate nature of reality.

Thales was the first of a group of philosophers—or rather, the first of several groups of philosophers, scattered around the various Greek islands and the coasts of Asia Minor who lived in the sixth and fifth centuries B.C., just before the time of Socrates. Accordingly, they are called *Pre-Socratics*. Their opinions varied greatly. Between them, they developed a wide range of systematic views of the universe and the ultimate nature of reality. Unlike Socrates

25

and most later philosophers, they were not very concerned with questions of method. They went straight to the heart of the question, to the nature of the universe itself. And some of them, as we shall see, came strikingly close to our modern scientific conceptions.

We are all aware that the way the world really is may not correspond to our everyday views of the world, the way it seems to be. For example, we casually talk of "sunrises" and "sunsets," and surely it does seem as if the sun goes "up" and "down," while we and our earth stay in place. It took several thousand years for people in general to recognize that, despite appearances, our earth actually moves around the sun. We now accept that without question, even if there is little in our everyday experience to support it. Similarly, consider the chair on which you are sitting: Does it seem to you that it is composed mostly of empty space and tiny electrically charged colorless particles whirling about at fantastic speeds? Of course not, but modern science has taught you that "solid" objects are indeed made up of just such spaces and particles. The world is not as it seems. And the beginnings of both philosophy and science were the first attempts of men and women to see beyond their "common sense" views of things and try to find the reality behind them.

What is the way the world really is? How would you answer that question? Very likely, you will appeal to the authority of modern science, and that is probably a reasonable beginning. But you know that the "science" of one generation is seen as the superstitions of another. (Once people believed that the earth was flat.) And you have probably, at least once in your school career, caught one of the "authorities"—perhaps a teacher, perhaps even a noted scientist—in a mistake. Can we simply accept what scientists tell us without question, any more than Descartes could accept the teachings of his teachers without question? Have you ever examined the evidence for the theory that the earth goes around the sun? If not, why should you believe it? Or, to take a very different example, scientists are generally agreed that some version of Darwin's theory of evolution is true. Does that mean that you have to believe it? There are many people who do not, because it seems to contradict the story of creation in the Bible. And so you have to decide which to believe. Even within science there are always disagreements and debates. There are different theories to answer the same questions, and you have to decide. Which are you to believe? You can always sit back and wait a few years or centuries until the problem is resolved, but if you can do that, you couldn't have been very interested in the problem to begin with. And, with some of the problems we shall be dealing with, you will agree that one can't simply wait around for somebody else's answer.

Your view of reality is influenced by modern science but it is also influenced by 2500 years of Western philosophy, even if you've never studied it before. We can say, with some confidence, that we know much more about the world than the ancient Greek philosophers. But we must not be too confident. Not only are there still many scientific problems unsolved, there are and always will be conflicting views of how we are to see our world in more general terms. How much faith should we have in religion? How much should we see the world as a world of people and how much as a world of physical objects? How much should we accept "common sense" (which changes all the time) and how much should we indulge in scientific and philosophical speculation (which change all the time also)? How far-fetched will we allow our views of the world to become? And how closely should we stick to the nitty-gritty facts of everyday life? These are questions which we all have tried to answer, whether in serious philosophical, scientific, or religious discussions or just in casual conversations and "bull sessions" with friends.

The first Greek philosophers did not have the advantage of either our scientific sophistication or a long history of philosophical thinking to give them support. Thus, Thales' answer, that ultimate reality is water, should not surprise us nearly so much as the fact that he attempted such a theory at all. Indeed, we should be impressed by the fact that he even asked the question, "What is the world really like?" because, as far as we know, no one had attempted to ask such a question before him. Of course, there were lots of opinions about reality; all of the ancient religions had them. But Thales' approach was different. He was not willing to accept the opinions and mythologies that had been handed down for generations. He insisted, instead, on observing the world for himself, in thinking out his own answer, and in discussing it with his friends and neighbors, many of whom, no doubt, thought that he was slightly peculiar. (It is also said, however, that his cosmic speculations helped him to make a fortune in the olive oil business. No doubt his neighbors respected that.)

The idea that everything was water did not satisfy Thales' friends and students. They appreciated his attempt to find the "One Reality," but they thought that it must be something else. Thales' first student, named Anaximander, argued against his teacher that some things, for example, the dry, dusty cliffs of Asia Minor, could not possibly be made of water, which was naturally wet and never dry. Anaximander was the first recorded student to talk back to his teacher (which in philosophy, unlike most other subjects, is considered a virtue rather than a discourtesy). Thales had made the first gigantic step, rejecting the "obvious" answers of common sense and trying to find out "the way the world really is." But notice that Thales' answer to that question still appeals to a common sense ingredient, water, which is so familiar to us. And Thales' defense of his thesis also depended on some very commonsensical claims: for example, the idea that, if you dig deep enough into the earth, you will eventually hit water.

Once Thales had made the break with common sense and said that the way the world really is need not be at all like the way it seems to us, it was no longer necessary to suppose that reality was anything like our experiences. Anaximander, consequently, argued that ultimate reality could not be composed of any of the then known elements—earth, air, fire or water—since these were each so different from the others. They might be mixed together, as when earth and water are mixed to make mud or clay, but it made no sense to suppose that any of them might really be made up of any of the others. So Anaximander suggested that the ultimate nature of reality was something else—let us simply call it "primordial stuff"—which is not like anything we could ever experience. This notion of "stuff" was a second major step in philosophy and science. Today, we feel comfortable with the idea that things are made of "stuff" (atoms and molecules) which we never experience in everyday life. But in the ancient world, this suggestion must have seemed extremely exciting.

Anaximander's student, Anaximenes, thought his teacher's notion of "stuff" was too mysterious, but he also rejected Thales' theory and replaced it with the idea that air is the basic "stuff" and makes up the other elements and the various things of the world by becoming thicker and thinner. (Think of steam condensing to form water, and then ice.) Heraclitus, another philosopher of the same period, defended the idea that fire was the fundamental "stuff" of the universe, arguing that the heat of living organisms and the constant changing of the things of this world could best be explained as manifestations of this fascinating element. (Think of a flame, constantly active, consuming itself and always changing.) Heraclitus' view of the importance of change brought him to the view of reality itself as flux, thereby placing him in opposition to the established notion that reality is unchanging. (The famous example, "you can't step twice into the same river," is often attributed to him because of his belief in reality as flux.) Heraclitus' view of reality was to have a profound effect on the philosophers of the nineteenth and twentieth centuries.

The attempt to reduce all of the varied things in the world to one kind of thing is called *monism*. It is the search for ultimate reality, which might be very different from the appearance of everyday life, that has motivated philosophy and science for two and a half thousand years. So the debate began: was the world really made of water? or air? or fire? or perhaps some other kind of "stuff" that we could never experience? Today, the debate continues: is everything made up of matter, or energy, or matter-energy? Are there basic particles that cannot be reduced to anything else? Scientists once thought that atoms were such particles; then they discovered electrons, protons, and neutrons that made up atoms. And since then, they have discovered dozens of other particles, and today they are debating a mysterious particle called the quark, which physicists now think may provide the ultimate answer to Thales' ancient question. But notice that all of these views are strictly physical. That is, they are concerned about basic questions of what we now call physics and chemistry, concerned about the material "stuff" of which all things are composed. This was true of Thales; and it is still true of modern "quark" theorists. Accordingly, the philosophies of all of these thinkers can be called *materialism,* the view that reality is ultimately composed of some kind of material "stuff." (In this context, "materialism" does not mean concern about the material things in life—money, cars, jewelry, or getting a new garbage disposal every year.)

Not all materialists thought that there was only one ultimate component of reality. A number of philosophers appeared in the ancient world who were *pluralists,* that is, they believed that more than one basic "stuff" made up the universe. The best known of the pluralists was Democritus, who suggested that the universe was made up of tiny bits of "stuff" which he called *atoms*. These combined together to form the many different things of the world. Other pluralists stressed the idea that these different bits of "stuff" were very different in kind as well, so that the bits of stuff that composed water, for example, would be very different from the bits of "stuff" that composed fire. You can appreciate how modern these are, given our current ideas in chemistry and physics. These ancient Greek issues and answers have not become obsolete; they have changed and become more refined. Some have been more in favor at one time and others at other times. But they are still very much with us.

If you think like a physical scientist, the idea that the universe is made up of some kind of material "stuff" sounds very plausible. In fact, you might wonder, what else could it be made of? Consider this; there are some things in the universe that could not plausibly be made of material "stuff." For example, what about your thoughts and feelings? Are they simply bits of matter, or are they composed of some entirely different kind of "stuff," perhaps some kind of mental or spiritual "stuff?" Heraclitus, who had argued that everything was made of fire, was already groping for some such conception of *immaterial* "stuff," something not material, but rather spiritual or non-physical. ("Immaterial," in a philosophical context, does not mean "unimportant.") Accordingly, he introduced the idea that, underlying all of the things and the changes in the universe is a *logos,* which might be called a logic. Thought had a role in the universe as well as material "stuff," and Heraclitus tried to argue that "thought is Being," in other words, that everything is composed of thought as well as of matter. People had (and still have) a very difficult time trying to understand what he meant by this, but it is at least clear what he was trying to do. Heraclitus was concerned to recognize something that had previously been neglected, namely, thought, which was not just another kind of material "stuff."

Another Pre-Socratic philosopher, Pythagoras, also attempted to defend a view of the world which did not depend upon the usual kinds of material "stuff." He taught that numbers were the real nature of things, and he taught his students to worship the mathematical order of the universe. (The term, "the music of the spheres," was part of his teachings.) Unlike the other Pre-Socratic philosophers we have met, Pythagoras was much more of a religious figure. He was a mystic and the leader of a powerful underground cult which believed in reincarnation and the immortality of the soul. In accordance with this religion, he gave the mind and the soul a much more prominent place in his view of the world than other Pre-Socratic philosophers. But despite the sometimes mysterious views of Pythagoras and his cult, he is still recognized as one of the most important thinkers of the ancient world. Together with Heraclitus, he was one of the first to defend a view of reality which depended more on logic and thought than purely material "stuff." (The theorem that you learned in high school, the "Pythagorean theorem," is named after him.)

These Ancient attempts to find out the way the world really is should not be thought of as clumsy attempts to find out the things that modern scientists now know. All the theories of "stuff" were indeed the precursors of modern physics and chemistry. But you can already see that these philosophers were also concerned with what we would call the mental and the spiritual aspects of the world. Even the most materialistic among them, for example, Thales, did not believe that the basic matter of the universe was cold and lifeless "stuff." All of these philosophers believed that the universe itself, as well as everything in it, was alive in at least some limited way. That is, they all believed in *animism,* the doctrine that everything, volcanoes and stones as well as elephants and flowers, are living things. Furthermore, animism has not disappeared because of the advances of science, though in certain periods (like our own) it has been treated less favorably than in others. But even in the nineteenth century, when physics and chemistry were making some of their most spectacular advances, animism was an extremely popular doctrine, even among scientists. And there are still a great many people today who accept a modified version of it. So don't think that the problems discussed by these ancient philosophers have been solved by science or simply gone away. The place of mind and spirit in a world of matter and energy is still among our basic problems. The ancient search for the way the world really is is still very much with us.

There were a great many philosophers in the "Pre-Socratic" period, but it is not our purpose to provide a history of them. We just want to get some idea of the questions and answers that have defined philosophy since ancient times. But before we can understand the truly magnificent breakthrough that comes with Socrates, Plato, and Aristotle, it is necessary to see how these earlier theories ran into troubles that they could not solve. First, what had been presupposed by everyone we have discussed is the idea that reality, whatever it is, must be eternal and unchanging. For Thales, water was the eternal and unchanging element, although the forms it took might be very different and change constantly. For Democritus, atoms were unchanging and indestructible, although the things they combined to compose might change and be destroyed. For Pythagoras, numbers, unlike the particular things in the world, were eternal and unchanging. Only Heraclitus seemed to have some reservations about this presupposition; because he believed that the ultimate nature of reality was fire, he appreciated the importance of change, as in the flickering of a flame. But even he insisted that the *logos* or logic that underlay the constant changes in the world was itself eternal and unchanging. And we shall see that this presupposition, that reality cannot change, however much things seem to change, will remain one of the most important beliefs in Western culture. (In Christianity, for example, the eternal and unchanging nature of God and the human soul are built upon the same philosophical foundation.)

But this insistence on the eternal and unchanging nature of ultimate reality raises a serious problem. The philosopher who brought it out most clearly was the Pre-Socratic Parmenides. He was an accomplished mathematician who thought far more of the eternal certainties of arithmetic than he did of the transient things of everyday experience. He too was a monist and believed in a single reality. Because he shared the assumption that reality must be eternal and unchanging, he came to an astonishing conclusion: this world, the world of our experience, cannot be real! Our world is constantly changing: objects are created and destroyed, organisms live and die, people grow old, change their appearance and move from place to place. And so this world, with all its changes, could not be the real world, nor could we ever know the real world, since we are as inconstant and changing as the other things of our experience. We are, at best, living in a kind of illusion, not in reality at all!

Ever since Thales, the main achievement of philosophy had been to break away from common sense and ordinary experience in order to find out the way the world really is. But now we can see how far away from common sense and ordinary experience this breaking away can lead us. In Parmenides' philosophy, if the results of his logic are incompatible with common sense and ordinary experience, so much the worse for common sense and ordinary experience. The followers of Parmenides, particularly the mathematician Zeno, carried these bizarre conclusions even further. Zeno argued, by means of a series of famous paradoxes, that all motion and change was nothing but an illusion.

The following generation of philosophers, who called themselves *Sophists* (who have ever since given "sophistry" a bad name because of their rhetorical debating tricks) went even further. They argued that there was no reality, and even if there were, we couldn't know anything about it anyway. (So argued the sophist Gorgias.) And the teaching of Protagoras, another sophist, is still well-known today; he said, "Man is the measure of all things," which means that there is no reality except for what we take to be reality. Wandering around the countryside, giving lessons in debating and rhetoric (the ancient equivalent of law school) the sophists used the accomplishments of the earlier philosophers to ridicule philosophy and to make fools of practically everyone. That is, until they met Socrates, whose arguments against them changed the course of philosophy and Western thought in general.

The second difficulty ancient theories ran into was this: all of the Pre-Socratic philosophers, including Heraclitus and Pythagoras, gave primary emphasis to material things and the relations between them; they gave only secondary and passing attention to immaterial objects, thoughts and numbers, for example. They were groping for a way of dealing with them, but their attempts were never satisfactory. Pythagoras did not view numbers as immaterial objects but only as aspects of material objects. It would remain for Socrates and his student Plato, in the fourth century B.C., to finally give the immaterial aspects of reality their full recognition.

These various theories about the way the world really is have a proper name. They are called *metaphysical doctrines,* and the attempt to develop such doctrines, in which we have been taking part for these past pages, is called *metaphysics.* The business of metaphysics is to ask and attempt to answer the most basic questions about the universe, its composition and the "stuff" of which it is composed, the role of man and mind and the nature of the im-

material aspects of the universe as well as its physical nature. But now that we
are about to discuss metaphysics in its maturity, with Plato and Aristotle, let
us also give "stuff" its proper name. It is called (first by Aristotle) *substance.*
Accordingly, metaphysics, the study of "the way the world really is," begins with
the answers to a series of questions about substance and how it is manifested in
particular things (such as people and trees).

1. How many substances are there? (Monism versus pluralism.)
2. What are they? (Water, air, fire, numbers, something unknown, minds,
   spirit, atoms?)
3. How are individual things composed? (And how do we tell them apart,
   identify them, re-identify them?)
4. How do different things and (if there is more than one) different substances interact?
5. How did substance come into being? (Created by God? or has it always
   been there?)
6. Are substances "in" space and time? Are space and time substances? (If
   not, what are they?)

The first four questions are usually referred to as *ontology,* the study of
being as such. The last questions are referred to as *cosmology,* the study of the
universe. (For the Pre-Socratics, these were the same.) Cosmological questions
are necessarily shared between philosophers, physicists, and astronomers, and it
is impossible for us to give them more than a cursory review within a strictly
philosophical book. Ontology, on the other hand, is still considered by many
philosophers to be the heart of metaphysics. It is with ontology, therefore, that
this chapter will be primarily concerned.

[Ontology and cosmology are not all there is to metaphysics. A further set
of problems must be singled out because they are of particular personal importance to us. (The division follows that of the great German metaphysician,
Immanuel Kant, whom we shall meet in later chapters.) Kant summarized
this second set of problems with the abbreviation "God, Freedom, and Immortality," problems which "the human mind will never give up." The
existence of God is both an ontological problem (God has been identified as the
"substance of the universe") and a cosmological problem (God as creator; God
as eternal). But the existence and nature of God quite obviously deserves
separate study, however intricately bound up that may be with other ontological
and cosmological problems. (We shall provide this separate study in Chapter
7.) The problem of the existence of the human soul is often tied to religious
questions, particularly in the Christian tradition (which is the context Kant
intended). But it is more than this: we shall see how Plato used the concept of
an immortal soul to explain our ability to know eternal truths. In a more
secular and transient context, there is the metaphysical problem of the relationship between mind and body (Ch. 9). Finally, the question of metaphysical
freedom (the only one of these questions not deeply considered by any of the
Greek philosophers) needs to be examined in detail before we can move on to
any more "practical" questions involving human action. (Ch. 10)]

TWO KINDS OF METAPHYSICS:
PLATO AND ARISTOTLE

The term "metaphysics" is relatively new (from about 70 B.C. or so), but it is generally agreed that the first great systematic metaphysicians were Plato (428–348 B.C.) and Aristotle (384–322 B.C.). Plato had been a student of Socrates and his most faithful recorder. (Almost all that we have of Socrates' teachings comes to us through Plato.) Yet Socrates was a moralist, not a metaphysician, and most of the metaphysical doctrines that Plato discusses using Socrates as his mouthpiece are probably Plato's own. Aristotle never tried to be a faithful disciple of Plato, and he turned into his teacher's most famous and harshest critic. It has been said of each of them that the history of philosophy is nothing more than a series of footnotes to their brilliant dialogues and treatises of 2400 years ago.

Metaphysics is what Aristotle called "first philosophy," the investigation of "Being as Being," or ultimate reality. What does it mean for something to exist? What is it for something to change? What makes one thing like another? Sometimes, these questions, or at least the answers to these questions, are presupposed in our everyday thinking, whether we actually think about them or not. For example, we "naturally" believe that a tree continues to exist when we aren't looking at it. Why do we believe this? But even when such questions are the creations of philosophers, they outline views of the world which nonphilosophers share with them. The problem is, as we shall see, that people disagree violently about these issues, even from one generation to the next (for example, from Plato to Aristotle). And what seems to be clear and obvious to one philosopher will seem obscure, merely metaphorical or downright paradoxical to another. But as we watch the warring history of metaphysics, we too should be humbled by it, for it cannot be that all of those geniuses got it wrong while we now have it right. We too, whether explicitly or not, have metaphysical views, and we too may have to be ready to give them up as we think more about them and face further arguments.

With Plato and Aristotle, metaphysics becomes a cautious, consuming enterprise, producing monumental systems of many volumes which require a lifetime of study to master. All we can do here is to present a thumbnail sketch, with some brief selections, of Plato's metaphysics and a very brief introduction to Aristotle's philosophy, which seems, at first glance, to be primarily a refutation of Plato. But like so many philosophers who seem to be attacking each other from completely opposed viewpoints, Plato and Aristotle have much in common. Both attempted to resolve the problems they inherited from the Pre-Socratics: to find the ultimate "stuff" of the universe, to understand what was eternal and unchanging, to understand change, and to show that the universe as a whole was intelligible to human understanding. Plato, following Parmenides and the other Pre-Socratics who trusted their reason more than common sense, gave reason a grander position in human life and in the universe in general than it had ever received before. Aristotle, although he too defended reason, insisted that philosophy return to common sense and have a respect for ordinary opinion, which many of the Greek philosophers seemed to have lost.

Plato

The most important single feature of Plato's philosophy is his emphasis on the importance of *Ideas*. But Plato does not mean "ideas" in a person's mind. He means *ideal forms*, or perfect examples—the perfect circle, perfect beauty. Plato's Ideas are also referred to as *Forms*, and we shall use both terms. Ideas or Forms are the ultimate "stuff" of reality. Things change, people grow old and die, but Ideas are eternal and unchanging. Thus Plato could agree with Heraclitus that the world of our experience is constantly changing; but he could also agree with Parmenides, who insisted that the real world, the eternal and unchanging world, was not the same as the world of our experience. According to Plato, it was a *world of forms*, a world of eternal truths. There were, in other words, two worlds, (1) the world in which we live, a world of constant change or a *world of becoming*, and (2) a world of ideas, an unchanging world, the real world or the *world of being*. Our only access to this latter world, the real world, was through our reason, our capacity for intellectual thought. Plato's "two-worlds" view was to have a direct and obvious influence on Christian theology. It would also affect philosophers, mathematicians, mystics, poets, and romantics of all kinds until the present day. But in his own time, it had a more immediate importance; it allowed him to reconcile Heraclitus and Parmenides, to resolve the problems of the Pre-Socratics, and to finally give ideas their proper place in human thought.

For Plato, it is the world of ideas, the world of being, that is real. But this is not to say (as Parmenides had argued) that the world we live in, the world of becoming, is unreal. It is, however, less than real, not an illusion, but without those qualities of eternity and necessity that were the marks of true reality. This might seem like a verbal trick; it is not. The idea of a hierarchy of realities was already familiar in religions that antedated Plato's philosophy by centuries. And we still use such notions in our own thinking, comparing, for example, the world of film and novels to "the real world," or the dreary humdrum of workingday life to "really living." But the best illustration of Plato's two-worlds view is his own, which he offers us in a parable, called "the Myth of the Cave":

> SOCRATES. Here is a parable to illustrate the degrees in which our nature may
> be enlightened or unenlightened. Imagine the condition of men living in
> a sort of cavernous chamber underground, with an entrance open to the
> light and a long passage all down the cave. Here they have been from
> childhood, chained by the leg and also by the neck, so that they cannot
> move and can see only what is in front of them, because the chains will
> not let them turn their heads. At some distance higher up is the light
> of a fire burning behind them; and between the prisoners and the fire is
> a track with a parapet built along it, like the screen at a puppet-show,

which hides the performers while they show their puppets over the top.

GLAUCON. I see.

SOCRATES. Now behind this parapet imagine persons carrying along various artificial objects, including figures of men and animals in wood or stone or other materials, which project above the parapet. Naturally, some of these persons will be talking, others silent.

GLAUCON. It is a strange picture, and a strange sort of prisoners.

SOCRATES. Like ourselves, for in the first place prisoners so confined would have seen nothing of themselves or of one another, except the shadows thrown by the fire-light on the wall of the Cave facing them, would they?

GLAUCON. Not if all their lives they had been prevented from moving their heads.

SOCRATES. And they would have seen as little of the objects carried past.

GLAUCON. Of course.

SOCRATES. Now, if they could talk to one another, would they not suppose that their words referred only to those passing shadows which they saw?

GLAUCON. Necessarily.

SOCRATES. And suppose their prison had an echo from the wall facing them? When one of the people crossing behind them spoke, they could only suppose that the sound came from the shadow passing before their eyes.

GLAUCON. No doubt.

SOCRATES. In every way, then, such prisoners would recognize as reality nothing but the shadows of those artificial objects.

GLAUCON. Inevitably.

SOCRATES. Now consider what would happen if their release from the chains and the healing of their unwisdom should come about in this way. Suppose one of them set free and forced suddenly to stand up, turn his head, and walk with eyes lifted to the light; all these movements would be painful, and he would be too dazzled to make out the objects whose shadows he had been used to see. What do you think he would say, if someone told him that what he had formerly seen was meaningless illusion, but now, being somewhat nearer to reality and turned towards more real objects, he was getting a truer view? Suppose further that he were shown the various objects being carried by and were made to say, in reply to questions, what each of them was. Would he not be perplexed and believe the objects now shown him to be not so real as what he formerly saw?

GLAUCON. Yes, not nearly so real.

SOCRATES. And if he were forced to look at the fire-light itself, would not his eyes ache, so that he would try to escape and turn back to the things which he could see distinctly, convinced that they really were clearer than these other objects now being shown to him?

GLAUCON. Yes.

SOCRATES. And suppose someone were to drag him away forcibly up the steep and rugged ascent and not let him go until he had hauled him out into the sunlight, would he not suffer pain and vexation at such treatment, and, when he had come out into the light, find his eyes so full of its radiance that he could not see a single one of the things that he was now told were real?

GLAUCON. Certainly he would not see them all at once.

SOCRATES. He would need, then, to grow accustomed before he could see things in that upper world. At first it would be easiest to make out shadows, and then the images of men and things reflected in water, and later on the things themselves. After that, it would be easier to watch the heavenly bodies and the sky itself by night, looking at the light of the moon and stars rather than the Sun and the Sun's light in the day-time.

GLAUCON. Yes, surely.

SOCRATES. Last of all, he would be able to look at the Sun and contemplate its nature, not as it appears when reflected in water or any alien medium, but as it is in itself in its own domain.

GLAUCON. No doubt.

SOCRATES. And now he would begin to draw the conclusion that it is the Sun that produces the seasons and the course of the year and controls everything in the visible world, and moreover is in a way the cause of all that he and his companions used to see.

GLAUCON. Clearly he would come at last to that conclusion.

SOCRATES. Then if he called to mind his fellow prisoners and what passed for wisdom in his former dwelling-place, he would surely think himself happy in the change and be sorry for them. They may have had a practice of honouring and commending one another, with prizes for the man who had the keenest eye for the passing shadows and the best memory for the order in which they followed or accompanied one another, so that he could make a good guess as to which was going to come next. Would our released prisoner be likely to covet those prizes or to envy the men exalted to honour and power in the Cave? Would he not feel like Homer's Achilles, that he would far sooner 'be on earth as a hired servant in the house of a landless man' or endure anything rather than go back to his old beliefs and live in the old way?

GLAUCON. Yes, he would prefer any fate to such a life.

SOCRATES. Now imagine what would happen if he went down again to take his former seat in the Cave. Coming suddenly out of the sunlight, his eyes would be filled with darkness. He might be required once more to deliver his opinion on those shadows, in competition with the prisoners who had never been released, while his eyesight was still dim and un-steady; and it might take some time to become used to the darkness. They would laugh at him and say that he had gone up only to come back with his sight ruined; it was worth no one's while even to attempt the ascent. If they could lay hands on the man who was trying to set them free and lead them up, they would kill him.

GLAUCON. Yes, they would.

SOCRATES. Every feature in this parable, my dear Glaucon, is meant to fit our earlier analysis. The prison dwelling corresponds to the region revealed to us through the sense of sight, and the fire-light within it to the power of the Sun. The ascent to see the things in the upper world you may take as standing for the upward journey of the soul into the region of the intelligible; then you will be in possession of what I surmise, since that is what you wish to be told. Heaven knows whether it is true; but this, at any rate, is how it appears to me. In the world of knowledge, the last thing to be perceived and only with great difficulty is the essential Form of Goodness. Once it is perceived, the conclusion must follow that, for all things, this is the cause of whatever is right and good; in the visible world it gives birth to light and to the lord of light, while it is itself sovereign in the intelligible world and the parent of intelligence and truth. Without having had a vision of this Form no one can act with wisdom, either in his own life or in matters of state.

GLAUCON. So far as I can understand, I share your belief.

SOCRATES. Then you may also agree that it is no wonder if those who have reached this height are reluctant to manage the affairs of men. Their souls long to spend all their time in that upper world—naturally enough, if here once more our parable holds true. Nor, again, is it at all strange that one who comes from the contemplation of divine things to the miseries of human life should appear awkward and ridiculous when, with eyes still dazed and not yet accustomed to the darkness, he is compelled, in a law-court or elsewhere, to dispute about the shadows of justice or the images that cast those shadows, and to wrangle over the notions of what is right in the minds of men who have never beheld Justice itself.

GLAUCON. It is not at all strange.

SOCRATES. No; a sensible man will remember that the eyes may be confused in two ways—by a change from light to darkness or from darkness to light; and he will recognize that the same thing happens to the soul. When he sees it troubled and unable to discern anything clearly, instead of laughing thoughtlessly, he will ask whether, coming from a brighter existence, its unaccustomed vision is obscured by the darkness, in which case he will think its condition enviable and its life a happy one; or whether, emerging from the depths of ignorance, it is dazzled by excess of light. If so, he will rather feel sorry for it; or, if he were inclined to laugh, that would be less ridiculous than to laugh at the soul which has come down from the light.

GLAUCON. That is a fair statement.

SOCRATES. If this is true, then, we must conclude that education is not what it is said to be by some, who profess to put knowledge into a soul which does not possess it, as if they could put sight into blind eyes. On the contrary, our own account signifies that the soul of every man does possess the power of learning the truth and the organ to see it with; and that, just as one might have to turn the whole body round in order that the eye should see light instead of darkness, so the entire soul must be turned away from this changing world, until its eye can bear to contemplate reality and that supreme splendour which we have called the Good. Hence there may well be an art whose aim would be to effect this very thing, the conversion of the soul, in the readiest way; not to put the power of sight into the soul's eye, which already has it, but to ensure that, instead of looking in the wrong direction, it is turned the way it ought to be.[1]

---

[1] Plato, *The Republic,* BK. VII, trans. Francis M. Cornford (Oxford: Oxford University Press, 1941).

Our world is like a set of shadows of the real world; that does not make it an illusion, but it does make it a mere imitation of the bright originals. Notice too, the savior-like role of the philosopher that Plato is setting up here. (His famous argument that philosophers should be kings, and kings philosophers, follows just after this.) Like Pythagoras, Plato believed that knowledge of pure Forms, knowledge of the world of "Being," is a person's only hope for salvation and the "good life."

Socrates had taught his students, Plato among them, that the truth, if we can know it at all, must be in us. Plato (using his teacher as his literary spokesman) gives this revelation a new twist. It begins with a puzzle. How is it possible to learn anything? If we don't already know it, how will we recognize it when we find it? And if we already do know it, it makes no sense to say that we "learn it." Now this puzzle sounds like nonsense if we think only of examples such as "What is the beer consumption rate in Omaha, Nebraska?" To answer such questions, obviously we can't simply "look into ourselves"; we have to go out into the world and get information. But Plato insists that he is after much bigger game than "information;" he wants Knowledge (with a capital K), knowledge of reality, to which we have access only through thinking. That world, unlike the world of change and "information" in which we live, is characterized by the fact that everything in it is eternal and necessary. In this eternal world, reality is not discoverable merely through observation and experience. For example, consider the simple truth, $2 + 2 = 4$; it never changes, no experience is necessary to know it; it is one of those eternal truths that deserves its place in Plato's world of Being. But then how do we know it? How can it already be "in us"?

The second principle of Plato's metaphysics, our bridge between the two worlds, is the immortality and immateriality of the human soul. Our souls contain knowledge of the world of Being which is already in us at birth. Such knowledge and ideas are called *innate*, "born into us." Experience only triggers them off and allows us to "remember" them. Here is the extravagant answer to Plato's puzzle, "How is it possible to learn a truth about the world of Being?" The answer is: we already "know" it; it's just a matter of recalling it. Consider his famous proof of this second doctrine in his dialogue, *Meno:*

> MENO. But how will you look for something when you don't in the least know what it is? How on earth are you going to set up something you don't know as the object of your search? To put it another way, even if you come right up against it, how will you know that what you have found is the thing you didn't know?
>
> SOCRATES. I know what you mean. Do you realize that what you are bringing up is the trick argument that a man cannot try to discover either what he knows or what he does not know? He would not seek what he knows, for since he knows it there is no need of the inquiry, nor what he does not know, for in that case he does not even know what he is to look for.
>
> MENO. Well, do you think it a good argument?
>
> SOCRATES. No.

MENO. Can you explain how it fails?

SOCRATES. I can. . . . Those who tell it are priests and priestesses of the sort who make it their business to be able to account for the functions which they perform. Pindar speaks of it too, and many another of the poets who are divinely inspired. What they say is this—see whether you think they are speaking the truth. They say that the soul of man is immortal: at one time it comes to an end—that which is called death—and at another is born again, but is never finally exterminated. . . .

Thus the soul, since it is immortal and has been born many times, and has seen all things both here and in the other world, has learned everything that is. So we need not be surprised if it can recall the knowledge of virtue or anything else which, as we see, it once possessed. All nature is akin, and the soul has learned everything, so that when a man has recalled a single piece of knowledge—*learned* it, in ordinary language—there is no reason why he should not find out all the rest, if he keeps a stout heart and does not grow weary of the search: for seeking and learning are in fact nothing but recollection.

We ought not then to be led astray by the contentious argument you quoted. It would make us lazy, and is music in the ears of weaklings. The other doctrine produces energetic seekers after knowledge. . . .

MENO. I see, Socrates. But what do you mean when you say that we don't learn anything, but that what we call learning is recollection? Can you teach me that it is so?

SOCRATES. I have just said that you're a rascal, and now you ask me if I can teach you, when I say there is no such thing as teaching, only recollection. Evidently you want to catch me contradicting myself straight away.

MENO. No, honestly, Socrates, I wasn't thinking of that. It was just habit. If you can in any way make clear to me that what you say is true, please do.

SOCRATES. It isn't an easy thing, but still I should like to do what I can since you ask me. I see you have a large number of retainers here. Call one of them, anyone you like, and I will use him to demonstrate it to you.

MENO. Certainly. (*To a slave-boy.*) Come here.

SOCRATES. He is a Greek and speaks our language?

MENO. Indeed yes—born and bred in the house.

SOCRATES. Listen carefully then, and see whether it seems to you that he is learning from me or simply being reminded.

MENO. I will.

SOCRATES. Now boy, you know that a square is a figure like this? (*Socrates begins to draw figures in the sand at his feet. He points to the square* ABCD.)

BOY. Yes.

SOCRATES. It has all these four sides equal?

BOY. Yes.

SOCRATES. And these lines which go through the middle of it are also equal? (The lines EF, GH.)

BOY. Yes.

SOCRATES. Such a figure could be either larger or smaller, could it not?

BOY. Yes.

SOCRATES. Now if this side is two feet long, and this side the same, how many

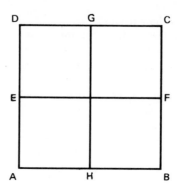

feet will the whole be? Put it this way. If it were two feet in this direction and only one in that, must not the area be two feet taken once?

BOY. Yes.

SOCRATES. But since it is two feet this way also, does it not become twice two feet?

BOY. Yes.

SOCRATES. And how many feet is twice two? Work it out and tell me.

BOY. Four.

SOCRATES. Now could one draw another figure double the size of this, but similar, that is, with all its sides equal like this one?

BOY. Yes.

SOCRATES. How many feet will its area be?

BOY. Eight.

SOCRATES. Now then, try to tell me how long each of its sides will be. The present figure has a side of two feet. What will be the side of the double-sized one?

BOY. It will be double, Socrates, obviously.

SOCRATES. You see, Meno, that I am not teaching him anything, only asking. Now he thinks he knows the length of the side of the eight-feet square.

MENO. Yes.

SOCRATES. But does he?

MENO. Certainly not.

SOCRATES. He thinks it is twice the length of the other.

MENO. Yes.

SOCRATES. Now watch how he recollects things in order—the proper way to recollect.

You say that the side of double length produces the double-sized figure? Like this I mean, not long this way and short that. It must be equal on all sides like the first figure, only twice its size, that is eight feet. Think a moment whether you still expect to get it from doubling the side.

BOY. Yes, I do.

SOCRATES. Well now, shall we have a line double the length of this (AB) if we add another the same length at this end (BJ)?

BOY. Yes.

SOCRATES. It is on this line then, according to you, that we shall make the eight-feet square, by taking four of the same length?

BOY. Yes.

SOCRATES. Let us draw in four equal lines (*i.e. counting* AJ, *and adding* JK, KL, *and* LA *made complete by drawing in its second half* LD), using the first as a base. Does this not give us what you call the eight-feet figure?

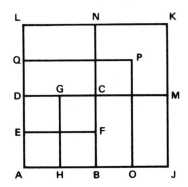

BOY. Certainly.

SOCRATES. But does it contain these four squares, each equal to the original four-feet one?

> (*Socrates has drawn in the lines* CM, CN *to complete the squares that he wishes to point out.*)

BOY. Yes.

SOCRATES. How big is it then? Won't it be four times as big?

BOY. Of course.

SOCRATES. And is four times the same as twice?

BOY. Of course not.

SOCRATES. So doubling the side has given us not a double but a fourfold figure?

BOY. True.

SOCRATES. And four times four are sixteen, are they not?

BOY. Yes.

SOCRATES. Then how big is the side of the eight-feet figure? This one has given us four times the original area, hasn't it?

BOY. Yes.

SOCRATES. And a side half the length gave us a square of four feet?

BOY. Yes.

SOCRATES. Good. And isn't a square of eight feet double this one and half that?

BOY. Yes.

SOCRATES. Will it not have a side greater than this one but less than that?

BOY. I think it will.

SOCRATES. Right. Always answer what you think. Now tell me: was not this side two feet long, and this one four?

BOY. Yes.

SOCRATES. Then the side of the eight-feet figure must be longer than two feet but shorter than four?

BOY. It must.

SOCRATES. Try to say how long you think it is.

BOY. Three feet.

SOCRATES. If so, shall we add half of this bit (BO, *half of* BJ) and make it three feet? Here are two, and this is one, and on this side similarly we have two plus one; and here is the figure you want.

(*Socrates completes the square* AOPQ.)

BOY. Yes.

SOCRATES. If it is three feet this way and three that, will the whole area be three times three feet?

BOY. It looks like it.

SOCRATES. And that is how many?

BOY. Nine.

SOCRATES. Whereas the square double our first square had to be how many?

BOY. Eight.

SOCRATES. But we haven't yet got the square of eight feet even from a three-feet side?

BOY. No.

SOCRATES. Then what length will give it? Try to tell us exactly. If you don't want to count it up, just show us on the diagram.

BOY. It's no use, Socrates, I just don't know.

SOCRATES. Observe, Meno, the stage he has reached on the path of recollection. At the beginning he did not know the side of the square of eight feet. Nor indeed does he know it now, but then he thought he knew it and answered boldly, as was appropriate—he felt no perplexity. Now however he does feel perplexed. Not only does he not know the answer; he doesn't even think he knows.

MENO. Quite true.

SOCRATES. Isn't he in a better position now in relation to what he didn't know?

MENO. I admit that too.

SOCRATES. So in perplexing him and numbing him like the sting-ray, have we done him any harm?

MENO. I think not.

SOCRATES. In fact we have helped him to some extent towards finding out the right answer, for now not only is he ignorant of it but he will be quite glad to look for it. Up to now, he thought he could speak well and fluently, on many occasions and before large audiences, on the subject of a square double the size of a given square, maintaining that it must have a side of double the length.

MENO. No doubt.

SOCRATES. Do you suppose then that he would have attempted to look for, or learn, what he thought he knew (though he did not), before he was thrown into perplexity, became aware of his ignorance, and felt a desire to know?

MENO. No.

SOCRATES. Then the numbing process was good for him?

MENO. I agree.

SOCRATES. Now notice what, starting from this state of perplexity, he will discover by seeking the truth in company with me, though I simply ask him questions without teaching him. Be ready to catch me if I give him any instruction or explanation instead of simply interrogating him on his own opinions.

(*Socrates here rubs out the previous figures and starts again.*)

Tell me, boy, is not this our square of four feet? (ABCD.) You understand?

BOY. Yes.

SOCRATES. Now we can add another equal to it like this? (BCEF.)

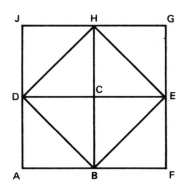

BOY. Yes.

SOCRATES. And a third here, equal to each of the others? (CEGH.)

BOY. Yes.

SOCRATES. And then we can fill in this one in the corner? (DCHJ.)

BOY. Yes.

SOCRATES. Then here we have four equal squares?

BOY. Yes.

SOCRATES. And how many times the size of the first square is the whole?

BOY. Four times.

SOCRATES. And we want one double the size. You remember?

BOY. Yes.

SOCRATES. Now does this line going from corner to corner cut each of these squares in half?

BOY. Yes.

SOCRATES. And these are four equal lines enclosing this area? (BEHD.)

BOY. They are.

SOCRATES. Now think. How big is this area?

BOY. I don't understand.

SOCRATES. Here are four squares. Has not each line cut off the inner half of each of them?

BOY. Yes.

SOCRATES. And how many such halves are there in this figure? (BEHD.)

BOY. Four.

SOCRATES. And how many in this one? (ABCD.)

BOY. Two.

SOCRATES. And what is the relation of four to two?

BOY. Double.

SOCRATES. How big is this figure then?

BOY. Eight feet.

SOCRATES. On what base?

BOY. This one.

SOCRATES. The line which goes from corner to corner of the square of four feet?

BOY. Yes.

SOCRATES. The technical name for it is 'diagonal'; so if we use that name, it is your personal opinion that the square on the diagonal of the original square is double its area.

BOY. That is so, Socrates.

SOCRATES. What do you think, Meno? Has he answered with any opinions that were not his own?

MENO. No, they were all his.

SOCRATES. Yet he did not know, as we agreed a few minutes ago.

MENO. True.

SOCRATES. But these opinions were somewhere in him, were they not?

MENO. Yes.

SOCRATES. So a man who does not know has in himself true opinions on a subject without having knowledge.

MENO. It would appear so.

SOCRATES. At present these opinions, being newly aroused, have a dream-like quality. But if the same questions are put to him on many occasions and in different ways, you can see that in the end he will have a knowledge on the subject as accurate as anybody's.

MENO. Probably.

SOCRATES. This knowledge will not come from teaching but from questioning. He will recover it for himself.

MENO. Yes.

SOCRATES. And the spontaneous recovery of knowledge that is in him is re-collection, isn't it?

MENO. Yes.

SOCRATES. Either then he has at some time acquired the knowledge which he now has, or he has always possessed it. If he always possessed it, he must always have known; if on the other hand he acquired it at some previous time, it cannot have been in this life. . . . And if the truth about reality is always in our soul, the soul must be immortal, and one must take courage and try to discover—that is, to recollect—what one doesn't happen to know, or (more correctly) remember, at the moment.

MENO. Somehow or other I believe you are right.

SOCRATES. I think I am.[2]

The doctrine of the immortality of the soul was not original with Plato, of course. The ancient Egyptians had believed in it many centuries before the first Greek philosophers, and Pythagoras had taught it to his students. But Plato's doctrine had more than religious significance; it was his answer to the skeptics and our bridge to the eternal world of Being. Of course, as a student of Socrates, he also appreciated the advantages of believing in an afterlife. Socrates could face death so calmly, he told his students, just because he believed in life

[2] Plato, *Meno,* in *Plato: Protagoras and Meno,* trans. W. K. C. Guthrie (Harmondsworth, Middlesex: Penguin, 1956).

after death. But for Plato it signified something more; it provided us with knowledge in this life as well as continued existence in another.

Plato's doctrines of the world of Being and the immortality of the soul introduce a clearly immaterialist conception of reality, as opposed to all of the more or less materialist conceptions we have encountered so far (the world as "stuff"). Even Pythagoras' numbers and Heraclitus' *logos* had their materialistic foundations, for neither philosopher was willing to grant these things independent existence, independent, that is, of the material things of this world. The things of Plato's world of Being can exist apart from anything in our world, but nothing in our world can exist apart from them (like shadows).

What is in this "other world," this world of Being? We have already met one of its inhabitants: the simple truth, $2 + 2 = 4$. In general, its inhabitants are Ideas or Forms. (The Greek word is *eidos*. Again, Plato does not mean what we ordinarily mean by "idea.") Consider the following familiar example: you are asked by your geometry teacher to prove that the internal angles of a triangle total 180°. Simple enough. You remember how; you extend the base of the triangle and draw a line parallel to the base through the apex, and then proceed with your proof. But now, how do you know that you have not only shown that the internal angles of *this* triangle total 180°? As a matter of fact, it is pretty obvious that what you have drawn isn't even a triangle; the sides sag, one of the angles is broken, and the lines are fat (after all, a real line has no width at all). But yet you claim to have proved something about all triangles. Well, it is clear that you needn't do the proof even twice, much less an infinite number of times, to make your claim. How come? Because, you will answer, what you have been working with is not this particular poorly drawn triangle in your notebook but an ideal triangle, the form of all and any triangles. And there it is—Plato's Form or Idea of a triangle. It is not identical to any particular triangle. (How could it be, for it would have to be acute, isoceles, right, and non-right all at the same time!) It is their ideal form, which each particular triangle approximates, that has its own existence in the world of Being. Plato says that every triangle that we can draw participates in the ideal form and that it is only through reason, not through observation of particular triangles, that we come into contact with these ideal Forms.

Ideas or Forms are what different things of the same kind have in common and what make them things of the same kind. For example, two horses have in common the form horse, and you recognize a horse, Plato would say, because of its form. Suppose that you've never seen a horse before. Is it possible for you to know what a horse is? The answer is, "of course." It is enough that you have learned what a horse is (from pictures or descriptions) even if you've never seen one. But how is such learning possible? According to Plato, it is possible because we have an Idea or recognize the form of a horse, like the ideal form of a triangle, and with it we are able to know what a horse is, even if we have never one, and to recognize horses when we do see them. In Plato's terms, we can recognize all horses, no matter what their age, shape, color, or peculiarities, just because they "participate" in the Form horse. And for Plato, the Form horse has even more reality than particular, flesh-and-blood horses.

The concept of Form allows Plato to explain what it is that one comes to understand when he or she learns that two or more things are of the same kind. But the notion of Form serves another purpose for Plato as well. In addition to what we know about things from experience, we also know some things independent of experience, and we know these things with certainty (the same certainty Descartes sought in our introduction). For example, we know that every horse is an animal. We know this not simply because every horse that we have seen has turned out to be an animal, but because we know, apart from any particular experiences with horses, that the very Form horse includes the Idea animal. (In our times, we would say that the meaning of the English word "horse" already includes the concept of "being an animal"; accordingly, philosophers refer to this kind of truth as "conceptual truth." But this term was not available to Plato.)

The world of Being is filled with Ideas and ideal Forms. Most importantly, it is filled with the ideals of human perfection: Wisdom, Justice, Beauty, and Goodness. It is to these ideals of perfection that each of us aspires, and it is the definition of these ideals that is the task of every philosopher. His or her job (and Socrates' main task in all of Plato's dialogues) is to sort out our common confusions about such vital matters. The business of the philosopher, in short, is to make us recognize eternal ideals and make it possible to achieve that heroic wisdom to which Plato's teacher Socrates had devoted his life.

I hope that you can appreciate, even from this brief sketch, the power of the metaphysical doctrines Plato has developed. You may also be aware of some of their difficulties. Most importantly, the gap between our world and the real world makes us exceedingly uncomfortable; none of us likes to think of ourselves living merely in the shadows. (And Plato himself warns, "wouldn't the prisoners who had never been released . . . laugh at him and even . . . kill" the philosopher who thus instructs them?) The connection between the world of Being and our own world of Becoming is not at all clear. Plato does say that the things of this latter world "participate" in the Ideas of the former, but one thing that we shall have to learn right away in philosophy (and in every other discipline) is that words that pretend to be explanations are often only cosmetic cover-ups. It looks as if we have a theory when in fact we have only a word. This is particularly true of Plato's word, "participates," and he himself raised serious doubts about it in his later dialogues. But the real attack comes, as it should come in philosophy, from his own students, and in particular, from one, perhaps the greatest of them all.

Aristotle

Aristotle claimed that he did not understand Plato's concept of "participation." (When a philosopher claims "not to understand" something, it means that he is pushing for a better account of it, that he is not at all satisfied so far. Aristotle probably understood Plato as well as anybody ever has.) Aristotle also wanted to determine the nature of reality. But Plato had argued that reality was something other than the world of our experience. Aristotle, a practical man of the earth, a great biologist, physicist, and worldly tutor to Alexander the Great, would have none of this. This world, our world, is reality. Accordingly, he brought metaphysics back home. But it must not be thought that he made it any simpler. The beginning student of Aristotle—as well as the trained scholar—will attest to the fact that he is among the most difficult authors in philosophy.

The doctrines of Aristotle's metaphysics sound as simple as they could be. This world, the world of our experience, is reality; there is no other world. The ultimate things of reality, which he calls substances, are individual things—men, horses, trees and butterflies. Change is real and reality changes (thus rejecting the chief presupposition of most who came before him). The soul is not immortal, and Ideas have no existence apart from the things that are instances of them. But don't think that Aristotle thereby rejected the 250 years of Greek philosophy preceding him. Aristotle, despite the common-sense quality of his metaphysics, knew better. He was not simply returning philosophy to "common sense." Quite the contrary, he was still answering the problems of Plato and his ancestors and making use of their answers as well.

Aristotle's methodology was analysis, in particular, a form of conceptual analysis. To the untrained reader, it sometimes looks as if Aristotle is simply making a tedious number of distinctions, analyzing the shortest words in the language (for example "is") into as many pieces as possible. Plato, of course, had also done a kind of analysis, but through the dramatic mechanism of his dialogue. But for Aristotle, this analysis had nothing to do with the eternal inhabitants of another world—it had solely to do with our understanding of this world. The Forms, Ideas and ideals he analyzed were the tangible forms, ideas, and ideals of our everyday, ordinary lives.

We can divide Aristotle's metaphysics into an ontology and a cosmology. For beginning philosophers, the latter is far more interesting, the former extremely difficult. Aristotle's ontology is based upon the all-important notion of substance, his technical term for the Pre-Socratic conceptions of the ultimate "stuff" of the universe. "The question that was asked long ago, is asked now, and always is a matter of difficulty, 'What is Being?' is now the question, 'What is Substance?' "[3]

For Aristotle, the primary substances are individual things; secondary substances (less real than individuals) were what he called the species and the genus to which a thing belonged. To return to our equestrian example, this particular horse, for Aristotle, is the primary substance. The species, "horse," and the even broader genus, "animal," are less real than the horse itself. Aristotle, like Plato, has a hierarchy of reality. But he turns Plato's hierarchy up-

[3] Aristotle, *Metaphysics,* trans. Hugh Tredennick (Cambridge, Mass.: Harvard University Press, 1933).

side down. Plato holds that the more abstract things are the more real; Aristotle argues that the more concrete things, individuals, are most real. For Aristotle, as in common sense, the more tangible things are considered to be the most real things.

What is a substance? Aristotle spends many pages giving a number of definitions, enough to keep the philosophers of the Middle Ages busy for a thousand years sorting them out. But we can summarize Aristotle's views in a few sentences. Most important is the idea that a substance is independent of anything else. (We shall see how important this becomes in the modern metaphysics of Spinoza and Leibniz.) Other things might depend upon a substance, but a substance does not depend upon them. The color of a horse, for example, could not exist without the horse, but the horse could surely exist without its being a particular color. (We could even paint him.) Another way of characterizing substance is to say that substance is what underlies all of the properties and changes in something. In this sense, you can say that you are the same person (that is, the same substance) that you were ten years ago, despite the fact that you are, quite obviously, very different in a great many ways. (Aristotle says, "Substance, while remaining the same, is capable of admitting contrary properties.") Combining these two characterizations, we can say that a substance is whatever is most basic to reality, like the Pre-Socratic philosophers notion of "stuff."

It is important to introduce one other technical term used by Aristotle, for it too will define the work of philosophers for years to follow. It is the concept of an essence or an essential property. An *essence* (or an *essential property*) is that aspect of an individual that identifies it as a particular individual. For example, it is part of the essence of being Socrates that he is a human being, that he lived in the fourth century B.C., and that he was wise. Anything that does not have these properties could not possibly be Socrates. There are other properties that Socrates has, of course, for example, the fact that he had a wart on his nose. But this is not an essential property. (Aristotle calls it an *accident* or an *accidental property*.) Socrates still would have been Socrates without it. But Socrates could not have been a centipede, for it is part of his essence to be human.

You may already anticipate certain troubles that will plague later philosophers. How much can we change a person, for example, and still have him or her be the same? Provide a haircut? a college education? a ten year jail sentence? a sex change operation? But before we worry about such problems, let us appreciate the importance of this notion of essence in Aristotle's philosophy. With it, he can do everything that Plato wanted to do with his special notion of Ideas, but without invoking anything other-worldly. According to Aristotle, we can know that Socrates is a man, for instance, just because the essence of Socrates includes the property of being a man. We can know that a horse is an animal because the essence of being a horse includes the property of being an animal. In Plato, a conceptual truth of this kind was a truth about Ideas; for Aristotle, it is a statement about essences.

Later, we shall see why these two concepts of substance and essence are so important to later philosophy. But for now, let us turn to a much more exciting aspect of Aristotle's philosophy, his cosmology. It has inspired literally thousands of great thinkers, notably Saint Thomas Aquinas, who used Aristotle's metaphysics to build one of the great theological systems of Christianity.

The problem is one that Aristotle inherited from his predecessors—the problem of change. Because the earlier philosophers had insisted that reality must be eternal and unchanging, they had concluded that the universe could not have come into being, but must have always existed. Aristotle found this to be absurd. He believed in changes in reality, and that every change had its sufficient natural cause.[4] (We shall see much more of this belief in later chapters.) But if every change in reality has its cause, then its cause must have a cause in turn, and that cause must have a cause, and so on. But it is the "and so on" that Aristotle finds just as absurd as the idea that there can be no change in reality. Of course reality changes, and of course these changes have causes, but the idea that these causes might go back in time indefinitely (philosophers call this "an *infinite regress*") was considered by Aristotle to be unintelligible. There must have been, he argued, a first cause, or what he called a "prime mover," that set the universe in motion but is itself not caused by anything else:

> Moreover, it is obvious that there is some first principle, and that the causes of things are not infinitely many either in a direct sequence or in kind. For the material generation of one thing from another cannot go on in an infinite progression (*e.g.* flesh from earth, earth from air, air from fire, and so on without a stop); nor can the source of motion (*e.g.* man be moved by air, air by the sun, the sun by Strife, with no limit to the series). In the same way neither can the Final Cause [that is, purposes] recede to infinity—walking having health for its object, and health happiness, and happiness something else: one thing always being done for the sake of another. And it is just the same with the Formal Cause [that is, the essence]. For in the case of all intermediate terms of a series which are contained between a first and last term, the prior term is necessarily the cause of those which follow it; because if we had to say which of the three is the cause, we should say "the first." At any rate it is not the last term, because what comes at the end is not the cause of anything. Neither, again, is the intermediate term, which is only the cause of one (and it makes no difference whether there is one intermediate term or several, nor whether they are infinite or limited in number). But of series which are infinite in this way, and in general of the infinite, all the parts are equally intermediate, down to the present moment. Thus if there is no first term, there is no cause at all.[5]

Aristotle says that the prime mover is "pure thought, thinking about itself." It is an obscure, but fascinating idea, which was taken up by Christian theology as an apt characterization of God. In fact, Aristotle himself called the

---

[4] The concept of "cause" is a complex one. See this term in the glossary.
[5] Aristotle, *Metaphysics*.

prime mover *theos,* or "God." But it is important to emphasize that virtually none of the characteristics which Christians, Jews, and Moslems attribute to their God are to be found in Aristotle's prime mover; it has no particular concern for man and no function as creator in the biblical sense. (Aristotle rather says that the prime mover is the guiding principle of the universe.) Aristotle's God, in other words, is more of a metaphysical necessity than a potential object of worship. But when we add to this tempting notion of the prime mover the fact that Aristotle was also (like most of the early Greek philosophers) an animist, who believed that the universe as a whole was a kind of living organism, we can appreciate how this cosmology would become a source of inspiration for a great many philosophers, poets, and religious people. In more recent centuries, for example, it was used as a welcome alternative to the "nuts and bolts" materialism of modern Newtonian science (as we shall see in Leibniz). Tied to the technical details of Aristotle's ontology is an extremely imaginative cosmology; the picture of a living universe, developing according to its own purposes. Aristotle's cosmology is therefore called a *teleology* (from the Greek word *telos* meaning purpose), for it gives everything a purpose and tries to explain everything in terms of purposes. For example, in answer to a question such as, "why do things fall down?" Aristotle would answer "in order to find their natural places." Everything that happens, on this teleological view, can be explained in a similar way, almost as if we were explaining human activities rather than natural phenomena. It is a fascinating picture and still an attractive alternative to the lifeless picture of the physical universe that is so central to our modern outlook.

TWO IMPORTANT ASSUMPTIONS

We have just reviewed the two greatest metaphysical theories in the history of human thought. With Plato, humanity first began to appreciate the extent to which its world was structured by Ideas and abstract Forms. With Aristotle, people began to realize the significance of language in structuring that world. But despite their intimate connections, Plato and Aristotle offer us very different *paradigms* (that is, ideal examples) of the nature of metaphysics. In Plato there is the leap into the realm of pure Ideas, the thrill of esoteric argument, and the elegance of the proofs against common sense. In Aristotle, there is always the anchor of common sense and everyday experience, the cautious and piecemeal analysis of the concepts we use every day in talking about our world, in Aristotle's view, the only world. In an important sense, the history of philosophy is the interplay of these two paradigms. And philosophy is still very much involved in a debate between the two.

Before we skip two millenia to modern times, it is important that we make explicit two assumptions or presuppositions that have been generally accepted until very recently. These were assumed by the Pre-Socratics from the very start of their venture; they were accepted by Plato and Aristotle and would be presupposed by most medieval and modern philosophers as well. Those assumptions are:

First, the world is intelligible. Every attempt to understand the world presupposes that it can be understood, and understood by us. Another way of stating this is to say that all metaphysics assumes that our thought is adequate to understanding the world, or at least, to understanding the limits of our understanding (as for example, in our attempts to understand God). It is this faith in thought as a guide to reality that Heraclitus was groping for with his *"logos,"* a first crude approximation of the doctrine that "thought" is a dependable guide to "Being." Plato assumed that thought could discover the world of Being. Aristotle, who didn't accept Plato's two-worlds view, nevertheless accepted Plato's confidence that an examination of the language we speak will allow us to discover truths about reality. So too, metaphysicians from Thales to Alfred North Whitehead in our own century have made the same assumption: language and thought are more or less accurate vehicles for representing and recognizing reality, and that reality is thereby intelligible to us.

It is only very recently that this assumption has been seriously questioned. Without this assumption an embarrassing doubt arises. Why should we suppose that what we describe as the way the world really is is anything more than an autobiographical account of the only way that we can describe it? Perhaps our view of the world is determined by the structures and limitations of the language we learned from our parents and peers? Moreover, how can we even know that reality has any "structure" at all, apart from those structures which we impose upon it with our language? For example, could it not be that the distinctions Aristotle applies to reality are nothing other than a reflection of the structure of the Greek language? And could not the necessary truths we discover about reality be nothing other than the conceptual truths that are built right into the meanings of our words? Here the skeptic is armed with a particularly powerful set of arguments. If we give up the assumption that our language mirrors reality, then we must face the skeptic and we can never be assured of having a grasp of "the way the world really is" at all. For this reason, most philosophers have always felt compelled to hold on to this important assumption. Descartes, for example, though he tried to doubt everything, never for a second doubted the trustworthiness of his own language. But today, such leading scientist-philosophers as Albert Einstein have insisted that the intelligibility of the universe is itself a problem, a problem surmounted only by faith.

Second, it is usually assumed that all statements about reality in metaphysics are necessary truths. We have several times mentioned the fact that metaphysical claims are not simply statements about "the way the world really is" but actually claims about "the way the world must be." Every statement in metaphysics, in other words, must be taken as if the reality it described could not be otherwise. This is what Descartes required of his "first principles." He demanded that they be "perfectly certain," and he insisted throughout his philosophy that the only truths really worth the honorific title of "knowledge" were those that could be known beyond all possible doubt. In Plato, we saw that necessary truth was the earmark of reality, eternal and unchanging. And in Aristotle, although the matter becomes more subtle, it is clear that he considered all of his principles—even his principles of natural science—as matters of necessity. This emphasis on necessity is of tremendous importance. We shall devote two later chapters to it (Chapters 4 and 5).

SUMMARY AND CONCLUSION

Metaphysics is the study of ultimate reality, the attempt to find out the way the world really is. The first recognized metaphysical theory in Western philosophy is Thales' suggestion that everything is ultimately made out of water. After Thales, a number of schools of metaphysics suggested alternative theories, all of them depending on the speculative powers of human reason and diverging in various and important ways from "common sense." But these thinkers were not only the first significant Western philosophers; they were also the first theoretical scientists, anticipating in many ways some of the most sophisticated theories of contemporary physics, astronomy, and chemistry.

The first turning point in Western metaphysics came with Socrates, although Socrates himself was more interested in moral issues than in metaphysics as such. Socrates' student, Plato, and his student in turn, Aristotle, became the first great systematic metaphysicians, and philosophy ever since has been deeply indebted to them. Plato introduced an elaborate theory in which ultimate reality consisted of Ideas or Forms, in contrast with the particular and changing things of everyday life. To support this "two-worlds" theory of Ideas or Forms versus individual things, he offered a theory of learning, a "theory of recollection," in which he argued that the human soul is immortal and that each of us already knows, in some sense, what we appear to learn in our lives. Aristotle argues instead that only individual things deserve the ultimate claim to reality, for these individual things are the primary substances. Since Aristotle, metaphysicians have typically used the term "substance" as the name of the basic "stuff" of reality.

GLOSSARY

animism: the view that things (or, at the extreme, all things) are alive. It may also be the view that the universe as a whole is one gigantic organism.

Becoming: change. In Plato, the "world of Becoming" is the world of our daily experience, in which things and people come into being and pass away.

Being: whatever exists. In Plato, the "world of Being" is the realm of abstract Ideas and eternal Forms, in which nothing ever changes. It is, for him, reality, and, in general, Being is used by philosophers to refer to whatever they consider ultimately real (e.g., substance, God).

cause: that which brings something about. Philosophers usually add, "as a matter of necessity." In Aristotle, "cause" means something like "reason," and he distinguishes four different kinds of "causes" of a change: (1) the *formal* cause, the principle or essential idea according to which a change comes about (think of a blueprint for a building, or the plans for a project); (2) the *material* cause, the matter which undergoes the change (think of the raw materials for building a house—lumber, bricks, cement); (3) the *efficient* cause, that which initiates the change (the construction workers and their tools); (4) the *final* cause, or the purpose of the change (to build a place where Socrates and his family can live, for example).

conceptual truth: a statement which is true and which we can see to be true just on the basis of the words (or we should say, the "concepts") that compose it. For example, "a horse is an animal" is a conceptual truth because anyone who speaks English and knows the meanings of the words "horse" and "animal" knows that such a statement must be true. (We shall discuss such statements in greater detail in Chapters 4 and 5.) In Plato, a conceptual truth is a truth about Ideas. In Aristotle, a conceptual truth is a matter of describing the essence of a thing. (See *Idea, essence.*)

cosmology: the study of the cosmos, or the universe in its entirety.

essence: (*essential characteristics* or *essential properties*) the necessary or defining characteristics or properties of a thing. "That which makes a thing what it is," in other words, those features which one must list in a definition or uniquely identifying description. (For example, the fact that Socrates is a man is part of his essence, the fact that he never smoked on Saturdays is not.)

Form: the structure of a thing, that which identifies it as a particular thing or kind of thing. In Plato, a Form is an independently existing entity in the world of Being, which determines the nature of the particular things of this world. In Aristotle, forms are merely the essential characteristics that identify a thing as what it is, without independent existence.

Idea: In Plato, a Form. In general, the word "idea" refers to a thought or any mental representation.

immaterialism: the metaphysical view that accepts the existence of nonmaterial entities. The weak version asserts merely that there are such entities. The strong version, Idealism, asserts that there are only such entities (that is, there are no material objects).

immortality: (of the soul) the idea that something immaterial in us survives death (and, in some belief systems, precedes birth).

infinite regress: a sequence going back endlessly. For example, "A is caused by B, and B by C, and C by D . . . and so on to infinity." Aristotle believed such a regress to be an intellectual absurdity.

innate ideas: knowledge which is "programmed" into us from birth and need not be learned. Experience may be necessary to "trigger off" such ideas, but they are already "in" all of us. In Plato, the theory of innate ideas is part of a general theory of the immortality of the soul.

materialism: the metaphysical view that only physical matter and its properties exist. Seemingly nonmaterial entities are really physical bodies: to talk about energy, for example, is, in a way, to talk about physical potential; to talk about minds is, as a kind of shorthand, to talk about behavior; to talk about ideas is, in a misleading way, to talk about the various structures and interrelationships between objects. Numbers have no existence of their own but only represent sets of sets of objects (the set of all sets of eight things is the number eight, for example). Materialism has always been a powerful world view in modern scientific culture. It was also the most common view among the Pre-Socratic philosophers.

metaphysics: most simply, the study of the most basic (or "first") principles. Traditionally, the study of ultimate reality, or "Being as such." Popularly, any kind of very abstract or obscure thinking. Most philosophers today would define metaphysics as the study of the most general concepts of science and human life, for example, "reality," "existence," "freedom," "God," "soul," "action," "mind." In general, we can divide metaphysics into: ontology, cosmology, and an ill-defined set of problems concerning God and the immortality of the human soul. Problems concerning human nature, freedom, and action are also sometimes included in metaphysical discussions. (See *ontology, cosmology,* and Chapters 7–10.)

monism: the metaphysical view that there is ultimately only one substance, that all reality is one. Less strictly, it may be applied to philosophers who believe in only one kind of substance.

necessary truth: true statements which could not possibly be false. (See Chapters 4 and 5.)

ontology: the study of being. That is, that part of metaphysics which asks such questions as "What is there?" "What is it for something to exist?" "What is an individual thing?" "How do things interact?" Traditionally, these questions were formulated as questions about substance (see p. 32). Today, much of ontology is part of logic and linguistics and is the study of the concepts we use to discuss such matters. Sometimes ontology is used as a synonym for metaphysics, but usually the latter is the broader discipline.

paradigm: an ideal example. Philosophers often talk about "a paradigm such-and-such" or "a paradigm case of. . . ." For example, "a paradigm case of will power is my getting up early on Sunday morning."

participation: Plato's obscure and unexplained relationship between the things of this world and the Forms of which they are manifestations. He tells us that individual things "participate" in their Forms.

pluralism: the metaphysical view that there are many distinct substances in the universe, and, perhaps, many different kinds of substances as well.

prime mover: in Aristotle, the "cause-of-itself," the first cause, which (Who) initiates all changes but is not itself (Himself) effected by anything prior. Aristotle believes there must be a prime mover if we are to avoid an infinite regress, which he considers an absurdity. Aristotle also refers to the prime mover as "God," and medieval philosophers (e.g., St. Thomas Aquinas) have developed these views into Christian theology.

property: any feature or characteristic of a thing. Properties are generally distinguished from the substances in which they "inhere" by pointing to the fact that a property cannot exist without being a property of something; for example, there can be any number of red things but no redness which exists independently. (Many philosophers have challenged this idea, but this problem, which is usually called the "problem of universals," will not be discussed in this introductory course.)

reason: in our introduction, we defined "reason" as simply "the ability to think abstractly." In metaphysics, however, it often has a more controversial meaning, namely, that human ability to go beyond experience to determine, through thought alone, what reality is really like.

substance: the essential reality of a thing or things which underlies the various properties and changes of properties. Its most common definitions: "that which is independent and can exist by itself," and "the essence of a thing which does not and cannot change." In traditional metaphysics, substance is the same as "ultimate reality," and the study of substance is that branch of metaphysics which studies reality, namely, ontology. (See *essence, ontology.*)

teleology (teleological): the belief that all phenomena have a purpose, end, or goal (from the Greek *telos,* meaning "purpose"). Aristotle's metaphysics is a teleology, which means that he believes that the universe itself—and consequently everything in it—operates for purposes and can be explained according to goals.

2

REALITY:
TWO MODERN VIEWS

The greatest good is the knowledge of the union which the mind has with the whole of nature.

Benedictus de Spinoza

The best way to learn modern metaphysics is to study the works of the great philosophers. One can also study the problems of ontology and cosmology as separate subjects, but then what is lost is the most striking aspect of metaphysics—the sense of system that ties these separate problems together and distinguishes the great metaphysicians from lesser philosophical technicians. It is within the scope of such all-encompassing sytems or world-views that these problems are unified into a matter of deep intellectual and cultural concern. Accordingly, our introduction to modern metaphysics can best begin by studying the works of two of the most systematic and brilliant philosophers from the late seventeenth century. The first is a Jewish philosopher, excommunicated for his heresies, who lived his life in poverty on the outskirts of Amsterdam. He is Benedictus[1] de Spinoza (1632–1677). The second is his slightly younger contemporary, Gottfried Wilhelm von Leibniz (1646–1716), Germany's first great modern philosopher. Together, they present us with the best possible lesson in modern metaphysics.

Modern metaphysics nominally begins with Descartes, his insistence upon perfect certainty and mathematical deduction as the legitimate methodology. But methodology aside, metaphysics is a continuous enterprise from the Greeks through medieval philosophy, with Descartes its direct heir. We should not be surprised, for example, to find that the central concept of Descartes' metaphysics is substance, and that his definition of it (and the term itself)

[1] Born Baruch: he changed his name after he was excommunicated from the Jewish faith.

comes straight from Aristotle: "a thing existing in such a manner that it has need of no other thing in order to exist." Both Spinoza and Leibniz follow Descartes in taking substance as their central concept, and they follow him also in their method. [The three philosophers are usually grouped together as a single school of thought often called *Rationalism*.]

At first glance, the problems of modern metaphysics appear to be the same that faced the Pre-Socratics: How many substances are there? What are they? How are individuals distinguished? How do different things (or substances) interact? How does substance come into being? Is there a beginning to the universe? But two momentous changes in the intervening centuries forced modern philosophers to deal with problems that had barely even occurred to Greek philosophers.

The long and powerful hold of Christianity had given immaterialism (including the immortality of the human soul and the existence of a spiritual God) a status it had only rarely enjoyed in materialistic Greece. Accordingly, few philosophers held to the ancient view that only material "stuff" existed, that is, the view we call materialism. It was now obligatory for any philosopher to account for those mysterious immaterial entities, minds. And, of course, God. Descartes' metaphysics, for example, began by acknowledging two kinds of "created substances," one physical, one mental. And then there was one (and only one) "uncreated substance"—God. Other philosophers, Leibniz for one, went so far as to argue that there were only immaterial substances. Such a position is now called *idealism*. In modern philosophy, materialism ("it's all matter, never mind") and idealism ("it's all in the mind, no matter") have been fighting it out for three centuries. Idealism typically carries with it a religious conviction, for the concept of mind and the concept of spirit are never far apart. (In German, for example, they are the same word, *Geist*.) Materialism, on the other hand, usually draws its power from the remarkable advancements in the sciences, and here we find our second momentous change.

With the rise of modern science, it became the generally accepted view that the universe was a giant machine, perhaps set up by God, but in any case a well-coordinated and predictable mechanism. Isaac Newton's discovery of the causal laws of motion and gravity only brought to a climax a scientific world-view that had been in the making for centuries. And though ancient animism was still alive and belief in God and spirituality was still virtually universal, the modern mechanical view of reality was an absolutely unavoidable consideration for any metaphysician.

Both Spinoza and Leibniz fully appreciated this modern scientific view, although they interpreted it very differently. They were both religious men. (Spinoza, ironically, was branded an atheist and his philosophy banned from most of Europe.) They both accepted Descartes' "rationalist," deductive method and both developed their thinking along the lines of a geometrical system. They both began by considering the concept of substance. Yet Spinoza emerged as a monist, Leibniz as a pluralist. In viewing their impressive systems of thought, it is important to keep in mind the long history we have quickly reviewed, the powerful influences of Christianity and science and, most importantly, the various metaphysical problems to which we were introduced in the preceding chapter.

BENEDICTUS DE SPINOZA

Spinoza's *Ethics* is one of the few modern works that is accepted as an unqualified classic by virtually everyone in philosophy. It is the author's only major work. Spinoza was an avid political reformer, particularly on the issue of religious toleration, and even in liberal Amsterdam, that made him a dangerous person to know. The following work, which, as you will see, is much more than a study in "ethics," was his most forceful contribution to the issue of tolerance. Spinoza introduced a shockingly radical re-interpretation of God and his relation to the universe (so radical he was branded an atheist). He also gave an equally shocking theory of our roles in the universe. So while you are attempting to comprehend these difficult statements and proofs about "substance," keep your mind open for the dramatic changes in the way Spinoza teaches us to look at our world.

As in geometry, Spinoza begins with a set of definitions:

DEFINITIONS

I. By that which is *self-caused,* I mean that of which the essence involves existence, or that of which the nature is only conceivable as existent.

II. A thing is called *finite after its kind,* when it can be limited by another thing of the same nature; for instance, a body is called finite because we always conceive another greater body. So, also, a thought is limited by another thought, but a body is not limited by thought, nor a thought by body.

III. By *substance,* I mean that which is in itself, and is conceived through itself: in other words, that of which a conception can be formed independently of any other conception.

IV. By *attribute,* I mean that which the intellect perceives as constituting the essence of substance.

V. By *mode,* I mean the modifications of substance, or that which exists in, and is conceived through, something other than itself.

VI. By *God,* I mean a being absolutely infinite—that is, a substance consisting in infinite attributes, in which each expresses eternal and infinite essentiality.

VII. That thing is called free, which exists solely by the necessity of its own nature, and of which the action is determined by itself alone. On the other hand, that thing is necessary, or rather constrained, which is determined by something external to itself to a fixed and definite method of existence or action.

VIII. By *eternity,* I mean existence itself, in so far as it is conceived necessarily to follow solely from the definition of that which is eternal.[2]

---

[2] Benedictus de Spinoza, *Ethics,* in *The Rationalists,* trans. R. H. M. Elwes (New York: Doubleday, 1960).

These definitions sound much more forbidding than they really are. Notice first how many of these terms and definitions are familiar to us from Aristotle: for example, the definition of substance as the basic "stuff" which has various properties but is dependent only on itself and can be thought of without thinking of anything else. *Attributes* and *modes,* on the other hand, are properties: attributes consist of essential characteristics of a substance; modes are modifications of attributes. (For example, having a body is an attribute of substance; being blonde and blue-eyed are merely modes.) The cause-of-itself is like Aristotle's prime mover, but with some very important differences. Spinoza's "mover" turns out to be identical to the universe, and Spinoza's "God" is much more than "thought thinking itself," as in Aristotle. But the basic starting point of the entire system, as summarized in these definitions and axioms, is the Aristotlean notion of substance. Like the ancient metaphysicians, Spinoza insists that whatever really exists, exists eternally (Def. VIII). But that also means—there can be no Creation and no Creator!

As in geometry, the definitions are followed by a set of *axioms,* that is, principles that are so obvious that they need no defense. In plane geometry, such an axiom would be "the shortest distance between two points is a straight line." Spinoza's axioms may not seem quite so obvious at first glance, partly because of the unfamiliarity of his metaphysical terminology.

AXIOMS

I. Everything which exists, exists either in itself or in something else.

II. That which cannot be conceived through anything else must be conceived through itself.

III. From a given definite cause an effect necessarily follows; and, on the other hand, if no definite cause be granted, it is impossible that an effect can follow.

IV. The knowledge of an effect depends on and involves the knowledge of a cause.

V. Things which have nothing in common cannot be understood, the one by means of the other; the conception of one does not involve the conception of the other.

VI. A true idea must correspond with its ideate or object.

VII. If a thing can be conceived as non-existing, its essence does not involve existence.[3]

You can see that the axioms follow approximately the same sequence as the definitions, and the axioms in most cases are based on the definitions, although they do not strictly follow from them. For example, Axiom 1, like Definition 1, concerns the idea that everything has an explanation. Definition 1, although stated in terms of "cause" ("self-caused"), concerns that which must exist if it can just be thought of. Axiom 1 says that everything must either be explainable through itself (that is, "self-caused") or through something else. Similarly, Definition 2 uses a technical term ("finite after its kind") to talk

[3] Spinoza, *Ethics.*

about things that can be explained only by reference to something greater, while Axiom 2 says that anything that cannot be so explained must be explained simply in terms of itself ("self-caused" again). Axioms 3 and 4 outline the basic principles of cause and effect, that is, that a cause makes its effect happen necessarily, and without the cause, there would be no effect, and that the knowledge of the effect depends on knowing the cause. (These principles have had a long and important history in both metaphysics and theories of science and knowledge. They will play a key role in Spinoza's theory of determinism [the idea that everything happens necessarily because of its causes] and in "deterministic" theories generally. These will be discussed in Chapter 10 in detail.) Axioms 5–7 return to the central theme of explanation begun in Axioms 1 and 2; Axiom 5 insists that one thing can be explained in terms of another only if they have "something in common." Thus you explain one physical event in terms of another physical event (since they have in common certain physical properties). Axiom 6 repeats the important assumption we made explicit at the end of Chapter 1, namely, that our ideas are capable of grasping reality. (This axiom also states a seemingly innocent theory of truth, often called "the correspondence theory of truth," which says that "a true idea corresponds with some actual fact [*ideate* or *object*] in the world." This is discussed in Chapter 5.) Axiom 7 returns to the idea of "essence involving existence," in other words, that which is self-caused, or substance or God. Axiom 7 is stated negatively, however, and says that if we can think of something as not existing (for example, we can imagine what it would be like to live in a world without freeways, or without stars, or even without other people) then "its essence does not involve existence." That is, existing is not one of its essential characteristics and it is not "self-caused."

The general theme of the axioms, therefore, is that everything has an explanation for its existence, either by reference to something else or because it is "self-caused" or self-explanatory, that is, its "essence involves its existence" or it is entirely "in itself and conceived through itself." This last phrase is from the definition of "substance" (Definition 3), so you can see how, even in his axioms and definitions, Spinoza is setting up his main thesis, that there can only be one substance.

Starting with these definitions and axioms, which he takes to be unobjectionable, Spinoza begins the "proofs" of his "propositions," which follow like the theorems of Euclidean geometry from the definitions of terms like "line," "point," and "parallel." Again, these look forbidding, but their philosophical relevance should be clear.

PROPOSITIONS

PROP. I. *Substance is by nature prior to its modifications.*

Proof.—This is clear from Deff. iii. and v.

PROP. II. *Two substances, whose attributes are different, have nothing in common.*

Proof.—Also evident from Def. iii. For each must exist in itself, and be conceived through itself; in other words, the conception of one does not imply the conception of the other.

PROP. III. *Things which have nothing in common cannot be one the cause of the other.*

Proof.—If they have nothing in common, it follows that one cannot be apprehended by means of the other (Ax. v.), and, therefore, one cannot be the cause of the other (Ax. iv.). *Q.E.D.* [Latin, *quod erat demonstrandum,* a phrase used in traditional logic meaning "thus it is proven."]

PROP. IV. *Two or more distinct things are distinguished one from the other either by the difference of the attributes of the substances, or by the difference of their modifications.*

Proof.—Everything which exists, exists either in itself or in something else (Ax. i.),—that is (by Deff. iii. and v.), nothing is granted in addition to the understanding, except substance and its modifications. Nothing is, therefore, given besides the understanding, by which several things may be distinguished one from the other, except the substances, or, in other words (see Ax. iv.), their attributes and modifications. *Q.E.D.*

PROP. V. *There cannot exist in the universe two or more substances having the same nature or attribute.*

Proof.—If several distinct substances be granted, they must be distinguished one from the other, either by the difference of their attributes, or by the difference of their modifications (Prop. iv.). If only by the difference of their attributes, it will be granted that there cannot be more than one with an identical attribute. If by the difference of their modifications—as substance is naturally prior to its modifications (Prop. i.),—it follows that setting the modifications aside, and considering substance in itself, that is truly, (Deff. iii. and vi.), there cannot be conceived one substance different from another,—that is (by Prop. iv.), there cannot be granted several substances, but one substance only. *Q.E.D.*

PROP. VI. *One substance cannot be produced by another substance.*

Proof.—It is impossible that there should be in the universe two substances with an identical attribute, *i.e.* which have anything common to them both (Prop. ii.), and, therefore (Prop. iii.), one cannot be the cause of another, neither can one be produced by the other. *Q.E.D.*

Corollary.—Hence it follows that a substance cannot be produced by anything external to itself. For in the universe nothing is granted, save substances and their modifications (as appears from Ax. i. and Deff. iii. and v.). Now (by the last Prop.) substance cannot be produced by another substance, therefore it cannot be produced by anything external to itself. *Q.E.D.* This is shown still more readily by the absurdity of the contradictory. For, if substance be produced by an external cause, the knowledge of it would depend on the knowledge of its cause (Ax. iv.), and (by Def. iii.) it would itself not be substance.[4]

So far, the main point is quite simple: if there is more than one substance, they could have no possible relation to each other. Therefore, by a kind

[4] Spinoza, *Ethics.*

of *reductio ad absurdum* argument, there can only be one substance. In the propositions that follow (and especially the note to Prop. VIII), this is demonstrated again:

PROP. VII. *Existence belongs to the nature of substance.*

Proof.—Substance cannot be produced by anything external (Corollary, Prop. vi.), it must, therefore, be its own cause—that is, its essence necessarily involves existence, or existence belongs to its nature.

PROP. VIII. *Every substance is necessarily infinite.*

Proof.—There can only be one substance with an identical attribute, and existence follows from its nature (Prop. vii.); its nature, therefore, involves existence, either as finite or infinite. It does not exist as finite, for (by Def. ii.) it would then be limited by something else of the same kind, which would also necessarily exist (Prop. vii.); and there would be two substances with an identical attribute, which is absurd (Prop. v.). It therefore exists as infinite. *Q.E.D.*

Note.—No doubt it will be difficult for those who think about things loosely, and have not been accustomed to know them by their primary causes, to comprehend the demonstration of Prop. vii.: for such persons make no distinction between the modifications of substances and the substances themselves, and are ignorant of the manner in which things are produced; hence they attribute to substances the beginning which they observe in natural objects. Those who are ignorant of true causes, make complete confusion—think that trees might talk just as well as men—that men might be formed from stones as well as from seed; and imagine that any form might be changed into any other. So, also, those who confuse the two natures, divine and human, readily attribute human passions to the deity, especially so long as they do not know how passions originate in the mind. But, if people would consider the nature of substance, they would have no doubt about the truth of Prop. vii. In fact, this proposition would be a universal axiom, and accounted a truism. For, by substance, would be understood that which is in itself, and is conceived through itself—that is, something of which the conception requires not the conception of anything else; whereas modifications exist in something external to themselves, and a conception of them is formed by means of a conception of the thing in which they exist. Therefore, we may have true ideas of non-existent modifications; for, although they may have no *actual* existence apart from the conceiving intellect, yet their essence is so involved in something external to themselves that they may through it be conceived. Whereas the only truth substances can have, external to the intellect, must consist in their existence, because they are conceived through themselves. Therefore, for a person to say that he has a clear and distinct—that is, a true—idea of a substance, but that he is not sure whether such substance exists, would be the same as if he said that he had a true idea, but was not sure whether or not it was false (a little consideration will make this plain); or if anyone affirmed that substance is created, it would be the same as saying that a false idea was true—in short, the height of absurdity. It must, then, necessarily be admitted that the existence of substance as its essence is an eternal truth. And we can hence conclude by another process of reasoning—that there is but one such substance.[5]

[5] Spinoza, *Ethics.*

This last phrase summarizes the key doctrine of the entire *Ethics,* that there can be but one substance. The argument in this note, which insists that the essence of substance includes its existence, was a very popular argument throughout the Middle Ages. It means, quite simply, that if you can even imagine something whose essence includes existence, then you know that thing necessarily exists. In a further digression (but it is the digressions that often contain the most philosophy), Spinoza adopts Aristotle's insistence (see p. 49) that everything (or every event) must have its cause:

> There is necessarily for each individual existent thing a cause why it should exist.
> This cause of existence must either be contained in the nature and definition of the thing defined, or must be postulated apart from such definition.[6]

It is such an assertion that gives Aristotle the basis for his "prime mover" argument. But Spinoza, unlike Aristotle, has no qualms about the idea of an "infinite regress"; and so, in his view, the universe extends back in time forever, has always existed, and at no time ever came into existence.

What then follows is the working out of the notion that there is one substance:

> PROP. IX. *The more reality or being a thing has, the greater the number of its attributes* (Def. iv.).
> PROP. X. *Each particular attribute of the one substance must be conceived through itself.*
> *Proof.*—An attribute is that which the intellect perceives of substance, as constituting its essence (Def. iv.), and, therefore, must be conceived through itself (Def. iii.). *Q.E.D.*[7]

Spinoza goes on to explain that, although we might think of different attributes separately (for example, think of minds and bodies as totally different from each other), we must not conclude that they are different substances. They are rather separate properties of one and the same substance. He then concludes that:

> Consequently it is abundantly clear, that an absolutely infinite being must necessarily be defined as consisting in infinite attributes, each of which expresses a certain eternal and infinite essence.
> If anyone now ask, by what sign shall he be able to distinguish different substances, let him read the following propositions, which show that there is but one substance in the universe, and that it is absolutely infinite, wherefore such a sign would be sought for in vain.[8]

Now this looks complicated, but we can appreciate its straightforward significance by looking at it through our earlier questions in ontology and cosmology: first, how many substances does Spinoza say that there are (and must be)? Only one—he is a monist, like the earliest pre-Socratics. Descartes, Spinoza's immediate predecessor, had argued that there are three kinds of

[6] Spinoza, *Ethics.*
[7] Spinoza, *Ethics.*
[8] Spinoza, *Ethics.*

substance: bodies, minds, and God. Spinoza, however, argues that the very definition of substance makes it necessary that there be only one substance, and that bodies and minds are attributes of this one substance, not substances themselves. So the answer to our second ontological question, "what kind of substances?" is "one infinite substance," the full nature of which we cannot know. But at least we know two of its properties, namely body and mind. Now notice that this gets around a problem that will plague Descartes (see Chapter 9); how can different substances, which by definition are independent, interact with one another (our fourth question)? If mind and body are separate substances, then how can they come together to form a person? For Spinoza, since there is only one substance, this problem does not arise. With regard to our third question, "how do we distinguish different things (attributes, bodies, and minds)?" Spinoza's answer is fantastic; there is ultimately only one body, namely the physical universe, and one mind, namely all of the thinking in the universe (which in turn are different attributes of the one substance). This means that distinctions between our bodies ("my" body and "your" body) and between our bodies and the rest of the physical universe are ultimately unwarranted, a humanistic pretention which has no basis in reality. But even more surprising is the idea that there is but a single mind, and that our individual minds are somehow only "part of it" (that is, particular modes) but not individual minds at all! Your pride in your "individuality," therefore, has no foundation in reality. You are only a part of that one cosmic substance, the universe.

But the universe is also God. Here is where the innocent-looking obscurity of Spinoza's system becomes the heresy which was banned throughout Europe. By Proposition X, Spinoza has proved that God, substance, and the cause-of-itself are all identical. In the next few propositions, he proves that God necessarily exists (we shall see similar proofs in Ch. 7). Then, Proposition XIV: *"Besides God, no substance can be granted or conceived."* This means that God and the universe are one and the same. This position, called *pantheism* (literally, "everything is God"), was considered sacrilege, even in liberal Amsterdam. It means, against all traditional Judeo-Christian teachings, that God has no existence independent of the universe and that he therefore cannot be its Creator. Look again at the explanation to Definition VIII and then at Proposition XV and those that follow:

PROP. XV. *Whatsoever is, is in God, and without God nothing can be, or be conceived.*

PROP. XVI. *From the necessity of the divine nature must follow an infinite number of things in infinite ways—that is, all things which can fall within the sphere of infinite intellect.*

PROP. XVII. *God acts solely by the laws of his own nature, and is not constrained by anyone.*

PROP. XVIII. *God is the indwelling and not the transient cause of all things.*

PROP. XIX. *God, and all the attributes of God, are eternal.*

PROP. XX. *The existence of God and his essence are one and the same.*

PROP. XXI. *All things which follow from the absolute nature of any attribute of God must always exist and be infinite, or, in other words, are eternal and infinite through the said attribute.*

PROP. XII. *Whatever follows from any attribute of God, in so far as it is modified by a modification, which exists necessarily and as infinite, through the said attribute, must also exist necessarily and as infinite.*

PROP. XXIII. *Every mode which exists both necessarily and as infinite must necessarily follow either from the absolute nature of some attribute of God, or from an attribute modified by a modification which exists necessarily and as infinite.*

PROP. XXIV. *The essence of things produced by God does not involve existence.*

PROP. XXV. *God is the efficient cause not only of the existence of things, but also of their essence.*[9]

Yes, Spinoza believes in God. But God is nothing other than the universe. He has few of the characteristics traditionally attributed to Him and worshipped in Him. For example, Spinoza goes on to argue, on the basis of what he has said already, that God has no will, that He doesn't do anything, and ultimately, He doesn't care about anything either, including humanity. Here is a scientific world view that is so unrelenting that even Newton himself would be shocked by it. This does not mean that Spinoza is a materialist; quite to the contrary, the importance of his constant insistence upon "the infinite attributes of God," of which we are capable of knowing only two (could you imagine what some of the others might be like?) is to say that God has not only physical existence but (at least) mental existence as well. But where the scientific outlook becomes most dramatic is in Spinoza's defense of the doctrine we shall call *determinism,* the thesis that every event in the universe necessarily occurs as the result of its cause. The ultimate cause is God, which is to say, the universe itself. Once again, the terms come from Aristotle, but it is therefore important to insist that Spinoza does not believe—with either Aristotle or Christendom—that the universe has any purpose whatsoever. Nor does he believe that the universe or God has any beginning or end, thus answering our two sets of cosmological questions with a single necessary truth, once again, derived directly from the definition of substance.

The ultimate meaning of Spinoza's arguments for determinism is that no action, whether of man or God, is ever free. Everything in the universe, according to Spinoza, is exactly as it must be; the universe couldn't be any other way. Nothing is so pointless as struggling against a universe in which everything, including our own natures and actions, is already determined.

PROP. XXVI. *A thing which is conditioned to act in a particular manner has necessarily been thus conditioned by God; and that which has not been conditioned by God cannot condition itself to act.*

PROP. XXVII. *A thing, which has been conditioned by God to act in a particular way, cannot render itself unconditioned.*

[9] Spinoza, *Ethics.*

PROP. XXVIII. *Every individual thing, or everything which is finite and has a conditioned existence, cannot exist or be conditioned to act, unless it be conditioned for existence and action by a cause other than itself, which also is finite and has a conditioned existence; and likewise this cause cannot in its turn exist or be conditioned to act, unless it be conditioned for existence and action by another cause, which also is finite and has a conditioned existence, and so on to infinity.*

PROP. XXIX. *Nothing in the universe is contingent, but all things are conditioned to exist and operate in a particular manner by the necessity of the divine nature.*[10]

PROP. XXX. *Intellect, in function finite, or in function infinite, must comprehend the attributes of God and the modifications of God, and nothing else.*

PROP. XXXI. *The intellect in function, whether finite or infinite, as will, desire, love, &c., should be referred to passive nature and not to active nature.*

PROP. XXXII. *Will cannot be called a free cause, but only a necessary cause.*

PROP. XXXIII. *Things could not have been brought into being by God in any manner or in any order different from that which has in fact obtained.* [God is determined too]

PROP. XXXIV. *God's power is identical with his essence.*

PROP. XXXV. *Whatsoever we conceive to be in the power of God, necessarily exists.*

PROP. XXXVI. *There is no cause from whose nature some effect does not follow.*[11]

Part II of the *Ethics* discusses "the Nature and Origin of the Mind." It begins with a further set of definitions and axioms, most importantly, the definition of body as "extended thing," that is, extended in space (which Spinoza got directly from Descartes and the medieval philosophers) and idea, "the mental conception which is formed by the mind as a thinking thing." Mind, unlike body, is defined as *unextended* (that is, it has no spacial dimensions). It is in this part that Spinoza argues those surprising doctrines that we have already summarized: mind and body are each one of an infinite number of attributes of God, not substance themselves (as they were for Descartes), and that our individual minds are really indistinguishable modifications of the one Great Mind of the One Substance. And Spinoza joins with all of his metaphysical colleagues in insisting that "the order and connection of ideas is the same as the order and connection of things" (Prop. VII). Here again is Spinoza's affirmation of his confidence in thought to grasp reality. (Remember Heraclitus, "thought is Being.")

The upshot of Part II, and the subject which dominates the *Ethics* for the remaining three Parts, is Spinoza's determinism.

[10] We are all determined by the nature of God or the universe. But then, here is a problem: are we not then compelled to struggle, and can't help but doing so? If so, what is the point of Spinoza's urging us not to. This Spinoza never answers.
[11] Spinoza, *Ethics.*

PROP. XLVIII. *In the mind there is no absolute or free will; but the mind is determined to wish this or that by a cause, which has been determined by another cause, and this last by another cause, and so on to infinity.*[12]

Spinoza has none of Aristotle's fears of an "infinite regress," and if he believes in a "cause-of-itself," that is not the same as a "first cause," for there is no such thing. We shall talk more about this "free will and determinism" problem in Chapter 10, but it is worth noting, as a way of summing up, Spinoza's drastic answer to the problem. As an unyielding determinist, he rejects every attempt to save some space for freedom of human action. But he assures us that we can, with heroic effort (Prop. XLVII), understand the nature of this determinism, and accept it gracefully. The folly is in the fighting, he tells us. The remainder of the *Ethics* is given over to the attempt to draw out the logical consequences of this stoic conclusion. Part III is a long argument against emotions and what we would call "emotional involvement" as the needless cause of suffering and vice. Against them, Spinoza argues the virtues of human reason, which penetrates the useless involvements of the emotions and allows us to understand the causes of our actions and feelings. And to understand an emotion, Spinoza believes, is to change and eliminate it. For example, to understand why one is angry, according to Spinoza, is sufficient to let us get rid of our anger. To realize that we are unable to change, according to Spinoza, is the only freedom we can really be said to have.

What you have just seen is modern metaphysics at its most brilliant. The geometrical method, however, is no longer fashionable, and much of Spinoza's language is, to us, antiquated and unnatural. But the intricacies of his system, the way he ties so many different ideas together, the answers he gave to ancient philosophical problems, and the boldness with which he sets out a new vision of the universe, have made Spinoza's philosophy widely appreciated despite his difficult style. What you are about to read, though, is no less astonishing, no less brilliant, and its author no less remarkable a genius. The work from which these excerpts come is a very short work (of about 90 paragraphs) written by Leibniz, who begins with much the same concepts and definitions as Spinoza, but ends up with a wholly different metaphysical system. (Leibniz and Spinoza met several times and discussed these issues. But Leibniz found Spinoza's opinions too shocking and acquaintanceship with him too dangerous.)

GOTTFRIED WILHELM VON LEIBNIZ

Leibniz begins with the same technical notion of substance, but from it he weaves an entirely different but equally fantastic picture of the universe. Where Spinoza's universe was mechanical and wholly dependent upon causes, Leibniz's

---

[12] Spinoza, *Ethics*.

universe is very much alive, and everything happens for a purpose (as in Aristotle's ancient teleology). The guiding principle of Leibniz's philosophy is called "The Principle of Sufficient Reason," which says, simply, that there must be a reason for everything. Even God, on this account, cannot act capriciously, but must have a reason for whatever He has created. We shall see that this principle is among the most important guidelines to Leibniz's philosophy. From it, he develops a radical alternative to Isaac Newton's physics and a spectacularly optimistic view that, because God acts according to this principle, this world that He created must be "the best of all possible worlds."

Where Spinoza argues that there can be at most one substance, Leibniz argues that there are many. He calls them *monads*. Every monad is different from every other, and God (who is something of a supermonad and the only "uncreated monad") has created them all. The work you are about to read, accordingly, is called the *Monadology* ("the study of monads"), written in 1714. It is a very condensed summary of Leibniz's metaphysics:

> 1. The Monad, of which we will speak here, is nothing else than a simple substance, which goes to make up composites; by simple, we mean without parts.
> 2. There must be simple substances because there are composites; for a composite is nothing else than a collection or *aggregatum* of simple substances.[13]

A simple substance is one that cannot be divided. The argument is curious: any "composite" is obviously divisible. That means that every composite must be "composed" of some simple substances that make it up. (There is a hidden infinite regress argument here: if there weren't ultimately simple substances, then we could go on dividing things forever.) But if the simple substances were extended in space, then they too would be further divisible, for anything that has length, for example, no matter how small, can be cut in two (at least in theory). Therefore, Leibniz concludes, these basic simple substances or monads must be immaterial and have no extension. They can have neither parts, nor extension, nor divisibility:

> 3. Now, where there are no constituent parts there is possible neither extension, nor form, nor divisibility. These Monads are the true Atoms of nature, and, in fact, the Elements of things.[14]

Here, in Leibniz's first three propositions, are the answers to our first two ontological questions: "How many substances are there?" Many. This answer makes Leibniz a pluralist. "What kind of substances are they?" Simple and immaterial substances, which makes Leibniz an *immaterialist*. (Don't be misled by the term "atoms": we are used to thinking of atoms as the smallest material substances, but Leibniz's atoms are *im*material.) And now, in three more propositions, Leibniz answers our first cosmological question: "Are these sub-

[13] Gottfried W. von Leibniz, *Monadology,* in *The Rationalists,* trans. George Montgomery (New York: Doubleday, 1960).
[14] Leibniz, *Monadology.*

stances eternal, or do they come into being at some time? How do they come into being? And are they destructible?":

> 4. Their dissolution, therefore, is not to be feared and there is no way conceivable by which a simple substance can perish through natural means.
>
> 5. For the same reason there is no way conceivable by which a simple substance might, through natural means, come into existence, since it can not be formed by composition.
>
> 6. We may say then, that the existence of Monads can begin or end only all at once, that is to say, the Monad can begin only through creation and end only through annihilation. Composites, however, begin or end gradually.[15]

Spinoza had argued that the one substance could neither be created nor destroyed; it had neither beginning nor end. Leibniz's substances, or "monads," can be created or destroyed, but not by any "natural" means. They can be created or destroyed only "all at once." Anticipating later propositions, we can guess that Leibniz will have God (who is something of a supermonad) create them. But notice that compounds of monads, for example, "material objects," can be created and destroyed "naturally."

Now our third question, "How do we distinguish different substances or monads?":

> 8. Still Monads must have some qualities, otherwise they would not even be existences. And if simple substances did not differ at all in their qualities, there would be no means of perceiving any change in things. Whatever is in a composite can come into it only through its simple elements and the Monads, if they were without qualities, since they do not differ at all in quantity, would be indistinguishable one from another. For instance, if we imagine *a plenum* or completely filled space, where each part receives only the equivalent of its own previous motion, one state of things would not be distinguishable from another.
>
> 9. Each Monad, indeed, must be different from every other. For there are never in nature two beings which are exactly alike, and in which it is not possible to find a difference either internal or based on an intrinsic property.[16]

Only God could actually know everything about every monad in order to compare and contrast them. But even God can distinguish different monads only because they in fact have differences between them. This leads Leibniz to suggest one of his most controversial principles, the so-called "Principle of the Identity of Indiscernibles": no two monads can have the same properties (Prop. 9). Why is this? According to the "Principle of Sufficient Reason" (Prop. 32) nothing can be without good reason. Even God, therefore, would have no good reason for duplicating any monad. If two monads were identical, Leibniz argues, God could have no reason for putting one in one place and

[15] Leibniz, *Monadology.*
[16] Leibniz, *Monadology.*

the other in another place, or for creating them both in the first place. Therefore, no two monads could be exactly alike. A strange kind of argument, but very much at the heart of Leibniz's philosophy, as we shall see later.

How does a monad, which is by definition "simple," alter or combine with other monads to form the changing and familiar universe of our experience? (Here you should be reminded of the similar problems that faced the ancient Pre-Socratics and Plato.) Here is our fourth question, and the most difficult Leibniz has to answer: "How do substances interact?" By definition, monads cannot literally "interact." And so Leibniz's answer is extremely speculative and imaginative:

> 7. There is also no way of explaining how a Monad can be altered or changed in its inner being by any other created thing, since there is no possibility of transposition within it, nor can we conceive of any internal movement which can be produced, directed, increased or diminished there within the substance, such as can take place in the case of composites where a change can occur among the parts. The Monads have no windows through which anything may come in or go out.[17]

The problem is that different substances, by definition, are independent and cannot, therefore, have anything to do with one another. Descartes, as we shall see in Chapter 9, had a terrible time getting together his two substances of mind and body. Spinoza, as a monist, solved the problem in the simplest possible way; since there is only one substance, no question of "interaction" is applicable. But Leibniz is a pluralist; there are many substances. They cannot interact as such. They cannot even perceive each other in the usual sense. They "have no windows," in his peculiar but now famous expression. "Nothing can come in or go out." And unlike the ancient (and modern) materialist atomists, Leibniz cannot have his monads simply combine and recombine to form new compounds in any usual sense. They cannot, in Leibniz's words, "be altered or changed in [their] inner being by any other created thing." So, how do monads change? They must have all changes already created (by God) within themselves.

Remember the animism that was so prevalent in the ancient Greek philosophers. For them, the phenomenon of life was the model for metaphysics. The idea of Newtonian mechanics would have been incomprehensible to them. Leibniz, we may now say, was vehemently anti-Newton. He was, we may also say, one of the outstanding modern animists. A monad is as different as can be from a Newtonian material atom; a monad is alive, and its changes come from within, never from without. (Except, that is, for its initial creation.) Think of a monad as a living being, "programmed" (to use a modern word) with all of the information and experiences it needs to develop in a certain way, like an acorn developing into an oak tree. Thus the changes in the monad are all internal, programmed by God at the creation. Now keep in mind that a monad is immaterial, and so its "growth" cannot be thought of as a develop-

[17] Leibniz, *Monadology*.

ment in the physical world. The growth too, therefore, must be internal, and the apparent interaction between monads must really be changes in the perceptions of the monads themselves.

10. I assume it as admitted that every created being, and consequently the created Monad, is subject to change, and indeed that this change is continuous in each.

11. It follows from what has just been said, that the natural changes of the Monad come from an internal principle, because an external cause can have no influence upon its inner being.

12. Now besides this principle of change there must also be in the Monad a manifoldness which changes. This manifoldness constitutes, so to speak, the specific nature and the variety of the simple substances.

13. This manifoldness must involve a multiplicity in the unity or in that which is simple. For since every natural change takes place by degrees, there must be something which changes and something which remains unchanged, and consequently there must be in the simple substance a plurality of conditions and relations, even though it has no parts.

14. The passing condition which involves and represents a multiplicity in the unity, or in the simple substance, is nothing else than what is called Perception. This should be carefully distinguished from Consciousness.[18]

Leibniz argues here that what we call interactions between things are really changes in perceptions; for example, what we are really talking about when we describe a squirrel climbing a tree is our perception of a squirrel climbing a tree. This makes Leibniz an idealist, for he is claiming that the sense in which material things exist in space is that we experience (*perceive*) them as existing. What is ultimately real, therefore, is perception, and it is perception that changes, within each monad, to create the appearance of a moving and changing material world. Notice that Leibniz carefully distinguishes "Perception" from what he calls "Consciousness." Perception is experience in general, and is present, in some degree, in every monad. Consciousness, on the other hand, is a very special kind of experience, reflective and articulate, and is to be found only in a few monads. (It is worth noting that, with this distinction, Leibniz precociously introduces the concept of "the unconscious" into German philosophy two hundred years before Freud.)

15. The action of the internal principle which brings about the change or the passing from one perception to another may be called Appetition. It is true that the desire is not always able to attain to the whole of the perception which it strives for, but it always attains a portion of it and reaches new perceptions.

16. We, ourselves, experience a multiplicity in a simple substance, when we find that the most trifling thought of which we are conscious involves a variety in the object. Therefore all those who acknowledge that the soul is a simple substance ought to grant this multiplicity in the Monad. . . .

17. It must be confessed, however, that Perception, and that which de-

18 Leibniz, *Monadology*.

pends upon it, are inexplicable by mechanical causes, that is to say, by figures and motions. Supposing that there were a machine whose structure produced thought, sensation, and perception, we could conceive of it as increased in size with the same proportions until one was able to enter into its interior, as he would into a mill. Now, on going into it he would find only pieces working upon one another, but never would he find anything to explain Perception.

Here is the attack on Newton's more materialist view of the universe. Such a view, Leibniz complains, cannot account for experience (perception), in other words, the immaterial aspects of the universe.

It is accordingly in the simple substance, and not in the composite nor in a machine that the Perception is to be sought. Furthermore, there is nothing besides perceptions and their changes to be found in the simple substance. And it is in these alone that all the internal activities of the simple substance can consist.

18. All simple substances or created Monads may be called Entelechies, because they have in themselves a certain perfection. There is in them a sufficiency which makes them the source of their internal activities, and renders them, so to speak, incorporeal Automations. [In other words, every monad is to a certain extent, alive.]

19. If we wish to designate as soul everything which has perceptions and desires in the general sense that I have just explained, all simple substances or created Monads could be called souls. But since feeling is something more than a mere perception I think that the general name of Monad or Entelechy should suffice for simple substances which have only perception, while we may reserve the term Soul for those whose perception is more distinct and is accompanied by memory. [Again, Leibniz insists that "Perception" is most primitive and is common to all monads.]

20. We experience in ourselves a state where we remember nothing and where we have no distinct perception, as in periods of fainting, or when we are overcome by a profound, dreamless sleep. In such a state the soul does not sensibly differ at all from a simple Monad. As this state, however, is not permanent and the soul can recover from it, the soul is something more.

21. Nevertheless it does not follow at all that the simple substance is in such a state without perception. This is so because of the reasons given above; for it cannot perish, nor on the other hand would it exist without some affection and the affection is nothing else than its perception. When, however, there are a great number of weak perceptions where nothing stands out distinctively, we are stunned; as when one turns around and around in the same direction, a dizziness comes on, which makes him swoon and makes him able to distinguish nothing. Among animals, death can occasion this state for quite a period. [!]

22. Every present state of a simple substance is a natural consequence of its preceding state, in such a way that its present is pregnant with its future. [Here is Leibniz's version of the thesis that one cause necessarily follows another.]

23. Therefore, since on awakening after a period of unconsciousness

we become conscious of our perceptions, we must, without having been conscious of them, have had perceptions immediately before; for one perception can come in a natural way only from another perception, just as a motion can come in a natural way only from a motion.

24. It is evident from this that if we were to have nothing distinctive, or so to speak prominent, and of a higher flavor in our perceptions, we should be in a continual state of stupor. This is the condition of Monads which are wholly bare.

25. We see that nature has given to animals heightened perceptions, having provided them with organs which collect numerous rays of light or numerous waves of air and thus make them more effective in their combination. Something similar to this takes place in the case of smell, in that of taste and of touch, and perhaps in many other senses which are unknown to us.

. . . . . .

29. It is the knowledge of eternal and necessary truths that distinguishes us from mere animals and gives us reason and the sciences, thus raising us to a knowledge of ourselves and of God. This is what is called in us the Rational Soul or the Mind.

30. It is also through the knowledge of necessary truths and through abstractions from them that we come to perform Reflective Acts, which cause us to think of what is called the I, and to decide that this or that is within us. It is thus, that in thinking upon ourselves we think of *being,* of *substance,* of the *simple* and *composite,* of a *material* thing and of *God* himself, conceiving that what is limited in us is in him without limits. These Reflective Acts furnish the principal objects of our reasonings.[19]

The answer to our fourth question is, "Monads don't interact." Each is locked into itself, and contains within itself its own view of the universe as a whole.

56. Now this interconnection, relationship, or this adaptation of all things to each particular one, and of each one to all the rest, brings it about that every simple substance has relations which express all the others and that it is consequently a perpetual living mirror of the universe.

57. And as the same city regarded from different sides appears entirely different, and is, as it were multiplied respectively, so, because of the infinite number of simple substances, there are a similar infinite number of universes which are, nevertheless, only the aspects of a single one as seen from the special point of view of each monad.

But, of course, the perspective of any one monad is extremely one-sided and confused.

60. Besides, in what has just been said can be seen the *a priori* reasons why things cannot be otherwise than they are. It is because God, in ordering the whole, has had regard to every part and in particular to each monad; and since the monad is by its very nature *representative,* nothing can limit it

[19] Leibniz, *Monadology.*

to represent merely a part of things. It is nevertheless true that this representation is, as regards the details of the whole universe, only a confused representation, and is distinct only as regards a small part of them, that is to say, as regards those things which are nearest or greatest in relation to each monad. If the representation were distinct as to the details of the entire universe, each monad would be a Deity. It is not in the object represented that the monads are limited, but in the modifications of their knowledge of the object. In a confused way they reach out to infinity or to the whole, but are limited and differentiated in the degree of their distinct perceptions.

Now Leibniz has an alternative to Newton: bodies (composite monads) only seem to interact; in fact, it all happens within each monad, programmed and created by God in "pre-established harmony."

61. In this respect composites are like simple substances, for all space is filled up; therefore, all matter is connected. And in a plenum or filled space every movement has an effect upon bodies in proportion to this distance, so that not only is every body affected by those which are in contact with it and responds in some way to whatever happens to them, but also by means of them the body responds to those bodies adjoining them, and their intercommunication reaches to any distance whatsoever. Consequently every body responds to all that happens in the universe, so that he who saw all could read in each one what is happening everywhere, and even what has happened and what will happen.

62. Thus although each created monad represents the whole universe, it represents more distinctly the body which specially pertains to it and of which it constitutes the entelechy. And as this body expresses all the universe through the interconnection of all matter in the plenum, the soul also represents the whole universe in representing this body, which belongs to it in a particular way.[20]

Every monad develops as a reflection of the development of all the other monads in the universe as well. If, for example, we are watching a squirrel climb around a tree, Leibniz's view is that the reality of the squirrel climbing around the tree is actually our perception of this. But you can see that this alone is not sufficient; we might simply dream or hallucinate this view, and it would then not be "real" at all. The difference between the dream and the reality is the changes in the other monads, for instance, the monads that constitute the squirrel, and any other observers of the same scene, including God. Reality is composed of the totality of all monads, each perceiving from its own perspective (although God, Leibniz insists, perceives from all perspectives at once). The "pre-established harmony" guarantees that all of these views from all of these perspectives are in agreement, so that our view of the squirrel, for example, is matched by the squirrel's view of us.

This view of the pre-established harmony between monads allows Leibniz to give a surprising answer to our fourth question, "How do different substances interact?" By definition, substances cannot interact as such. But they

[20] Leibniz, *Monadology.*

can seem to interact if their perceptions are coordinated. Thus, the collision of two billiard balls is in fact a harmony of perceptions about the collision of two billiard balls. Two people fighting is in fact a harmony of perceptions by each of the two people (and anyone else who is watching) about those two people fighting. This answer may seem to be extreme, but given Leibniz's conception of the universe as composed of a great number of immaterial substances, it is an answer that is necessary for his philosophy to be consistent. It is an answer which is also necessary, however, to enable him to reject Newton's cosmology, which he and many of his contemporaries found even more extreme and difficult to understand that Leibniz's own strange view of interaction.

The last of our initial set of questions about substance and our second cosmological question is, "are space and time themselves substances?" According to Leibniz, the anwer to this question is an emphatic "no!" It is on this question that Leibniz makes his sharpest break with Newton's physics. Are monads "in" space? Leibniz would have said "no." But he also seems to give the surprising answer that not only are monads not "in" space (since they are immaterial) but they are, strictly speaking, not "in" time either. The monad does not change in time, but rather, time is in the monad. That is, time is a relation between experiences of the monad. It is not something independent. This view of space and time are intimately tied to Leibniz's analysis of the only seeming "interaction" between monads. Both are rejections of Newton's theory, and an attempt to offer an alternative.

To our way of thinking, Leibniz's views seem bizarre, compared to the almost common sense character of Newton's theory. Newton had argued that the universe was the motion of (material) atoms in empty space, acting against each other according to the laws of motion, force, and gravity that he had so elegantly formulated. But Newton's theories, which seem almost quaintly obvious to us now, contained what most people of his and Leibniz's time—including Newton himself—considered to be manifest absurdities. One, relating to our fourth ontological question, was the idea of action at a distance, the idea that one object could affect another although the two were not even in contact. (For example, the idea that the moon and the earth have gravitational attraction for each other.) Thus Leibniz's conception of windowless monads, each seeming to interact with others but in fact only developing within itself, would have seemed to his contemporaries no less absurd than Newton's view of causality. Leibniz didn't need causality, he had his "pre-established harmony." Newton, meanwhile, had a great deal of trouble reconciling his mechanistic theories with the traditional ideas of God and Creation, which he continued to hold for the rest of his life.

The most famous disagreement between Leibniz and Newton concerns the nature of space and time, a topic that is still being debated because of the impact of Einstein's theory of relativity at the beginning of this century. Newton's mechanical theory seemed to presuppose the existence of some permanent container, namely space, in which the material atoms of his theory could mutually attract and bounce against each other. This container, which could exist independently of its contents is called *absolute space*. In itself, this sounds entirely reasonable; we talk about things "moving in space" and "taking up space." But then, can we also talk about the entire universe being "in" space, the way a basketball can be said to be "in" the basket? This idea has some absurd consequences which led Leibniz and many of his contemporaries to reject it. The idea that space could exist apart from all things in it, perhaps even entirely empty (or what many philosophers called the *void*) would mean that it makes sense to talk about movement or location in space even when there isn't anything in space, not even points and rulers with which to measure distances or dimensions. Bertrand Russell, one of Leibniz's most famous followers, pointed out the absurdity of this idea by asking, "if space is absolute, then wouldn't it make sense to suggest that the universe might have doubled in size last night?" But what would it mean to say that the universe has gotten larger. An elephant or a planet or even a galaxy can get larger, but only in comparison to some measuring stick and a frame of reference. It is only by such comparisons that such "size" talk makes sense. But to say that the universe doubles in size is to say that our measuring stick, and we ourselves, double in size also. So all comparisons remain the same. Similarly, what would it mean to say that the universe in its entirety moved one foot to the left? All of the one-foot measurements are in the universe. There is no way to talk about the universe itself moving. On the basis of such considerations, Leibniz rejected Newton's idea of absolute space as absurd. In its place, he insisted that space is relative, that is, relative to measurements and things that are measured. There is no absolute space; there is only space relative to the various positions of the monads, that is, to observers.

The same is true of time. Newton believed in *absolute time* also, time as existing apart from anything happening "in" it. But the same consequences follow this initially reasonable idea. If time is absolute, it seems to make sense to ask, "when did the universe begin?" (In fact, astronomers are again asking this question.) But what could this "when" refer to? It can't refer to any measurement in the universe (clocks, the age of rocks or stars) for it is the universe itself that is being measured. And, there aren't any measures of time outside of the universe. Consequently, Leibniz rejected absolute time along with absolute space. Both are relative to the monads and have no possible existence of their own. This means, among other things, that there could be no void or empty space, nor could there be any sense of time in which literally nothing happened. Space and time, according to Leibniz, are relative to our own perceptions.

Now I said many pages ago that such cosmological issues were never the domain of philosophy alone, and you are well aware that current physics and astronomy are still very much involved with these questions. And both alternatives, from Newton and from Leibniz, are still very much alive. Scientists indeed do still talk about the beginning of the universe, and with awesome sophistication; and of course they also talk in strictly relativistic terms, like Leibniz, but now à la Einstein. To delve into these issues any further, therefore, we should have to leave eighteenth century metaphysics and move into twentieth century physics. What is often relevant to these philosophical debates are the new and sometimes strange experimental findings that are always emerging from the sciences. Recently, for example, experiments with the speed of light have brought about startling changes in our views of space and time. One consequence of this changed view is the idea that we cannot intelligibly talk about two events happening "at the same time" if they are a sufficiently great distance apart, say several billion light years. The discovery of radiation from outer space and the expansion of galaxies has raised old issues about creation in a new way: whether the universe was created all at once and then started to expand and change (the "big-bang theory") or whether there is continuous creation going on even now (the "steady-state theory"). Because of recent theories in science, philosophers are now willing to say things that would have seemed like utter nonsense to both Newton and Leibniz—for example, that "space is curved."

These are not issues to be settled by scientists alone, however; it is philosophical theories that give structure and meaning to the scientific experiments. But neither can philosophers simply cut themselves off from science and pretend that they can solve these problems "just in their heads." At the outer reaches of science, you will find philosophy; just as, at the beginnings of philosophy, you will find the unanswered problems of science.

In an earlier chapter, we stressed the importance of a basic assumption of all metaphysics, that the universe is intelligible. In Leibniz's philosophy, this assumption is presented as one of the basic presuppositions of all thinking; he calls it,

> 32. . . . the Principle of Sufficient Reason, in virtue of which we believe that no fact can be real and no statement true unless it has a sufficient reason why it should be thus and not otherwise. Most frequently, however, these reasons cannot be known to us.[21]

They can, however, be known to God, who knows everything. It is on the basis of this principle, for example, that Leibniz defends the claim he made in Prop. 9, that two monads can never be identical ("the identity of indiscernibles"). The reasoning is this: since God is the supremely rational Being (monad), He must have a reason for all that He does. But Leibniz also argues (Prop. 58) that God must have created the universe "with the greatest possible variety together with the greatest order that may be." Here is the reason why God would not have created any two monads alike. But the Principle of Sufficient Reason has a further implication; it also serves as a principle of divine ethics. Among the various possible worlds (that is, among the infinitely many ways in which the world might have been), God chooses the most perfect, that is, "the best of all possible worlds." Here is the doctrine of cosmic optimism that Voltaire so brilliantly lampooned in his play, Candide. But Leibniz took this concept of "the best of all possible worlds" very seriously. In the next century,

---

[21] Leibniz, Monadology.

it was to provide a foundation for much of the optimism of the Enlightenment. And in Leibniz's own metaphysics, it provides the concluding propositions of the *Monadology*, a joyous optimism that creates as close to a "happy ending" as one can expect to find in a serious philosophical treatise.

> 85. Whence it is easy to conclude that the totality of all spirits must compose the city of God, that is to say, the most perfect state that is possible under the most perfect monarch.

· · · · ·

> 90. Finally, under this perfect government, there will be no good action unrewarded and no evil action unpunished; everything must turn out for the well-being of the good; that is to say, of those who are not disaffected in this great state, who, after having done their duty, trust in Providence and who love and imitate, as is meet, the Author of all Good, delighting in the contemplation of his perfections according to the nature of that genuine, pure love which finds pleasure in the happiness of those who are loved. It is for this reason that wise and virtuous persons work in behalf of everything which seems comformable to presumptive or antecedent will of God, and are, nevertheless, content with what God actually brings to pass through his secret, consequent and determining will, recognizing that if we were able to understand sufficiently well the order of the universe, we should find that it surpasses all the desires of the wisest of us, and that it is impossible to render it better than it is, not only for all in general, but also for each one of us in particular, provided that we have the proper attachment for the author of all, not only as the Architect and the efficient cause of our being [our Creator] but also as our Lord and the Final Cause [purpose of our existence] who ought to be the whole goal of our will, and who alone can make us happy.[22]

This theological "happy ending" is not an afterthought for Leibniz; it is the heart of his philosophy. Like his older contemporary Spinoza, his involvement in metaphysics is ultimately a very personal concern for religion and for his own view of himself and his place in the world. From this perspective, it is revealing to see the vast differences between the two philosophers. Spinoza's view of humanity is extremely anti-individualistic, and each individual is wholly submerged in the concept of the one substance. In Leibniz, however, even his pluralism reinforces the view that each individual is a world in him or herself, and his idealism places an emphasis on mind and thought that is in sharp contrast with Spinoza's balance between thought and body (although many critics have charged Spinoza with emphasizing body to an alarming degree). Spinoza's determinism and his view that ultimately we can do nothing but understand is surely a gloomy view compared to Leibniz's happy confidence that this is the "best of all possible worlds." And, of course, Spinoza's heretical view of God as the one substance (sometimes called *pantheism*) is very different from Leibniz's more traditional and pious view.

[22] Leibniz, *Monadology.*

Of equal importance, however, are the more technical issues that are raised by Leibniz and Spinoza, for these have preoccupied scientists and metaphysicians alike for over two centuries. The nature of ultimate reality ("substance") and the nature of space and time are still unresolved questions. These questions are still the subject of some of the most current investigations in science and philosophy. And many of the current answers are modeled after those of Spinoza and Leibniz. In addition to the content of their theories, the methods of Spinoza and Leibniz also continue to dominate much of modern philosophy. Leibniz's logic, for example is considered by many modern logicians, Bertrand Russell for one, to be one of the most important advances in modern thinking.

Our concern in this chapter has been to study the best modern examples of a metaphysical system. For this purpose, Spinoza's *Ethics* and Leibniz's *Monadology* serve excellently. But now that we have investigated these two systems and come to appreciate their admirable intelligence as well as some of their obscurities, it is necessary to end on a note of doubt. We have seen two of the most brilliant minds in the history of philosophy begin with the same basic concept, "substance," and use similar methods of deduction to arrive at wholly different views of reality. How could they disagree so radically? And, thinking of ourselves, how are we to decide which of them to agree with? How can we defend one system against the other? Since the systems flatly contradict each other on several points (for example, whether there is only one or whether there are many substances), we cannot logically agree with both of them. Thus the question arises, how can one prove a metaphysical theory? How can we know the way the world really is? Or, more skeptically, can we know the way the world really is?

SUMMARY AND CONCLUSION

In this chapter we have summarized the thought of two of the greatest metaphysical thinkers of modern times. Both begin from the concept of "substance" and attempt to use deduction as a method for proving the ultimate nature of reality. Their answers, however, are extremely different. Spinoza argues that there can only be one substance; Leibniz argues that there are many. For Spinoza, God is identical to the universe, to the one substance; for Leibniz, God is distinct from all other substances, which He created. For Spinoza, mind and body are but two of an infinite number of attributes of God, the only two that we can know; for Leibniz, all substances are ultimately immaterial. But beneath these technical concerns is a struggle by both philosophers to answer the most important problems of human existence: the nature of God and proper religion, the place of man and woman in the universe, and the role and foundations of science.

GLOSSARY

absolute (space and time): the view that space and time exist independently of objects and events "in" them, a view defended by Newton. In general, absolute, as used in philosophy, means independent and nonrelative, unqualified and all-inclusive. Accordingly, it is often used as a way of referring to reality, or substance, or God.

action-at-a-distance: the idea that one object can have a causal effect on another from a distance, as in Newton's laws of gravitational attraction. Leibniz's rejection of this idea as "absurd" led him to develop a noncausal interpretation of the same phenomena.

animism: (see Glossary, Ch. 1)

attribute: in Spinoza, an essential property of God; for example, having a physical nature, having thoughts. In general, an attribute is a property (as in Aristotle).

best of all possible worlds: Leibniz's view that God demands a perfect universe and makes it "the best possible," all things considered.

cause-of-itself (*causa sui*): that which explains its own existence, often said of God. It also follows from the usual definitions of substance.

determinism: the view that every event in the universe is dependent upon other events which are its causes. On this view, all human actions and decisions, even those which we would normally describe as "free" and "undetermined," are totally dependent on prior events which cause them. (This problem will be examined in Ch. 10.)

extended: having spacial dimensions. Philosophers (for example, Descartes, Leibniz, and Spinoza) often define bodies as "extended," minds and ideas as "unextended."

idealism: the metaphysical view that only minds and their ideas exist.

Identity of Indiscernibles: a principle of Leibniz's philosophy according to which no two things can possibly have all of the same properties, or be absolutely identical in all respects.

modes: in Spinoza, inessential properties or modifications of attributes.

monad: in Leibniz, the simple immaterial substances that are the ultimate constituents of all reality. God, the one uncreated monad, created all of the others as self-enclosed ("windowless") predetermined entities.

Principle of Sufficient Reason: in Leibniz, the insistence that all events must have their "reasons," and that ultimately all events must have their explanations in God's reasons. The principle is sometimes invoked to assert that everything must have some explanation, whether or not God is involved. (For example, scientists use such a principle in their work, as we shall see in the following chapter.)

pre-established harmony: the belief that the order of the universe is pre-arranged by God. In Leibniz, this view allows him an alternative to Newton's theory of causal relationships.

unextended: not having spacial dimensions. Philosophers (for example, Descartes, Leibniz and Spinoza) often define mind and ideas as unextended.

void: empty space.

3

KNOWLEDGE

The Chinese philosopher awakened with a start, for he had been dreaming that he was a butterfly. And for the rest of his days, he did not know whether he was a Chinese philosopher dreaming that he was a butterfly, or a butterfly who was now dreaming that he was a Chinese philosopher.

Chuang-Tzu

After an evening of heated but fruitless metaphysical debate with a number of his friends, the British physician John Locke turned to them and asked, "shouldn't we first determine whether we are capable of answering such questions?" They agreed. Perhaps you are thinking much the same thing. These great metaphysical systems are surely monuments to human intelligence. But do they achieve what they are intended to? Do they tell us "the way the world really is?" Since each of the contending systems claims that it does, how can it be that they disagree? Which is right? And how can we decide?

In 1690, Locke took philosophy around a sharp turn, one that had been suggested by Descartes a half century before. But Descartes had broached the question "what can we know?" only as a preface to his metaphysics. Locke, on the other hand, decided to put questions about reality on the shelf until he could develop an adequate theory of human knowledge. Accordingly, his great book is not primarily an inquiry into substance or reality or God or truth (although all of these enter in); it is *An Essay Concerning Human Understanding*. From metaphysics, the study of ultimate reality, we now turn to *epistemology*, the study of human knowledge—how we get it, what it is, whether we have it, or why we don't.

Even before Plato, Parmenides had seen that between knowledge and reality are the appearances of reality, which might be very different from the reality itself. Plato's "Parable of the Cave" is a graphic illustration of this distinction. Descartes, although he distrusted his senses and wasn't certain that they gave accurate representations of reality, at least could be certain of the appearances themselves—he could not be mistaken about them. And here is the problem that has defined modern epistemology, the seeming abyss between reality and mere appearance. Perhaps we know the appearances of things, but how can we know that we know the reality "behind" them?

Let us return for a moment to the central idea of traditional metaphysics, that of substance. Substance is that which underlies all of the various properties of a thing (or things); and it is the properties, never the substance itself, that are experienced by us. Now, presumably, there can be no properties unless they are properties of something. That seems to be a platitude. But yet, we cannot experience the nature of the substance itself. And here begins the embarrassment of metaphysics.

The problem was stated succinctly by the best-known British philosopher of this century, Bertrand Russell, in a little volume called *The Problems of Philosophy*. He says:

> In daily life, we assume as certain many things which, on a closer scrutiny, are found to be so full of apparent contradictions that only a great amount of thought enables us to know what it is that we really may believe. In the search for certainty, it is natural to begin with our present experiences, and in some sense, no doubt, knowledge is to be derived from them. But any statement as to what it is that our immediate experiences make us know is very likely to be wrong. It seems to me that I am now sitting in a chair, at a table of a certain shape, on which I see sheets of paper with writing or print. By turning my head I see out of the window buildings and clouds and the sun. I believe that the sun is about ninety-three million miles from the earth; that it is a hot globe many times bigger than the earth; that, owing to the earth's rotation, it rises every morning, and will continue to do so for an indefinite time in the future. I believe that, if any other normal person comes into my room, he will see the same chairs and tables and books and papers as I see, and that the table which I see is the same as the table which I feel pressing against my arm. All this seems to be so evident as to be hardly worth stating, except in answer to a man who doubts whether I know anything. Yet all this may be reasonably doubted, and all of it requires much careful discussion before we can be sure that we have stated it in a form that is wholly true.
>
> To make our difficulties plain, let us concentrate attention on the table. To the eye it is oblong, brown and shiny, to the touch it is smooth and cool and hard; when I tap it, it gives out a wooden sound. Any one else who sees and feels and hears the table will agree with this description, so that it might seem as if no difficulty would arise; but as soon as we try to be more precise our troubles begin. Although I believe that the table is 'really' of the same colour all over, the parts that reflect the light look much brighter than the other parts, and some parts look white because of reflected light. I know that, if I move, the parts that reflect the light will be different, so that the apparent distribution of colours on the table will change. It follows that if several people are looking at the table at the same moment, no two of them will see exactly the same distribution of colours, because no two can see

it from exactly the same point of view, and any change in the point of view makes some change in the way the light is reflected.

For most practical purposes these differences are unimportant, but to the painter they are all-important: the painter has to unlearn the habit of thinking that things seem to have the colour which common sense says they 'really' have, and to learn the habit of seeing things as they appear. Here we have already the beginning of one of the distinctions that cause most trouble in philosophy—the distinction between 'appearance' and 'reality', between what things seem to be and what they are. The painter wants to know what things seem to be, the practical man and the philosopher want to know what they are; but the philosopher's wish to know this is stronger than the practical man's, and is more troubled by knowledge as to the difficulties of answering the question.

To return to the table. It is evident from what we have found, that there is no colour which preeminently appears to be *the* colour of the table, or even of any one particular part of the table—it appears to be of different colours from different points of view, and there is no reason for regarding some of these as more really its colour than others. And we know that even from a given point of view the colour will seem different by artificial light, or to a colour-blind man, or to a man wearing blue spectacles, while in the dark there will be no colour at all, though to touch and hearing the table will be unchanged. This colour is not something which is inherent in the table, but something depending upon the table and the spectator and the way the light falls on the table. When, in ordinary life, we speak of *the* colour of the table, we only mean the sort of colour which it will seem to have to a normal spectator from an ordinary point of view under usual conditions of light. But the other colours which appear under other conditions have just as good a right to be considered real; and therefore, to avoid favouritism, we are compelled to deny that, in itself, the table has any one particular colour.

The same thing applies to the texture. With the naked eye one can see the grain, but otherwise the table looks smooth and even. If we looked at it through a microscope, we should see roughnesses and hills and valleys, and all sorts of differences that are imperceptible to the naked eye. Which of these is the 'real' table? We are naturally tempted to say that what we see through the microscope is more real, but that in turn would be changed by a still more powerful microscope. If, then, we cannot trust what we see with the naked eye, why should we trust what we see through a microscope? Thus, again, the confidence in our senses with which we began deserts us.

The *shape* of the table is no better. We are all in the habit of judging as to the 'real' shapes of things, and we do this so unreflectingly that we come to think we actually see the real shapes. But, in fact, as we all have to learn if we try to draw, a given thing looks different in shape from every different point of view. If our table is 'really' rectangular, it will look, from almost all points of view, as if it had two acute angles and two obtuse angles. If opposite sides are parallel, they will look as if they converged to a point away from the spectator; if they are of equal length, they will look as if the nearer side were longer. All these things are not commonly noticed in looking at a table, because experience has taught us to construct the 'real' shape from the apparent shape, and the 'real' shape is what interests us as practical men. But the 'real' shape is not what we see; it is something inferred from what we see. And what we see is constantly changing in shape as we move about the room; so that here again the senses seem not to give us the truth about the table itself, but only about the appearance of the table.

Similar difficulties arise when we consider the sense of touch. It is true that the table always gives us a sensation of hardness, and we feel that it resists pressure. But the sensation we obtain depends upon how hard we press the table and also upon what part of the body we press with; thus the various sensations due to various pressures or various parts of the body cannot be supposed to reveal *directly* any definite property of the table, but at most to be *signs* of some property which perhaps *causes* all the sensations, but is not actually apparent in any of them. And the same applies still more obviously to the sounds which can be elicited by rapping the table.

Thus it becomes evident that the real table, if there is one, is not the same as what we immediately experience by sight or touch or hearing. The real table, if there is one, is not *immediately* known to us at all, but must be an inference from what is immediately known. Hence, two very difficult questions at once arise; namely, (1) Is there a real table at all? (2) If so, what sort of object can it be?[1]

In these few pages, Russell succeeds in summarizing the problems that have dominated British philosophy since Locke's original epistemological studies. But why say "British philosophy?" Why should this problem have been more serious there than on the continent of Europe, where most of the great metaphysicians were working? Why should it have had more impact on Locke and his followers than on Descartes, Spinoza, Leibniz and their latter-day followers? Because of a single profound difference, which has always created a general gap in understanding between British-American philosophy and European philosophy. Descartes, Spinoza, and Leibniz retained their faith in human reason's ability to give us knowledge of reality, despite the fact that reality was beyond our every possible experience. Because of their confidence in the powers of reason, they are usually called rationalists. And because it happens that all three were Europeans (Descartes was French, Spinoza, Dutch, and Leibniz, German), they are often called *continental rationalists*. The movement developed by John Locke, on the other hand, is generally called *empiricism*, because of its insistence upon the data of experience (or *empirical* data) as the source of all knowledge. (A *datum* [plural, *data*] is a bit of "given" information; modern empiricist philosophers sometimes talk of *sense-data*, that is, the information immediately given by the senses.) Also included in this group of empiricists are Bishop George Berkeley[2] and David Hume, whom we shall also meet in this chapter. And because they were all from Great Britain, they are often called *British empiricists*. (Berkeley was Irish; Hume, Scottish; Bertrand Russell is generally considered a more contemporary member of this same movement.)

[1] Bertrand Russell, *The Problems of Philosophy* (Oxford: Oxford University Press, 1912).
[2] Bishop Berkeley traveled to America; Berkeley, California is named after him.

So, how are we to know reality? By retaining traditional confidence in our own powers of abstract reason? or by appeal to experience, which carries with it the threat that we may never know reality beyond our experience at all?

THE RATIONALIST'S CONFIDENCE: DESCARTES

Let's return to the philosopher who began the modern emphasis on methodology, René Descartes. We have already seen his "method of doubt," but the goal of this method is not to defend the doubts but, quite to the contrary, to move from doubt to knowledge and certainty. Descartes' doubt is intended only to separate what is doubtful from what is not. He never doubted, nor did his followers, that he would be able to find beliefs that were beyond doubt and use them to prove all sorts of other beliefs about reality. These beliefs would be "clear and distinct" and "perfectly certain." (Spinoza refers to such ideas as "adequate ideas"; Leibniz calls them "truths of reason.") Once Descartes had found even one such belief, he could use it as a premise, from which he could deduce all of his other beliefs about reality. And none of this depends upon the data of experience; it is entirely a process of reason, of examining the clarity of his beliefs and the logical connections between them.

When we left him in the Introduction, Descartes had completed his first "Meditation," in which he resolved to doubt everything, supposing for the sake of argument that an evil demon was causing him to believe a great many falsehoods. Given such a supposition (which he did not really believe for a second, of course) could there be any belief that would still be beyond doubt and "perfectly certain?" Descartes believes that there is, and it is at this point that we rejoin him in the second of his *Meditations*. Having watched him work his way into Plato's Cave, it is only proper that we now watch him work his way out again:

MEDITATION II

Of the nature of the human mind; and
that it is more easily known than the body

The Meditation of yesterday filled my mind with so many doubts that it is no longer in my power to forget them. And yet I do not see in what manner I can resolve them; and, just as if I had all of a sudden fallen into very deep water, I am so disconcerted that I can neither make certain of setting my feet on the bottom, nor can I swim and so support myself on the surface. I shall nevertheless make an effort and follow anew the same path as that on which I yesterday entered, i.e. I shall proceed by setting aside all that in which the least doubt could be supposed to exist, just as if I had discovered that it was absolutely false; and I shall ever follow in this road until I have met with something which is certain, or at least, if I can do nothing else, until I have learned for certain that there is nothing in the world that is certain. Archimedes, in order that he might draw the terrestrial globe out of its place, and transport it elsewhere, demanded only that one point should be fixed and immovable; in the same way I shall have the right to conceive high hopes if I am happy enough to discover one thing only which is certain and indubitable.

I suppose, then, that all the things that I see are false; I persuade myself that nothing has ever existed of all that my fallacious memory represents to me. I consider that I possess no senses; I imagine that body, figure, extension, movement and place are but the fictions of my mind. What, then, can be esteemed as true? Perhaps nothing at all, unless that there is nothing in the world that is certain.

But how can I know there is not something different from those things that I have just considered, of which one cannot have the slightest doubt? Is there not some God, or some other being by whatever name we call it, who puts these reflections into my mind? That is not necessary, for is it not possible that I am capable of producing them myself? I myself, am I not at least something? But I have already denied that I had senses and body. Yet I hesitate, for what follows from that? Am I so dependent on body and senses that I cannot exist without these? But I was persuaded that there was nothing in all the world, that there was no heaven, no earth, that there were no minds, nor any bodies: was I not then likewise persuaded that I did not exist? Not at all; of a surety I myself did exist since I persuaded myself of something [or merely because I thought of something]. But there is some deceiver or other, very powerful and very cunning, who ever employs his ingenuity in deceiving me. Then without doubt I exist also if he deceives me, and let him deceive me as much as he will, he can never cause me to be nothing so long as I think that I am something. So that after having reflected well and carefully examined all things, we must come to the definite conclusion that this proposition: I am, I exist, is necessarily true each time that I pronounce it, or that I mentally conceive it.[3]

But I do not yet know clearly enough what I am, I who am certain that I am; and hence I must be careful to see that I do not imprudently take some other object in place of myself, and thus that I do not go astray in respect of this knowledge that I hold to be the most certain and most evident of all that I have formerly learned. That is why I shall now consider anew what I believed myself to be before I embarked upon these last reflections; and of my former opinions I shall withdraw all that might even in a small degree be invalidated by the reasons which I have just brought forward, in order that there may be nothing at all left beyond what is absolutely certain and indubitable.

What then did I formerly believe myself to be? Undoubtedly I believed myself to be a man. But what is a man? Shall I say a reasonable animal? Certainly not; for then I should have to inquire what an animal is, and what is reasonable; and thus from a single question I should insensibly fall into an infinitude of others more difficult; and I should not wish to waste the little time and leisure remaining to me in trying to unravel subtleties

[3] The more famous formulation of this proposition, *cogita, ergo sum,* "I think, therefore I am," occurs in his earlier *Discourse on Method* (1637). It is worth mentioning that St. Augustine had used this argument over 1000 years before.

like these. But I shall rather stop here to consider the thoughts which of themselves spring up in my mind, and which were not inspired by anything beyond my own nature alone when I applied myself to the consideration of my being. In the first place, then, I considered myself as having a face, hands, arms, and all that system of members composed of bones and flesh as seen in a corpse which I designated by the name of body. In addition to this I considered that I was nourished, that I walked, that I felt, and that I thought, and I referred all these actions to the soul: but I did not stop to consider what the soul was, or if I did stop, I imagined that it was something extremely rare and subtle like a wind, a flame, or an ether, which was spread throughout my grosser parts. As to body I had no manner of doubt about its nature, but thought I had a very clear knowledge of it; and if I had desired to explain it according to the notions that I had then formed of it, I should have described it thus: By the body I understand all that which can be defined by a certain figure: something which can be confined in a certain place, and which can fill a given space in such a way that every other body will be excluded from it; which can be perceived either by touch, or by sight, or by hearing, or by taste, or by smell: which can be moved in many ways not, in truth, by itself, but by something which is foreign to it, by which it is touched [and from which it receives impressions]: for to have the power of self-movement, as also of feeling or of thinking, I did not consider to appertain to the nature of body: on the contrary, I was rather astonished to find that faculties similar to them existed in some bodies.

But what am I, now that I suppose that there is a certain genius which is extremely powerful, and, if I may say so, malicious, who employs all his powers in deceiving me? Can I affirm that I possess the least of all those things which I have just said pertain to the nature of body? I pause to consider, I revolve all these things in my mind, and I find none of which I can say that it pertains to me. It would be tedious to stop to enumerate them. Let us pass to the attributes of soul and see if there is any one which is in me? What of nutrition or walking [the first mentioned]? But if it is so that I have no body it is also true that I can neither walk nor take nourishment. Another attribute is sensation. But one cannot feel without body, and besides I have thought I perceived many things during sleep that I recognized in my waking moments as not having been experienced at all. What of thinking? I find here that thought is an attribute that belongs to me; it alone cannot be separated from me. I am, I exist, that is certain. But how often? Just when I think; for it might possibly be the case if I ceased entirely to think, that I should likewise cease altogether to exist. I do not now admit anything which is not necessarily true: to speak accurately I am not more than a thing which thinks, that is to say a mind or a soul, or an understanding, or a reason, which are terms whose significance was formerly unknown to me. I am, however, a real thing and really exist; but what thing? I have answered: a thing which thinks. . . . What is a thing which thinks? It is a thing which doubts, understands, [conceives], affirms, denies, wills, refuses, which also imagines and feels.[4]

---

[4] René Descartes, "Meditation II," in *Meditations on First Philosophy,* in *The Philosophical Works of Descartes,* trans. Elizabeth S. Haldane and G. R. T. Ross (Cambridge: Cambridge University Press, 1911).

Descartes has his premise, the fact of his own existence as a "thinking thing." What must follow, then, is the use of this premise in an argument that will "prove" the beliefs he began by doubting: the existence of his own body, the existence of the "external" world, and the existence of God. And, finally, he must somehow get rid of his tentative supposition of the evil demon. But first, he raises once again the old metaphysical question of substance. In a very famous example, he argues:

> Let us begin by considering the commonest matters, those which we believe to be the most distinctly comprehended, to wit, the bodies which we touch and see; not indeed bodies in general, for these general ideas are usually a little more confused, but let us consider one body in particular. Let us take, for example, this piece of wax: it has been taken quite freshly from the hive, and it has not yet lost the sweetness of the honey which it contains; it still retains somewhat of the odour of the flowers from which it has been culled; its colour, its figure, its size are apparent; it is hard, cold, easily handled, and if you strike it with the finger, it will emit a sound. Finally all the things which are requisite to cause us distinctly to recognize a body, are met with in it. But notice that while I speak and approach the fire what remained of the taste is exhaled, the smell evaporates, the colour alters, the figure is destroyed, the size increases, it becomes liquid, it heats, scarcely can one handle it, and when one strikes it, no sound is emitted. Does the same wax remain after this change? We must confess that it remains; none would judge otherwise. What then did I know so distinctly in this piece of wax? It could certainly be nothing of all that the senses brought to my notice, since all these things which fall under taste, smell, sight, touch, and hearing, are found to be changed, and yet the same wax remains.
>
> Perhaps it was what I now think, viz. that this wax was not that sweetness of honey, nor that agreeable scent of flowers, nor that particular whiteness, nor that figure, nor that sound, but simply a body which a little while before appeared to me as perceptible under these forms, and which is now perceptible under others. But what, precisely, is it that I imagine when I form such conceptions? Let us attentively consider this, and, abstracting from all that does not belong to the wax, let us see what remains. Certainly nothing remains excepting a certain extended thing which is flexible and movable. But what is the meaning of flexible and movable? Is it not that I imagine that this piece of wax being round is capable of becoming square and of passing from a square to a triangular figure? No, certainly it is not that, since I imagine it admits of an infinitude of similar changes, and I nevertheless do not know how to compass the infinitude of my imagination, and consequently this conception which I have of the wax is not brought about by the faculty of imagination. What now is this extension? Is it not also unknown? For it becomes greater when the wax is melted, greater when it is boiled, and greater still when the heat increases; and I should not conceive [clearly] according to truth what wax is, if I did not think that even this piece that we are considering is capable of receiving more variations in extension than I have ever imagined. We must then grant that I could not even understand through the imagination what this piece of wax is, and that it is

my mind alone which perceives it. I say this piece of wax in particular, for as to wax in general it is yet clearer. But what is this piece of wax which cannot be understood excepting by the [understanding or] mind? It is certainly the same that I see, touch, imagine, and finally it is the same which I have always believed it to be from the beginning. But what must particularly be observed is that its perception is neither an act of vision, nor of touch, nor of imagination, and has never been such although it may have appeared formerly to be so, but only an intuition of the mind, which may be imperfect and confused as it was formerly, or clear and distinct as it is at present, according as my attention is more or less directed to the elements which are found in it, and of which it is composed.[5]

This "intuition of mind" is the key to all rationalist thinking. Intuition is where the rationalist obtains his premises, from which he argues to all other conclusions. And the difference between the rationalist and the empiricist, at least in what they say that they are doing, is the rationalist's heavy reliance on nonempirical intuition. Both would agree on the legitimacy of the deductions which follow; it is the source of the premises that is in dispute. And intuition, according to the rationalists, has its source in reason alone. (Notice that "reason" refers not only to the activity of reasoning but to unreasoned intuitions and insights as well.) Accordingly, it is this source of intuition that will be the center of the dispute rather than the actual arguments which Descartes then uses to "prove" his other beliefs. The strategy of Descartes' argument is as follows. First, there is the premise, which you have seen,

I exist (as a thinking thing).

Then (in "Meditation III"), Descartes uses this premise to prove the existence of God. So,

God exists. (We shall look at his "proof" in Chapter 7.)

And, by His very nature (another intuition), God is good, in fact, perfectly good. And so,

Since He has given me a very strong inclination to believe that these ideas (of trees, houses, etc.) arise from corporeal objects, I do not see how He could be vindicated from the charge of deceit, if in truth they proceeded from any other source, or were produced by other causes than corporeal things? [For example, by the evil demon, or in dreams.]

Therefore:

We cannot be deceived [whether by the evil demon or whatever else.]

. . . I cannot doubt but that there is in me a certain passive faculty of perception, that is, of receiving and taking knowledge of the ideas of sensible things; but this would be useless to me, if there did not also exist in me, or in some other thing, another active faculty capable of forming and producing those ideas. But this active faculty cannot be in me [in as far as I am but a thinking thing], seeing that it does not presuppose thought, and also that those ideas are frequently produced in my mind without my contributing to

5 Descartes, "Meditation II."

it in any way, and even frequently contrary to my will. This faculty must therefore exist in some substance different from me, in which all the objective reality of the ideas that are produced by this faculty is contained formally or eminently, as I before remarked: and this substance is either a body, that is to say, a corporeal nature in which is contained formally [and in effect] all that is objectively [and by representation] in those ideas; or it is God himself, or some other creature, of a rank superior to body, in which the same is contained eminently. But as God is no deceiver, it is manifest that he does not of himself and immediately communicate those ideas to me, nor even by the intervention of any creature in which their objective reality is not formally, but only eminently, contained. For as he has given me no faculty whereby I can discover this to be the case, but, on the contrary, a very strong inclination to believe that those ideas arise from corporeal objects, I do not see how he could be vindicated from the charge of deceit, if in truth they proceeded from any other source, or were produced by other causes than corporeal things: and accordingly it must be concluded, that corporeal objects exist. Nevertheless they are not perhaps exactly such as we perceive by the senses, for their comprehension by the senses is, in many instances, very obscure and confused; but it is at least necessary to admit that all which I clearly and distinctly conceive as in them, that is, generally speaking, all that is comprehended in the object of speculative geometry, really exists external to me.[6]

The argument is not convincing, as Descartes' critics were very quick to point out. Where does Descartes get his confidence in reason to begin with, such that he feels confident in his own abilities to prove God's existence? Descartes' answer is that we get that confidence from God Himself. But with this answer he has begged the question, that is, he has presumed the existence of God in order to get the confidence with which he then proves God's existence. (This circularity of argument is often called "the Cartesian Circle.") Another way of criticizing the same strategy is to say that, having once introduced the evil demon, Descartes has no way of getting rid of him, since that supposition undermines his confidence in his own reason just as thoroughly as his confidence in God bolsters it.

Our primary concern, however, is with Descartes' claim that certain beliefs are self-evident or "clear and distinct" on the basis of intuition and reason alone. These are beliefs which we don't have to learn—in fact, couldn't learn—from experience. It is not just Descartes' "I exist" premise that is such a belief; all of the rules of inference, which he uses in his arguments, are also beliefs of this kind. And, ultimately, his confidence in reason itself is one too. But how does one defend these beliefs, for not every philosopher agrees with them. In particular, John Locke, in his disillusionment with metaphysics, begins his philosophy with an assault on the very idea of knowledge that is independent of experience. Thus he begins with an attack on the heart of the rationalist methodology.

[6] Descartes, "Meditation VI."

CONCERNING HUMAN UNDERSTANDING
JOHN LOCKE

Regarding metaphysics, John Locke is reported to have commented to a f.
"you and I have had enough of this kind of fiddling." Against the somet?
fantastic claims of the metaphysicians, Locke sought a restoration of comm
sense.[7] Just as Aristotle had acted as a healthy slap in the face to Plato
extravagant two-worlds view, Locke acted as a corrective to the metaphysical
enthusiasm of the medieval and modern worlds. He accepted Descartes' method
of tentative skepticism, but he questioned his French predecessor's urge to
metaphysics as well as his confidence in the insights of pure reason. He rejected
the unsupportable "intuitions" that provided Descartes with his rules and his
premises, and he turned instead to the data of experience as the ultimate
source of all knowledge. He therefore rejected Descartes' exclusively deductive
method and supplanted it with a method appropriate to generalizations from
experience, or *induction*. In inductive reasoning, the conclusion always goes
beyond the premises and therefore, unlike deduction, is always less certain
than they are. (For example, from the observed fact that all the philosophy
professors that you have met have been absent-minded (the premise), you
conclude, by *inductive generalization,* that all philosophy professors are probably absent-minded.) Accordingly, Locke also modified Descartes' demand for
"perfect certainty" and allowed for probability and "degrees of assent." But
it must not be thought that Locke therefore rejected reason as such. He still
accepted the certainty of mathematical reasoning and the validity of deductive
inferences; but he also expanded the concept of rationality to include inductive
reasoning and probability as well as deduction and certainty.

Locke's *Essay Concerning Human Understanding* (1689) is built on a
single premise, namely, that all our knowledge comes from experience. This
means, in his view, that there cannot possibly be ideas that are prior to
experience, ideas that are "born into" us, as suggested so vividly by Plato. In
other words, Locke refuses to accept the notion of innate ideas, by which he
means not only those ideas that are literally "born into us" but all ideas that
are derived without appeal to experience. This includes, in his opinion,
Descartes' "clear and distinct ideas," Spinoza's "adequate ideas," and Leibniz's
"truths of reason."

> 1. *The way shown how we come by any knowledge, sufficient to prove
> it not innate.*—It is an established opinion among some men, that there
> are in the understanding certain innate principles; some primary notions,
> κοιναί ᾽έννοιαι, characters, as it were, stamped upon the mind of man

---

[7] British empiricism has traditionally considered itself the defender of "common sense"
against the excesses of metaphysics. This was even true of Berkeley and Hume, who
reached conclusions more outrageous than any metaphysician. And it is also true of
Bertrand Russell and G. E. Moore in this century.

oul receives in its very first being, and brings into the world with
which would be sufficient to convince unprejudiced readers of the falseness
it. Opposition, if I should only show (as I hope I shall in the following
of this discourse) how men, barely by the use of their natural faculties may attain to all the knowledge they have, without the help of any
the impressions, and may arrive at certainty, without any such original
ions or principles. . . .

2. *General Assent the great Argument.*—There is nothing more commonly taken for granted, than that there are certain principles both speculative and practical (for they speak of both), universally agreed upon by all
mankind, which therefore, they argue, must needs be constant impressions
which the souls of men receive in their first beings, and which they bring
into the world with them, as necessarily and really as they do any of their
inherent faculties.

3. *Universal Consent proves nothing innate.*—This argument, drawn
from universal consent, has this misfortune in it, that if it were true in matter of fact that there were certain truths wherein all mankind agreed, it
would not prove them innate, if there can be any other way shown how men
may come to that universal agreement in the things they do consent in,
which I presume may be done.

4. *"What is, is," and "it is impossible for the same Thing to be and not
to be," not universally assented to.*—But, which is worse, this argument of
universal consent, which is made use of to prove innate principles, seems to
me a demonstration that there are none such; because there are none to
which all mankind give an universal assent. I shall begin with the speculative, and instance in those magnified principles of demonstration, "Whatsoever is, is," and "It is impossible for the same thing to be, and not to be";
which, of all others, I think, have the most allowed title to innate. These
have so settled a reputation of maxims universally received that it will no
doubt be thought strange if anyone should seem to question it. But yet I take
liberty to say that these propositions are so far from having an universal
assent that there are a great part of mankind to whom they are not so much
as known.

5. *Not on the Mind naturally imprinted, because not known to Children, Idiots, &.*—For, first, it is evident that all children and idiots have not
the least apprehension or thought of them; and the want of that is enough
to destroy that universal assent which must needs be the necessary concom-
itant of all innate truths: it seeming to me near a contradiction to say that
there are truths imprinted on the soul which it perceives or understands not;
imprinting, if it signify anything, being nothing else but the making certain
truths to be perceived. For to imprint anything on the mind without the
mind's perceiving it, seems to me hardly intelligible. If therefore children
and idiots have souls, have minds, with those impressions upon them, they
must unavoidably perceive them, and necessarily know and assent to these
truths; which since they do not, it is evident that there are no such impressions. For if they are not notions naturally imprinted, how can they be innate? And if they are notions imprinted, how can they be unknown? To say
a notion is imprinted on the mind, and yet at the same time to say that the
mind is ignorant of it, and never yet took notice of it, is to make this impres-

sion nothing. No proposition can be said to be in the mind which it never yet knew, which it was never yet conscious of.[8]

The argument is straightforward; there is in fact no universal agreement regarding supposedly "innate" principles, and even if there were, that would not prove their "innateness." Rather, he argues:

> Let us suppose the mind to be, as we say, a blank tablet (*tabula rasa*) of white paper, void of all characters, without any ideas; how comes it to be furnished? Whence comes it by that vast store, which the busy and boundless fancy of man has painted on it with almost endless variety? Whence has it all the materials of reason and knowledge? To this I answer in one word, from *experience:* in that all our knowledge is founded, and from that it ultimately derives itself.[9]

It is this premise that Locke is concerned to defend and use, and his attack on innate ideas is by way of introduction. But Locke fails to succeed in proving that the human mind does not have inborn potentials and limitations, and more importantly, he fails to recognize that inference from experience might itself require principles which are not drawn from experience. In fact, Leibniz, one of the chief targets of Locke's attack, was not long in providing what we might call "the rationalist's reply." Turning Locke against himself, Leibniz argued that, by his own principles, he could not attack the concept of innate ideas.

> . . . The question at issue is whether the soul in itself is entirely empty, like the tablet upon which nothing has yet been written [*tabula rasa*], as is the view of Aristotle and the author of the *Essay* [Locke], and whether all that is traced on it comes solely from the senses and from experience; or whether the soul contains originally the principles of various notions and doctrines which external objects merely awaken from time to time, as I believe, with Plato and even with the Schoolmen, and with all those who take in this sense the passage of St. Paul (Romans, 2:15) where he remarks that the law of God is written in the heart. . . . From this there arises another question, whether all truths depend on experience, that is to say, on induction and examples, or whether there are some that have some other basis. For if some events can be foreseen before any trial has been made of them, it is clear that we must here contribute something of our own. The senses, although necessary for all our actual knowledge, are not sufficient to give us the whole of it, since the senses never give anything except examples, that is to say, particular or individual truths. All examples which confirm a general truth, however numerous they may be, are not enough to establish the universal necessity of this same truth; for it does not follow that what has happened will happen again in the same way.
>
> . . . It would seem that necessary truths, such as are found in pure mathematics, and especially in arithmetic and in geometry, must have principles the proof of which does not depend on examples, nor, consequently,

---

[8] John Locke, *An Essay Concerning Human Understanding*, ed. A. C. Fraser (Oxford: Clarendon Press, 1894).

[9] Locke, *An Essay Concerning Human Understanding*.

on the testimony of the senses, although without the senses it would never have occurred to us to think of them. This ought to be well recognised; Euclid has so well understood it that he often demonstrates by reason what is obvious enough through experience and by sensible images. Logic also, together with metaphysics and ethics, one of which forms natural theology and the other natural jurisprudence, are full of such truths; and consequently their proof can only come from internal principles, which are called innate. It is true that we must not imagine that these eternal laws of the reason can be read in the soul as in an open book, as the edict of the praetor can be read in his *album* without difficulty or research; but it is enough that they can be discovered in us by dint of attention, for which opportunities are given by the senses. The success of experiments serves also as confirmation of the reason, very much as proofs serve in arithmetic for better avoiding error of reckoning when the reasoning is long. . . .

It seems that our able author claims that there is nothing potential in us and nothing even of which we are not at any time actually conscious; but he cannot mean this strictly, or his opinion would be too paradoxical; for acquired habits and the contents of our memory are not always consciously perceived and do not even always come to our aid at need, although we often easily bring them back to mind on some slight occasion which makes us remember them, just as we need only the beginning of a song to remember the song. Also he modifies his assertion in other places by saying that there is nothing in us of which we have not been at least formerly conscious. But besides the fact that no one can be sure by reason alone how far our past apperceptions, which we may have forgotten, may have gone, especially in view of the Platonic doctrine of reminiscence, which, mythical as it is, is not, in part at least, incompatible with bare reason; in addition to this, I say, why is it necessary that everything should be acquired by us through the perceptions of external things, and that nothing can be unearthed in ourselves? Is our soul, then, such a blank that, besides the images borrowed from without, it is nothing? . . . there are a thousand indications that lead us to think that there are at every moment numberless perceptions in us, but without apperception and without reflection; that is to say, changes in the soul itself of which we are not conscious, because the impressions are either too slight and too numerous, or too even, so that they have nothing sufficient to distinguish them one from the other; but, joined to others, they do not fail to produce their effect and to make themselves felt at least confusedly in the mass. . . .[10]

Locke himself did not continue the debate; he was already convinced of his own position and had more urgent problems to worry about (the political chaos in London following the "Glorious Revolution" of 1688). But the debate continued in different forms. The rise of anthropology in the nineteenth century, with the discoveries of societies whose basic ideas were radically different from our own, seemed to support Locke's claim that no one will believe in innate universal principles if they "ever look beyond the smoke of their own chimneys." But in the nineteenth century, there were also a great many philos-

[10] Gottfried von Leibniz, *New Essays on the Human Understanding*, trans. A. G. Langley (La Salle, Ill.: Open Court, 1949).

ophers who still argued for the existence of universal principles not learned through experience. (Immanuel Kant did this in a very powerful set of arguments which we shall view in the next several chapters.) In the early twentieth century, opinion was in general accord with Locke, but recently it has taken another swing back to Leibniz, this time, ironically, supported by anthropology. A major movement in the social sciences, usually called structuralism (whose main proponent is Claude Levi-Strauss in France) has argued that, underneath the many superficial differences between very different societies, there are certain basic "structures" which are universal and innate. And in America, the notion of innate ideas has appeared once again in the work of the well-known linguist, Noam Chomsky. According to Chomsky, certain capacities for language are built into us from birth, and this allows him to explain, not only the similarities of human thinking (which was the view that Locke attacked), but also the enormous capacity for learning different languages quickly. (The average three year old learns a language in six months.) The Locke-Leibniz debate is still very much alive.

THE EMPIRICIST THEORY OF KNOWLEDGE

The *tabula rasa* or "blank tablet" view of the mind is Locke's most famous epistemological concept. Leaving aside those special concerns which involve only "the relations between ideas" (as in mathematics, logic, and trivial conceptual truths such as "a horse is an animal"), all of our ideas are derived from experience. Epistemology (and philosophy in general) now became a kind of psychology (indeed, the two disciplines were not yet distinguished), a study of the history of our common experiences in order to discover where we get our ideas, particularly such ideas as substance, God and our various conceptions of reality. In his theory, Locke uses three familiar terms; *sensation* (or what more modern empiricists call sense-data), *ideas*, not in the Platonic sense but simply "the immediate object of perception, thought, or understanding," and *quality*, or what we have so far been calling property (for example, being red, being round, being heavy).

> 1. Concerning the simple ideas of Sensation, it is to be considered—that whatsoever is so constituted in nature as to be able, by affecting our senses, to cause any perception in the mind, doth thereby produce in the understanding a simple idea; which, whatever be the external cause of it, when it comes to be taken notice of by our discerning faculty, it is by the mind looked on and considered there to be a real positive idea in the understanding, as much as any other whatsoever; though, perhaps, the cause of it be but a privation of the subject.
>
> 2. Thus the ideas of heat and cold, light and darkness, white and black, motion and rest, are equally clear and positive ideas in the mind; though, perhaps, some of the causes which produce them are barely privations, in

those subjects from whence our senses derive those ideas. These the under-standing, in its view of them, considers all as distinct positive ideas, without taking notice of the causes that produce them: which is an inquiry not be-longing to the idea, as it is in the understanding, but to the nature of the things existing without us. These are two very different things, and carefully to be distinguished; it being one thing to perceive and know the idea of white or black, and quite another to examine what kind of particles they must be, and how ranged in the superficies, to make any object appear white or black. . . .

7. To discover the nature of our *ideas* the better, and to discourse of them intelligibly, it will be convenient to distinguish them *as they are ideas or perceptions in our minds;* and *as they are modifications of matter in the bodies that cause such perceptions in us:* that so we may not think (as per-haps usually is done) that they are exactly the images and resemblances of something inherent in the subject; most of those of sensation being in the mind no more the likeness of something existing without us, than the names that stand for them are the likeness of our ideas, which yet upon hearing they are apt to excite in us.

8. Whatsoever the mind perceives *in itself,* or is the immediate object of perception, thought, or understanding, that I call *idea;* and the power to produce any idea in our mind, I call *quality* of the subject wherein that power is. Thus a snowball having the power to produce in us the ideas of white, cold, and round,—the power to produce those ideas in us, as they are in the snowball, I call qualities; and as they are sensations or perceptions in our understandings, I call them ideas; which *ideas,* if I speak of sometimes as in the things themselves, I would be understood to mean those qualities in the objects which produce them in us.[11]

Notice that the basis of Locke's theory is the "common sense" distinction between physical objects in the world and sensations and ideas in our minds. Accordingly, we may talk of the qualities or properties inherent in the objects in the world and the qualities or properties that they cause in us. Locke refers to the first, namely those properties which are properties of the objects them-selves, as *primary qualities;* he calls the second, those properties "of the object" which are caused in us, *secondary qualities.* A paradigm of a primary quality would be the shape of an object; a paradigm of a secondary quality would be its color.

Primary qualities:

Qualities thus considered in bodies are, *First,* such as are utterly insepa-rable from the body, in what state soever it be; and such as in all the altera-tions and changes it suffers, all the force can be used upon it, it constantly keeps; and such as sense constantly finds in every particle of matter which has bulk enough to be perceived; and the mind finds inseparable from every particle of matter, though less than to make itself singly be perceived by our senses: e.g. Take a grain of wheat, divide it into two parts; each part has still solidity, extension, figure, and mobility: divide it again, and it retains still the same qualities; and so divide it on, till the parts become insensible;

[11] Locke, *An Essay Concerning Human Understanding.*

they must retain still each of them all those qualities. For division (which is all that a mill, or pestle, or any other body, does upon another, in reducing it to insensible parts) can never take away either solidity, extension, figure, or mobility from any body, but only makes two or more distinct separate masses of matter, of that which was but one before; all which distinct masses, reckoned as so many distinct bodies, after division, make a certain number. These I call *original* or *primary qualities* of body, which I think we may observe to produce simple ideas in us, viz. solidity, extension, figure, motion or rest, and number.

Secondary qualities:

Secondly, such qualities which in truth are nothing in the objects themselves but powers to produce various sensations in us by their primary qualities, i.e. by the bulk, figure, texture, and motion of their insensible parts, as colours, sounds, tastes, &c. These I call *secondary qualities*. To these might be added a *third* sort, which are allowed to be barely powers; though they are as much real qualities in the subject as those which I, to comply with the common way of speaking, call qualities, but for distinction, secondary qualities. For the power in fire to produce a new colour, or consistency, in *wax* or *clay*,—by its primary qualities, is as much a quality in fire, as the power it has to produce in *me* a new idea or sensation of warmth or burning, which I felt not before,—by the same primary qualities, viz. the bulk, texture, and motion of its insensible parts.[12]

The question, then, is how physical objects cause us to have sensations and ideas. Locke's answer, (which, like his theory as a whole is very strongly influenced by the physical theories of his contemporary Isaac Newton) is, by impulse. This might not seem illuminating, until you try to think of the Newtonian theory of force as a product of particles and masses in motion. And on this model, Locke develops what is now called his "Causal Theory of Perception." First, for the primary qualities:

If then external objects be not united to our minds when they produce ideas therein; and yet we perceive these *original* qualities in such of them as singly fall under our senses, it is evident that some motion must be thence continued by our nerves, or animal spirits, by some parts of our bodies, to the brains or the seat of sensation, there to produce in our minds the particular ideas we have of them. And since the extension, figure, number, and motion of bodies of an observable bigness, may be perceived at a distance by the sight, it is evident some singly imperceptible bodies must come from them to the eyes, and thereby convey to the brain some motion; which produces these ideas which we have of them in us.

Then, for secondary qualities:

After the same manner that the ideas of these original qualities are produced in us, we may conceive that the ideas of *secondary* qualities are also produced, viz. by the operation of insensible particles on our senses. For, it being manifest that there are bodies and good store of bodies, each whereof

[12] Locke, *An Essay Concerning Human Understanding.*

are so small, that we cannot by any of our senses discover either their bulk, figure, or motion,—as is evident in the particles of the air and water, and others extremely smaller than those; perhaps as much smaller than the particles of air and water, as the particles of air and water are smaller than peas or hail-stones;—let us suppose at present that the different motions and figures, bulk and number, of such particles, affecting the several organs of our senses, produce in us those different sensations which we have from the colours and smells of bodies; e.g. that a violet, by the impulse of such insensible particles of matter, of peculiar figures and bulks, and in different degrees and modifications of their motions, causes the ideas of the blue colour, and sweet scent of that flower to be produced in our minds. It being no more impossible to conceive that God should annex such ideas to such motions, with which they have no similitude, than that he should annex the idea of pain to the motion of a piece of steel dividing our flesh, with which that idea hath no resemblance.

What I have said concerning colours and smells may be understood also of tastes and sounds, and other the like sensible qualities; which, whatever reality we by mistake attribute to them, are in truth nothing in the objects themselves, but powers to produce various sensations in us; and depend on those primary qualities, viz. bulk, figure, texture, and motion of parts [as I have said].

Therefore:

I think it easy to draw this observation,—that the ideas of primary qualities of bodies are resemblances of them, and their patterns do really exist in the bodies themselves, but the ideas produced in us by these secondary qualities have no resemblance of them at all. There is nothing like our ideas, existing in the bodies themselves. They are, in the bodies we denominate from them, only a power to produce those sensations in us: and what is sweet, blue, or warm in idea, is but the certain bulk, figure, and motion of the insensible parts, in the bodies themselves, which we call so.

Flame is denominated hot and light; snow, white and cold; and manna, white and sweet, from the ideas they produce in us. Which qualities are commonly thought to be the same in those bodies that those ideas are in us, the one the perfect resemblance of the other, as they are in a mirror, and it would by most men be judged very extravagant if one should say otherwise. And yet he that will consider that the same fire that, at one distance produces in us the sensation of warmth, does, at a nearer approach, produce in us the far different sensation of pain, ought to bethink himself what reason he has to say—that this idea of warmth, which was produced in him by the fire, is *actually in the fire;* and his idea of pain, which the same fire produced in him the same way, is *not* in the fire. Why are whiteness and coldness in snow, and pain not, when it produces the one and the other idea in us; and can do neither, but by the bulk, figure, number, and motion of its solid parts?

The particular bulk, number, figure, and motion of the parts of fire or snow are really in them,—whether any one's senses perceive them or no: and therefore they may be called *real* qualities, because they really exist in those bodies. But light, heat, whiteness, or coldness, are no more really in them than sickness or pain is in manna. Take away the sensation of them; let not the eyes see light or colours, nor the ears hear sounds; let the palate not taste, nor the nose smell, and all colours, tastes, odours, and sounds, *as they are such particular ideas,* vanish and cease, and are reduced to their causes, i.e. bulk, figure, and motion of parts.[13]

This is the basic theory. Its logical consequences, as we shall see when we study Berkeley and Hume, are not nearly so palatable. But how does the "causal theory of perception" allow Locke to approach the traditional questions of metaphysics? Significantly, the first two steps in the argument are identical with those we traced in Descartes,—one's own existence and the existence of God—and Locke even includes the problematic notion of "intuition."

1. The knowledge of our own being we have by intuition. The existence of a God, reason clearly makes known to us.

But then, the strict empiricist reemerges and insists:

The knowledge of the existence of *any other thing* we can have only by *sensation:* for there being no necessary connexion of real existence with any *idea* a man hath in his memory; nor of any other existence but that of God with the existence of any particular man: no particular man can know the existence of any other being, but only when, by actual operating upon him, it makes itself perceived by him. For, the having the idea of anything in our mind, no more proves the existence of that thing, than the picture of a man evidences his being in the world, or the visions of a dream make thereby a true history.

2. It is therefore the *actual receiving* of ideas from without that gives us notice of the existence of other things, and makes us know, that something doth exist at that time without us, which causes that idea in us; though per-haps we neither know nor consider how it does it. For it takes not from the certainty of our senses, and the ideas we receive by them, that we know not the manner wherein they are produced: e.g. whilst I write this, I have, by the paper affecting my eyes, that idea produced in my mind, which, what-ever object causes, I call *white;* by which I know that that quality or acci-dent (i.e. whose appearance before my eyes always causes that idea) doth really exist, and hath a being without me. And of this, the greatest assur-ance I can possibly have, and to which my faculties can attain, is the testi-mony of my eyes, which are the proper and sole judges of this thing; whose testimony I have reason to rely on as so certain, that I can no more doubt, whilst I write this, that I see white and black, and that something really exists that causes that sensation in me, than that I write or move my hand; which is a certainty as great as human nature is capable of, concerning the ex-istence of anything, but a man's self alone, and of God.

And here Locke asserts his alternative to the strict Cartesian limitation of knowledge to matters of certainty and deduction:

3. The notice we have by our senses of the existing of things without us, though it be not altogether so certain as our intuitive knowledge, or the de-

---

[13] Locke, *An Essay Concerning Human Understanding.*

ductions of our reason employed about the clear abstract ideas of our own minds; yet it is an assurance that deserves the name of *knowledge*. If we persuade ourselves that our faculties act and inform us right concerning the existence of those objects that affect them, it cannot pass for an ill-grounded confidence: for I think nobody can, in earnest, be so sceptical as to be uncertain of the existence of those things which he sees and feels. At least, he that can doubt so far, (whatever he may have with his own thoughts,) will never have any controversy with me; since he can never be sure I say anything contrary to his own opinion. As to myself, I think God has given me assurance enough of the existence of things without me: since, by their different application, I can produce in myself both pleasure and pain, which is one great concernment of my present state. This is certain: the confidence that our faculties do not herein deceive us, is the greatest assurance we are capable of concerning the existence of material beings. For we cannot act anything but by our faculties; nor talk of knowledge itself, but by the help of those faculties which are fitted to apprehend even what knowledge is.

Experience has its own supports:

. . . besides the assurance we have from our senses themselves, that they do not err in the information they give us of the existence of things without us, when they are affected by them, we are further confirmed in this assurance by other concurrent reasons:—

4. I. It is plain those perceptions are produced in us by exterior causes affecting our senses: because those that want the *organs* of any sense, never can have the ideas belonging to that sense produced in their minds. This is too evident to be doubted: and therefore we cannot but be assured that they come in by the organs of that sense, and no other way. The organs themselves, it is plain, do not produce them: for then the eyes of a man in the dark would produce colours, and his nose smell roses in the winter: but we see nobody gets the relish of a pineapple, till he goes to the Indies, where it is, and tastes it.

5. II. Because sometimes I find that *I cannot avoid having those ideas produced in my mind.* For though, when my eyes are shut, or windows fast, I can at pleasure recall to my mind the ideas of light, or the sun, which former sensations had lodged in my memory; so I can at pleasure lay by *that* idea, and take into my view that of the smell of a rose, or taste of sugar. But, if I turn my eyes at noon towards the sun, I cannot avoid the ideas which the light or sun then produces in me. So that there is a manifest difference between the ideas laid up in my memory, (over which, if they were there only, I should have constantly the same power to dispose of them, and lay them by at pleasure,) and those which force themselves upon me, and I cannot avoid having. And therefore it must needs be some exterior cause, and the brisk acting of some objects without me, whose efficacy I cannot resist, that produces those ideas in my mind, whether I will or no. Besides, there is nobody who doth not perceive the difference in himself between contemplating the sun, as he hath the idea of it in his memory, and actually looking upon it: of which two, his perception is so distinct, that few of his ideas are more distinguishable one from another. And therefore he hath certain

knowledge that they are not *both* memory, or the actions of his mind, and fancies only within him; but that actual seeing hath a cause without.

6. III. Add to this, that many of those ideas are *produced in us with pain,* which afterwards we remember without the least offence. Thus, the pain of heat or cold, when the idea of it is revived in our minds, gives us no disturbance; which, when felt, was very troublesome; and is again, when actually repeated: which is occasioned by the disorder the external object causes in our bodies when applied to them: and we remember the pains of hunger, thirst, or the headache, without any pain at all; which would either never disturb us, or else constantly do it, as often as we thought of it, were there nothing more but ideas floating in our minds, and appearances entertaining our fancies, without the real existence of things affecting us from abroad. The same may be said of *pleasure,* accompanying several actual sensations. And though mathematical demonstration depends not upon sense, yet the examining them by diagrams gives great credit to the evidence of our sight, and seems to give it a certainty approaching to that of demonstration itself. For, it would be very strange, that a man should allow it for an undeniable truth, that two angles of a figure, which he measures by lines and angles of a diagram, should be bigger one than the other, and yet doubt of the existence of those lines and angles, which by looking on he makes use of to measure that by.

7. IV. Our *senses* in many cases *bear witness to the truth of each other's report,* concerning the existence of sensible things without us. He that *sees* a fire, may, if he doubt whether it be anything more than a bare fancy, *feel* it too; and be convinced, by putting his hand in it. Which certainly could never be put into such exquisite pain by a bare idea or phantom, unless that the pain be a fancy too: which yet he cannot, when the burn is well, by raising the idea of it, bring upon himself again.

Thus I see, whilst I write this, I can change the appearance of the paper; and by designing the letters, tell *beforehand* what new idea it shall exhibit the very next moment, by barely drawing my pen over it: which will neither appear (let me fancy as much as I will) if my hands stand still; or though I move my pen, if my eyes be shut: nor, when those characters are once made on the paper, can I choose afterwards but see them as they are; that is, have the ideas of such letters as I have made. Whence it is manifest, that they are not barely the sport and play of my own imagination, when I find that the characters that were made at the pleasure of my own thoughts, do not obey them; nor yet cease to be, whenever I shall fancy it, but continue to affect my senses constantly and regularly, according to the figures I made them. To which if we will add, that the sight of those shall, from another man, draw such sounds as I beforehand design they shall stand for, there will be little reason left to doubt that those words I write do really exist without me, when they cause a long series of regular sounds to affect my ears, which could not be the effect of my imagination, nor could my memory retain them in that order.

8. But yet, if after all this any one will be so sceptical as to distrust his senses, and to affirm that all we see and hear, feel and taste, think and do, during our whole being, is but the series and deluding appearances of a long dream, whereof there is no reality; and therefore will question the ex-

istence of all things, or our knowledge of anything: I must desire him to consider, that, if all be a dream, then he doth but dream that he makes the question, and so it is not much matter that a waking man should answer him. But yet, if he pleases, he may dream that I make him this answer, That the certainty of things existing in *rerum natura* when we have the testimony of our senses for it is not only as great as our frame can attain to, but as our condition needs. For, our faculties being suited not to the full extent of being, nor to a perfect, clear, comprehensive knowledge of things free from all doubt and scruple; but to the preservation of us, in whom they are; and accommodated to the use of life: they serve to our purpose well enough, if they will but give us certain notice of those things, which are convenient or inconvenient to us. For he that sees a candle burning, and hath experimented the force of its flame by putting his finger in it, will little doubt that this is something existing without him, which does him harm, and puts him to great pain: which is assurance enough, when no man requires greater certainty to govern his actions by than what is as certain as his actions themselves. And if our dreamer pleases to try whether the glowing heat of a glass furnace be barely a wandering imagination in a drowsy man's fancy, by putting his hand into it, he may perhaps be wakened into a certainty greater than he could wish, that it is something more than bare imagination. So that this evidence is as great as we can desire, being as certain to us as our pleasure or pain, i.e. happiness or misery; beyond which we have no concernment, either of knowing or being. Such an assurance of the existence of things without us is sufficient to direct us in the attaining the good and avoiding the evil which is caused by them, which is the important concernment we have of being made acquainted with them.

9. In summary, then, when our senses do actually convey into our understanding any idea, we cannot but be satisfied that there doth something *at that time* really exist without us, which doth affect our senses, and by them give notice of itself to our apprehensive faculties, and actually produce that idea which we then perceive.[14]

We are now ready to return to the traditional metaphysical notion of substance—that which underlies both the primary and the secondary qualities of a thing:

1. *Ideas of Substances, how made.*—The mind being, as I have declared, furnished with a great number of the simple ideas conveyed in by the senses, as they are found in exterior things, or by reflection on its own operations, takes notice, also, that a certain number of these simple ideas go constantly together; which being presumed to belong to one thing, and words being suited to common apprehensions, and made use of for quick dispatch, are called, so united in one subject, by one name; which, by inadvertency, we are apt afterward to talk of and consider as one simple idea, which indeed is a complication of many ideas together: because, as I have said, not imagining how these simple ideas can subsist by themselves, we

---

[14] Locke, *An Essay Concerning Human Understanding.*

accustom ourselves to suppose some substratum wherein they do subsist, and from which they do result; which therefore we call "substance."

2. *Our Idea of Substance in general.*—So that if anyone will examine himself concerning his notion of pure substance in general, he will find he has no other idea of it at all, but only a supposition of he knows not what support of such qualities which are capable of producing simple ideas in us; which qualities are commonly called "accidents." If anyone should be asked, "What is the subject wherein colour or weight inheres?" he would have nothing to say but, "The solid extended parts." And if he were demanded "What is it that solidity and extension inhere in?" he would not be in a much better case than the Indian before mentioned, who, saying that the world was supported by a great elephant, was asked what the elephant rested on? to which his answer was, "A great tortoise"; but being again pressed to know what gave support to the broad-backed tortoise, replied—something, he knew not what. And thus here, as in all other cases where we use words without having clear and distinct ideas, we talk like children, who, being questioned what such a thing is which they know not, readily give this satisfactory answer, that it is something, which in truth signifies no more, when so used, either by children or men, but that they know not what; and that the thing they pretend to know and talk of is what they have no distinct idea of at all, and so are perfectly ignorant of it, and in the dark. The idea, then, we have, to which we give the general name "substance" being nothing but the supposed, but unknown, support of those qualities we find existing, which we imagine cannot subsist *sine re substante,* "without something to support them," we call that support *substantia;* which, according to the true import of the word, is, in plain English, "standing under," or "upholding."

. . . . .

Hence, when we talk or think of any particular sort of corporeal substances, as horse, stone, &c., though the idea we have of either of them be but the complication or collection of those several simple ideas of sensible qualities which we used to find united in the thing called "horse" or "stone"; yet because we cannot conceive how they should subsist alone, nor one in another, we suppose them existing in, and supported by, some common subject; which support we denote by the name "substance," though it be certain we have no clear or distinct idea of that thing we suppose a support.[15]

Substance is "we know not what." Yet Locke hesitates to reject the notion, for he cannot escape the suspicion that talk of "qualities" makes no sense unless the qualities are the qualities of something. But this suspicion is dispensable according to Locke's own principles. And so, it turns out, is his central distinction between primary and secondary qualities, as Bishop Berkeley is soon to point out. And the consequence of these simple, technical moves will be shocking, to say the least.

[15] Locke, *An Essay Concerning Human Understanding.*

COMMON SENSE UNDONE:
BISHOP BERKELEY

Beginning from John Locke's common sense philosophy, Bishop Berkeley developed the most provocative thesis in all of philosophy. Berkeley's thesis is called *subjective idealism;* it is the doctrine that there are no material substances, no physical objects, only minds and ideas in minds. (His concept of "idea" comes directly from Locke.) This surprising position emerges directly from Locke's thesis by three simple steps. First, it accepts the argument that we have no idea whatsoever what a substance might be, and agrees that all that we can ever know of a thing are its sensible properties (or "qualities"). Second, it is shown that the distinction between primary and secondary qualities cannot be, as Locke had argued, a distinction between properties inherent in the objects themselves as opposed to properties which the objects simply cause in us. And third, once one has agreed that all knowledge of the world (except for knowledge of one's own existence and of God) must be based upon experience, the question becomes why we should ever think that there is anything other than our experiences. Locke had argued that our experiences were caused by the physical objects; but how could this claim be justified by experience? Since we have no experience of either the objects themselves or their causation, but only of their effects (that is, the ideas they cause in us) a consistent empiricist must give up not only the causal theory of perception but the notion of physical objects as well.

Bishop Berkeley is an exceptionally clear writer, and the following excerpts from his *Treatise Concerning the Principles of Human Knowledge* (1710) should not be difficult to understand:

> 1. It is evident to anyone who takes a survey of the objects of human knowledge, that they are either ideas (1) actually imprinted on the senses, or else such as are (2) perceived by attending to the passions and operations of the mind, or lastly (3) ideas formed by help of memory and imagination, either compounding, dividing, or barely representing those originally perceived in the aforesaid ways. By sight I have the ideas of lights and colors, with their several degrees and variations. By touch I perceive hard and soft, heat and cold, motion and resistance, and of all these more and less either as to quantity or degree. Smelling furnishes me with odors, the palate with tastes, and hearing conveys sounds to the mind in all their variety of tone and composition. And as several of these are observed to accompany each other, they come to be marked by one name, and so to be reputed as one thing. Thus, for example, a certain color, taste, smell, figure, and consistence, having been observed to go together, are accounted one distinct thing, signified by the name "apple." Other collections of ideas constitute a stone, a tree, a book, and the like sensible things; which, as they are pleasing or disagreeable, excite the passions of love, hatred, joy, grief, and so forth.

2. But besides all that endless variety of ideas or objects of knowledge, there is likewise something which knows or perceives them, and exercises divers operations, as willing, imagining, remembering, about them. This perceiving, active being is what I call *mind, spirit, soul,* or *myself.* By which words I do not denote any one of my ideas, but a thing entirely distinct from them wherein they exist, or, which is the same thing, whereby they are perceived; for the existence of an idea consists in being perceived.

3. That neither our thoughts, nor passions, nor ideas formed by the imagination, exist without the mind, is what everybody will allow. And it seems no less evident that the various sensations or ideas imprinted on the sense, however blended or combined together (that is, whatever objects they compose), cannot exist otherwise than in a mind perceiving them. I think an intuitive knowledge may be obtained of this by anyone that shall attend to what is meant by the term "exist" when applied to sensible things. The table I write on I say exists—that is, I see and feel it; and if I were out of my study I should say it existed—meaning thereby that if I was in my study I might perceive it, or that some other spirit actually does perceive it. There was an odor, that is, it was smelt; there was a sound, that is, it was heard; a color or figure, and it was perceived by sight or touch. This is all that I can understand by these and the like expressions. For as to what is said of the absolute existence of unthinking things without any relation to their being perceived, that seems perfectly unintelligible. Their *esse* is *percipi,*[16] nor is it possible they should have any existence out of the minds or thinking things which perceive them.

4. It is indeed an opinion strangely prevailing amongst men, that houses, mountains, rivers, and in a word all sensible objects, have an existence, natural or real, distinct from their being perceived by the understanding. But with how great an assurance and acquiescence so ever this principle may be entertained in the world, yet whoever shall find in his heart to call it in question may, if I mistake not, perceive it to involve a manifest contradiction. For what are the forementioned objects but the things we perceive by sense? and what do we perceive *besides our own ideas or sensations?* and is it not plainly repugnant that any one of these, or any combination of them, should exist unperceived?

5. If we thoroughly examine this tenet it will perhaps be found at bottom to depend on the doctrine of *abstract ideas.* For can there be a nicer strain of abstraction than to distinguish the existence of sensible objects from their being perceived, so as to conceive them existing unperceived? Light and colors, heat and cold, extension and figures—in a word the things we see and feel—what are they but so many sensations, notions, ideas, or impressions on the sense? And is it possible to separate, even in thought, any of these from perception? For my part, I might as easily divide a thing from itself. I may, indeed, divide in my thoughts, or conceive apart from each other, those things which perhaps I never perceived by sense so divided. Thus I imagine the trunk of a human body without the limbs, or conceive the smell of a rose without thinking on the rose itself. So far, I will not deny, I can abstract, if that may properly be called abstraction which extends only to

---

[16] *to be* is *to be perceived*

the conceiving separately such objects as it is possible may really exist or be actually perceived asunder. But my conceiving or imagining power does not extend beyond the possibility of real existence or perception. Hence, as it is impossible for me to see or feel anything without an actual sensation of that thing, so it is impossible for me to conceive in my thoughts any sensible thing or object distinct from the sensation or perception of it.

6. Some truths there are so near and obvious to the mind that a man need only open his eyes to see them. Such I take this important one to be, to wit, that all the choir of heaven and furniture of the earth, in a word all those bodies which compose the mighty frame of the world, have not any subsistence without a mind, that their *being* is to be perceived or known; that consequently so long as they are not actually perceived by me, or do not exist in my mind or that of any other created spirit, they must either have no existence at all, or else subsist in the mind of some Eternal Spirit; it being perfectly unintelligible, and involving all the absurdity of abstraction, to attribute to any single part of them an existence independent of a spirit. To be convinced of which, the reader need only reflect and try to separate in his own thoughts the *being* of a sensible thing from its *being perceived*.

7. From what has been said it follows there is not any other substance than *spirit,* or that which perceives. But for the fuller proof of this point, let it be considered the sensible qualities are color, figure, motion, smell, taste, etc.—that is, the ideas perceived by sense. Now, for an idea to exist in an unperceiving thing is a manifest contradiction, for to have an idea is all one as to perceive; that therefore wherein color, figure, and the like qualities exist must perceive them; hence it is clear there can be no unthinking substance or *substratum* of those ideas.

8. But, say you, though the ideas themselves do not exist without the mind, yet there may be things *like* them, whereof they are copies or resemblances, which things exist without the mind in an unthinking substance. I answer, an idea can be like nothing but an idea; a color or figure can be like nothing but another color or figure. If we look but never so little into our thoughts, we shall find it impossible for us to conceive a likeness except only between our ideas. Again, I ask whether those supposed originals or external things, of which our ideas are the pictures or representations, be themselves perceivable or no? If they are, then they are ideas and we have gained our point; but if you say they are not, I appeal to anyone whether it be sense to assert a color is like something which is invisible, hard or soft, like something which is intangible; and so of the rest.

9. Some there are who make a distinction betwixt *primary* and *secondary* qualities. By the former they mean extension, figure, motion, rest, solidity or impenetrability, and number; by the latter they denote all other sensible qualities, as colors, sounds, tastes, and so forth. The ideas we have of these they acknowledge not to be the resemblances of anything existing without the mind, or unperceived, but they will have our ideas of the primary qualities to be patterns or images of things which exist without the mind, in an unthinking substance which they call *matter.* By *matter,* therefore, we are to understand an inert, senseless substance, in which extension, figure, and motion do actually subsist. But it is evident from what we have already shown, that extension, figure, and motion are only ideas existing in the mind, and that an idea can be like nothing but another idea, and that consequently

neither they nor their archetypes can exist in an unperceiving substance. Hence, it is plain that the very notion of what is called *matter,* or *corporeal substance,* involves a contradiction in it.

10. They who assert that figure, motion, and the rest of the primary or original qualities do exist without the mind in unthinking substances, do at the same time acknowledge that color, sounds, heat, cold, and suchlike secondary qualities, do not; which they tell us are sensations existing in the mind alone, that depend on and are occasioned by the different size, texture, and motion of the minute particles of matter. This they take for an undoubted truth, which they can demonstrate beyond all exception. Now, if it be certain that those original qualities are inseparably united with the other sensible qualities, and not, even in thought, capable of being abstracted from them, it plainly follows that they exist only in the mind. But I desire anyone to reflect and try whether he can, by any abstraction of thought, conceive the extension and motion of a body without all other sensible qualities. For my own part, I see evidently that it is not in my power to frame an idea of a body extended and moving, but I must withal give it some color or other sensible quality which is acknowledged to exist only in the mind. In short, extension, figure, and motion, abstracted from all other qualities, are inconceivable. Where therefore the other sensible qualities are, there must these be also, to wit, in the mind and nowhere else. . . .

14. I shall farther add that, after the same manner as modern philosophers prove certain sensible qualities to have no existence in matter, or without the mind, the same thing may be likewise proved of all other sensible qualities whatsoever. Thus, for instance, it is said that heat and cold are affections only of the mind, and not at all patterns of real beings, existing in the corporeal substances which excite them, for that the same body which appears cold to one hand seems warm to another. Now, why may we not as well argue that figure and extension are not patterns or resemblances of qualities existing in matter, because to the same eye at different stations, or eyes of a different texture at the same station, they appear various, and cannot therefore be the images of anything settled and determinate without the mind? Again, it is proved that sweetness is not really in the sapid thing, because the thing remaining unaltered the sweetness is changed into bitter, as in case of a fever or otherwise vitiated palate. Is it not as reasonable to say that motion is not without the mind, since if the succession of ideas in the mind become swifter, the motion, it is acknowledged, shall appear slower without any alteration in any external object?

15. In short, let anyone consider those arguments which are thought manifestly to prove that colors and tastes exist only in the mind, and he shall find they may with equal force be brought to prove the same thing of extension, figure, and motion—though it must be confessed this method of arguing does not so much prove that there is no extension or color in an outward object, as that we do not know by sense which is the true extension or color of the object. But the arguments foregoing plainly show it to be impossible that any color or extension at all, or other sensible quality whatsoever, should exist in an unthinking subject without the mind, or in truth, that there should be any such thing as an outward object.

16. But let us examine a little the received opinion. It is said extension is a mode or accident of matter, and that matter is the *substratum* that

supports it. Now I desire that you would explain to me what is meant by matter's *supporting* extension. Say you, I have no idea of matter and therefore cannot explain it. I answer, though you have no positive, yet, if you have any meaning at all, you must at least have a relative idea of matter; though you know not what it is, yet you must be supposed to know what relation it bears to accidents, and what is meant by its supporting them. It is evident "support" cannot here be taken in its usual or literal sense—as when we say that pillars support a building; in what sense therefore must it be taken?

17. If we inquire into what the most accurate philosophers declare themselves to mean by *material substance,* we shall find them acknowledge they have no other meaning annexed to those sounds but the idea of *Being in general,* together with the relative notion of its supporting accidents. The general idea of Being appeareth to me the most abstract and incomprehensible of all other; and as for its supporting accidents, this, as we have just now observed, cannot be understood in the common sense of those words; it must therefore be taken in some other sense, but what that is they do not explain. So that when I consider the two parts or branches which make the signification of the words *material substance,* I am convinced there is no distinct meaning annexed to them. But why should we trouble ourselves any farther, in discussing this material *substratum* or support of figure and motion, and other sensible qualities? Does it not suppose they have an existence without the mind? And is not this a direct repugnancy, and altogether inconceivable?

18. But though it were possible that solid, figured, movable substances may exist without the mind, corresponding to the ideas we have of bodies, yet how is it possible for us to know this? Either we must know it by sense or by reason. As for our senses, by them we have the knowledge only of our sensations, ideas, or those things that are immediately perceived by sense, call them what you will; but they do not inform us that things exist without the mind, or unperceived, like to those which are perceived. This the materialists[17] themselves acknowledge. It remains therefore that if we have any knowledge at all of external things, it must be by reason, inferring their existence from what is immediately perceived by sense. But what reason can induce us to believe the existence of bodies without the mind, from what we perceive, since the very patrons of matter themselves do not pretend there is any necessary connection betwixt them and our ideas? I say it is granted on all hands (and what happens in dreams, frenzies, and the like, puts it beyond dispute) that *it is possible we might be affected with all the ideas we have now, though there were no bodies existing without, resembling them.* Hence, it is evident the supposition of external bodies is not necessary for the producing our ideas; since it is granted they are produced sometimes, and might possibly be produced always in the same order we see them in at present, without their concurrence.

19. But, though we might possibly have all our sensations without them, yet perhaps it may be thought easier to conceive and explain the manner of their production by supposing external bodies in their likeness rather than otherwise; and so it might be at least probable there are such things as bodies that excite their ideas in our minds. But neither can this be said; for though we give the materialists their external bodies, they by their own confession

---

[17] Berkeley uses "materialist" to refer to those who believe in the existence of matter, not to those who believe in only matter, its usual meaning.

are never the nearer knowing how our ideas are produced, since they own themselves unable to comprehend in what manner body can act upon spirit, or how it is possible it should imprint any idea in the mind. Hence it is evident the production of ideas or sensations in our minds can be no reason why we should suppose matter or corporeal substances, since that is acknowledged to remain equally inexplicable with or without this supposition. If therefore it were possible for bodies to exist without the mind, yet to hold they do so, must needs be a very precarious opinion; since it is to suppose, without any reason at all, that God has created innumerable things that are entirely useless, and serve to no manner of purpose.

20. In short, if there were external bodies, it is impossible we should ever come to know it; and if there were not, we might have the very same reasons to think there were that we have now. Suppose (what no one can deny possible) an intelligence without the help of external bodies, to be affected with the same train of sensations or ideas that you are, imprinted in the same order and with like vividness in his mind. I ask whether that intelligence hath not all the reason to believe the existence of corporeal substances, represented by his ideas, and exciting them in his mind, that you can possibly have for believing the same thing? Of this there can be no question; which one consideration were enough to make any reasonable person suspect the strength of whatever arguments he may think himself to have for the existence of bodies without the mind. . . .

23. But, say you, surely there is nothing easier than for me to imagine trees, for instance, in a park, or books existing in a closet, and nobody by to perceive them. I answer, you may so, there is no difficulty in it; but what is all this, I beseech you, more than framing in your mind certain ideas which you call books and trees, and the same time omitting to frame the idea of anyone that may perceive them? But do not you yourself perceive or think of them all the while? This therefore is nothing to the purpose; it only shews you have the power of imagining or forming ideas in your mind: but it doth not shew that you can conceive it possible the objects of your thought may exist without the mind. To make out this, it is necessary that you conceive them existing unconceived or unthought of, which is a manifest repugnancy. When we do our utmost to conceive the existence of external bodies, we are all the while only contemplating our own ideas.[18]

But what, then, can explain the fact that we cannot simply "think" things into existence by imagining them? And how can we say that a thing exists when no one is there to perceive it? ("If a tree falls in the forest, and there's no one there to hear it, does it make a sound?") It is here that God enters the picture as a matter of necessity.

29. But, whatever power I may have over my own thoughts, I find the ideas actually perceived by Sense have not a like dependence on my will. When in broad daylight I open my eyes, it is not in my power to choose whether I shall see or no, or to determine what particular objects shall present themselves to my view; and so likewise as to the hearing and other

18 George Berkeley, *Treatise Concerning the Principles of Human Knowledge* (New York: Bobbs-Merrill, 1957).

senses, the ideas imprinted on them are not creatures of my will. There is therefore some *other* Will or Spirit that produces them.

30. The ideas of Sense are more strong, lively, and distinct than those of the Imagination; they have likewise a steadiness, order, and coherence, and are not excited at random, as those which are the effects of human wills often are, but in a regular train or series—the admirable connexion whereof sufficiently testifies the wisdom and benevolence of its Author. Now the set rules or established methods wherein the Mind we depend on excites in us the ideas of sense, are called the *laws of nature;* and these we learn by experience, which teaches us that such and such ideas are attended with such and such other ideas, in the ordinary course of things.

31. This gives us a sort of foresight which enables us to regulate our actions for the benefit of life. And without this we should be eternally at a loss; we could not know how to act anything that might procure us the least pleasure, or remove the least pain of sense. That food nourishes, sleep refreshes, and fire warms us; that to sow in the seedtime is the way to reap in the harvest; and in general that to obtain such or such ends, such or such means are conducive—all this we know, not by discovering any *necessary connexion* between our ideas, but only by the *observation* of the settled laws of nature, without which we should be all in uncertainty and confusion, and a grown man no more know how to manage himself in the affairs of life than an infant just born. . . .

33. The ideas imprinted on the senses by the Author of nature are called *real things;* and those excited in the imagination, being less regular, vivid, and constant, are more properly termed *ideas,* or *images* of *things,* which they copy and represent. But then our sensations, be they never so vivid and distinct, are nevertheless ideas, that is, they exist in the mind, or are perceived by it, as truly as the ideas of its own framing. The ideas of sense are allowed to have more reality in them, that is, to be more strong, orderly, and coherent than the creatures of the mind; but this is no argument that they exist without the mind. They are also less dependent on the spirit, or thinking substance which perceives them, in that they are excited by the will of another and more powerful spirit; yet still they are *ideas,* and certainly no idea, whether faint or strong, can exist otherwise than in a mind perceiving it.[19]

[19] This final formulation, that the things of the world are nothing other than ideas in the mind of God, is the subject of a limerick by Ronald Knox, quoted for us by Bertrand Russell.

> There was a young man who said, "God
> Must think it exceedingly odd
>   If he finds that this tree
>   Continues to be
> When there's no one about in the Quad."

> REPLY

> Dear Sir:
>   Your astonishment's odd:
> *I* am always about in the Quad.
>   And that's why the tree
>   Will continue to be,
> Since observed by
>   *Yours faithfully,*
>   GOD.

And, finally, the defense against common sense:

> 38. But after all, say you, it sounds very harsh to say we eat and drink ideas, and are clothed with ideas. I acknowledge it does so; the word "idea" not being used in common discourse to signify the several combinations of sensible qualities which are called "things"; and it is certain that any expression which varies from the familiar use of language will seem harsh and ridiculous. But this doth not concern the truth of the proposition, which in other words is no more than to say, we are fed and clothed with those things which we perceive immediately by our senses.
>
> 39. If it be demanded why I make use of the word "idea," and do not rather in compliance with custom call them "thing"; I answer, I do it for two reasons:—first, because the term "thing" in contradistinction to "idea," is generally supposed to denote somewhat existing without the mind; secondly, because "thing" hath a more comprehensive signification than "idea," including spirit or thinking things as well as ideas. Since therefore the objects of sense exist only in the mind, and are withal thoughtless and inactive, I chose to mark them by the word "idea," which implies those properties.[20]

Is this where Locke was leading us? If so, it looks as if the "new metaphysics" is every bit as fantastic as the old ones. But the controversial development of Locke's empiricism has still another step to go.

THE ULTIMATE SKEPTIC:
DAVID HUME

It isn't very far from Berkeley's subjective idealism to David Hume's unacceptable but seemingly irrefutable skepticism. Bertrand Russell, writing about Hume two hundred years later (1945), says,

> To refute him has been, ever since he wrote, a favorite pastime among metaphysicians. For my part, I find none of their refutations convincing; nevertheless, I cannot but hope that something less skeptical than Hume's system may be discoverable.

and

> Hume's skeptical conclusions . . . are equally difficult to refute and to accept. The result was a challenge to philosophers, which, in my opinion, has still not been adequately met.[21]

There have been many philosophers who have said—or feared—that Hume's skepticism is the last word in philosophy. But in any case, it is one of those positions that no philosophy student can avoid taking seriously.

Hume's *Treatise of Human Nature* (1739) was written when he was in

[20] Berkeley, *Treatise Concerning the Principles of Human Knowledge.*
[21] Bertrand Russell, *A History of Western Philosophy* (New York: Simon and Schuster, 1945).

his early twenties; his ambition was no less than to be the Isaac Newton of philosophy and psychology, following but outdoing John Locke. The book failed to attract attention (he said "it fell stillborn from the press"), and Hume turned his attention to other matters, making himself famous as a historian. Later, in 1748, he wrote a more popular version of his earlier *Treatise,* which he called *An Enquiry Concerning Human Understanding.* It was extremely successful, and Hume became widely known as a "devil's advocate" during his lifetime, a position he generally enjoyed. Both the *Treatise* and the *Enquiry* are firmly committed to Locke's empiricist methodology, but where Locke was generous with doubtful ideas with no clear experiential basis (notably, substance and God), Hume was ruthless. In a famous threatening passage, he had bellowed:

> When we run over libraries, persuaded of these [empiricist] principles, what havoc must we make? If we take in our hand any volume of divinity or school metaphysics, for instance, let us ask, Does it contain any abstract reasoning concerning quantity or number? No. Does it contain any experimental reasoning concerning matter of fact and existence? No, Commit it to the flames, for it can contain nothing but sophistry and illusion.[22]

In this unveiled threat to traditional metaphysics we can see in a glance Hume's formidable tactics—the insistence that every justifiable belief must be either a "relation of ideas," for example, a statement of mathematics, logic, or a trivial conceptual truth, or a "matter of fact," which can be confirmed by appeal to our experience. (This "either-or" is sometimes called "Hume's fork.") Of course, most of the modern philosophers we have discussed shared this insistence upon justifiability by either reason ("relation of ideas") or by experience. But it is only Hume who realizes the severity of this demand, and the embarrassing number of our fundamental beliefs which do not allow justification by either reason or experience.

Like his empiricist predecessor, Hume insists that all knowledge begins with basic units of sensory experience. Hume's "impressions" (Locke's "sensations") are these basic units (what we would still call "sensations" or "sense-data").

> ALL the perceptions of the human mind resolve themselves into two distinct kinds, which I shall call IMPRESSIONS and IDEAS. The difference betwixt these consists in the degrees of force and liveliness with which they strike upon the mind, and make their way into our thought or consciousness. Those perceptions, which enter with most force and violence, we may name *impressions;* and under this name I comprehend all our sensations, passions and emotions, as they make their first appearance in the soul. By *ideas* I mean the faint images of these in thinking and reasoning; such as, for instance, are all the perceptions excited by the present discourse, excepting only, those which arise from the sight and touch, and excepting the imme-

---

[22] David Hume, *An Enquiry Concerning Human Understanding,* 2nd ed., ed. L. A. Selby-Bigge (Oxford: Oxford University Press, 1902).

diate pleasure or uneasiness it may occasion. I believe it will not be very necessary to employ many words in explaining this distinction. Every one of himself will readily perceive the difference betwixt feeling and thinking. The common degrees of these are easily distinguished; tho' it is not impossible but in particular instances they may very nearly approach to each other. Thus in sleep, in a fever, in madness, or in any very violent emotions of soul, our ideas may approach to our impressions: As on the other hand it sometimes happens, that our impressions are so faint and low, that we cannot distinguish them from our ideas. But notwithstanding this near resemblance in a few instances, they are in general so very different, that no-one can make a scruple to rank them under distinct heads, and assign to each a peculiar name to mark the difference.

There is another division of our perceptions, which it will be convenient to observe, and which extends itself both to our impressions and ideas. This division is into SIMPLE and COMPLEX. Simple perceptions or impressions and ideas are such as admit of no distinction nor separation. The complex are the contrary to these, and may be distinguished into parts. Tho' a particular colour, taste, and smell are qualities all united together in this apple, 'tis easy to perceive they are not the same, but are at least distinguishable from each other.

Having by these divisions given an order and arrangement to our objects, we may now apply ourselves to consider with the more accuracy their qualities and relations. The first circumstance, that strikes my eye, is the great resemblance betwixt our impressions and ideas in every other particular, except their degree of force and vivacity. The one seem to be in a manner the reflexion of the other; so that all the perceptions of the mind are double, and appear both as impressions and ideas. When I shut my eyes and think of my chamber, the ideas I form are exact representations of the impressions I felt, nor is there any circumstance of the one, which is not to be found in the other. In running over my other perceptions, I find still the same resemblance and representation. Ideas and impressions appear always to correspond to each other. This circumstance seems to me remarkable, and engages my attention for a moment.

Upon a more accurate survey I find I have been carried away too far by the first appearance, and that I must make use of the distinction of perceptions into *simple and complex,* to limit this general decision, *that all our ideas and impressions are resembling.* I observe, that many of our complex ideas never had impressions, that corresponded to them, and that many of our complex impressions never are exactly copied in ideas. I can imagine to myself such a city as the *New Jerusalem,* whose pavement is gold and walls are rubies, tho' I never saw any such. I have seen *Paris;* but shall I affirm I can form such an idea of that city, as will perfectly represent all its streets and houses in their real and just proportions?

I perceive, therefore, that tho' there is in general a great resemblance betwixt our *complex* impressions and ideas, yet the rule is not universally true, that they are exact copies of each other. We may next consider how the case stands with our *simple* perceptions. After the most accurate examination, of which I am capable, I venture to affirm, that the rule here holds without any exception, and that every simple idea has a simple impression, which resembles it; and every simple impression a correspondent idea. That idea of red, which we form in the dark, and that impression, which strikes our eyes in sun-shine, differ only in degree, not in nature. That the case is the same with all our simple impressions and ideas, 'tis impossible to prove by a particular enumeration of them. Every one may satisfy himself in this point by running over as many as he pleases. But if any one should deny this universal resemblance, I know no way of convincing him, but by desiring him to shew a simple impression that has not a correspondent idea, or a simple idea, that has not a correspondent impression. If he does not answer this challenge, as 'tis certain he cannot, we may from his silence and our own observation establish our conclusion.

Thus we find, that all simple ideas and impressions resemble each other; and as the complex are formed from them, we may affirm in general, that these two species of perception are exactly correspondent. Having discover'd this relation, which requires no farther examination, I am curious to find some other of their qualities. Let us consider how they stand with regard to their existence, and which of the impressions and ideas are causes, and which effects.

The *full* examination of this question is the subject of the present treatise; and therefore we shall here content ourselves with establishing one general proposition. *That all our simple ideas in their first appearance are deriv'd from simple impressions, which are correspondent to them, and which they exactly represent.*[23]

According to Hume, simple ideas are derived from simple impressions. A simple idea would be something like a red, round image; the simple impression would be seeing a red, round image. More complex ideas, for example, the idea of an apple, are complex arrangements and associations of simple ideas. To justify a belief as knowledge, therefore, we must break up its complex ideas into simple ideas and then find the impressions upon which those ideas are based. If I claim to see an apple, for example, I analyze my experience; my idea that there is an apple out there depends upon my seeing several red, round images from different angles, feeling something smooth, tasting something fruity and tart, and so on. If I claim that there are objects of a certain kind (apples for example), I must identify the simple ideas and impressions upon which my supposed knowledge is based. And if I make a metaphysical claim, about the existence of God or substances, I must either be prepared to identify the ideas and impressions upon which such a claim is based, or I must show that it is nothing other than a "relation of ideas"; otherwise, the claim cannot be justified ("commit it to the flames").

But, to the embarrassment of most metaphysical doctrines, they cannot be defended by either of the methods allowed by Hume. They are, by their very nature, about things (for example God, substance) beyond everyday experience, and so not based upon "impressions"; nor are they "relations of ideas" which can be demonstrated by a simple logical or mathematical proof. Therefore, they cannot be justified. The problem, however, is that the same argu-

[23] Hume, *An Enquiry Concerning Human Understanding.*

ment extends far beyond the debatable claims of metaphysics and undermines some of the beliefs that are most essential to our everyday experiences as well. In Hume's philosophy, three such beliefs in particular are singled out for analysis. On the one hand, they are so fundamental to our daily experience and common knowledge that no sane man or woman could possibly doubt them; but on the other hand, they are completely without justification. As Hume argues, first, there is our idea of causation (or causality), of one event bringing about or causing another event. From this idea, which provides what Hume calls "the strongest connections" of our experience and, elsewhere, "the cement of the universe," we derive a most important principle, the principle of universal causation, which states that every event has its cause (or causes). It is evident that we invoke such a principle every time that we explain anything; for example, the car won't start. We search for the cause, but everything seems to check out—the carburetor, the electrical system and so on. Now we might search for hours without finding the cause, but there is one thing that we know for certain, and that is that there must be a cause somewhere—even if it is a very complex cause. What is not possible is that there be no cause. Presupposed in our everyday thinking is this principle, that every event has its cause. (You may recognize this principle as a version of Leibniz's Principle of Sufficient Reason, but substituting the more Newtonian notion of "cause'" for the notion of "reason.")

Second, because of our presupposed belief in causation and its universal applicability, we are able to think beyond our immediate "ideas" and predict the future and explain the past. But to do so, we must also believe that our observations of the present will have some relevance in the future, that we can in fact draw valid inductive generalizations from our experience. Of course, we do so all of the time; for example, when I wake up at 6:00 in the morning, I expect the sun to rise within the hour. Why? Because it has always done so, because it is February 26th and the almanac says it will. In making every such prediction, we presuppose a *principle of induction,* that is, that the laws of nature that have always held in the past will continue to hold in the future. The principle of induction is sometimes summarized as "the future will be like the past," which is all right only so long as it is not taken too literally; for of course the future is never just like the past (you are now fifteen seconds older, for example, and have added a whole new expression to your knowledge, and, (unless you are eating while you read) lost a tiny bit of weight as well). But the laws of nature, at least, do not change from moment to moment.

And third, there is our belief in the "external world," that is, a physical or material world that exists independently of our impressions and ideas, which it presumably causes in us. Bishop Berkeley had already done Hume's work for him here. Hume, following Berkeley, also rejects all notions of substance as unintelligible, including even that minimal "we know not what" of John Locke. But where Berkeley turned the rejection of matter and substance into a metaphysics (namely, his subjective idealism) and used it to defend the existence of God, Hume rejects this idealist metaphysics as well and remains wholly skeptical, refusing to accept the existence of God. He remains firm in his insistence that our belief in the existence of anything is no different from "the idea of what we conceive to be existent."

We can see that these three basic beliefs are intimately tied together; it is the notion of cause that supports the principle of induction,[24] and it is the causal theory of perception that supports our belief in the "external world." Accordingly, Hume takes causation to be the central idea of all reasoning,[25] that is, all attempts to connect separate ideas together in a single belief. Hume's arguments are both elegant and extremely simple to follow. He refutes both the principle of universal causation and the principle of induction by showing that neither can be defended either as a "relation of ideas" or as a "matter of fact." He begins with a statement that all human knowledge must be one or the other, explains what he means by "relations of ideas" and "matters of fact," shows how it is that "cause and effect" are the basis of all reasoning, and then proceeds to show that such reasoning can be neither a relation of ideas nor a simple matter of fact:

> All the objects of human reason or enquiry may naturally be divided into two kinds, to wit, *Relations of Ideas,* and *Matters of Fact.* Of the first kind are the sciences of Geometry, Algebra, and Arithmetic; and in short, every affirmation which is either intuitively or demonstratively certain. *That the square of the hypothenuse is equal to the square of the two sides,* is a proposition which expresses a relation between these figures. *That three times five is equal to the half of thirty,* expresses a relation between these numbers. Propositions of this kind are discoverable by the mere operation of thought, without dependence on what is anywhere existent in the universe. Though there never were a circle or triangle in nature, the truths demonstrated by Euclid would for ever retain their certainty and evidence.
>
> Matters of fact, which are the second objects of human reason, are not ascertained in the same manner; nor is our evidence of their truth, however great, of a like nature with the foregoing. The contrary of every matter of fact is still possible; because it can never imply a contradiction, and is conceived by the mind with the same facility and distinctness, as if ever so conformable to reality. *That the sun will not rise to-morrow* is no less intelligible a proposition, and implies no more contradiction than the affirmation, *that it will rise.* We should in vain, therefore, attempt to demonstrate its falsehood. Were it demonstratively false, it would imply a contradiction, and could never be distinctly conceived by the mind.
>
> It may, therefore, be a subject worthy of curiosity, to enquire what is the nature of that evidence which assures us of any real existence and matter of fact, beyond the present testimony of our senses, or the records of our memory. This part of philosophy, it is observable, has been little cultivated,

---

[24] Modern philosophers have given a great deal of attention to inductive inferences which are not based upon any obvious causes, for example, statistical probabilities (as in genetics or gambling).

[25] It is important to remember that Hume, like Locke, models his philosophy-psychology after Newton's physics. So even if he rejects Locke's "causal theory of perception," the Newtonian model, in which causality is central, remains at the heart of his theories.

either by the ancients or moderns; and therefore our doubts and errors, in the prosecution of so important an enquiry, may be the more excusable; while we march through such difficult paths without any guide or direction. They may even prove useful, by exciting curiosity, and destroying that implicit faith and security, which is the bane of all reasoning and free enquiry. The discovery of defects in the common philosophy, if any such there be, will not, I presume, be a discouragement, but rather an incitement, as is usual, to attempt something more full and satisfactory than has yet been proposed to the public.

All reasonings concerning matter of fact seem to be founded on the relation of *Cause and Effect.* By means of that relation alone we can go beyond the evidence of our memory and senses. If you were to ask a man, why he believes any matter of fact, which is absent; for instance, that his friend is in the country, or in France; he would give you a reason; and this reason would be some other fact; as a letter received from him, or the knowledge of his former resolutions and promises. A man finding a watch or any other machine in a desert island, would conclude that there had once been men in that island. All our reasonings concerning fact are of the same nature. And here it is constantly supposed that there is a connexion between the present fact and that which is inferred from it. Were there nothing to bind them together, the inference would be entirely precarious. The hearing of an articulate voice and rational discourse in the dark assures us of the presence of some person: Why? because these are the effects of the human make and fabric, and closely connected with it. If we anatomize all the other reasonings of this nature, we shall find that they are founded on the relation of cause and effect, and that this relation is either near or remote, direct or collateral. Heat and light are collateral effects of fire, and the one effect may justly be inferred from the other.

If we would satisfy ourselves, therefore, concerning the nature of that evidence, which assures us of matters of fact, we must enquire how we arrive at the knowledge of cause and effect.

I shall venture to affirm, as a general proposition, which admits of no exception, that the knowledge of this relation is not, in any instance, attained by reasonings *a priori;* but arises entirely from experience, when we find that any particular objects are constantly conjoined with each other. Let an object be presented to a man of ever so strong natural reason and abilities; if that object be entirely new to him, he will not be able, by the most accurate examination of its sensible qualities, to discover any of its causes or effects. Adam, though his rational faculties be supposed, at the very first, entirely perfect, could not have inferred from the fluidity and transparency of water that it would suffocate him, or from the light and warmth of fire that it would consume him. No object ever discovers, by the qualities which appear to the senses, either the causes which produced it, or the effects which will arise from it; nor can our reason, unassisted by experience, ever draw any inference concerning real existence and matter of fact.

This proposition, *that causes and effects are discoverable, not by reason but by experience,* will readily be admitted with regard to such objects, as we remember to have once been altogether unknown to us; since we must be conscious of the utter inability, which we then lay under, of foretelling what would arise from them. Present two smooth pieces of marble to a man who has no tincture of natural philosophy; he will never discover that they will adhere together in such a manner as to require great force to separate them in a direct line, while they make so small a resistance to a lateral pressure. Such events, as bear little analogy to the common course of nature, are also readily confessed to be known only by experience; nor does any man imagine that the explosion of gunpowder, or the attraction of a lode-stone, could ever be discovered by arguments *a priori*. In like manner, when an effect is supposed to depend upon an intricate machinery or secret structure of parts, we make no difficulty in attributing all our knowledge of it to experience. Who will assert that he can give the ultimate reason, why milk or bread is proper nourishment for a man, not for a lion or a tiger?

But the same truth may not appear, at first sight, to have the same evidence with regard to events, which have become familiar to us from our first appearance in the world, which bear a close analogy to the whole course of nature, and which are supposed to depend on the simple qualities of objects, without any secret structure of parts. We are apt to imagine that we could discover these effects by the mere operation of our reason, without experience. We fancy, that were we brought on a sudden into this world, we could at first have inferred that one Billiard-ball would communicate motion to another upon impulse; and that we needed not to have waited for the event, in order to pronounce with certainty concerning it. Such is the influence of custom, that, where it is strongest, it not only covers our natural ignorance, but even conceals itself, and seems not to take place, merely because it is found in the highest degree.

But to convince us that all the laws of nature, and all the operations of bodies without exception, are known only by experience, the following reflections may, perhaps, suffice. Were any object presented to us, and were we required to pronounce concerning the effect, which will result from it, without consulting past observation; after what manner, I beseech you, must the mind proceed in this operation? It must invent or imagine some event, which it ascribes to the object as its effect; and it is plain that this invention must be entirely arbitrary. The mind can never possibly find the effect in the supposed cause, by the most accurate scrutiny and examination. For the effect is totally different from the cause, and consequently can never be discovered in it. Motion in the second Billiard-ball is a quite distinct event from motion in the first; nor is there anything in the one to suggest the smallest hint of the other. A stone or piece of metal raised into the air, and left without any support, immediately falls: but to consider the matter *a priori*, is there anything we discover in this situation which can beget the idea of a downward, rather than an upward, or any other motion in the stone or metal?

And as the first imagination or invention of a particular effect, in all natural operations, is arbitrary, where we consult not experience; so must we also esteem the supposed tie or connexion between the cause and effect, which binds them together, and renders it impossible that any other effect could result from the operation of that cause. When I see, for instance, a Billiard-ball moving in a straight line towards another; even suppose motion in the second ball should by accident be suggested to me, as the result of their contact or impulse; may I not conceive, that a hundred different events might as well follow from that cause? May not both these balls remain at absolute rest? May not the first ball return in a straight line, or leap off from the second in any line or direction? All these suppositions are consistent and conceivable. Why then should we give the preference to one, which is no more consistent or conceivable than the rest? All our reasonings *a priori* will never be able to show us any foundation for this preference.

In a word, then, every effect is a distinct event from its cause. It could not, therefore, be discovered in the cause, and the first invention or conception of it, *a priori*, must be entirely arbitrary. And even after it is suggested, the conjunction of it with the cause must appear equally arbitrary; since there are always many other effects, which, to reason, must seem fully as consistent and natural. In vain, therefore, should we pretend to determine any single event, or infer any cause or effect, without the assistance of observation and experience.

Hence we may discover the reason why no philosopher, who is rational and modest, has ever pretended to assign the ultimate cause of any natural operation, or to show distinctly the action of that power, which produces any single effect in the universe. It is confessed, that the utmost effort of human reason is to reduce the principles, productive of natural phenomena, to a greater simplicity, and to resolve the many particular effects into a few general causes, by means of reasonings from analogy, experience, and observation. But as to the causes of these general causes, we should in vain attempt their discovery; nor shall we ever be able to satisfy ourselves, by any particular explication of them. These ultimate springs and principles are totally shut up from human curiosity and enquiry. Elasticity, gravity, cohesion of parts, communication of motion by impulse; these are probably the ultimate causes and principles which we shall ever discover in nature; and we may esteem ourselves sufficiently happy, if, by accurate enquiry and reasoning, we can trace up the particular phenomena to, or near to, these general principles. The most perfect philosophy of the natural kind only staves off our ignorance a little longer: as perhaps the most perfect philosophy of the moral or metaphysical kind serves only to discover larger portions of it. Thus the observation of human blindness and weakness is the result of all philosophy, and meets us at every turn, in spite of our endeavours to elude or avoid it.

Nor is geometry, when taken into the assistance of natural philosophy, ever able to remedy this defect, or lead us into the knowledge of ultimate causes, by all that accuracy of reasoning for which it is so justly celebrated. Every part of mixed mathematics proceeds upon the supposition that certain laws are established by nature in her operations; and abstract reasonings are employed, either to assist experience in the discovery of these laws, or to determine their influence in particular instances, where it depends upon any precise degree of distance and quantity. Thus, it is a law of motion, discovered by experience, that the moment or force of any body in motion is in the compound ratio or proportion of its solid contents and its velocity; and consequently, that a small force may remove the greatest obstacle or raise the greatest weight, if, by any contrivance or machinery, we can increase the velocity of that force, so as to make it an overmatch for its antagonist. Geometry assists us in the application of this law, by giving us the just dimensions of all the parts and figures which can enter into any species of machine; but still the discovery of the law itself is owing merely to experience, and all the abstract reasonings in the world could never lead us one step towards the knowledge of it. When we reason *a priori,* and consider merely any object or cause, as it appears to the mind, independent of all observation, it never could suggest to us the notion of any distinct object, such as its effect; much less, show us the inseparable and inviolable connexion between them. A man must be very sagacious who could discover by reasoning that crystal is the effect of heat, and ice of cold, without being previously acquainted with the operation of these qualities.[26]

Hume's argument against the principle of universal causation is also an argument against rationalism in general. What he is saying is that reasoning alone, without information from experience, cannot tell us anything whatever about the world. Reasoning *a priori,* that is, thinking without any appeal to experience, is incapable of proving any of those theorems so important to the rationalists, such as the nature of substance, the existence of God or a "first cause," or even, Hume argues, of the reality of any causes of any kind.

His argument against induction takes precisely the same form. Again he begins with his "fork" between "relations of ideas" and "matters of fact," and again he proves that one of the basic assumptions of all of our thinking, the principle of induction, cannot be established either way:

> But we have not yet attained any tolerable satisfaction with regard to the question first proposed. Each solution still gives rise to a new question as difficult as the foregoing, and leads us on to farther enquiries. When it is asked, *What is the nature of all our reasonings concerning matter of fact?* the proper answer seems to be, that they are founded on the relation of cause and effect. When again it is asked, *What is the foundation of all our reasonings and conclusions concerning that relation?* it may be replied in one word, Experience. But if we still carry on our sifting humour, and ask, *What is the foundation of all conclusions from experience?* this implies a new question, which may be of more difficult solution and explication. Philosophers, that give themselves airs of superior wisdom and sufficiency, have a hard task when they encounter persons of inquisitive dispositions, who push them from every corner to which they retreat, and who are sure at last to bring them to some dangerous dilemma. The best expedient to prevent this confusion, is to be modest in our pretensions; and even to discover the difficulty ourselves before it is objected to us. By this means, we may make a kind of merit of our very ignorance.
>
> I shall content myself, in this section, with an easy task, and shall pretend only to give a negative answer to the question here proposed. I say then, that, even after we have experience of the operations of cause and effect, our conclusions from that experience are *not* founded on reasoning, or any process of the understanding. This answer we must endeavour both to explain and to defend.
>
> It must certainly be allowed, that nature has kept us at a great distance

[26] Hume, *An Enquiry Concerning Human Understanding.*

from all her secrets, and has afforded us only the knowledge of a few superficial qualities of objects; while she conceals from us those powers and principles on which the influence of those objects entirely depends. Our senses
inform us of the colour, weight, and consistence of bread; but neither sense
nor reason can ever inform us of those qualities which fit it for the nourishment and support of a human body. Sight or feeling conveys an idea of the
actual motion of bodies; but as to that wonderful force or power, which
would carry on a moving body for ever in a continued change of place, and
which bodies never lose but by communicating it to others; of this we cannot form the most distant conception. But notwithstanding this ignorance of
natural powers and principles, we always presume, when we see like sensible qualities, that they have like secret powers, and expect that effects, similar to those which we have experienced, will follow from them. If a body of
like colour and consistence with that bread, which we have formerly eat,
be presented to us, we make no scruple of repeating the experiment, and
foresee, with certainty, like nourishment and support. Now this is a process
of the mind or thought, of which I would willingly know the foundation.
It is allowed on all hands that there is no known connexion between the
sensible qualities and the secret powers; and consequently, that the mind is
not led to form such a conclusion concerning their constant and regular
conjunction, by anything which it knows of their nature. As to past *Experience,* it can be allowed to give *direct* and *certain* information of those precise objects only, and that precise period of time, which fell under its cog-
nizance: but why this experience should be extended to future times, and
to other objects, which for aught we know, may be only in appearance similar; this is the main question on which I would insist. The bread, which I
formerly eat, nourished me; that is, a body of such sensible qualities was, at
that time, endued with such secret powers: but does it follow, that other
bread must also nourish me at another time, and that like sensible qualities
must always be attended with like secret powers? The consequence seems
nowise necessary. At least, it must be acknowledged that there is here a
consequence drawn by the mind; that there is a certain step taken; a process of thought, and an inference, which wants to be explained. These two
propositions are far from being the same, *I have found that such an object
has always been attended with such an effect,* and *I foresee, that other objects, which are, in appearance, similar, will be attended with similar effects.*
I shall allow, if you please, that the one proposition may justly be inferred
from the other: I know, in fact, that it always is inferred. But if you insist
that the inference is made by a chain of reasoning, I desire you to produce
that reasoning. The connexion between these propositions is not intuitive.
There is required a medium, which may enable the mind to draw such an
inference, if indeed it be drawn by reasoning and argument. What that
medium is, I must confess, passes my comprehension; and it is incumbent
on those to produce it, who assert that it really exists, and is the origin of
all our conclusions concerning matter of fact.

This negative argument must certainly, in process of time, become altogether convincing, if many penetrating and able philosophers shall turn their
enquiries this way and no one be ever able to discover any connecting proposition or intermediate step, which supports the understanding in this con-

clusion. But as the question is yet new, every reader may not trust so far to his own penetration, as to conclude, because an argument escapes his enquiry, that therefore it does not really exist. For this reason it may be requisite to venture upon a more difficult task; and enumerating all the branches of human knowledge, endeavour to show that none of them can afford such an argument.

All reasonings may be divided into two kinds, namely, demonstrative reasoning, or that concerning relations of ideas, and moral reasoning, or that concerning matter of fact and existence. That there are no demonstrative arguments in the case seems evident; since it implies no contradiction that the course of nature may change, and that an object, seemingly like those which we have experienced, may be attended with different or contrary effects. May I not clearly and distinctly conceive that a body, falling from the clouds, and which, in all other respects, resembles snow, has yet the taste of salt or feeling of fire? Is there any more intelligible proposition than to affirm, that all the trees will flourish in December and January, and decay in May and June? Now whatever is intelligible, and can be distinctly conceived, implies no contradiction, and can never be proved false by any demonstrative argument or abstract reasoning *a priori*.

If we be, therefore, engaged by arguments to put trust in past experience, and make it the standard of our future judgement, these arguments must be probable only, or such as regard matter of fact and real existence, according to the division above mentioned. But that there is no argument of this kind, must appear, if our explication of that species of reasoning be admitted as solid and satisfactory. We have said that all arguments concerning existence are founded on the relation of cause and effect; that our knowledge of that relation is derived entirely from experience; and that all our experimental conclusions proceed upon the supposition that the future will be conformable to the past. To endeavour, therefore, the proof of this last supposition by probable arguments, or arguments regarding existence, must be evidently going in a circle, and taking that for granted, which is the very point in question.

In reality, all arguments from experience are founded on the similarity which we discover among natural objects, and by which we are induced to expect effects similar to those which we have found to follow from such objects. And though none but a fool or madman will ever pretend to dispute the authority of experience, or to reject that great guide of human life, it may surely be allowed a philosopher to have so much curiosity at least as to examine the principle of human nature, which gives this mighty authority to experience, and makes us draw advantage from that similarity which nature has placed among different objects. From causes which appear *similar* we expect similar effects. This is the sum of all our experimental conclusions. Now it seems evident that, if this conclusion were formed by reason, it would be as perfect at first, and upon one instance, as after ever so long a course of experience. But the case is far otherwise. Nothing so like as eggs; yet no one, on account of this appearing similarity, expects the same taste and relish in all of them. It is only after a long course of uniform experiments in any kind, that we attain a firm reliance and security with regard to a particular event. Now where is that process of reasoning which, from one instance, draws a conclusion, so different from that which it infers from a hundred instances that are nowise different from that single one? This question I propose as much for the sake of information, as with an intention of raising difficulties. I cannot find, I cannot imagine any such reasoning. But I keep my mind still open to instruction, if any one will vouchsafe to bestow it on me.

Should it be said that, from a number of uniform experiments, we *infer* a connexion between the sensible qualities and the secret powers; this, I must confess, seems the same difficulty, couched in different terms. The question still recurs, on what process of argument this *inference* is founded? Where is the medium, the interposing ideas, which join propositions so very wide of each other? It is confessed that the colour, consistence, and other sensible qualities of bread appear not, of themselves, to have any connexion with the secret powers of nourishment and support. For otherwise we could infer these secret powers from the first appearance of these sensible qualities, without the aid of experience; contrary to the sentiment of all philosophers, and contrary to plain matter of fact. Here, then, is our natural state of ignorance with regard to the powers and influence of all objects. How is this remedied by experience? It only shows us a number of uniform effects, resulting from certain objects, and teaches us that those particular objects, at that particular time, were endowed with such powers and forces. When a new object, endowed with similar sensible qualities, is produced, we expect similar powers and forces, and look for a like effect. From a body of like colour and consistence with bread we expect like nourishment and support. But this surely is a step or progress of the mind, which wants to be explained. When a man says, *I have found, in all past instances, such sensible qualities conjoined with such secret powers:* And when he says, *Similar sensible qualities will always be conjoined with similar secret powers,* he is not guilty of a tautology, nor are these propositions in any respect the same. You say that the one proposition is an inference from the other. But you must confess that the inference is not intuitive; neither is it demonstrative: Of what nature is it, then? To say it is experimental, is begging the question. For all inferences from experience suppose, as their foundation, that the future will resemble the past, and that similar powers will be conjoined with similar sensible qualities. If there be any suspicion that the course of nature may change, and that the past may be no rule for the future, all experience becomes useless, and can give rise to no inference or conclusion. It is impossible, therefore, that any arguments from experience can prove this resemblance of the past to the future; since all these arguments are founded on the supposition of that resemblance. Let the course of things be allowed hitherto ever so regular; that alone, without some new argument or inference, proves not that, for the future, it will continue so. In vain do you pretend to have learned the nature of bodies from your past experience. Their secret nature, and consequently all their effects and influence, may change, without any change in their sensible qualities. This happens sometimes, and with regard to some objects: Why may it not happen always, and with regard to all objects? What logic, what process of argument secures you against this supposition? My practice, you say, refutes my doubts. But you mistake the purport of my question. As an agent, I am quite satisfied in the point;

but as a philosopher, who has some share of curiosity, I will not say scepticism, I want to learn the foundation of this inference. No reading, no enquiry has yet been able to remove my difficulty, or give me satisfaction in a matter of such importance. Can I do better than propose the difficulty to the public, even though, perhaps, I have small hopes of obtaining a solution? We shall at least, by this means, be sensible of our ignorance, if we do not augment our knowledge.

I must confess that a man is guilty of unpardonable arrogance who concludes, because an argument has escaped his own investigation, that therefore it does not really exist. I must also confess that, though all the learned, for several ages, should have employed themselves in fruitless search upon any subject, it may still, perhaps, be rash to conclude positively that the subject must, therefore, pass all human comprehension. Even though we examine all the sources of our knowledge, and conclude them unfit for such a subject, there may still remain a suspicion, that the enumeration is not complete, or the examination not accurate. But with regard to the present subject, there are some considerations which seem to remove all this accusation of arrogance or suspicion of mistake.

It is certain that the most ignorant and stupid peasants—nay infants, nay even brute beasts—improve by experience, and learn the qualities of natural objects, by observing the effects which result from them. When a child has felt the sensation of pain from touching the flame of a candle, he will be careful not to put his hand near any candle; but will expect a similar effect from a cause which is similar in its sensible qualities and appearance. If you assert, therefore, that the understanding of the child is led into this conclusion by any process of argument or ratiocination, I may justly require you to produce that argument; nor have you any pretence to refuse so equitable a demand. You cannot say that the argument is abstruse, and may possibly escape your enquiry; since you confess that it is obvious to the capacity of a mere infant. If you hesitate, therefore, a moment, or if, after reflection, you produce any intricate or profound argument, you, in a manner, give up the question, and confess that it is not reasoning which engages us to suppose the past resembling the future, and to expect similar effects from causes which are, to appearance, similar. This is the proposition which I intended to enforce in the present section. If I be right, I pretend not to have made any mighty discovery. And if I be wrong, I must acknowledge myself to be indeed a very backward scholar; since I cannot now discover an argument which, it seems, was perfectly familiar to me long before I was out of my cradle.[27]

What is the solution to these skeptical doubts? If we seek a justification or defense, there is none, according to Hume. But in everyday life, such philosophical doubts need have no effect at all, for though there is no justification of our beliefs, we can yet remain confident that, at least, there is an explanation for them:

Suppose a person, though endowed with the strongest faculties of reason and reflection, to be brought on a sudden into this world; he would,

[27] Hume, *An Enquiry Concerning Human Understanding.*

indeed, immediately observe a continual succession of objects and one event following another, but he would not be able to discover anything further. He would not at first, by any reasoning, be able to reach the idea of cause and effect, since the particular powers by which all natural operations are performed never appear to the senses; nor is it reasonable to conclude, merely because one event in one instance precedes another, that therefore the one is the cause, the other the effect. The conjunction may be arbitrary and casual. There may be no reason to infer the existence of one from the appearance of the other: and, in a word, such a person without more experience could never employ his conjecture or reasoning concerning any matter of fact or be assured of anything beyond what was immediately present to his memory or senses.

Suppose again that he has acquired more experience and has lived so long in the world as to have observed similar objects or events to be constantly conjoined together—what is the consequence of this experience? He immediately infers the existence of one object from the appearance of the other, yet he has not, by all his experience, acquired any idea or knowledge of the secret power by which the one object produces the other, nor is it by any process of reasoning he is engaged to draw this inference; but still he finds himself determined to draw it, and though he should be convinced that his understanding has no part in the operation, he would nevertheless continue in the same course of thinking. There is some other principle which determines him to form such a conclusion.

This principle is *custom* or *habit*. For wherever the repetition of any particular act or operation produces a propensity to renew the same act or operation without being impelled by any reasoning or process of the understanding, we always say that this propensity is the effect of *custom*. By employing that word we pretend not to have given the ultimate reason of such a propensity. We only point out a principle of human nature which is universally acknowledged, and which is well known by its effects. Perhaps we can push our inquiries no further or pretend to give the cause of this cause, but must rest contented with it as the ultimate principle which we can assign of all our conclusions from experience. It is sufficient satisfaction that we can go so far without repining at the narrowness of our faculties, because they will carry us no further. And it is certain we here advance a very intelligible proposition at least, if not a true one, when we assert that after the constant conjunction of two objects, heat and flame, for instance, weight and solidity, we are determined by custom alone to expect the one from the appearance of the other. This hypothesis seems even the only one which explains the difficulty why we draw from a thousand instances an inference which we are not able to draw from one instance that is in no respect different from them. Reason is incapable of any such variation. The conclusions which it draws from considering one circle are the same which it would form upon surveying all the circles in the universe. But no man, having seen only one body move after being impelled by another, could infer that every other body will move after a like impulse. All inferences from experience, therefore, are effects of custom, not of reasoning.[28]

[28] Hume, *An Enquiry Concerning Human Understanding.*

In other words, there is no "solution to these skeptical doubts," but, at most, what Hume calls "a skeptical solution." It means an end, not only to philosophy, but to all rational inquiry and all claims that we can know anything (even that the sun will rise tomorrow, or that there is a typewriter now in front of me). You might think that such conclusions would have driven Hume mad, or caused him such confusion that he would have been incapable of coping with the most everyday chores. Yet we know that he was the most practical and jolliest sort of fellow. As a philosopher, he has been driven right up against the wall of Plato's Cave. But he remains unperturbed. In a famous passage at the end of the *Treatise,* he simply remarks:

> Most fortunately it happens, that since reason is incapable of dispelling these clouds, nature herself suffices to that purpose, and cures me of this philosophical melancholy and delirium, either by relaxing this bent of mind, or by some avocation, and lively impression of my senses, which obliterate all these chimeras. I dine, I play a game of back-gammon, I converse, and am merry with my friends; and when after three or four hours' amusement, I wou'd return to these speculations, they appear so cold, and strain'd, and ridiculous, that I cannot find in my heart to enter into them any farther.[29]

Perhaps you too find "these speculations cold, strained and ridiculous." If so, however, this is not the time to run off to dinner and an evening of games and conversation. Something has gone very wrong. The empiricist attempt to restore common sense to philosophy has ended in the least commonsensical philosophy imaginable. A person who really believed that there might be no material world, or that the future will not resemble the past (and therefore, having been hit by a truck last week, steps into the street confident that it will not happen again) would be crazy! How can our intellects be so out of joint with our experience? or our philosophy so far away from practical life? Not only for the sake of philosophy, therefore, but for the sake of our sanity, we must find a way around Hume's intolerable skepticism.

SUMMARY AND CONCLUSION

Epistemology is the study of human knowledge—what we can know, how we can know it, and what we cannot know. In this sense, epistemology and metaphysics are complementary disciplines. Epistemology becomes the method or approach to the knowledge of the way the world really is. For some philosophers, this approach places its primary trust in reason, accordingly, they are called rationalists. For other philosophers, the preferred approach is to trust the senses and experience, they are called empiricists. The problem for both of them is to get beyond the mere appearance of things to the reality behind

[29] David Hume, *Treatise of Human Nature,* ed. L. A. Selby-Bigge (Oxford: Oxford University Press, 1888).

them. The rationalist tries to do this by appealling to intuition and certain principles from which he can deduce the way the world really is. The Empiricist, on the other hand, appeals to his experiences, trying to find there his evidence for the nature of reality. For both views, however, the danger is that their methods do not always seem to achieve as much as they would like. Rationalists disagree about which principles to start with and which intuitions to trust. Empiricists find that their own method of experience makes it impossible to say anything about what lies beyond experience. Thus Bishop Berkeley argues that only our ideas and the minds that have these ideas exist (including God), and David Hume concludes that we can never know anything about reality, but only about our own associations of ideas. Epistemologists are still working on more satisfactory answers to the questions of knowledge, and still trying to defeat once and for all the skeptical conclusions so brilliantly argued by Hume two centuries ago.

GLOSSARY

appearance: the way something seems to us, through our senses. Usually philosophers worry about something's being a mere appearance, such that it bears no faithful resemblance to the reality of which it is the appearance.

association of ideas: a central idea of empiricist psychology, according to which all knowledge is composed of separate ideas which are connected by their resemblance to one another (e.g., "this one looks exactly like that one"), by their contiguity in space and time (e.g., "every time I see this, I see that as well") and causality (e.g., "every time a thing of that sort happens it is followed by something of this sort"). (The three different "associations" here are Hume's.)

causation or **causality:** the relation of cause and effect, one event's bringing about another according to natural law. In Hume, (1) one event's following another necessarily (or so it seems to us); (2) one type of event regularly following another (See *association of ideas* above).

cause: that which produces an effect; an event (or state of affairs, object, art, or person) which brings about another event.

causal theory of perception: the view that our experience (our sensations and ideas) are the effects of physical objects acting upon our sense organs (which are thereby the causes).

cogito, ergo sum: or "I think, therefore I am" is Descartes' only principle which he finds "beyond doubt" and "perfectly certain." ("Think" here refers to any kind of idea or experience in the mind, not just what we would normally call "thinking.") It is the premise of his entire philosophy.

datum: Latin, literally, "what is given." (plural, *data*)

empiricism: that philosophy that demands that all knowledge, except for certain logical truths and principles of mathematics, comes from experience. British empiricism is often used to refer specifically to the three philosophers Locke, Berkeley, and Hume. It is still very much an alive movement, however, and includes Bertrand Russell in our own century and a great many philosophers of the past forty years who have called themselves "logical empiricists" (better known as logical positivists).

epistemology: the study of human knowledge, its nature, its sources, its justification.

explanation: an account—usually a causal account—of something; it is opposed to *justification,* which also defends. One can, for example, explain one's action (say, by claiming that he or she was drunk) without thereby justifying it, that is, showing it to be right. Hume ultimately explains our knowledge but does not justify it.

generalization from experience or **inductive generalization:** inference from observation, experience, and experiment to a generalization about all members of a certain class. For example, in a laboratory, a researcher finds that certain experiments on tobacco plants always have the same result. He or she generalizes, through induction, from experimental observations to a claim (or *hypothesis*) about all tobacco plants. But notice that this generalization is never certain (like the generalization in geometry from a proof of a theorem about this triangle to a theorem about all triangles). It might always turn out that there was a fluke in the experiment or that he/she chose a peculiar sample of plants.

Hume's fork: Hume's insistence that every belief be justified either as a "relation between ideas" or as a "matter of fact."

idea: in epistemology, almost any mental phenomenon (not, as in Plato, with existence independent of individual minds). The terminology varies slightly; Locke uses "idea" to refer to virtually any "mental content"; Hume reserves "idea" for those mental atoms which are derived by the mind from impressions.

impression: Hume's word for sensations or sense-data, that which is given to the mind through the senses.

induction; inductive reasoning; inductive generalization: induction is the process of inferring general conclusions (for example, "all swans are white") from a sufficiently large sample of particular observations ("this swan is white, that swan is white, and that one, and that one, and that one . . ."). It is usually contrasted with *deduction* (see Ch. 1), in that, while deductive reasoning guarantees that the conclusion shall be as certain as the premises, induction never gives us a conclusion as certain as the premises. Its conclusions are, at most, merely probable. (There might always be some black swan somewhere; and there are, in Western Australia.)

innate ideas: literally, ideas that are "born into the mind." Locke's famous attack on such ideas took them to be literally ideas which all men share from birth. The rationalist philosophers he was supposedly attacking, however, held a much more sophisticated notion; they did not believe that ideas were literally "born into us," but they did believe that we are born with certain "innate" capacities and dispositions, which will develop with proper education (and mental health). And these ideas, most importantly, can be defended or justified without appeal to any particular experiences or experiments. This is the claim that Locke ultimately rejected.

intuition: immediate knowledge, without the aid of reasoning or inference. It must be stressed, however, that intuition is often (even usually) argued to be a function of reason, and capable of rational insights even if they are, by their very nature, not defensible by any arguments.

justification: an attempt to defend a position or an act, to show that it is correct (or at least reasonable). (Cf. *explanation* above.)

primary qualities: in Locke, those properties ("qualities") that inhere in the object.

principle of induction: the belief that the laws of nature will continue to hold in the future as they have in the past. (Crudely, "the future will be like the past.")

principle of universal causation: the belief that every event has its cause (or causes). In scientific circles, it is usually added, "its sufficient natural cause," in order to eliminate the possibility of miracles and divine intervention (which are allowed in Leibniz's similar but broader Principle of Sufficient Reason.

probable: likely; or supported by the evidence (but not conclusively). The empiricist's middle step between the extremities of certainty and doubt. (Probability is the measure of how probable something is.)

quality: in Locke (and other authors), a property.

rationalism: that philosophy which is characterized by its confidence in reason, and intuition in particular, to know reality independently of experience. (See *reason* and *intuition*.) Continental rationalism is usually reserved for the three great European philosophers, Descartes, Spinoza, and Leibniz.

reason: in rationalism, the faculty which allows us to know reality through intuition. In empiricism, simply the ability to recognize certain principles which are "relations of ideas," for example, trivial truths ("a cat is an animal") and, more complicated, principles of arithmetic and geometry. Empiricists deny that reason allows us special insight into reality, however; it tells us only relations between ideas.

relations of ideas: in empiricism, knowledge which is restricted to the logical and conceptual connections between ideas, not to the correspondence of those ideas to experience or to reality.

secondary qualities: in Locke, those properties ("qualities") that are caused in us by objects, but do not inhere in the objects themselves (for example, color).

sensation: the experiential result of the stimulation of a sense organ, for example, *seeing* red, *hearing* a ringing noise, *smelling* something burning. The simplest of mental phenomena.

sense-data: that which is given to the senses, prior to any reasoning or organization on our part.

skepticism: the philosophical belief (or fear) that knowledge is not possible, and that no rational arguments will succeed in overcoming our doubts.

subjective idealism: the view that only ideas and minds exist, and that there are no substances, matter, or material objects. In particular, the philosophy of Bishop Berkeley.

tabula rasa: in Locke's philosophy, the "blank tablet" metaphor of the mind, in opposition to the doctrine that there are innate ideas. In other words, the mind is a "blank" at birth, and everything we know must be "stamped in" through experience.

4

NECESSITY

It is the common fate of human reason to complete its speculative structures as speedily as may be, and only afterwards to enquire whether the foundations are reliable.

Immanuel Kant

Surely there are some things that we can know with certainty! Even Hume, for example, granted that some of our beliefs are beyond the range of his skeptical doubts, namely, those which he calls "relations of ideas," such as the basic principles of arithmetic. Nothing could make us doubt that two plus two equals four. Descartes may have suggested that it was possible that an evil demon was fooling him about even this; but what would it mean to be "fooled" about such matters? How could he have been wrong about that? Of course, he could always say that he might be wrong about two plus two equalling four, just as we could always say that two plus two equals five. But what could we possibly mean by that? We can understand what it would be like to be wrong about some factual belief, such as "there are no Chinese paratroopers in Cuba"; perhaps it even makes sense, however implausible, to suggest that we might be dreaming right now. But one can't even imagine, no matter how hard one tries, what it would be for "two plus two equals four" to be false.

Beliefs that we cannot even imagine being false and which lie beyond the range of all possible doubt and refutation are called *necessary truths*. In short, they must be true. Necessary truth is contrasted with *contingent truth*, which is a belief that is in fact true but might not have been. It is true, for example, that I am now wearing a sweater, but we can easily imagine what it would be for me not to wear one. That is a contingent truth. Necessary truths, because we cannot even imagine what it would be like for them to be false, are always "perfectly certain"; contingent truths, because we can always imagine that they might be false (and that we are possibly fooled or misled in believing them) are never "perfectly certain" but always merely probable. We can always think of some way, no matter how implausible, in which we might be wrong. (I might be dreaming that I'm wearing a sweater, for example.) But one cannot be mistaken about a necessary truth. (There is a curious but important exception to this distinction that is already familiar to you: Descartes' "I exist" is both necessary [it can't be intelligibly doubted] and contingent [since it is possible that he might not have existed].)

A partial distinction between necessary truth and contingent truth is this: contingent truths are based upon experience and necessary truths are not. Accordingly, contingent truths allow for some further experience that would change our minds. We may be sure that there are no armadillos on the upper east side of Manhattan, but because that is a contingent truth, it is always possible that we shall see an armadillo crossing 86th Street, and thereby have to give up our belief. Because of this essential link between contingent truths and experience, philosophers often refer to our knowledge of them as *empirical knowledge*. Necessary truths, on the other hand, are not based upon experience, and there is no possible experience—real or imagined—that could change our minds about them. For this reason, philosophers talk about these truths as being prior to experience or *a priori* and knowledge of them is also considered to be *a priori*, in other words, to be knowledge that is independent of experience. It is important to stress that the "prior" or "before" here does not mean "earlier in time." For example, it does not mean that we know *a priori* that "two plus two equals four" before we ever have experience of two things adding up with two other things to give us four things. It means rather that the justification of *a priori* knowledge does not depend on any possible experience. You cannot refute "two plus two equals four" through experience. But neither can you justify it through experience. You could spend a year adding up different pairs of things, walnuts, elephants, pieces of chalk, people and scoops of ice cream; you would then have the general claim that "whenever I add two things to two things I get four things," but you would fail to prove the necessity of that truth.

There are philosophers, as we have seen, who do take *a priori* to mean literally "before"; that is, those philosophers who believe in innate ideas believe that we actually do have certain knowledge before we have any experience at all. We are born with it, and that would explain, if you accept this theory, how it is that *a priori* knowledge is possible. But it is important to emphasize that the belief in innate ideas is not essential to the notion of either necessary truth or *a priori* knowledge, and most philosophers talk about the latter without ever mentioning the former.

What then, is the source of *a priori* knowledge? For those philosophers who believe in innate ideas, the answer is that we are born with it. But even this is not enough, for it is necessary to say how it is that we are born with such knowledge. Even if it is "stamped in our minds by God," as some philosophers have held, how do we recognize it? The traditional answer, for those who believe in innate ideas and for those who do not, is through reason. In fact, reason is traditionally defined (for example, by Plato, Aristotle, Spinoza and Leibniz) as our ability to know necessary truths. But our account is circular; we are told that we can know necessary truths because of reason but reason is defined as our ability to know necessary truths. So, in this chapter we must ask, what is this ability? How do we have it? How is *a priori* knowledge possible?

Although we shall be exclusively concerned with necessary and contingent truths, it is important to say that there is a similar distinction between necessary and contingent falsehoods. "Every triangle has at least five sides" is a necessary falsehood: it could not possibly be true. "There are no eagles in America" is a contingent falsehood: it is in fact false, but we can (too easily) imagine that it might be true.

THE NOTION OF NECESSITY

For convenience, we can divide up necessary truths into three categories:

1) *Analytic truths* or *logical truths:* these are, for example, trivial statements such as "either it is raining or it is not raining" and "a horse is an animal." Analytic truths can be known to be true just by analyzing the form of the statement and the meanings of the words of the statement.

2) *Truths of arithmetic and geometry:* these do not seem to be analytic, that is, known to be true just because of the form of the statement. "413 plus 2785 = 3198," for example does not seem to be true because of the meanings of the terms, "413," "2785," etc., yet this would seem to be a necessary truth if anything is. The same would be true of "the internal angles of a triangle equal two right triangles."

3) *Truths of metaphysics:* these are the principles of metaphysics formulated by the great metaphysicians (Plato, Aristotle, Leibniz, Spinoza), which were claimed to be necessary truths. It has also been suggested that the principles Hume claimed could not be justified, the principle of universal causation and the principle of induction, are necessary truths. (You can guess that this category of necessary truths will be far more controversial than the first two.)

Analytic truths

Consider the utterly trivial statement, "all bachelors are unmarried." Not very interesting, to be sure, but it is, obviously, a necessary truth. We can be perfectly certain that this statement is true and we know in advance that no study of bachelors could possibly turn up an instance of one who was married.

We cannot even imagine a situation in which this statement would be false, and there is no sense in wondering "well, we've only looked at the bachelors in our neighborhood, what about the bachelors in southern California?" All we have to know to know that "all bachelors are unmarried" is the meaning of the English sentence, nothing else.

Now consider the contingent claim, "all bachelors are happy." Of course, in order to find out whether that is true or not, you have to know the meanings of the words, but you cannot tell whether or not it is true just by looking at the words. This statement raises an empirical question. That is, in order to know whether or not it is true you have to go out into the world and interview bachelors. To falsify the claim that all bachelors are happy, you would have to find only one unhappy bachelor. But even if you never found one, you could never be perfectly certain of the truth of the claim. There might always be one unhappy bachelor, living in a cave off the coast of Madagascar. A contingent claim, therefore, is never perfectly certain. One can always at least imagine some circumstance that would prove it to be false, even if it seems, on the basis of the present evidence, to be true.

The example, "all bachelors are unmarried" is an analytic truth: its truth can be demonstrated just by referring to the meanings of the words in the sentence. This particular example is what we referred to in earlier chapters as a conceptual truth (such as, "a horse is an animal"). Conceptual truths are a special class of analytic truths. Aristotle discussed such truths in terms of essences, he would say that "the essence of a bachelor is to be unmarried." More modern philosophers would talk about concepts, they would say that "the concept 'bachelor' includes the concept of being unmarried." Today, most philosophers would rather say that "bachelor means unmarried person." But these different formulations all point to the same fact, that conceptual truths are necessary truths because of the meanings of the words in the sentence.

Not all analytic truths are conceptual truths, however. Consider the statement, "either it is raining or it is not raining." Now obviously you don't have to look out the window to see whether this is true or not. It is true just because of the form of the sentence, which is "P or not—P." Such sentences are called *tautologies*. They are true by virtue of the form of the sentence alone, and it doesn't matter what phrase you substitute for "P." For example, you know that "either there are exactly 7,500 comets in our galaxy or there are not," even if you don't know anything about astronomy, or exactly what a "comet" or a "galaxy" is.

Tautologies are not very interesting. They are the most boring and uninformative sentences in our language, but they are also very important. Every tautology gives us what we called (in the Introduction) a rule of inference, one of those basic rules that we use in all our thinking. (This is true even for people who claim "not to be logical" or actually attack logic.) It is according to these rules of inference that we define the validity of our arguments. But here a problem arises. How can we defend a rule of inference itself? We cannot say that it is valid, since we have to use such rules in order to say that any-thing is valid. And you can't use a rule to prove itself. (That would be the same as appointing a magistrate to judge his own alleged corruption.) To answer this question, many philosophers appeal to intuition as a defense of our basic rules of inference. Rationalists feel comfortable with this, since they have confidence in reason to show us such basic truths through intuition. Empiricists tend to feel very uncomfortable, however, for they would rather either that these rules are based upon experience (but they are not) or that they are matters of reasoning (but this can't be either, since they are the basis of all reasoning). So what empiricists try to do is to find as small a set of basic rules as possible, from which they can derive all of the others. The problem then becomes, how do you defend that basic set of rules?

The most basic of these rules is called the *law of contradiction*. That law says: a statement and its denial cannot both be true. For example, it cannot be true that it is raining and that it is not raining at the same place at the same time. This law has been used by many philosophers (for example, Leibniz and Hume) to define analytic truths in general. They say that a statement is analytic if, when you deny it, you get a contradiction. The recognition of the importance of this law, however, goes as far back as Aristotle, who worried about this law and what makes it true. After con-siderable thought, he concluded:

> This is the most certain of all principles, for it is impossible for anyone to suppose that the same thing is and is not . . . then clearly it is impossible for the same man to suppose at the same time that the same thing is and is not; for the man who made this error would entertain two contrary opinions at the same time. Hence all men who are demonstrating anything refer back to this as an ultimate belief; for it is by nature the starting-point of all the other axioms as well.
>
> . . . . .
>
> Some, indeed, demand to have the law proved, but this is because they lack education; for it shows lack of education not to know of what we should require proof, and of what we should not. For it is quite impossible that everything should have a proof; the process would go on to infinity, so that even so there would be no proof. If on the other hand there are some things of which no proof need be sought, they cannot say what principle they think to be more self-evident. Even in the case of this law, however, we can demon-strate the impossibility of refutation, if only our opponent makes some state-ment. If he makes none, it is absurd to seek for an argument against one who has no arguments of his own about anything, in so far as he has none; for such a person, in so far as he is such, is really no better than a vegetable.[1]

Aristotle's answer is still accepted by most philosophers. This one principle, at least, cannot be defended except to say that it would be utterly absurd to

[1] Aristotle, *Metaphysics*, BK. IV, trans. Hugh Tredennick (Cambridge, Mass.: Harvard University Press, 1933).

deny it. Even if a philosopher will not accept the appeal to intuition in any other case, it seems that he must at least in this one.

There are many other kinds of analytic truths, but it would take a course in logic to adequately discuss them. But what they all have in common is that they are necessary truths which can be known simply by the analysis of the form of the sentence or the meanings of the words within the sentence. But will this account of analytic truths cover all cases of necessary truths? For example, will it work for the truths of arithmetic and geometry too?

The truths of arithmetic and geometry

Ever since ancient times, the principles of arithmetic and geometry have been considered necessary truths. The explanations of them varied, from religious laws of the cosmos (as in Pythagoras and many ancient cults of astrology) to Plato's theory of ideal forms. But this much has seemed obvious to almost everyone who has thought about the nature of these principles: no stretch of the imagination could describe a circumstance in which they would not be true. No matter how the world changed, and no matter what else people came to believe, two plus two would still equal four, and the principles of Euclidean geometry would still be true. No matter what could ever happen, it seems, these principles would always hold.

Think, for a moment, about the simple truth of arithmetic, "two plus two equals four." It is not the case that two things plus two things of the same kind always result in four things: two drops of ink added to two more drops of ink give you one big drop, not four. But this doesn't give us a counter-example to the laws of arithmetic, since the volume of the large drop would still have to equal the total volume of the two plus two smaller drops. Similarly, you can draw a triangle whose interior angles do not equal two right angles, as Euclid shows they must, by drawing the triangle on the curved surface of a globe. But this does not show that Euclid's principles, which are specifically concerned with figures drawn on a flat surface, could possibly be false. In general, people have believed that, even if there are apparent counter-examples to the truths of arithmetic and geometry, those truths themselves are absolutely necessary and cannot be challenged.

The defense of this necessary truth, however, and all such truths of mathematics, Euclidean geometry and arithmetic, does not simply appeal to the meanings of the words involved. The truth of "two plus two equals four" does not depend on replacing one synonym with another, as in "all bachelors are unmarried." The number four, for example, can be described in many ways, as "two plus two," as "one plus three," as "the number following three" or "the number preceding five," as "the number which is the first non-prime," and as "the square root of sixteen." This list could be extended indefinitely (for example, "one half of eight," "one third of twelve," "one fourth of sixteen"). Consequently, it is difficult to see how "two plus two equals four" is true just because the meaning of "four" is "two plus two." If the symbolic system that we call arithmetic makes its principles necessarily true by some system of interconnected definitions, they would have to be infinitely more complicated than any of the analytic truths we have seen thus far.

There is another consideration, however, that has often been argued as a reason for thinking that the truths of arithmetic and geometry cannot be merely analytic. The argument was originally formulated by Immanuel Kant. He pointed out, against Hume and his other predecessors who so glibly spoke of "relations of ideas" and "truths of reason," that the truths of arithmetic and geometry are not just abstract formulas which we accept as true because we accept the overall system of which they are a part. We also apply these principles to the world in concrete ways, to give us new knowledge of things. For example, we count things, "one, two, three . . ." and this means that our number system must be linked up with the world of experience as well as being a self-contained system of necessary truths. (Logicians refer to any logical system of abstract symbols as a *calculus;* a system which is applied to the world, such as arithmetic, is an *interpreted calculus.*) Analytic truths, as we have described them, do not tell us anything about the world; logical principles tell us how we reason, but they say nothing of what we reason about. Conceptual truths tell us something about the meanings of words, but (except for teaching young children the categories to which things belong, as for example, "a horse is an animal, but a tree is a plant"), they too tell us nothing about the world itself. But arithmetic and geometry, it seems, give us new information which we did not have before. This is obviously true of the principles of physics and of "higher" mathematics. Perhaps it is also true of the simplest truths of arithmetic.

In elementary education, there are some problems in which we learn to calculate, given the basic principles of arithmetic. "Long" division, for example, presupposes the simple truths of "short" division, multiplication and subtraction. These simple truths, however, like the simple truths of multiplication, subtraction, and addition "tables," are not calculated but memorized. The important question, then, is whether these basic principles can themselves be proved or calculated, or whether they can only be memorized. How do we defend these basic truths? Can we only say, "by intuition?" Further, there are some evident truths of arithmetic that no mathematicians have ever been able to prove. There is now a general proof, developed only a few years ago by a contemporary logician named Kurt Gödel, which shows that there can never be a system of proofs which can succeed in proving all the truths of arithmetic without proving some false claims as well. The same is true in Euclidean geometry. You may remember from high school that problematic theorem, that one and only one line can be drawn through a point parallel to a given line. It is obviously true, necessarily true, but no one can develop a valid proof for it.

THE EMPIRICIST ARGUMENT: The basic principles of arithmetic would seem to be necessary truths if anything is. But are they logical truths, true by virtue of their logical form? or conceptual truths, true by virtue of their symbolic meanings? It is here that the arguments about the nature of necessary truth become most violent, and most brilliant. Once again, the rationalist need not be particularly disturbed, for his confidence in reason allows him to agreeably accept the idea that certain non-analytic truths may yet be necessary, and known by intuition. For him, it is enough to say, along with Plato, Descartes, and Leibniz, that certain principles of mathematics are "self-evident," "intuitively obvious," or even "innate ideas." But for the empiricist, who insists that all knowledge is based upon either experience or analytic sentences, the foundations of arithmetic prove to be an embarrassing problem. It is worth noting that all three traditional empiricists, Locke, Berkeley, and Hume, simply accepted the idea that the truths of arithmetic were "relations of ideas," without looking any further. Modern empiricists, however, have not been so negligent. The most famous of the British "logical positivists," A. J. Ayer, for example, states the empiricist problem in the following way:

Where the empiricist does encounter difficulty is in connection with the truths of formal logic and mathematics. For whereas a scientific generalization is readily admitted to be fallible, the truths of mathematics and logic appear to everyone to be necessary and certain. But if empiricism is correct no proposition which has a factual content can be necessary or certain. Accordingly the empiricist must deal with the truths of logic and mathematics in one of the two following ways: he must say either that they are not necessary truths, in which case he must account for the universal conviction that they are; or he must say that they have no factual content, and then he must explain how a proposition which is empty of all factual content can be true and useful and surprising.

If neither of these courses proves satisfactory, we shall be obliged to give way to rationalism. We shall be obliged to admit that there are some truths about the world which we can know independently of experience; that there are some properties which we can ascribe to all objects, even though we cannot conceivably observe that all objects have them. And we shall have to accept it as a mysterious inexplicable fact that our thought has this power to reveal to us authoritatively the nature of objects which we have never observed. . . . It is vital, therefore, for us to be able to show that one or other of the empiricist accounts of the propositions of logic and mathematics is correct. If we are successful in this, we shall have destroyed the foundations of rationalism. For the fundamental tenet of rationalism is that thought is an independent source of knowledge, and is moreover a more trustworthy source of knowledge than experience; indeed some rationalists have gone so far as to say that thought is the only source of knowledge. And the ground for this view is simply that the only necessary truths about the world which are known to us are known through thought and not through experience. So that if we can show either that the truths in question are not necessary or that they are not "truths about the world," we shall be taking away the support on which

rationalism rests. We shall be making good the empiricist contention that there
are no "truths of reason" which refer to matters of fact.[2]

The alternatives are few, but the variety of ways in which they have been
developed is dazzling. One possibility is to simply deny what we have seemingly
accepted as obvious all along, namely, that the truths of arithmetic are necessary truths. The fact that they are not analytic does not therefore appear as a
problem. They are rather, according to this empiricist position, very well-
confirmed matters of fact (and therefore not "relations of ideas" at all).
John Stuart Mill, the most famous British philosopher of the nineteenth
century, argued this position as follows:

> Why are mathematics by almost all philosophers, and (by some) even those
> branches of natural philosophy which, through the medium of mathematics,
> have been converted into deductive sciences, considered to be independent
> of the evidence of experience and observation, and characterized as systems
> of Necessary Truth?
>
> The answer I conceive to be, that this character of necessity, ascribed
> to the truths of mathematics, and (even with some reservations to be here-
> after made) the peculiar certainty attributed to them, is an illusion; in order
> to sustain which, it is necessary to suppose that those truths relate to, and
> express the properties of, purely imaginary objects. It is acknowledged that
> the conclusions of geometry are deduced, partly at least, from the so-called
> Definitions, and that those definitions are assumed to be correct representa-
> tions, as far as they go, of the objects with which geometry is conversant.
> Now we have pointed out that, from a definition as such, no proposition,
> unless it be one concerning the meaning of a word, can ever follow; and that
> what apparently follows from a definition, follows in reality from an implied
> assumption that there exists a real thing conformable thereto. This assumption,
> in the case of the definitions of geometry, is not strictly true: there exist no
> real things exactly conformable to the definitions. There exist no points with-
> out magnitude; no lines without breadth, nor perfectly straight; no circles
> with all their radii exactly equal, nor squares with all their angles perfectly
> right. It will perhaps be said that the assumption does not extend to the
> actual, but only to the possible, existence of such things. I answer that,
> according to any test we have of possibility, they are not even possible. Their
> existence, so far as we can form any judgment, would seem to be inconsistent
> with the physical constitution of our planet at least, if not of the universe. To
> get rid of this difficulty, and at the same time to save the credit of the sup-
> posed system of necessary truth, it is customary to say that the points, lines,
> circles, and squares which are the subject of geometry, exist in our concep-
> tions merely, and are part of our minds; which minds, by working on their
> own materials, construct an *a priori* science, the evidence of which is purely
> mental, and has nothing whatever to do with outward experience. By howso-
> ever high authorities this doctrine may have been sanctioned, it appears to me
> psychologically incorrect. The points, lines, circles, and squares which any
> one has in his mind, are (I apprehend) simply copies of the points, lines,

[2] A. J. Ayer, *Language, Truth and Logic,* 2nd ed. (London: Victor Gollancz, 1936 and
New York: Dover, 1946).

circles, and squares which he has known in his experience. Our idea of a point, I apprehend to be simply our idea of the *minimum visible,* the smallest portion of surface which we can see. A line, as defined by geometers, is wholly inconceivable. We can reason about a line as if it had no breadth; because we have a power, which is the foundation of all the control we can exercise over the operations of our minds; the power, when a perception is present to our senses, or a conception to our intellects, of *attending* to a part only of that perception or conception, instead of the whole. But we can not *conceive* a line without breadth; we can form no mental picture of such a line: all the lines which we have in our minds are lines possessing breadth. If any one doubts this, we may refer him to his own experience. I much question if any one who fancies that he can conceive what is called a mathematical line, thinks so from the evidence of his consciousness: I suspect it is rather because he supposes that unless such a conception were possible, mathematics could not exist as a science: a supposition which there will be no difficulty in showing to be entirely groundless.

Since, then, neither in nature, nor in the human mind, do there exist any objects exactly corresponding to the definitions of geometry, while yet that science can not be supposed to be conversant about nonentities; nothing remains but to consider geometry as conversant with such lines, angles, and figures, as really exist; and the definitions, as they are called, must be regarded as some of our first and most obvious generalizations concerning those natural objects. The correctness of those generalizations, *as* generalizations, is without a flaw: the equality of all the radii of a circle is true of all circles, so far as it is true of any one: but it is not exactly true of any circle; it is only nearly true; so nearly that no error of any importance in practice will be incurred by feigning it to be exactly true. . . .

When, therefore, it is affirmed that the conclusions of geometry are necessary truths, the necessity consists in reality only in this, that they correctly follow from the suppositions from which they are deduced. Those suppositions are so far from being necessary, that they are not even true; they purposely depart, more or less widely, from the truth. The only sense in which necessity can be ascribed to the conclusions of any scientific investigation, is that of legitimately following from some assumption, which, by the conditions of the inquiry, is not to be questioned. In this relation, of course, the derivative truths of every deductive science must stand to the inductions, or assumptions, on which the science is founded, and which, whether true or untrue, certain or doubtful in themselves, are always supposed certain for the purposes of the particular science. . . .

From these considerations it would appear that Deductive or Demonstrative Sciences are all, without exception, Inductive Sciences; that their evidence is that of experience; but that they are also, in virtue of the peculiar character of one indispensable portion of the general formulae according to which their inductions are made, Hypothetical Sciences. Their conclusions are only true on certain suppositions, which are, or ought to be, approximations to the truth, but are seldom, if ever, exactly true; and to this hypothetical character is to be ascribed the peculiar certainty, which is supposed to be inherent in demonstration.

What we have now asserted, however, can not be received as universally true of Deductive or Demonstrative Sciences, until verified by being applied to the most remarkable of all those sciences, that of Numbers; the theory of the Calculus; Arithmetic and Algebra. It is harder to believe of the doctrines of this science than of any other, either that they are not truths a priori, but experimental truths, or that their peculiar certainty is owing to their being not absolute but only conditional truths.

.   .   .   .   .

One theory attempts to solve the difficulty apparently inherent in the case, by representing the propositions of the science of numbers as merely verbal, and its processes as simple transformations of language, substitutions of one expression for another. The proposition, Two and one is equal to three, according to these writers, is not a truth, is not the assertion of a really existing fact, but a definition of the word three; a statement that mankind have agreed to use the name three as a sign exactly equivalent to two and one; to call by the former name whatever is called by the other more clumsy phrase. According to this doctrine, the longest process in algebra is but a succession of changes in terminology, by which equivalent expressions are substituted one for another; a series of translations of the same fact, from one into another language; though how, after such a series of translations, the fact itself comes out changed (as when we demonstrate a new geometrical theorem by algebra), they have not explained; and it is a difficulty which is fatal to their theory.

It must be acknowledged that there are peculiarities in the processes of arithmetic and algebra which render the theory in question very plausible, and have not unnaturally made those sciences the stronghold of Nominalism. The doctrine that we can discover facts, detect the hidden processes of nature, by an artful manipulation of language, is so contrary to common sense, that a person must have made some advances in philosophy to believe it: men fly to so paradoxical a belief to avoid, as they think, some even greater difficulty, which the vulgar do not see. What has led many to believe that reasoning is a mere verbal process is, that no other theory seemed reconcilable with the nature of the Science of Numbers. For we do not carry any ideas along with us when we use the symbols of arithmetic or of algebra. In a geometrical demonstration we have a mental diagram, if not one on paper; AB, AC, are present to our imagination as lines, intersecting other lines, forming an angle with one another, and the like; but not so a and b. These may represent lines or any other magnitudes, but those magnitudes are never thought of; nothing is realized in our imagination but a and b. The ideas which, on the particular occasion, they happen to represent, are banished from the mind during every intermediate part of the process, between the beginning, when the premises are translated from things into signs, and the end, when the conclusion is translated back from signs into things. Nothing, then, being in the reasoner's mind but the symbols, what can seem more inadmissible than to contend that the reasoning process has to do with any thing more?

Nevertheless, it will appear on consideration, that this apparently so decisive instance is no instance at all; that there is in every step of an arithmetical or algebraical calculation a real induction, a real inference of facts from facts; and that what disguises the induction is simply its comprehensive nature, and the consequent extreme generality of the language. All numbers must be numbers of something; there are no such things as numbers in the abstract. *Ten* must mean ten bodies, or ten sounds, or ten beatings of the pulse. But though numbers must be numbers of something, they may be numbers of any thing. Propositions, therefore, concerning numbers, have the remarkable peculiarity that they are propositions concerning all things whatever; all objects, all existences of every kind, known to our experience. All things possess quantity; consist of parts which can be numbered; and in that character possess all the properties which are called properties of numbers. That half of four is two, must be true whatever the word four represents, whether four hours, four miles, or four pounds weight. We need only conceive a thing divided into four equal parts (and all things may be conceived as so divided), to be able to predicate of it every property of the number four, that is, every arithmetical proposition in which the number four stands on one side of the equation. Algebra extends the generalization still farther: every number represents that particular number of all things without distinction, but every algebraical symbol does more, it represents all numbers without distinction. As soon as we conceive a thing divided into equal parts, without knowing into what number of parts, we may call it a or x, and apply to it, without danger of error, every algebraical formula in the books. The proposition, $2(a + b) = 2a + 2b$, is a truth co-extensive with all nature. Since then algebraical truths are true of all things whatever, and not, like those of geometry, true of lines only or of angles only, it is no wonder that the symbols should not excite in our minds ideas of any things in particular.

. . . . .

There is another circumstance, which, still more than that which we have now mentioned, gives plausibility to the notion that the propositions of arithmetic and algebra are merely verbal. That is, that when considered as propositions respecting Things, they all have the appearance of being identical propositions. The assertion, Two and one is equal to three, considered as an assertion respecting objects, as for instance, "Two pebbles and one pebble are equal to three pebbles," does not affirm equality between two collections of pebbles, but absolute identity. It affirms that if we put one pebble to two pebbles, those very pebbles are three. The objects, therefore, being the very same, and the mere assertion that "objects are themselves" being insignificant, it seems but natural to consider the proposition, Two and one is equal to three, as asserting mere identity of signification between the two names.

This, however, though it looks so plausible, will not bear examination. The expression "two pebbles and one pebble," and the expression "three pebbles," stand indeed for the same aggregation of objects, but they by no means stand for the same physical fact. They are names of the same objects, but of those objects in two different states: though they *de*note the same things, their *con*notation is different. Three pebbles in two separate parcels, and three pebbles in one parcel, do not make the same impression on our senses; and the assertion that the very same pebbles may by an alteration of place and arrangement be made to produce either the one set of sensations or the other, though a very familiar proposition, is not an identical one. It is a truth known to us by early and constant experience: an inductive truth;

and such truths are the foundation of the science of Number. The fundamental truths of that science all rest on the evidence of sense; they are proved by showing to our eyes and our fingers that any given number of objects—ten balls, for example—may by separation and re-arrangement exhibit to our senses all the different sets of numbers the sums of which is equal to ten. All the improved methods of teaching arithmetic to children proceed on a knowledge of this fact. All who wish to carry the child's *mind* along with them in learning arithmetic; all who wish to teach numbers, and not mere ciphers—now teach it through the evidence of the senses, in the manner we have described.

We may, if we please, call the proposition, "Three is two and one," a definition of the number three, and assert that arithmetic, as it has been asserted that geometry, is a science founded on definitions. But they are definitions in the geometrical sense, not the logical; asserting not the meaning of a term only, but along with it an observed matter of fact. The proposition, "A circle is a figure bounded by a line which has all its points equally distant from a point within it," is called the definition of a circle; but the proposition from which so many consequences follow, and which is really a first principle in geometry, is, that figures answering to this description exist. And thus we may call "Three is two and one" a definition of three; but the calculations which depend on that proposition do not follow from the definition itself, but from an arithmetical theorem presupposed in it, namely, that collections of objects exist, which while they impress the senses thus, $^{\circ}{}_{\circ}{}^{\circ}$, may be separated into two parts, thus, o o o. This proposition being granted, we term all such parcels Threes, after which the enunciation of the above-mentioned physical fact will serve also for a definition of the word Three.

The Science of Number is thus no exception to the conclusion we previously arrived at, that the processes even of deductive sciences are altogether inductive, and that their first principles are generalizations from experience. It remains to be examined whether this science resembles geometry in the further circumstance, that some of its inductions are not exactly true; and that the peculiar certainty ascribed to it, on account of which its propositions are called Necessary Truths, is fictitious and hypothetical, being true in no other sense than that those propositions legitimately follow from the hypothesis of the truth of premises which are avowedly mere approximations to truth.[3]

In this selection, John Stuart Mill challenges what has been one of the best established beliefs in the history of Western thought, the belief that arithmetical and geometrical truths are necessary and could not be otherwise. He argues that these truths, like all truths, are nothing other than generalizations from experience, and that they differ only in the degree of confirmation, not in kind. He uses the Kantian argument that arithmetic is never simply abstract calculation, but also applicable to the world. And this means, according to Mill (but not according to Kant) that there must always be some inference from facts about the world. Numbers are never simply numbers, he

[3] John Stuart Mill, *A System of Logic*, 8th ed. (New York: Harper & Row, 1874).

argues, they are always numbers of something, and this means that the meaning of a number (for example, "four") always extends beyond the language of arithmetic alone. The truths of arithmetic and geometry, in other words, are just like the truths of science, generalizations about the world.

Most empiricists, however, have not taken Mill's alternative of arguing that these truths are not necessary. Like A. J. Ayer, they have generally agreed that the principles of arithmetic and geometry are indeed necessary truths, and therefore, they conclude, they must be analytic. Mill refers to several such attempts in his own day. The problem, however, is to show how these truths are derivable either from principles of logic or from the meanings of arithmetical or geometrical terms. The attempt to derive arithmetic from logic was begun by Gottlob Frege in Germany, who attacked the defenders of Mill's empirical interpretation in his own country. The project was fully developed in England by Bertrand Russell and Alfred North Whitehead in their *Principia Mathematica*. In what has been called the most brilliant single philosophical campaign in the twentieth century, they proved that the principles of arithmetic could be deduced from a small set of axioms (developed by an Italian mathematician named Giuseppe Peano), which could in turn be defined and defended in logical terms alone.

In what follows, the basic empiricist position is presented in two different forms. The first, by A. J. Ayer, summarizes the empiricist position in simple non-technical language. The second, by the contemporary American philosopher C. G. Hempel, will provide you with a more detailed account of the logic and mathematics involved. (The second excerpt may prove difficult for students who have not had mathematics in college. Even so, I believe that you will get the idea of the general empiricist project, even if you don't master the details.)

Here is Ayer's argument that the truths of mathematics are tautological and hence analytic.

> We have already explained how it is that these analytic propositions are necessary and certain. We saw that the reason why they cannot be confuted in experience is that they do not make any assertion about the empirical world. They simply record our determination to use words in a certain fashion. We cannot deny them without infringing the conventions which are presupposed by our very denial, and so falling into self-contradiction. And this is the sole ground of their necessity. As Wittgenstein puts it, our justification for holding that the world could not conceivably disobey the laws of logic is simply that we could not say of an unlogical world how it would look. And just as the validity of an analytic proposition is independent of the nature of the external world, so is it independent of the nature of our minds. It is perfectly conceivable that we should have employed different linguistic conventions from those which we actually do employ. But whatever these conventions might be, the tautologies in which we recorded them would always be necessary. For any denial of them would be self-stultifying.
>
> We see, then, that there is nothing mysterious about the apodeictic cer-

tainty of logic and mathematics. Our knowledge that no observation can ever confute the proposition "7 + 5 = 12" depends simply on the fact that the symbolic expression "7 + 5" is synonymous with "12," just as our knowledge that every oculist is an eye-doctor depends on the fact that the symbol "eye-doctor" is synonymous with "oculist." And the same explanation holds good for every other *a priori* truth.

What is mysterious at first sight is that these tautologies should on occasion be so surprising, that there should be in mathematics and logic the possibility of invention and discovery. As Poincaré says: "If all the assertions which mathematics puts forward can be derived from one another by formal logic, mathematics cannot amount to anything more than an immense tautology. Logical inference can teach us nothing essentially new, and if everything is to proceed from the principle of identity, everything must be reducible to it. But can we really allow that these theorems which fill so many books serve no other purpose than to say in a round-about fashion 'A = A'?" Poincaré finds this incredible. His own theory is that the sense of invention and discovery in mathematics belongs to it in virtue of mathematical induction, the principle that what is true for the number 1, and true for $n + 1$ when it is true for n, is true for all numbers. And he claims that this is a synthetic *a priori* principle. It is, in fact, *a priori*, but it is not synthetic. It is a defining principle of the natural numbers, serving to distinguish them from such numbers as the infinite cardinal numbers, to which it cannot be applied. Moreover, we must remember that discoveries can be made, not only in arithmetic, but also in geometry and formal logic, where no use is made of mathematical induction. So that even if Poincaré were right about mathematical induction, he would not have provided a satisfactory explanation of the paradox that a mere body of tautologies can be so interesting and so surprising.

The true explanation is very simple. The power of logic and mathematics to surprise us depends, like their usefulness, on the limitations of our reason. A being whose intellect was infinitely powerful would take no interest in logic and mathematics. For he would be able to see at a glance everything that his definitions implied, and, accordingly, could never learn anything from logical inference which he was not fully conscious of already. But our intellects are not of this order. It is only a minute proportion of the consequences of our definitions that we are able to detect at a glance. Even so simple a tautology as "91 × 79 = 7189" is beyond the scope of our immediate apprehension. To assure ourselves that "7189" is synonymous with "91 × 79" we have to resort to calculation, which is simply a process of tautological transformation—that is, a process by which we change the form of expressions without altering their significance. The multiplication tables are rules for carrying out this process in arithmetic, just as the laws of logic are rules for the tautological transformation of sentences expressed in logical symbolism or in ordinary language. As the process of calculation is carried out more or less mechanically, it is easy for us to make a slip and so unwittingly contradict ourselves. And this accounts for the existence of logical and mathematical "falsehoods," which otherwise might appear paradoxical. Clearly the risk of error in logical reasoning is proportionate to the length and the complexity of the process of calculation. And in the same way, the more complex an analytic proposition is, the more chance it has of interesting and surprising us.

It is easy to see that the danger of error in logical reasoning can be minimized by the introduction of symbolic devices, which enable us to express highly complex tautologies in a conveniently simple form. And this gives us an opportunity for the exercise of invention in the pursuit of logical enquiries. For a well-chosen definition will call our attention to analytic truths, which would otherwise have escaped us. And the framing of definitions which are useful and fruitful may well be regarded as a creative act.

Having thus shown that there is no inexplicable paradox involved in the view that the truths of logic and mathematics are all of them analytic, we may safely adopt it as the only satisfactory explanation of their *a priori* necessity. And in adopting it we vindicate the empiricist claim that there can be no *a priori* knowledge of reality. For we show that the truths of pure reason, the propositions which we know to be valid independently of all experience, are so only in virtue of their lack of factual content. To say that a proposition is true *a priori* is to say that it is a tautology. And tautologies, though they may serve to guide us in our empirical search for knowledge, do not in themselves contain any information about any matter of fact.[4]

C. G. Hempel also argues that mathematical truths are necessary and analytic, but he employs some of the very sophisticated logical machinery that had been developed by Peano, Frege, Russell, and Whitehead. He goes beyond Ayer in trying to show how mathematical truths can be derived from simpler logical rules, thus demonstrating their analyticity. He begins, however, by first attacking the rationalist's belief that mathematical truths are "self-evident" as well as Mill's belief that mathematics is a form of empirical knowledge. He then goes on to show how mathematical truths can be derived by logical inference from a limited number of axioms.

ARE THE PROPOSITIONS OF MATHEMATICS SELF-EVIDENT TRUTHS?

One of the several answers which have been given to our problem asserts that the truths of mathematics, in contradistinction to the hypotheses of empirical science, require neither factual evidence nor any other justification because they are "self-evident." This view, however, which ultimately relegates decisions as to mathematical truth to a feeling of self-evidence, encounters various difficulties. First of all, many mathematical theorems are so hard to establish that even to the specialist in the particular field they appear as anything but self-evident. Secondly, it is well known that some of the most interesting results of mathematics—especially in such fields as abstract set theory and topology—run counter to deeply ingrained intuitions and the customary kind of feeling of self-evidence. Thirdly, the existence of mathematical conjectures such as those of Goldbach and of Fermat, which are quite elementary in content and yet undecided up to this day, certainly shows that not all mathematical truths can be self-evident. And finally, even if self-evidence were attributed only to the basic postulates of mathematics, from which all other mathematical propositions can be deduced, it would be

---

[4] Ayer, *Language, Truth and Logic.*

pertinent to remark that judgments as to what may be considered as self-evident are subjective; they may vary from person to person and certainly cannot constitute an adequate basis for decisions as to the objective validity of mathematical propositions.

IS MATHEMATICS THE MOST GENERAL EMPIRICAL SCIENCE?

According to another view, advocated especially by John Stuart Mill, mathematics is itself an empirical science which differs from the other branches such as astronomy, physics, chemistry, etc., mainly in two respects: its subject matter is more general than that of any other field of scientific research, and its propositions have been tested and confirmed to a greater extent than those of even the most firmly established sections of astronomy or physics. Indeed, according to this view, the degree to which the laws of mathematics have been borne out by the past experiences of mankind is so overwhelming that—unjustifiably—we have come to think of mathematical theorems as qualitatively different from the well-confirmed hypotheses or theories of other branches of science: we consider them as certain, while other theories are thought of as at best "very probable" or very highly confirmed.

But this view, too, is open to serious objections. From a hypothesis which is empirical in character—such as, for example, Newton's law of gravitation—it is possible to derive predictions to the effect that under certain specified conditions certain specified observable phenomena will occur. The actual occurrence of these phenomena constitutes confirming evidence, their non-occurrence disconfirming evidence for the hypothesis. It follows in particular that an empirical hypothesis is theoretically disconfirmable; i.e., it is possible to indicate what kind of evidence, if actually encountered, would disconfirm the hypothesis. In the light of this remark, consider now a simple "hypothesis" from arithmetic: $3 + 2 = 5$. If this is actually an empirical generalization of past experiences, then it must be possible to state what kind of evidence would oblige us to concede the hypothesis was not generally true after all. If any disconfirming evidence for the given proposition can be thought of, the following illustration might well be typical of it: We place some microbes on a slide, putting down first three of them and then another two. Afterwards we count all the microbes to test whether in this instance 3 and 2 actually added up to 5. Suppose now that we counted 6 microbes altogether. Would we consider this as an empirical disconfirmation of the given proposition, or at least as a proof that it does not apply to microbes? Clearly not; rather, we would assume we had made a mistake in counting or that one of the microbes had split in two between the first and the second count. But under no circumstances could the phenomenon just described invalidate the arithmetical proposition in question; for the latter asserts nothing whatever about the behavior of microbes; it merely states that any set consisting of $3 + 2$ objects may also be said to consist of 5 objects. And this is so because the symbols "$3 + 2$" and "5" denote the same number: they are synonymous by virtue of the fact that the symbols "2," "3," "5," and "$+$" are *defined* (or tacitly understood) in such a way that the above identity holds as a consequence of the meaning attached to the concepts involved in it.

THE ANALYTIC CHARACTER OF MATHEMATICAL PROPOSITIONS

The statement that $3 + 2 = 5$, then, is true for similar reasons as, say, the assertion that no sexagenarian is 45 years of age. Both are true simply by virtue of definitions or of similar stipulations which determine the meaning of the key terms involved. Statements of this kind share certain important characteristics: Their validation naturally requires no empirical evidence; they can be shown to be true by a mere analysis of the meaning attached to the terms which occur in them. In the language of logic, sentences of this kind are called analytic or true *a priori*, which is to indicate that their truth is logically independent of, or logically prior to, any experiential evidence. And while the statements of empirical science, which are synthetic and can be validated only *a posteriori*, are constantly subject to revision in the light of new evidence, the truth of an analytic statement can be established definitely, once and for all. However, this characteristic "theoretical certainty" of analytic propositions has to be paid for at a high price: An analytic statement conveys no factual information. Our statement about sexagenarians, for example, asserts nothing that could possibly conflict with any factual evidence: it has no factual implications, no empirical content; and it is precisely for this reason that the statement can be validated without recourse to empirical evidence.

Let us illustrate this view of the nature of mathematical propositions by reference to another, frequently cited, example of a mathematical—or rather logical—truth, namely the proposition that whenever $a = b$ and $b = c$ then $a = c$. On what grounds can this so-called "transitivity of identity" be asserted? Is it of an empirical nature and hence at least theoretically disconfirmable by empirical evidence? Suppose, for example, that a, b, c, are certain shades of green, and that as far as we can see, $a = b$ and $b = c$, but clearly $a \neq c$. This phenomenon actually occurs under certain conditions; do we consider it as disconfirming evidence for the proposition under consideration? Undoubtedly not; we would argue that if $a \neq c$, it is impossible that $a = b$ and also $b = c$; between the terms of at least one of these latter pairs, there must obtain a difference, though perhaps only a subliminal one. And we would dismiss the possibility of empirical disconfirmation, and indeed the idea that an empirical test should be relevant here, on the grounds that identity is a transitive relation by virtue of its definition or by virtue of the basic postulates governing it. Hence, the principle in question is true *a priori*.

MATHEMATICS AS AN AXIOMATIZED DEDUCTIVE SYSTEM

I have argued so far that the validity of mathematics rests neither on its alleged self-evidential character nor on any empirical basis, but derives from the stipulations which determine the meaning of the mathematical concepts, and that the propositions of mathematics are therefore essentially "true by definition." This latter statement, however, is obviously oversimplified and needs restatement and a more careful justification.

For the rigorous development of a mathematical theory proceeds not simply from a set of definitions but rather from a set of non-definitional propositions which are not proved within the theory; these are the postulates or axioms of the theory. They are formulated in terms of certain basic or primitive concepts for which no definitions are provided within the theory. It is sometimes asserted that the postulates themselves represent "implicit definitions" of the primitive terms. Such a characterization of the postulates, however, is misleading. For while the postulates do limit, in a specific sense, the meanings that can possibly be ascribed to the primitives, any self-consistent postulate system admits, nevertheless, many different interpretations of the primitive terms (this will soon be illustrated), whereas a set of definitions in the strict sense of the word determines the meanings of the definienda in a unique fashion.

Once the primitive terms and the postulates have been laid down, the entire theory is completely determined; it is derivable from its postulational basis in the following sense: Every term of the theory is definable in terms of the primitives, and every proposition of the theory is logically deducible from the postulates. To be entirely precise, it is necessary also to specify the principles of logic which are to be used in the proof of the propositions, i.e., in their deduction from the postulates. These principles can be stated quite explicitly. They fall into two groups: Primitive sentences, or postulates, of logic (such as: If p and q is the case, then p is the case), and rules of deduction or inference (including, for example, the familiar *modus ponens* rule and the rules of substitution which make it possible to infer, from a general proposition, any one of its substitution instances). A more detailed discussion of the structure and content of logic would, however, lead too far afield in the context of this article.

PEANO'S AXIOM SYSTEM AS A BASIS FOR MATHEMATICS

Let us now consider a postulate system from which the entire arithmetic of the natural numbers can be derived. This system was devised by the Italian mathematician and logician G. Peano (1858–1932). The primitives of this system are the terms "0," "number," and "successor." While, of course, no definition of these terms is given within the theory, the symbol "0" is intended to designate the number 0 in its usual meaning, while the term "number" is meant to refer to the natural numbers 0, 1, 2, 3 . . . exclusively. By the successor of a natural number n, which will sometimes briefly be called n', is meant the natural number immediately following n in the natural order. Peano's system contains the following 5 postulates:

P1. 0 is a number
P2. The successor of any number is a number
P3. No two numbers have the same successor
P4. 0 is not the successor of any number
P5. If P is a property such that (a) 0 has the property P, and (b) whenever a number n has the property P, then the successor of n also has the property P, then every number has the property P.

The last postulate embodies the principle of mathematical induction and illustrates in a very obvious manner the enforcement of a mathematical "truth" by stipulation. The construction of elementary arithmetic on this basis begins with the definition of the various natural numbers. 1 is defined as the successor of 0, or briefly as $0'$; 2 as $1'$, 3 as $2'$, and so on. By virtue of P2, this process can be continued indefinitely; because of P3 (in combination with P5), it never leads back to one of the numbers previously defined, and in view of P4, it does not lead back to 0 either.

As the next step, we can set up a definition of addition which expresses in a precise form the idea that the addition of any natural number to some given number may be considered as a repeated addition of 1; the latter operation is readily expressible by means of the successor relation. This definition of addition runs as follows:

D1.   (a) $n + 0 = n$;   (b) $n + k' = (n + k)'$.

The two stipulations of this recursive definition completely determine the sum of any two integers. Consider, for example, the sum $3 + 2$. According to the definitions of the numbers 2 and 1, we have $3 + 2 = 3 + 1' = 3 + (0')'$; by D1 (b), $3 + (0')' = (3 + 0')' = ((3 + 0)')'$; but by D1 (a), and by the definitions of the numbers 4 and 5, $((3 + 0)')' = (3')' = 4' = 5$. This proof also renders more explicit and precise the comments made earlier in this paper on the truth of the proposition that $3 + 2 = 5$: Within the Peano system of arithmetic, its truth flows not merely from the definition of the concepts involved, but also from the postulates that govern these various concepts. (In our specific example, the postulates P1 and P2 are presupposed to guarantee that 1, 2, 3, 4, 5 are numbers in Peano's system; the general proof that D1 determines the sum of any two numbers also makes use of P5.) If we call the postulates and definitions of an axiomatized theory the "stipulations" concerning the concepts of that theory, then we may say now that the propositions of the arithmetic of the natural numbers are true by virtue of the stipulations which have been laid down initially for the arithmetical concepts. (Note, incidentally, that our proof of the formula "$3 + 2 = 5$" repeatedly made use of the transitivity of identity; the latter is accepted here as one of the rules of logic which may be used in the proof of any arithmetical theorem; it is, therefore, included among Peano's postulates no more than any other principle of logic.)

Now, the multiplication of natural numbers may be defined by means of the following recursive definition, which expresses in a rigorous form the idea that a product nk of two integers may be considered as the sum of k terms each of which equals n.

D2.   (a) $n \cdot 0 = 0$;   (b) $n \cdot k' = n \cdot k + n$.

It now is possible to prove the familiar general laws governing addition and multiplication, such as the commutative, associative, and distributive laws $(n + k = k + n;\ n \cdot k = k \cdot n;\ n + (k + l) = (n + k) + l;\ n \cdot (k \cdot l) = (n \cdot k) \cdot l;\ n \cdot (k + l) = (n \cdot k) + (n \cdot l))$. In terms of addition and multiplication, the inverse operations of subtraction and division can then be defined. But it turns out that these "cannot always be performed"; i.e., in contradistinction to the sum and the product, the difference and the quotient are not defined for every couple of numbers; for example, $7 - 10$ and $7 \div 10$ are undefined. This situation suggests an enlargement of the number system by the introduction of negative and of rational numbers.

It is sometimes held that in order to effect this enlargement, we have to "assume" or else to "postulate" the existence of the desired additional kinds of numbers with properties that make them fit to fill the gaps of subtraction and division. This method of simply postulating what we want has its advantages; but, as Bertrand Russell puts it, they are the same as the advantages of theft over honest toil; and it is a remarkable fact that the negative as well as the rational numbers can be obtained from Peano's primitives by the honest toil of constructing explicit definitions for them, without the introduction of any new postulates or assumptions whatsoever. Every positive and negative integer (in contradistinction to a natural number which has no sign) is definable as a certain set of ordered couples of natural numbers; thus, the integer $+ 2$ is definable as the set of all ordered couples (m, n) of natural numbers where $m = n + 2$; the integer $- 2$ is the set of all ordered couples (m, n) of natural numbers with $n = m + 2$. (Similarly, rational numbers are defined as classes of ordered couples of integers.) The various arithmetical operations can then be defined with reference to these new types of numbers, and the validity of all the arithmetical laws governing these operations can be proved by virtue of nothing more than Peano's postulates and the definitions of the various arithmetical concepts involved.

The much broader system thus obtained is still incomplete in the sense that not every number in it has a square root, and more generally, not every algebraic equation whose coefficients are all numbers of the system has a solution in the system. This suggests further expansions of the number system by the introduction of real and finally of complex numbers. Again, this enormous extension can be effected by mere definition, without the introduction of a single new postulate. On the basis thus obtained, the various arithmetical and algebraic operations can be defined for the numbers of the new system, the concepts of function, of limit, of derivative and integral can be introduced, and the familiar theorems pertaining to these concepts can be proved, so that finally the huge system of mathematics as here delimited rests on the narrow basis of Peano's system: Every concept of mathematics can be defined by means of Peano's three primitives, and every proposition of mathematics can be deduced from the five postulates enriched by the definitions of the non-primitive terms. These deductions can be carried out, in most cases, by means of nothing more than the principles of formal logic; the proof of some theorems concerning real numbers, however, requires one assumption which is not usually included among the latter. This is the so-called axiom of choice. It asserts that given a class of mutually exclusive classes, none of which is empty, there exists at least one class which has exactly one element in common with each of the given classes. By virtue of this principle and the rules of formal logic, the content of all of mathematics can thus be derived from Peano's modest system—a remarkable achievement in systematizing the content of mathematics and clarifying the foundations of its validity.

MATHEMATICS AS A BRANCH OF LOGIC

As was pointed out earlier, all the theorems of arithmetic, algebra, and analysis can be deduced from the Peano postulates and the definitions of those mathematical terms which are not primitives in Peano's system. This deduction requires only the principles of logic plus, in certain cases, the axiom of choice. By combining this result with what has just been said about the Peano system, the following conclusion is obtained, which is also known as *the thesis of logicism concerning the nature of mathematics:*

Mathematics is a branch of logic. It can be derived from logic in the following sense:

a. All the concepts of mathematics, i.e., of arithmetic, algebra, and analysis, can be defined in terms of four concepts of pure logic.

b. All the theorems of mathematics can be deduced from those definitions by means of the principles of logic (including the axioms of infinity and choice).[5]

THE RATIONALIST RESPONSE: What kinds of truths are the truths of arithmetic and geometry? We just watched various empiricists try to show that (1) the truths of mathematics are not necessary and not analytic and therefore not known *a priori* (Mill) and (2) they are necessary and analytic and therefore known *a priori* (Ayer, Hempel).

Against both of these empiricist projects, the rationalist continues to insist that the truths of arithmetic and mathematics are neither empirical nor analytic, but matters of necessity in some other way. Traditionally, particularly in the philosophy of Descartes, this "other way" is through intuition, the anathema of the empiricist. The empiricist does not trust the appeal to intuition, for, by its very nature, it cannot be defended either by rational argument nor by appeal to ordinary experience. The rationalist, with his or her confidence in reason, feels no qualms about this. The problem belongs to the empiricist, the price for the lack of confidence in reason. But even the empiricist may be eventually forced back to intuition, if there is no further justification of ultimate principles and "relations of ideas." Unlike the traditional rationalist, the empiricist believes these intuitions follow from our use of language or our adopting a certain logic. He or she might say (here quoting A. J. Ayer) : "these principles simply record our determination to use words in a certain fashion." The rationalist has said all along that some such appeal to self-evidence is ultimately necessary, for there must be some principles which have to be accepted without proof. The empiricist just restricts the scope within which such appeals must be made. But there must be a third possibility if the rationalist is right, for he/she insists that these truths are certainly necessary but yet not analytic. What kind of truth could this be?

In historical terms, the discovery of this third alternative precedes the empiricist attempts of the nineteenth and twentieth centuries (by Mill and later by Frege, Russell, Whitehead, Hempel, and Ayer). It was discovered by Immanuel Kant, in the 1770s, as an answer to both the traditional rationalists and the empiricists. He found their theories all unacceptable. Both Leibniz and Hume, for example, had simply distinguished necessary from contingent

[5] C. G. Hempel, "On the Nature of Mathematical Truth," in *American Mathematical Monthly*, vol. 52, 1945.

truths, without further distinction. And we so far have done the same thing, only using more sophisticated terminology. But are all necessary truths analytic, known by analysis of the sentence alone? Or might there be some *a priori* knowledge of the world rather than just of language? The rationalist believes that there is, and Kant, a new kind of rationalist, shows what it would be.

It is one thing to say that knowledge is either *a priori* or *empirical*. It is quite another to say that sentences are either analytic or not analytic. The first distinguishes two kinds of knowledge; the second distinguishes two kinds of sentences. The term Kant uses for "not analytic" is *synthetic;* so we have two sets of distinctions, *a priori* versus empirical and analytic versus synthetic.

We have been talking as if all *a priori* knowledge was based on analytic sentences. But then, we have also been talking as if only empirical knowledge could be stated in non-trivial or synthetic sentences: for example, "not all trees are green all year." But isn't it possible that there might be synthetic sentences whose truth can be known *a priori?* Kant thinks that there can be, and he calls such knowledge *synthetic a priori knowledge*. Arithmetic and geometry are his most important examples, but he also uses this notion of "the synthetic *a priori*" to provide a generally new conception of the problems and principles of philosophy.

So far, we haven't resolved anything. You remember (in our discussion of Plato's word "participation") that we insisted we must always be careful not to mistake a new word for an explanation, and, so far, that's all that we have. The words, "synthetic *a priori*," though very impressive, only tell us that the truths of arithmetic are neither analytic nor empirical. In other words, it is a restatement of the problem, which still remains. How does one justify synthetic *a priori* principles?

The last two centuries have seen a great many rationalist attempts to work out their problematic notion of "intuition" and to display the viability of their confidence in human reason. (Rationalism, like empiricism, is still very much a living philosophy.) In this chapter, we shall mention only two of them. One is by Immanuel Kant. The other, which emerged only in this century, is called *phenomenology*. It was invented by a German-Czech philosopher-mathematician named Edmund Husserl, and it is one of those philosophies which has enormous influence in both Europe and the United States. (England, it seems, has remained far more committed to empiricism.)

Kant is the man whom most contemporary philosophers—whether they agree with him or not—would call the greatest philosopher since Plato and Aristotle. In what follows, Kant makes his distinctions between *a priori* and empirical (*a posteriori*) knowledge and between analytic and synthetic sentences (or "judgments"). Then he introduces the idea of synthetic *a priori* knowledge. And, finally, he gives us his radically new way of defending the truths of arithmetic and geometry.

THE DISTINCTION BETWEEN PURE AND EMPIRICAL KNOWLEDGE

There can be no doubt that all our knowledge begins with experience. For how should our faculty of knowledge be awakened into action did not objects affecting our senses partly of themselves produce representations, partly arouse the activity of our understanding to compare these representations, and, by combining or separating them, work up the raw material of the sensible impressions into that knowledge of objects which is entitled experience? In the order of time, therefore, we have no knowledge antecedent to experience, and with experience all our knowledge begins.

But though all our knowledge begins with experience, it does not follow that it all arises out of experience. For it may well be that even our empirical knowledge is made up of what we receive through impressions and of what our own faculty of knowledge (sensible impressions serving merely as the occasion) supplies from itself. If our faculty of knowledge makes any such addition, it may be that we are not in a position to distinguish it from the raw material, until with long practice of attention we have become skilled in separating it.

This, then, is a question which at least calls for closer examination, and does not allow of any off-hand answer:—whether there is any knowledge that is thus independent of experience and even of all impressions of the senses. Such knowledge is entitled *a priori*, and distinguished from the *empirical,* which has its sources *a posteriori,* that is, in experience.

THE DISTINCTION BETWEEN
ANALYTIC AND SYNTHETIC JUDGMENTS

In all judgments in which the relation of a subject to the predicate is thought (I take into consideration affirmative judgments only, the subsequent application to negative judgments being easily made), this relation is possible in two different ways. Either the predicate B belongs to the subject A, as something which is (covertly) contained in this concept A; or B lies outside the concept A, although it does indeed stand in connection with it. In the one case I entitle the judgment analytic, in the other synthetic. Analytic judgments (affirmative) are therefore those in which the connection of the predicate with the subject is thought through identity; those in which this connection is thought without identity should be entitled synthetic. The former, as adding nothing through the predicate to the concept of the subject, but merely breaking it up into those constituent concepts that have all along been thought in it, although confusedly, can also be entitled explicative. The latter, on the other hand, add to the concept of the subject a predicate which has not been in any wise thought in it, and which no analysis could possibly extract from it; and they may therefore be entitled ampliative. If I say, for instance, 'All bodies are extended', this is an analytic judgment. For I do not require to go beyond the concept which I connect with 'body' in order to find extension as bound up with it. To meet with this predicate, I have merely to analyse the concept, that is, to become conscious to myself of the manifold which I always think in that concept. The judgment is therefore analytic. But when I say, 'All bodies are heavy', the predicate is something quite different from anything that I think in the mere concept of body in general; and the addition of such a predicate therefore yields a synthetic judgment.

Judgments of experience, as such, are one and all synthetic. For it would be absurd to found an analytic judgment on experience. Since, in framing the judgment, I must not go outside my concept, there is no need to appeal to the testimony of experience in its support. That a body is extended is a proposition that holds *a priori* and is not empirical. For, before appealing to experience, I have already in the concept of body all the conditions required for my judgment. I have only to extract from it, in accordance with the principle of contradiction, the required predicate, and in so doing can at the same time become conscious of the necessity of the judgment—and that is what experience could never have taught me.

And then the problem, "How are synthetic *a priori* judgments possible?"

It cannot be experience, because the suggested principle has connected the second representation with the first, not only with greater universality, but also with the character of necessity, and therefore completely *a priori* and on the basis of mere concepts. Upon synthetic, that is, ampliative principles, all our *a priori* speculative knowledge must ultimately rest; analytic judgments are very important, and indeed necessary, but only for obtaining that clearness in the concepts which is requisite for such a sure and wide synthesis as will lead to a genuinely new addition to all previous knowledge.

In particular, "How is pure mathematics possible?"

All mathematical judgments, without exception, are synthetic. This fact, though incontestably certain and in its consequences very important, has hitherto escaped the notice of those who are engaged in the analysis of human reason, and is, indeed, directly opposed to all their conjectures. For as it was found that all mathematical inferences proceed in accordance with the principle of contradiction (which the nature of all apodeictic certainty requires), it was supposed that the fundamental propositions of the science can themselves be known to be true through that principle. This is an erroneous view. For though a synthetic proposition can indeed be discerned in accordance with the principle of contradiction, this can only be if another synthetic proposition is presupposed, and if it can then be apprehended as following from this other proposition; it can never be so discerned in and by itself.

First of all, it has to be noted that mathematical propositions, strictly so called, are always judgments *a priori,* not empirical; because they carry with them necessity, which cannot be derived from experience. If this be demurred to, I am willing to limit my statement to *pure* mathematics, the very concept of which implies that it does not contain empirical, but only pure *a priori* knowledge.

We might, indeed, at first suppose that the proposition $7 + 5 = 12$ is a merely analytic proposition, and follows by the principle of contradiction from the concept of a sum of 7 and 5. But if we look more closely we find that the concept of the sum of 7 and 5 contains nothing save the union of the two numbers into one, and in this no thought is being taken as to what that single number may be which combines both. The concept of 12 is by no means already thought in merely thinking this union of 7 and 5; and I may analyse my concept of such a possible sum as long as I please, still I shall never find the 12 in it. We have to go outside these concepts, and call in the aid of the intuition which corresponds to one of them, our five fingers, for instance, or, as Segner does in his *Arithmetic,* five points, adding to the concept of 7, unit by unit, the five given in intuition. For starting with the number 7, and for the concept of 5 calling in the aid of the fingers of my hand as intuition, I now add one by one to the number 7 the units which I previously took together to form the number 5, and with the aid of that finger [the hand] see the number 12 come into being. That 5 should be added to 7, I have indeed already thought in the concept of a sum = 7 + 5, but not that this sum is equivalent to the number 12. Arithmetical propositions are therefore always synthetic. This is still more evident if we take larger numbers. For it is then obvious that, however we might turn and twist our concepts, we could never, by the mere analysis of them, and without the aid of intuition, discover what [the number is that] is the sum.

Just as little is any fundamental proposition of pure geometry analytic. That the straight line between two points is the shortest, is a synthetic proposition. For my concept of *straight* contains nothing of quantity, but only of quality. The concept of the shortest is wholly an addition, and cannot be derived, through any process of analysis, from the concept of the straight line. Intuition, therefore, must here be called in; only by its aid is the synthesis possible. What here causes us commonly to believe that the predicate of such apodeictic judgments is already contained in our concept, and that the judgment is therefore analytic, is merely the ambiguous character of the terms used. We are required to join in thought a certain predicate to a given concept, and this necessity is inherent in the concepts themselves. But the question is not what we *ought* to join in thought to the given concept, but what we *actually* think in it, even if only obscurely; and it is then manifest that, while the predicate is indeed attached necessarily to the concept, it is so in virtue of an intuition which must be added to the concept, not as thought in the concept itself.

Some few fundamental propositions, presupposed by the geometrician, are, indeed, really analytic, and rest on the principle of contradiction. But, as identical propositions, they serve only as links in the chain of method and not as principles; for instance, $a = a$; the whole is equal to itself; or $(a + b) > a$, that is, the whole is greater than its part. And even these propositions, though they are valid according to pure concepts, are only admitted in mathematics because they can be exhibited in intuition.[6]

And the answer to "how is pure mathematics possible?"

Here is a great and established branch of knowledge, encompassing even now a wonderfully large domain and promising an unlimited extension in the future, yet carrying with it thoroughly apodictic certainty, that is, absolute necessity, and therefore resting upon no empirical grounds. Consequently it is a pure product of reason; and, moreover, it is thoroughly synthetical. [Hence the question arises:] "How then is it possible for human reason to produce such knowledge entirely *a priori?*"

. . . We find that all mathematical cognition has this peculiarity: it must first exhibit its concept in intuition and indeed *a priori;* therefore in an intuition which is not empirical but pure. Without this mathematics cannot take a single step; hence its judgments are always intuitive. . . . This ob-

---

[6] Immanuel Kant, *The Critique of Pure Reason,* trans. Norman Kemp Smith (London: St. Martin's Press, 1933).

servation on the nature of mathematics gives us a clue to the first and highest condition of its possibility, which is that some pure intuition must form
its basis, in which all its concepts can be exhibited or constructed, *in concreto*
and yet *a priori*. If we can uncover this pure intuition and its possibility, we
may thence easily explain how synthetical propositions *a priori* are possible
in pure mathematics.

. . . In one way only can my intuition anticipate the actuality of the
object, and be a cognition *a priori*, namely: *if my intuition contains nothing
but the form of sensibility, antedating in my mind all the actual impressions
through which I am affected by objects.*

. . . Accordingly, it is only the form of sensuous intuition by which we
can intuit things *a priori*, but by which we can know objects only as they
appear to us (to our senses), not as they are in themselves; and this assumption is absolutely necessary if synthetical propositions *a priori* be granted as
possible or if, in case they actually occur, their possibility is to be comprehended and determined beforehand.

Now, the intuitions which pure mathematics lays at the foundation of
all its cognitions and judgments which appear at once apodictic and necessary are space and time. For mathematics must first present all its concepts
in intuition, and pure mathematics in pure intuition; that is, it must construct them. If it proceeded in any other way, it would be impossible to take
a single step; for mathematics proceeds, not analytically by dissection of concepts, but synthetically, and if pure intuition be wanting there is nothing in
which the matter for synthetical judgments *a priori* can be given. Geometry
is based upon the pure intuition of space. Arithmetic achieves its concept of
number by the successive addition of units in time, and pure mechanics
cannot attain its concepts of motion without employing the representation
of time. Both representations, however, are only intuitions; for if we omit
from the empirical intuitions of bodies and their alterations (motion) everything empirical, that is, belonging to sensation, space and time still remain, which are therefore pure intuitions that lie *a priori* at the basis of the
empirical.

. . . . .

The problem of the present section is therefore solved. Pure mathematics, as synthetical cognition *a priori*, is possible only by referring to no
other objects than those of the senses. At the basis of their empirical intuition lies a pure intuition (of space and of time) which is *a priori*, because
the latter intuition is nothing but the mere form of sensibility, which precedes
the actual appearance of the objects, since in fact it makes them possible.
Yet this faculty of intuiting *a priori* affects not the matter of the phenomenon (that is, the sensation in it, for this constitutes that which is empirical),
but its form, namely, space and time. . . . . Consequently, the basis of mathematics actually is pure intuitions, which make its synthetical and apodictically
valid propositions possible.[7]

Kant's solution to the problem of mathematical truth is colossal. He is
defending the claim that the truths of arithmetic depend upon certain intui-

[7] Immanuel Kant, *Prolegomena to Any Future Metaphysics*, trans. Lewis White Beck
(New York: Bobbs-Merrill, 1950).

tions which can give us *a priori* knowledge. But, for Kant, these intuitions are nothing other than the forms of space and time, by which we organize our perceptual experiences; geometry is nothing other than a formalized set of descriptions about the way we must experience space, and the same is true of arithmetic and time. Now notice two things about this theory. First, in addition to explaining something about the nature of arithmetic and geometry, it also provides a middle way between Newton and Leibniz's theories of space and time which we mentioned in Chapter 2 (p. 75). In agreement with Newton, Kant says that space and time are absolute, but he also agrees with Leibniz that they don't exist outside of experience. But second, and much more important, here is an example of Kant's philosophical strategy, which he will use to carry out a revolution in philosophy no less radical than those of Thales, Plato, Descartes, and Locke. What he is saying, in effect, is that the necessary truths of arithmetic and geometry are true because they describe the *essential structures of the human mind,* in this case, the ways in which we are aware of space and time. In the next chapter, we shall see what a powerful strategy this is. But for now, we shall turn to the contemporary response of rationalism to the problem of mathematical truth.

Husserl's phenomenology has become a general philosophy with ramifications in ethics, esthetics, politics, and literature as well as the austere problems of epistemology and necessary truth. But it is the "phenomenological" approach to necessary truth that concerns us here, and, in particular, Husserl's answer to the problems of arithmetic and geometry. How does one justify these necessary truths? Husserl, very much a modern rationalist, says, "by intuition."

Husserl began as a mathematician, and his first theory (and his first book) was a defense of the empiricist approach of John Stuart Mill. That is, he thought that the truths of arithmetic and geometry were simply well-confirmed empirical generalizations. An argument with Frege changed his mind, and he turned to the position that such truths must be what they seem to be, namely necessary. But he refused to accept the idea that they were also trivial analytic truths, true by linguistic convention or derivable from basic logical truths, the positions defended during his lifetime by Frege, Russell and Whitehead. He held, like Kant before him, that such truths were synthetic *a priori*. And he held that these truths were known through a special kind of intuition. Husserl spent his life, and many tens of thousands of pages, trying to say precisely what this special kind of "intuition" amounted to.

The heart of Husserl's phenomenology is this: There are two very different kinds of "experience": (1) ordinary "experience," which he calls "individual intuition," such as my present awareness that there are three bananas and two cats on my desk, and (2) a special kind of intuition, which Husserl calls *essential* (or, when he uses the Greek, *eidetic*) *intuition*. In this second kind of intuition, we do not see particular things but rather universal truths, or essences (the Greek here is *eidos*). Now this theory, and even its Greek terminology, ought to seem very familiar to you. From where? From Plato and Aristotle! For what Husserl is doing here is to revise a very old theory, in which such things as numbers and triangles and the various truths of arithmetic and geometry are ideal objects and laws, like Plato's Forms or Ideas. (The word Plato uses is also *Eidos,* and the title of Husserl's best known work is *Ideas.*) But Husserl, unlike Plato, does not believe that these special entities have an existence independent of human consciousness. Here he shares Aristotle's criticisms of Plato. These essences, such as numbers and triangles and the laws of arithmetic and geometry, are "in consciousness," and *phenomenology* is the attempt to study consciousness in order to determine what these essences are.

What Husserl is doing, then, is to give an overall theory of the rationalist's important appeal to intuition. And how can we defend this appeal to intuition? Phenomenologists still don't agree on the defense of intuition. Well, at least this much is clear, we can reject a claim based on intuition if not everyone shares that intuition, since the most important characteristic of rational intuitions and essences is that everyone shares them. Properly described, everyone in the world will agree about a rational intuition. But here we recall Locke's argument, that even universal agreement among men would not prove that an idea was *necessarily* common to all men. And the phenomenologist must respond again to this old argument. You can see that these are still very much living issues, now formulated in more sophisticated language, but still much the same as they were when Leibniz and Locke debated them centuries ago.

Husserl is a notoriously difficult author, but it is important to include at least a small sample of his work for you to read directly. What follows is from *Ideas* (vol. I) and outlines his distinction between two kinds of intuition, "individual," contingent and particular, and "essential," necessary and universal.

> Individual Being of every kind is, to speak quite generally, *"acciden-tal."* It is so-and-so, but essentially it could be other than it is. . . . But the import of this contingency, which is there called matter-of-factness, is limited in this respect that the contingency is correlative to a *necessity* which does not carry the mere actuality-status of a valid rule of connexion obtaining between temporo-spatial facts, but has the character of *essential necessity,* and therewith a relation to *essential universality.* Now when we stated that every fact could be "essentially" other than it is, we were already expressing thereby *that it belongs to the meaning of everything contingent that it should have essential being and therewith an Eidos to be apprehended in all its purity;* and this Eidos comes under *essential truths of varying degrees of universality.*

ESSENTIAL INSIGHT AND INDIVIDUAL INTUITION

> *At first* "essence" indicated that which in the intimate self-being of an individual discloses to us *"what"* it is. But every such What can be "set out as Ideas." *Empirical or individual intuition* can be transformed into *essential insight* (ideation)—a possibility which is itself not to be understood as em-

pirical but as essential possibility. The object of such insight is then the corresponding *pure* essence or eidos, whether it be the highest category or one of its specializations, right down to the fully "concrete."

Of whatever kind the individual intuition may be, whether adequate or not, it can pass off into essential intuition, and the latter, whether correspondingly adequate or not, has the character of a dator act. And this means that—

The essence (Eidos) is an object of a new type. Just as the datum of individual or empirical intuition is an individual object, so the datum of essential intuition is a pure essence.

Here we have not a mere superficial analogy, but a radical community of nature. *Essential insight is still intuition,* just as the eidetic object is still an object. . . . It is an intuition of a fundamentally *unique* and *novel* kind, namely in contrast to the types of intuition which belong as correlatives to the object-matters of other categories, and more specifically to intuition in the ordinary narrow sense, that is, individual intuition.

It lies undoubtedly in the intrinsic nature of essential intuition that it should rest on what is a chief factor of individual intuition, namely the striving for this, the visible presence of individual fact, though it does not, to be sure, presuppose any apprehension of the individual or any recognition of its reality. Consequently it is certain that no essential intuition is possible without the free possibility of directing one's glance to an individual *counterpart* and of shaping an illustration; just as contrariwise no individual intuition is possible without the free possibility of carrying out an act of ideation and therein directing one's glance upon the corresponding essence which exemplifies itself in something individually visible; but that does not alter the fact that *the two kinds of intuition differ in principle,* and in assertions of the kind we have just been making it is only the essential relations between them that declare themselves. Thus, to the essential differences of the intuitions correspond the essential relations between "existence" (here clearly in the sense of individual concrete being) and "essence," between *fact* and *eidos.*[8]

Husserl begins with the very old distinction, taken from Aristotle and medieval philosophers, between "essence" and "accident." An "accident," according to this usage, could possibly be other than it is, an essence could not. For example, it is possible that some particular triangle might have been drawn acute rather than isoceles, but it is not possible that it could have been drawn as a triangle with five angles. Having three angles is essential to being a triangle, being isoceles is not. This essence is what Husserl calls the *eidos,* and an *eidos,* within a certain description ("various degrees of universality") provides us with a necessary truth. Thus the *eidos* of this particular figure drawn as a triangle includes having three angles. It's *eidos* as a geometric figure, however, does not include having any particular number of angles, but it does require that it consist of lines on a plane. Husserl insists that the essence or *eidos* makes something "what" it is; in other words, it defines it as

[8] Edmund Husserl, *Ideas,* trans. W. R. Boyce Gibson (New York: Collier, Macmillan, 1962).

a certain kind of thing. The distinction between individual intuition and essential intuition is then a difference between (1) *particular* things, which might be different or might not exist at all, and (2) essence or *eidos,* which enables us to talk about a *kind* of thing (for example, centaurs or unicorns) even if they do not, never have, and never will exist.

The most important claim of Husserl's argument is his insistence that the *eidos* is itself "an object of a new type." In other words, it is something which can be intuited itself, apart from particular examples of it. (In medieval philosophy and since, these entities which represent "kinds of things" are called "universals." The problems of necessary truth are sometimes called "the problem of universals.") A geometer can talk about the properties of a right triangle, for example, without using or thinking of any particular right triangle. He is talking about the type, about the *eidos.* And Husserl's central claim is that, through phenomenology, we learn to recognize the essence or *eidos* by special sorts of intuition. It is such intuitions that make necessary truths possible. In other words, where Kant insisted that it is the form of our intuitions (as space and time) that makes the principles of arithmetic and geometry necessarily true, Husserl says that it is the content of our intuitions that makes these principles true. That content is what he calls the *eidos* or essence. This is his way of developing the rationalist's belief that necessary truths can be known by intuition.

THE TRUTHS OF METAPHYSICS

Because the principles of metaphysics are so very basic to all human thought and experience, it has often been argued that they too, like the principles of logic and mathematics, must be necessary truths. As the foundation principles of all of our knowledge, they must have as much certainty as possible, just as a building must have the strongest foundations possible. Without such foundations, everything built on top will be rickety and uncertain. Furthermore, traditional rationalists have claimed that the way in which we come to understand these basic principles, namely, through reason, guarantees us precisely this certainty. The principles of reason, unlike principles drawn from experience, are by their very nature necessary truths.

The various principles of metaphysics advanced by Plato, Aristotle, Spinoza and Leibniz were all supposed to be necessary truths by virtue of reason. Spinoza's argument that there can only be one substance, for instance, was based upon definitions and axioms which were necessarily true by virtue of reason and derived in the form of theorems (or "propositions") in much the same way that geometrical theorems are derived from the definitions and axioms of Euclidean geometry. The idea that there could be but one substance was not drawn from experience and was not intended to be merely a hypothesis or a viewpoint. It had to be true in exactly the same sense that the principles of arithmetic had to be true, as necessary truths.

But if Spinoza's principle is a necessary truth, then how is it possible that Leibniz, using a similar set of definitions and a similar deductive method arrived at the very opposite conclusion, that there are many substances? He too claimed this as a necessary truth about the universe. But obviously these cannot both be true; either there is only one substance or there is more than one substance. There cannot be both only one and more than one. But this means (assuming that the systems of Spinoza and Leibniz are consistent within themselves) that either one of them is wrong and the other right, or else that they have each given us a view of the world without giving us necessary truths at all. Each is giving us a possible, not a necessary principle, nothing more. How can one decide which of these great philosophers is correct? Or should we rather say that neither of them has in fact given us a necessary truth and that each has given us an elegant but only speculative idea about the way the world really is? Reason alone seems not to be enough.

The problem of justifying supposedly necessary truths of metaphysics arises even in those cases in which there is no such direct disagreement. The basic principles of our knowledge, for example, the principle of universal causation, which states that every event has its cause, or the principle of induction, which asserts that the future will be like the past, display the same problem of justification. The problem here is not so much whether or not we should accept these principles (although a few philosophers might reject them, as Leibniz rejects the first principle). We do in fact accept them and use them virtually every moment of our lives. The problem is showing that they are necessarily true, and not merely habitual or useful to us. Yet it is clear, as David Hume argued, that such principles can be neither analytic ("relations of ideas") nor straightforward "matters of fact," since it is upon these principles that all "matters of fact" are based. Because of this, Hume suggested that such principles were only matters of habit and custom, that we had become so accustomed to using these principles that we now assumed (wrongly) that they were necessary. But because they could not be defended either as principles of reason—as analytic truths or as principles like those of arithmetic and geometry—or as principles drawn from experience, they could not be justified at all. It is largely against Hume, therefore, that modern metaphysics has had to defend itself.

There is a sense in which the entire history of metaphysics, from Plato until the present day, revolves around the various attempts to establish metaphysical principles as necessary truths based on a foundation that is certain. Traditionally, confidence in reason itself, as divinely inspired and capable of grasping necessary truths, was sufficient to justify confidence in metaphysics. In modern times, this tradition is continued by many rationalists, but it has also been subjected to critical scrutiny and rejected by a great many empiricists and others. This critical scrutiny reaches its extremes with Hume, who dismisses not only the whole of traditional metaphysics and theology as "sophistry and illusion" but the basic principles of all human knowledge as unjustifiable as well. It is at this point in history that Kant steps into the picture, attempting to reestablish the traditional claims of metaphysicians to be able to provide necessary truths. This is not to say that he accepts all of the suggestions of the metaphysicians in the past. It is clear that he prefers Leibniz to Spinoza on many issues, for example. Moreover, there are some metaphysical disputes, such as the dispute between Leibniz and Spinoza about whether there can be only one substance or more than one, which he dismisses as irresolvable and useless. There are still other metaphysical principles, for example, belief in God and the immortality of the human soul, which he defends as necessary, but as necessary on practical grounds, not as necessary truths or necessary knowledge. But at least some of the principles which Hume rejected as unjustifiable are defended by Kant in his unique way as synthetic *a priori* truths, truths which are neither analytic nor empirical (as Hume had also argued) but which are nevertheless necessary truths (which Hume had denied). Kant argued that these principles are, like the principles of arithmetic and geometry, basic to the structure of the human mind. What makes them necessarily true, therefore, is just the fact that they represent the only possible way in which we can conceive and perceive the world. Here is a third way of defending metaphysical claims which earlier philosophers had not anticipated. By showing that such principles as the principle of universal causation and the principle of induction are necessary for any human knowledge whatever, Kant succeeds in providing a new way of looking at metaphysics and a new way of defending its principles as necessary truths.

SUMMARY AND CONCLUSION

Do we know some things for certain, for example, the basic principles of logic and arithmetic and geometry? The answer isn't as sure as we would like. On the one hand, it is clear that we can't even imagine what it would be like for such necessary truths to be false or for us to be mistaken about them. But on the other hand, it is not clear how these truths can be justified. We can appeal to intuition, but can we absolutely trust our intuitions? We can deduce some of these truths from other truths, but then how do we justify the truths which act as premises? And then some philosophers (for example, Mill) argue that these are not necessary truths at all, but only very well confirmed generalizations from experience, which could possibly (but not likely) turn out to be false.

Although philosophers do not agree about how to justify the basic principles of logic and arithmetic and geometry, most would agree that they are the most certain principles of our knowledge. A much more difficult problem arises with the necessary truths of metaphysics, however. Everyone agrees that two plus two equals four, even if they don't agree about why they so confidently agree. But not everyone agrees that there is only one substance, or that God exists, or that human acts are free from causal determination. In this chapter, we have discussed the difficulties that are involved in defending even those necessary truths which we all agree about. In the chapters that follow, we shall find it even more difficult to defend those claims which people don't agree about. Yet they would still argue that what they believe is necessarily true.

GLOSSARY

analytic (of a sentence or truth): demonstrably true (and necessarily true) by virtue of the logical form or the meanings of the component words. The concept was introduced by Kant, who defined it in terms of a sentence (he called it a "judgment") in which the "predicate was contained in the subject" and "added nothing to it." For example, in "a horse is an animal," he would say that the concept of "horse" already includes the concept of being an animal; we would say that "horse" means "an animal which . . ." and thus "is an animal" adds nothing to what we already know just from "horse." Kant also says that the *criterion* or test for analytic sentences (or *analyticity*) is the principle of contradiction; an analytic sentence is one whose denial yields a self-contradiction.

a posteriori (knowledge): "after experience," or empirical. (See *empirical*.)

a priori (knowledge): "before experience," or more accurately, independent of all experience. *A priori* knowledge is always necessary, for there can be no imaginable instances that would refute it and no intelligible doubting of it. One might come to know something *a priori* through experience (for example, you might find out that no parallel lines ever touch each other by drawing tens of thousands of parallel lines) but what is essential to *a priori* knowledge is that no such experience is needed. Knowledge is *a priori* if it can be proven independently of experience. The most obvious examples of *a priori* knowledge are analytic sentences, such as "a horse is an animal" and "If all men are mammals and Socrates is a man, then Socrates is a mammal."

calculus: any logical system of abstract symbols, whether interpreted or not.

conceptual truth: an analytic sentence which is true by virtue of the meanings of its component words, or concepts. The example, "a horse is an animal," is a conceptual truth.

confirmation: the successful justification of an empirical claim as knowledge through experiment, observation, and experience. For example, counting the number of sheep and people in New Zealand confirms my hypothesis that there are more sheep in New Zealand than people.

contingent (truth): not necessary, and could have been otherwise. What we believe (or a state of affairs) is contingent if we can imagine its being other than it is. It is contingent, therefore, that heavy objects fall towards the earth, since we easily imagine what it would be like if they did not. This is so even though, in another sense, we say that it is (physically) necessary that heavy objects fall. The philosophical terms, "contingent" and "necessary," refer to logical possibility, whether we can even imagine alternatives, whatever the facts of the matter happen to be.

counter-example: a refuting instance. For example, one white crow is a counter-example to the claim, "all crows are black."

criterion (of an analytic sentence or truth): a sentence is analytic if its denial yields a self-contradiction. This is Kant's test (also Leibniz's and Hume's).

definition: the meaning of a word or phrase. Some definitions, called stipulative definitions, actually introduce the meaning of a word with rigor and distinct boundaries (for example, the logician's definition of "validity"). But, most of the time, a definition is an attempt to capture the not very exact ways in which we ordinarily use a word. In conceptual truths, we can say that they are true "by definition," that is, they are true by virtue of the meanings of the component words, for one word (the subject) contains another (the predicate) in its definition; for example, "a cow is an animal" and the definition of "cow" is "the female *animal* of the genus *Bos*."

eidos: (in Husserl), see *essence*.

empirical (knowledge): derived from and to be defended by appeal to experience. Empirical knowledge can only be so derived and so defended (as opposed to *a priori* knowledge, which need not be).

essence: (in Husserl), an ideal object (e.g., a number) or an ideal law (e.g., of arithmetic).

falsify: to show that an empirical claim is not justified by appeal to experience.

form: the structure of a sentence, that is, the logical form, without reference to the meaning of its component substantial words or "what it says." Analytic sentences are formally true when their truth can be determined solely by looking at the logical form. Formal logic is that part of logic that is concerned only with logical forms and the deductive relations between sentences with logical forms.

grammar: the formal aspects of a sentence. In logic, this means the **logical form** or **syntax.** (In linguistics, "grammar" is sometimes given a more general sense, including the phonetics and semantics of a sentence as well.)

hypothesis: a provisional suggestion which must be confirmed (or falsified) through experience. Hypotheses are the bulwark of all empirical knowledge and the end point of all inductive reasoning.

intuition: immediate knowledge of the truth, without the aid of any reasoning and without appeal to experience. Intuition, as rational intuition (there are other kinds), is a central concern of the rationalist philosophers, who consider intuition one of the main functions of reason. But because of its very nature, intuition cannot be argued for, nor can it be defended by experience. Accordingly, many philosophers, especially empiricists, reject the notion of intuition and accept it only when absolutely unavoidable. In this century, Edmund Husserl has defended the appeal to intuition in his phenomenology.

law of contradiction: that basic rule of logic which demands that a sentence and its denial cannot both be true. This law is used by many philosophers (Kant, Leibniz and Hume, for example) as a criterion for analyticity or analytic truth.

law of the excluded middle: that rule of logic that says that every sentence must be either true or false, there being no "middle" ground. An alternative characterization is this: either a sentence or its denial must be true. In formal logic, this law, together with the law of contradiction, forms the basis of a great many arguments (for example, that form of *reductio ad absurdum* argument in which the consequences of one premise are shown to be absurd, and therefore its denial is accepted. Many logicians are now reconsidering this law, for it is becoming evident that not all sentences are either true or false. For example, consider Russell's famous example, "the King of France is bald" (when there is no king of France); is that true or false? It surely isn't true, but neither can it be false, for there is no king of France who is not bald. Or what of, "green ideas sleep furiously"? Many philosophers would say that these are neither true nor false, thus rejecting the law of the excluded middle.

logic: that part of philosophy which studies the rules of valid inference and (we now add) the rules of inductive generalization. It is also, however, the study of the form of sentences, their grammar or syntax, or logical form. More loosely, "logic" sometimes means simply "order."

logical truth: a sentence that can be shown to be true by virtue of its logical form alone, (by virtue of the little words, "and," "or," etc.).

logicism: the thesis that all necessary truths are reducible to logical or analytic truths.

matter of fact: in Hume's philosophy, an empirical claim, to be confirmed or falsified through experience.

necessary (truth): cannot be otherwise and cannot be imagined to be otherwise. In philosophy, it is not enough that something be "necessary" according to physical laws (for example the law of gravity) or "necessary" according to custom or habit (for example, the "necessity" of laws against rape or the felt necessity of having a cigarette after dinner). Necessary allows for not even imaginary counter-examples; thus it is a necessary truth that two plus two equals four; not only do we believe this with certainty and find ourselves incapable of intelligibly doubting it, but we cannot even suggest what it might be for it to be false, no matter how wild our imaginations.

necessity: in accordance with a necessary truth.

phenomenology: the philosophy of Edmund Husserl, a twentieth-century rationalism which defends appeals to intuition in the defense of necessary truths.

relation of ideas: in traditional empiricist philosophy, analytic truths, which can be demonstrated without appeal to experience. Arithmetic and geometry were taken to be paradigm examples of "relations of ideas."

rules of inference: those rules of logic according to which validity is defined. All such rules are analytic, but there is considerable disagreement whether all are so by virtue of their own logical form or whether some are so because they are derived from other, more basic rules. There is also the following question; given that these rules define correct logical form, how is it possible to say that they have correct logical form?

semantics: the meanings of a sentence and its various components. Also, the study of those meanings. (So, we can talk about the semantics of a sentence, and we can talk about doing semantics.) "Merely semantic" is a nasty way of referring to conceptual truths, analytic sentences which are true just by virtue of meanings.

synonym: "meaning the same." Two words are synonymous if they are interchangeable in a sentence, without losing the meaning of the sentence. For example, "criminal" and "felon" are synonyms in most contexts. The test of a supposedly conceptual truth is to replace certain words with synonyms, and then see if its denial yields a self-contradiction. In other words, substituting synonyms turns a conceptual truth into an analytic truth. For example, "ferns are plants"; substituting for "fern" its synonym (or, in this case, also its definition) "a primitive plant that bears spors, etc." we have "a plant is a plant," whose denial is a contradiction ("a plant is not a plant") and thus is analytic.

syntax: the grammar or logical form of a sentence. (In linguistics, it may also refer to the various linguistic components of the sentence, its phonetics and word order, for example.)

synthetic (of a sentence): not analytic. A synthetic sentence cannot be shown to be true by appeal to the logical form or the meanings of the component words. Kant defined a "synthetic" sentence as one which "adds an idea to the subject which is not already contained in it." For example, "a horse is the source of a large income for some people" is a strictly synthetic sentence. No appeal to the meaning of "horse" will help you find out whether it is true or not, and its denial surely does not result in self-contradiction. But, according to Kant, it must not be concluded that all synthetic sentences can be shown to be true solely by appeal to experience. Some, he claimed, are known *a priori*.

synthetic a priori (knowledge): knowledge which is necessary and known independently of experience (and thus *a priori*), but which does not derive its truth from the logic or meaning of sentences (thus synthetic). This is the focal concept of Kant's philosophy.

tautology: a trivial truth which is true by virtue of logical form alone and tells us nothing about the world. (Popularly, a bit of repetitive nonsense, for example, "a rose is a rose is a rose." Technically, (in logic) a sentence that can be shown to be true no matter what the truth or falsity of its component parts.)

truth of reason: in traditional rationalism, a belief which can be justified solely by appeal to reason, through intuition or by deduction from premises based upon intuition. Arithmetic and geometry were, for the rationalists as for the empiricists, a paradigm case of such truths. They disagreed mainly on the scope of such truths, and the restrictions to be placed on the problematic appeal to intuition.

5

TRUTH
AND RATIONALITY

What is truth?
Pontius Pilate

We turned from metaphysics to epistemology because we began to question our ability to know "the way the world really is." Hence, we thought we should first find out what we can know. But then, after Hume, it seemed that not only were we incapable of doing metaphysics but we could not justify even the most ordinary and obvious principles of our everyday lives. With a hint of desperation, we turned to the notion of necessary truth, attempting to find out whether there was anything we could know for certain. But the results were not entirely satisfying; the basic rules of our thinking, by their very nature, seemed to be unarguable. The necessary truths of arithmetic and geometry, though true beyond doubt, were not clearly provable. And the whole topic of "necessity" was haunted by the specter of what we shall call *relativism*: That is, these "truths" seem necessary to us, but a totally different set of "truths" might seem equally necessary to someone else. Perhaps our "necessary truths" are but habits so engrained in us that we cannot even envision any alternatives. We are haunted by Hume, in other words. But does that mean that we shall never know the truth? Is any belief as justifiable as another? Are all of our beliefs uncertain?

We have reached that point in our thinking where we must upset everything that we have done. The weapon we shall use in this revolution, as we anticipated in the last chapter, is Immanuel Kant. It is really his revolution, and with it, we will bring philosophy up to our own times.

167

What must be over-thrown? Nothing less than the very basic assumptions of metaphysics and common sense that have ruled philosophy since Plato:

First, there is Plato's "two-worlds" view: the "world of Being," which is the real world, and the "world of Becoming," the world of our daily experience which, though perhaps not unreal, is less real than the world of Being. Now, the actual model Plato uses, the real world as the world of Ideas, our world as the world of material objects and change, has certainly not been accepted by all modern philosophers, and it is certainly out of line with common sense. What has been accepted by many philosophers, especially empiricists, is the distinction between appearance and reality. Ironically, this view is precisely the reverse of Plato's view. According to empiricism, it is the material world that becomes the real world, and the world of ideas—our mental "ideas" and experiences—becomes the less real world. And the problem, in Descartes, Locke, Hume, and Russell, is always how to know that our "ideas" or experiences in fact match up to the real world. The fact that Descartes is confident that he can know that his experiences "match up" while Hume believes that we can never know even if there is such a world must not hide from us the "two-worlds" model that both of them presuppose: reality (if there is one) on the one side, our experience on the other. How do we move from experience to reality?

Second, there are the two assumptions we mentioned in Chapter 2, common not only to Plato and Aristotle but to most modern thinkers as well, Spinoza and Leibniz, for example. They were: 1) faith in our language to capture the structures of reality and the idea that the world in itself is intelligible to us; 2) the idea that all knowledge of reality (that is, metaphysical knowledge) must consist of necessary truths. The first assumption seems to presuppose the "two-worlds" model in some sense, since something (our language) can't be "faithful" unless it is faithful to something else, outside of itself (reality). And our discussion in the last chapter raised the haunting Humean question: How do we know that what we believe to be necessary—because of the structure of our language—is not just necessary for us, and not true of reality at all? And, if you remember, all of those necessary truths which we called analytic, rules of inference, tautologies, and conceptual truths, were no more than displays of our use of language and "told us nothing about the world." So we have to ask, "are we trapped inside of our language? Is it impossible for us to know anything about reality which we have not ourselves imposed through language?"

The second assumption has already begun to bother us, since John Locke and his empiricist followers insisted that all of our knowledge of the world must consist of truths based upon experience, and since, by the very nature of inductive arguments from experience, we could not actually be certain of anything. Descartes had insisted that any belief worth the honorific title "knowledge" had to be certain ("perfectly certain," he said). But now, let us ask, wasn't he demanding a bit too much? In fact, much too much! Surely I have the right to say that I know that I'm not dreaming right now, even if it's true that I might be wrong. In other words, it is time to weaken our demands; perhaps it will be enough if we believe what is rational to believe, even if it is not certain, and even if it does not "match up" with some unexperienceable reality. You might even say, "perhaps it is not necessary to believe what is true," but notice that you would already have presupposed that what makes our belief true is some reality beyond our experience. But it is just this notion that we must examine in this chapter, particularly the key notion of truth, and the related notion of rationality.

WHAT IS TRUTH?

That familiar question was raised by Pontius Pilate as he dismissed Christ's case from his court. He was just a politician; he did not take the question seriously. Philosophers do. It is their business to find the truth, to expose fraudulent beliefs and superstitions, and to assure us that we can know, at least most of the time, what is true from what is false.

What indeed is truth? Should we say, as we have so far, that our beliefs are true if and only if they "match up" with reality? Or, in accordance with our present suspicions, should we not perhaps hold out for some different conception of "truth," one which does not place such emphasis on "matching up" and the separation of reality on the one hand from our beliefs and experiences on the other?

The proper philosophical name for this notion of "matching up" our beliefs and experiences with reality is the *correspondence theory of truth.* On the one hand, it is an obvious truism: for example, when I tell you "there is beer in the refrigerator," what I tell you is true if and only if there is in fact beer in the refrigerator. So obvious is this "correspondence" criterion of truth—that a belief or a statement is true if and only if it "corresponds" to the facts—that no one would have thought of calling it a "theory" at all, until recently. In his *Metaphysics,* Aristotle dismissed the whole "problem of truth" in a single sentence: "To say of what is that it is not, or of what is not that it is, is false, while to say of what is that it is, or of what is not that it is not, is true." As long as philosophers (and everyone else) believed themselves unquestionably capable of knowing reality as such, this common sense platitude was as appropriate for the investigations of metaphysics as it was for the daily task of checking to see whether or not there was beer in the refrigerator. But as empiricism and Hume's skepticism grew in persuasiveness, and the confidence that we could know reality was thrown into question, the platitude became a problem.

For Descartes, the correspondence between our ideas and reality had to be demonstrated. Locke expressed his doubts; Berkeley rejected the "external world" altogether, leaving only God (and other minds like Berkeley's own); and Hume left us with the seemingly irrefutable argument that we could never know reality outside of us, or even if there was a reality to be known. Hume had given us a *reductio ad absurdum* argument; one of his premises— perhaps not an explicit one—has brought us to the absurdity of not being able to defend the most common sense beliefs. But all of these philosophers presuppose the correspondence theory of truth, the idea that knowledge is the correspondence of our ideas to reality and that the only knowledge worthy of the name is our being certain of this correspondence. It is here that Kant returns to the beginnings of Hume's arguments, and everyone else's, and roots out the correspondence theory of truth as the implicit premise that is the cause of all the trouble.

Now it will probably seem odd to you to even question something so obviously "true" as the correspondence theory of truth. Of course, one cannot deny that "there is beer in the refrigerator" is true if and only if there is beer in the refrigerator. But we have already seen some of the limitations to this view in our discussion of "necessary truth" in Chapter 4. What does "two plus two equals four" correspond to, that makes it true? As we have already seen argued (by Hempel, Ayer, and others) it cannot simply be that it corresponds to all combinations in the world of two things (walnuts, elephants, acres or apples) and two other things of the same kind. "Two plus two equals four" would still be true even if there were no such combinations in the universe. The same is true of analytic truths in general. A tautology does not correspond to anything; it "tells us nothing about the world." A conceptual truth tells us only about the meanings of the words in our language. A rule of inference tells us how to think. But none of these "correspond" to anything. So, at most, we shall have to say that the correspondence theory is good as an account of empirical knowledge only! (This is the conclusion of most empiricists, including more contemporary "logical positivists.")

But there are more serious problems, even within the domain of empirical knowledge. Let's look again at the truism, " 'there's beer in the refrigerator' is true if and only if there is beer in the refrigerator." That's good enough for a friend's dropping over in the late afternoon for a beer, but you can't leave it at that in a philosophical analysis. Let's ask, first of all, in what sense the noises you utter (the sounds, "there's beer . . .") correspond to the fact that there is beer in the refrigerator. If you think of one thing corresponding to another, you might think of a map corresponding to the terrain it is a map of: smaller scale with many omissions, but at least it is the same shape, same proportions, and has representations of things in that terrain which you can recognize. But how do those sounds coming out of your mouth (which, now that you listen to them, might sound strange indeed) "correspond" to that six-pack of Schlitz in the kitchen? Now you will say that it is not merely "the sounds" that correspond but rather what you are saying or mean. And, of course, this is correct. But notice that what those words mean is not a matter of their use in this particular instance; they depend upon their role in a language (American English), which you happen to speak. (If you spoke only Eskimo, and pronounced the same sounds, it would be a remarkable coincidence, but wouldn't mean anything.) And the "correspondence" between those words with their meanings and the fact that there is beer in the refrigerator depends not only on the whole American-English language and your knowledge of it but also on a set of conventions which both you and your friend must understand as referring to the beer in the refrigerator. In class, for example, your teacher says, "there is beer in the refrigerator" as an example of an English sentence. But you do not get up and look for a refrigerator. You know that, although your teacher has said the same words that you say to your friend when offering a beer, he/she is not directly referring to anything. And the statement does not "correspond" to a fact that there is beer in the refrigerator. It is clear that what you've said (and the same is true of what you've thought) cannot correspond to anything by itself. In a sense, you might say that what corresponds to the fact that there is beer in the refrigerator when you offer your friend a beer is the whole of the English language, with all of its conventions and everything that you and your friend know that is relevant to the meaning of your statement in this particular case.

And, from the other side of this "correspondence," matters are no less complicated. What is "the fact" that there is beer in the refrigerator? Sounds like an easy question. The answer is—that there is beer in the refrigerator!! But how do we pick out this fact, except by using our language to distinguish this fact from any number of others. Suppose, instead of saying anything, you were to simply point towards the refrigerator for your friend. Now, of course, knowing you, your friend knows what you mean. In this case, the pointing is shorthand for the statement, and presupposes it. But suppose your friend is a New Guinea headhunter who had no idea what a refrigerator was, or a beer for that matter? Would he pick out the right "fact?" How would he know whether you were pointing to the kitchen, to the door of the refrigerator or to its contents? And which contents? Even if you point to the beer, is it the can or the contents? Is the "beer" to be drunk or to be poured on one's feet? How do we even understand the pointing gesture? (When I point my finger towards the cat food, my cats smell my finger!) So, if it seems obvious to you that "the facts" are simply there, waiting to be corresponded to by our verbal or gestural pointing, think again. One distinguishes the facts of the world only by picking them out by language. The language then can't be said to "correspond" to the world, for it is language which "carves up" our world into those individually identifiable "facts."

Now none of this is to say that your statement, "there's beer in the refrigerator" isn't true if and only if there is beer in the refrigerator. It is rather to say that this simple "correspondence" is possible only because of the enormous number of systematic assumptions we share within our language and about the world and about the way we refer to particular "facts" in the world by use of certain statements. In everyday life, we don't have to think about such things. But in philosophy, they make us marvel at what complex and clever creatures we are. Bertrand Russell, certainly one of the smartest among us, spent forty years trying to make sense out of the "common sense" correspondence theory. He never did. He never succeeded in formulating an adequate defense of the idea that some single unit of language could "correspond" to discrete "facts" in the world. And today, most philosophers would agree, no matter what kind of method they follow, that the correspondence theory—no matter how common sensical—cannot make sense of the notion of truth. A statement means something only within a language, and a "fact" is "corresponded to" only after it has been picked out by language. And that means that truth can't be correspondence.

And so, the seemingly simple act of "saying what is true" turns out to be enormously complicated. And against the "correspondence theory of truth," there are three telling arguments:

1) it is, at best, limited. All cases of necessary truth, and perhaps some others, cannot be accounted for by it at all.
2) there is no such thing as a statement or a belief which, by itself, is capable of "corresponding" to anything.
3) there is no such thing as a "fact," which can be picked out independently of the language used to describe it.

Next time you say or think that there is beer in the refrigerator, you might marvel at the complex that has just come into action. That won't, unfortunately, guarantee that your statement or thought will be true. For despite all this sophisticated, intellectual apparatus, we still occasionally forget to buy the beer.

THEORIES OF TRUTH

Now what? We find ourselves with some ill-defined complex in which our language and reality are tied together and mutually depend on each other. But what we have been leading up to, finally, is that we need something more than the naive common sense "correspondence theory of truth," one which takes into account this complexity of interrelations. Three such theories have achieved prominence in this century, although all three of them, remarkably, were anticipated by Immanuel Kant a hundred years earlier. They are:

1) *The coherence theory of truth:* which says that a statement or a belief is true if and only if it "coheres" or ties in with other statements and beliefs.
2) *The pragmatic theory of truth:* which says that a statement or a belief is true if and only if "it works," if it allows us to predict certain results, if it allows us to function effectively in everyday life, and if it encourages further inquiry or helps us lead better lives.
3) *The semantic theory of truth:* which says that a statement or a belief is true because the rules of our language set up a correspondence be-

tween certain statements and "the facts" which our language picks out in the world. Superficially, this theory looks like the correspondence theory, but it is very different. The correspondence theory accepts facts as "already there," independent of our language. The semantic theory explains this apparent correspondence by telling us that it is our language that sets it up in the first place.

We shall deal with each of these theories briefly, in turn. To represent the coherence theory, I have chosen a selection from the American philosopher, Brand Blandshard.

To think is to seek understanding. And to seek understanding is an activity of mind that is marked off from all other activities by a highly distinctive aim. This aim . . . is to achieve systematic vision, so to apprehend what is now unknown to us as to relate it, and relate it necessarily, to what we know already. We think to solve problems; and our method of solving problems is to build a bridge of intelligible relation from the continent of our knowledge to the island we wish to include in it. Sometimes this bridge is causal, as when we try to explain a disease; sometimes teleological, as when we try to fathom the move of an opponent over the chess board; sometimes geometrical, as in Euclid. But it is always systematic; thought in its very nature is the attempt to bring something unknown or imperfectly known into a sub-system of knowledge, and thus also into that larger system that forms the world of accepted beliefs. That is what explanation is.

. . . . .

But may it not be that what satisfies thought fails to conform to the real world? Where is the guarantee that when I have brought my ideas into the form my ideal requires, they should be *true?* . . . In our long struggle with the relation of thought to reality we saw that if thought and things are conceived as related only externally, then knowledge is luck; there is no necessity whatever that what satisfies intelligence should coincide with what really is. It may do so, or it may not; on the principle that there are many misses to one bull's-eye, it more probably does not. But if we get rid of the misleading analogies through which this relation has been conceived, of copy and original, stimulus and organism, lantern and screen, and go to thought itself with the question what reference to an object means, we get a different and more hopeful answer. To think of a thing is to get that thing itself in some degree within the mind. To think of a color or an emotion is to have that within us which if it *were developed and completed,* would identify itself with the object. In short, if we accept its own report, thought is related to reality as the partial to the perfect fulfillment of a purpose. The more adequate its grasp the more nearly does it approximate, the more fully does it realize in itself, the nature and relations of its objects.

. . . . .

. . . We may look at the growth of knowledge, individual or social, either as an attempt by our own minds to return to union with things as they are in their ordered wholeness, or the affirmation through our minds of the ordered whole itself. And if we take this view, our notion of truth is marked out for us. Truth is the approximation of thought to reality. It is thought on its way home. Its measure is the distance thought has travelled, under guidance of its inner compass, toward that intelligible system which unites its ultimate object with its ultimate end. Hence at any given time the degree of truth in our experience as a whole is the degree of system it has achieved. The degree of truth of a particular proposition is to be judged in the first instance by its coherence with experience as a whole, ultimately by its coherence with that further whole, all-comprehensive and fully articulated, in which thought can come to rest.

Does acceptance of coherence as a test commit us to a view about the nature of truth? There have been some highly reputable philosophers who have held that the answer to "what is the test of truth?" is "coherence" while the answer to "what is the nature of truth?" is "Correspondence." These questions are plainly distinct. Nor does there seem to be any direct path from the acceptance of coherence as the test of truth to its acceptance as the nature of truth. Nevertheless there is an indirect path. If we accept coherence as our test, we must use it everywhere. We must therefore use it to test the suggestion that truth *is* other than coherence. But if we do, we shall find that we must reject the suggestion as leading to *in*coherence. Coherence is a pertinatious concept and, like the well-known camel, if one lets it get its nose under the edge of the tent, it will shortly walk off with the whole.

Suppose that, accepting coherence as the test, one rejects it as the nature of truth in favor of some alternative; and let us assume, for example, that this alternative is correspondence. This, we have said, is incoherent; why? Because if one holds that truth is correspondence, one cannot intelligibly hold either that it is tested by coherence or that there is any dependable test at all. Consider the first point. Suppose that we construe experience into the most coherent picture possible, remembering that among the elements included will be such secondary qualities as colors, odors and sounds. Would the mere fact that such elements as these are coherently arranged prove that anything precisely corresponding to them exists "out there"? I cannot know that it would, even if we knew that the two arrangements had closely corresponding patterns. If on one side you have a series of elements a, b, c . . . , and on the other a series of elements α, β, γ . . . , arranged in patterns that correspond, you have no proof as yet that the *natures* of these elements correspond. It is therefore impossible to argue from a high degree of coherence within experience to its correspondence in the same degree with anything outside. And this difficulty is typical. If you place the nature of truth in one sort of character and its test in something quite different, you are pretty certain, sooner or later, to find the two falling apart. In the end, the only test of truth that is not misleading is the special nature or character that is itself constitutive of truth.

Feeling that this is so, the adherents of correspondence sometimes insist that correspondence shall be its own test. But then the second difficulty arises. If truth does consist in correspondence, no test can be sufficient. For in order to know that experience corresponds to fact, we must be able to get at that fact, unadulterated with idea, and compare the two sides with each other. And we have seen . . . that such fact is not accessible. When we try to lay hold of it, what we find in our hands is a judgment which is obviously not itself the indubitable fact we are seeking, and which must be checked by some fact beyond it. To this process there is no end. And even if we did get at the fact directly, rather than through the veil of our ideas, that would be no less fatal to correspondence. This direct seizure of fact presumably gives us truth, but since that truth no longer consists in correspondence of idea with fact, the main theory has been abandoned. In short, if we can know fact only through the medium of our own ideas, the original forever eludes us; if we can get at the facts directly, we have knowledge whose truth is not correspondence. The theory is forced to choose between scepticism and self-contradiction.

Thus the attempt to combine coherence as the test of truth with correspondence as the nature of truth will not pass muster by its own test. The result is *in*coherence. We believe that an application of the test to other theories of truth would lead to a like result. The argument is: Assume coherence as the test, and you will be driven by the incoherence of your alternatives to the conclusion that it is also the nature of truth.

· · · · ·

Coherence means more than consistency. It means not only that the various constituents entering into the system of truth are compatible with each other, but also that they necessitate each other. The system assumed is a system ideally perfect, for nothing less than this would satisfy intelligence as stable beyond rectification. In such a system there would be no loose ends. Difference anywhere would be reflected in difference everywhere.[1]

The coherence theory of truth, according to Blandshard, begins with the observation that we test the truth of a belief by seeing its implications and other logically connected beliefs. But the theory is not confined to this test. Truth itself, he insists, is nothing other than the interconnectedness of our various beliefs. The truth of a particular belief is nothing other than how well it fits in with everything else that we believe.

The pragmatic theory of truth makes a similar move, but instead of insisting that truth concerns only connections between beliefs, it insists that connections with practical concerns are equally important. The following selection is from the American "pragmatist," William James:

I fully expect to see the pragmatist view of truth run through the classic stages of a theories career. First, you know, a new theory is attacked as absurd; then it is admitted to be true, but obvious and insignificant; finally it is seen to be so important that its adversaries claim that they themselves discovered it. Our doctrine of truth is at present in the first of these three stages, with symptoms of the second stage having begun in certain quarters. . . . Truth, as any dictionary will tell you, is a property of certain of our ideas. It means their "agreement," as falsity means their disagreement, with "reality." Pragmatism and intellectualists both accept this definition as a matter of course. They begin to quarrel only after the question is raised as to what may precisely be meant by the term "agreement," and what by the

[1] Brand Blanshard, *The Nature of Thought* (New York: Macmillan, 1941).

term "reality," when reality is taken as something for our ideas to agree with.

In answering these questions the pragmatists are more analytic and painstaking, the intellectualists more offhand and irreflective. The popular notion is that a true idea must copy its reality. Like other popular views, this one follows the analogy of the most usual experience. Our true ideas of sensible things do indeed copy them. Shut your eyes and think of yonder clock on the wall, and you get just such a true picture or copy of its dial. But your idea of its "works" (unless you are a clock-maker) is much less of a copy, yet it passes muster, for it in no way clashes with the reality. Even though it should shrink to the mere word "works," that word still serves you truly; and when you speak of the "time-keeping function" of the clock, or of its spring's "elasticity," it is hard to see exactly what your ideas can copy.

You perceive that there is a problem here. Where our ideas cannot copy definitely their object, what does agreement with that object mean? Some idealists seem to say that they are true whenever they are what God means that we ought to think about that object. Others hold the copy-view all through, and speak as if our ideas possessed truth just in proportion as they approach to being copies of the Absolute's eternal way of thinking.

These views, you see, invite pragmatistic discussion. But the great assumption of the intellectualists is that truth means essentially an inert static relation. When you've got your true idea of anything, there's an end of the matter. You're in possession: you *know;* you have fulfilled your thinking destiny. You are where you ought to be mentally; you have obeyed your categorical imperative; and nothing more need follow on that climax of your rational destiny. Epistemologically you are in stable equilibrium.

Pragmatism, on the other hand, asks its usual question. "Grant an idea or belief to be true," it says, "what concrete difference will its being true make in any one's actual life? How will the truth be realized? What experiences will be different from those which would obtain if the belief were false? What, in short, is the truth's cash-value in experiential terms?"

The moment pragmatism asks this question, it sees the answer: *True ideas are those that we can assimilate, validate, corroborate and verify. False ideas are those that we can not.* That is the practical difference it makes to us to have true ideas; that, therefore, is the meaning of truth, for it is all that truth is known as.

This thesis is what I have to defend. The truth of an idea is not a stagnant property inherent in it. Truth *happens* to an idea. It *becomes* true, is *made* true by events. Its verity *is* in fact an event, a process: the process namely of its verifying itself, its veri-*fication.* Its validity is the process of its valid-*ation.*

But what do the words verification and validation themselves pragmatically mean? They again signify certain practical consequences of the verified and validated idea. It is hard to find any one phrase that characterizes these consequences better than the ordinary agreement-formula— just such consequences being what we have in mind whenever we say that our ideas "agree" with reality. They lead us, namely, through the acts and other ideas which they instigate, into or up to, or towards, other parts of experience with which we feel all the while—such feeling being among our potentialities—that the original ideas remain in agreement. The connexions and transitions come to us from point to point as being progressive, harmonious, satisfactory. This function of agreeable leading is what we mean by an idea's verification. Such an account is vague and it sounds at first quite trivial, but it has results which it will take the rest of my hour to explain.

Let me begin by reminding you of the fact that the possession of true thoughts means everywhere the possession of invaluable instruments of action; and that our duty to gain truth, so far from being a blank command from out of the blue, or a "stunt" self-imposed by our intellect, can account for itself by excellent practical reasons.

The importance to human life of having true beliefs about matters of fact is a thing too notorious. We live in a world of realities that can be infinitely useful or infinitely harmful. Ideas that tell us which of them to expect count as the true ideas in all this primary sphere of verification, and the pursuit of such ideas is a primary human duty. The possession of truth, so far from being here an end in itself, is only a preliminary means towards other vital satisfactions. If I am lost in the woods and starved, and find what looks like a cow-path, it is of the utmost importance that I should think of a human habitation at the end of it, for if I do so and follow it, I save myself. The true thought is useful here because the house which is its object is useful. The practical value of true ideas is thus primarily derived from the practical importance of their objects to us. Their objects are, indeed, not important at all times. I may on another occasion have no use for the house; and then my idea of it, however verifiable, will be practically irrelevant, and had better remain latent. Yet since almost any object may some day become temporarily important, the advantage of having a general stock of *extra* truths, of ideas that shall be true of merely possible situations, is obvious. We store such extra truths away in our memories, and with the overflow we fill our books of reference. Whenever such an extra truth becomes practically relevant to one of our emergencies, it passes from cold-storage to do work in the world and our belief in it grows active. You can say of it then either that "it is useful because it is true" or that "it is true because it is useful." Both these phrases mean exactly the same thing, namely that here is an idea that gets fulfilled and can be verified. True is the name for whatever idea starts the verification-process, useful is the name for its completed function in experience. True ideas would never have been singled out as such, would never have acquired a class-name, least of all a name suggesting value, unless they had been useful from the outset in this way.

. . . . .

To 'agree' in the widest sense with a reality *can only mean to be guided either straight up to it or into its surroundings, or to be put into such working touch with it as to handle either it or something connected with it better than if we disagreed.*

. . . . .

'The true,' *to put it very briefly, is only the expedient in the way of our thinking, just as 'the right' is only the expedient way of our behaving.*[2]

[2] William James, *Pragmatism: A New Name for Some Old Ways of Thinking* (New York: Longmans, Green, 1907).

In other words, truth, according to the pragmatic theory, is what allows us to handle situations better, what is expedient, what "works." This includes, however, not isolated tasks (in which a "false" belief might occasionally work better) but the entire process of scientific verification, so that the truth of a belief depends not only on its workability on some particular occasion, but, as in the coherence theory, on its connection in the process of scientific testing with the whole of our beliefs.

The semantic theory is most difficult of all, partly because of its misleadingly superficial resemblance to the correspondence theory, but mainly because it has been a purely formal theory. That is, it concerns only the artificial systems of the logician and not ordinary, "natural" languages (for example, English or French). In a sense, it is a theory that has been developing in many ways since the Kantian turn in philosophy. In its formal "semantic" version, however, it is generally credited to the American logician, Alfred Tarski.

> . . . we must always relate the notion of truth, like that of a sentence, to a specific language; for it is obvious that the same expression which is a true sentence in one language can be false or meaningless in another.
>
> Let us start with a concrete example. Consider the sentence *"snow is white."* We ask the question under what conditions this sentence is true or false. It seems clear that if we base ourselves on the classical conception of truth, we shall say that the sentence is true if snow is white, and that it is false if snow is not white. Thus, if the definition of truth is to conform to our conception, it must imply the following equivalence:
>
> *The sentence "snow is white" is true, if, and only if, snow is white.*
>
> We shall now generalize the procedure which we have applied above. Let us consider an arbitrary sentence; we shall replace it by the letter *"p."* We form the name of this sentence and we replace it by another letter, say *"X."* We ask now what is the logical relation between the two sentences *"X is true"* and *"p."* It is clear that from the point of view of our basic conception of truth these sentences are equivalent. In other words, the following equivalence holds:
>
> (T)   *X is true if, and only if, p.*
>
> We shall call any such equivalence (with *"p"* replaced by any sentence of the language to which the word *"true"* refers, and "X" replaced by a name of this sentence) an *"equivalence of the form* (T)."
>
> Now at last we are able to put into a precise form the conditions under which we will consider the usage and the definition of the term *"true"* as adequate from the material point of view: we wish to use the term *"true"* in such a way that all equivalences of the form (T) can be asserted, and *we shall call a definition of truth "adequate" if all these equivalences follow from it.*
>
> I should like to propose the name *"the semantic conception of truth"* for the conception of truth which has just been discussed.
>
> *Semantics* is a discipline which, speaking loosely, *deals with certain rela-*

tions between expressions of a language and the objects (or "states of affairs") *"referred to" by those expressions.* As typical examples of semantic concepts we may mention the concepts of *designation, satisfaction,* and *definition* as these occur in the following examples:

> the expression "the father of his country" designates (denotes) George Washington;
> snow satisfies the sentential function (the condition) "x is white";
> the equation "2 • x = 1" defines (uniquely determines) the number ½

While the words *"designates," "satisfies,"* and *"defines"* express relations (between certain expressions and the objects "referred to" by these expressions), the word *"true"* is of a different logical nature: it expresses a property (or denotes a class) of certain expressions, viz., of sentences. However, it is easily seen that all the formulations which were given earlier and which aimed at the meaning of this word ("true") referred not only to sentences themselves, but also to objects "talked about" by these sentences, or possibly to "states of affairs" described by them. . . . A definition of truth can be obtained in a very simple way from that of another semantic notion, namely, of the notion of *satisfaction.*[3]

Very simply explained, Tarski's semantic theory picks out a "class" of "individuals" (objects, states of affairs, or "facts") and specifies, for every sentence in the language, which individuals will or will not "satisfy" it, that is, make it "true" or not. But since the logician must "set up" each pair of sentences and individuals that will satisfy it, it is obvious that this formula will work only for a relatively small number of basic sentences with a manageable class of individuals. Here is the problem in extending the theory to natural languages (such as American English), which have a potentially infinite number of sentences and have to deal with an indefinite number of individuals. (This extension is being attempted today, however, by several leading philosophers, particularly Donald Davidson.) But for our purposes, the theory comes to this: we must set up the rules of satisfaction according to which our sentences become true or false. "Correspondence" is not a relation for which we supply only the appropriate sentences. In developing a language, we must also specify the relation of the language to the world, and thus "set up" the world to correspond to our language.

Taken individually, each of these theories has its opponents. We have attacked the correspondence theory sufficiently. Against the coherence theory, other philosophers have objected that: a system of statements and beliefs can be "coherent" but yet not be true. For example, take a simple system of true beliefs and deny them all. They will still form a coherent system, but they will all be false. Similarly, we said in Chapter 1 that an argument can be valid (which makes it coherent) but yet have false premises and false conclusions.

[3] Alfred Tarski, "The Semantic Theory of Truth," in *Philosophy and Phenomenological Research,* vol. 4, no. 3, March 1944.

Two opposed systems of statements and beliefs can be equally "coherent," but surely both cannot be true, for they claim opposite things about the world. (Think of the metaphysical systems of Spinoza and Leibniz.) So, truth must be more than mere coherence.

Against the pragmatic theory, philosophers have objected that: a belief might "work" but not be true. Scientists have often made great headway with false hypotheses. Political demagogues have often obtained great power and even achieved positive results with lies. And false beliefs often make us happier than the truth. ("What you don't know won't hurt you" and "the truth hurts.")

The reason why some beliefs "work" better than others, it has been argued (for example, by Bertrand Russell), is because they are true. They are true, therefore, not because they "work," but they work because they are true to the facts.

And against the semantic theory, philosophers have objected that: ultimately, it is still a restatement of the correspondence theory (" 'snow is white' is true if and only if snow is white"). Although the semantic theory is an improvement because it emphasizes the role of language in picking out the facts that make our statements true, it still leaves the nature of the "picking out" as obscure as ever. We are not in the position of a logician, who can make up his semantic models and languages at will. (Consider the following silly but profoundly philosophical joke: Eve says to Adam, "Let's call that one a hippopotamus. Adam: "Why 'hippopotamus'?" Eve: "Because it looks more like a hippopotamus than anything else we've seen so far.")

An adequate semantic theory of truth must be far more than merely formal. It must specify how such a theory would apply to natural (unformalized and open-ended) languages. Truth cannot be only formally defined. If the semantic theory is true, then translations between languages are impossible, since the rules of satisfaction are unique to each language.

The debate between these theories continues, but the likeliest outcome is usually a combination of theories rather than the exclusive victory of any particular one. Each makes up for the deficiencies in the others. But one of the most important consequences of this debate, ironically, has been the loss of interest in the very concept of Truth (with a capital "T"). In everyday contexts, of course, philosophers, like everyone else, will talk about statements and beliefs being "true" and "false" on the basis of a primitive "correspondence" notion, that is, "correspondence to the facts." But philosophically, the power of the word "Truth" has always dwelled in its strong metaphysical linkage to "the way the world really is." And having given up on that grandiose conception of Truth, many philosophers are sometimes inclined to give up the word "truth" altogether. They concern themselves only with what we ordinarily mean when we say that a statement is "true."[4] Other philosophers,

---

[4] J. L. Austin, for example, begins an essay on "Truth" by declaring, "*In vino veritas,* ('in wine, truth') perhaps, but in a sober symposium, *verum* ('true')."

however, refuse to give up the traditional search for truth, and new and improved versions of the traditional and newer theories are still appearing.

RATIONALITY

If the correspondence theory of truth loses ground and interest in "Truth" moves to a secondary position, other philosophical notions become more central. Kant, for example, rarely mentions "Truth," he prefers to talk only about "knowledge" and "reason." And, since Kant, philosophers have often talked about rationality rather than truth. Where truth carries with it the heavy metaphysical linkage to the "way the world really is," rationality makes milder claims about our ways of thinking. Of course, "being rational" might still be said to be the best approach to the truth. But, more importantly, "being rational" refers to a way of thinking (and acting) that can be justified even if there is no truth (in the correspondence sense).

Of course, the goal of philosophy has always been to make us more rational, as with Socrates, for example. But "rationality," like "reason," has meant many things to many thinkers. For Plato, Aristotle, and most modern "rationalists," "rationality" applied to our ability to know necessary truths, calculate arithmetic problems, and prove God's existence. For the empiricists, to be rational meant rather to obey the laws of inductive reasoning. Today, "be rational" often means "be scientific" or, in certain contexts, "don't be emotional." And because the concepts of "truth" and "rationality" have always been closely tied, we must expect that the problems of the first will infect the second as well.

What is rationality? One suggestion is that rationality is thinking in accordance with the three alternative theories of truth outlined in the previous section. In evaluating our beliefs, we have to ask, do they "cohere"? Are they "practical"? And, how are we to understand the role of our own mental and linguistic activities in providing the concepts with which we understand the world? The ideal of philosophy is no longer the straightforward but problematic attempt to say "the way the world really is." According to the correspondence theory, this would be stated as "giving up on truth." But this is misleading. "Truth" is not necessarily wedded to the correspondence theory, and what is going on in philosophy is still the search for truth. But truth is now understood in a very different way than before, as rationality. Because, to be rational does not only depend on what you believe but rather how you believe it, the way you have thought it out, the reasons you have provided, and the clarity and courage with which you have approached your problems.

Rationality means "thinking and acting in accordance with reason." But that isn't too helpful, given the very loaded definitions of "reason" we have seen in the history of metaphysics. Perhaps this will help; *rationality* is thinking with reasons, good reasons. What is a "good reason?" If thinking is based on "facts," then the facts must be well-confirmed, not simply hearsay or wild guesses. (We do not have to say that the facts must be "true" in the correspondence sense; someone might have every good reason to accept them but, by some twist of circumstances, they turn out not to be true.) If thinking is based upon deductive reasoning, then the reasoning must be valid. Of course, a "good reason" must make sense; unspecifiable appeals to mysterious forces or mystical insights will not do in rational argument. And a good reason must be relevant to the case at hand; a brilliant argument and a welter of facts do not constitute rationality if they are not directed at the matter under consideration. But this last point is derived from the most important general characteristic of rationality: rationality depends most of all upon coherence. To be rational is to think of as many reasons, dig up as many facts, and call up as many beliefs as are necessary to provide a comprehensive logical web in support of any given belief. To be rational in philosophy is to develop as comprehensive and coherent a system as possible. This does not mean that it must be an extravagant metaphysical system like those of Spinoza and Leibniz; it may be enough that our quite ordinary, everyday beliefs are thought out and tied together in a thorough and thoughtful way.

Since Kant, this ideal of rationality has ruled philosophy in place of the traditional ("correspondence") notion of truth. But what is the relationship between rationality and truth? In one sense, it is important that we insist that rationality does not require that our beliefs be true. For example, you might think that the belief that the earth is flat, or motionless, or made of water, is a false belief, and, in terms of the system of beliefs which we all share today, any of these beliefs certainly is irrational. But had you lived in earlier times, in ancient Greece for example, these would not have seemed false at all, but completely rational. And had you suggested that the earth is a (flattened) sphere, whirling about its axis and around the sun at incredible speeds, composed of tiny charged particles which themselves are whirling about at even more incredible speeds, you surely would have been branded the village idiot, or chased out of town. For, in the context of their system of beliefs, what you now believe would have been utterly irrational. This does not mean that it is always rational to believe what everyone around you believes and irrational not to; it is possible that everyone's beliefs are irrational, founded on bad reasons, lack of evidence, refusal to think about it clearly or carefully, and unspoken prejudice or superstition. But this is not always or even usually the case. In the above example, we may suppose that the Greeks had the best of reasons for believing what they did about the earth. Rationality, therefore, does not require truth; it requires only that one make the best possible use of all of the information and "reason" at his or her disposal.

This distinction between rationality (clear and coherent thinking) and truth (the way the world really is) is debatable because it too presupposes a correspondence theory with our thinking on the one side and reality on the other. But the upshot of our discussion in this chapter has been to discredit precisely this distinction. Therefore, although we can distinguish between rational thinking and truth in some particular cases (for example, the ancient belief that the world is flat and motionless) we believe that our rational thinking is the truth. In other words, the truth is that which is most rational to believe at a given time and in a given situation, on the basis of the best available evidence and the most careful thinking possible. There is no other sense to be given to the words "true" and "truth," unless we are to fall back again into the intolerable and absurd doubts of Hume's skepticism.

But now, you might well ask, why be rational? And a great many serious philosophers have asked this question as well. But first, we have to distinguish several conceptions of rationality (just as we distinguished several conceptions of truth). Sometimes, "rational" has a familiar negative connotation, such as when you accuse your friend or lover of "being too rational," meaning insensitive, not "in touch" with his or her emotions, or abusing thought as a way of escaping from an emotionally charged situation. In this sense, we can quickly agree that there is good reason not to be rational. Similarly, if you think of rationality as "thinking something into the ground," such that you never act upon it at all, or always too late, then, again, we can willingly give up rationality, in that sense. But these are not the conceptions of rationality that are at stake here. First, there is the answer, "it is as close as you will ever get to the truth." (Once we have given up the correspondence theory of truth we can say, "rationality *is* the truth.") To be rational is to use our abilities to sift evidence and weigh arguments and formulate reasons in the most efficient way. Accordingly, the answer to the question "why be rational?" is simply, it is the most efficient way to comprehend the world, and the best guarantee that you know what is going on around you. But if this answer isn't convincing to you, the following should be: it is a mistake to talk about "rationality" as purely a matter of understanding. It is also a matter of action and of living, acting rationally and living rationally. (This is a further advantage in talking about rationality rather than truth.) And as soon as we add this pragmatic dimension (which, according to the pragmatic theory of truth, is truth), the answer to the question "why be rational?" becomes extremely persuasive. To act rationally is to act in such a way that you are more likely to get what you want (including knowledge as well as enjoyment, satisfaction, and an occasional ego boost). "Well, why should I want what I want?" you might ask. But if you say you don't want to want what you want, or that you'd rather not be rational in getting it, then that is only to say that you want something else, and to be rational then means only to get that in the best way possible. The best way to get something is not always the most "rational" in the narrow sense of "most efficient." In this machine-and-consumer society, it is often more efficient to buy something than to make it with your own hands. That doesn't make it more rational. And it is not necessarily rational to think everything out and plan ahead, for sometimes what we want is novelty and adventure, in which case, it may be most rational not to think it all out and plan ahead. But, in any case, rationality, in this sense, is hardly objectionable.

Rationality is tying our knowledge and our lives together in the most coherent and effective way. But here we come back to the dilemma facing philosophy since Kant. If we have separated truth and rationality from the question of "the way the world really is," it is apparent that different societies and even different individuals can tie their experiences and their lives together in very different ways. Take the most extreme example, a paranoid schizophrenic believes that not only friends and family are out to get him, but also all sorts of strange creatures, which are visible only to him, are determined to harm him in ways that are not apparent to anyone else. He ties together his world in an airtight package, with an enormous amount of evidence interpreted consistently with his overall paranoid picture of the world. Now if rationality meant only coherence, we should have to say that the thoughtful paranoid is as rational as any of us, perhaps even more so, for he has thought about his experience more and developed an elegantly simple and coherent world picture which few of us could match. And if we add our pragmatic considerations, it might still turn out that (as R. D. Laing and other recent psychiatrists have argued) the paranoid is, given his situation and personality, acting out his life in the most efficient way possible for getting what he wants (although what he wants may seem, to us, a bit bizarre). Is there a "refutation" of the paranoid? Is he "irrational?" Or does he just seem that way to us, in the context of our (but not his) beliefs? This is an extreme case, but the problem is clear. According to our account of rationality, are we going to be forced to accept any system, no matter how bizarre, as rational and even true, just because it is coherent and satisfies the person or the people who believe in it?

KANT'S REVOLUTION

We have seen that almost every philosopher before Kant accepted, in some form or other, the correspondence theory of truth. At first, this was innocent enough, and combined with the rationalist's confidence in reason, was enough to produce some monumental metaphysics. But as philosophers found their differences irreconcilable, and as their confidence eroded, skepticism and bickering began to take over. Finally, Hume argued that we couldn't even know that the sun will rise tomorrow, or that one billiard ball causes the movement of another, or if there is a material world—or whether he was just dreaming. And this was too much for Kant, who, in his own words, "was awakened from his dogmatic slumbers" by Hume's skepticism. The problem, as he diagnosed it, was the unquestioned belief that our ideas (thoughts, beliefs, and statements) were true (or false) insofar as they corresponded (or failed to correspond) to reality. Kant saw, what most modern philosophers now accept, that our "ideas" (our language and our concepts) and reality are so intertwined that they are inseparable, and that our language "sets up" the facts of reality. The word Kant used was "constitutes." *Reality has no existence* that we can understand *other than as we constitute it with our language and our concepts.* Previous philosophers had asked, "How can we know that our ideas correspond with the way the world really is?" Kant rejected that question. Instead, he asked, *"how do our ideas constitute the world?"* "What is the structure, and what are the rules (the *concepts* or *categories*) of the human mind according to which we "set up" our world, the world of our experience?" No more correspondence, except within that world as we "set it up!" Rationality (knowledge and truth) means obeying the rules. (Think of it this way, you take a number of pieces of wood and a checkered board and "set up" the game by making up rules about what can be moved where, how and when. Then, within the game, you are free to make any number of moves, some brilliant, some stupid, but you are always bound by the rules that you yourself have "set up.")

Kant's revolution (for it was nothing less than that) changed our conception of truth, and, along with it, our conception of reality, our conception of knowledge, and, most importantly, our conception of ourselves. Truth is no longer correspondence between our ideas and reality, but our own system of rules (concepts or categories) by which we constitute our reality. Knowledge, accordingly, is no longer the comprehending of a reality beyond our experience, but knowledge of our experience. But this does not mean, "knowledge of only our experience," for the objects of our experience are all there is to reality. Moreover, in making this move, Kant gives the philosophers something which they thought they had lost, a renewed ideal of certainty, for, he argued, we can be certain of the rules of our own experience. Kant defended the truths of arithmetic and geometry as the rules of our experience, in particular, those rules that have to do with the forms of our intuitions of space and time. According to Kant's philosophy in general, reality is the world of our experience, as we constitute it. Therefore, we can know it with certainty, for truth, in general, is our own construction.

You might at first think that there is some trick here, as if Kant is saying, "well if we can't have knowledge in the hard sense, then I'll simply re-define the words 'knowledge,' 'reality' and 'truth.'" But this isn't it at all. What he has done is to point to the difficulty of the picture that other philosophers had accepted and shown that what we normally mean by "truth," "knowledge," and "reality" is not an insatiable appeal to a world beyond our experience. My everyday statement, "there's beer in the refrigerator" is true, whatever any philosopher might say, if there is beer in the refrigerator—if I can go and look, see it, pick it up, open the can and drink it. As for some beer beyond my experience that is the real beer, what kind of absurdity is that? Underneath Kant's spectacular pronouncements, there is, once again, a return to common sense. This world, the one I stand in, touch and see, is the real world. But what makes it real, according to Kant, is not just that I stand in, touch and see it, but that I actively constitute it as the way it is, apply my own rules for understanding it, and structure it through my own experience.

In 1781 Kant already anticipated all three of those "theories of truth" which would become so powerful in the twentieth century. In his emphasis on our constitution of reality through interconnected rules and concepts, Kant anticipates the coherence theory of truth, which stresses precisely these interconnections. In his emphasis on the workability of these rules, he anticipates the pragmatic theory. And in his theory that it is our concepts and rules which "set up" reality, Kant anticipates Tarski's semantic theory. But what is of equal importance is the fact that Kant does not endorse any single one of these theories, but embraces them all.

We now have a general way of giving an account of all of those necessary but nonempirical beliefs that we described in the last chapter. Using Kant's terminology, we can say they are forms of synthetic *a priori* knowledge. If a truth is not true because of our experiences, nor is it true because of the grammar or meanings of the sentences of our language, how else could it be defended? This was Hume's dilemma, and with his two-test system of justification, he eliminated many of our most important beliefs as "unjustifiable." But now, we have our third way: a belief can be true, necessarily true, if it is one of those rules which we impose to constitute our experience. Thus we saw that Kant defended the truths of arithmetic and geometry by showing that they were the "(*a priori*) forms of intuition," the ways in which we must experience our world. So too will he defend all of those truths which Hume had thrown out of court. The principle of universal causation is neither a generalization from experience nor an analytic truth, but rather a *rule* for "setting up" our world. And that rule is, "always look for regular (or 'lawlike') connections between events, so that you can explain an event as an *effect* of previous events, and therefore predict future events as well." Like a rule in chess, this is not a move within the game but one of those rules that defines the game. So too with the principle of induction: it is neither based upon experience nor a trivial truth but a rule with which we govern all of our experience. And so too for our belief in the "external" or material world, which Berkeley and Hume found so problematic. Our experience alone will not tell us whether we are dreaming or not, and the idea of the material ("external") world is not a tautology or a conceptual truth. It too is one of the rules that we use to constitute our experience, namely, that we shall *always* interpret our experience of objects in space as external to us and as material or *substantial*. But notice, our metaphysical notion of substance is no longer that which is, by definition, outside of our experience. It is now part of the rules by which we set up our experience.

Kant also gives us a way of resolving the age-old disputes of metaphysics. Since the claims of the metaphysicians are all synthetic *a priori*, Kant provides us with the following policy:

1) Those claims which are rules by which we must interpret our experience are true—necessarily true.
2) Those claims which contradict rules by which we must interpret our experience are false—necessarily false.
3) Those which are not rules by which we must interpret our experience are either analytic, contingently true, or contingently false.

4) Finally, those claims which cannot be decided by appeal to the rules of our experience and make no difference to our experience one way or the other, are to be rejected as possible topics of knowledge.

The logical positivists, whom we met in the last chapter, took this last part of Kant's policy as a program for a devastating attack on metaphysics in general. Although the logical positivists, as empiricists in the tradition of David Hume, did not accept much of Kant's theory, they whole-heartedly endorsed his rejection of claims which made no difference whatever to our experience. They said that any claim that makes no difference to our experience—that cannot be tested in any way—is meaningless.

Some of the metaphysician's claims will be upheld. For example, Kant saves Newton's (and Spinoza's) determinism in his rule of causality, thus rejecting Leibniz's "pre-established harmony" view as necessarily false. With some revisions, he accepts a large part of Leibniz's view of space and time as relative, that is, relative to our experience. He saves the notion of substance because he says that one of the most important rules of our experience is that we see objects as substantial (that is, as "real"). But he does not accept the view that substance is something independent of human experience, for such a view, by definition, means that substance would be irrelevant to our experience. Nor does he accept the central dispute between Spinoza and Leibniz, whether there is but one substance or many, for no rule of our experience is concerned one way or another. It makes no difference to our experience. It is a metaphysician's game and not a possible topic for knowledge.

Kant's revolution is the elimination of the correspondence theory, the elimination of "reality" and "truth" as external to ourselves. Since Kant, many philosophers no longer view human knowledge as the passive reception of sensations or intuitions. And, needless to say, the problems of philosophy have become radically changed.

SUMMARY AND CONCLUSION

Philosophers have always seen their main business as the search for truth. But the notion of truth has itself become a problem and several competing theories of truth have emerged. The traditional theory is the correspondence theory of truth, which claims that a belief (or statement) is true if it "matches up" or corresponds to the facts of reality. But there have been many arguments to show that this view is inadequate. Accordingly, philosophers have defended the coherence theory of truth, which says that a belief or statement is true if it is logically connected to other beliefs and statements, the pragmatic theory of truth, which says that a belief or statement is true if it helps us in practice with our work and our lives, and a semantic theory of truth, which says that truth is a function of our language as well as a question about the "facts" of the world.

Philosophers have also always seen themselves—at least most of them—as defenders of rationality. The desire to be rational is a more modest enterprise than the search for truth because rationality is concerned only with the way we think and act, without necessarily committing us to claim that we know the truth. It is possible to be completely rational and still not know the truth, just as scientists of any given period may rationally believe one thing that is known to be false by their successors. But some of the more recent theories of truth tend to blur the distinction between rationality and truth. If truth is coherence or pragmatism, for example, to think and act rationally and to know what is true cannot be distinguished.

GLOSSARY

coherence theory of truth: a statement or a belief is true if and only if it "coheres" with a system of statements or beliefs. A truth of mathematics is "true" because it forms part of the nexus in the complex of mathematical truths. A geometrical theorem is "true" because it can be proven from other theorems (axioms, definitions) of the geometrical system. A "factual" statement is true insofar as other "factual" statements, including general statements about experience which are logically relevant to the original statement, support it. Since we can never get "outside" our experience, the only sense in saying that a belief is true (according to this theory) is that it "coheres" with the rest of our experience.

constitution: Kant's word for "set up": our concepts constitute our experience.

correspondence theory of truth: a statement or belief is true if and only if it "corresponds" with "the facts." Even when restricting our attention to statements of fact, however, this common sensical "theory" gets into trouble as soon as it tries to pick out what corresponds to what. How can we identify a "fact," for example, apart from the language we use to identify it? And what does it mean to say that a statement "corresponds" to a fact? (Do they look the same? Not a bit!)

conventions (of language): those rules of usage which are shared by the speakers of a linguistic community and make it possible for us to use language to refer to something particular, to be insulting or sarcastic, and to mean something by making certain sounds in the language.

irrational: going against the rules of reason. (Not the same as *non*rational, such as when we say that worms and fish are "not rational animals.") Only rational (that is, thinking, planning, calculating) creatures can be *irrational*.

pragmatic theory of truth: a statement or a belief is true if and only if it "works," that is, if it allows us to predict certain results, function effectively in everyday life, and encourages further inquiry and helps us lead better lives.

rational: in accordance with the rules of effective thought: coherence, consistency, practicability, simplicity, comprehensiveness, looking at the evidence and weighing it carefully, not jumping to conclusions etc. Rationality may not guarantee truth; all of the evidence and everything we believe may point to one conclusion, while later generations, who know things that we do not, may see that our conclusion was incorrect. Yet it would still be, for us, the rational conclusion. Rationality points to the manner of thinking rather than its ultimate conclusions. Philosophically, the stress on rationality takes the emphasis off reality and places it on our manner of philosophizing.

reference: in everyday talk, we loosely say that this word (e.g. "pumpkin") refers to that actual thing, a pumpkin. In philosophy, this is the beginning of serious mistakes, for example, thinking that the word has some "natural connection" with the thing. But once we say that it is not the word but the user of the word who refers to the thing, we can see how complicated matters must become. Reference is not a simple connection between word and thing; it is an extremely complex set of activities and conventions which surround certain persons making certain sounds in certain contexts. The naive theory of reference is often the first step in the equally naive correspondence theory of truth. Giving up that theory of reference is a major step in giving up that theory of truth.

semantic theory of truth: a formal theory best known from the work of Alfred Tarski, which defines "true" in terms of a technical notion of *satisfaction*. According to the theory, every sentence in the language is either satisfied or not by a distinct class of individuals. This is adequate, however, only for artificially constructed languages. Generalizing the theory to natural languages (e.g. American English), we can say that the theory suggests that we (but not each of us personally) set up the rules according to which our sentences do or do not "correspond with the facts" of the world.

6

IS IT ALL RELATIVE?

Different strokes for different folks.
                                        Anonymous

Kant destroyed the old problems, resolved the old disputes, and answered Hume's skepticism, at least for a while. In rejecting the correspondence theory of truth and the idea of an "external" reality, he eliminated the basis of those problems, disputes, and doubts. But I expect that you can already see a new and even more virulent version of those problems, disputes, and doubts on the horizon. By denying us our anchor in reality, Kant launches philosophy in a bold new direction, and he creates the dilemma that still defines philosophy today: is there any uniquely correct way of describing the way the world is?

The basis of Kant's theory is that we supply the rules according to which we constitute our experience. Truth can be talked about only within our experience and according to those rules. But you can see what happens when we raise the following question: what about people (or creatures) who are very different from us? Will they use the same rules? Will they have the same experiences? And, if we do differ from them, who is "right"? Whose rules are "better"? Whose experience is "true"? You can see here the problems of the coherence theory of truth coming to haunt Kant's philosophy. Suppose there are two (or more) sets of rules, equally coherent? Can they both be "true"? And the problems of the semantic theory too: what if there are different languages with different basic concepts or categories, constituting different "facts?" Are they all "true?" You can appreciate how easily the German Romantic philosophers who immediately followed Kant replaced his notion of "constitution" with the more exciting notion of "creation." We create our realities, they announced. We are all artists, building our worlds. And notice the words "realit*ies*" and "world*s*"; there is no longer confidence, much less a guarantee, that there is only one reality or one world.

Kant's most immediate follower, a German named Johann Gottlieb Fichte, used the pragmatic theory of truth to come to the same conclusion; the truth is, according to him, that which is most practical, most conducive to the good life, and the evaluation of different realities depends wholly on the practical consequences. (He said, in his most famous dictum: "the kind of philosophy a man chooses depends upon the kind of man one is.") With Kant's revolution, the Truth seems destined to be replaced by many truths.

But before we go on to explore these intriguing complications, let us make it clear that Kant himself never accepted a word of all this. According to him, there was still but one possible set of rules, and therefore only one way of constituting our experience, whoever we are, wherever we're from, and no matter what kind of conscious creature we happen to be. And this means: one world, one science, one reality and one truth. Kant tries to prove this in the central section of his *Critique of Pure Reason,* in a formidable argument which he calls a "transcendental deduction."

Like so much philosophical jargon, Kant's term is easily explained, and is used often enough to make it worth explaining. You already know what a deduction is, an inference from one statement to another according to a set of rules of inference. In this case, Kant attempts to infer, from various statements which we believe, the basic rules (concepts, categories) of human experience. And this is what *"transcendental"* means, the basic rules of human experience. But a transcendental deduction is not satisfied with simply deducing some such rules; it also proves that they are the only rules which we are able to use to constitute our experience. That is why it is so important to Kant. It allows him his revolution without its anarchist consequences.

The argument itself is enormously complicated and scholars who have studied it for half their lives still do not agree what it is or whether it is a valid argument. So, obviously, we won't try to summarize it for you here. What can and must be said is this, however: Kant believed that such a transcendental deduction would prove that, although it is we ourselves who supply the rules of our experience and determine what can be true for us, we don't have a choice in the matter. There still is only one reality for all of us.

Philosophers are still arguing whether any such transcendental argument (Kant's or not) might succeed. If one does, then people must, in their basic rules, all agree. (Of course, they will always disagree about particular matters; no two chess players make all the same moves.) But if there is no successful transcendental argument, then there need be no such universal agreement. It then makes sense to talk about different truths for different people. This, we may say, is the dominant battle of twentieth-century philosophy, in America and in Europe.[1] Those who believe that there is only one set of rules and one

[1] It is important to recognize that there are many possible perspectives from which to summarize the more recent developments in philosophy since the turn of the nineteenth

truth are often called *absolutists* (though many philosophers find that name repulsive, since it sounds so dogmatic). Others, who believe that there are different rules for different people, and therefore different "truths," are called *relativists*. Kant was an absolutist. Most of his followers were relativists. (This is obscured by the confusing fact that many of them talked about "the Absolute" all the time. But, they were still relativists, and to avoid confusion, we shall not talk about "the Absolute" at all in this book.)

THE BATTLE IN EUROPE AFTER KANT: RELATIVISM AND ABSOLUTISM

The story of philosophy in Europe since Kant is largely the story of a war between relativism and absolutism, in which even the politics and arts of the times play a continuing role. The philosophers immediately following Kant, as we have already mentioned, pursued relativism with a relish, developing alternative systems of philosophy as fast as they could find publishers. The philosopher Friedrich Schelling, for example, produced about one system a year at the turn of the century. He became the best known "Romantic" philosopher of a large group of "Romantic" intellectuals, poets, and critics throughout Europe who turned to the virtual worship of individual "genius" and competed for the most extravagant and creative views of the world.

The virtually undisputed winner of this contest, however, was not Schelling but one of his schoolmates, Georg Wilhelm Friedrich Hegel. Hegel developed, in his first book, one of the most colossal systems of thought since Plato, easily outdoing even Leibniz and Spinoza. But where Leibniz and Spinoza were telling us "the way the world really is," Hegel gave us a long series of alternative ways of viewing (and living in) the world. He called these different views, "forms of consciousness," and the series itself a "phenomenology of spirit," that is, the long road over which human consciousness has traveled in its adoption of one view of the world (or "form of consciousness") and then another.

Starting from a clearly Kantian perspective, Hegel taught that we have to stop talking about "true" and "false" philosophies, and "true" and "false" religions, political systems, societies, scientific theories, and values. There are only different "forms of consciousness," some more sophisticated and perspicacious than others, but none wholly true (or false) to the exclusion of others. Hegel wholly endorsed the Kantian thesis that the world is nothing

---

century and this is one of them. The dual purpose of this chapter is (1) to bring into the present day one of the most controversial aspects of the entire history of Western metaphysics and epistemology discussed in the preceding five chapters, and (2) to give a brief survey of some of the major movements in recent philosophy.

other than the way in which we constitute it. Or rather, the ways, for Hegel no longer believes that there is only one. And that means that seemingly opposed philosophies are not really contradictory; they are just alternative views of reality. But, didn't we just claim that there is a reality, which exists independently of these various "views" of it? Not at all, according to Hegel. "Reality" is nothing other than the totality of these different human views of it, that comprehensive consciousness that sees not just this view or that view but sees them all as bits and pieces of the truth. And what is that "truth"? Just that there is no reality other than the reality we constitute with our concepts.

Hegel had his own favorite world views, which were in themselves extravagant and admirable creations. For example, he developed a conception he called *Geist* (the German word for "Spirit" in the title of his *"Phenomenology"*), which was his view of a God who could not be distinguished from mankind. (You will recognize a heavy debt to Spinoza here.) He also argued, as Napoleon was marching across Europe, for the importance of internationalism. He was an arch enemy of what he considered vulgar individualism (for example, in his friends, the Romantics) and defended a sense of community spirit, which very strongly influenced Karl Marx, and formed the philosophical foundations of both socialism and fascism. But most famously, he developed the old idea of dialectic (which we found in Socrates), and suggested that the various "forms of consciousness" he catalogued were linked to one another in a progressive logical chain. He resurrected the old Aristotelian animism with a picture of the universe which, through human consciousness, was evolving towards a goal. But like Heraclitus, to whom the concept of "dialectic" is often attributed, Hegel believed that this evolution was anything but a smooth progression: it was violent, depending on a constant battle of opposites and reconciliations that would last only a moment, until the next battle. It is from this notion of dialectic that Marx develops his powerful and influential view of history as class conflict, replacing Hegel's abstract "forms of consciousness" with the day-to-day battles of wages, jobs, exploitation, and profits.[2]

After Hegel, relativism became ever more sophisticated. In Marx, differences in philosophical world views were explained in terms of different economic and social circumstances. The question was no longer "which view of the world was true?" but rather, "what circumstances would make a person believe that?" A few years later, a similar view was defended by the eccentric but brilliant iconoclast, Friedrich Nietzsche. He too attacked the traditional notions of truth with a vengeance and argued that there could be as many equally "true" (or equally "false"—it doesn't matter) world views as there were creative people and societies. He also urged that every person adopt for him or herself as many different world views as possible, at one time or another, as a matter of "experiment." And, like Marx, he replaced the old

[2] The familiar doctrine of Hegel's dialectic is often known only in terms of "thesis-antithesis-synthesis." In fact these categories are rarely used by either Hegel or Marx.

question, "which view of the world is true?" with a question of circumstances. But Nietzsche was not interested in economic or social circumstances so much as psychological factors. And so he asked, "what kind of personality would need to believe that?" Truth is no longer even an issue. In fact, even rationality is starting to feel the threat of relativism. For, with Nietzsche, not only is truth out the window, but coherence and pragmatism are forced to take second place as well. What comes first? Excitement, adventure, heroism, creativity, and what Nietzsche generally calls "the will to power." Of course, one must still act rationally if he or she is to achieve these things, but thinking, in Nietzsche's view, plays at most a secondary role in our lives. With Nietzsche, the philosophy that will later be called existentialism receives its most powerful impetus; the emphasis on action rather than protracted deliberation, the emphasis on the individual rather than the group, and the demand that each person and each society create reality for themselves.

The turn of this century saw the introduction of a powerful doctrine that is still immensely influential in Europe and, to a lesser degree, in the U.S.A. It is called *historicism,* and the man who is best known for defending it is a philosopher named Wilhelm Dilthey. Historicism is Hegel's dialectic of forms of consciousness, pinned down to precise social and historical periods. It is the thesis, simply, that truth and rationality are relative to particular peoples at particular times in history, and that overall comparison of them, with the intention of finding out which is "true," is totally mistaken. It is, obviously, a very strong relativist doctrine, so strong, and so influential, that the absolutists in philosophy, who had had much less publicity and success than the relativists for the last century, started looking around for a champion. They found him, (and we have met him) in the phenomenologist, Edmund Husserl.

When we met Husserl last time, it was in our discussion of necessary truth. Husserl was a new kind of rationalist, who believed that the truths of arithmetic and geometry are known—and known with certainty—by appeal to a certain kind of intuition, which he called "essential" intuition. Believing that such intuitions are adequate for arithmetic and geometry, Husserl turned his theory elsewhere, to philosophy in general. Husserl, as much as any philosopher of his time (the early twentieth century), was horrified by what he saw as rampant relativism. He saw it, in fact, not only as a crisis in philosophy but as "a crisis in European civilization." And so he turned his phenomenology to attack it. Turning against Dilthey, for example, he argued that:

> Historicism takes its position in the factual sphere of the empirical life of the spirit. To the extent that it posits this latter absolutely, without exactly naturalizing it (the specific sense of nature in particular lies far from historical thinking and in any event does not influence it by determining it in general), there arises a relativism that has a close affinity to naturalistic psychologism and runs into similar sceptical difficulties.
>   . . . In view of this constant change in scientific views we would actually have no right to speak of sciences as objectively valid unities instead

of merely as cultural formations. It is easy to see that historicism, if consistently carried through, carries over into extreme sceptical subjectivism. The ideas of truth, theory, and science would then, like all ideas, lose their absolute validity. That an idea has validity would mean that it is a factual construction of spirit which is held as valid and which in its contingent validity determines thought. There would be no unqualified validity, or validity-in-itself, which is what it is even if no one has achieved it and though no historical humanity will ever achieve it. Thus too there would then be no validity to the principle of contradiction nor to any logic, which latter is nevertheless still in full vigor in our time. The result, perhaps, will be that the logical principles of noncontradiction will be transformed into their opposites.[3]

Using both Kant's terminology and his absolutist intentions, Husserl attacked all forms of relativism and attempted to develop a *transcendental phenomenology*, in other words, a phenomenology which discovers the basic rules of all experience (just as he had discovered them for arithmetic and geometry before). And because these rules (or "ideal laws") were discovered to be essential, they were, Husserl concluded, the only rules possible. In Husserl as in Kant, the word "transcendental" means the basic and the only rules with which we "constitute" our world. (Husserl used the notion of "constitution" also, with much the same meaning that Kant did.) But what is *phenomenology?* Briefly, it is the study of human consciousness. These essential rules of experience, in other words, were to be found in consciousness, not in a mysterious Platonic "world of being" nor simply in our language. Consciousness itself, with the objects of its own constitution, becomes our new anchor.

Husserl's battle, from beginning to end, was a battle against relativism, against all of those philosophies that held that there can be different equally true or equally rational world-views. And it must be said that his phenomenology, for all of its internal struggles, was immensely successful, and still attracts the attention of a great many philosophers today. But phenomenology was not the solution to relativism. Husserl thought that phenomenology could be transcendental and prove that certain rules were basic and essential to all human thinking. But just as Kant opened the door to relativism with his view that we constitute our world, Husserl opened it wider with his view that a study of consciousness was the way to do philosophy. For were there not, his followers asked, many different forms of consciousness? (Thus returning to Hegel rather than Kant.) And phenomenology as it developed in France, rather than Germany, became the source of a new phenomenological relativism. Its most famous expositor was the French philosopher Jean-Paul Sartre, and he gave it the name of the best-known philosophy in this century. He called it, *existentialism* (or more properly, "existential phenomenology"). We shall see more of it in later chapters.

[3] Edmund Husserl, "Philosophy as Rigorous Science," in *Phenomenology and the Crisis of Philosophy,* trans. Quentin Lauer (New York: Harper & Row, 1965).

LANGUAGE, TRUTH, AND LOGIC:
ANALYTIC PHILOSOPHY

The first and most important assumption of traditional metaphysics was the trustworthiness of our language in describing reality. Until the end of the eighteenth century, this was rarely doubted, even by those who tried to doubt everything else. But with Kant, that assumption hits the rocks. If we use our concepts to constitute the world, then of course our language will fit reality, but not because of any "trustworthiness." We have carved out reality to fit our language as well as adjusted our language to suit that reality. And, once we have taken a relativist's step beyond Kant to suggest that different languages might "carve out" different realities, the very idea of knowing reality apart from the language we use to describe it becomes utter nonsense.

But this idea has a flip side. If our world reflects the language we use to describe it, then we can also describe the basic features and structures of the world by examining the features and structures of our language. Kant tried to find the rules by which we constitute our experience by looking at our "concepts"; but what are concepts? They are, according to many modern philosophers, nothing other than functions of our language. Accordingly, the most powerful single movement in twentieth-century philosophy (though, like all "movements," it consists of a great many distinct sub-groups and doctrines,) shifts the focus of philosophy from reality and knowledge to language. The technique used by these philosophers is the analysis of our language. They are therefore called (and usually call themselves) *analytic* (or sometimes *linguistic*) philosophers.

It is often wrongly objected that analytic philosophers are concerned only with language ("only semantics"), but this is a misunderstanding. Their concern with language is based on the belief that our language is our only intellectual handle on reality, and that a study of the structures of language is therefore the study of reality. A physicist studies tiny particles by studying their paths in a cloudy chamber; a virologist studies viruses by studying their reflections in a complicated electron microscope. Analytic philosophers study reality by studying its reflection in our language. It is as much a true philosophy (and not mere "semantics") as anything else we have studied, whether it is the piecemeal analysis of Aristotle (which it often resembles) or the elaborate intuitionism of Husserl's phenomenology.

The history of analytic philosophy is usually traced back to Frege and Russell at the turn of this century. It parallels the development of the various conceptions of truth we discussed in the last chapter, but now as different theories of meaning. This is not to say that all analytic philosophers at any given time accepted the same theory of meaning. Nor is it to say that analytic philosophy is only concerned with theories of meaning. Just as important are the various metaphysical, epistemological, and other topics which we have discussed and will discuss in this book. But a certain view of meaning, that is, the relationship between our language and reality, underlies every problem they decide to tackle with their methods.

The analytic tradition began as a revolt (like most traditions) against well-established doctrines that were becoming increasingly absurd. In this instance, the revolt was a British revolt against European metaphysics (much as, two hundred years before, John Locke had led the British empiricist revolt against the European metaphysics of that period). The revolt was given considerable support by the German logician, Gottlob Frege, whose impressive logical techniques were to provide many of the basic tools of philosophical analysis. But the movement was primarily British, an appeal to common sense and empiricism, and its "prime mover" was a philosopher already familiar to us, Bertrand Russell. Together with his colleague at Cambridge University, G. E. Moore, Russell attacked the prevalent coherence theory of truth that derived from the post-Kantians in Europe and replaced it with a common-sensical correspondence theory of truth and an accompanying reference theory of meaning: that is, the meaning of a statement is the fact that it refers to. The opposing metaphysical view at the time (defended primarily by the philosopher F. H. Bradley) was monism and idealism. Russell later comments:

> Moore took the lead in the rebellion, and I followed with a sense of emancipation. . . . We believed that grass is green, that the sun and stars would exist if no one was aware of them. The world which had been thin and logical now became rich and varied.[4]

Moore's and Russell's rebellion became the first stage of analytic philosophy. It was based on a correspondence theory of truth and, against Bradley, it was realistic rather than idealistic. But it was the realism of John Locke rather than of the metaphysicians. Against Bradley's monism, Russell defended a pluralism, a view that proposed the existence of many different facts in the universe. Accordingly, he called his philosophy *atomism*. It was not a pluralism of substances but of facts (more like Leibniz than Democritus). Ultimately, the facts were facts of our own experience (like Locke's "ideas"). Russell also assumed that our language provided a perfect mirror of the structure of reality. Accordingly, this first analytic philosophy was called, *logical atomism*. Its technique, which borrowed its elegant logical apparatus from Frege and from Russell's own earlier *Principia Mathematica,* was to give a logical analysis of the basic bits of our language ("atomic propositions") which corresponded to the structures of the basic bits of reality ("atomic facts"), and then to discover how the logically more complex bits of language are put together to correspond to (or construct) the more complex bits of reality. The details of Russell's analyses are often ingenious, but we cannot go into them here.

Logical atomism was developed by not only one but two geniuses of the highest order. The other was a Viennese student of Russell's, Ludwig Wittgen-

---

[4] Bertrand Russell, "My Mental Development," in *The Philosophy of Bertrand Russell,* ed. Paul A. Schilpp (La Salle, Ill.: Open Court, 1975).

stein. Wittgenstein, while still a student but sitting in the trenches of Europe during World War One, wrote a remarkable book, called *Tractatus Logico–Philosophicus,* or just *Tractatus* for short. It is generally agreed to be one of the great philosophical works of this century and it is still the subject of tremendous debates.[5] The book was very short and unusually written, divided into seven "propositions," the rest of the book being simply explanations and extensions of these. The main propositions are (excluding those of primarily logical interest) :

1) The world is everything that is the case.
   (1.1) The world is the totality of facts, not things.
2) What is the case—a fact—is the existence of states of affairs.
   (2.1) We picture facts to ourselves.
   (2.2) A picture has a logico-pictorial form in common with what it depicts.
3) A logical picture of facts is a thought.
   (3.1) In a proposition, a thought finds an expression that can be perceived by the senses.
4) A thought is a proposition with a meaning.
   (4.1) Propositions represent the existence or non-existence of states of affairs.
   (4.5) The general form of a proposition is: This is how things stand.
5) A proposition is a truth function of elementary propositions. (An elementary proposition is a truth function of itself.)
   (5.6) The limits of my language mean the limits of my world.
6) [on the general form of truth functions]
   (6.4) All propositions are of equal value.
   (6.5) When the answer cannot be put into words, the question cannot either. *The riddle* does not exist. If a question can be framed at all, it is also *possible* to answer it.
7) What we cannot speak about we must pass over in silence.[6]

Again, the work is worth a full term of study, but we can only try to appreciate Wittgenstein's intentions. It is clearly a statement of logical atomism, combined with a mystical touch at the end; namely, that there are all-important human experiences that cannot be talked about. It is an attempt to deal with the basic question of all analytic philosophy, "how does language relate to the world?" And in the *Tractatus,* Wittgenstein's answer is very similar to Russell's. There are bits of language, and there are bits of reality (facts), and the first "matches up" to the second. If they don't "match up," they are false. Sometimes, however, we try to use language when there are no "facts"

[5] G. E. Moore, who was also Wittgenstein's teacher, wrote him a letter of recommendation when Wittgenstein tried to get a Ph.D. using the *Tractatus* as his thesis. Moore said "it is a work of genius, but even so, it is good enough for a Ph.D. thesis."
[6] Ludwig Wittgenstein, *Tractatus Logico-Philosophicus,* trans. D. F. Pears and B. F. McGuinness (London: Routledge and Kegan Paul, 1961).

at all. That is when we had better "keep silent" (Prop. 7). But just when Wittgenstein's book was beginning to have its full impact, and stimulated the most powerful movement in analytic philosophy, namely, *logical positivism,* Wittgenstein changed his mind. (We'll meet him again in a few pages.)

Logical positivism was the second stage of the development of analytic philosophy. We have already met this powerful modern movement twice: once as a renewed version of Hume's empiricist attack on metaphysics (Ch. 3) and once as an (also Humean) theory regarding the nature of necessary truths as all analytic (or "relations of ideas") (Hempel, Ayer, Ch. 4). The central feature of logical positivism is a theory of meaning, which is, quite simply, that every meaningful statement about the world must be verifiable (or falsifiable) through experience, and that the meaning of a statement is its method of verification. Accordingly, the theory is called the *verifiability theory of meaning.* For example, the statement, "there are no rabbits in Australia" is meaningful because there is a well-established method of verification (namely, take a boat to Australia and look for rabbits) ; the statement's meaning is that set of operations and circumstances by which it is verified (or falsified; note, a false statement is still meaningful, because it can be tested through experience). On the other hand, a statement such as "substance is infinitely divisible" would be said by the logical positivists to be meaningless, because there are no operations or circumstances in which its truth could be tested. Nothing would falsify it (not even slicing up everything in sight into the tiniest bits; for substance in this metaphysical sense cannot be experimentally "sliced up," and no amount of "slicing up" would be sufficient to show that anything could be infinitely divided or not). And nothing could verify it, for the same reasons. It is therefore meaningless; here is Hume modernized, and with a vengeance. The logical positivists (or "logical empiricists") have borrowed "Hume's fork" and turned it into a formidable weapon; every statement is either an analytic truth, trivially true by virtue of its own language and capable of telling us nothing about the world, or it is an empirically verifiable statement with specifiable tests for its truth or falsity. Everything else is meaningless.

The logical positivists' major single philosophical ancestor (in addition to Hume) was Wittgenstein (in the *Tractatus*). That mysterious book's final proposition was just what the positivists were looking for, a way to keep the metaphysicians silent. And the main theme of the *Tractatus,* philosophy as the clarification of our thinking rather than the advancement of any new proposals about "the way the world really is," appealed to the positivists very much. For there was also a non-philosophical determinant of their work, no less powerful, which is too rarely appreciated in the often negative publicity that the movement still receives. That was their resolution to combat the rise of irrationality in Europe, and in Germany and Austria in particular. Fanaticism was on the rampage, and these philosophers, virtually all of whom were German or Austrian (Ayer joined them later) sought a place of refuge and sanity from which to explode the pretensions of absolutist fascism and relativism alike. That "place" of refuge was science, and most of the so-called

"Vienna Circle," the heart of the movement, was composed of scientists and philosophers of science. For them, the rigors of empirical verification were the antidote against the wild and far from merely academic metaphysics that was popular in Europe at the time. This is the reason for their great success, and the reason for Hitler's condemnation of them. Positivism still tends to regain its strength in times of careless metaphysical extravagance and intellectual confusion. (The social sciences, for example, whenever they feel the need to give themselves some solid and respectable ground, turn to positivism, often in extreme forms, as in behaviorism or operationalism.) So before we take a quick look at some of its serious deficiencies, we should appreciate its enormous strength. Positivism is not simply scientific fetishism, as its more metaphysical critics have often charged, nor is it anti-humanist, as its humanist critics have objected. In its time, it was the strongest intellectual defense of humanism available.

But there were problems. First, there were technical problems with the verifiability theory of meaning in particular. Consider the statement, "there are tiny life forms on the dark side of the second planet of the distant star M." Given current technology, it is hard to specify a "method of verification." Yet it is clearly a meaningful statement. The theory was amended, so that a statement is meaningful if it is verifiable in principle (that is, even if we can't imagine how to do it). The theory was further amended to include statistical probability in place of the excessive demand for actual verification and to quiet troublesome questions about what kind of "experience" would count in the verification. But none of this was satisfactory: the phrase "in principle" turned out to be a nightmare, the complexities of probability theory gave rise to paradoxes, and the notion of "experience" was never adequately developed. But the problem that most disturbed positivism's critics was not a technical problem at all. It was of much broader scope. Not only the statements of the metaphysicians, but it turns out, every statement in ethics, religion, esthetics, and every area of concern or value is neither verifiable nor falsifiable. Accordingly, the positivists were left with the limp theory that such matters were "merely emotional" and not meaningful topics of debate at all. Hardly a satisfying conclusion for a movement whose purpose is to fight irrationalism.

In reaction to this unwelcome conclusion, and in order to overcome the problems inherent in the verifiability theory of meaning, British analytic philosophy took a new turn, still concerned with language and meaning but no longer restricted to the verifiability theory. The architect of this new turn was again Ludwig Wittgenstein. For, as we mentioned, Wittgenstein had become dissatisfied with his own logical atomist theory only a short time after he wrote it, and just when it was having its most powerful success among the logical positivists. Moreover, Wittgenstein never did agree with the positivists' anti-metaphysical interpretation of his final proposition. "Silent," yes, but not thereby to be rejected. He had clarified the logic of language in order to make room for the less logical aspects of human experience, art, religion, and ethics. In reaction to his own old theories, he completely revised his conception of language and its role in human life. Language remains central, but its primary role is no longer to describe and make scientific-type statements. "Language," he told his small seminars in Cambridge, "defines forms of life," and particular uses of language, or what he called "language-games." You can see how his reaction to his earlier work is like Kant's reaction to Hume. Wittgenstein replaced his earlier atomistic dualism with a notion of "constituting reality" through language. He can now be said to have a "theory of meaning," which is, "the meaning of a word or sentence is its use." But Wittgenstein was, by this time, vehemently anti-theoretical, and his project was not to develop a "theory of meaning" but rather to attend with extreme care to the everyday "games" we play with language and see how philosophers tend to abuse that language and get themselves in bizarre corners. His aim is as anti-metaphysical as the positivists, but with an entirely new technique. All philosophical problems, Wittgenstein tells us, are due to "language going on holiday," being plucked out of ordinary contexts and made to do work that it is not capable of doing. Accordingly, he looked at philosophy as a kind of "psychoanalysis," in which philosophers try to help each other out of the traps they have set for themselves. "A picture held us captive, and we could not get outside it, for it lay in our language and language seemed to repeat it to us inexorably. . . ."

After the Second World War, the center of attention moved from Cambridge to Oxford. Wittgenstein's view of philosophy developed into a program, which is alternatively called "ordinary language philosophy" or simply "Oxford philosophy." Its twin purposes are well summarized in titles of early works by its two leading practitioners, an article by Gilbert Ryle called "Systematically Misleading Expressions" and a piece by J. L. Austin called "How to Do Things with Words." Ordinary expressions, innocent in themselves, lead philosophers to make unwarranted metaphysical leaps. And language, however useful for science and description, is primarily a tool for doing things, for insulting people, for asking for the salt, and for having uninformative but polite conversation. Consequently, "ordinary language philosophy" began a piecemeal intensive project to understand, in many particular areas, how we use language and how philosophers, by over-simplifying or otherwise abusing ordinary language, raise problems that are not really problems at all.

But therapy, even when it cures, is rarely inspiring. Having had considerable success in cleaning up the refuse still remaining after the positivists' onslaught, ordinary language philosophy gave way to that age-old quest for comprehensive metaphysical understanding. British metaphysics, however, could not again return to the old substance metaphysics and the illusory quest for "the way the world really is." The new metaphysics was modest. It claimed only to be a comprehensive description (therefore, "descriptive metaphysics") of the way we conceive of our world through our use of language. Not surprisingly, the leading metaphysical system builder, P. F. Strawson, is also an expert on the philosophy of Kant. For you can see that the development of analytic philosophy, throughout its variations, might also be viewed as a renewed approach to Kant, beginning with the influence of Hume and empiricism and developing, through Wittgenstein in particular, into the very Kantian thesis, now fully developed in terms of linguistic analysis, that through our language we "constitute" the world.

MAKING DO: PRAGMATISM
AND EXISTENTIALISM

The analytic movement we have just described took place almost entirely in England. Young American philosophers traveled to Oxford and Cambridge and sat at the feet of Wittgenstein in his tiny apartment, took seminars and degrees with Ryle and Austin at Oxford, and returned home with enthusiasm. They soon became the dominant influence in American philosophy, but always looking across the Atlantic for their latest cues. America had its own native philosophy, however, and it is this native philosophy that has finally emerged as the capstone of the analytic movement. This philosophy is *pragmatism,* the same philosophy that was made popular by William James at the turn of the century, combined with the borrowed tools of British analysis. In the 1940's, pragmatism was defended by John Dewey at Columbia and C. I. Lewis at Harvard. Today, two of Lewis' students, W. V. O. Quine and Nelson Good-man are continuing the pragmatist tradition in America.

Even before we go on to describe contemporary pragmatism, however, it is important to point out a parallel in European philosophy that is often overlooked. The central thesis of pragmatism, in both its classical (James, Dewey) and contemporary formulations (Quine, Goodman), is the importance of practical constraints and considerations in all questions of belief and knowledge. But this question of "practical constraints" has had a long and distinguished history in Europe as well. The philosopher Fichte (see p. 191), reacting to Kant, made practical (in particular, moral) considerations definitive in all questions of knowledge. Hegel refused to separate "practical" from "theoretical" concerns, and Karl Marx insisted on the concept of *praxis,* the indissoluble union of theory and practice. Friedrich Nietzsche did not believe in "pure knowledge," but explained all human endeavors, including the "will to truth," by the practical drive that he called "the will to power." And, in this century, there is the philosophy of existentialism, best represented by Jean-Paul Sartre. What do contemporary pragmatism and existentialism have in common? First, a turn towards relativism, in reaction against the absolutism of logical positivism and Husserl's phenomenology respectively. And second, their insistence on the vital importance of the practical dimension in human knowledge. It happens that American pragmatism, like positivism, is extremely devoted to the scientific outlook while European existentialism is often dedicated to a wholesale attack on science and technology. But this important difference should not blind us to the fact that the philosophies themselves are very similar contemporary reactions which have taken place in very different cultural contexts.

To understand pragmatism, we must return to a problem that has been haunting us ever since Chapter 3—the battle between the rationalists and the empiricists. The rationalists, we insisted, were to be characterized by their faith in reason and their appeal to (rational) intuition in particular. The empiricists, on the other hand, rejected any such appeal, and insisted that all of our knowledge about the world must come from experience alone. The empiricists could not help but rely on intuition (or something very much like it) in the defense of the basic rules of logic (Chapter 4). Moreover, the empiricists were forced to put an immense weight on their conception of the "relations of ideas," which now included, as merely "trivial principles which could tell us nothing about the world," all of the complex truths of arithmetic and geometry. Perhaps you accepted the claim of more modern empiricists to deduce such truths from the rules of logic, perhaps not. In either case, without a strong rationalist conception of "intuition," you are forced to the view that the fundamental rules are relative to the persons or societies who accept them. And now, when we bring in all those problematic principles of knowledge, such as the principle of universal causation, what are we to say of them? If we accept Hume's arguments, then we must say that we accept them through habit or custom, but we cannot justify them. Do we know them through intuition? Or can we prove, as Kant tried to prove in his "transcendental deduction," that such a principle is an universal rule of experience? But, what if there are alternative rules? Why should we accept this one rather than that one? And the answer always seems to drive us back towards *intuition*.

It is important to emphasize that our being pushed to intuition need not make us rationalists. The final appeal to intuition may not be a justification of our beliefs at all, but only an explanation to the effect that "we can go no further." But you can see what has happened; we are always pushed back to some inexplicable stopping point. "Why accept these principles?" The rationalist justifies them through intuition; the empiricist just says, "we have to stop here." Ultimately, there is not much difference between them, except that the rationalist feels good about it and the empiricist does not.

Here enters the pragmatist with a simple answer: we choose one set of principles rather than another, because it works for us. There is no need to appeal to intuition, and no need for skepticism. Both the rationalist and the empiricist programs suffer from their attempts to restrict their inquiries to knowledge alone, without adequate attention to the practical dimension of human experience. The rules we accept, including the basic law of contradiction, the other rules of inference that guide our thinking, the axioms of arithmetic and geometry and the various principles of knowledge, have long proven effective in our experience. If they started to fail us, we would give them up. The principle of induction, for example, has an obvious practical advantage. Suppose you face a choice between principles, the principle of induction, "the future will be like the past," and the principle that "the future will not be like the past." Yesterday, you were knocked down by a pickup truck while crossing the street against the light, today, you decide whether or not to try the same thing again. If you accept the principle of induction, you can expect that it is likely to happen again (and decide accordingly). If you accept the other principle, you will figure, "since I was knocked down by a truck yesterday, then it is very unlikely that it will happen today." Is there any question which principle will turn out to be more practical? Or why we continue to accept the one rather than the other? (But then again, why should we suppose that the principle will continue to be more practical, unless we presuppose the principle?)

The contemporary pragmatist solution to these problems includes a number of radical proposals directed against the traditions of modern philosophy. First, notice that it is a rejection of the most enduring distinctions in philosophy. On the pragmatist's account, there is no distinction between purely theoretical and purely practical considerations and no distinction between necessary and contingent truths. All are justified in basically the same way, by their practicality. Most striking of all, this view rejects the very idea of "the way the world really is" and accepts a conception of truth that rests wholly on the basis of coherence and, of course, pragmatic considerations. Nelson Goodman, for example, in an essay entitled "The Way the World Is," concludes that "there is no way the world is." And W. V. O. Quine, in a much celebrated passage, offers us his picture of human knowledge, not a rigid structure of analytic truths[7] filled in by empirical stuffing, but rather:

> The totality of our so-called knowledge or beliefs, from the most casual matters of geography and history to the profoundest laws of atomic physics or even of pure mathematics and logic, is a man-made fabric which impinges on experience only along the edges. Or, to change the figure, total science is like a field of force whose boundary conditions are experience. A conflict with experience at the periphery occasions readjustments in the interior of the field. Truth values have to be redistributed over some of our statements. Reevaluation of some statements entails reevaluation of others, because of their logical interconnections—the logical laws being in turn simply certain further statements of the system, certain further elements of the field. Having reevaluated one statement we must reevaluate some others, which may be statements logically connected with the first or may be the statements of logical connections themselves. But the total field is so underdetermined by its boundary conditions, experience, that there is much latitude of choice as to what statements to reevaluate in the light of any single contrary experience. No particular experiences are linked with any particular statements in the interior of the field, except indirectly through considerations of equilibrium affecting the field as a whole.

---

[7] One of Quine's most celebrated arguments is aimed at the very idea of any such distinctions, between analytic and synthetic sentences, or between *a priori* and empirical knowledge.

If this view is right, it is misleading to speak of the empirical content of an individual statement—especially if it is a statement at all remote from the experiential periphery of the field. Furthermore it becomes folly to seek a boundary between synthetic statements, which hold contingently on experience, and analytic statements, which hold come what may. Any statement can be held true come what may, if we make drastic enough adjustments elsewhere in the system. Even a statement very close to the periphery can be held true in the face of recalcitrant experience by pleading hallucination or by amending certain statements of the kind called logical laws. Conversely, by the same token, no statement is immune to revision. Revision even of the logical law of the excluded middle has been proposed as a means of simplifying quantum mechanics; and what difference is there in principle between such a shift and the shift whereby Kepler superseded Ptolemy, or Einstein Newton, or Darwin Aristotle?

For vividness I have been speaking in terms of varying distances from a sensory periphery. Let me try now to clarify this notion without metaphor. Certain statements, though *about* physical objects and not sense experience, seem peculiarly germane to sense experience—and in a selective way: some statements to some experiences, others to others. Such statements, especially germane to particular experiences, I picture as near the periphery. But in this relation of "germaneness" I envisage nothing more than a loose association reflecting the relative likelihood, in practice, of our choosing one statement rather than another for revision in the event of recalcitrant experience.[8]

It might seem, at first glance, as if the pragmatist's general answer does not differ significantly from Hume's reference to habit or custom. But there is a major difference, one, appropriately, of tremendous practical importance. Where Hume's skepticism stops us short, pragmatism encourages us to seek out new rules and experiment with them. Instead of making philosophy into a futile game, it makes it into an invigorating challenge, one no longer distinguished from the scientist's explorations or the radical theorist's adventures in thought. To do this, it rejects the alienating distinctions between uniquely philosophical necessary truths (as in metaphysics) and plain empirical knowledge, which was thought before to lie outside of the philosophers' domain.

The same advantage is to be found in existentialism. Because existentialism is far more concerned with questions of morality and "human nature" than it is with questions of knowledge, we shall save most of our discussion of it until later chapters. Its advantage over other forms of philosophy is also that it encourages us to search and experiment, rather than settle back with the structures of the past. In particular, the existentialists emphasize the importance of human freedom and choice, and insist that in knowledge as in morality, we make our own rules. We do so, they say, in order to live as we choose most effectively. But existentialism, like pragmatism, has finally given up the age-old search for certainty, embraced relativism as not only an unavoidable but also as a desirable philosophical position, and replaced the

[8] W. V. O. Quine, "Two Dogmas of Empiricism," in *From a Logical Point of View* (Cambridge, Mass.: Harvard University Press, 1961).

traditional concern for "the way the world really is" with practical demands and experiments for a more coherent and satisfying life.

SUMMARY AND CONCLUSION

In this chapter, we have outlined some of the main developments of the past 150 years in Western philosophy. The central figure in this development was Immanuel Kant, and virtually every important movement in the past century and a half can be linked, directly or indirectly, to his work. One of the outstanding features of Kant's philosophy is his bold attack on relativism, the idea that knowledge and values are relative to a given society and might be different—but equally valid—from one society to another. One way of summarizing philosophy since Kant (and of course there are many other ways) is to see the various defenses of relativism that have been raised against him, ironically, while often employing the principles and theories which he invented. The emphasis in this chapter is epistemological, but it has also brought to a conclusion our discussion of metaphysics, beginning with Thales in Chapter 1. It has been necessary to say little about moral theories (which will be discussed in Chapter 11) and social-political theories (such as Marxism, which will be discussed in Ch. 13). In the modern tradition, we can trace the influence of Kant through Hegel to Marxism and existentialism in one direction and through Anglo-American analytic philosophy to pragmatism in another. All of these movements will appear again in the following chapters of the book.

GLOSSARY

absolutism: the thesis that there is but one correct view of reality. Opposed to *relativism.*

analytic philosophy: the movement in twentieth-century philosophy, particularly in America and Britain, that focuses its primary attention on language and linguistic analysis. Also called "linguistic philosophy."

categories: Kant's word (borrowed from Aristotle) for those most basic and *a priori* concepts of human knowledge, for example, "causality," "substance."

constitute: the putting together, "setting up," or synthesis of experience through categories or concepts. First used by Kant, later by Husserl.

dialectic: a "logic" developed by Hegel in which different forms or philosophies are arranged according to increasing sophistication and scope. The "logic" is a development from one form, whose inadequacies are demonstrated, to another, which corrects these inadequacies, and so on. Marx borrows this "dialectic" and gives it a social interpretation. (The "logic" need not be anything like the form "thesis-antithesis-synthesis.")

essence (essential intuition): in Husserl, those ideal objects and laws which constitute necessary truths. The term "essence" is borrowed from Aristotle (and the medieval philosophers) and used in much the same way. Except that Husserl's notion of essence is always tied to "intuition" and consciousness.

existentialism: a twentieth-century philosophical movement which developed in France and Germany through the work of Martin Heidegger, Jean-Paul Sartre and others. Its basic theme is human freedom and responsibility, the lack of any given rules and the need for us to be responsible for our actions.

forms of consciousness: in Hegel, different views of the world. Many contemporary philosophers would call them "conceptual frameworks" or, giving the term a more "practical" twist, different "lifestyles." Hegel chooses the term "form of consciousness" because it includes both of these.

forms of life: like the above in Hegel. A term made popular by Wittgenstein in his discussion of language as defining various "forms of life." His intention was to break down the rigidly descriptive model of language he had defended in his earlier work.

historicism: a philosophy that localizes truth and different views of reality to particular times, places, and peoples in history. It is generally linked to a very strong relativist thesis as well, that there is no truth apart from these various historical commitments.

language games: Wittgenstein's way of referring to the variety of employments, with very different rules and goals, to which we apply our language.

logical atomism: early analytic philosophy, developed by Bertrand Russell and Ludwig Wittgenstein, which taught that atomic propositions, the smallest bits of language (as a simple declarative sentence), corresponded to "atomic facts," the smallest bits of reality. According to this theory, complicated facts were constructed out of these "atoms." In the development of this simple thesis, they built up the logical repertoire which is still the basis of virtually all analytic philosophy.

meaningful/meaningless: an important pair of terms in logical positivism, in which a statement could be said to be meaningful only if conditions could be specified under which it could be empirically verified (or falsified). If no such conditions could be specified, the statement was dismissed as meaningless.

phenomenology: a contemporary European philosophy, founded by the German-Czech philosopher Edmund Husserl, which begins with a "pure description of consciousness." Originally developed as an answer to certain questions of necessary truth in the foundations of arithmetic, it was later expanded to answer more general philosophical questions and, in the hands of its later practitioners, it became a "philosophy of man" as well as a theory of knowledge.

pragmatism: a distinctly American philosophical movement founded by Charles Sanders Pierce at the turn of this century and popularized by William James and John Dewey. Its central thesis is obvious in its name, that truth (etc.) is always to be determined by reference to practical (pragmatic) considerations. Only those metaphysical distinctions that make some difference in practice are worth considering. And the only ultimate defense of any belief is, that "it works."

praxis: term used by Marx to refer to the synthesis of theory and practice, a synthesis urged by Fichte, Hegel, and many other philosophers both before and after Marx.

relativism: the thesis that there is no single correct view of reality, no single truth. Relativists often talk about the possibility of "different conceptual frameworks," "alternative lifestyles," and various "forms of consciousness." They are opposed, often violently, to absolutists (although most of their opponents do not go by that name).

transcendental: referring to the basic rules of human knowledge, usually with an absolutist suggestion that there can be but a single set of such basic rules. Thus Kant's "transcendental deduction" attempted to deduce the one possible set of basic rules for human understanding, and Husserl's transcendental phenomenology attempted to lay bare the one set of basic ("essential") laws of human consciousness. Contemporary philosophers sometimes talk about "the transcendental turn" in philosophy, in other words, the attempt to move beyond claims which might apply only to ourselves and our way of viewing things to the way that things must be viewed.

transcendental deduction: Kant's elaborate attempt to prove that there is but one set of categories (basic rules or *a priori* concepts) which all rational creatures must use in constituting their experience.

verifiability (theory of meaning): in logical positivism, the claim that the meaning of a sentence is its method of verification (or falsification).

7

RELIGION

*Now faith is the substance of things hoped for, the evidence
of things not seen.*

Heb. 11:1

The age-old efforts of metaphysicians to know the way the world really is have
rarely been motivated by curiosity or the scientific spirit alone. Most often,
metaphysics and philosophy in general have been motivated by religious devotion. The search for truth and the concern with what we can know has often
been tied to the very personal concern about the nature of God and our relationship to Him. For many people, there is no more powerful an experience
than the religious experience and they have no more important beliefs than
their religious beliefs. Religion defines their lives, and their religious views
define reality. Although religion is philosophically within the domain of metaphysics and epistemology, its importance demands special attention. It involves
experiences of a kind which are not common to other ontological and cosmological concerns. Religious beliefs involve emotions which are not relevant to
the technical concerns with substance and science. And it is this emotional
involvement in religion which has inspired some of the greatest art, the
bloodiest wars, and the most brilliant philosophy in Western history.

THE TRADITIONAL CONCEPTION OF GOD

There have been many conceptions of God and many different gods in the
history of religion. But whatever the variations in belief and however broad

209

modern interest in religion has become, our dominant conception of God is inherited from the Old and New Testaments and the Jewish and Christian religions. This is not to say that the dominant conception is final or "the best," or even that it is a single conception rather than a summary of a great many conceptions. But it is necessarily the starting point of virtually any discussion of God and religion in our culture.

The power of religious experience does not mean that one cannot be rational and philosophical where religious matters are concerned. Some of the greatest philosophical thought in history can be found in the devoted rationalism of the medieval philosophers, especially in their attempts to understand religious experience and clarify the Christian conception of God. Their rationalism and analysis in no way interfered with their piety. Examination of our religious beliefs clearly does not necessarily entail a change in those beliefs. A moment's reflection reveals that our beliefs, no matter how personal, have much in common and require examination. The God of Judaism and Christianity has many characteristics that must be identified for our understanding. Most importantly, it is generally believed that God is an independent Being, the Creator of the universe and distinct from the universe He created. It is generally agreed that God is the supremely rational and moral Being, with concern for human justice and human suffering. It is agreed that He is all-powerful (*omnipotent*), all-knowing (*omniscient*), and that He is everywhere at once (*omnipresent*). In the Old Testament, it is made evident that God has emotions: for example, we read of God as "a jealous God" and we hear of "the wrath of God." It is also worth noting that we traditionally think of God as male, as in "God the Father," who created man (Adam, not Eve) "in His own image." It is the attempt to understand the Being who has these characteristics that defines Western theology and a great deal of Western metaphysics.

To insist that God is an independent Being, the Creator of the universe but distinct from that universe is of the utmost importance for traditional Western religion. You will appreciate why this belief is so important if you recall Spinoza's pantheism, in which he argues that God is nothing other than the universe. When people try to reinterpret God so that he is nothing other than some universal quality, as in "God is love," or "God is ultimate force," or "God is life," or "God is the universe," there is a very real possibility that they are actually denying that God exists as an independent Being. One can say "God is love" as shorthand for "God loves us and wants us to love each other" without this danger. But if one believes that God simply is identical to people's loving one another, then it is evident that this belief is no different from that of a person who might not believe in God at all, but just believes in love. Similarly, it is one thing to believe that God is a "force," among other things, who created the universe; but if you believe that God is just nothing other than a force that created the universe, without consciousness or concern, then your belief does not differ from someone who also believes that some force created the universe, but does not believe in God. Of course, there are alternative conceptions of God, some of which we shall discuss in this chapter. But in traditional Western religion, the independence of God from the uni-

[handwritten annotation at top: transcendence of God is the same as God being separate from the universe he created. (He transcends the universe)]

verse he created is an all-important belief. Philosophers and theologians refer to this independence as the *transcendence* of God. (Don't confuse this word with the adjective "transcendental" we used in Ch. 6.) We say that God "transcends" the universe and mankind. We also say that he "transcends" all human experience. It is this notion of transcendence which raises an immediate epistemological problem. If God transcends our experience, how can we know that He exists at all?

In some ancient religions, gods and goddesses were very much like human beings. They were usually stronger and perhaps smarter. They lived forever and had powers of special kinds (for example, they could change into animals at will, or cause changes in the weather with a snap of their fingers). The Greek and Roman gods, for example, were like this. They took sides and even fought in the Trojan War; they often misbehaved and became jealous or furious at one another. Philosophers use the word *anthropomorphism* when they refer to the perception of gods as more or less human. It is quite natural, when people try to envision their deities, that they should endow them with those characteristics they understand best, human characteristics.

The God of Judaism and Christianity is much less anthropomorphic than the gods and goddesses of ancient Greece and Rome. But it would be a mistake to deny that God is conceived in certain anthropomorphic ways as well. The God of the Hebrews frequently took their side in battle in the Old Testament, helping them to fell the walls of Jericho, keeping the sun still for extra hours or holding apart the waters of the Red Sea. The God of the Old Testament has many human emotions: he becomes jealous or angry when his commands are not carried out, having people swallowed by whales and sometimes destroying whole cities. Even the notion that God is a loving God carries with it anthropomorphism. It is often said that these are mere approximations, based on the fact that we can never really know or understand what God is like. (For example, it is often said that we cannot understand divine love, and use our all too human conception of love as the only example we can find.) But it must also be said that such anthropomorphic projections are in no way an objection to a belief in God; it is only to be expected that people will try to understand religion in those terms they know best. The biblical emphasis on God's sense of justice and his concern for mankind also demonstrates anthropomorphic characteristics, even if it is true, as we are so often told, that God's conception of justice may be very different from our own. And these characteristics are so important that, if a person does not believe that God is a merciful and concerned Being with a strong sense of justice, then that person probably does not believe in God at all. (For example, a person might believe in something like Aristotle's "prime mover," a first force that gets the universe moving, but it is highly debatable whether that should count as a "belief in God.") Prayer is meaningful only on the assumption that God listens to us and understands us; faith is intelligible only on the assumption that God cares about us. Without these characteristics, God would not be a moral force in our lives.

The traditional conception of God has been varied in so many ways that we can't even begin to consider them. The differences between the God of the Old Testament and the God of the New Testament have been often discussed. Then there are the obvious differences between the various sects of Judaism and Christianity. And the differences between the Judeo-Christian God and other gods (Zeus, Krishna, Isis) are so enormous that traditional Christians and Jews would hesitate to call these "God" at all. Furthermore, there are religions which do not have any god at all. But for our purposes in this chapter, it will be more than enough to stay within the bounds of our own traditions. Without considering the more modern variations of Judaism and Christianity or the sometimes considerable differences between their various sects, let us say that a person who believes in God with our previously enumerated characteristics (an independent Being, who is the Creator of the universe, all-powerful and all-knowing, and is rational, moral, concerned for man, with a perfect sense of justice) is a *theist*, a believer, whether Jewish, Catholic, Protestant, or Muslim. To refuse to believe in God is to be an *atheist*. (Spinoza was treated as an atheist in his time, even though he believed in something he called "God" because it lacked most of the characteristics just described.) To admit one's ignorance, and simply accept the fact that one does not know and perhaps has no way of knowing whether there is such a Being or not, is to be an *agnostic*.

CAN WE KNOW THAT GOD EXISTS?

It is one thing to be taught that there is a God, it is another thing to believe in God for good reason, rationality, and to know what one believes. Of course, there have been many people who have insisted that belief in God is not a matter of rationality or knowledge at all, but only of faith. But the turn to faith logically comes after attempts to know. The early Jews and Christians would not talk simply of "faith"; they claimed to know. So before we turn to examine faith, let us ask whether or not we can know that God exists.

The problem is a familiar one. Since God by definition transcends our experience, how can we have evidence for his existence? It is the same problem we faced with substance (and it is for that reason that God and substance are so easily interchanged in metaphysics, as for example, in Spinoza). There are people who claim to have been direct witnesses to miracles or to have heard God's own voice. But, assuming that none of us is one of them, our problem remains: should we believe their reports? Might they have been victims of imagination or hallucination? Is there any evidence in our experience that would allow us to know of God's existence? And if not, what reasons can we give for a belief in God?

In the long history of Christian theology, three major sets of "proofs" have emerged as attempts to demonstrate God's existence. Each has received various formulations, and all are still being discussed today. Their proper names are forebidding, but their logic can be easily explained. The first is the most difficult, for it is a purely logical proof; it attempts to argue from the idea of God to His necessary existence. It is this argument that Descartes used in his *Meditations* to prove God's existence from the idea that he (Descartes) had of Him. Similar arguments were to be found in both Spinoza and Leibniz. But the man who is generally credited with the invention of the argument is an eleventh century monk named Saint Anselm. Because the argument depends wholly on the idea of God's existence, it is called the *ontological argument*. Here is how Anselm presents it:

> Some time ago, at the urgent request of some of my brethren, I published a brief work, as an example of meditation on the grounds of faith. I wrote it in the role of one who seeks, by silent reasoning with himself, to learn what he does not know. But when I reflected on this little book, and saw that it was put together as a long chain of arguments, I began to ask myself whether *one* argument might possibly be found, resting on no other argument for its proof, but sufficient in itself to prove that God truly exists, and that he is the supreme good, needing nothing outside himself, but needful for the being and well-being of all things. I often turned my earnest attention to this problem, and at times I believed that I could put my finger on what I was looking for, but at other times it completely escaped my mind's eye, until finally, in despair, I decided to give up searching for something that seemed impossible to find. But when I tried to put the whole question out of my mind, so as to avoid crowding out other matters, with which I might make some progress, by this useless preoccupation, then, despite my unwillingness and resistance, it began to force itself on me more persistently than ever. Then, one day, when I was worn out by my vigorous resistance to the obsession, the solution I had ceased to hope for presented itself to me, in the very turmoil of my thoughts, so that I enthusiastically embraced the idea which in my disquiet, I had spurned.

. . . . .

GOD TRULY IS

And so, O Lord, since thou givest understanding to faith, give me to understand—as far as thou knowest it to be good for me—that thou dost exist, as we believe, and that thou art what we believe thee to be. Now we believe that thou art a being than which none greater can be thought. Or can it be that there is no such being, since "the fool hath said in his heart, 'There is no God' "? But when this same fool hears what I am saying—"A being than which none greater can be thought"—he understands what he hears, and what he understands is in his understanding, even if he does not understand that it exists. For it is one thing for an object to be in the understanding, and another thing to understand that it exists. When a painter considers beforehand what he is going to paint, he has it in his understanding, but he does not suppose that what he has not yet painted already exists. But when he has painted it, he both has it in his understanding and understands that what he has now produced exists. Even the fool, then, must be convinced that a being than which none greater can be thought exists at least in his understanding, since when he hears this he understands it, and whatever is understood is in the understanding. But clearly that than which a greater cannot be thought cannot exist in the understanding alone. For if it is actually in the understanding alone, it can be thought of as existing also in reality, and this is greater. Therefore, if that than which a greater cannot be thought is in the understanding alone, this same thing than which a greater cannot be thought is that than which a greater can be thought. But obviously this is impossible. Without doubt, therefore, there exists, both in the understanding and in reality, something than which a greater cannot be thought.

GOD CANNOT BE THOUGHT OF AS NONEXISTENT

And certainly it exists so truly that it cannot be thought of as nonexistent. For something can be thought of as existing, which cannot be thought of as not existing, and this is greater than that which *can* be thought of as not existing. Thus, if that than which a greater cannot be thought can be thought of as not existing, this very thing than which a greater cannot be thought is *not* that than which a greater cannot be thought. But this is contradictory. So, then, there truly is a being than which a greater cannot be thought—so truly that it cannot even be thought of as not existing.

And *thou* art this being, O Lord our God. Thou so truly are, then, O Lord my God, that thou canst not even be thought of as not existing. And this is right. For if some mind could think of something better than thou, the creature would rise above the Creator and judge its Creator; but this is altogether absurd. And indeed, whatever is, except thyself alone, can be thought of as not existing. Thou alone, therefore, of all beings, has being in the truest and highest sense, since no other being so truly exists, and thus every other being has less being. Why, then, has "the fool said in his heart, 'There is no God,'" when it is so obvious to the rational mind that, of all beings, thou dost exist supremely? Why indeed, unless it is that he is a stupid fool?

HOW THE FOOL HAS SAID IN HIS HEART
WHAT CANNOT BE THOUGHT

But how did he manage to say in his heart what he could not think? Or how is it that he was unable to think what he said in his heart? After all, to say in one's heart and to think are the same thing. Now if it is true—or, rather, since it is true—that he thought it, because he said it in his heart, but did not say it in his heart, since he could not think it, it is clear that something can be said in one's heart or thought in more than one way. For we think of a thing, in one sense, when we think of the word that signifies it, and in another sense, when we understand the very thing itself. Thus, in the first sense God can be thought of as nonexistent, but in the second sense this is quite impossible. For no one who understands what God is can think that God does not exist, even though he says these words in his heart—perhaps without any meaning, perhaps with some quite extraneous meaning. For God is that than which a greater cannot be thought, and whoever understands this rightly must understand that he exists in such a way that he cannot be nonexistent even in thought. He, therefore, who understands that God thus exists cannot think of him as nonexistent.

Thanks be to thee, good Lord, thanks be to thee, because I now understand by thy light what I formerly believed by thy gift, so that even if I were to refuse to believe in thy existence, I could not fail to understand its truth.[1]

The logic of the argument is deceptively simple: God is defined, innocently enough, as "a being greater than which none can be thought." Then, Anselm asks, "which would be greater, a being who is merely thought, or a being who actually exists?" The answer, of course, is a being who actually exists. But since God is, by definition, the greatest being who can be thought, he must therefore exist. "God cannot be nonexistent even in thought." It is a lightening-quick bit of reasoning. The argument has had a long, influential history, and logicians are still arguing about it. In the seventeenth century, Descartes (in his *Meditations*) argued another variation of the ontological argument:

But now, if just because I can draw the idea of something from my thought, it follows that all which I know clearly and distinctly as pertaining to this object does really belong to it, may I not derive from this an argument demonstrating the existence of God? It is certain that I no less find the idea of God, that is to say, the idea of a supremely perfect Being, in me, than that of any figure or number whatever it is; and I do not know any less clearly and distinctly that an [actual and] eternal existence pertains to this nature than I know that all that which I am able to demonstrate of some figure or number truly pertains to the nature of this figure or number, and therefore, although all that I concluded in the preceding Meditations were found to be false, the existence of God would pass with me as at least as certain as I have ever held the truths of mathematics (which concern only numbers and figures) to be.

This indeed is not at first manifest, since it would seem to present some appearance of being a sophism. For being accustomed in all other things to make a distinction between existence and essence, I easily persuade myself that the existence can be separated from the essence of God, and that we can thus conceive God as not actually existing. But, nevertheless, when I think of it with more attention, I clearly see that existence can no more be separated from the essence of God than can its having its three angles equal to two right angles be separated from the essence of a [rectilinear] triangle, or the idea of a mountain from the idea of a valley; and so there is not any less repugnance to our conceiving a God (that is, a Being supremely perfect) to whom existence is lacking (that is to say, to whom a certain perfection is lacking), than to conceive of a mountain which has no valley.

But although I cannot really conceive of a God without existence any more than a mountain without a valley, still from the fact that I conceive of a mountain with a valley, it does not follow that there is such a mountain in the world; similarly although I conceive of God as possessing existence, it would seem that it does not follow that there is a God which exists; for my thought does not impose any necessity upon things, and just as I may

[1] St. Anselm, *Proslogion,* in *A Scholastic Miscellany,* vol. 10, The Library of Christian Classics, ed. and trans. Eugene R. Fairweather (Philadelphia: Westminster Press, 1956).

imagine a winged horse, although no horse with wings exists, so I could perhaps attribute existence to God, although no God existed.

But a sophism is concealed in this objection; for from the fact that I cannot conceive a mountain without a valley, it does not follow that there is any mountain or any valley in existence, but only that the mountain and the valley, whether they exist or do not exist, cannot in any way be separated one from the other. While from the fact that I cannot conceive God without existence, it follows that existence is inseparable from Him, and hence that He really exists; not that my thought can bring this to pass, or impose any necessity on things, but, on the contrary, because the necessity which lies in the thing itself, i.e. the necessity of the existence of God determines me to think in this way. For it is not within my power to think of God without existence (that is of a supremely perfect Being devoid of a supreme perfection) though it is in my power to imagine a horse either with wings or without wings.

And we must not here object that it is in truth necessary for me to assert that God exists after having presupposed that He possesses every sort of perfection, since existence is one of these, but that as a matter of fact my original supposition was not necessary, just as it is not necessary to consider that all quadrilateral figures can be inscribed in the circle; for supposing I thought of this, I should be constrained to admit that the rhombus might be inscribed in the circle since it is a quadrilateral figure, which, however, is manifestly false. Although it is not necessary that I should at any time entertain the notion of God, nevertheless whenever it happens that I think of a first and a sovereign Being, and, so to speak, derive the idea of Him from the storehouse of my mind, it is necessary that I should attribute to Him every sort of perfection, although I do not get so far as to enumerate them all, or to apply my mind to each one in particular. And this necessity suffices to make me conclude (after having recognised that existence is a perfection) that this first and sovereign Being really exists; just as though it is not necessary for me ever to imagine any triangle, yet, whenever I wish to consider a rectilinear figure composed only of three angles, it is absolutely essential that I should attribute to it all those properties which serve to bring about the conclusion that its three angles are not greater than two right angles, even although I may not then be considering this point in particular. But when I consider which figures are capable of being inscribed in the circle, it is in no way necessary that I should think that all quadrilateral figures are of this number; on the contrary, I cannot even pretend that this is the case, so long as I do not desire to accept anything which I cannot conceive clearly and distinctly. And in consequence there is a great difference between the false suppositions such as this, and the true ideas born within me, the first and principal of which is that of God. For really I discern in many ways that this idea is not something factitious, and depending solely on my thought, but that it is the image of a true and immutable nature; first of all, because I cannot conceive anything but God himself to whose essence existence [necessarily] pertains; in the second place because it is not possible for me to conceive two or more Gods in this same position; and, granted that there is one such God who now exists, I see clearly that it is necessary that He should have existed from all eternity, and that He must exist eternally; and finally, because I know an infinitude of other properties in God, none of which I can either diminish or change.[2]

Descartes' version is:

> I cannot conceive of a God without the property of existence.
> ("His existence cannot be separated from His essence.")
> Therefore, God exists.

and then he adds,

> My conception of God is such that He has every sort of perfection.
> Existence is a perfection.
> Therefore, God necessarily exists.

These arguments are valid as stated, but are they also sound? Consider the following argument, which has been proposed in the same form as the above arguments. Define the devil as, "the worst imaginable creature." Now, which is "worse," a horrible creature that does exist, or one which does not? Obviously the one that exists. Therefore, the devil exists.

This unacceptable argument would seem to have the same form as the ontological argument; for that reason, we must be suspicious. If the argument form is valid, then how can it be that some instance of it is absurd? The answer must lie in the propositions involved.

The great philosopher Kant suggested that the problem lies in the central idea, shared by the ontological argument and the unacceptable argument that follows the same form, that existence is one of the essential properties, that is, part of the definition of a thing. But existence, Kant argues, is not a property and cannot be part of a definition. In an often quoted passage of his *Critique of Pure Reason*, he argues:

> My answer is as follows. There is already a contradiction in introducing the concept of existence—no matter under what title it may be disguised— into the concept of a thing which we profess to be thinking solely in reference to its possibility. If that be allowed as legitimate, a seeming victory has been won; but in actual fact nothing at all is said: the assertion is a mere tautology. We must ask: Is the proposition that *this or that thing* (which, whatever it may be, is allowed as possible) *exists*, an analytic or a synthetic proposition? If it is analytic, the assertion of the existence of the thing adds nothing to the thought of the thing; but in that case either the thought, which is in us, is the thing itself, or we have presupposed an existence as belonging to the realm of the possible, and have then, on that pretext, inferred its existence from its internal possibility—which is nothing but a miserable tautology. The word 'reality', which in the concept of the thing sounds other than the word 'existence' in the concept of the predicate, is of no avail in meeting this objection. For if all positing (no matter what it may be that is posited) is entitled reality, the thing with all its predicates is already posited in the

---

[2] René Descartes, "Meditation III," in *Meditations on First Philosophy*, in *The Philosophical Works of Descartes*, trans. Elizabeth S. Haldane and G. R. T. Ross (Cambridge: Cambridge University Press, 1911).

concept of the subject, and is assumed as actual; and in the predicate this is merely repeated. But if, on the other hand, we admit, as every reasonable person must, that all existential propositions are synthetic, how can we profess to maintain that the predicate of existence cannot be rejected without contradiction? This is a feature which is found only in analytic propositions, and is indeed precisely what constitutes their analytic character.

'*Being*' is obviously not a real predicate; that is, it is not a concept of something which could be added to the concept of a thing. It is merely the positing of a thing, or of certain determinations, as existing in themselves. Logically, it is merely the copula of a judgment. The proposition, 'God is omnipotent', contains two concepts, each of which has its object—God and omnipotence. The small word 'is' adds no new predicate, but only serves to posit the predicate *in its relation* to the subject. If, now, we take the subject (God) with all its predicates (among which is omnipotence), and say 'God is', or 'There is a God', we attach no new predicate to the concept of God, but only posit the subject in itself with all its predicates, and indeed posit it as being an *object* that stands in relation to my *concept*. The content of both must be one and the same; nothing can have been added to the concept, which expresses merely what is possible, by my thinking its object (through the expression 'it is') as given absolutely. Otherwise stated, the real contains no more than the merely possible. A hundred real dollars do not contain the least coin more than a hundred possible dollars. For as the latter signify the concept, and the former the object and the positing of the object, should the former contain more than the latter, my concept would not, in that case, express the whole object, and would not therefore be an adequate concept of it. My financial position is, however, affected very differently by a hundred real dollars than it is by the mere concept of them (that is, of their possibility). For the object, as it actually exists, is not analytically contained in my concept, but is added to my concept (which is a determination of my state) synthetically; and yet the conceived hundred dollars are not themselves in the least increased through thus acquiring existence outside my concept.[3]

What Kant is arguing is that the existence of a thing can never be merely a matter of logic. (This is what he means when he says that the proposition that a thing exists cannot be analytic.) "Existence" or "being," he argues, isn't a "real predicate" (though it is a grammatical predicate), because it does not tell us anything more about whatever is said to have existence or being. In other words, there is something odd about the statement, "this apple is red, round, ripe, and exists." What is odd is that "exists" does not give a characteristic of the apple, but rather says that there is an apple with these characteristics. The proper characterization of God, therefore, includes the various characteristics we discussed earlier in this chapter, but it should not include, according to Kant, any characteristic that implies God's existence. It is one thing to say that God, if he exists, has such-and-such characteristics,

---

[3] Immanuel Kant, *The Critique of Pure Reason,* trans. Norman Kemp Smith (London: St. Martin's Press, 1933).

it is something more to say that such a God exists. (This is what Kant means by his example about the 100 real versus 100 possible dollars; they both have exactly the same number of cents, but only the 100 real dollars are worth anything.)

Many contemporary philosophers agree with Kant's argument. But many do not. Furthermore, contemporary logicians have developed versions of the ontological argument that can even dispense with this controversial notion of existence as a property. For example, with just the seemingly innocent premise, "if God exists, then he necessarily exists," some logicians have recently argued according to the sophisticated rules of modern logic that the conclusion that "God exists" does follow. The premise is innocent because you can grant that "if God exists" without in anyway admitting that God in fact exists. Yet the argument works.

But even if the argument does not succeed in its classical form, it can be understood in another way, which clearly distinguishes it from all the absurd arguments which apparently have the same form. If you believe in God, then the argument might be taken in a very different way, not as a "proof" but as an attempt to articulate your belief. It has often been said that this is what Anselm's argument really tries to do, and as you read over his argument a second or third time it becomes clear that he is expressing his faith as much as he is offering a logical proof. In general, the "proofs" of God's existence have been such articulations and expressions as well as proper logical arguments. And even if they fail as proofs, they often succeed in this other and perhaps more important function.

It is clear that, considered simply as a logical argument, the ontological argument does not have the power to convert nonbelievers into believers. Or, if you are a believer, it is clear that an objection to the "proof" is not going to shake your faith in any way whatsoever. So the significance of the proof is ambiguous; as a logical exercise it is brilliant, as an expression of faith it may be edifying, but as an actual proof that God exists or as a means of converting atheists, it seems to have no power at all.

The second "proof" of God's existence is a set of arguments which date back to Aristotle's argument for the prime mover. The basis of all these arguments is the unthinkability of an infinite regress and the need for some ultimate explanation. Together, they are called the *cosmological argument,* and their best-known formulation is by Saint Thomas Aquinas as the first three of his "five ways" of proving God's existence.

> The first and more manifest way is the argument from motion. It is certain, and evident to our senses, that in the world some things are in motion. Now whatever is moved is moved by another, for nothing can be moved except it is in potentiality to that towards which it is moved whereas a thing moves inasmuch as it is in act. For motion is nothing else than the reduction of something from potentiality to actuality. But nothing can be reduced from potentiality to actuality, except by something in a state of actuality. Thus that which is actually hot, as fire, makes wood, which is

potentially hot, to be actually hot, and thereby moves and changes it. Now it is not possible that the same thing should be at once in actuality and potentiality in the same respect, but only in different respects. For what is actually hot cannot simultaneously be potentially hot; but it is simultaneously potentially cold. It is therefore impossible that in the same respect and in the same way a thing should be both mover and moved, i.e., that it should move itself. Therefore, whatever is moved must be moved by another. If that by which it is moved be itself moved, then this also must needs be moved by another, and that by another again. But this cannot go on to infinity, because then there would be no first mover, and consequently, no other mover, seeing that subsequent movers move only inasmuch as they are moved by the first mover, as the staff moves only because it is moved by the hand. Therefore, it is necessary to arrive at a first mover, moved by no other; and this everyone understands to be God.

The second way is from the nature of efficient cause.[4] In the world of sensible things we find there is an order of efficient causes. There is no case known (neither is it, indeed, possible) in which a thing is found to be the efficient cause of itself; for so it would be prior to itself, which is impossible. Now in efficient causes it is not possible to go on to infinity, because in all efficient causes following in order, the first is the cause of the intermediate cause, and the intermediate is the cause of the ultimate cause, whether the intermediate cause be several, or one only. Now to take away the cause is to take away the effect. Therefore, if there be no first cause among efficient causes, there will be no ultimate, nor any intermediate, cause. But if in efficient causes it is possible to go on to infinity, there will be no first efficient cause, neither will there be an ultimate effect, nor any intermediate efficient causes; all of which is plainly false. Therefore it is necessary to admit a first efficient cause, to which everyone gives the name of God.

The third way is taken from possibility and necessity, and runs thus. We find in nature things that are possible to be and not to be, since they are found to be generated, and to be corrupted, and consequently, it is possible for them to be and not to be. But it is impossible for these always to exist, for that which can not-be at some time is not. Therefore, if everything can not-be, then at one time there was nothing in existence. Now if this were true, even now there would be nothing in existence, because that which does not exist begins to exist only through something already existing. Therefore, if at one time nothing was in existence, it would have been impossible for anything to have begun to exist; and thus even now nothing would be in existence—which is absurd. Therefore, not all beings are merely possible, but there must exist something the existence of which is necessary. But every necessary thing either has its necessity caused by another, or not. Now it is impossible to go on to infinity in necessary things which have their necessity caused by another, as has been already proved in regard to efficient causes. Therefore we cannot but admit the existence of some being having of itself its own necessity, and not receiving it from another, but rather causing in others their necessity. This all men speak of as God.

---

[4] An *efficient cause* is an event (or an agent) that brings something about. The term comes from Aristotle. See glossary to Ch. 2, "cause."

And, in his "fourth way," Aquinas combines the form of the cosmological argument with some of the ideas from the ontological argument:

> The fourth way is taken from the gradation to be found in things. Among beings there are some more and some less good, true, noble, and the like. But *more* and *less* are predicated of different things according as they resemble in their different ways something which is the maximum, as a thing is said to be hotter according as it more nearly resembles that which is hottest; so that there is something which is truest, something best, something noblest, and, consequently, something which is most being, for those things that are greatest in truth are greatest in being, as it is written in [Aristotle's] *Metaphysics*. . . . Now the maximum in any genus is the cause of all in that genus, as fire, which is the maximum of heat, is the cause of all hot things, as is said in the same book. Therefore, there must also be something which is to all beings the cause of their being, goodness, and every other perfection; and this we call God.[5]

The cosmological argument, in all of these versions, is also both an attempt at "proof" and an expression of one's belief in God. Accordingly, it must be appreciated for its role in articulating the concept of God in traditional Christianity and evaluated as a logical argument. As a logical argument, there are two modern objections which seem to have considerable weight. First, even if the argument is formally valid, it proves only that there is some "first mover" or "first cause" or "necessary being." It does not prove that this being has any of the other attributes which allow us to recognize God. (Aquinas' fourth "way," however, includes moral attributes of perfection as well.) Taken at face value, the first three versions of the ontological argument are similar to Aristotle's argument for the "prime mover" (Chapter 1) and prove no more. In other words, one might accept the argument and believe only in a "first cause," but deny the existence of God. Or, if it is accepted that there must be a first cause, why could the universe itself not be its own cause? In current physics, scientists would argue that this idea is just as plausible as the idea that there must have been something else which caused our universe to exist. And this leads us to the second objection, which would have been unthinkable to Aquinas (or Aristotle), but is generally accepted today. The idea of an "infinite regress," that the universe did not have a beginning but has always existed, seemed like an obvious absurdity until the last century. But now, even though scientists and mathematicians talk about the beginning of the universe and the relativity of time, they no longer consider an infinite regress as necessarily impossible. And without the idea that every infinite regress is an absurdity, the cosmological argument loses its main premise.

The third "proof" of God's existence is the one that is probably most familiar to you. It is usually called "the argument from design" or, to give it its more technical name, *the teleological argument*. It is often the most universally appealing of the three arguments because it depends as much on our emotions and our sense of wonder as it does on logical principles. The classical form of the argument goes like this. Suppose you are walking across a deserted beach and come across a watch, lying in the sand. You immediately conclude, "people have been here." Why? Because it is highly unlikely that a mechanism as intricately designed as a watch might be thrown together by the chancy forces of nature. A pebble on the beach might be curiously shaped, but anything approaching the complexity of a tool or a piece of sculpture, much less a complex mechanism, would strike us as proof of some intelligent being. Now, looking at the universe, it is easy to wonder at its complexity, the intricate workings of the heavens or even a single-celled organism and the grand variety and interconnection of all living things. And from this, one concludes that the universe as a whole must have been rationally designed. No less a scientist than Albert Einstein, for example, has argued that it is this religious awe and appreciation for the complex regularities and "design" of nature that has spawned the great efforts of science to understand it.

> It is easy to see why the churches have always fought science and persecuted its devotees. On the other hand, I maintain that the cosmic religious feeling is the strongest and noblest motive for scientific research. Only those who realize the immense efforts and, above all, the devotion without which pioneer work in theoretical science cannot be achieved are able to grasp the strength of the emotion out of which alone such work, remote as it is from the immediate realities of life, can issue. What a deep conviction of the rationality of the universe and what a yearning to understand, were it but a feeble reflection of the mind revealed in this world, Kepler and Newton must have had to enable them to spend years of solitary labor in disentangling the principles of celestial mechanics! Those whose acquaintance with scientific research is derived chiefly from its practical results easily develop a completely false notion of the mentality of the men who, surrounded by a skeptical world, have shown the way to kindred spirits scattered wide through the world and the centuries. Only one who has devoted his life to similar ends can have a vivid realization of what has inspired these men and given them the strength to remain true to their purpose in spite of countless failures. It is cosmic religious feeling that gives a man such strength. A contemporary has said, not unjustly, that in this materialistic age of ours the serious scientific workers are the only profoundly religious people.[6]

And, classically, the teleological argument is Aquinas' "fifth way":

> The fifth way is taken from the governance of the world. We see that things which lack knowledge, such as natural bodies, act for an end, and this is evident from their acting always, or nearly always in the same way, so as to obtain the best result. Hence it is plain that they achieve their end, not fortuitously, but designedly. Now whatever lacks knowledge cannot move towards an end, unless it be directed by some being endowed with knowledge and intelligence; as the arrow is directed by the archer. Therefore

[6] Albert Einstein, "Religion and Science," in *Ideas and Opinions*, trans. Sonia Bargmann (New York: Crown, 1954).

some intelligent being exists by whom all natural things are directed to their end; and this being we call God.[7]

The argument is powerful psychologically, but it too has its problems. Like the earlier two arguments, it may prove much less about God than the theist needs to be proven. The God who has rationally designed the universe need not have the slightest concern for mankind, for example. He may well consider us just one of those little curiosities of evolution which, for a few thousand years, interfered with His other interests. But there are other problems, peculiar to this argument. It is easily mocked, and Voltaire, who was around when the argument was most popular, parodied its logic in *Candide* by suggesting that, among other things, it was marvelous that God designed our noses such that they would support spectacles. About the same time, the German Enlightenment-writer Georg Christoph Lichtenberg commented that it was clever of God to put holes in the cat's skin right where his eyes are. These nonsense-comments point to an important point, however. The "design" in nature appears as such only to one who is already predisposed to believe in a designer. This is most powerfully presented by David Hume in his blasphemous (and therefore posthumous) *Dialogues on Natural Religion:*

> In a word, Cleanthes, a man who follows your hypothesis is able, perhaps, to assert or conjecture that the universe sometime arose from something like design; but beyond that position he cannot ascertain one single circumstance and is left afterwards to fix every point of his theology by the utmost license of fancy and hypothesis. This world, for aught he knows, is very faulty and imperfect compared to a superior standard and was only the first rude essay of some infant deity who afterwards abandoned it, ashamed of his lame performance; it is the work only of some dependent, inferior deity and is the object of derision to his superiors; it is the production of old age and dotage in some superannuated deity and, ever since his death, has run on at adventures from the first impulse and active force which it received from him. You justly give signs of horror, Demea, at these strange suppositions; but these, and a thousand more of the same kind, are Cleanthes' suppositions, not mine. From the moment the attributes of the Deity are supposed finite, all these have place. And I cannot, for my part, think that so wild and unsettled a system of theology is, in any respect, preferable to none at all.
>
> These suppositions I absolutely disown, cried Cleanthes. They strike me, however, with no horror, especially when proposed in that rambling way in which they drop from you. On the contrary, they give me pleasure when I see that, by the utmost indulgence of your imagination, you never get rid of the hypothesis of design in the universe, but are obliged at every turn to have recourse to it. To this concession I adhere steadily; and this I regard as a sufficient foundation for religion.[8]

The credibility of the argument from design has suffered enormously from the shock of Darwin's theory of evolution. Accordingly, the Christian

[7] Aquinas, *Summa Theologica.*
[8] David Hume, *Dialogues on Natural Religion,* ed. Norman Kemp Smith (Oxford: Oxford University Press, 1935).

Church has combatted the latter with all of the resources at its command. But the battle has been largely unnecessary and, if anything, has falsely overemphasized the conflict between science and religion, weakening the credibility of the Church. For evolution does not deny the argument from design. It only changes the argument from the traditional idea that God created the universe all at once (though even in Genesis, He spread it out over several days) to the idea that He created it over a long period of time, using "natural selection" as one of His tools.

But the logic of evolution does undermine the argument from design in a more subtle way. The power of the argument is, boiled down to essentials, "isn't it marvelous that things are as they are!" But our "marvel" depends on our putting some premium on "the way things are." We place a high premium on "the way things are" because according to the laws of probability (or chance) the odds against this way are enormous. Now consider the following analogy: you are playing cards, stud poker, and the dealer gives you, twice in a row, excellent hands. You would be suspicious. The odds are against it. And, particularly if you lose both times, you will be certain that some "design" (namely the dealer's) is behind it. But now, why would you not have the same suspicions given any two consecutive hands, for the odds are exactly the same against any combination of cards? (The odds against receiving any one hand of five cards twice are 2,600,000:1.) The answer, of course, has nothing to do with the "likelihood" of getting one set of hands rather than another, but on the significance you place on the one combination rather than the other. So too, with the argument from design. Evolution has given the world many different "ways that things are," and will give it many more. The reason for our marveling at this particular "way that things are" is the fact that we suppose that the odds against it are uniquely high. But they are not. They are equally high against every other possible "way that things are," and so this "way" seems to deserve no special explanation.

Wittgenstein summed up this view towards the argument from design in a phrase; "what is remarkable is not how things are, but that they are at all." (This turns us back to the cosmological argument.) Or consider the following parable by one of Wittgenstein's students, John Wisdom:

> Two people return to their long neglected garden and find among the weeds a few of the old plants surprisingly vigorous. One says to the other "It must be that a gardener has been coming and doing something about these plants." Upon inquiry they find that no neighbor has ever seen anyone at work in their garden. The first man says to the other "He must have worked while people slept." The other says "No, someone would have heard him and besides, anybody who cared about the plants would have kept down these weeds." The first man says "Look at the way these are arranged. There is purpose and a feeling for beauty here. I believe that someone comes, someone invisible to mortal eyes. I believe that the more carefully we look the more we shall find confirmation of this." They examine the garden ever so carefully and sometimes they come on new things suggesting that a

gardener comes and sometimes they come on new things suggesting the contrary and even that a malicious person has been at work. Besides examining the garden carefully they also study what happens to gardens left without attention. Each learns all the other learns about this and about the garden. Consequently, when after all this, one says "I still believe a gardener comes" while the other says "I don't" their different words now reflect no difference as to what they have found in the garden, no difference as to what they would find in the garden if they looked further, and no difference about how fast untended gardens fall into disorder. At this stage, in this context, the gardener hypothesis has ceased to be experimental; the difference between one who accepts and one who rejects it is now not a matter of the one expecting something the other does not expect. What is the difference between them? The one says: "A gardener comes unseen and unheard. He is manifested only in his works with which we are all familiar." The other says "There is no gardener." And with this difference in what they say about the gardener goes a difference in how they feel toward the garden, in spite of the fact that neither expects anything of it which the other does not expect.

But is this the whole difference between them—that the one calls the garden by one name and feels one way toward it, while the other calls it by another name and feels in another way toward it? And if this is what the difference has become, then is it any longer appropriate to ask "Which is right?" or "Which is reasonable?"[9]

In other words, the main force of the teleological argument may not be as a proper "proof" of God's existence so much as an expression of belief in him. So considered, the argument may be extremely important even if it is not formally valid. And the religious answer may be just as reasonable as the non-religious one.

KNOWLEDGE AND FAITH

Can we know that God exists? The three traditional forms of "proof" don't seem to be adequate as literal proofs. In order to accept any of them, it looks as if one has to begin by believing in God. Moreover, what each of them proves is not the existence of *God,* but at most the existence of something; something that is defined by its existence, something that is a first cause, or something that is an intelligent "designer." But the most important attribute of the traditional Western God—the reason why men and women have worshipped Him, prayed to Him, feared Him, fought wars and died for Him—is their belief in God's divine justice. The single most important attributes of God in Western religion are his moral qualities. Without them, our belief in God would be very different than it is.

The importance of God in Western thought is his role as the source of our moral laws, as the judge of our actions and feelings, and as the sanction

[9] John Wisdom, "Gods," in *Proceedings of the Aristotelean Society,* XLV (London: Harrison & Sons, 1944–45).

that stands behind those laws and judgments. The preceding "proofs" of
God's existence are not wholly convincing, even if they are valid, just because
they leave out this all-important moral aspect of belief in God. What distinguishes theists from atheists is not a matter of mere theory or argument
("a mere hypothesis," the French philosopher La Place called it), but a
difference in lifestyle and confidence. The theist believes in a divine source of
morality, in a judgment of his actions that transcends everyday life, and the
promise (or threat) of reward (or punishment) after death. The atheist also
believes in morality, but not in divine morality, and he believes that all
judgments of our actions and all rewards and punishments must take place in
this life, or not at all. Accordingly, the question of our knowledge of God's
existence has a distinctly moral dimension.

Immanuel Kant, after attempting to refute all three of the traditional
arguments for God's existence, offered one of his own. He no longer tried to
"prove" God's existence as such, and even said that, strictly speaking, we
could have no knowledge of God at all, since God, as transcendent, cannot be
the object of any possible experience. So Kant, following a long tradition in
Christianity, said that belief in God is a matter of faith. But this does not
mean, as people so often take it to mean, that it was an irrational belief. Quite
to the contrary, Kant insisted that it was the most rational belief of all. For
without it, we would not have the anchor for our morality, nor would we
have any reason to suppose that our good deeds would in fact be eventually
rewarded or evil deeds punished. For it was obvious to Kant, as it has been
to every person with his or her eyes open since ancient times, that justice is
not always delivered in this life. Innocent children are butchered in wars; evil
men live grand lives well into old age. Therefore, according to Kant, it was
rational to believe in God, rational to have faith, even if faith was not,
strictly speaking, a matter of knowledge. It is, he says, a "Postulate of Practical Reason."

> The moral law led, in the foregoing analysis, to a practical problem
> which is assigned solely by pure reason and without any concurrence of
> sensuous incentives. It is the problem of the completeness of the first and
> principal part of the highest good, viz., morality; since this problem can be
> solved only in eternity, it led to the postulate of immortality. The same law
> must also lead us to affirm the possibility of the second element of the highest
> good, i.e., happiness proportional to that morality; it must do so just as
> disinterestedly as heretofore, by a purely impartial reason. This it can do on
> the supposition of the existence of a cause adequate to this effect, i.e., it
> must postulate the existence of God as necessarily belonging to the possibility
> of the highest good (the object of our will which is necessarily connected
> with the moral legislation of pure reason). We proceed to exhibit this con-
> nection in a convincing manner.
>
> Happiness is the condition of a rational being in the world, in whose
> whole existence everything goes according to wish and will. It thus rests on
> the harmony of nature with his entire end and with the essential determining

ground of his will. But the moral law commands as a law of freedom through motives wholly independent of nature and of its harmony with our faculty of desire (as incentives). Still, the acting rational being in the world is not at the same time the cause of the world and of nature itself. Hence there is not the slightest ground in the moral law for a necessary connection between the morality and proportionate happiness of a being which belongs to the world as one of its parts and as thus dependent on it. Not being nature's cause, his will cannot by its own strength bring nature, as it touches on his happiness, into complete harmony with his practical principles. Nevertheless, in the practical task of pure reason, i.e., in the necessary endeavor after the highest good, such a connection is postulated as necessary: we *should* seek to further the highest good (which therefore must be at least possible). Therefore also the existence is postulated of a cause of the whole of nature, itself distinct from nature, which contains the ground of the exact coincidence of happiness with morality. This supreme cause, however, must contain the ground of the agreement of nature not merely with a law of the will of rational beings but with the idea of this law so far as they make it the supreme ground of determination of the will. Thus it contains the ground of the agreement of nature not merely with actions moral in their form but also with their morality as the motives to such actions, i.e., with their moral intention. Therefore, the highest good is possible in the world only on the supposition of a supreme cause of nature which has a causality corresponding to the moral intention. Now a being which is capable of actions by the idea of laws is an intelligence (a rational being), and the causality of such a being according to this idea of laws is his will. Therefore, the supreme cause of nature, in so far as it must be presupposed for the highest good, is a being which is the cause (and consequently the author) of nature through understanding and will, i.e., God. As a consequence, the postulate of the possibility of a highest derived good (the best world) is at the same time the postulate of the reality of a highest original good, namely, the existence of God. Now it was our duty to promote the highest good; and it is not merely our privilege but a necessity connected with duty as a requisite to presuppose the possibility of this highest good. This presupposition is made only under the condition of the existence of God, and this condition inseparably connects this supposition with duty. Therefore, it is morally necessary to assume the existence of God.[10]

The key to Kant's argument is the obvious fact that good deeds are not always rewarded in this life and evil deeds are often not punished. Why then, he asks, should a person be moral and do what is right? If we are to rationally decide to be moral, therefore, we must also believe that happiness and morality will be in harmony (what Kant calls "the highest good"), that good people will be rewarded with happiness and evil people will be punished. But if this does not happen in this life, then we must believe that it happens in another life (". . . this problem can be solved only in eternity"). Furthermore, we must believe in some ultimate source of justice, a divine judge who will weigh good against evil and make certain that eternal happiness and

[10] Immanuel Kant, *Critique of Practical Reason,* trans. Lewis White Beck (New York: Bobbs-Merrill, 1956).

punishment is meted out fairly. This argument is at one and the same time a defense of the Christian belief in the immortality of the human soul and in God. It is necessary to believe in both, according to Kant, in order to sustain our willingness to be moral. "Therefore, it is morally necessary to assume the existence of God."

A similar position was argued more recently by the pragmatist William James. His position is a "pragmatic" one, that is, believing in God is "rational" insofar as it doesn't conflict with our other beliefs (for example, our beliefs in science, a matter which Kant stressed also) and if it tends to make us lead better lives. He argues:

> Science says things are; morality says some things are better than other things; and religion says essentially two things.
>
> First, she says that the best things are the more eternal things, the overlapping things, the things in the universe that throw the last stone, so to speak, and say the final word. "Perfection is eternal"—this phrase of Charles Secrétan seems a good way of putting this first affirmation of religion, an affirmation which obviously cannot yet be verified scientifically at all.
>
> The second affirmation of religion is that we are better off even now if we believe her first affirmation to be true.
>
> Now, let us consider what the logical elements of this situation are *in case the religious hypothesis in both its branches be really true.* (Of course, we must admit that possibility at the outset. If we are to discuss the question at all, it must involve a living option. If for any of you religion be a hypothesis that cannot, by any living possibility be true, then you need go no farther. I speak to the "saving remnant" alone.) So proceeding, we see, first, that religion offers itself as a *momentous* option. We are supposed to gain, even now, by our belief, and to lose by our nonbelief, a certain vital good. Secondly, religion is a *forced* option, so far as that good goes. We cannot escape the issue by remaining sceptical and waiting for more light, because, although we do avoid error in that way *if religion be untrue,* we lose the good, *if it be true,* just as certainly as if we positively chose to disbelieve. It is as if a man should hesitate indefinitely to ask a certain woman to marry him because he was not perfectly sure that she would prove an angel after he brought her home. Would he not cut himself off from that particular angel-possibility as decisively as if he went and married someone else? Scepticism, then, is not avoidance of option; it is option of a certain particular kind of risk. *Better risk loss of truth than chance of error*—that is your faith-vetoer's exact position. He is actively playing his stake as much as the believer is; he is backing the field against the religious hypothesis, just as the believer is backing the religious hypothesis against the field. To preach scepticism to us as a duty until "sufficient evidence" for religion be found, is tantamount therefore to telling us, when in presence of the religious hypothesis, that to yield to our fear of its being error is wiser and better than to yield to our hope that it may be true. It is not intellect against all passions, then; it is only intellect with one passion laying down its law. And by what, forsooth, is the supreme wisdom of this passion warranted? Dupery for dupery, what proof is there that dupery through hope is so much worse

than dupery through fear? I, for one, can see no proof; and I simply refuse obedience to the scientist's command to imitate his kind of option, in a case where my own stake is important enough to give me the right to choose my own form of risk. If religion be true and the evidence for it be still insufficient, I do not wish, by putting your extinguisher upon my nature (which feels to me as if it had after all some business in this matter), to forfeit my sole chance in life of getting upon the winning side—that chance depending, of course, on my willingness to run the risk of acting as if my passional need of taking the world religiously might be prophetic and right.

All this is on the supposition that it really may be prophetic and right, and that, even to us who are discussing the matter, religion is a live hypothesis which may be true. Now, to most of us religion comes in a still further way that makes a veto on our active faith even more illogical. The more perfect and more eternal aspect of the universe is represented in our religions as having personal form. The universe is no longer a mere *It* to us, but a *Thou*, if we are religious; and any relation that may be possible from person to person might be possible here. For instance, although in one sense we are passive portions of the universe, in another we show a curious autonomy, as if we were small active centres on our own account. We feel, too, as if the appeal of religion to us were made to our own active good-will, as if evidence might be forever withheld from us unless we met the hypothesis half-way. To take a trivial illustration: just as a man who in a company of gentlemen made no advances, asked a warrant for every concession, and believed no one's word without proof, would cut himself off by such churlishness from all the social rewards that a more trusting spirit would earn—so here, one who should shut himself up in snarling logicality and try to make the gods extort his recognition willy-nilly, or not get it at all, might cut himself off forever from his only opportunity of making the gods' acquaintance. This feeling, forced on us we know not whence, that by obstinately believing that there are gods (although not to do so would be so easy both for our logic and our life) we are doing the universe the deepest service we can, seems part of the living essence of the religious hypothesis. If the hypothesis *were* true in all its parts, including this one, then pure intellectualism, with its veto on our making willing advances, would be an absurdity; and some participation of our sympathetic nature would be logically required. I, therefore, for one, cannot see my way to accepting the agnostic rules of truth-seeking, or willfully agree to keep my willing nature out of the game. I cannot do so for this plain reason, that *a rule of thinking which would absolutely prevent me from acknowledging certain kinds of truth if those kinds of truth were really there, would be an irrational rule.* That for me is the long and short of the formal logic of the situation, no matter what the kinds of truth might materially be.[11]

This "practical" argument for belief in God ruled philosophy from the time of Kant until the present century. It has its origins in a short but brilliant argument by the French philosopher Blaise Pascal. Pascal offered an argument which he called a wager, literally a bet about God. It isn't a proof of God's

[11] William James, "The Will to Believe," in *The Will to Believe and Other Essays in Popular Philosophy* (New York: Longmans, Green, 1896).

existence in any sense; in fact, one of its explicit terms is the fact that we can't know whether God exists or not. But then, he says, if God exists, and we believe in Him, we are entitled to an infinite reward. If he exists and we don't believe in him, on the other hand, we are really in for it—eternal damnation. If he doesn't exist, however, the only difference is the small effort of piety or the small transient enjoyments of impiety that we expend or gain in the meantime. So, if we treat this as a betting situation, in which our option is simply to believe or not believe, our betting odds look like this.

IF WE BELIEVE	AND GOD EXISTS Then eternal reward	AND GOD DOESN'T EXIST We've wasted a little piety and missed some good times
IF WE DON'T BELIEVE	Then eternal damnation	Then we're O.K.; we've had some good times.

Looking at the odds as a betting person, it is obvious which option we ought to choose. The risk of eternal damnation overwhelms the promise of a few good times; and the promise of eternal reward is well worth the risk that we shall waste a little piety and miss a few good times. The conclusion, then, on strictly practical grounds, is that we ought to believe in God.

All three of these arguments by Kant, James and Pascal are based on the same all-important assumption, that "God is good." On the basis of this assumption, they then argue that it is rational to believe in God, even if it is not possible to prove (or even know) that he exists. Accordingly, belief in God is a matter of faith, but this faith can be argued and justified as rational belief. Just because it is faith and not knowledge, it does not follow that it is "blind faith" or irrational, beyond argument or arbitrary. To insist that belief in God is a matter of faith, therefore, is not to say that it is beyond the reach of philosophy or rational consideration.

The problem of evil

These "moral" arguments for believing in God are sound only as long as we accept the assumption that "God is good." There have been few theists who have actually denied this, of course, but there have been a great many, particularly in modern times, who have worried about it considerably. The problem is called "the problem of evil." It can be stated very simply, but the solution, if you believe in God, is not simple at all. The problem is this: if

Evil in the world

God is all-powerful (omnipotent), all-knowing (omniscient), and just, then how is it possible that there is so much unearned suffering and unpunished wickedness in the world? Or simply, if God exists, how can the world be so full of evil? It cannot be that He does not know of these misfortunes, for he is all-knowing. Nor can it be that he is unable to do anything about them, for he is all-powerful. And, if he is just and has concern for human beings, then he must care about protecting the innocent and punishing or preventing evil.

The problem of evil is a problem because no theist is willing to give up any of these vital attributes of God. The idea that God is not all-powerful, or that He doesn't know what is going on, or that He is not wholly just, is intolerable to traditional Christianity. So the problem is to show how there can be evil in the world without denying God any of his essential attributes. A partial solution is this: since God created men and women with "free will" and thereby the power to choose between good and evil, the evil and suffering in the world is not due to God's inability to do anything about it or His lack of knowledge or any injustice on His part. It is the fault of people, who misuse their freedom and create their own hardships. Having given humanity freedom of choice, it is argued, there is no reason why God should be blamed for human mistakes resulting from that freedom. It can even be argued that, having once given people freedom of choice, God ought not to interfere with their choices. Accordingly, evil is explained and the problem of evil seems solved, at least partially.

The problem arises once again, however, if we ask, "how could God have given people free will, knowing—as He must—that they would misuse it so badly?" Would everyone be much better off if we had a bit less "free will," or at least if we would have more desires to do good and fewer impulses to cause trouble and suffering? There are several traditional responses to this: one is that God has allowed us moral latitude to provide a test of our virtue, for if we were all "naturally" good, there would be little question of good versus evil or salvation versus damnation. But, it is open to question whether these distinctions are themselves desirable; wouldn't it have been better for humanity to have stayed in the Garden of Eden? Why did God have to create temptation, and what would have been lost from the world if Adam and Eve had been created with a bit more fortitude and obedience? And then there is the familiar defense, "but doesn't the world need some evil, in order that we recognize the good?" But it isn't at all obvious that we need anything like the amount of evil and suffering we have in the world in order to recognize what is good. You can see that the argument has a great many familiar defenses and rejoinders, and it would take a long chapter at least just to spell out the various objections and replies just to this "free will" solution to the problem of evil. But even if we were to agree on this "free will" defense of the traditional conception of God as omnipotent, omniscient, and perfectly just, laying the blame for suffering to people's own choices, that would not solve the problem of evil. This is why we said that the "free will" defense is, at best, a partial solution. For the obvious truth of the matter is that not all human

natural disaster

hardships and sufferings are our own doing, and that much of the evil in the world does not depend on human action in any way.

During the Enlightenment, the European world found itself in a state of theological confusion because of a monstrous earthquake that killed thousands of people, including many children, in Lisbon, Portugal. And to make matters worse, the earthquake struck on a Sunday morning, just as people were in church worshipping, so that the pious people were more likely to be killed than the atheists who had drunken themselves to sleep on the beach. And today, theists are forced to ask the same question after every such "natural" disaster: "Does it even make sense to say that God is punishing us or testing our faith?" What could justify a punishment that killed innocent children and spared the guilty? And what could justify a "test" in which people are killed just to see if they are still faithful? (The Job story is relevant here too. In general, ask yourself if the same actions would even be tolerable on a human scale. For example, what would we say of a father who punished his youngest child when the older children got into trouble? And what would we say of a father who spanked his children just to "test" their loyalty to him?)

A popular response at this point is to refer to "God's mysterious ways" and to argue that we cannot possibly understand God's ultimate purposes. This response does succeed in answering the problem of evil, but only at considerable cost. In all of the arguments we have considered so far, and in most of the history of Western religion, belief in God, and belief in God's omnipotence, omniscience, and perfect justice, has been a matter of rational belief (whether or not it was considered a matter of knowledge or of faith). But with the reference to "God's mysterious ways," we mark a major breach with this rational tradition, and we admit that, not only can we not know about God, but we cannot even understand or rationally argue these matters. In other words, the phrase "God's mysterious ways" solves the problem of evil only at the cost of ending discussion altogether.

There are many philosophers and religious people who do not object to this costly consequence. It is costly, they would argue, only to the interests of those who insist on arguing and understanding these religious matters; it need have no effect on religious belief itself. In the next section, we shall discuss some of these nonrational alternatives to the philosophy of religion. But it is first important to appreciate that there is a long history of efforts to solve the problem of evil and save a more or less traditional conception of God which do not take this drastic alternative. Spinoza's pantheism, for example, is one of these many attempts to save at least a nominal belief in God while getting around the problem of evil, in this case, by denying that God is just and by denying that he has any moral characteristics at all. On Spinoza's theory, God is identical to the universe. He is not its creator, and so is not responsible for the existence of evil in it. He is not a moral agent, so he has neither concern nor ability for the misfortunes and suffering of the world. He has no special concern for people, and no concern for justice. And, since Spinoza defends a strict determinism, in which no one—not even God—has "free will," questions of moral responsibility, reward and punishment, are irrelevant, a matter of human vanity, nothing more.

This way of avoiding the problem of evil was quite common in the Enlightenment, in that adolescence of Western thought in which people were rebelling against their medieval parents but not yet confident enough to stand on their own without God. The best example of this adolescent attitude was the French genius Voltaire. He was a vehement opponent of Christianity. ("I have heard enough how it took only 12 men to establish Christianity; I should like to prove that only one can destroy it.") But he couldn't give up God, so he invented a new religion (that he in many ways borrowed from the English), which sheered the concept of God of all His moral attributes, thus avoiding the problem of evil by denying God his attribute of "justice." "It makes no more sense to say that God is just or unjust than it does to say that he is blue or green." For Voltaire, God was just a "hypothesis," the creator who turned on the giant Newtonian machine, but then left it to go on its own. This peculiarly truncated version of theism is usually called *Deism*. It believes in God, but not much of a one. It is, essentially, an appeal to the cosmological argument; and it is satisfied with a minimal deity, which stops so far short of our traditional conception of God. Needless to say, Voltaire despised the "argument from design," with all of its hidden moralizing. The world is full of evil, Voltaire insisted, and there is no denying it. And since there is evil, there cannot be an all-powerful, all-knowing God who is also just. And there can be no appeal to his "mysterious ways." He has no "mysterious ways"; in fact, He has no "ways" at all.

The number of alternative religions during this intellectually creative period in our history was truly astounding. But virtually all had approximately the same purpose: to continue to believe in God, at least nominally, but to avoid the problem of evil by cutting out at least one of God's traditional attributes. It was during this period that Kant invented his "moral proof," attempting to plug up the problem of evil by postponing all judgments of justice until some indefinite future date. It was also during this period that many of the still popular formulas, "God is the energy of the universe," "God is life," and "God is universal love" became influential and respectable. The problem with these moves is already familiar: it is not clear whether they are, as they seem, revisions of the concept of God or rather subtle denials of God's existence. Many people have doubts about their religion at one time or another, but very few people are willing to jump immediately from theism to atheism (although people often jump from atheism to theism in a single "revelation"). Accordingly, people who are torn between religious belief on the one hand and arguments against such belief on the other often adopt an ambiguous intermediary position, holding onto the name of God explicitly but sometimes giving up much of the substance of their traditional belief. And just as this is an important crisis in individual lives, it is also a crisis in history. The Enlightenment was one such period in history. The outcome is by no means inevitable atheism; it might just as well be a renewed commitment to religion. But at least, such crises require rigorous thinking and a renewed attempt to understand and justify beliefs that were once taken for granted.

Faith and irrationality

Whenever you can defend your belief rationally, it is obviously desirable to do so. The move from rationality to irrationality in the defense of religion, therefore, is a serious step. Kant, who defended belief in God as a matter of faith, nevertheless defended this belief as rational. But there have always been religious people who have defended faith against reason, emphasizing the impossibility of rational justification and the irrelevance of the usual forms of understanding and knowledge where religion is concerned. In some cases, particularly in modern times, this step away from rationality may be a convenient escape from arguments and doubts that have become too overpowering. But it is not always, or even usually, taken for this reason. Instead, there has always been an enthusiastic movement within the sometimes overly formal confines of organized religion and dogma to emphasize the experience of religious belief. Such experience may well be indescribable and incommunicable. (Philosophers would thereby say it is *ineffable*.) But it is precisely the fact that it defies description and contradicts our everyday rational beliefs that makes such experiences so important to those who have had them.

Among the ancient Hebrews, there were already a considerable number of mystics who rejected the solid and conscientiously rational teachings of the religion in favor of its more mysterious and less describable experiences. And Christianity has always been powerfully motivated by its mystics; sometimes they were burned as heretics, others have been celebrated as saints. The history of Western religion has always had its nonrational side, in which faith depended upon passion and experience rather than argument and reason, even through those many centuries in which theism was generally accepted as the rational thing to believe and when the justification of this belief as knowledge had not yet been seriously challenged.

GOD AS EXPERIENCE: In earlier chapters, we discussed the rationalist notion of intuition, a special kind of experience which allows us to know some things for certain without argument and without abstraction from experience in the usual sense. According to the rationalists, we know the basic principles of logic and arithmetic in this way, and perhaps the basic principles of metaphysics as well. But when we introduced intuition, however, we emphasized that not everyone believed that intuition was part of rationality. In addition to rational insight, there may also be, according to most religious mystics, extra-rational or even irrational insight. Their epistemology is often ambiguous at this point. On the one hand, mystics want to deny the rational nature of their intuitions. But, at the same time, they want to insist that what they experience is true. You can see how this will generate considerable confusion.

When the mystic insists that his experience is true, he has made a claim which is on a par with the rationalist's claim (whether they agree or disagree in their conclusions). If they disagree, that is, if the mystic insists that there is a God (perhaps he has even "seen" Him) and the rationalist denies it, it should be obvious to you that there will be little room for constructive argument. The mystic considers the rationalist's arguments irrelevant; the rationalist considers the mystic to be obstinate and unwilling to argue rationally. It is at this point that, assuming the discussion does not degenerate to name-calling and fisticuffs, the rationalist will probably storm out of the room in frustration and the mystic, like a Zen master, may just shrug his shoulders. In such a case, that is probably the most rational response for both of them.

The mystic need not argue that what he has experienced is true, however. He might insist only that what he has "seen" is extremely important to him personally. And if he does so, it is clear that he need have no disagreement whatsoever with the rationalist, either in conclusions or in methods. They are different, of course; but not at odds. The mystic may simply be satisfied with saying that his experience is what it is, and not be concerned with claims about the nature of reality. This is rare, of course, since it is a rare person indeed who does not yield to the temptation to insist that his or her experience is the truth about reality as well. But whether the mystical experience is an intuition of the (more-or-less) traditional Judeo-Christian God, whether it is a vision of the Virgin, or simply a "feeling of oneness with the universe," whether the experience is the result of twenty years of prayer and meditation, or induced in an evening with peyote or mescaline, the philosophical question that follows is always one of interpretation. Without denying the reality of the experience, the question is always whether one ought to interpret the experience as the knowledge of reality. Is it just an experience? perhaps beautiful, worth repeating, even worth building your life around. But it is very different to claim that the experience is true, a breakthrough in our normal perceptions (or, perhaps, our everyday illusions) to the reality behind them. This is not to say that the mystic must be wrong. It is only to say that, given the impossibility of argument, there is no way to decide the issue. Just because the mystic is "irrational," doesn't mean that he is wrong.

The retreat to personal experience was the natural strategy for those many believers who saw the substance of their beliefs hard to defend against rational criticism. Following the Enlightenment, particularly in Germany, religion took a dramatic swing to the subjective. Attempts at rational defense were given up entirely. The German Romantic philosopher Friedrich Schliermacher insisted that religion was simply a matter of intense feelings of dependence, nothing more. (His contemporary Hegel wryly commented that this would make a dog a better Christian than most of us.) Other philosophers turned to modernized mysticism, including very contemporary experiments with drug-induced experiences, in an attempt to save their religion from all rational criticism. The point, always, was to make religion a personal experience, and valid as a personal experience, without making any claims that could be destroyed through rational argument.

THE LEAP OF FAITH: The best and most famous of all of these "new" Christians was an eccentric Danish philosopher, Søren Kierkegaard, who is often considered the father of both the "new" Christianity and that nonreligious philosophy called "existentialism." Kierkegaard was born into a society in which everyone was a Christian; they all believed the same dogmas, without thinking about them. They all went to the same (Lutheran) churches for Sunday services and Friday afternoon bingo games, and enjoyed these social gatherings immensely. They were all entitled to call themselves "Christians," just by virtue of the fact that they had been born of certain parents, brought as children to certain churches, and continued to mouth certain doctrines which they didn't understand or care to understand in the slightest. What they all lacked was passion. Their religion and they themselves, according to Kierkegaard, were boring through and through. Whatever happened to the phrase "the fear of God in their hearts?" These people felt no "fear"; just the comfort of a comfortable and self-righteous society and the warm swill of beer in their bellies, he complained. And Kierkegaard, who had been brought up in an unusually devout Lutheran home, was disgusted with them. This isn't Christianity, he insisted, and the sophisticated disputes over doctrine and dogma had nothing more to do with being religious than the calculations of an accountant at tax time.

Accordingly, Kierkegaard offered his alternative—a new (in fact very old) way of seeing oneself as a Christian. Rational argument was irrelevant. The doctrines of Christianity, he admitted, were absolutely absurd. But that didn't matter. In fact, it was the very absurdity of these beliefs that made the passion of Christianity possible. After all, if it were simply a matter of accepting some proposition, why should we feel anything. And "proofs" of God's existence, needless to say, were as irrelevant—in fact offensive—as you could imagine. "Christianity is passion!" he insisted. "Religion is feeling and commitment." No talk of "truth," unless you mean simply subjective truth, truth for me alone. No talk of "proof" and no talk of "rationality." There is simply, to use his most famous phrase, *the leap of faith,* across the borders of rationality and thinking to the passion-filled life of old-fashioned Christian fear and awe of God. "My only analogy is Socrates. My task is a Socratic task—to revise the conception of what it means to be a Christian."

Kierkegaard's move away from rationality is characterized as a rejection of "objectivity." Being a Christian, he says, is not a matter of "objective faith" (consisting of reason, doctrines, and "proofs") but of subjectivity, passion, and "inwardness."

> . . . The objective faith, what does that mean? It means a sum of doctrinal propositions. But suppose Christianity were nothing of the kind; suppose on the contrary it were inwardness, and hence also the paradox, so as to thrust the individual away objectively, in order to obtain significance

for the existing individual in the inwardness of his existence, in order to place him as decisively as no judge can place an accused person, between time and eternity in time, between heaven and hell in the time of salvation. The objective faith—it is as if Christianity also had been promulgated as a little system, if not quite so good as the Hegelian; it is as if Christ—aye, I speak without offense—it is as if Christ were a professor, and as if the Apostles had formed a little scientific society. Verily, if it was once difficult to become a Christian, now I believe it becomes increasingly difficult year by year, because it has now become so easy that the only ambition which stirs any competition is that of becoming a speculative philosopher. And yet the speculative philosopher is perhaps at the farthest possible remove from Christianity, and it is perhaps far preferable to be an offended individual who nevertheless sustains a relation to Christianity than a speculative philosopher who assumes to have understood it.

. . . . .

Suppose, on the other hand, that subjectivity is the truth, and that subjectivity is an existing subjectivity, then, if I may so express myself, Christianity fits perfectly into the picture. Subjectivity culminates in passion, Christianity is the paradox, paradox and passion are a mutual fit, and the paradox is altogether suited to one whose situation is, to be in the extremity of existence. Aye, never in all the world could there be found two lovers so wholly suited to one another as paradox and passion, and the strife between them is like the strife between lovers, when the dispute is about whether he first aroused her passion, or she his. And so it is here; the existing individual has by means of the paradox itself come to be placed in the extremity of existence. And what can be more splendid for lovers than that they are permitted a long time together without any alteration in the relationship between them, except that it becomes more intensive in inwardness?[12]

Religion is a confrontation with the unknown, not something knowable.

But what is this unknown something with which the Reason collides when inspired by its paradoxical passion, with the result of unsettling even man's knowledge of himself? It is the Unknown. It is not a human being, in so far as we know what man is; nor is it any other known thing. So let us call this unknown something: *the God.* It is nothing more than a name we assign to it. The idea of demonstrating that this unknown something (the God) exists, could scarcely suggest itself to the Reason. For if the God does not exist it would of course be impossible to prove it; and if he does exist it would be folly to attempt it. For at the very outset, in beginning my proof, I would have presupposed it, not as doubtful but as certain (a presupposition is never doubtful, for the very reason that it is a presupposition), since otherwise I would not begin, readily understanding that the whole would be impossible if he did not exist. But if when I speak of proving the God's existence I mean that I propose to prove that the Unknown, which exists, is the God, then I express myself unfortunately. For in that case I do not prove anything, least of all an existence, but merely develop the content of a con-

[12] Søren Kierkegaard, *Concluding Unscientific Postscript,* trans. David F. Swenson and Walter Lowrie (Princeton, N.J.: Princeton University Press, 1941).

ception. Generally speaking, it is a difficult matter to prove that anything exists; and what is still worse for the intrepid souls who undertake the venture, the difficulty is such that fame scarcely awaits those who concern themselves with it. The entire demonstration always turns into something very different and becomes an additional development of the consequences that flow from my having assumed that the object in question exists. Thus I always reason from existence, not toward existence, whether I move in the sphere of palpable sensible fact or in the realm of thought. I do not for example prove that a stone exists, but that some existing thing is a stone. The procedure in a court of justice does not prove that a criminal exists, but that the accused, whose existence is given, is a criminal. Whether we call existence an *accessorium* [something predicated] or the eternal *prius* [first given or assumed], it is never subject to demonstration. Let us take ample time for consideration. We have no such reason for haste as have those who from concern for themselves or for the God or for some other thing, must make haste to get existence demonstrated. Under such circumstances there may indeed be need for haste, especially if the prover sincerely seeks to appreciate the danger that he himself, or the thing in question, may be nonexistent unless the proof is finished and does not surreptitiously entertain the thought that it exists whether he succeeds in proving it or not.

If it were proposed to prove Napoleon's existence from Napoleon's deeds, would it not be a most curious proceeding? His existence does indeed explain his deeds, but the deeds do not prove *his* existence, unless I have already understood the word "his" so as thereby to have assumed his existence. But Napoleon is only an individual, and in so far there exists no absolute relationship between him and his deeds; some other person might have performed the same deeds. Perhaps this is the reason why I cannot pass from the deeds to existence. If I call these deeds the deeds of Napoleon the proof becomes superfluous, since I have already named him; if I ignore this, I can never prove from the deeds that they are Napoleon's, but only in a purely ideal manner that such deeds are the deeds of a great general, and so forth. But between the God and his works there is an absolute relationship; God is not a name but a concept. Is this perhaps the reason that his *essentia involvit existentiam* [essence entails existence]? The works of God are such that only the God can perform them. Just so, but where then are the works of the God? The works from which I would deduce his existence are not directly and immediately given. The wisdom in nature, the goodness, the wisdom in the governance of the world—are all these manifest, perhaps, upon the very face of things? Are we not here confronted with the most terrible temptations to doubt, and is it not impossible finally to dispose of all these doubts? But from such an order of things I will surely not attempt to prove God's existence; and even if I began I would never finish, and would in addition have to live constantly in suspense, lest something so terrible should suddenly happen that my bit of proof would be demolished. From what works then do I propose to derive the proof? From the works as apprehended through an ideal interpretation, i.e., such as they do not immediately reveal themselves. But in that case it is not from the works that I make the proof; I merely develop the ideality I have presupposed, and because of my confidence in *this* I make so bold as to defy all objections, even those that have not yet been made. In beginning my proof I presuppose the ideal interpretation, and also that I will be successful in carrying it through; but what else is this but to presuppose that the God exists, so that I really begin by virtue of confidence in him?[13]

You can see how little Kierkegaard thinks of the ingenious "proofs" of God's existence, as well as all attempts to "know" Him. The point of religion, he says, is precisely not to know, but rather to feel. And it is the absurdity and the irrationality of Christian doctrines, he insists, that makes this rare intensity of feeling possible.

> . . . The absurd is precisely by its objective repulsion the measure of the intensity of faith in inwardness. Suppose a man who wishes to acquire faith; let the comedy begin. He wishes to have faith, but he wishes also to safeguard himself by means of an objective inquiry and its approximation-process. What happens? With the help of the approximation-process the absurd becomes something different; it becomes probable, it becomes increasingly probable, it becomes extremely and emphatically probable. Now he is ready to believe it, and he ventures to claim for himself that he does not believe as shoemakers and tailors and simple folk believe, but only after long deliberation. Now he is ready to believe it; and lo, now it has become precisely impossible to believe it. Anything that is almost probable, or probable, or extremely and emphatically probable, is something he can almost know, or as good as know, or extremely and emphatically almost *know*—but it is impossible to *believe*. For the absurd is the object of faith, and the only object that can be believed.[14]

Christianity, Kierkegaard concludes, is suffering, the suffering that comes with the anticipation of our own death and our feeling of smallness and insignificance when we consider the eternal order of things. And for those who try to minimize this suffering through professional "understanding" and knowledge, Kierkegaard has little but sarcasm: "*The two ways.* One is to suffer; the other is to become a professor of the fact that another suffered."

GOD AS ULTIMATE CONCERN: Following Kierkegaard, Christian "irrationalism" changed the complexion of Western religion and gave faith a meaning that is not vulnerable to rational arguments. Recently, Paul Tillich proposed an extremely powerful form of Christianity that also gives up the traditional view of God and moves the focus of the religion to purely personal concerns and commitments. These are our religion, and we don't need anything more:

RELIGIOUS SYMBOLS

We have discussed the meaning of symbols generally because, as we said, man's ultimate concern must be expressed symbolically! One may ask: Why

[13] Søren Kierkegaard, *Philosophical Fragments,* trans. David Swenson (Princeton, N.J.: Princeton University Press, 1936).
[14] Kierkegaard, *Concluding Unscientific Postscript.*

can it not be expressed directly and properly? If money, success, or the nation is someone's ultimate concern, can this not be said in a direct way without symbolic language? Is it not only in those cases in which the content of the ultimate concern is called "God" that we are in the realm of symbols? The answer is that everything which is a matter of unconditional concern is made into a god. If the nation is someone's ultimate concern, the name of the nation becomes a sacred name and the nation receives divine qualities which far surpass the reality of the being and functioning of the nation. The nation then stands for and symbolizes the true ultimate, but in an idolatrous way. Success as ultimate concern is not the natural desire of actualizing potentialities, but is readiness to sacrifice all other values of life for the sake of a position of power and social predominance. The anxiety about not being a success is an idolatrous form of the anxiety about divine condemnation. Success is grace; lack of success, ultimate judgment. In this way concepts designating ordinary realities become idolatrous symbols of ultimate concern.

The reason for this transformation of concepts into symbols is the character of ultimacy and the nature of faith. That which is the true ultimate transcends the realm of finite reality infinitely. Therefore, no finite reality can express it directly and properly. Religiously speaking, God transcends his own name. This is why the use of his name easily becomes an abuse or a blasphemy. Whatever we say about that which concerns us ultimately, whether or not we call it God, has a symbolic meaning. It points beyond itself while participating in that to which it points. In no other way can faith express itself adequately. The language of faith is the language of symbols. If faith were what we have shown that it is not, such an assertion could not be made. But faith, understood as the state of being ultimately concerned, has no language other than symbols. When saying this I always expect the question: Only a symbol? He who asks this question shows that he has not understood the difference between signs and symbols nor the power of symbolic language, which surpasses in quality and strength the power of any nonsymbolic language. One should never say "only a symbol," but one should say "not less than a symbol." With this in mind we can now describe the different kinds of symbols of faith.

The fundamental symbol of our ultimate concern is God. It is always present in any act of faith, even if the act of faith includes the denial of God. Where there is ultimate concern, God can be denied only in the name of God. One God can deny the other one. Ultimate concern cannot deny its own character as ultimate. Therefore, it affirms what is meant by the word "God." Atheism, consequently, can only mean the attempt to remove any ultimate concern—to remain unconcerned about the meaning of one's existence. Indifference toward the ultimate question is the only imaginable form of atheism. Whether it is possible is a problem which must remain unsolved at this point. In any case, he who denies God as a matter of ultimate concern affirms God, because he affirms ultimacy in his concern. God is the fundamental symbol for what concerns us ultimately. Again it would be completely wrong to ask: So God is nothing but a symbol? Because the next question has to be: A symbol for what? And then the answer would be: For God! God is symbol for God. This means that in the person of God we must distinguish two elements: the element of ultimacy, which is a matter of im-

mediate experience and not symbolic in itself, and the element of concreteness, which is taken from our ordinary experience and symbolically applied
to God. The man whose ultimate concern is a sacred tree has both the ultimacy of concern and the concreteness of the tree which symbolizes his relation to the ultimate. The man who adores Apollo is ultimately concerned,
but not in an abstract way. His ultimate concern is symbolized in the divine
figure of Apollo. The man who glorifies Jahweh, the God of the Old Testament, has both an ultimate concern and a concrete image of what concerns
him ultimately. This is the meaning of the seemingly cryptic statement that
God is the symbol of God. In this qualified sense God is the fundamental
and universal content of faith.

It is obvious that such an understanding of the meaning of God makes
the discussions about the existence or nonexistence of God meaningless. It is
meaningless to question the ultimacy of an ultimate concern. This element
in the idea of God is in itself certain. The symbolic expression of this element varies endlessly through the whole history of mankind. Here again it
would be meaningless to ask whether one or another of the figures in which
an ultimate concern is symbolized does "exist." If "existence" refers to something which can be found within the whole of reality, no divine being exists.
The question is not this, but: Which of the innumerable symbols of faith is
most adequate to the meaning of faith? In other words, which symbol of
ultimacy expresses the ultimate without idolatrous elements? This is the problem, and not the so-called "existence of God"—which is in itself an impossible combination of words. God as the ultimate in man's ultimate concern
is more certain than any other certainty, even that of oneself. God as symbolized in a divine figure is a matter of daring faith, of courage and risk.

God is the basic symbol of faith, but not the only one. All the qualities
we attribute to him, power, love, justice, are taken from finite experiences
and applied symbolically to that which is beyond finitude and infinity. If
faith calls God "almighty," it uses the human experience of power in order
to symbolize the content of its infinite concern, but it does not describe a
highest being who can do as he pleases. So it is with all the other qualities
and with all the actions, past, present, and future, which men attribute to
God. They are symbols taken from our daily experience, and not information about what God did once upon a time or will do sometime in the
future. Faith is not the belief in such stories, but it is the acceptance of
symbols that express our ultimate concern in terms of divine actions.

Another group of symbols of faith are manifestations of the divine in
things and events, in persons and communities, in words and documents. This
whole realm of sacred objects is a treasure of symbols. Holy things are not
holy in themselves, but they point beyond themselves to the source of all
holiness, that which is of ultimate concern.[15]

Notice how far Tillich has moved from the traditional Judeo-Christian
conception of God. Yet he is still a theist and a Christian. But "God" for him
does not mean that divine being discussed in the Old and New Testaments
but a symbol of "ultimate concern." The belief in God is now expanded to

[15] Paul Tillich, *Dynamics of Faith* (New York: Harper & Row and London: George
Allen and Unwin, 1957).

represent the fact that one finds his or her life meaningful. Tillich says that this "makes the discussions about the existence or non-existence of God meaningless." It also undercuts the traditional idea that God is a single kind of Being with precisely the characteristics we discussed in the beginning of this chapter. God is whatever concerns us ultimately, whatever is most important in our lives. This is even true, Tillich says, when one denies the existence of God. "Where there is ultimate concern, God can be denied only in the name of God."

DOUBT

One can still be religious and be an atheist. A Zen Buddhist, for example, may be extremely religious, but he or she does not believe in God. One can be religious as a humanist—as a lover of humanity—and not believe in God. Religion, in general, is the sense that something, at least, is sacred. But, in the context of traditional Western religion, being an *atheist* means one thing in particular, not believing in God. For some, atheism is not merely an intellectual position, it is a tragedy. For others, it is simply the logical conclusion of contemporary rationality and a proper antidote for centuries of superstition. In the following two selections, we will see the difference between these views. The first is a selection from the great Russian novelist, Fyodor Dostoevsky, who found himself facing unwelcome and terrifying doubts about Christianity. He reflects his despair in all of his works. His doubts begin with the problem of evil, but develop to such a pitch that he begins to wonder whether the whole of Christianity has been nothing more than a sham, so much so that, if Christ were to return as promised, he would be burned as a heretic. The second selection, as different as possible, is by A. J. Ayer, the British logical positivist, who, in the cool and logical style of that movement, dismantles religion like an old piece of machinery that has never worked correctly.

Here is Dostoevsky.

"It will reduce the scope of my argument to about a tenth of the total, but I still prefer to restrict myself to the subject of children. Not that that restriction is to my advantage. But, in the first place, it *is* possible to love children, at close quarters, even if they are dirty, even if they have ugly faces, although to me a child's face is never really ugly. In the second place, I also will not speak of adults at the moment, because, besides being disgusting and undeserving of love, they have something to compensate them for their suffering: they have eaten their apple of knowledge, they know about good and evil and are like gods themselves. And they keep eating the apple. But little children haven't eaten it. They're not yet guilty of anything. Do you like small children, Alyosha? I know you do and that you'll understand why I have chosen to speak exclusively of them. Well then, if they suffer here in this world, it's because they're paying for the sins of their fathers who ate the apple. But that is the reasoning of another world and it's incomprehensible to the human heart here on earth. No innocent should be made to suffer for another man's sins, especially innocents such as these!

. . . . .

"Do you understand this . . . my dear friend, my brother, you gentle novice who is so eager to spend his life in the service of God? Tell me, do you understand the purpose of this absurdity? Who needs it and why was it created? They say that man could not do without it on earth, for otherwise he would not be able to learn the difference between good and evil. But I say I'd rather not know about their damned good and evil than pay such a terrible price for it. I feel that all universal knowledge is not worth that child's tears when she was begging 'gentle Jesus' to help her! I'm not even talking about the sufferings of adults: they, at least, have eaten their apple of knowledge, so the hell with them. But it's different when it comes to children. It seems I'm hurting you, Alyosha, my boy. You don't look very well. I won't go on if you don't want me to."

"Never mind. I want to suffer too," Alyosha mumbled.

"One more little sketch then, the last, and that only because it's a rather curious little story and a very typical one.

"Well, this happened early in our nineteenth century, during the darkest days of serfdom—and, by the way, long live our Tsar Alexander II, the Liberator of the People! Well then, at the turn of this century, there lived a retired general, a man with the highest connections, a big landowner, one of those, you know (although even at that time there were only a few such left), who, upon retiring from the service of their country, feel sure that they have earned the right of life and death over those subjected to them. Yes, there used to be such people then. This general lived on his estate, which had two thousand serfs. He strutted around, feeling immensely important, and bullying his lesser neighbors as if they were hangers-on and clowns obliged to amuse him. He had hundreds of hounds and just about as many kennel attendants, all dressed in special livery and every one of them mounted.

"It so happened that one day an eight-year-old boy, playing in the courtyard, threw a stone and inadvertently hit the General's favorite hound in the leg, injuring it. 'Why is my favorite hound limping?' the General demanded, and he was informed that the boy had hit it with a stone. 'So it was you,' the General said, looking the boy up and down. 'Lock him up.' They took the boy away from his mother and locked him up in the guardroom for the whole night. The next day, at dawn, the General rode out to the hunt in full dress, surrounded by his obsequious neighbors, hounds, kennel attendants, huntsmen, every one of them on horseback. All the serfs of the estate were summoned too, for their edification, and so was the boy's mother. They brought the boy out of the guardroom. It was a bleak, foggy, raw day—an ideal day for hunting. The General ordered the boy stripped naked. The boy was shivering. He seemed paralyzed with fear. He didn't dare utter a sound. 'Off with him now, chase him!' 'Hey, you, run, run!' a flunkey yelled, and the boy started to run. 'Sic 'im!' the General roared. The whole pack was set on the boy and the hounds tore him to pieces before his mother's eyes. I believe that, as a result of this, the General was later declared incompetent to administer his own estates without an appointed supervisory body. . . . But perhaps you could tell me what should have been done in this case? Perhaps he ought to have been shot, to satisfy the moral indignation that such an act arouses in us? Well, speak up, my boy, go on!"

"Yes, shot . . ." Alyosha murmured, raising his eyes to his brother with a strange, faint, twisted grin.

"Good!" Ivan cried with affected delight. "Now, if you say so, it really shows that . . . Ah, you little novice, so there is that devil lurking in your heart too, you wicked Alyosha Karamazov, you!"

"What I said was pretty stupid, but. . . ."

"Yes, that 'but' is just the thing!" Ivan cried. "I want you to know, novice, that absurdity is very much needed on this earth of ours. Indeed, the whole universe is founded on absurdity, and, perhaps, without absurdity there would be nothing at all. There are a few things we do know, after all."

. . . . .

Ivan remained silent for a moment and suddenly his face grew very sad.

"I want you to understand me," he said. "I spoke only of small children to make my point more obvious. I didn't mention the other human tears with which our earth is soaked from crust to core, because I was deliberately narrowing the subject. I'm nothing but a bug and I most humbly admit that it's quite beyond me why things are arranged the way they are. I suppose that men themselves are to blame for it: they were given a paradise on earth, but they wanted freedom and they stole fire from heaven, although they knew that it would bring them unhappiness. So there's no reason to be sorry for them. All that my puny, Euclidean, earthling's mind can grasp is that there is such a thing as suffering, that no one can be blamed for it, that quite uncomplicatedly cause precedes effect, that everything that flows finds its proper level—but then all that is just Euclidean gibberish, and, being aware of that fact, I cannot agree to live by it! What good does it do me to know that no one is to blame, that every effect is determined by a cause, which itself is an effect of some other cause, and so on, and that, therefore, no one should ever be blamed for anything? For, even though I may know it, I still need retribution. Without it I'd rather destroy myself. And I must have that retribution not somewhere far off in infinity but here, on earth. I want to see it myself. I believe in justice and I want to see justice done with my own eyes; if I should be dead by that time, I want to be brought back to life, because the idea that, when justice finally does triumph, I won't even be there to witness it is too abhorrent to me. No, I want to see with my own eyes the lamb lie down with the lion and the resurrected victim rise and embrace his murderer. I want to be here when everyone understands why the world has been arranged the way it is. It is on that craving for understanding that all human religions are founded, so I am a believer. But then, what about the children? How will we ever account for their sufferings? For the hundredth time I repeat, there are many questions that could be asked, but I ask you only one—about the children—because I believe it conveys fully and clearly what I am trying to tell you. Listen, even if we assume that every person must suffer because his suffering is necessary to pay for eternal harmony, still do tell me, for God's sake, where the children come in. If the suffering of little children is needed to complete the sum total of suffering required to pay for the truth, I don't want that truth, and I declare in advance that all the truth in the world is not worth the price! And finally, I don't really want to see the mother of the little boy embrace the man who set the hounds on him to tear him apart! She won't be able to forgive him. If she wants to, she may forgive him for herself, for having caused her, the mother, infinite suffering. But she has no right to forgive him for her child torn to pieces. She may not forgive him, even if the child chooses to forgive him himself. And if I am right, if they cannot forgive, what harmony can there be? Is there one single creature in the whole world who could forgive or would have the right to do so? No, I want no part of any harmony; I don't want it, out of love for mankind. I prefer to remain with my unavenged suffering and my unappeased anger—*even if I happen to be wrong*. I feel, moreover, that such harmony is rather overpriced. We cannot afford to pay so much for a ticket. And so I hasten to return the ticket I've been sent. If I'm honest, it is my duty to return it as long as possible before the show. And that's just what I'm trying to do, Alyosha. It isn't that I reject God; I am simply returning Him most respectfully the ticket that would entitle me to a seat."

"That's rebellion," Alyosha said softly, lowering his eyes.

"Rebellion? I wish you hadn't used that word," Ivan said feelingly. "I don't believe it's possible to live in rebellion, and I want to live! Tell me yourself—I challenge you: let's assume that you were called upon to build the edifice of human destiny so that men would finally be happy and would find peace and tranquility. If you knew that, in order to attain this, you would have to torture just one single creature, let's say the little girl who beat her chest so desperately in the outhouse, and that on her unavenged tears you could build that edifice, would you agree to do it? Tell me and don't lie!"

"No, I would not," Alyosha said softly.

"And do you find acceptable the idea that those for whom you are building that edifice should gratefully receive a happiness that rests on the blood of a tortured child and, having received it, should continue to enjoy it eternally?"

"No, I do not find that acceptable," Alyosha said and his eyes suddenly flared up. "But a moment ago you asked whether there was in the world 'a single creature who could forgive.' Well, there is. And He can forgive everyone for everything, because He Himself gave His innocent blood for everyone's sins and for everyone's sake. You forgot to mention Him, although it is on Him that the edifice must be founded, it is to Him that they will sing, 'You were right, O Lord, for Your ways have now been revealed to us!' "

"You mean 'the one without sin' and His blood! No, Alyosha, I hadn't forgotten about Him. Indeed, I was wondering how long it would take you to bring Him into our discussion, because the people on your side usually make use of Him above all else in their arguments. You know—well, don't laugh now—about a year or so ago I composed a sort of poem and, if

you're willing to waste, say, another ten minutes with me, I could recite it
to you."

"You? You wrote a poem?"

"Why should an author forego even one listener, after all?" Ivan said with
a grin. "So, are you willing to hear it?"

"I'm listening attentively."

"My poem is called 'The Grand Inquisitor.' It's a ridiculous piece really,
but I'd like you to hear it."

THE GRAND INQUISITOR

"Fifteen centuries have passed since He promised to come in His glory,
fifteen centuries since His prophet wrote, 'Behold, I come quickly.' 'Of that
day and hour knoweth no man, neither the Son, but the Father,' as He Himself announced when He was still on earth. But men still wait for Him with
the same faith, with the same love. Nay, with even greater faith, for fifteen
centuries have passed without a sign from heaven to mankind.

". . . He decided to show Himself, if only for a moment, to His people,
long-suffering, tormented, sinful people who loved Him with a child-like
love. My story takes place in Spain, in Seville, during the grimmest days of
the Inquisition, when throughout the country fires were burning endlessly
to the greater glory of God and

> In autos-da-fé resplendent
> Wicked heretics were burned.

"Of course, this was not the coming in which He had promised to appear
in all His heavenly glory at the end of time and which would be as sudden
as a bolt of lightning cutting the sky from east to west. No, He wanted to
come only for a moment to visit His children and He chose to appear where
the fires were crackling under the heretics.

"In His infinite mercy He came among men in human form, just as He
had walked among them fifteen centuries before. He came down to that sun-
baked Southern city the day after nearly a hundred heretics had been burned
all at once *ad majorem gloriam Dei,* in a resplendent auto-da-fé by the
order of the Cardinal, the Grand Inquisitor, and in the presence of the King,
the royal court, knights, beautiful ladies-in-waiting, and the entire population
of Seville.

"He came unobserved and moved about silently but, strangely enough,
those who saw Him recognized Him at once. This might, perhaps, be the
best part of my poem—I mean if I could explain what made them recognize
Him . . . People are drawn to Him by an irresistible force, they gather
around Him, follow Him, and soon there is a crowd. He walks among them
in silence, a gentle smile of infinite compassion on His lips. The sun of love
burns in His heart; light, understanding, and spiritual power flow from His
eyes and set people's hearts vibrating with love for Him. He holds His hands
out to them, blesses them, and just from touching Him, or even His clothes,
comes a healing power. An old man who has been blind from childhood
suddenly cries out to Him: 'Cure me, O Lord, so that I may see You too!'

And it is as if scales had fallen from his eyes, and the blind man sees Him. People weep and kiss the ground on which He walks. Children scatter flowers in His path and cry out to Him, 'Hosannah!' 'It is He, He Himself!' people keep saying. 'Who else could it be!' He stops on the steps of the cathedral of Seville at a moment when a small white coffin is carried into the church by weeping bearers. In it lies a girl of seven, the only daughter of a prominent man. She lies there amidst flowers. 'He will raise your child from the dead!' people shout to the weeping mother. The priest, who has come out of the cathedral to meet the procession, looks perplexed and frowns. But now the mother of the dead child throws herself at His feet, wailing, 'If it is truly You, give me back my child!' and she stretches out her hands to Him. The procession stops. They put the coffin down at His feet. He looks down with compassion, His lips form the words *Talitha cumi*—arise, maiden—and the maiden arises. The little girl sits up in her coffin, opens her little eyes, looks around in surprise, and smiles. She holds the white roses that had been placed in her hand when they had laid her in the coffin. There is confusion among the people, shouting and weeping . . .

"Just at that moment, the Cardinal, the Grand Inquisitor himself, crosses the cathedral square. He is a man of almost ninety, tall and erect. His face is drawn, his eyes are sunken, but they still glow as though a spark smoldered in them. Oh, now he is not wearing his magnificent cardinal's robes in which he paraded before the crowds the day before, when they were burning the enemies of the Roman Church; no, today he is wearing just the coarse cassock of an ordinary monk. He is followed by his grisly assistants, his slaves, his 'holy guard.' He sees the crowd gathered, stops, and watches from a distance. He sees everything: the placing of the coffin at His feet and the girl rising from it. His face darkens. He knits his thick white brows; his eyes flash with an ominous fire. He points his finger and orders his guards to seize Him.

"The Grand Inquisitor's power is so great and the people are so submissive and tremblingly obedient to him that they immediately open up a passage for the guards. A death-like silence descends upon the square and in that silence the guards lay hands on Him and lead Him away.

"Then everyone in the crowd, to a man, prostrates himself before the Grand Inquisitor. The old man blesses them in silence and passes on.

"The guards take their prisoner to an old building of the Holy Inquisition and lock Him up there in a dark, narrow, vaulted prison cell. The day declines and is replaced by the stifling, black Southern night of Seville. The air is fragrant with laurel and lemon.

"Suddenly, in the complete darkness, the iron gate of the cell opens and there stands the Grand Inquisitor himself, holding a light in his hand. The old man enters the cell alone and, when he is inside, the door closes behind him. He stops and for a long time—one or even two minutes—he looks at Him. At last he sets the light down on the table and says: 'You? Is it really You?' Receiving no answer, he continues in great haste:

" 'You need not answer me. Say nothing. I know only too well what You could tell me now. Besides, You have no right to add anything to what You said before. Why did You come here, to interfere and make things difficult for us? For You came to interfere—You know it. But shall I tell You what will happen tomorrow? Well, I do not know who You really are, nor do I want to know whether You are really He or just a likeness of Him, but no later than tomorrow I shall pronounce You the wickedest of all heretics and sentence You to be burned at the stake, and the very people who today were kissing Your feet will tomorrow, at a sign of my hand, hasten to Your stake to rake the coals. Don't You know it? Oh yes, I suppose You do,' he added, deeply immersed in thought, his eyes fixed for a moment on his prisoner."

"And the prisoner—He just looks at him and says nothing?"

"Why, yes," Ivan laughed once more, "and that's as it should be in any case. Besides, the old man himself reminds Him that He may not add a single word to what He has said before. I might add that this may be the most crucial feature of Roman Catholicism, at least the way I see it. It's as if the Grand Inquisitor said to Him: 'You have transmitted all Your authority to the Pope and now he wields it. As to You, You had better stay away or, at any rate, not interfere with us for the time being.' They don't just say that, they even have it in writing, at least the Jesuits have. I've read it myself in the works of their theologians.

" 'Do You think You have the right to reveal even a single mystery of the world from which You come?' the Grand Inquisitor asks Him and then answers himself: 'No, You do not, for You may not add anything to what has been said before and You may not deprive men of the freedom You defended so strongly when You were on earth. Anything new that You might reveal to them now would encroach upon the freedom of their faith, for it would come to them as a miracle, and fifteen centuries ago it was freely given faith that was most important to You. Didn't You often tell them then that You wanted to make them free. Well, then,' the old man adds with a grin, 'so now You have seen *free* men. Yes, that business cost us a great deal,' he continues, looking sternly at Him, 'but at last, in Your name, we saw it through. For fifteen hundred years we were pestered by that notion of freedom, but in the end we succeeded in getting rid of it, and now we are rid of it for good. You don't believe that we got rid of it, do You? You look at me so gently, and You do not even consider me worthy of Your anger? I want You to know, though, that on this very day men are convinced that they are freer than they have ever been, although they themselves brought us their freedom and put it meekly at our feet. This is what we have achieved, but was it really what You wanted, was this the freedom that You wanted to bring them?' "

"I'm afraid I'm lost again," Alyosha interrupted Ivan, "is he being sarcastic? Is he laughing at Him?"

"He certainly is not. Indeed, he is claiming for himself and his church the credit for having done away with freedom and having thus given happiness to mankind.

" 'It is only now,' he says, obviously thinking of the Inquisition, 'that it has become possible, for the first time, to think of men's happiness. Man is a rebel by nature and how can a rebel be happy? You were warned,' he says to Him. 'There was no lack of warnings and signs, but You chose to ignore them. You spurned the only way that could have brought happiness to men. Fortunately, though, You allowed us to take over from You when You left. You made commitments to us, You sealed them with Your word, You gave us the right to loosen and to bind their shackles, and, of course, You cannot think of depriving us of that right now.' "[16]

And, in a completely different mood, A. J. Ayer:

It is now generally admitted, at any rate by philosophers, that the existence of a being having the attributes which define the god of any non-animistic religion cannot be demonstratively proved. To see that this is so, we have only to ask ourselves what are the premises from which the existence of such a god could be deduced. If the conclusion that a god exists is to be demonstratively certain, then these premises must be certain; for, as the conclusion of a deductive argument is already contained in the premises, any uncertainty there may be about the truth of the premises is necessarily shared by it. But we know that no empirical proposition can ever be anything more than probable. It is only *a priori* propositions that are logically certain. But we cannot deduce the existence of a god from an *a priori* proposition. For we know that the reason why *a priori* propositions are certain is that they are tautologies. And from a set of tautologies nothing but a further tautology can be validly deduced. It follows that there is no possibility of demonstrating the existence of a god.

What is not so generally recognised is that there can be no way of proving that the existence of a god, such as the God of Christianity, is even probable. Yet this also is easily shown. For if the existence of such a god were probable, then the proposition that he existed would be an empirical hypothesis. And in that case it would be possible to deduce from it, and other empirical hypotheses, certain experiential propositions which were not deducible from those other hypotheses alone. But in fact this is not possible. It is sometimes claimed, indeed, that the existence of a certain sort of regularity in nature constitutes sufficient evidence for the existence of a god. But if the sentence "God exists" entails no more than that certain types of phenomena occur in certain sequences, then to assert the existence of a god will be simply equivalent to asserting that there is the requisite regularity in nature; and no religious man would admit that this was all he intended to assert in asserting the existence of a god. He would say that in talking about God, he was talking about a transcendent being who might be known through certain empirical manifestations, but certainly could not be defined in terms of those manifestations. But in that case, the term "god" is a metaphysical term. And if "god" is a metaphysical term, then it cannot be even probable that a god exists. For to say that "God exists" is to make a metaphysical utterance which cannot be either true or false. And by the same criterion, no sentence which purports to describe the nature of a transcendent god can possess any literal significance.

It is important not to confuse this view of religious assertions with the view that is adopted by atheists, or agnostics. For it is characteristic of an agnostic to hold that the existence of a god is a possibility in which there is no good reason either to believe or disbelieve; and it is characteristic of an atheist to hold that it is at least probable that no god exists. And our view that all utterances about the nature of God are nonsensical, so far from being

[16] Fyodor Dostoevsky, *The Brothers Karamazov*, trans. Andrew R. MacAndrew (New York: Bantam, 1970).

identical with, or even lending any support to, either of these familiar contentions, is actually incompatible with them. For if the assertion that there is a god is nonsensical, then the atheist's assertion that there is no god is equally nonsensical, since it is only a significant proposition that can be significantly contradicted. As for the agnostic, although he refrains from saying either that there is or that there is not a god, he does not deny that the question whether a transcendent god exists is a genuine question. He does not deny that the two sentences "There is a transcendent god" and "There is no transcendent god" express propositions one of which is actually true and the other false. All he says is that we have no means of telling which of them is true, and therefore ought not to commit ourselves to either. But we have seen that the sentences in question do not express propositions at all. And this means that agnosticism is also ruled out.

Thus we offer the theist the same comfort as we gave to the moralist. His assertions cannot possibly be valid, but they cannot be invalid either. As he says nothing at all about the world, he cannot justly be accused of saying something false, or anything for which he has insufficient grounds. It is only when the theist claims that in asserting the existence of a transcendent god be in expressing a genuine proposition that we are entitled to disagree with him.

It is to be remarked that in cases where deities are identified with natural objects, assertions concerning them may be allowed to be significant. If, for example, a man tells me that the occurrence of thunder is alone both necessary and sufficient to establish the truth of the proposition that Jehovah is angry, we may conclude that, in his usage of words, the sentence "Jehovah is angry" is equivalent to "It is thundering." But in sophisticated religions, though they may be to some extent based on men's awe of natural processes which they cannot sufficiently understand, the "person" who is supposed to control the empirical world is not himself located in it; he is held to be superior to the empirical world, and so outside it; and he is endowed with super-empirical attributes. But the notion of a person whose essential attributes are non-empirical is not an intelligible notion at all. We may have a word which is used as if it named this "person," but, unless the sentences in which it occurs express propositions which are empirically verifiable, it cannot be said to symbolise anything. And this is the case with regard to the word "god," in the usage in which it is intended to refer to a transcendent object. The mere existence of the noun is enough to foster the illusion that there is a real, or at any rate a possible entity corresponding to it. It is only when we inquire what God's attributes are that we discover that "God," in this usage, is not a genuine name.

It is common to find belief in a transcendent god conjoined with belief in an after-life. But, in the form which it usually takes, the content of this belief is not a genuine hypothesis. To say that men do not ever die, or that the state of death is merely a state of prolonged insensibility, is indeed to express a significant proposition, though all the available evidence goes to show that it is false. But to say that there is something imperceptible inside a man, which is his soul or his real self, and that it goes on living after he is dead, is to make a metaphysical assertion which has no more factual content than the assertion that there is a transcendent god.

It is worth mentioning that, according to the account which we have given of religious assertions, there is no logical ground for antagonism between religion and natural science. As far as the question of truth or falsehood is concerned, there is no opposition between the natural scientist and the theist who believes in a transcendent god. For since the religious utterances of the theist are not genuine propositions at all, they cannot stand in any logical relation to the propositions of science. Such antagonism as there is between religion and science appears to consist in the fact that science takes away one of the motives which make men religious. For it is acknowledged that one of the ultimate sources of religious feeling lies in the inability of men to determine their own destiny; and science tends to destroy the feeling of awe with which men regard an alien world, by making them believe that they can understand and anticipate the course of natural phenomena, and even to some extent control it. The fact that it has recently become fashionable for physicists themselves to be sympathetic towards religion is a point in favour of this hypothesis. For this sympathy towards religion marks the physicists' own lack of confidence in the validity of their hypotheses, which is a reaction on their part from the antireligious dogmatism of nineteenth-century scientists, and a natural outcome of the crisis through which physics has just passed.

It is not within the scope of this enquiry to enter more deeply into the causes of religious feeling, or to discuss the probability of the continuance of religious belief. We are concerned only to answer those questions which arise out of our discussion of the possibility of religious knowledge. The point which we wish to establish is that there cannot be any transcendent truths of religion. For the sentences which the theist uses to express such "truths" are not literally significant.

An interesting feature of this conclusion is that it accords with what many theists are accustomed to say themselves. For we are often told that the nature of God is a mystery which transcends the human understanding. But to say that something transcends the human understanding is to say that it is unintelligible. And what is unintelligible cannot significantly be described. Again, we are told that God is not an object of reason but an object of faith. This may be nothing more than an admission that the existence of God must be taken on trust, since it cannot be proved. But it may also be an assertion that God is the object of a purely mystical intuition, and cannot therefore be defined in terms which are intelligible to the reason. And I think there are many theists who would assert this. But if one allows that it is impossible to define God in intelligible terms, then one is allowing that it is impossible for a sentence both to be significant and to be about God. If a mystic admits that the object of his vision is something which cannot be described, then he must also admit that he is bound to talk nonsense when he describes it.

For his part, the mystic may protest that his intuition does reveal truths to him, even though he cannot explain to others what these truths are; and that we who do not possess this faculty of intuition can have no ground for denying that it is a cognitive faculty. For we can hardly maintain a priori that there are no ways of discovering true propositions except those which we ourselves employ. The answer is that we set no limit to the number of ways in which one may come to formulate a true proposition. We do not in any way deny that a synthetic truth may be discovered by purely intuitive methods as well as by the rational method of induction. But we do say that every synthetic proposition, however it may have been arrived at, must be subject to the test of actual experience. We do not deny *a priori* that the mystic is able to discover truths by his own special methods. We wait to hear what are the propositions which embody his discoveries, in order to see whether they are verified or confuted by our empirical observations. But the mystic, so far from producing propositions which are empirically verified, is unable to produce any intelligible propositions at all. And therefore we say that his intuition has not revealed to him any facts. It is no use his saying that he has apprehended facts but is unable to express them. For we know that if he really had acquired any information, he would be able to express it. He would be able to indicate in some way or other how the genuineness of his discovery might be empirically determined. The fact that he cannot reveal what he "knows," or even himself devise an empirical test to validate his "knowledge," shows that his state of mystical intuition is not a genuinely cognitive state. So that in describing his vision the mystic does not give us any information about the external world; he merely gives us indirect information about the condition of his own mind.

These considerations dispose of the argument from religious experience which many philosophers still regard as a valid argument in favour of the existence of a god. They say that it is logically possible for men to be immediately acquainted with God, as they are immediately acquainted with a sense content, and that there is no reason why one should be prepared to believe a man when he says that he is seeing a yellow patch, and refuse to believe him when he says that he is seeing God. The answer to this is that if the man who asserts that he is seeing God is merely asserting that he is experiencing a peculiar kind of sense-content, then we do not for a moment deny that his assertion may be true. But, ordinarily, the man who says that he is seeing God is saying not merely that he is experiencing a religious emotion, but also that there exists a transcendent being who is the object of this emotion; just as the man who says that he sees a yellow patch is ordinarily saying not merely that his visual sense-field contains a yellow sense-content, but also that there exists a yellow object to which the sense-content belongs. And it is not irrational to be prepared to believe a man when he asserts the existence of a yellow object, and to refuse to believe him when he asserts the existence of a transcendent god. For whereas the sentence "There exists here a yellow-coloured material thing" expresses a genuine synthetic proposition which could be empirically verified, the sentence "There exists a transcendent god" has, as we have seen, no literal significance.

We conclude, therefore, that the argument from religious experience is altogether fallacious. The fact that people have religious experiences is interesting from the psychological point of view, but it does not in any way imply that there is such a thing as religious knowledge, any more than our having moral experiences implies that there is such a thing as moral knowledge. The theist, like the moralist may believe that his experiences are cognitive experiences, but, unless he can formulate his "knowledge" in propositions that are empirically verifiable, we may be sure that he is deceiving himself. It follows that those philosophers who fill their books with assertions that they intuitively "know" this or that moral or religious "truth" are merely providing material for the psycho-analyst. For no act of intuition can be said to reveal a truth about any matter of fact unless it issues in verifiable propositions. And all such propositions are to be incorporated in the system of empirical propositions which constitutes science.[17]

It is important to notice that neither of these positions is "atheist" in the literal sense—neither denies the existence of God as such. Dostoevsky's character Ivan speaks for his author in what might be called an extremely sentimental and traumatic agnosticism, filled with the doubts that arise from the problem of evil and from a general cynicism about humanity. "If there is not God," he worries, "then everything is permitted." But even if there is God, the Grand Inquisitor tells us, the purpose of religion has little to do with Him. It is instead an instrument of unfreedom, and a way to keep people ignorant and hopeful. Ayer explicitly rejects atheism as well as theism, but he does this not as an agnostic (that is, one who does not know) but as a philosopher who claims that the very notion of "God" is ultimately meaningless. This too is atheism, if by that word we mean not believing in God. What Ayer rejects under that name is the assertion that something with certain characteristics that might exist does indeed exist. Ayer insists that there is no sense even in suggesting that God might exist. (Notice the difference between Ayer and Tillich. For Ayer, the notion that it makes no sense to discuss the existence of God is an argument for atheism, for Tillich the same notion is an argument for theism.) And finally, the last word of confusion, from Harold Pinter's play, *The Dwarfs:*

LEN. Do you believe in God?
MARK. What?
LEN. Do you believe in God?
MARK. Who?
LEN. God.
MARK. God?
LEN. Do you believe in God?
MARK. Do I believe in God?
LEN. Yes.
MARK. Would you say that again?[18]

THE ATTACK ON RELIGION:
MARX, NIETZSCHE, AND FREUD

But even if religion is a matter of personal viewpoint, beyond rational argument and mere passion or "experience," this is not to say that it is immune

---

[17] A. J. Ayer, *Language, Truth and Logic,* 2nd ed. (London: Victor Gollancz, 1936 and New York: Dover 1946).
[18] Harold Pinter, *The Dwarfs,* in *Three Plays* (New York: Grove Press, 1961).

from attack. The truth and falsity of religious doctrines may not be subject to rational scrutiny, but the motivation of religious thinking might be. Why do people turn to religion? Is it just for edification? or to give them hope? or as a rationalization for the lack of justice in this world? Or is it an escape, a kind of irresponsible reaction to a world we cannot cope with, perhaps a childish unwillingness to give up an illusion of security we ought to have outgrown in adolescence?

Karl Marx is often quoted for his incisive critique of religion. His point is simple, and he makes it powerfully. Humans invent religion to escape their intolerable social conditions. And once we see this, we should reject religion as an escape and turn instead to the correction of those conditions that make such an escape necessary.

The basis of irreligious criticism is this: *man makes religion;* religion does not make man. Religion is indeed man's self-consciousness and self-awareness so long as he has not found himself or has lost himself again. But *man* is not an abstract being, squatting outside the world. Man is *the human world*, the state, society. This state, this society, produce religion which is an *inverted world consciousness,* because they are an *inverted world.* Religion is the general theory of this world, its encyclopedic compendium, its logic in popular form, its spiritual *point d'honneur,* its enthusiasm, its moral sanction, its solemn complement, its general basis of consolation and justification. It is *the fantastic realization* of the human being inasmuch as the *human being* possesses no true reality. The struggle against religion is, therefore, indirectly a struggle against *that world* whose spiritual *aroma* is religion.

Religious suffering is at the same time an *expression* of real suffering and a *protest* against real suffering. Religion is the sigh of the oppressed creature, the sentiment of a heartless world, and the soul of soulless conditions. It is the *opium* of the people.

The abolition of religion as the *illusory* happiness of men, is a demand for their *real* happiness. The call to abandon their illusions about their condition is a *call to abandon a condition which requires illusions.* The criticism of religion is, therefore, *the embryonic criticism of this vale of tears* of which religion is the *halo.*

Criticism has plucked the imaginary flowers from the chain, not in order that man shall bear the chain without caprice or consolation but so that he shall cast off the chain and pluck the living flower. The criticism of religion disillusions man so that he will think, act and fashion his reality as a man who has lost his illusions and regained his reason; so that he will revolve about himself as his own true sun. Religion is only the illusory sun about which man revolves so long as he does not revolve about himself.

· · · · ·

It is clear that the arm of criticism cannot replace the criticism of arms. Material force can only be overthrown by material force; but theory itself becomes a material force when it has seized the masses. Theory is capable of seizing the masses when it demonstrates *ad hominem,* and it demonstrates *ad hominem* as soon as it becomes radical. To be radical is to grasp things by the root. But for man the root is man himself. What proves beyond doubt the radicalism of Germany theory, and thus its practical energy, is that it begins from the resolute *positive* abolition of religion. The criticism of religion ends with the doctrine that *man is the supreme being for man.* It ends, therefore, with the *categorical imperative to overthrow all those conditions* in which man is an abased, enslaved, abandoned, contemptible being— conditions which can hardly be better described than in the exclamation of a Frenchman on the occasion of a proposed tax upon dogs: "Wretched dogs! They want to treat you like men!"[19]

Fifty years later, Friedrich Nietzsche opened an even more blistering attack, on religion in general, on Christianity in particular. Christianity is accused of being nothing other than rationalizations for impotence, an expression of everything that is most contemptible in human nature.

In the Jewish "Old Testament," the book of divine justice, there are men, things, and speeches in so grand a style that Greek and Indian literature have nothing to compare with it. One stands in awe and reverence before these tremendous remnants of what man once was, and sad thoughts come to one about ancient Asia and its jutting peninsula, Europe, which wants so definitely to signify, as against Asia, the "progress of man." Of course, those who are merely wretched tame domestic animals and know only the wants of domestic animals (like our cultivated people of today, including the Christians of "cultivated" Christianity) need neither be amazed nor even sorry when faced with these ruins: the taste for the Old Testament is a touchstone of "greatness" and "smallness." Perhaps they will even find the New Testament, the book of grace, more to their taste (it is full of the odor of the real, effeminate, stupid canter and petty soul). To have glued this New Testament, a kind of rococo of taste in every respect, to the Old Testament to form one book—the "Bible," *the* book—that is perhaps the greatest audacity and "sin against the spirit" which literary Europe has on its conscience.[20]

. . . . .

Christianity should not be beautified and embellished: it has waged deadly war against this higher type of man; it has placed all the basic instincts of this type under the ban; and out of these instincts it has distilled evil and the Evil One: the strong man as the typically reprehensible man, the "reprobate." Christianity has sided with all that is weak and base, with all failures; it has made an ideal of whatever *contradicts* the instinct of the strong life to preserve itself; it has corrupted the reason even of those strongest in spirit . . . it has in fear of them bred the opposite type—the domestic animal, the herd animal, the sick human animal—the Christian.

As long as the priest is considered a *higher* type of man—this *professional* negator, slanderer, and poisoner of life—there is no answer to the question: what *is* truth? For truth has been stood on its head when the

[19] Karl Marx, *Critique of Hegel's Philosophy of Right,* in *Early Writings,* trans. T. Bottomore (New York: McGraw-Hill, 1963).
[20] Friedrich Nietzsche, *Beyond Good and Evil,* trans. Walter Kaufmann (New York: Random House, 1966).

conscious advocate of nothingness and negation is accepted as the representative of "truth."

In Christianity neither morality nor religion has even a single point of contact with reality. Nothing but imaginary *causes* ("God," "soul," "ego," "spirit," "free will"—for that matter, "unfree will"), nothing but imaginary *effects* ("sin," "redemption," "grace," "punishment," "forgiveness of sins"). Intercourse between imaginary *beings* ("God," "spirits," "souls"); an imaginary *natural* science (anthropocentric; no trace of any concept of natural causes); an imaginary *psychology* (nothing but self-misunderstandings, interpretations of agreeable or disagreeable general feelings—for example, of the states of the *nervus sympathicus*—with the aid of the sign language of the religio-moral idiosyncrasy: "repentance," "pangs of conscience," "temptation by the devil," "the presence of God"); an imaginary *teleology* ("the kingdom of God," "the Last Judgment," "eternal life").

This *world of pure fiction* is vastly inferior to the world of dreams insofar as the latter *mirrors* reality, whereas the former falsifies, devalues, and negates reality. Once the concept of "nature" had been invented as the opposite of "God," "natural" had to become a synonym of "reprehensible": this whole world of fiction is rooted in *hatred* of the natural (of reality!); it is the expression of a profound vexation at the sight of reality.

But this explains everything. Who alone has good reason to lie his way out of reality? He who suffers from it. But to suffer from reality is to be a piece of reality that has come to grief. The preponderance of feelings of displeasure over feelings of pleasure is the cause of this fictitious morality and religion; but such a preponderance provides the very formula for decadence.

·   ·   ·   ·   ·

The deity of decadence, gelded in his most virile virtues and instincts, becomes of necessity the god of the physiologically retrograde, of the weak. Of course, they do not *call* themselves the weak; they call themselves "the good."

·   ·   ·   ·   ·

The Christian conception of God—God as god of the sick, God as a spider, God as spirit—is one of the most corrupt conceptions of the divine ever attained on earth. It may even represent the low-water mark in the descending development of divine types. God degenerated into the *contradiction* of life, instead of being its transfiguration and eternal Yes! God as the declaration of war against life, against nature, against the will to live! God—the formula for every slander against "this world," for every lie about the "beyond"! God—the deification of nothingness, the will to nothingness pronounced holy!

·   ·   ·   ·   ·

This pitiful god of Christian monotono-theism! This hybrid product of decay, this mixture of zero, concept, and contradiction, in which all the instincts of decadence, all cowardices and wearinesses of the soul, find their sanction![21]

[21] Friedrich Nietzsche, *The Antichrist,* in *The Portable Nietzsche,* ed. and trans. Walter Kaufmann (New York: Viking, 1954).

Not surprisingly, Nietzsche sees the decline of Christianity and religion in general with great enthusiasm. It is Nietzsche who popularized the old Lutheran phrase, "God is dead," but with an anti-religious twist and a shout of delight that declared open war on all remaining forms of religious "weaknesses."

> The most important of more recent events—that "God is dead," that the belief in the Christian God has become unworthy of belief—already begins to cast its first shadows over Europe. To the few at least whose eye, whose *suspecting* glance, is strong enough and subtle enough for this drama, some sun seems to have set, some old, profound confidence seems to have changed into doubt: our old world must seem to them daily more darksome, distrustful, strange and "old." In the main, however, one may say that the event itself is far too great, too remote, too much beyond most people's power of apprehension, for one to suppose that so much as the report of it could have *reached* them; not to speak of many who already knew *what* had taken place, and what must all collapse now that this belief had been undermined,— because so much was built upon it, so much rested on it, and had become one with it: for example, our entire European morality. This lengthy, vast and uninterrupted process of crumbling, destruction, ruin and overthrow which is now imminent: who has realised it sufficiently to-day to have to stand up as the teacher and herald of such a tremendous logic of terror, as the prophet of a period of gloom and eclipse, the like of which has probably never taken place on earth before? . . . Even we, the born riddle-readers, who wait as it were on the mountains posted 'twixt to-day and to-morrow, and engirt by their contradiction, we, the firstlings and premature children of the coming century, into whose sight especially the shadows which must forthwith envelop Europe *should* already have come—how is it that even we, without genuine sympathy for this period of gloom, contemplate its advent without any *personal solicitude or fear?* Are we still, perhaps, too much under the *immediate effects* of the event—and are these effects, especially as regards *ourselves,* perhaps the reverse of what was to be expected—not at all sad and depressing, but rather like a new and indescribable variety of light, happiness, relief, enlivenment, encouragement, and dawning day? . . . In fact, we philosophers and "free spirits" feel ourselves irradiated as by a new dawn by the report that the "old God is dead"; our hearts overflow with gratitude, astonishment, presentiment and expectation. At last the horizon seems open once more, granting even that it is not bright; our ships can at last put out to sea in face of every danger; every hazard is again permitted to the discerner; the sea, *our* sea, again lies open before us; perhaps never before did such an "open sea" exist.—[22]

Finally, in our own century, the attack has been given a psychoanalytic foundation by Sigmund Freud, who also reduces the grand aspirations of

---

[22] Friedrich Nietzsche, *The Joyful Wisdom,* trans. Thomas Common, in *The Complete Works of Friedrich Nietzsche,* Oscar Levy, General Editor (1909–11) (New York: Russell & Russell, 1964).

religion to mere illusions, but, even worse, the illusions of an insecure child who has never properly grown up; in *The Future of an Illusion,* he says:

> . . . if we turn our attention to the psychical origin of religious ideas. These, which are given out as teachings, are not precipitates of experience or end results of thinking: they are illusions, fulfilments of the oldest, strongest and most urgent wishes of mankind. The secret of their strength lies in the strength of those wishes. As we already know, the terrifying impression of helplessness in childhood aroused the need for protection—for protection through love— which was provided by the father; and the recognition that this helplessness lasts throughout life made it necessary to cling to the existence of a father, but this time a more powerful one. Thus the benevolent rule of a divine Prov- idence allays our fear of the dangers of life; the establishment of a moral world-order ensures the fulfilment of the demands of justice, which have so often remained unfulfilled in human civilization; and the prolongation of earthly existence in a future life provides the local and temporal framework in which these wish-fulfilments shall take place. Answers to the riddles that tempt the curiosity of man, such as how the universe began or what the relation is between body and mind, are developed in conformity with the underlying assumptions of this system. It is an enormous relief to the individual psyche if the conflicts of its childhood arising from the father- complex—conflicts which it has never wholly overcome—are removed from it and brought to a solution which is universally accepted.
>
> When I say that these things are all illusions, I must define the meaning of the word. An illusion is not the same thing as an error; nor is it necessarily an error. Aristotle's belief that vermin are developed out of dung (a belief to which ignorant people still cling) was an error; so was the belief of a former generation of doctors that *tabes dorsalis* is the result of sexual excess. It would be incorrect to call these errors illusions. On the other hand, it was an illusion of Columbus's that he had discovered a new sea-route to the Indies. The part played by his wish in this error is very clear. One may describe as an illusion the assertion made by certain nationalists that the Indo-Germanic race is the only one capable of civilization; or the belief, which was only destroyed by psycho-analysis, that children are creatures without sexuality. What is charac- teristic of illusions is that they are derived from human wishes. In this respect they come near to psychiatric delusions. But they differ from them, too, apart from the more complicated structure of delusions. In the case of delusions, we emphasize as essential their being in contradiction with reality. Illusions need not necessarily be false—that is to say, unrealizable or in contradiction to reality. . . . Thus we call a belief an illusion when a wish-fulfilment is a prominent factor in its motivation, and in doing so we disregard its relations to reality, just as the illusion itself sets no store by verification.[23]

In conclusion, Freud agrees with Marx and Nietzsche, that the only proper concern of man is humanity. But is this necessarily an indictment of religion? Freud was fascinated by Jewish mysticism, and Nietzsche offered

---

[23] Sigmund Freud, *The Future of An Illusion,* ed. and trans. James Strachey (New York: Norton, 1961).

extravagant praise of Buddhism. There have been many Christians, Muslims, and Jews who have used their religion as a metaphysical support for concerted social activism and humanism (as well as "holy" wars), and there are many people for whom religion is an emotional support without which they could not even function as human beings. The balance is precarious. No one can deny that there have been thousands of atrocities—to both spirit and body— in the name of religion. But neither has it been proved that such cruelty is necessary for religion, or that religion is as easily dispensable as some of its critics have suggested. (Even Nietzsche had his serious doubts.)

SUMMARY AND CONCLUSION

Religion is one of the most important, and therefore one of the most controversial and sensitive parts of our lives. It is therefore also one of the most important, controversial, and sensitive areas of philosophy. Initially, religion seems to be part of metaphysics, an examination of the way the world really is, and the answer of religion, in a word, is that reality is divine. But we have seen that religion is much more than a search for knowledge; it is also a search for meaning, for morality, for ultimate justice, and for a type of experience that is like no other. Philosophy of religion begins as a metaphysical discipline, attempting to define a supreme entity of a certain type (God) and to demonstrate His existence through rational arguments and proofs. But many philosophers and religious people deny that such a metaphysical approach is either possible or appropriate. Some philosophers deny that we can know God but insist that it is necessary to have faith. But while some philosophers interpret this faith as a form of rationality, others claim that it is strictly an emotional commitment, beyond the domain of rational argument and understanding.

These various approaches to the philosophy of religion are all very much alive, and so too are the doubts that accompany each approach. Those who believe that we can know God are at odds with those who deny that we can know Him. Those who insist on faith disagree among themselves whether this faith can be or ought to be justified. There are those who want to believe in God but find that certain problems (for example, the problem of evil) make it difficult or impossible for them to do so. There are those who see belief in God as an outmoded belief, left over from the inadequate science and metaphysics of previous centuries. And there are those who attack religion as not only out-moded but as insidious, as a symptom of decadence, weakness, or immaturity. But in the face of these various doubts and attacks, the traditional religious beliefs of Judaism and Christianity seem to be barely disturbed. Religion is humanity's oldest philosophy, and it is still the most controversial area of philosophical concern.

GLOSSARY

agnosticism: the refusal to believe either that God exists or that He does not exist, usually on the grounds that there can be no sufficient evidence for either belief.

anthropomorphic: human-like. An anthropomorphic conception of God attributes human attributes to Him.

argument from design: see *teleological argument*

atheism: the belief that there is no God. A person who doesn't believe in God is an *atheist*.

cosmological argument: an argument (or set of arguments) that undertakes to "prove" that God exists on the basis of the idea that there must have been a first cause or an ultimate reason for the existence of the universe (the cosmos).

deism: a variation of the Judeo-Christian religion that was extremely popular in the science-minded eighteenth century. Deism holds that God must have existed to create the universe with all of its laws (and thereby usually accepts some form of the cosmological argument) but also holds that there is no justification for our belief that God has any special concern for man, any concern for justice, or any of those anthropomorphic attributes for which we worship Him, pray to Him, and believe in biblical stories about Him.

faith: in the popular sense, believing in something for which you have inadequate evidence or little good reason. In theology, faith usually refers to the trust which a believer should have in God's ultimate grace and fairness. Sometimes, faith is defended as a rational belief in God (for example, in Kant). More often, faith is defended against rationality (as in Kierkegaard).

God: in traditional Judeo-Christian theology, that Being who created the universe and exists independently of it, who is all-powerful, all-knowing, everywhere at once, and concerned with justice and the ultimate welfare of humankind. When spelled with a small "g" the word refers to any supernatural being worthy of worship or at least extraordinary respect.

illusion: a false belief motivated by intense wishes. According to Marx, religion is an illusion which is intended to compensate for an intolerable social situation. According to Freud, religion is an illusion which attempts to hold onto our childhood desires for fatherly protection and security.

ineffable: indescribable.

mysticism: the belief that one can come to grasp certain fundamental religious truths (the existence of God, the oneness of the universe) through direct experience, but of a very special kind, different from ordinary understanding and often at odds with reason.

omnipotent: all-powerful, usually said of God.

omniscient: all-knowing, usually said of God.

ontological argument: an argument (or set of arguments) that tries to "prove" the existence of God from the very concept of "God." For example, "God," by definition, is that Being with all possible perfection; existence is a perfection; therefore, God exists.

pantheism: the belief that everything is God. Spinoza, for example, was a *pantheist*. Hinduism is, in part, a form of pantheism.

problem of evil: the dilemma that emerges from trying to reconcile the belief that God is omnipotent, omniscient, and just with the suffering and evil in the world.

teleological argument (for God's existence): an argument that attempts to "prove" that God exists because of the intricacy and "design" of nature. It is sometimes called the "argument from design," since the basis of the argument is that, since the universe is evidently designed, it must have a designer. The analogy most often used is our inference from finding a complex mechanism on the beach (for example, a watch) that there must have been some intelligent being who created it.

theism: belief in God.

transcendent: independent of. In the philosophy of religion, a *transcendent God* is one who is distinct and separate from the universe he created. This is contrasted with the concept of an immanent God, for example, in pantheism, where God is identical with his creation, or, to take a different example, in certain forms of humanism, in which God is identical with humankind. (Hegel argued some such thesis.)

PART TWO

perspectives and values

8

SELF-IDENTITY

"I'm not myself today, you see," Alice said to the caterpillar.
"I don't see," said the caterpillar.

Lewis Carroll

"Just be yourself!" How often have you heard that? And have you ever really understood what it meant? What is it to be a "self"? And what does it mean to be your particular self? In the abstract, the question seems to have a certain obscurity to it. But think of yourself in an office, applying for a job or a scholarship for professional school or just filling out one of those dozens of forms that bombard you during the year; you dutifully answer—your birthdate, where you were born, your grades in school, your service in the army if any, awards you have received, arrests and other troubles, whether you're married or not, male or female, perhaps your race and religion. Is this you? Is this your identity—this list of dates, grades, official distinctions and social circumstances? At some point, I am sure you too have felt that sense of absurdity and rebellion, "this isn't me!" or "this is all irrelevant!" Well, what is being challenged at that point is precisely the bureaucratic conception of self-identity that we have been raised with.

In everything that we do, we adopt some conception of our identity, whether we are called upon to articulate it or not. You walk into a classroom with certain conceptions of your own abilities and intelligence, your status among other students, your role vis-à-vis the professor, the haunting memory of a previous embarrassment and a certain vanity about your looks, your grades, or just your new pair of shoes. But what are these self-identities? Are they just concerned with status and roles among other people? Or is there something that can truly be called "your self," without reference to anyone

265

else? Should we think of ourselves as individuals? Or should we rather see ourselves as components of a larger organism, society or, perhaps, humanity? How should we identify ourselves? And how do we?

SELF-IDENTITY AND SELF-CONSCIOUSNESS: FROM DESCARTES TO KANT

Your *self-identity* is the way you characterize yourself, whether in general (as a human being, as a man or as a woman, as a creature before God, or as one among many animals fighting for survival) or in particular (as the tallest person in your class, as the ex-boy scout who could tie the fastest timberline hitch ever, as someone who can't get rid of acne). Sometimes these characterizations are explicit, when we talk about them or are forced to think about them on some special occasion. But even if we don't make them explicit, we often use them in our behavior, choosing our actions and our manners on the basis of our self-identities. Accordingly, we should also introduce the notion of *self-consciousness*. Sometimes, we act out our identities without being aware of it at all. At other times, particularly when we talk about ourselves or are placed in a situation in which we are forced to "look at ourselves as others see us," we are very much aware—even painfully aware—of our identities. At such times we say that we are self-conscious.[1] In general, most modern philosophers and psychologists would argue that you can't have a concept of self-identity unless you are also sometimes (not necessarily always—as Descartes suggests) self-conscious. Conversely, you can't ever be self-conscious unless you have some sense of identity, no matter how crude. The two concepts, in other words, go hand in hand, and cannot be separated from each other.

In this chapter, we shall explore a number of different questions and conceptions about self-identity. First, it is necessary to further examine the connection between self-identity and self-consciousness. An important and still influential tradition in philosophy, from Descartes and Locke to Hume and Kant, focuses on self-consciousness as the sole key to personal identity. But then we shall look at a number of general questions. Whether self-identity is a matter of personal choice or whether certain facts, factors, or other people define our identity for us? Whether each person can have only one self or whether a single "person" might in fact have several or many selves? Whether there is a self at all? Or, as many Eastern philosophers have argued, whether the self is an illusion and the ideal self-identity is rather selflessness? And

---

[1] It is worth commenting that, in American English, "self-conscious" usually means "embarrassed." In other languages, however, it has very different connotations. Descartes' use of "self-consciousness" was a purely logical one, meaning "consciousness of the self," without any suggestion of embarrassment. And many German philosophers (for example, Hegel) use "self-conscious" as a rough synonym for "proud".

whether we ought to conceive of ourselves as individuals or instead as organic components of a larger community or society?

It all begins with a flash of insight, a shock of recognition. It can be a moment of pride, when you are receiving applause for something you've just said or done; or it can be a moment of vanity, when you've just been praised or propositioned, or you're looking at yourself in a photograph or in a new pair of levis. It might be an excruciating moment of embarrassment (being "self-conscious," we sometimes say); or it might be a moment when you are caught by a stranger in the middle of an awkward situation, trapped in a social situation for which you are totally unprepared, or found out in the midst of a little lie. Or it might be a purely philosophical flash, such as we saw in Descartes' second "Meditation"—his sudden realization of his own existence as the indubitable premise for which he had been searching. Or it might just be the shock of being forced to "see yourself"; you walk into a room, and everyone turns around to look at you. Or, your friend walks in with a new movie camera, starts it going and says, "do something!" Of course, you were already "doing something," but, in the light of your new self-consciousness, it doesn't quite seem adequate. You were polishing your car, but that isn't how you see yourself. That isn't essential to your identity. (You wouldn't want to think of "the car-polisher" as part of your "essence" the way, for example, "being wise" is part of Socrates' "essence.") The philosophical problem of self-identity ultimately comes down to precisely this experience of self-consciousness; when we are forced to become conscious of ourselves, what is it that we consider essential to being ourselves?

What is it about you without which you wouldn't be you? Presumably you would still be you even if you never polished your car. But what if you had a sex change operation? Or what if you completely lost your memory, all recollection of your family and friends? Or what if you physically disappeared altogether, remaining only a whispy consciousness, a spirit or a ghost without a body? Would it then make sense to say that you are still you?

There are philosophers who have argued that self-consciousness alone is the key to self-identity. Descartes is an example. Remember how he characterized himself:

> But what then am I? A thing which thinks. What is a thing which thinks?
> It is a thing which doubts, understands, affirms, denies, wills, refuses, which
> also imagines and feels.

And, he goes on to say, I am a thing with desires, who perceives light and noise and feels heat. But he also shows, by his method of doubt, that all of this might be so even if he were not to have a body at all. Perhaps, he argues, I am fooled about my "having" a body just as I might be fooled about all sorts of other things. Therefore, he concludes, it is not my body that provides me with an identity or with the self from which I begin my philosophy. It follows from this that the particular aspects of my body—whether I am male or female, black or white, tall or short, handsome or ugly, strong or weak—cannot be essential to my identity either. My self-identity is in my mind, in my thinking, doubting, feeling, perceiving, imagining and desiring. I am, essentially, "a thing that thinks."

> And first of all, because I know that all things which I apprehend clearly and distinctly can be created by God as I apprehend them, it suffices that I am able to apprehend one thing apart from another clearly and distinctly in order to be certain that the one is different from the other, since they may be made to exist in separation at least by the omnipotence of God; and it does not signify by what power this separation is made in order to compel me to judge them to be different: and, therefore, just because I know certainly that I exist, and that meanwhile I do not remark that any other thing necessarily pertains to my nature or essence, excepting that I am a thinking thing, I rightly conclude that my essence consists solely in the fact that I am a thinking thing [or a substance whose whole essence or nature is to think]. And although possibly (or rather certainly, as I shall say in a moment) I possess a body with which I am very intimately conjoined, yet because, on the one side, I have a clear and distinct idea of myself inasmuch as I am only a thinking and unextended thing, and as, on the other, I possess a distinct idea of body, inasmuch as it is only an extended and unthinking thing, it is certain that this I [that is to say, my soul by which I am what I am], is entirely and absolutely distinct from my body, and can exist without it. . . .[2]

It is important to appreciate the kind of step Descartes has taken here. What he is saying is that self-identity depends wholly on self-consciousness, and that human identity is therefore different from the identity of anything else in the world.

Compare this view with the following argument from David Hume, in which he talks about the identity or sameness of objects, and argues that human identity is ultimately no different.

> We now proceed to explain the nature of *personal identity,* which has become so great a question in philosophy, especially of late years in *England,* where all the abstruser sciences are study'd with a peculiar ardour and application. And here 'tis evident, the same method of reasoning must be continu'd, which has so successfully explain'd the identity of plants, and animals, and ships, and houses, and of all the compounded and changeable productions either of art or nature. The identity, which we ascribe to the mind of man, is only a fictitious one, and of a like kind with that which we ascribe to vegetables and animal bodies. It cannot, therefore, have a different origin, but must proceed from a like operation of the imagination upon his objects.
>
> We have a distinct idea of an object, that remains invariable and uninterrupted thro' a suppos'd variation of time; and this idea we call that of *identity* or *sameness.* We have also a distinct idea of several different objects

---

[2] René Descartes, "Meditation VI," in *Meditations on First Philosophy,* in *The Philosophical Works of Descartes,* trans. Elizabeth S. Haldane and G. R. T. Ross (Cambridge: Cambridge University Press, 1911).

existing in succession, and connected together by a close relation; and this to an accurate view affords as perfect a notion of *diversity,* as if there was no manner of relation among the objects. But tho' these two ideas of identity, and a succession of related objects be in themselves perfectly distinct, and even contrary, yet 'tis certain, that in our common way of thinking they are generally confounded with each other. That action of the imagination, by which we consider the uninterrupted and invariable object, and that by which we reflect on the succession of related objects, are almost the same to the feeling, nor is there much more effort to thought requir'd in the latter case than in the former. The relation facilitates the transition of the mind from one object to another, and renders its passage as smooth as if it contemplated one continu'd object. This resemblance is the cause of the confusion and mistake, and makes us substitute the notion of identity, instead of that of related objects.

Our last resource is to . . . boldly assert that these different related objects are in effect the same, however interrupted and variable. In order to justify to ourselves this absurdity, we often feign some new and unintelligible principle, that connects the objects together, and prevents their interruption or variation. Thus we feign the continu'd existence of the perceptions of our senses, to remove the interruption; and run into the notion of a *soul,* and *self,* and *substance,* to disguise the variation. But we may farther observe, that where we do not give rise to such a fiction, our propension to confound identity with relation is so great, that we are apt to imagine something unknown and mysterious connecting the parts, beside their relation; and this I take to be the case with regret to the identity we ascribe to plants and vegetables. And even when this does not take place, we still feel a propensity to confound these ideas, tho' we are not able fully to satisfy ourselves in that particular, nor find any thing invariable and uninterrupted to justify our notion of identity. . . .

Suppose any mass of matter, of which the parts are contiguous and connected, to be plac'd before us; 'tis plain we must attribute a perfect identity to this mass, provided all the parts continue uninterruptedly and invariably the same, whatever motion or change of place we may observe either in the whole or in any of the parts. But supposing some very *small* or *inconsiderable* part to be added to the mass, or substracted from it; tho' this absolutely destroys the identity of the whole, strictly speaking; yet as we seldom think so accurately, we scruple not to pronounce a mass of matter the same, where we find so trivial an alteration. The passage of the thought from the object before the change to the object after it, is so smooth and easy, that we scarce perceive the transition, and are apt to imagine, that 'tis nothing but a continu'd survey, of the same object.[3]

Hume's argument is familiar to us from our discussion of empiricism in Chapter 3. All we perceive, he says, is a sequence of impressions. What right do we have, therefore, to identify the object of this impression with the object of another? This tree, for example: what justifies our claiming that this is the same tree we saw five years ago, or even five minutes ago? As a matter of

[3] David Hume, *A Treatise of Human Nature,* ed. L. A. Selby-Bigge (Oxford: Oxford University Press, 1888).

fact, we know that the cells and parts of the tree are continuously being replaced, so that at no time is it ever literally the same tree. But Hume's argument goes further than this; even if that were not so, we would still have no way of justifying our belief that this tree is the same one we saw some time ago, rather than another, reasonably similar to it, but yet different. How do we know, for example, that someone has not come along and replaced it with another? Like so many other crucial concepts, the notion of identity is a "fiction," Hume argues. And the same is true of our concept of a person being the same from one time to another—even when that person is oneself.

On what basis do we create the "fiction" of identity? First, there is the spacio-temporal continuity of the thing; the tree is in the same place at different times. People, however, have the troublesome habit of moving around, going away to Europe for the summer or college for the semester. But we still see the continuity of his or her movement, receive postcards from appropriate places at the appropriate times, and so we conclude that it is the same person. (Consider what you would think if your new-found friend suddenly vanished "into thin air," or casually replaced the lower two-thirds of his or her body with another, as you might change your pants.) As Hume says, we still call something the same if it changes only a "small part" at a time; but what about Dr. Jekyll and Mr. Hyde, in Robert Louis Stevenson's story; what if your friend were to undergo a total change of appearance and personality, right before your eyes? Would he or she be the same person, radically changed? Or would you rather say that it is a different person, who has replaced your friend?

In addition to spacio-temporal continuity, we also use resemblance as a criterion for identity. We can tolerate small changes, a haircut or a new scar or a blackened eye, perhaps even a lost leg or a bit of plastic surgery. But a Jekyll and Hyde change! Is there any way of saying that we now have the same person as before? How could Dr. Jekyll, having turned back from being Mr. Hyde, say that he and Hyde are in fact the same person?

It is considerations such as this that have led philosophers to reject bodily continuity and resemblance as criteria for self-identity and turn instead to purely mental criteria. In Descartes, not only the particulars of one's body, but even having a body becomes irrelevant to the essentials of self-identity. A milder argument can be found in Descartes' empiricist counterpart, John Locke. In his *Essay Concerning Human Understanding*, Locke argues:

> In the state of living creatures, their identity depends not on a mass of the same particles, but on something else. For in them the variation of great parcels of matter alters not the identity: an oak growing from a plant to a great tree, and then lopped, is still the same oak; and a colt grown up to a horse, sometimes fat, sometimes lean, is all the while the same horse: though, in both these cases, there may be a manifest change of the parts; so that truly they are not either of them the same masses of matter, though they be truly one of them the same oak, and the other the same horse.
>
> *Identity of Animals.*——The case is not so much different in *brutes*

but that any one may hence see what makes an animal and continues it the same. Something we have like this in machines, and may serve to illustrate it. For example, what is a watch? It is plain it is nothing but a fit organization or construction of parts to a certain end, which, when a sufficient force is added to it, it is capable to attain. If we would suppose this machine one continued body, all whose organized parts were repaired, increased, or diminished by a constant addition or separation of insensible parts, with one common life, we should have something very much like the body of an animal. . . .

    The Identity of Man.—This also shows wherein the identity of the same *man* consists; viz. in nothing but a participation of the same continued life, by constantly fleeting particles of matter, in succession vitally united to the same organized body.[4]

Locke then distinguishes between the soul, which might be found in any number of different individuals (even animals), the "man," who is to be identified in the same way as animals or things, by its external characteristics, and the "person," which is what we mean by "personal" self-identity.

If the identity of *soul alone* makes the same *man;* and there be nothing in the nature of matter why the same individual spirit may not be united to different bodies, it will be possible that those men, living in distant ages, and of different tempers, may have been the same man: which way of speaking must be from a very strange use of the word man, applied to an idea out of which body and shape are excluded. And that way of speaking would agree yet worse with the notions of those philosophers who allow of transmigration, and are of opinion that the souls of men may, for their miscarriages, be detruded into the bodies of beasts, as fit habitations, with organs suited to the satisfaction of their brutal inclinations. But yet I think nobody, could he be sure that the *soul* of Heliogabalus were in one of his hogs, would yet say that hog were a *man* or *Heliogabalus.*

. . . . .

    To find wherein personal identity consists, we must consider what *person* stands for;—which, I think, is a thinking intelligent being, that has reason and reflection, and can consider itself as itself, the same thinking thing, in different times and places; which it does only by that consciousness which is inseparable from thinking, and, as it seems to me, essential to it: it being impossible for any one to perceive without *perceiving* that he does perceive. When we see, hear, smell, taste, feel, meditate, or will anything, we know that we do so. Thus it is always as to our present sensations and perceptions: and by this every one is to himself that which he calls *self:*—it not being considered, in this case, whether the same self be continued in the same or divers substances. For, since consciousness always accompanies thinking, and it is that which makes every one to be what he calls self, and thereby distinguishes himself from all other thinking things, in this alone consists personal identity, i.e. the sameness of a rational being: and as far as this con-

---

[4] John Locke, *An Essay Concerning Human Understanding,* ed. A. C. Fraser (Oxford: Clarendon Press, 1894).

sciousness can be extended backwards to any past action or thought, so far reaches the identity of that person; it is the same self now it was then; and it is by the same self with this present one that now reflects on it, that that action was done.

Consciousness makes personal Identity.——But it is further inquired, whether it be the same identical substance. This few[5] would think they had reason to doubt of, if these perceptions, with their consciousness, always remained present in the mind, whereby the same thinking thing would be always consciously present, and, as would be thought, evidently the same to itself. But that which seems to make the difficulty is this, that this consciousness being interrupted always by forgetfulness, there being no moment of our lives wherein we have the whole train of all our past actions before our eyes in one view, but even the best memories losing the sight of one part whilst they are viewing another; and we sometimes, and that the greatest part of our lives, not reflecting on our past selves, being intent on our present thoughts, and in sound sleep having no thoughts at all, or at least none with that consciousness which remarks our waking thoughts,—I say, in all these cases, our consciousness being interrupted, and we losing the sight of our past selves, doubts are raised whether we are the same thinking thing, i.e. the same *substance* or no. Which, however reasonable or unreasonable, concerns not *personal* identity at all. The question being what makes the same person; and not whether it be the same identical substance, which always thinks in the same person, which, in this case, matters not at all: different substances, by the same consciousness (where they do partake in it) being united into one person, as well as different bodies by the same life are united into one animal, whose identity is preserved in that change of substances by the unity of one continued life. For, it being the same consciousness that makes a man be himself to himself, personal identity depends on that only, whether it be annexed solely to one individual substance, or can be continued in a succession of several substances. For as far as any intelligent being *can* repeat the idea of any past action with the same consciousness it had of it at first, and with the same consciousness it has of any present action; so far it is the same personal self. For it is by the consciousness it has of its present thoughts and actions, that it is *self to itself* now, and so will be the same self, as far as the same consciousness can extend to actions past or to come; and would be by distance of time, or change of substance, no more two persons, than a man be two men by wearing other clothes to-day than he did yesterday, with a long or a short sleep between: the same consciousness uniting those distant actions into the same person, whatever substances contributed to their production.

Personal Identity in Change of Substance.——That this is so, we have some kind of evidence in our very bodies, all whose particles, whilst vitally united to this same thinking conscious self, so that *we feel* when they are touched, and are affected by, and conscious of good or harm that happens to them, are a part of ourselves; i.e. of our thinking conscious self. Thus, the limbs of his body are to every one a part of himself; he sympathizes and is concerned for them. Cut off a hand, and thereby separate it from that consciousness he had of its heat, cold, and other affections, and it is then no

[5] Locke refers here to Descartes.

longer a part of that which is himself, any more than the remotest part of matter. Thus, we see the *substance* whereof personal self consisted at one time may be varied at another, without the change of personal identity; there being no question about the same person, though the limbs which but now were a part of it, be cut off.

. . . . .

If the same consciousness (which, as has been shown, is quite a different thing from the same numerical figure or motion in body) can be transferred from one thinking substance to another, it will be possible that two thinking substances may make but one person. For the same consciousness being preserved, whether in the same or different substances, the personal identity is preserved. Whether the same immaterial being, being conscious of the action of its past duration, may be wholly stripped of all the consciousness of its past existence, and lose it beyond the power of ever retrieving it again: and so as it were beginning a new account from a new period, have a consciousness that *cannot* reach beyond this new state. All those who hold pre-existence are evidently of this mind; since they allow the soul to have no remaining consciousness of what it did in that pre-existing state, either wholly separate from body, or informing any other body; and if they should not, it is plain experience would be against them. So that personal identity, reaching no further than consciousness reaches, a pre-existent spirit not having continued so many ages in a state of silence, must needs make different persons. Suppose a Christian Platonist or a Pythagorean should, upon God's having ended all his works of creation the seventh day, think his soul hath existed ever since; and should imagine it has revolved in several human bodies; as I once met with one, who was persuaded his had been the *soul* of Socrates (how reasonably I will not dispute; this I know, that in the post he filled, which was no inconsiderable one, he passed for a very rational man, and the press has shown that he wanted not parts or learning;)—would any one say, that he, being not conscious of any of Socrates's actions or thoughts, could be the same *person* with Socrates? Let any one reflect upon himself, and conclude that he has in himself an immaterial spirit, which is that which thinks in him, and, in the constant change of his body keeps him the same: and is that which he calls *himself*.

The body, as well as the soul, goes to the making of a Man.——And thus may we be able, without any difficulty, to conceive the same person at the resurrection, though in a body not exactly in make or parts the same which he had here,—the same consciousness going along with the soul that inhabits it. But yet the soul alone, in the change of bodies, would scarce to any one but to him that makes the soul the man, be enough to make the same man. For should the soul of a prince, carrying with it the consciousness of the prince's past life, enter and inform the body of a cobbler, as soon as deserted by his own soul, every one sees he would be the same *person* with the prince, accountable only for the prince's actions: but who would say it was the same *man?* The body too goes to the making the man, and would, I guess, to everybody determine the man in this case, wherein the soul, with all its princely thoughts about it, would not make another man: but he would be the same cobbler to every one besides himself. I know that, in the ordinary way of speaking, the same person, and the same man, stand for one and the same thing.

Consciousness alone unites actions into the same Person.——But though the same immaterial substance or soul does not alone, wherever it be, and in whatsoever state, make the same *man;* yet it is plain, consciousness, as far as ever it can be extended—should it be to ages past—unites existences and actions very remote in time into the same *person,* as well as it does the existences and actions of the immediately preceding moment: so that whatever has the consciousness of present and past actions, is the same person to whom they both belong. Had I the same consciousness that I saw the ark and Noah's flood, as that I saw an overflowing of the Thames last winter, or as that I write now, I could no more doubt that I who write this now, that saw the Thames overflowed last winter, and that viewed the flood at the general deluge, was the same *self,*—place that self in what *substance* you please—than that I who write this am the same *myself* now whilst I write (whether I consist of all the same substance, material or immaterial, or no) that I was yesterday. For as to this point of being the same self, it matters not whether this present self be made up of the same or other substances— I being as much concerned, and as justly accountable for any action that was done a thousand years since, appropriated to me now by this self-consciousness, as I am for what I did the last moment.

Self depends on Consciousness, not on Substance.——*Self* is that conscious thinking thing,—whatever substance made up of, (whether spiritual or material, simple or compounded, it matters not)—which is sensible or conscious of pleasure and pain, capable of happiness or misery, and so is concerned for itself, as far as that consciousness extends. Thus every one finds that, whilst comprehended under that consciousness, the little finger is as much a part of himself as what is most so. Upon separation of this little finger, should this consciousness go along with the little finger, and leave the rest of the body, it is evident the little finger would be the person, the same person; and self then would have nothing to do with the rest of the body. As in this case it is the consciousness that goes along with the substance, when one part is separate from another, which makes the same person, and constitutes this inseparable self: so it is in reference to substances remote in time. That with which the consciousness of this present thinking thing *can* join itself, makes the same person, and is one self with it, and with nothing else; and so attributes to itself, and owns all the actions of that thing, as its own, as far as that consciousness reaches, and no further.[6]

The main thesis of Locke's argument is this: personal self-identity is based upon self-consciousness, in particular, upon memories about one's former experiences. In this, he argues, man is different from animals, whose identity (that is, "the same dog" or "the same horse") is based on the continuity of the body, just as you would say that you have had "the same car" for ten years even if almost every part except the chassis has been replaced during that time. The identity of "man" as a biological organism is the same as the

[6] Locke, *An Essay Concerning Human Understanding.*

identity of animals, but the identity of a "person," that is, "personal" identity, depends on self-consciousness. Notice Locke's curious discussion of the possibility of a migrating soul, moving from body to body. He rejects the idea of the soul being the seat of self-identity, for the soul alone provides none of the characteristics that allow for the identity of either man (as the same organism) or of people (as the same persons). Thus he comments that even if the soul of Heliogabalus, an ancient Roman emperor, could move into one of his pigs, the pig would neither become the man (animal) Heliogabalus nor the person Heliogabalus. What makes Heliogabalus the person Heliogabalus is his memories of himself as young Heliogabalus, his memories of his exploits in battle, and the fact, for example, that he does not remember any of Socrates' exploits and thoughts, for he is not Socrates. But what makes Heliogabalus Heliogabalus nevertheless requires both personal identity as consciousness and bodily identity as a man.

This way of equating personal self-identity with self-consciousness has been the main theory of modern thought. It is worth mentioning (though we shall deal with it in the following chapter) that ancient philosophers, Aristotle for example, did not believe this, and probably would not even have understood much of what Descartes and Locke were arguing about. For Aristotle, self-identity was essentially bodily identity, without any particular reference to self-consciousness. But neither must it be thought that the modern thesis has been without its critics, in fact, its devastating critics. Continuing with Hume, for example, we can see him turning his skeptical eye to the concept of the self, declaring that the self is not only a "fiction" but a philosophical illusion based on those other fictions of metaphysics, substance and causation.

> There are some philosophers, who imagine we are every moment intimately conscious of what we call our SELF; that we feel its existence and its continuance in existence and are certain, beyond the evidence of a demonstration, both of its perfect identity and simplicity. The strongest sensation, the most violent passion, say they, instead of distracting us from this view, only fix it the more intensely, and make us consider their influence on *self* either by their pain or pleasure. To attempt a farther proof of this were to weaken its evidence; since no proof can be deriv'd from any fact, of which we are so intimately conscious; nor is there any thing, of which we can be certain, if we doubt of this.
>
> Unluckily all these positive assertions are contrary to that very experience, which is pleaded for them, nor have we any idea of *self*, after the manner it is here explain'd. For from what impression cou'd this idea be deriv'd? This question 'tis impossible to answer without a manifest contradiction, and absurdity; and yet 'tis a question, which must necessarily be answer'd, if we wou'd have the idea of self pass for clear and intelligible. It must be some one impression, that gives rise to every real idea. But self or person is not any one impression, but that to which our several impressions and ideas are suppos'd to have a reference. If any impression gives rise to the idea of self, that impression must continue invariably the same, thro'

the whole course of our lives; since self is suppos'd to exist after that manner. But there is no impression constant and invariable. Pain and pleasure, grief and joy, passions and sensations succeed each other, and never all exist at the same time. It cannot, therefore, be from any of these impressions, or from any other, that the idea of self is deriv'd; and consequently there is no such idea.

But farther, what must become of all our particular perceptions upon this hypothesis? All these are different, and distinguishable, and separable from each other and may be separately consider'd, and may exist separately, and have no need of any thing to support their existence. After what manner, therefore, do they belong to self and how are they connected with it? For my part, when I enter most intimately into what I call *myself,* I always stumble on some particular perception or other, of heat or cold, light or shade, love or hatred, pain or pleasure. I never can catch *myself* at any time without a perception, and never can observe any thing but the perception. When my perceptions are remov'd for any time, as by sound sleep; so long am I insensible of myself, and may truly be said not to exist. And were all my perceptions remov'd by death, and cou'd I neither think, nor feel, nor see, nor love, nor hate after the dissolution of my body, I shou'd be entirely anni-hilated, nor do I conceive what is further requisite to make me a perfect non-entity. If any one upon serious and unprejudiced reflexion, thinks he has a different notion of *himself,* I must confess I can reason no longer with him. All I can allow him is, that he may be in the right as well as I, and that we are essentially different in this particular. He may, perhaps, perceive something simple and continu'd, which he calls *himself;* tho' I am certain there is no such principle in me.

But setting aside some metaphysicians of this kind, I may venture to affirm of the rest of mankind, that they are nothing but a bundle or collection of different perceptions, which succeed each other with an inconceivable rapidity, and are in a perpetual flux and movement. Our eyes cannot turn in their sockets without varying our perceptions. Our thought is still more variable than our sight; and all our other senses and faculties contribute to this change; nor is there any single power of the soul, which remains unalterably the same, perhaps for one moment. The mind is a kind of theatre, where several perceptions successively make their appearance; pass, re-pass, glide away, and mingle in an infinite variety of postures and situations. There is properly no *simplicity* in it at one time, nor *identity* in different; whatever natural propension we may have to imagine that simplicity and identity. The comparison of the theatre must not mislead us. They are the successive perceptions only, that constitute the mind: nor have we the most distant notion of the place, where these scenes are represented, or of the materials, of which it is compos'd.

What then gives us so great a propension to ascribe an identity to these successive perceptions, and to suppose ourselves possest of an invariable and uninterrupted existence thro' the whole course of our lives? In order to answer this question, we must distinguish betwixt personal identity, as it regards our thought or imagination, and as it regards our passions or the concern we take in ourselves. The first is our present subject; and to explain it perfectly we must take the matter pretty deep, and account for that identity, which we attribute to plants and animals; there being a great analogy betwixt it, and the identity of a self or person.

· · · · ·

The whole of this doctrine leads us to a conclusion, which is of great importance in the present affair, *viz.* that all the nice and subtile questions concerning personal identity can never possibly be decided, and are to be regarded rather as grammatical than as philosophical difficulties.[7]

But Hume's argument, that "I never can catch myself . . ." suffers from a peculiar but obvious form of self-contradiction. He can't even deny that there is a self without in some sense pointing to himself in order to do it. This point was not missed by Immanuel Kant, who saw that Hume's error, as in other matters, was in confusing the supposed experience of self-consciousness with the transcendental rules with which we tie these various experiences together. Accordingly, Kant argues, Descartes and Locke are both correct in equating self-identity and self-consciousness, but it must not be thought that the self is therefore a "thing" (as Descartes said) that we find in experience.

According to Kant, the self is the activity of consciousness, in particular the activity of organizing our various experiences. Kant borrows Hume's argument, but he turns it towards the opposite conclusion: true, I never find a self "in" my experiences, but I can always find myself in that "I" which has the experience. Kant's "self," in other words, is the act of having experiences rather than anything which we experience itself. But for Kant this self is not merely the passive recipient of experiences, and here is where the notion of self as activity becomes all-important. The self is the activity of applying the rules by which we organize our experience. Moreover, Kant argues that one of the most basic rules of this activity is that the self organize its experience in such a way that it always recognizes them as its own experience. The rule is that we must always "synthesize" our various experiences into a unity, for we could not come to have any knowledge whatever of a scattering of various impressions and sensations without this synthesis. (Think, for example, of the slightly painful and generally meaningless sensations you have when someone sets off a camera flashbulb in your eyes.) This basic rule of synthesis allows Kant to say that, not only is the self the activity that applies the various rules to experience but its existence as a unified self with a unified synthesis of experiences is itself a rule. Kant gives this curious idea of the self as a rule a formidable name, "the transcendental unity of apperception." What is important in this concept is that the self for Kant is indeed essential to self-consciousness, but it is not "in" self-consciousness. Metaphorically, it is often said that it is "behind" self-consciousness, that is, it is the activity of bringing our various experiences together in accordance with the basic rules of our experience. Accordingly, Kant refers to this self as the *transcendental ego,* "transcendental" because, as we discussed in Chapter five, it is basic and necessary for all possible human experience. The difference between Hume

[7] Hume, *A Treatise of Human Nature.*

and Kant is sometimes illustrated in this way: Hume looks for the self among our experiences, and doesn't find it. Kant agrees with Hume, but argues that he looked in the wrong place. The self, Kant says, is the thread that ties together our various experiences. Accordingly, it is not in the bundle of our experiences, but, as the "transcendental" thread that holds them all together, is as real as any experience.

Kant returns to Descartes and challenges his main theses, even while agreeing with parts of them. First, while Descartes thought that we had to be self-conscious all the time, Kant insists that it is only necessary for "the 'I think' to be able to accompany all experiences." It is not necessary to be always conscious of our selves, but only to be, at any point in our experience, capable of becoming self-conscious; we can turn our attention when we want to from whatever we are doing and watch ourselves doing what we are doing. This is an important point: our concern with self-consciousness is given impetus just because we are often not self-conscious. In fact, there have been several philosophers (and many mystics) who have argued that self-consciousness is bad, a useless thing, and should be avoided as much as possible. According to Descartes, this is not possible, for to exist at all as a human being is to exist self-consciously. According to Kant, on the other hand, to exist as a human being is "to be able" to be self-conscious.

Second, Kant objects to Descartes' belief that the thinking self is a thinking thing. He objects to this, first of all, because of his insistence (as a result of Hume's argument) that the self (or "transcendental ego") is not in our experience but rather "behind" it and responsible for it. More literally, he says that the self must be thought of as an activity. You can see what a radical move this is when you recall the traditional doctrine of the soul, in Plato, in Christianity, and in much of modern thought. The soul, quite simply, is the self conceived of as a thing, an enduring thing that can survive the death of the body. By saying that the self is an activity, Kant undermines (as Hume had intended to undermine) the traditional concept of soul.[8]

> Pure reason requires us to seek for every predicate of a thing its own subject, and for this subject, which is itself necessarily nothing but a predicate, its subject, and so on indefinitely (or as far as we can reach). But hence it follows that we must not hold anything at which we can arrive to be an ultimate subject.
>
> Now we appear to have this substance in the consciousness of ourselves (in the thinking subject), and indeed in an immediate intuition; for all the predicates of an internal sense refer to the *ego*, as a subject, and I cannot conceive myself as the predicate of any other subject. Hence completeness in the reference of the given concepts as predicates to a subject—not merely an Idea, but an object—that is, the absolute subject itself, seems to be given in experience. But this expectation is disappointed. For the ego is

[8] It is worth mentioning, however, that Kant held onto the Christian concept of soul; but to do so, he could defend it only as a "postulate of practical reason," in other words, as a strictly moral claim, much as he had defended his belief in God. Later philosophers borrowed Kant's arguments to get rid of the soul altogether.

not a concept, but only the indication of the object of the inner sense, so far as we know it by no further predicate. Consequently it cannot indeed be itself a predicate of any other thing; but just as little can it be a definite concept of an absolute subject, but is, as in all other cases, only the reference of the inner phenomena to their unknown subject. Yet this idea (which serves very well as a regulative principle totally to destroy all materialistic explanations of the internal phenomena of the soul) occasions by a very natural misunderstanding a very specious argument, which infers its nature from this supposed knowledge of the substance of our thinking being. This is specious so far as the knowledge of it falls quite without the complex of experience.

But though we may call this thinking self (the soul) "substance," as being the ultimate subject of thinking which cannot be further represented as the predicate of another thing, it remains quite empty and without significance if permanence—the quality which renders the concept of substances in experience fruitful—cannot be proved of it.

But permanence can never be proved of the concept of a substance as a thing in itself, but for the purposes of experience only.

If, therefore, from the concept of the soul as a substance we would infer its permanence, this can hold good as regards possible experience only, not of the soul as a thing in itself and beyond all possible experience. Life is the subjective condition of all our possible experience; consequently we can only infer the permanence of the soul in life, for the death of a man is the end of all experience which concerns the soul as an object of experience, except the contrary be proved—which is the very question in hand. The permanence of the soul can therefore only be proved (and no one cares to do that) during the life of man, but not, as we desire to do, after death. The reason for this is that the concept of substance, so far as it is to be considered necessarily with the concept of permanence, can be so combined only according to the principles of possible experience, and therefore for the purposes of experience only.[9]

Third, Kant argued that we need two very different conceptions of self. He saw that this conception of self as self-consciousness was not sufficient to do the whole job that philosophers had wanted it to do. One part of Descartes' enterprise was to find out what was essential to his existence, what could not be doubted and so could serve as a first premise for his *Meditations*. So too Locke and Hume had tried to find (though Locke did and Hume didn't) that self which defined us through our various changes, which identified Jekyll and Hyde and identifies us from year to year, day to day, and

---

[9] Immanuel Kant, *Prolegomena to Any Future Metaphysics,* trans. Lewis White Beck (New York: Bobbs-Merrill, 1950). Ludwig Wittgenstein, for example, used a Kantian thesis to deny the existence of the subject altogether. In his *Tractatus Logico-Philosophicus,* he tells us:

The thinking, presenting subject—there is no such thing. *In an important sense* there is no subject. The subject does not belong to the world, but is a limit of the world. There is [therefore] really a sense in which in philosophy we can talk non-psychologically of the I. The I occurs in philosophy through the fact that the 'world is my world.' The philosophical I is not the man, not the human body, or the human soul of which psychology treats, but the metaphysical subject, the limit—not a part of the world.

mood to mood. But the function of the self was also to serve as a way of identifying ourselves in distinction from other people and other things. Thus Descartes' concept of the self as a thinking thing was not sufficient to tell us what made one person different from another, and he found it necessary to supplement his concept of self with an account of how a person was composed of a self and a body in some special way. Similarly, Locke distinguishes between personal identity and identity as a man (that is, as a biological example of the species *homo sapiens*) and tells us that both are necessary for us to understand how one particular person is different from another particular person. We can see that the question of self-identity now divides into two questions: (1) what is essential to being a self? and (2) what is essential to being a particular self? Kant's conception of self as that which has experiences, the transcendental self, only answers the first question. There is nothing in the notion of transcendental self that allows us to distinguish between different people and tell them apart. Accordingly, he identifies another "self" that he calls the *empirical self,* which includes all of those particular things about us that make us different people. Differences in our bodies, our looks, our size, our strength would be such differences. So too would our different personalities, our different thoughts and memories. (Thus the distinction between Kant's transcendental and empirical selves is not the same as Locke's distinction between "person" and "man"; most of the characteristics of both of Locke's distinctions would be part of what Kant calls the empirical self.) It is the empirical self that identifies us as individual persons. It is the transcendental self that makes us human.

These have been the traditional answers to the philosophical problem of self-identity. What is it that makes one "the same person" from moment to moment and year to year? The spacio-temporal continuity of the body would seem to be a part of the answer. But philosophers since (and before) Descartes have seen quite clearly that this is never enough, that it is also self-consciousness that provides the key to self-identity. But even this has not solved the problem. To see this, consider the following two bizarre but illuminating examples:

Jones has an emergency brain operation. His own brain is removed and replaced by the brain of Brown (who is recently deceased). "Jones" still looks like Jones, still carries the same driver's license and lives in the same house, but all of his memories and personality traits are those of Brown. Is he still Jones? Or is he Brown in Jones' body? Suppose you had been (or are?) Brown, could you claim to be still alive in Jones' body?

Smith undergoes a personality split, of the most radical kind imaginable. Like the one-celled animal, the amoeba, Smith splits, head to toe, each half of him forming an exact duplicate of the original, same memories and personality, same habits, knowledge, likes and dislikes, skills etc. Which of the two is Smith? Does it make any sense to say that both are? Suppose you are now one of the two resultant Smiths: Would you—could you—intelligibly say that the other Smith is also you? That would surely violate the concept of the transcendental self, which must always be oneself. It would also violate common sense. But, given your common origins and exact similarities, could you say that the other Smith was merely someone else?

None of what we have discussed so far would seem to provide us with satisfactory answers to these two puzzles. Granting that the examples are strange, they still show us that our traditional conceptions of self-identity are not as adequate as they might be. And given the increasing possibility of such examples in real life with some of the advances in modern science, we must expect that our conceptions of self-identity may well change in the near future just in order to make sense of these cases.

FACTS AND FANTASIES: EXISTENTIALISM AND BEYOND

Let's return to common experience again. You are once again filling out one of those many forms that ask for the facts about you—age, place of birth, marital status, grades and such. And you are once again experiencing that familiar sense of revolt and disgust which says, "this is all irrelevant." But is it? What are you, if anything, over and above all the facts about you? Of course, job and scholarship applications rarely ask what is more personal about you. They won't dare ask about your sexual exploits and drinking habits, what you dream about or how you like your pizza. But suppose you were to supply all of that information too. Would that be you?

This problem of concrete self-identity has always been a practical problem for self-conscious people. Who am I? It isn't enough to say that a person is the sum total of facts about him or her. Surely some such "facts" are simply irrelevant, like the fact that you had a mole on your knee when you were three or the fact that, in last week's chemistry exam, you got number 18 wrong but luckily guessed number 23 correctly. So, we want to say that some facts are more essential than others. The fact that you are "devastatingly good looking" is probably much more important to you than the fact that you own exactly fourteen kitchen forks; or the fact that you are a straight "A" student is far more essential to your self-identity than the fact that you once failed a driving test. But what of other facts? Is the fact that you are white, or black, or Chinese, or congenitally bald, or male, or female an essential fact about you? Does it also constitute your identity, the way you essentially think about yourself? Do you think it should? Or do you think it is irrelevant, like the number of forks in your kitchen or the fact that you happened to be born in a taxicab?

This problem has long troubled European philosophers. In the Middle Ages, Christian philosophers argued forcefully that all of this, except for one's individual religious attitudes and the soul, was irrelevant. One's identity was or should be simply a soul seeking salvation before God. Contemporary philosophers, enamored by the growth of science, often talked as if our ultimate self-identity was or should be what we know. The self was considered nothing other than the locus of knowledge; other things—our looks, athletic abilities, enjoyments and actions—might be amusing or curious distractions but not the essence of self-identity. It is not at all unusual for people who are exceptional in one area rather than another to use their own abilities or vanities as a standard for everyone; athletes tend to admire athletes, intellectuals tend to admire intellectuals. But there is nothing necessary about this, or even desirable. The problem of self-identity, both in each individual case and as a general problem, is the problem of deciding which of the many possible characteristics (not necessarily one) should be chosen as our own standards for self-identity.

"What difference does it make?" Well, it makes an enormous difference. A self-identity isn't simply a label you throw on yourself in the casual discussion of a philosophy class. It is a mask and a role that you wear in every social encounter (though perhaps slightly different masks and roles for significantly different encounters). It is the way you think of yourself and the standards by which you judge yourself in every moment of reflection and self-evaluation. It is the self-image you follow in every action, when you decide that one thing is "worth doing" more than another or when you decide how to act in a given circumstance. Because of it, you feel proud, guilty, ashamed or delighted after you have done something. The problem of self-identity is not just a problem for philosophers; it is a problem we all face, either explicitly or implicitly, every self-conscious minute of our lives.

But, you might say, why make it sound as if there is a correct self-identity? The way in which a contemporary Chinese farmer will think of himself and judge himself is very different from that of a contemporary American college student. And a very handsome but stupendously dumb bully type will surely have a very different conception of self-identity than an extremely intelligent and talented coed studying art in college. This will not stop the medieval scholastic, for he will immediately declare all of that irrelevant, and insist that, "before God" all of us are the same, and our identities are to be judged accordingly. And most of us, despite the glib relativism we usually defend, would insist on a category that transcends all such individual considerations; we call it "being a good person." Ultimately, we would judge the dumb bully and the budding young artist according to the same criterion, and, in doing so, we would think that they should share the criterion "being a good person." Even where cultural differences would seem to demand entirely different conceptions of self-identity, we might still insist on applying the same criterion. For example, a South Sea Islander might well think of him or herself in terms that would be wholly unacceptable to us, but we can always reduce any variance from our norms to mere "accidental differences," insisting that we are essentially the same. And then we can always say, if another person does not agree with us, that he or she is mistaken, or "primitive," or "immature," or "neurotic." Of course people are different and think differently of themselves; but it does not follow that those differences are essential, nor does it follow that relativism is true. Ultimately, when you say that all people are "essentially the same" then you believe that there are, indeed, universal criteria for self-identity, and that the differences between people, though we need not deny them, are merely superficial.

One of the most powerful schools of contemporary thought, however, has been dedicated to the idea that self-identity, in every case, is a matter of individual choice. This school, which we have briefly met before, is *existentialism*. Its most powerful contemporary advocate is the French philosopher Jean-Paul Sartre. According to Sartre, there are no set standards for self-identity, either for individuals, or for people in general. There is, he argues, no such thing as "human nature," and what we are—and what it means to be a human being—are always matters of decision. There is no correct choice; there are only choices. In a well-known essay from the late 1940's, he argues:

What existentialists have in common is simply the fact that they believe that *existence* comes before *essence*—or, if you will, that we must begin from the subjective. What exactly do we mean by that?

If one considers an article of manufacture—as, for example, a book or a paper-knife—one sees that it has been made by an artisan who had a conception of it; and he has paid attention, equally, to the conception of a paper-knife and to the pre-existent technique of production which is a part of that conception and is, at bottom, a formula. Thus the paper-knife is at the same time an article producible in a certain manner and one which, on the other hand, serves a definite purpose, for one cannot suppose that a man would produce a paper-knife without knowing what it was for. Let us say, then, of the paper-knife that its essence—that is to say the sum of the formulae and the qualities which made its production and its definition possible—precedes its existence. The presence of such-and-such a paper-knife or book is thus determined before my eyes. Here, then, we are viewing the world from a technical standpoint, and we can say that production precedes existence.

When we think of God as the creator, we are thinking of him, most of the time, as a supernal artisan. Whatever doctrine we may be considering, whether it be a doctrine like that of Descartes, or of Leibnitz himself, we always imply that the will follows, more or less, from the understanding or at least accompanies it, so that when God creates he knows precisely what he is creating. Thus, the conception of man in the mind of God is comparable to that of the paper-knife in the mind of the artisan: God makes man according to a procedure and a conception, exactly as the artisan manufactures a paper-knife, following a definition and a formula. Thus each individual man is the realisation of a certain conception which dwells in the divine understanding. In the philosophic atheism of the eighteenth century, the notion of God is suppressed, but not, for all that, the idea that essence is prior to existence; something of that idea we still find everywhere, in Diderot, in Voltaire and even in Kant. Man possesses a human nature; that "human nature," which is the conception of human being, is found in every man; which means that each man is a particular example of an universal conception, the conception of Man. In Kant, this universality goes so far that the wild man of the woods, man in the state of nature and the bourgeois are all contained in the same definition and have the same fundamental qualities. Here again, the essence of man precedes that historic existence which we confront in experience.

.   .   .   .   .

What do we mean by saying that existence precedes essence? We mean that man first of all exists, encounters himself, surges up in the world—and defines himself afterwards. If man as the existentialist sees him is not definable, it is because to begin with he is nothing. He will not be anything until later, and then he will be what he makes of himself. Thus, there is no human nature, because there is no God to have a conception of it. Man simply is. Not that he is simply what he conceives himself to be, but he is what he wills, and as he conceives himself after already existing—as he wills to be after that leap towards existence. Man is nothing else but that which he makes of himself. That is the first principle of existentialism. And this is what people call its "subjectivity," using the word as a reproach against us. But what do we mean to say by this, but that man is of a greater dignity than a stone or a table? For we mean to say that man primarily exists—that man is, before all else, something which propels itself towards a future and is aware that it is doing so. Man is, indeed, a project which possesses a subjective life, instead of being a kind of moss, or a fungus or a cauliflower. Before that projection of the self nothing exists; not even in the heaven of intelligence: man will only attain existence when he is what he purposes to be. Not, however, what he may wish to be. For what we usually understand by wishing or willing is a conscious decision taken—much more often than not—after we have made ourselves what we are. I may wish to join a party, to write a book or to marry—but in such a case what is usually called my will is probably a manifestation of a prior and more spontaneous decision. If, however, it is true that existence is prior to essence, man is responsible for what he is. Thus, the first effect of existentialism is that it puts every man in possession of himself as he is, and places the entire responsibility for his existence squarely upon his own shoulders. And, when we say that man is responsible for himself, we do not mean that he is responsible only for his own individuality, but that he is responsible for all men.

When we say that man chooses himself, we do mean that every one of us must choose himself; but by that we also mean that in choosing for himself he chooses for all men. For in effect, of all the actions a man may take in order to create himself as he wills to be, there is not one which is not creative, at the same time, of an image of man such as he believes he ought to be.[10]

But this existentialist doctrine of choice doesn't make the problem of self-identity any easier. In fact, it complicates it enormously. Earlier in this section, we began by asking whether the facts about a person are sufficient to determine his or her identity. And we said, surely not all of them are neces-

[10] Jean-Paul Sartre, *Existentialism As a Humanism,* trans. Philip Mairet (New York: Philosophical Library, 1949).

sary, some are more essential than others. But this isn't yet an answer to the question, for it may be that all the essential facts are still not sufficient to determine a person's identity. According to the existentialist, this is made even more complex by the fact that a person chooses which facts are to be considered as essential. Are the facts alone ever sufficient to determine our identity? Sartre's answer, which he adapted from a German existentialist follower of Husserl named Martin Heidegger, is "never!" The facts that are true of a person are always, at least so long as a person is alive, only indicative of what a person has been and done so far. In judging a person's identity, we must always consider more than the facts that are true of him or her (which Sartre and Heidegger collectively name, somewhat technically, a person's *facticity*); we must also consider their projections into the future, their ambitions, plans, intentions, hopes and fantasies. (Sartre calls these considerations a person's *transcendence*. Notice that this is the third different way in which "transcendence" has been used, so be careful.) This way of viewing the person makes the question of self-identity impossibly complex, in fact, irresolvable. For example, consider Sartre's example of what he calls "bad faith" in one of his most important works, *Being and Nothingness* (1943). Bad faith, quite simply,[11] is refusing to accept yourself. This means, refusing to accept the facts about yourself. Or, to state Sartre's position differently, this means, accepting the facts about yourself as *conclusive* of your identity, thus ignoring the decisions that you now might make to change your intentions and ambitions, your resolutions and fantasies.

> Let us take an example: A homosexual frequently has an intolerable feeling of guilt, and his whole existence is determined in relation to this feeling. One will readily foresee that he is in bad faith. In fact it frequently happens that this man, while recognizing his homosexual inclination, while avowing each and every particular misdeed which he has committed, refuses with all his strength to consider himself *"a homosexual."* His case is always "different," peculiar; there enters into it something of a game, of chance, of bad luck; the mistakes are all in the past; they are explained by a certain conception of the beautiful which women cannot satisfy; we should see in them the results of a restless search, rather than the manifestations of a deeply rooted tendency, *etc., etc.* Here is assuredly a man in bad faith who borders on the comic since, acknowledging all the facts which are imputed to him, he refuses to draw from them the conclusion which they impose. His friend, who is his most severe critic, becomes irritated with this duplicity. The critic asks only one thing—and perhaps then he will show himself indulgent: that the guilty one recognize himself as guilty, that the homosexual declare frankly—whether humbly or boastfully matters little—"I am a homosexual." We ask here: Who is in bad faith? The homosexual or the champion of sincerity?
>
> The homosexual recognizes his faults, but he struggles with all his strength against the crushing view that his mistakes constitute for him a

[11] This is, however, the main concept of *Being and Nothingness,* and takes well over 700 pages to analyze correctly.

destiny. He does not wish to let himself be considered as a thing. He has an obscure but strong feeling that a homosexual is not a homosexual as this table is a table or as this red-haired man is red-haired. It seems to him that he has escaped from each mistake as soon as he has posited it and recognized it; he even feels that the psychic duration by itself cleanses him from each misdeed, constitutes for him an undetermined future, causes him to be born anew. Is he wrong? Does he not recognize in himself the peculiar, irreducible character of human reality? His attitude includes then an undeniable comprehension of truth. But at the same time he needs this perpetual rebirth, this constant escape in order to live; he must constantly put himself beyond reach in order to avoid the terrible judgment of collectivity. Thus he plays on the word *being.* He would be right actually if he understood the phrase "I am not a homosexual" in the sense of "I am not what I am." That is, if he declared to himself, "To the extent that a pattern of conduct is defined as the conduct of a paederast and to the extent that I have adopted this conduct, I am a homosexual. But to the extent that human reality cannot be finally defined by patterns of conduct, I am not one." But instead he slides surreptitiously toward a different connotation of the word "being." He understands "not being" in the sense of "not-being-in-itself." He lays claim to "not being a homosexual" in the sense in which this table *is not* an inkwell. He is in bad faith.[12]

And then, Sartre lays bare the heart of his theory. Bad faith points to the most important single fact about personal self-identity—there isn't any. In somewhat paradoxical terminology, Sartre tells us, "one is what one is not, and one is not what one is." In other words, whatever the facts about you, you are always something more than those facts. As long as a person is alive, he or she is identified by intentions, plans, dreams and hopes as much as what is already true by virtue of the facts.

Bad faith is possible only because sincerity is conscious of missing its goal inevitably, due to its very nature. I can try to apprehend myself as *"not being cowardly,"* when I *am* so, only on condition that the "being cowardly" is itself "in question" at the very moment when it exists, on condition that it is itself *one* question, that at the very moment when I wish to apprehend it, it escapes me on all sides and annihilates itself. The condition under which I can attempt an effort in bad faith is that in one sense, I *am not* this coward which I do not wish to be. But if I *were not* cowardly in the simple mode of not-being-what-one-is-not, I would be "in good faith" by declaring that I am not cowardly. Thus this inapprehensible coward is evanescent; in order for me not to be cowardly, I must in some way also be cowardly. That does not mean that I must be "a little" cowardly, in the sense that "a little" signifies "to a certain degree cowardly—and not cowardly to a certain degree." No. I must at once both be and not be totally and in all respects a coward. Thus in this case bad faith requires that I should not be what I am; that is,

---

[12] Jean-Paul Sartre, *Being and Nothingness,* trans. Hazel E. Barnes (New York: Philosophical Library, 1956).

that there be an imponderable difference separating being from non-being in the mode of being of human reality.[13]

And, given this complexity, the problem of deciding "who I am" takes on dramatic and extravagant complications. Consider the following scene from Sartre's famous play, *No Exit,* in which one of the characters (now dead and "living" in hell) tries to justify his image of himself as a hero, despite the facts of his life, which would indicate that he was a coward.

GARCIN. They shot me.

ESTELLE. I know. Because you refused to fight. Well, why shouldn't you?

GARCIN. I—I didn't exactly refuse. [*In a far-away voice*] I must say he talks well, he makes out a good case against me, but he never says what I should have done instead. Should I have gone to the general and said: "General, I decline to fight"? A mug's game; they'd have promptly locked me up. But I wanted to show my colors, my true colors, do you understand? I wasn't going to be silenced. [*To* ESTELLE] So I—I took the train. . . . They caught me at the frontier.

ESTELLE. Where were you trying to go?

GARCIN. To Mexico. I meant to launch a pacifist newspaper down there. [*A short silence.*] Well, why don't you speak?

ESTELLE. What could I say? You acted quite rightly, as you didn't want to fight. [GARCIN *makes a fretful gesture.*] But, darling, how on earth can I guess what you want me to answer?

INEZ. Can't you guess? Well, *I* can. He wants you to tell him that he bolted like a lion. For "bolt" he did, and that's what's biting him.

GARCIN. "Bolted," "went away"—we won't quarrel over words.

ESTELLE. But you *had* to run away. If you'd stayed they'd have sent you to jail, wouldn't they?

GARCIN. Of course. [*A pause.*] Well, Estelle, am I a coward?

ESTELLE. How can I say? Don't be so unreasonable, darling. I can't put myself in your skin. You must decide that for yourself.

GARCIN [*wearily*]. I can't decide.

ESTELLE. Anyhow, you must remember. You must have had reasons for acting as you did.

GARCIN. I had.

ESTELLE. Well?

GARCIN. But were they the real reasons?

ESTELLE. You've a twisted mind, that's your trouble. Plaguing yourself over such trifles!

GARCIN. I'd thought it all out, and I wanted to make a stand. But was that my real motive?

INEZ. Exactly. That's the question. Was that your real motive? No doubt you argued it out with yourself, you weighed the pros and cons, you found good reasons for what you did. But fear and hatred and all the dirty little instincts one keeps dark—they're motives too. So carry on, Mr. Garcin, and try to be honest with yourself—for once.

[13] Sartre, *Being and Nothingness.*

GARCIN. Do I need you to tell me that? Day and night I paced my cell, from the window to the door, from the door to the window. I pried into my heart, I sleuthed myself like a detective. By the end of it I felt as if I'd given my whole life to introspection. But always I harked back to the one thing certain—that I had acted as I did, I'd taken that train to the frontier. But why? Why? Finally I thought: My death will settle it. If I face death courageously, I'll prove I am no coward.

INEZ. And how did you face death?

GARCIN. Miserably. Rottenly. [INEZ *laughs*.] Oh, it was only a physical lapse— that might happen to anyone; I'm not ashamed of it. Only everything's been left in suspense, forever. [*To* ESTELLE] Come here, Estelle. Look at me. I want to feel someone looking at me while they're talking about me on earth. . . . I like green eyes.

INEZ. Green eyes! Just hark to him! And you, Estelle, do you like cowards?

ESTELLE. If you knew how little I care! Coward or hero, it's all one— provided he kisses well.

GARCIN. There they are, slumped in their chairs, sucking at their cigars. Bored they look. Half-asleep. They're thinking: "Garcin's a coward." But only vaguely, dreamily. One's got to think of something. "That chap Garcin was a coward." That's what they've decided, those dear friends of mine. In six months' time they'll be saying: "Cowardly as that skunk Garcin." You're lucky, you two; no one on earth is giving you another thought. But I—I'm long in dying.

· · · · ·

GARCIN [*putting his hands on* (INEZ'S) *shoulders*]. Listen! Each man has an aim in life, a leading motive; that's so, isn't it? Well, I didn't give a damn for wealth, or for love. I aimed at being a real man. A tough, as they say. I staked everything on the same horse. . . . Can one possibly be a coward when one's deliberately courted danger at every turn? And can one judge a life by a single action?

INEZ. Why not? For thirty years you dreamt you were a hero, and con- doned a thousand petty lapses—because a hero, of course, can do no wrong. An easy method obviously. Then a day came when you were up against it, the red light of real danger—and you took the train to Mexico.

GARCIN. I "dreamt," you say. It was no dream. When I chose that hardest path, I made my choice deliberately. A man is what he wills himself to be.

INEZ. Prove it. Prove it was no dream. It's what one does, and nothing else, that shows the stuff one's made of.

GARCIN. I died too soon. I wasn't allowed time to—to do my deeds.

INEZ. One always dies too soon—or too late. And yet one's whole life is complete at that moment, with a line drawn neatly under it, ready for the summing up. You are—your life, and nothing else.[14]

[14] Jean-Paul Sartre, *No Exit,* trans. Stuart Gilbert (New York: Vintage, 1948).

ONE SELF? ANY SELF?:
THE EASTERN ALTERNATIVE

So, "who am I"? How does one decide? It looks like one of those questions that, on the one hand, we can't ever avoid asking, but, at the same time, we can never succeed in answering. It gets more complicated yet. So far, we have talked as if, even if it is a matter of personal choice, self-identity is something singular, a unified set of ideals and characteristics according to which one identifies him or herself. There are, however, other ways of viewing the self. In his novel *Steppenwolf* Hermann Hesse argues a very different ideal, one taken from the Orient. It is not the ideal of selflessness, but rather the ideal of the *multiple* or *pluralistic* self, the self as a collection of "selves," with no one of them "real" or "essential." The "hero" of *Steppenwolf* (Harry Haller) is a man of extraordinary talents, but he is immensely unhappy. Like many of us, he lives with the myth of "two selves," one human, rational, and well-behaved, the other beastly, wild, and wolf-like. He is torn between the two. But, Hesse tells us, Harry's unhappiness is not, as he thinks, a result of this "war between the selves" at all, but rather of an oversimplified notion of self:

> The Steppenwolf is a fiction. When Harry feels himself to be a werewolf, and chooses to consist of two hostile and opposed beings, he is merely availing himself of a mythological simplification. He is no werewolf at all, and if we appeared to accept without scrutiny this lie which he invented for himself and believes in, and tried to regard him literally as a twofold being and a Steppenwolf, and so designated him, it was merely in the hope of being more easily understood with the assistance of a delusion, which we must now endeavor to put in its true light.
>
> The division into wolf and man, flesh and spirit, by means of which Harry tries to make his destiny more comprehensible to himself is a very great simplification. It is a forcing of the truth to suit a plausible, but erroneous, explanation of that contradiction which this man discovers in himself and which appears to himself to be the source of his by no means negligible sufferings. Harry finds in himself a "human being," that is to say, a world of thoughts and feelings, of culture and tamed or sublimated nature, and besides this he finds within himself also a "wolf," that is to say, a dark world of instinct, of savagery and cruelty, of unsublimated or raw nature. In spite of this apparently clear division of his being between two spheres, hostile to one another, he has known happy moments now and then when the man and the wolf for a short while were reconciled with one another. Suppose that Harry tried to ascertain in any single moment of his life, any single act, what part the man had in it and what part the wolf, he would find himself at once in a dilemma, and his whole beautiful wolf theory would go to pieces. For there is not a single human being . . . not even the idiot, who is so conveniently simple that his being can be explained as the sum of two or three principal elements; and to explain so complex a man as Harry by the artless

division into wolf and man is a hopelessly childish attempt. Harry consists of a hundred or a thousand selves, not of two. His life oscillates, as everyone's does, not merely between two poles, such as the body and the spirit, the saint and the sinner, but between thousand and thousands.

We need not be surprised that even so intelligent and educated a man as Harry should take himself for a Steppenwolf and reduce the rich and complex organism of his life to a formula so simple, so rudimentary and primitive. Man is not capable of thought in any high degree, and even the most spiritual and highly cultivated of men habitually sees the world and himself through the lenses of delusive formulas and artless simplifications—and most of all himself. For it appears to be an inborn and imperative need of all men to regard the self as a unit. However often and however grievously this illusion is shattered, it always mends again. The judge who sits over the murderer and looks into his face, and at one moment recognizes all the emotions and potentialities and possibilities of the murderer in his own soul and hears the murderer's voice as his own, is at the next moment one and indivisible as the judge, and scuttles back into the shell of his cultivated self and does his duty and condemns the murderer to death. And if ever the suspicion of their manifold being dawns upon men of unusual powers and of unusually delicate perceptions, so that, as all genius must, they break through the illusion of the unity of the personality and perceive that the self is made up of a bundle of selves, they have only to say so and at once the majority puts them under lock and key, calls science to aid, establishes schizomania and protects humanity from the necessity of hearing the cry of truth from the lips of these unfortunate persons. Why then waste words, why utter a thing that every thinking man accepts as self-evident, when the mere utterance of it is a breach of taste? A man, therefore, who gets so far as making the supposed unity of the self twofold is already almost a genius, in any case a most exceptional and interesting person. In reality, however, every ego, so far from being a unity, is in the highest degree a manifold world, a constellated heaven, a chaos of forms, of states and stages, of inheritances and potentialities. It appears to be a necessity as imperative as eating and breathing for everyone to be forced to regard this chaos as a unity and to speak of his ego as though it were a onefold and clearly detached and fixed phenomenon. Even the best of us share the delusion.

The delusion rests simply upon a false analogy. As a body everyone is single, as a soul never. In literature, too, even in its ultimate achievement, we find this customary concern with apparently whole and single personalities. Of all literature up to our days the drama has been the most highly prized by writers and critics, and rightly, since it offers (or might offer) the greatest possibilities of representing the ego as a manifold entity, but for the optical illusion which makes us believe that the characters of the play are manifold entities by lodging each one in an undeniable body, singly, separately and once and for all. An artless aesthetic criticism, then, keeps its highest praise for this so-called character drama in which each character makes his appearance unmistakably as a separate and single entity. Only from afar and by degrees the suspicion dawns here and there that all this is perhaps a cheap and superficial aesthetic philosophy and that we make a mistake in attributing to our great dramatists those magnificent conceptions of beauty that come to us from antiquity. These conceptions are not native to us, but are merely picked up at second hand, and it is in them, with their common source in the visible body, that the origin of the fiction of an ego, an individual, is really to be found. There is no trace of such a notion in the poems of ancient India. The heroes of the epics of India are not individuals, but whole reels of individualities in a series of incarnations. And in modern times there are poems, in which, behind the veil of a concern with individuality and character that is scarcely, indeed, in the author's mind, the motive is to present a manifold activity of soul. Whoever wishes to recognize this must resolve once and for all not to regard the characters of such a poem as separate beings, but as the various facets and aspects of a higher unity, in my opinion, of the poet's soul. If "Faust" is treated in this way, Faust, Mephistopheles, Wagner and the rest form a unity and a supreme individuality; and it is in this higher unity alone, not in the several characters, that something of the true nature of the soul is revealed. When Faust, in a line immortalized among schoolmasters and greeted with a shudder of astonishment by the Philistine, says, "Two souls, alas, inhabit in my breast!" he has forgotten Mephisto and a whole crowd of other souls that he has in his breast likewise. The Steppenwolf, too, believes that he bears two souls (wolf and man) in his breast and even so finds his breast disagreeably cramped because of them. The breast and the body are indeed one, but the souls that dwell in it are not two, nor five, but countless in number. Man is an onion made up of a hundred integuments, a texture made up of many threads. The ancient Asiatics knew this well enough, and in the Buddhist Yoga an exact technique was devised for unmasking the illusion of the personality. The human merry-go-round sees many changes: The illusion that cost India the efforts of thousands of years to unmask is the same illusion that the West has labored just as hard to maintain and strengthen.

· · · · ·

That man is not yet a finished creation but rather a challenge of the spirit; a distant possibility dreaded as much as it is desired; that the way toward it has only been covered for a very short distance and with terrible agonies and ecstasies even by those few for whom it is the scaffold today and the monument tomorrow—all this the Steppenwolf, too, suspected. What, however, he calls the "man" in himself, as opposed to the wolf, is to a great extent nothing else than this very same average man of the bourgeois convention.

· · · · ·

Man designs for himself a garden with a hundred kinds of trees, a thousand kinds of flowers, a hundred kinds of fruit and vegetables. Suppose, then, that the gardener of this garden knew no other distinction than between edible and inedible, nine-tenths of this garden would be useless to him. He would pull up the most enchanting flowers and hew down the noblest trees and even regard them with a loathing and envious eye. This is what the

Steppenwolf does with the thousand flowers of his soul. What does not stand classified as either man or wolf he does not see at all.[15]

Hesse refers to Buddhist concepts of the self with praise. Although he remains entrenched in Western ideas as well, Hesse is already more than half way to a very Eastern conception of self, which is essentially a denial of the self as we think of it. The Buddhist says, "give up your self-identity," "give up your self-consciousness," and, finally, "give up your self." This is a familiar refrain among many Eastern mystics, although Zen Buddhists have been the best-known advocates of selflessness in recent years in America. It may also be an ideal secular aspiration, however, for example, in contemporary China, and it is the goal of a large variety of ancient and contemporary forms of meditation.

Buddha says (notice a certain similarity to Hume) :

> Though both body and mind appear because of cooperating causes, it does not follow that there is an ego-personality. As the body of flesh is an aggregate of elements, it is, therefore, impermanent.
>
> If the body were an ego-personality, it could do this and that as it would determine.
>
> A king has the power to praise or punish as he wishes, but he becomes ill despite his intent and desire, he comes to old age unwillingly, and his fortune and his wishes often have little to do with each other.
>
> Neither is the mind the ego-personality. The human mind is also an aggregate of causes and conditions. It is in constant change.
>
> If the mind were an ego-personality it could do this and that as it would determine, but the mind often flies from what it knows is right and chases after evil unwillingly. Nothing seems to happen exactly as the ego desires.
>
> If one is asked whether the body is constant or impermanent, he will be obliged to answer "impermanent."
>
> If one is asked whether impermanent existence is happiness or suffering, he will generally have to answer "suffering."
>
> If a man believes that such an impermanent thing, so changeable and replete with suffering is the ego-personality, it is a serious mistake.
>
> The human mind is also impermanent and suffering; it has nothing that can be called an ego-personality.
>
> Therefore, both body and mind, which make up an individual life, and the external world which seems to surround it, are far apart from both the conceptions of "me" and "mine".
>
> It is simply the mind clouded over by impure desires, and impervious to wisdom, that obstinately persists in thinking of "me" and "mine."
>
> Since both body and its surroundings are originated by cooperating causes and conditions, they are continually changing and never can come to an end.

[15] Hermann Hesse, *Steppenwolf*, trans. Basil Creighton and rev. Joseph Mileck (New York: Holt, Rinehart and Winston, 1929).

The human mind, in its never-ending changes, is like the moving water of a river, or the burning flame of a candle; like an ape, it is forever jumping about, not ceasing for even a moment.

A wise man, seeing and hearing such, should break away from any attachment to body or mind, if he is ever to attain Enlightenment.

· · · · ·

. . . there is nothing that can be called an "ego," and there is no such thing as "mine" in all the world.

. . . everything is impermanent and passing and egoless. . . .

But even this call to "selflessness" is not simply a negative teaching. It has a positive counterpart, called "Buddha-nature."

We have been speaking of Buddha-nature as though it were something that could be described, as though it were similar to the "soul" of other teachings, but it is not.

The concept of an "ego-personality" is something that has been imagined by a discriminating mind which first grasped it and then became attached to it, but which must abandon it. On the contrary, Buddha-nature is something indescribable that must first be discovered. In one sense, it resembles an "ego-personality" but it is not the "ego" in the sense of "I am" or "mine."

To believe in the existence of an ego is an erroneous belief, that supposes non-existence; to deny Buddha-nature is wrong, for it supposes that existence is non-existence.

This can be explained in a parable. A mother took her sick child to a doctor. The doctor gave the child medicine and instructed the mother not to nurse the child until the medicine was digested.

The mother anointed her breast with something bitter so that the child would keep away from her of his own volition. After the medicine had time enough to be digested, the mother cleansed her breast and let the child suck her. The mother took this method of saving her child out of kindness because she loved the child.

Like the mother in the parable, Buddha, in order to remove misunderstanding and to break up attachments to an ego-personality, denies the existence of an ego; and when the misunderstanding and attachments are done away with, then He explains the reality of the true mind that is Buddha-nature.

Attachment to an ego-personality leads people into delusions, but faith in their Buddha-nature leads them to Enlightenment.

It is like the woman in a story, to whom a chest was bequeathed. Not knowing that the chest contained gold, she continued to live in poverty until another person opened it and showed her the gold. Buddha opens the minds of people and shows them the purity of their Buddha-nature.[16]

The Buddhist position offers us a paradoxical answer to the question of self-identity. On the one hand, it denies that there is a self and rejects the

[16] *The Teaching of Buddha,* rev. ed. (Tokyo: Bukkyo Deudo Kyokai, 1976).

views of self-identity that have become so familiar in Western philosophy, on the other, this too is a conception of self-identity. That is, if self-identity is a way of conceiving of oneself, then a denial that one has a self, a denial that one ought to think of oneself as a self, and a denial that one ought to see oneself as an individual rather than as part of Universal Mind is itself a form of self-identity. In the next section, we shall see that the concept of self need not be a concept of individual self. In Buddhism, the concept of self is expanded to the point at which it includes everything. (There have been similar moves in Western thought, for example, in the work of the German philosopher Hegel, whom we shall discuss in the following section.) The paradoxical answer of the Buddhist is the denial of self as individual self on the one hand and the expansion of the concept of self to include everything. We may seriously disagree whether or not this should still be called a "self" at all. But its importance in any discussion of self-identity is beyond argument. To deny the self is as important an option as to define the self in the individualistic ways we discussed in Descartes, Locke, and Kant.

The Buddhist conception of self introduces another very important alternative to our usual Western conceptions. Our Western conceptions are typically concerned with striving and ambition, status and planning for the future, "making something of yourself." Existentialism is one form of this conception. The American dream and the Protestant and capitalist ethics in general are another. But from the Buddhist conception of self comes a very different picture—of unqualified acceptance of things as they are rather than struggling to change them, which involves a rejection of such notions as "status" and "making something of yourself."

Once again, we must not confuse this rejection of traditional Western conceptions of the self with a rejection of the philosophical question of self-identity. "Who am I?" is as important a question for the Buddhist as it is for the Western philosopher. It is just that his answer to the question is radically different. Does it make sense to say that the one is more "correct" than the other? This too is part of the question of self-identity. Must there be a single "correct" answer for everyone?

THE INDIVIDUAL AND THE COMMUNITY

In Buddhism, we saw a concept of self that was not, like everything else we have been discussing, an individual self. But even within discussions of the individual self, it becomes evident that the individual self is largely, if not entirely, a social product and a self defined by society. We have all had the experience of finding ourselves in company in which we "could not be ourselves" or, even worse, in which we acted according to an identity which was wholly imposed upon us by other people. When going to school, for example, we long played the role of "student," ingratiating and oppressed, much before we started to recognize that it is a role, and not a very pleasant one at that. Now we see it as a role that has been formulated solely for the advantage of other people—teachers, administrators, parents—so that we could be forced to "behave." Have you started to wonder how many other aspects of your identity have been similarly imposed upon you, not chosen at all, much less created by you? How much of your behavior has been "programmed" or "conditioned" by parents, society, television, movies, friends, and schoolmates? The suspicion deepens. And soon you start to see a split developing in your thinking about yourself: first, there is your conception of your own identity; second, there is the identity that has been imposed upon you. The two drift apart like boat and dock, and you find yourself falling between. No wonder, then, that one of the leading psychiatrists of our times, R. D. Laing, has looked at this problem as not only the basis of much of our everyday unhappiness, but as the cause of some of our most serious psychological breakdowns as well.

> Self-consciousness, as the term is ordinarily used, implies two things: an awareness of oneself by oneself, and *an awareness of oneself as an object of someone else's observation.*
>
> These two forms of awareness of the self, as an object in one's own eyes and as an object in the other's eyes, are closely related to each other. In the schizoid individual both are enhanced and both assume a somewhat compulsive nature. The schizoid individual is frequently tormented by the compulsive nature of his awareness of his own processes, and also by the equally compulsive nature of his sense of his body as an object in the world of others. The heightened sense of being always seen, or at any rate of being always potentially seeable, may be principally referable to the body, but the preoccupation with being seeable may be condensed with the idea of the mental self being penetrable, and vulnerable, as when the individual feels that one can look right through him into his 'mind' or 'soul'. Such 'plate-glass' feelings are usually spoken about in terms of metaphor or simile, but in psychotic conditions the gaze or scrutiny of the other can be experienced as an actual penetration into the core of the 'inner' self.
>
> The heightening or intensifying of the awareness of one's own being, both as an object of one's own awareness and of the awareness of others, is practically universal in adolescents, and is associated with the well-known accompaniments of shyness, blushing, and general embarrassment. One readily invokes some version of 'guilt' to account for such awkwardness. But to suggest, say, that the individual is self-conscious 'because' he has guilty secrets (e.g. masturbation) does not take us far. Most adolescents masturbate, and not uncommonly they are frightened that it will show in some way in their faces. But why, if 'guilt' is the key to this phenomenon, does guilt have these particular consequences and not others, since there are many ways of being guilty, and a heightened sense of oneself as an embarrassed or ridiculous object in the eyes of others is not the only way. 'Guilt' in itself is inadequate to help us here. Many people with profound and crushing guilt do not feel unduly self-conscious. Moreover, it is possible, for instance, to tell a lie and feel guilt at doing so without being frightened that the lie will show

in one's face, or that one will be struck blind. It is indeed an important achievement for the child to gain the assurance that the adults have no means of knowing what he does, if they do not see him; that they cannot do more than guess at what he thinks to himself if he does not tell them; that actions that no one has seen and thoughts that he has 'kept to himself' are in no way accessible to others unless he himself 'gives the show away'. The child who *cannot* keep a secret or who *cannot* tell a lie because of the persistence of such primitive magical fears has not established his full measure of autonomy and identity. No doubt in most circumstances good reasons can be found against telling lies, but the *inability* to do so is not one of the best reasons.

The self-conscious person feels he is more the object of other people's interest than, in fact, he is. Such a person walking along the street approaches a cinema queue. He will have to 'steel himself' to walk past it: preferably, he will cross to the other side of the street. It is an ordeal to go into a restaurant and sit down at a table by himself. At a dance he will wait until two or three couples are already dancing before he can face taking the floor himself, and so on.

Curiously enough, those people who suffer from intense anxiety when performing or acting before an audience are by no means necessarily 'self-conscious' in general, and people who are usually extremely self-conscious may lose their compulsive preoccupations with this issue when they are performing in front of others—the very situation, on first reflection, one might suppose would be most difficult for them to negotiate.

· · · · ·

An understanding of self-consciousness in some such terms eludes, I believe, the central issue facing the individual whose basic existential position is one of ontological insecurity and whose schizoid nature is partly a direct expression of, and occasion for, his ontological insecurity, and partly an attempt to overcome it; or, putting the last remark in slightly different terms, partly an attempt to defend himself against the dangers to his being that are the consequences of his failure to achieve a secure sense of his own identity.

The 'self-conscious' person is caught in a dilemma. He may *need* to be seen and recognized, in order to maintain his sense of realness and identity. Yet, at the same time, the other represents a threat to his identity and reality. One finds extremely subtle efforts expended in order to resolve this dilemma in terms of the secret inner self and the behavioural false-self systems already described. James, for instance, feels that 'other people provide me with my existence'. On his own, he feels that he is empty and nobody. 'I can't feel real unless there is someone there. . . .' Nevertheless, he cannot feel at ease with another person, because he feels as 'in danger' with others as by himself.

He is, therefore, driven compulsively to seek company, but never allows himself to 'be himself' in the presence of anyone else. He avoids social anxiety by never really *being with* others. He never quite says what he means or means what he says. The part he plays is always not quite himself. He takes care to laugh when he thinks a joke is *not* funny, and look bored when he is amused. He makes friends with people he does not really like and is rather cool to those with whom he would 'really' like to be friends. No one, therefore, really knows him, or understands him. He can be *himself* in safety only in isolation, albeit with a sense of emptiness and unreality. With others, he plays an elaborate game of pretence and equivocation. His social self is felt to be false and futile. What he longs for most is the possibility of 'a moment of recognition', but whenever this by chance occurs, when he has by accident 'given himself away', he is covered in confusion and suffused with panic.

The more he keeps his 'true self' in hiding, concealed, unseen, and the more he presents to others a false front, the more compulsive this false presentation of himself becomes. He appears to be extremely narcissistic and exhibitionistic. In fact he hates himself and is terrified to reveal himself to others. Instead, he compulsively exhibits what he regards as mere extraneous trappings to others; he dresses ostentatiously, speaks loudly and insistently. He is constantly drawing attention to himself, and at the same time drawing attention *away* from his self. His behaviour is compulsive. All his thoughts are occupied with being seen. His longing is to be known. But this is also what is most dreaded.[17]

The idea that self-identity is really social-identity flies in the face of that whole Cartesian tradition—and much of Western thinking—that begins with the autonomy of the self and self-consciousness. Nietzsche, for example, goes so far as to suggest that self-consciousness is simply superfluous.

The "Genius of the Species."—The problem of consciousness (or more correctly: of becoming conscious of oneself) meets us only when we begin to perceive in what measure we could dispense with it: and it is at the beginning of this perception that we are now placed by physiology and zoology (which have thus required two centuries to overtake the hint thrown out in advance by Leibnitz). For we could in fact think, feel, will and recollect, we could likewise "act" in every sense of the term, and nevertheless nothing of it all need necessarily "come into consciousness" (as one says metaphorically). The whole of life would be possible without its seeing itself as it were in a mirror: as in fact even at present the far greater part of our life still goes on without this mirroring,—and even our thinking, feeling, volitional life as well, however painful this statement may sound to an older philosopher. *What* then is *the purpose* of consciousness generally, when it is in the main *superfluous?*—Now it seems to me, if you will hear my answer and its perhaps extravagant supposition, that the subtlety and strength of consciousness are always in proportion to the *capacity for communication* of a man (or an animal), the capacity for communication in its turn being in proportion to the *necessity for communication:* the latter not to be understood as if precisely the individual himself who is master in the art of communicating and making known his necessities would at the same time have to be most dependent upon others for his necessities. It seems to me, however, to be so in relation to whole races and successions of generations: where necessity and need have long compelled men to communicate with their fellows and understand one another rapidly and subtly, a surplus of the power and art of communication is at last acquired, as if it were a fortune which had gradually

17 R. D. Laing, *The Divided Self* (New York: Pantheon, 1969).

accumulated, and now waited for an heir to squander it prodigally (the so-called artists are these heirs, in like manner the orators, preachers and authors: all of them men who come at the end of a long succession, "late-born" always, in the best sense of the word, and as has been said, *squanderers* by their very nature). Granted that this observation is correct, I may proceed further to the conjecture that *consciousness generally has only been developed under the pressure of the necessity for communication,*—that from the first it has been necessary and useful only between man and man (especially between those commanding and those obeying), and has only developed in proportion to its utility. Consciousness is properly only a connecting network between man and man,—it is only as such that it has had to develop; the recluse and wild-beast species of men would not have needed it. The very fact that our actions, thoughts, feelings and motions come within the range of our consciousness—at least a part of them—is the result of a terrible, prolonged "must" ruling man's destiny: as the most endangered animal he *needed* help and protection; he needed his fellows, he was obliged to express his distress, he had to know how to make himself understood—and for all this he needed "consciousness" first of all: he had to "know" himself what he lacked, to "know" how he felt, and to "know" what he thought. For, to repeat it once more, man, like every living creature, thinks unceasingly, but does not know it; the thinking which is becoming *conscious of itself* is only the smallest part thereof, we may say, the most superficial part, the worst part:—for this conscious thinking alone *is done in words, that is to say, in the symbols for communication,* by means of which the origin of consciousness is revealed. In short, the development of speech and the development of consciousness (not of reason, but of reason becoming self-conscious) go hand in hand. Let it be further accepted that it is not only speech that serves as a bridge between man and man, but also the looks, the pressure and the gestures; our becoming conscious of our sense impressions, our power of being able to fix them, and as it were to locate them outside of ourselves, has increased in proportion as the necessity has increased for communicating them to *others* by means of signs. The sign-inventing man is at the same time the man who is always more acutely self-conscious; it is only as a social animal that man has learned to become conscious of himself,—he is doing so still, and doing so more and more.—As is obvious, my idea is that consciousness does not properly belong to the individual existence of man, but rather to the social and gregarious nature in him; that, as follows therefrom, it is only in relation to communal and gregarious utility that it is finely developed; and that consequently each of us, in spite of the best intention of *understanding* himself as individually as possible, and of "knowing himself," will always just call into consciousness the non-individual in him, namely, his "averageness";—that our thought itself is continuously as it were *outvoted* by the character of consciousness—by the imperious "genius of the species" therein—and is translated back into the perspective of the herd. Fundamentally our actions are in an incomparable manner altogether personal, unique, and absolutely individual—there is no doubt about it; but as soon as we translate them into consciousness, they *do not appear so any longer.* . . . This is the proper phenomenalism and perspectivism as I understand it: the nature of *animal consciousness* involves the notion that the world of which we can become conscious is only a superficial and symbolic world, a generalised and vulgarised world;—that everything which becomes conscious *becomes* just thereby shallow, meagre, relatively stupid,—a generalisation, a symbol, a characteristic of the herd; that with the evolving of consciousness there is always combined a great, radical perversion, falsification, superficialisation and generalisation. Finally, the growing consciousness is a danger, and whoever lives among the most conscious European knows even that it is a disease. As may be conjectured, it is not the antithesis of subject and object with which I am here concerned: I leave that distinction to the epistemologists who have remained entangled in the toils of grammar (popular metaphysics). It is still less the antithesis of "thing in itself" and phenomenon, for we do not "know" enough to be entitled even to *make such a distinction.* Indeed, we have not any organ at all for *knowing*, or for "truth": we "know" (or believe, or fancy) just as much as may be of *use* in the interest of the human herd, the species; and even what is here called "usefulness" is ultimately only a belief, a fancy, and perhaps precisely the most fatal stupidity by which we shall one day be ruined.[18]

Our response to this split between what some philosophers call the "self for itself" and the "self for others" has been varied. For some, particularly those who have been called existentialists, the response has been wholesale rebellion, the demand that we break away from "the masses" and our given social identities and create our selves. Nietzsche, for example, attacks what he calls "the herd" in the above passage, and urges us to develop ourselves as unique individuals. Indeed, this is the main point of Nietzsche's entire philosophy, and underlies his attack on religion and morality.

> *Herd-Instinct.*—Wherever we meet with a morality we find a valuation and order of rank of the human impulses and activities. These valuations and orders of rank are always the expression of the needs of a community or herd: that which is in the first place to *its* advantage—and in the second place and third place—is also the authoritative standard for the worth of every individual. By morality the individual is taught to become a function of the herd, and to ascribe to himself value only as a function. As the conditions for the maintenance of one community have been very different from those of another community, there have been very different moralities; and in respect to the future essential transformations of herds and communities, states and societies, one can prophesy that there will still be very divergent moralities. Morality is the herd-instinct in the individual.[19]

A similar attempt at individual rebellion was attempted even earlier by Kierkegaard, the religious philosopher who has often been called the father of existentialism. Like Nietzsche, he deplores what he sarcastically calls "the public," and urges an end to collective identity and social roles in favor of renewed respect for the individual.

[18] Friedrich Nietzsche, *The Joyful Wisdom*, trans. Thomas Common, in *The Complete Works of Friedrich Nietzsche*, Oscar Levy, General Editor (1909–11) (New York: Russell & Russell, 1964).
[19] Nietzsche, *The Joyful Wisdom.*

In spite of all his exertion the subjective thinker enjoys only a meager reward. The more the collective idea comes to dominate even the ordinary consciousness, the more forbidding seems the transition to becoming a particular existing human being instead of losing oneself in the race, and saying "we," "our age," "the nineteenth century." That it is a little thing merely to be a particular existing human being is not to be denied; but for this very reason it requires considerable resignation not to make light of it. For what does a mere individual count for? Our age knows only too well how little it is, but here also lies the specific immorality of the age. Each age has its own characteristic depravity. Ours is perhaps not pleasure or indulgence or sensuality, but rather a dissolute pantheistic contempt for the individual man. In the midst of all our exultation over the achievements of the age and the nineteenth century, there sounds a note of poorly conceived contempt for the individual man; in the midst of the self-importance of the contemporary generation there is revealed a sense of despair over being human. Everything must attach itself so as to be a part of some movement; men are determined to lose themselves in the totality of things, in world-history, fascinated and deceived by a magic witchery; no one wants to be an individual human being.

In fact, so adamant is Kierkegaard on this issue that he argues that a person who "follows the crowd" and does not choose his or her own identity and live passionately as an individual cannot even be said to really exist.

It is impossible to exist without passion, unless we understand the word "exist" in the loose sense of a so-called existence. Every Greek thinker was therefore essentially a passionate thinker. I have often reflected how one might bring a man into a state of passion. I have thought in this connection that if I could get him seated on a horse and the horse made to take fright and gallop wildly, or better still, for the sake of bringing the passion out, if I could take a man who wanted to arrive at a certain place as quickly as possible, and hence already had some passion, and could set him astride a horse that can scarcely walk—and yet this is what existence is like if one is to become consciously aware of it. Or if a driver were otherwise not especially inclined toward passion, if someone hitched a team of horses to a wagon for him, one of them a Pegasus and the other a worn-out jade, and told him to drive—I think one might succeed. And it is just this that it means to exist, if one is to become conscious of it. Eternity is the winged horse, infinitely fast, and time is a worn-out jade; the existing individual is the driver. That is to say, he is such a driver when his mode of existence is not an existence loosely so called; for then he is no driver, but a drunken peasant who lies asleep in the wagon and lets the horses take care of themselves. To be sure, he also drives and is a driver; and so there are perhaps many who—also exist.[20]

And in this century, borrowing from both Kierkegaard and Nietzsche, the German existentialist Martin Heidegger has argued against collective social identity in terms of what he (also ironically) calls das Man, an extremely

[20] Søren Kierkegaard, *Concluding Unscientific Postscript*, trans. David F. Swenson and Walter Lowrie (Princeton, N.J.: Princeton University Press, 1941).

useful German expression that roughly translates as "they" in "*they* say that garlic cures colds." Who are "they?" No one at all, Heidegger says, just an anonymous no one. In extremely dense philosophical prose,[21] he argues:

> Dasein, as everyday Being-with-one-another, stands in *subjection* to Others. It itself *is* not; its Being has been taken away by the Others. Dasein's everyday possibilities of Being are for the Others to dispose of as they please. These Others, moreover, are not *definite* Others. On the contrary, any Other can represent them. What is decisive is just that inconspicuous domination by Others which has already been taken over unawares from Dasein as Being-with. One belongs to the Others oneself and enhances their power. 'The Others' whom one thus designates in order to cover up the fact of one's belonging to them essentially oneself, are those who proximally and for the most part '*are there*' in everyday Being-with-one-another. The "who" is not this one, not that one, not oneself, not some people, and not the sum of them all. The 'who' is the neuter, *the "they"* [*das Man*].

> . . . . .

> Everyone is the other, and no one is himself. The *"they,"* which supplies the answer to the question of the *"who"* of everyday Dasein, is the *"nobody"* to whom every Dasein has already surrendered itself in Being-among-one-other.

And against this "surrender," Heidegger urges us to "take hold of ourselves" as individuals and find our "authentic" selves.

> The Self of everyday Dasein is the *they-self,* which we distinguish from the *authentic Self*—that is, from the Self which has been taken hold of in its own way.[22]

This individualist movement is not unique to existentialism, it is in the mainstream of Western thinking, from ancient Socrates through Reformation Christianity to contemporary Capitalism. Socrates' rebellion was, in a very important way, an existential rebellion. He stood up for his principles against the opinions of the age. And Luther's Reformation was, among other things, very much a reassertion of the individual (individual conscience, individual actions) against the all-embracing spirit of the Catholic church. And today, virtually every American would agree that every individual deserves at least some individual rights and respect. But individualism has always had its doubters. Individualism arises largely as a reaction against the awareness of how socially conditioned we really are. As an instrument of personal growth and as a defense against excessive socialization (to the point, for example, where individual rights and values are no longer meaningful), individualism is extremely valuable. But when individualism becomes so powerful that personal interests eclipse the interests of everyone else and individual values

---

21 For "Dasein," read, "individual human being"; for "Being-with," read "being around other people."

22 Martin Heidegger, *Being and Time,* trans. J. MacQuarrie and E. Robinson (New York: Harper & Row, 1962).

begin to destroy the community, then it may be time to bring the limits of individualism into question as well. Furthermore, there are limits to the degree to which we can challenge the values and customs of our upbringing. Some rebellion is required for growth and change, of the society as well as of the individual. But too much rebellion can be self-destructive as well as destructive to the community. For our self-identities, no matter how hard we try to think of ourselves as total individuals, are inextricably tied to the communities and values in which we were raised.

The American sociologist David Reisman looks again at individualism in the light of these considerations and defends it as follows:

> Social science has helped us become more aware of the extent to which individuals, great and little, are the creatures of their cultural conditioning; and so we neither blame the little nor exalt the great. But the same wisdom has sometimes led us to the fallacy that, since all men have their being in culture and as the result of the culture, they owe a debt to that culture which even a lifetime of altruism could not repay. (One might as well argue, and in fact many societies in effect do, that since we are born of parents, we must feel guilt whenever we transcend their limitations!) Sometimes the point is pushed to the virtual denial of individuality: since we arise in society, it is assumed with a ferocious determinism that we can never transcend it. All such concepts are useful correctives of an earlier solipsism. But if they are extended to hold that conformity with society is not only a necessity but also a duty, they destroy that margin of freedom which gives life its savor and its endless possibility for advance.[23]

But the argument for individualism is often stated as a form of mutual conflict (as in the existentialists and Reisman), which many philosophers would not accept. Why need there be a conflict? Kant, for example, while very much the champion of individual autonomy, yet insisted that the only individuality worth defending was the ability of the individual to participate in universal morality. The same argument is to be found in Socrates, Plato, and Aristotle. And, in more recent times, this argument has found a large following among thinkers who have seen the disastrous results of overly-individual thinking (what Reisman refers to as "solipsism"). The German philosopher Hegel, for example, writing in the midst of the great international movements of the early nineteenth century, argued:

> . . . at a time when the universal nature of spiritual life has become so very much emphasized and strengthened, and the mere individual aspect has become, as it should be, correspondingly a matter of indifference, when, too, that universal aspect holds, by the entire range of its substance, the full measure of the wealth it has built up, and lays claim to it all, the share in the total work of mind that falls to the activity of any particular individual can only be very small. Because this is so, the individual must all the more forget himself, as in fact the very nature of science implies and requires that he should; and he must, moreover, become and do what he can. But all

[23] David Reisman, *Individualism Reconsidered* (New York: Doubleday, 1954).

the less must be demanded of him, just as he can expect the less from him-self, and may ask the less for himself.[24]

And elsewhere, in a famous passage, he argues that individuals in history are significant only insofar as they contribute to movements far greater than themselves:

> . . . in contemplating history as the slaughter-bench at which the hap-piness of peoples, the wisdom of states, and the virtue of individuals have been sacrificed, a question necessarily arises: To what principle, to what final purpose, have these monstrous sacrifices been offered?
>
> . . . human agents have before them limited aims, special interests. But they are also intelligent, thinking beings. Their purposes are interwoven with general and essential considerations of law, the good, duty, etc. For mere desire, volition in its raw and savage form, falls outside the scene and sphere of world history. These general considerations, which at the same time form norms for directing purposes and actions, have a definite content. For such empty abstractions as "good for its own sake" have no place in living actuality.
>
> . . . Each individual has his position; he knows, on the whole, what a lawful and honorable course of conduct is. To assert in ordinary private relations that it is difficult to choose the right and good, and to regard it as mark of an exalted morality to find difficulties and raise scruples on that score indicates an evil and perverse will. It indicates a will that seeks to evade obvious duties or, at least, a petty will that gives its mind too little to do. The mind, then, in idle reflection, busies itself with itself and indulges in moral smugness.
>
> . . . *each individual is also the child of a people at a definite stage of its development. One cannot skip over the spirit of his people any more than one can skip over the earth. The earth is the center of gravity; a body imagined as leaving this center can only be imagined as exploding into the air. So it is with an individual. But only through his own effort can he be in harmony with his substance; he must bring the will demanded by his people to his own consciousness, to articulation. The individual does not invent his own content; he is what he is by acting out the universal as his own content.*
>
> *In the course of history two factors are important. One is the preservation of a people, a state, of the well-ordered spheres of life. This is the activity of individuals participating in the common effort and helping to bring about its particular manifestations. It is the preservation of ethical life. The other important factor, however, is the decline of a state. The existence of a national spirit is broken when it has used up and exhausted itself. World history, the World Spirit, continues on its course.*

. . . . .

This universal is an essential phase in the development of the creating Idea, of truth striving and urging toward itself. The historical men, *world-historical individuals*, are those [*who grasp just such a higher universal, make it their*

---

[24] G. W. F. Hegel, *The Phenomenology of Mind*, trans. J. B. Baillie (New York: Harper & Row, 1966).

own purpose, and realize this purpose in accordance with the higher law of the spirit].[25]

In the midst of the international upheavals led by Napoleon, you can appreciate the appropriateness of such a brutal philosophy. "The slaughter-bench of history" is not a pleasant concept! And the idea that each of us is virtually insignificant in our tiny place in history also hurts our grander conceptions of ourselves. But Hegel argues that no other view of ourselves is defensible. Even the greatest among us is nothing more than an expression of the "universal," the monumental forces of society and of mankind as a whole (these are what Hegel refers to as "the Creating Idea" and elsewhere as "the cunning of Reason").

But however appropriate in times of international warfare, Hegel's conception is bound to raise hackles among the individualists in peacetime. Consider Kierkegaard's ironic retort to Hegel's philosophy:

> Hence perhaps the many attempts to continue clinging to Hegel, even by men who have reached an insight into the questionable character of his philosophy. It is a fear that if they were to become particular existing human beings, they would vanish tracelessly, so that not even the daily press would be able to discover them, still less critical journals, to say nothing at all of speculative philosophers immersed in world-history. As particular human beings they fear that they will be doomed to a more isolated and forgotten existence than that of a man in the country; for if a man lets go of Hegel he will not even be in a position to have a letter addressed to him.[26]

Karl Marx was a student of Hegel's philosophy. In his "early writings" of 1844, he too argues for a view of self as essentially social, a part of a community, a "species-being":

> It follows from the character of this relationship [the human family] how far *man* has become, and has understood himself as, a *species-being*, a *human being*. The relation of man to woman is the *most natural* relation of human being to human being. It indicates, therefore, how far man's *natural* behaviour has become *human*, and how far his *human* essence has become a *natural* essence for him, how far his *human nature* has become *nature* for him. It also shows how far man's needs have become *human* needs, and consequently how far the other person, as a person, has become one of his needs, and to what extent he is in his individual existence at the same time a social being.[27]

We are painfully cut off from our own "nature" or natural identity, according to Marx, by the institution of "private property," which sets people against each other and creates unnecessary conflict between man and man, and man and nature. The solution to this conflict (or "alienation"), according to Marx, is the abolition of private property, or "communism."

[25] G. W. F. Hegel, *Reason in History,* trans. Robert S. Hartman (New York: Bobbs-Merrill, 1953).
[26] Kierkegaard, *Concluding Unscientific Postscript.*
[27] Karl Marx, *Early Writings,* trans. T. Bottomore (New York: McGraw-Hill, 1963).

Communism is the *positive* abolition of *private property*, of *human self-alienation*, and thus the real *appropriation* of *human* nature through and for man. It is, therefore, the return of man himself as a *social*, i.e. really human, being, a complete and conscious return which assimilates all the wealth of previous development. Communism as a fully developed naturalism is humanism and as a fully developed humanism is naturalism. It is the *definitive* resolution of the antagonism between man and nature, and between essence, between objectification and self-affirmation, between freedom and necessity, between individual and species. It is the solution of the riddle of history and knows itself to be this solution.

Marx also argues that our particular selves are socially determined:

We have seen how, on the assumption that private property has been positively superseded, man produces man, himself and then other men; how the object which is the direct activity of his personality is at the same time his existence for other men and their existence for him. Similarly, the material of labour and man himself as a subject are the starting-point as well as the result of this movement (and because there must be this starting-point private property is a historical necessity). Therefore, the *social* character is the universal character of the whole movement; *as* society itself produces *man* as *man*, so it is *produced* by him. Activity and mind are social in their content as well as in their *origin*; they are *social* activity and social mind. The *human* significance of nature only exists for *social* man, because only in this case is nature a *bond* with other *men*, the basis of his existence for others and of their existence for him. Only then is nature the *basis* of his own *human* experience and a vital element of human reality. The *natural* existence of man has here become his *human* existence and nature itself has become human for him. Thus *society* is the accomplished union of man with nature, the veritable resurrection of nature, the realized naturalism of man and the realized humanism of nature.

. . . . .

It is above all necessary to avoid postulating "society" once again as an abstraction confronting the individual. The individual *is* the *social being*. The manifestation of his life—even when it does not appear directly in the form of a communal manifestation, accomplished in association with other men—is, therefore, a manifestation and affirmation of *social life*. Individual human life and species-life are not different things, even though the mode of existence of individual life is necessarily either a more *specific* or a more *general* mode of species-life, or that of species-life a *specific* or more *general* mode of individual life.

In his *species-consciousness* man confirms his real *social life*, and reproduces his real existence in thought; while conversely, species-life confirms itself in species-consciousness and exists for itself in its universality as a thinking being. Though man is a unique individual—and it is just his particularity which makes him an individual, a really *individual* communal being—he is equally the *whole*, the ideal whole, the subjective existence of society as thought and experienced. He exists in reality as the representation and the real mind of social existence, and as the sum of human manifestations of life.[28]

It is important to emphasize that neither Marx nor Hegel (nor Socrates nor Kant) is actually denying the individual, or individual respect or individual rights. They are, however, insisting that an individual deserves such respect or such rights only insofar as he or she is a member of a community. This does not mean that a person cannot be eccentric, like the weirdo artist or the spaced-out rock musician, but it does mean that even their eccentricity, as well as their talents, must be viewed as social contributions. What they are denying, in other words, is what has sometimes been called "vulgar" individualism," that form of self-identity which denies all social relevance and social obligations.

SUMMARY AND CONCLUSION

Self-identity is a question of essential properties: What is it about you that makes you yourself? In this chapter we have reviewed a series of different answers to this question. The tradition from Descartes and Locke until Kant stresses the importance of consciousness in our conception of ourselves. (Even Hume, who denies that there is a self, is part of this tradition.) Then there is the general question, how much is the self something that we can choose, and how much is it something that is determined for us? Does each person have just one self, one set of essential properties, or might a single "person" be several people, with several selves? Or might there really be no self at all, as argued by Hume and Sartre, and in a very different way, by several influential Eastern philosophies? And how much should we conceive of ourselves as individuals, and how much as organic components of a larger community? None of these questions have any firmly agreed upon answers, but all of us adopt one view or another, even if just for a short time, every time we attempt to define ourselves or just "be ourselves."

GLOSSARY

bad faith: Sartre's characterization of a person's refusal to accept him or herself; this sometimes means not accepting the facts that are true about you. More often, it means accepting the facts about you as conclusive about your identity, as in the statement, "Oh, I couldn't do that, I'm too shy."

continuity (spacio-temporal continuity): the uninterrupted identifiability of an object over time in the same location or in a sequence of tangent locations.

criterion: test or standard.

[28] Marx, *Early Writings.*

empirical ego: all those characteristics of a person that can be discovered through experience and which distinguish each of us from other persons qualitatively; that which makes each of us a particular man or woman and gives us a particular "character." Cf. *transcendental ego*.

essence: that which is necessary for something to be what it is. The essence of a person is that without which we would not say one is *that* particular person (Fred rather than Mary, for example).

existentialism: in Sartre's terms, the philosophy that teaches that "man's existence precedes his essence." That is, people have no given self-identity, they have to choose their identities and work for them through their actions. (Neglect and omission, however, are also actions. One can be a certain type of person just by not bothering to do the appropriate activities.)

facticity: Sartre's term (borrowed from Heidegger) for the totality of facts that are true of a person at any given time.

resemblance: having the same features. All people resemble each other (or at least most do) in having one and only one head; you resemble yourself five years ago in (perhaps) having the same texture hair, the same color eyes, the same fear of spiders, and the same skill at chess.

self-consciousness: being aware of oneself, whether "as others see you" (looking in a mirror or "watching yourself play a role" at a party) or just "looking into yourself" (as when you reflect on your goals in life or wonder, in a moment of philosophical perversity, whether you really exist or not). Self-consciousness requires having some concept of your "self." Accordingly, it is logically tied to questions of self-identity.

self-identity: the way you characterize yourself, either in general (as a human being, as a man or as a woman, as a creature before God or as one among many animals) or in particular (as the person who can run the fastest mile, as an all-"C" student, or as the worst dressed slob in your class). Self-identity, on this characterization, requires self-consciousness. The self-identity of a person, in other words, is not merely the same as the identity of a "thing," for example, the identity of a human body.

transcendence: Sartre's term for a person's plans, ambitions, intentions and hopes for the future. (Do not confuse this use of the word with those introduced in Chapters 5 and 7.)

transcendental ego: the bare, logical fact of one's own self-consciousness: Descartes' "I think"; the self "behind" all of our experiences, the mental activity that unifies our various thoughts and sensations. (The term comes from Kant's *Critique of Pure Reason*.)

9

MIND AND BODY

*It is certain that I (that is, my mind, by which I am what I am) is
entirely and truly distinct from my body, and may exist without it.*

René Descartes

Whatever our attempts to answer the problems of self-identity, they begin
with a single "fact," our own consciousness. This was the logical beginning for
Descartes, who used the fact of his own consciousness as the starting point for
his whole philosophy. It was true for Locke, who argued that our identity is
to be found in the continuity of our consciousness rather than in the continuity
of our bodies. It was even used by Hume, who used his own consciousness as
the basis of his denial that there was any such thing as the self. It was the
starting point of Kant's philosophy; his transcendental ego, like Descartes' "I
think," gave him the basis for the rest of his philosophy. And even those
philosophers who have not been interested in these logical arguments—Buddhists, Marxists and existentialists—have begun with at least one of a variety
of considerations of consciousness; the fact of our own self-consciousness, the
facts of consciousness, or just the fact that only people seem capable of or
interested in asking the question "who am I?" But now, what is this "consciousness?" As soon as we ask the question, we find ourselves once again up
to our eyeballs in the labyrinth of traditional metaphysics.

WHAT IS CONSCIOUSNESS?

We can begin to appreciate the problems of consciousness by returning to the
attempts of the eighteenth-century rationalist metaphysicians to be clear about

308

and stands in need of food and drink when I experience the sensations of hunger and thirst, etc. And therefore I ought not to doubt but that there is some truth in these informations.

Nature likewise teaches me by these sensations of pain, hunger, thirst, etc., that I am not only lodged in my body as a pilot in a vessel, but that I am besides so intimately conjoined, and as it were intermixed with it, that my mind and body compose a certain unity. For if this were not the case, I should not feel pain when my body is hurt, seeing I am merely a thinking thing, but should perceive the wound by the understanding alone, just as a pilot perceives by sight when any part of his vessel is damaged; and when my body has need of food or drink, I should have a clear knowledge of this, and not be made aware of it by the confused sensations of hunger and thirst: for, in truth, all these sensations of hunger, thirst, pain, etc., are nothing more than certain confused modes of thinking, arising from the union and apparent fusion of mind and body.

Besides this, nature teaches me that my own body is surrounded by many other bodies. . . . some are agreeable, and others disagreeable, there can be no doubt that my body, or rather my entire self, in as far as I am composed of body and mind, may be variously affected, both beneficially and hurtfully, by surrounding bodies.[2]

But, how can two different substances, particularly two such different kinds of substances, interact? We know what it is for two bodies to interact: but how can a body make contact with a mind, which seems so intangible and "ghostly?" Descartes never answers this problem to his or to his critics' satisfaction. Spinoza, seeing Descartes' troubles, insists that there is only one substance, and that body and mind are but different "attributes" of that one substance. That avoids the metaphysical problem, for there is no problem about interaction within a substance. But it still leaves a sizable problem, namely, how these two attributes are coordinated. That is a problem Spinoza never answers. And Leibniz, attacking the same problem, finds it preferable to deny the reality of physical substance altogether. There are only mental substances, monads, each locked into its own experience. The extravagance of these two solutions should give you some idea of the difficulty of the problem.

We can get a more specific clue to the mysterious quality of "consciousness" if we consider the following. Descartes, Spinoza, and Leibniz, you recall, define mind as "unextended," that is, unextended in space. (Bodies, on the other hand, are defined as extended in space.) In other words, it is essential that minds, unlike bodies, cannot be said to be "this large" or to be located in such and such a place. But despite this definition, notice how much of our talk about consciousness consists of metaphors of a spatial form; we talk about something being "in" our minds. We talk about something "slipping (out of) our minds." Philosophers often talk about the "contents" of consciousness, and a popular phrase from William James is the "stream of consciousness." Now

[2] René Descartes, "Meditation VI," in *Meditations on First Philosophy,* in *The Philosophical Works of Descartes,* trans. Elizabeth S. Haldane and G. R. T. Ross (Cambridge: Cambridge University Press, 1911).

we might say, "those are just metaphors"; but why are such metaphors necessary?

How would you answer the question, "what is it to be conscious?" You might say something about "awareness" or "feelings," but that only restates the problem with different words. When we try to describe an image we do so in terms appropriate to physical things (namely, what it is an image *of*). We try to describe a pain, and come out with metaphors ("it's as if a vice were closing on my head") or comparisons ("it feels the same as when . . ."). The retreat to spatial metaphors reflects this difficulty. We talk about our experiences as if we were describing other things but then qualify our descriptions by saying that they are "in" consciousness rather than in the world.

How can we describe consciousness itself? There is a further difficulty: if I can talk about my mind only with difficulty, how can I talk about your mind at all? I can experience only what is "in" my mind. I can't feel your pain. Even if I feel "sympathy pains" with you, it is my pain I feel. So I can't describe your mind at all; and evidently I have difficulty describing my mind as well. Therefore, how can we talk about "mind" at all? Not suprisingly, many psychologists and philosophers have rejected the idea of "mind" altogether, preferring to talk only about what is mutually observable and "extended" in physical space (for example, neurology and overt behavior).

We shall later consider some of these attempts to reject the idea of "mind" altogether. But what should seem fairly obvious to you is that this idea can be rejected only with reference to other people, not with reference to ourselves. Why? Because of Descartes' first premise, to put it bluntly. The same logic that allows him to assert with certainty "I am thinking" and "I exist as a thinking thing" now forces us to admit that "I am not thinking" and "I am not a thinking thing" are utterly absurd and unintelligible statements. They are self-refuting in exactly the same sense that "I am thinking" is self-confirming. (This isn't to say that you are thinking clearly, or well, or enjoying it; only that, in some minimal sense, you are thinking.) And, therefore, you must have a mind. In one's own case, the fact that a person is conscious is the last thing one could ever deny.

The special relationship we have to our own consciousness has been the subject of considerable debate among philosophers, as you can well imagine. In their various attempts to get clear about the nature of consciousness, they have used this special relationship as a way of defining what they mean by "mind." Descartes claimed that he knew what was going on in his mind with an immediate certainty that he could never have about what was going on in the world "outside" him. In his first "Meditation," he talks about his seeming to be sitting in front of the fire and the fact that he might be wrong (if he were in bed asleep at the time). But what he could not be wrong about is his seeming to be sitting in front of the fire. Similarly, you think you see a friend walking across the street. You are wrong, for your friend is in fact in Alaska this week. But you can still be certain that you thought that you saw him, even if you didn't. Philosophers often refer to this special kind of "immediate" certainty in the case of our own conscious experiences as *incorrigibility*. You might make a mistake in any factual claim about the world, for you might be hallucinating, or dreaming, or simply fooled by circumstances. But nothing could lead you to suspect that you might be mistaken about your own experiences. Given enough evidence against you, you might be willing to change from "but I know that I saw it" to "well, I thought I saw it." But nothing could convince you that you were wrong in thinking that you saw whatever it was. That claim, the claim about your experience, is incorrigible. Your claim about what you saw, however, is always open to further questioning.

For many years, this notion of incorrigibility served as part of the definition of "mind"; whatever was mental could be described incorrigibly. But doubts have begun to creep in recently. Part of the problem was Freud's introduction of the notion of "the Unconscious." According to his famous "psychoanalytic" theory, not everything mental is knowable, and, therefore, surely not everything "in the mind" can be described incorrigibly. In a famous passage from his "Introductory Lectures," Freud says:

There is no need to discuss what is to be called conscious: it is removed from all doubt. The oldest and best meaning of the word 'unconscious' is the descriptive one; we call a psychical process unconscious whose existence we are obliged to assume—for some such reason as that we infer it from its effects—, but of which we know nothing. In that case we have the same relation to it as we have to a physical process in another person, except that it is in fact one of our own. If we want to be still more correct, we shall modify our assertion by saying that we call a process unconscious if we are obliged to assume that it is being activated *at the moment* though *at the moment* we know nothing about it. This qualification makes us reflect that the majority of conscious processes are conscious only for a short time; very soon they become *latent*, but can easily become conscious again. We might also say that they had become unconscious, if it were at all certain that in the condition of latency they are still something psychical. So far we should have learnt nothing new; nor should we have acquired the right to introduce the concept of an unconscious into psychology. But then comes the new observation that we were already able to make in parapraxes. In order to explain a slip of the tongue, for instance, we find ourselves obliged to assume that the intention to make a particular remark was present in the subject. We infer it with certainty from the interference with his remark which has occurred; but the intention did not put itself through and was thus unconscious. If, when we subsequently put it before the speaker, he recognizes it as one familiar to him, then it was only temporarily unconscious to him; but if he repudiates it as something foreign to him, then it was permanently unconscious. From this experience we retrospectively obtain the right also to pronounce as something unconscious what had been described as latent. A consideration of these dynamic relations permits us now to distinguish two kinds of unconscious— one which is easily, under frequently occurring circumstances, transformed into something conscious, and another with which this transformation is difficult and takes place only subject to a considerable expenditure of effort or possibly never at all. In order to escape the ambiguity as to whether we mean the one or the other unconscious, whether we are using the word in the descriptive or in the dynamic sense, we make use of a permissible and simple way out. We call the unconscious which is only latent, and thus easily becomes conscious, the 'preconscious' and retain the term 'unconscious' for the other. We now have three terms, 'conscious,' 'preconscious' and 'unconscious,' with which we can get along in our description of mental phenomena. Once again: the preconscious is also unconscious in the purely descriptive sense, but we do not give it that name, except in talking loosely or when we have to make a defence of the existence in mental life of unconscious processes in general.[3]

Notice that Freud starts from a Cartesian position, the idea that "conscious is removed from all doubt." But then he suggests what no Cartesian can tolerate, the idea that there are ideas (experiences, intentions) in our minds which we do not and sometimes cannot know, much less know with certainty. And if we accept this notion of "the unconscious" (or even the weaker notion of "preconscious"), the traditional notion of the "incorrigibility" of the mental is seriously challenged.

The argument, however, cuts both ways. Many philosophers have rejected Freud just because his notion of "the unconscious" goes against the notion of incorrigibility. "If it isn't knowable incorrigibly," these philosophers have said, "then it can't be mental at all." And even Freud himself was forced to admit that his theory flew in the face of our normal "manner of speaking." And the debate continues. Can you be wrong about what is going on in your own mind? For a long time, it was generally agreed that you could not be. Now, we aren't so sure. You are certain that you are over an old love affair, but, without too much difficulty, a friend or a psychologist convinces you that you have been thinking about it constantly. You are certain that you are angry, but, on closer examination, and in retrospect, you decide that you really felt guilty. You thought that you were thinking about your professor, when suddenly you realize that in fact it was the face of your father!

Can you be wrong about what you feel? Can you be wrong about what is going on in your own mind? It isn't clear. We now admit (as few philosophers had before) that at least there are some things we can be wrong about. Is there anything about which we could not be mistaken? What of those basic bits of data that the empiricists talked about—sensations or impressions? Could we possibly be wrong in our confidence that "right now, I am experiencing a cold feeling in my hand?" The empiricists assumed that one could not be wrong about this, for it was on the basis of such certainties that we were able to construct, through inductive reasoning, our theories about the world. Could we be wrong even about our own sensations? Consider this example (it comes from Bishop Berkeley); a mischievous friend tells you that he is going to touch your hand with a very hot spoon. When you aren't looking, he touches you with a piece of ice. You scream, and claim, with seeming certainty,

[3] Sigmund Freud, *New Introductory Lectures on Psychoanalysis,* ed. and trans. James Strachey (New York: Norton, 1964).

that he has given you an uncomfortable sensation of heat. But you're wrong. What you felt was cold. What you seemed to feel was heat. But even your "seeming," in this case, was mistaken.

Philosophers have also pointed out that what is unique to mind as opposed to body is the fact that one and only one person can (and must) experience what is going on. I can (and must) feel only my pains, I can't experience your pains. Philosophers have referred to this as *privileged access,* sometimes as the privacy of mental events. The "privilege" is the fact that, whatever is going on in your mind, you are not only the first but the only one to know of it directly. The "privacy" refers to the fact that, if you decide not to tell anyone or betray yourself (through your facial expressions or your behavior), no one else need ever know. If you have a wart on your thighs, you can keep it contingently "private" by choosing suitable clothing. But if you have a "dirty little secret" in your mind, you have a logical guarantee of its privacy—it is private necessarily.

"Incorrigible" means "beyond correction"; "privileged access" means "known in a special way." (These concepts must be kept separate.) Because of privileged access and the "privacy" of consciousness, our states of mind have the very peculiar status of being always knowable to ourselves (though whether we want to say "knowable with certainty" or not depends on our views about incorrigibility) and yet possibly unknowable to anyone else. That is why, as you learned in grade school, you could always fake a headache to stay home for the day but you couldn't fake a fever or a sore. As long as it was purely mental, it was also purely private. Your success depended wholly upon how good (or bad) an actor you were. But when it came to your body, you were in no privileged position. It was the thermometer, not your opinions, that told whether you had a fever or not. And it was the doctor, not you, who decided how serious your "sore" really was. But when it came to your own consciousness, you were in a truly privileged and irrefutable position.

HOW IS THE MIND RELATED TO THE BODY?

Defining consciousness is not easy, but what is even more difficult is giving any plausible account of how consciousness is connected to your body. You decide to raise your hand, and your hand goes up. You formulate an answer to your friend's question, and it comes out of your mouth. How does what takes place "in your mind" determine what happens with your body? A familiar image, borrowed from untold numbers of cartoons, is the little man (or woman) in your head, operating your body as a construction worker operates a giant steam shovel. But this is no answer at all. First, there is no little man. But even if there were, the same problem would then focus on him (or her). How does he or she move a body by making certain mental decisions? The same problem arises in the other direction, from body to mind. A friend steps on your toe—your physiology teacher can explain to you what happens—nerves are pinched and signals are sent through your central nervous system into that huge complex of fat cells called your brain. But then, at some point, there is something else, the feeling, the pain. How does this happen? How does a feeling emerge from that complex and still unknown network of neurological reactions going on in your body?

You can see that this problem of mind-body interaction is no longer just a technical metaphysical problem having to do with the special notion of substance. The problem of "interaction" is the same for Spinoza with his one substance as it is for Descartes with his dualism. And even if you don't want to talk of substances at all, there is still the problem of explaining how your mind effects your body and how your body effects your mind. For whether or not you accept the special problems of the eighteenth-century metaphysicians, you have to admit that your mind is very different from your body. And that is the source of the trickiest of all modern philosophy problems, the "mind-body problem." How are mind and body related?

The human body, like any other physical body, can be described in terms of its size, weight, chemical composition and movements in space. The workings of the human nervous system, although very complex and not yet adequately understood, can be described just like any other biological reaction, in terms of the changes in cell membranes and chemical reactions, the procession of chemo-electric nerve "impulses" and the computer-like network of different nerve components that are stimulated at any given time. The human brain can be seen as a complex machine, like a gooey computer. The human mind, however, is not to be characterized in any such spacial or chemical terms. The mind is not the same as the brain. It has no shape, no weight and has the awkward property of being observable—in any particular case—by one and only one person. (Anyone can see my brain if they can get inside my skull.) We can understand how a body might interact with another body, even when the "forces" involved are hard to picture (for example, the gravitational attraction between two distant planets). But how does a body interact with something that has none of the crucial characteristics of a body? You might think of "energy" here, for energy would seem to have at least some of the intangible and "unextended" features of mind. It too, in a very limited sense "has no size or weight." But energy is a function of physical bodies, force is a function of mass and acceleration. They are not, like our experiences, "private": a lightning bolt is observable to anyone who looks. And no one has ever claimed that descriptions of energy states, like descriptions of our ideas, are incorrigible. And while it has often been demonstrated (by Einstein) that energy and mass are interconvertible, any such "interconvertibility" of mind and matter is still at the highly speculative stage, limited to freak performances by a few isolated and not wholly dependable "psychics" and such. We may well talk about "mental energy," but it is far from clear what we mean. (And the fact that transcendental meditation gives us more of "whatever it is" only proves that we don't yet know what meditation is either.)

How can something so different as ideas and sensations interact with nervous systems and brain cells? Philosophers have proposed a number of solutions, all of them controversial and none of them yet satisfactory. But even before we look at some of them, it is important to stress the following point: the "mind-body problem" is not simply a matter of how little we still know about the human nervous system. No matter how our knowledge develops, we will still be faced with that mysterious gap between the last known neurological occurrence and the experience. Right now, we can trace our neural impulses only so far, and the "last known neurological occurrence" is not very far along. But even when we have complete "brain maps" and can say, for every mental occurrence, what is going on in the brain at the same time, the problem will still remain: how are the two related?[4]

The classic attempt to resolve the problem of dualism is by Descartes. The following selection is from his essay "The Passions of the Soul":

But in order to understand all these things more perfectly, we must know that the soul is really joined to the whole body, and that we cannot, properly speaking, say that it exists in any one of its parts to the exclusion of the others, because it is one and in some manner indivisible, owing to the disposition of its organs, which are so related to one another that when any one of them is removed, that renders the whole body defective; and because it is of a nature which has no relation to extension, nor dimensions, nor other properties of the matter of which the body is composed, but only to the whole conglomerate of its organs, as appears from the fact that we could not in any way conceive of the half or the third of a soul, nor of the space it occupies, and because it does not become smaller owing to the cutting off of some portion of the body, but separates itself from it entirely when the union of its assembled organs is dissolved.

It is likewise necessary to know that although the soul is joined to the whole body, there is yet in that a certain part in which it exercises its functions more particularly than in all the others; and it is usually believed that this part is the brain, or possibly the heart: the brain, because it is with it that the organs of sense are connected, and the heart because it is apparently in it that we experience the passions. But, in examining the matter with care, it seems as though I had clearly ascertained that the part of the body in which the soul exercises its functions immediately is in nowise the heart, nor the whole of the brain, but merely the most inward of all its parts, to wit, a certain very small gland which is situated in the middle of its substance and so suspended above the duct whereby the animal spirits in its anterior cavities have communication with those in the posterior, that the slightest movements which take place in it may alter very greatly the course

---

[4] Scientific research could show, although it is extremely unlikely, that the brain and our minds have very little to do with each other, that the presumed coordination between the two does not exist. It once was thought, for example, that the heart had to do with emotions (Aristotle and Descartes, for example). Science has proved them wrong. But science cannot do more than lay the ground for the problem. It cannot solve it.

of these spirits; and reciprocally that the smallest changes which occur in the course of the spirits may do much to change the movements of this gland.[5]

. . . . .

Let us then conceive here that the soul has its principal seat in the little gland which exists in the middle of the brain, from whence it radiates forth through all the remainder of the body by means of the animal spirits, nerves, and even the blood, which, participating in the impressions of the spirits, can carry them by the arteries into all the members. And recollecting what has been said above about the machine of our body, i.e. that the little filaments of our nerves are so distributed in all its parts, that on the occasion of the diverse movements which are there excited by sensible objects, they open in diverse ways the pores of the brain, which causes the animal spirits contained in these cavities to enter in diverse ways into the muscles, by which means they can move the members in all the different ways in which they are capable of being moved; and also that all the other causes which are capable of moving the spirits in diverse ways suffice to conduct them into diverse muscles; let us here add that the small gland which is the main seat of the soul is so suspended between the cavities which contain the spirits that it can be moved by them in as many different ways as there are sensible diversities in the object, but that it may also be moved in diverse ways by the soul, whose nature is such that it receives in itself as many diverse impressions, that is to say, that it possesses as many diverse perceptions as there are diverse movements in this gland. Reciprocally, likewise, the machine of the body is so formed that from the simple fact that this gland is diversely moved by the soul, or by such other cause, whatever it is, it thrusts the spirits which surround it towards the pores of the brain, which conduct them by the nerves into the muscles, by which means it causes them to move the limbs.[6]

The technical name given to this theory is *causal interactionism*, in other words, mental changes cause bodily changes and vice verse. Descartes did not take as seriously as his followers the problem of separate substances or radically different changes causally effecting one another. He apparently felt satisfied, if not exactly comfortable, with such a causal account. He was vigorously attacked in this by most of his immediate followers, including Spinoza, Leibniz and many of the empiricists. "Different substances cannot interact," they insisted. Or, in more modern dress, they argued that only physical bodies can causally interact, not anything so different as physical bodies and minds. Yet, one thing remains obvious. And that is that the familiar coordination of our mental activities and the movements of our bodies must be accounted for. And to do so, without bringing in causal interaction, required considerable ingenuity on the part of Descartes' critics.

[5] The gland Descartes is referring to is what is now called the Pineal Gland, a small endocrine gland at the base of the brain. It had only recently been discovered in Descartes' time, and its functions are still not adequately understood. It is currently hypothesized that it controls mating cycles in higher animals, and possibly any number of other activity cycles.
[6] René Descartes, "The Passions of the Soul," in *The Philosophical Works of Descartes*.

We have already seen the two metaphysical alternatives that immediately followed Descartes. The first was formulated by Leibniz as part of his overall theory of monads. He insisted that there could be no causal interaction between monads, and, specifically, there could be no sense made out of the claim that mental substances interacted with anything which we call "physical bodies." So what could he suggest as an alternative? His answer to the problem was that God, who had created monads in the first place, had also "programmed" them in such a way that our mental activities and what we call our bodily activities are exactly coordinated. Leaving aside the rest of Leibniz's theory and looking just at the mind-body problem, we can restate his solution as a form of what is called *parallelism*. His "pre-established harmony" between monads can now be viewed as the somewhat strange theory that our mental lives and the movements of our bodies are exactly coordinated (so that I feel pain when you step on my toe and so that my hand goes up just when I "'decide" that it should). Yet there is no causal interaction between them whatsoever. It is like the sound and visual tracks of a movie film, moving along exactly parallel but never in fact interacting. (That is, the character who appears to be talking in the movie does not cause the sounds which you hear as if he or she were producing them. The sounds are actually produced separately and would continue even if the projector bulb burned out and the figure on the screen disappeared altogether.) Of course, to accept this theory, you must also accept the considerable metaphysical and theological supports that it requires. If you don't believe in a God who could set up this complex system, there is absolutely no way of explaining the remarkable coordination of mind and body. And even if you do believe in God, you may well think that the mind-body problem requires some more plausible and secular solution.

Spinoza's theory need not be kept in the "one substance" metaphysics that he used to present it. In fact, much the same theory was defended only a few years ago by Bertrand Russell, without reference to the metaphysical notion of substance at all. Russell said, as Spinoza had said centuries before, that mind and body, mental events and physical changes, were different aspects of one and the same "something." For Spinoza, the "something" was "the one substance" and the aspects were what he called "attributes." Russell claimed only that our experiences and ideas were one aspect of some events or activities of which the various chemical reactions of the brain were another aspect. Accordingly, the theory has often been called the *dual aspect theory*, whether or not it is specifically addressed to the problem of substances and their attributes. Since we are now talking about two "aspects" of the same thing rather than two different things, the problem of interaction doesn't arise. But, as we complained before, this only hides the problem rather than solves it. What is this mysterious "something" of which mind and body are merely "aspects"? It is neither brain nor mind, so what could it be? By the nature of the case, we could one and the same thing have such different aspects?" You might say, can't find out. And it leaves us with the equally embarrassing question, "how "well, a hot coal has both 'aspects' of being heavy and being hot." But that we can explain. What are we to say of a "something" that is neither brain nor mind but both?

THE REJECTION OF DUALISM

If the problem is dualism, then perhaps the answer is the rejection of dualism. Of course, we still have to account for the obvious facts of the case, the fact that we feel something when certain things happen to our bodies, the fact that we do something when we mentally decide to. But philosophers of recent years—and nearly all psychologists—have taken a dim view towards dualism in all of the above forms.

A first, still timid step towards eliminating dualism consists of minimizing, though not rejecting, the mental side of dualism. This theory is usually called *epiphenomenalism* and William James was one of its best-known defenders. Epiphenomenalism allows for causal interaction, but only in one direction. Bodies and changes in bodies cause mental events. You might think of a boiler system or automobile engine equipped with various gauges to tell us how the machine is functioning at any given time. The machine works on, registering certain results on the attached gauges. But notice that, the gauge is relatively unimportant to the working of the machine. In fact, the gauge can break and the machine can function for years. What is the significance of such a theory? Many philosophers and psychologists are interested primarily in the continuity of physical and physiological laws without the problematic disruption of mysterious "mental causes." For them, such a theory allows them to concentrate wholly on the physical side of the matter and ignore "the mind" completely. If an objection is raised one can always insist: "Oh, I'm not denying that you feel something too." But this is an unimportant detail, a side-product, an epiphenomenon, which need not be taken all that seriously.

Epiphenomenalism is a timid rejection of dualism. It doesn't actually reject dualism, but it minimizes one half the duality. Other forms of attack are not so timid. In psychology, it has long been accepted by many authors that all talk of "the mental" is a hopeless tangle of confusions which, by the nature of the case, cannot be resolved through any experiment whatsoever. (That is, only one person could observe the results of the experiment in any given case, and the very nature of a scientific experiment is that it must be observable by anyone.) Accordingly, many psychologists have followed the American theorist John Watson in practicing what they call *behaviorism*. (Today, the best-known behaviorist is the Harvard psychologist B. F. Skinner.) Behaviorism, as a form of science, refuses to even consider any events which cannot be publicly witnessed, and that immediately and logically excludes mental events. Notice that behaviorism is primarily a scientific method, and need not deny the existence of mental events. Most behaviorists, however, have gone beyond the method—which only says that they will not scientifically study such events—and have done a bit of metaphysics as well: they also deny that there can be any mental events. What follows is a selection from Watson's *Behaviorism.*

Behaviorism . . . holds that the subject matter of human psychology *is the behavior of the human being.* Behaviorism claims that consciousness is neither a definite nor a usable concept. The behaviorist, who has been trained always as an experimentalist, holds, further, the belief in the existence of consciousness goes back to the ancient days of superstition and magic.

The extent to which most of us are shot through with a savage background is almost unbelievable. Few of us escape it. Not even a college education seems to correct it. If anything, it seems to strengthen it, since the colleges themselves are filled with instructors who have the same background. Some of our greatest biologists, physicists, and chemists, when outside of their laboratories, fall back upon folk lore which has become crystallized into religious concepts. These concepts—these heritages of a timid savage past—have made the emergence and growth of scientific psychology extremely difficult.

The great mass of the people even today has not yet progressed very far away from savagery—it wants to believe in magic. The savage believes that incantations can bring rain, good crops, good hunting, that an unfriendly voodoo doctor can bring disaster to a person or to a whole tribe; that an enemy who has obtained a nail paring or a lock of your hair can cast a harmful spell over you and control your actions. There is always interest and news in magic. Almost every era has its new magic, black or white, and its new magician. Moses had his magic: he smote the rock and water gushed out. Christ had his magic: he turned water into wine and raised the dead to life. Coué had his magic word formula. Mrs. Eddy had a similar one.

One example of such a religious concept is that every individual has a soul which is separate and distinct from the *body.* This soul is really a part of a supreme being. This ancient view led to the philosophical platform called "dualism." This dogma has been present in human psychology from earliest antiquity. No one has ever touched a soul, or seen one in a test tube, or has in any way come into relationship with it as he has with the other objects of his daily experience. Nevertheless, to doubt its existence is to become a heretic and once might possibly even have led to the loss of one's head. Even today the man holding a public position dare not question it.

. . . . .

Psychology and philosophy . . . in dealing as they thought with nonmaterial objects, found it difficult to escape the language of the church, and hence the concept of mind or soul as distinct from the body came down almost unchanged in essence to the latter part of the nineteenth century.

Wundt, the real father of experimental psychology, unquestionably wanted in 1879 a scientific psychology. He grew up in the midst of a dualistic philosophy of the most pronounced type. He could not see his way clear to a solution of the mind-body problem. His psychology, which has reigned supreme to the present day, is necessarily a compromise. He substituted the term *consciousness* for the term soul. Consciousness is not quite so unobservable as soul. We observe it by peeking in suddenly and catching it unawares as it were (*introspection*).

Wundt had an immense following. Just as now it is fashionable to go to Vienna to study psycho-analysis under Freud, just so was it fashionable some 40 years ago to study at Leipzig with Wundt. The men who returned founded the laboratories at Johns Hopkins University, the University of Pennsylvania, Columbia, Clark and Cornell. All were equipped to do battle with the elusive (almost soul-like) thing called consciousness.

To show how unscientific is the main concept behind this great German-American school of psychology, look for a moment at William James' definition of psychology. "Psychology is the description and explanation of states of consciousness as such." Starting with a definition which *assumes* what he starts out to prove, he escapes his difficulty by an *argumentum ad hominem*. Consciousness—Oh, yes, everybody must know what this "consciousness" is. When we have a sensation of red, a perception, a thought, when we *will* do something, or when we *purpose* to do something, or when we desire to do something, we are being *conscious*.

(Watson here clearly misreads James. Compare with the James selection later in this chapter.)

As a result of this major assumption that there is such a thing as consciousness and that we can analyze it by introspection, we find as many analyses as there are individual psychologists. There is no way of experimentally attacking and solving psychological problems and standardizing methods.

The behaviorist asks: Why don't we make what we can *observe* the real field of psychology? Let us limit ourselves to things that can be observed, and formulate laws concerning only those things. Now what can we observe? We can observe behavior—*what the organism does or says*. And let us point out at once: that *saying* is doing—that is, *behaving*. Speaking overtly or to ourselves (thinking) is just as objective a type of behavior as baseball.

The rule, or measuring rod, which the behaviorist puts in front of him always is: Can I describe this bit of behavior I see in terms of "stimulus and response?" By stimulus we mean any object in the general environment or any change in the tissues themselves due to the physiological condition of the animal, such as the change we get when we keep an animal from sex activity, when we keep it from feeding, when we keep it from building a nest. By response we mean anything the animal does—such as turning toward or away from a light, jumping at a sound, and more highly organized activities such as building a skyscraper, drawing plans, having babies, writing books.

.   .   .   .   .

After so brief a survey of the behavioristic approach to the problems of psychology, one is inclined to say: "Why, yes, it is worth while to study human behavior in this way, but the study of behavior is not the whole of psychology. It leaves out too much. Don't I have sensations, perceptions, conceptions? Do I not forget things and remember things, imagine things, have visual images and auditory images of things I once have seen and heard? Can I not see and hear things that I have never seen or heard in nature? Can I not be attentive or inattentive? Can I not will to do a thing or will not do it, as the case may be? Do not certain things arouse pleasure in me, and others displeasure? Behaviorism is trying to rob us of everything we have believed in since earliest childhood."

Having been brought up on introspective psychology, as most of us have, you naturally ask these questions and you will find it hard to put away the old terminology and begin to formulate your psychological life in terms of behaviorism. Behaviorism is new wine and it will not go into old bottles. It is advisable for the time being to allay your natural antagonism and accept the behavioristic platform at least until you get more deeply into it. Later you will find that you have progressed so far with behaviorism that the questions you now raise will answer themselves in a perfectly satisfactory natural science way. Let me hasten to add that if the behaviorist were to ask you what you mean by the subjective terms you have been in the habit of using he could soon make you tongue-tied with contradictions. He could even convince you that you do not know what you mean by them.[7]

Philosophers, too, have turned to behaviorism as a way of escaping the problems of Cartesian dualism. Gilbert Ryle, the "ordinary language" philosopher we mentioned briefly in Chapter 6, established this behaviorist viewpoint at the center of analytic philosophy with his book *The Concept of Mind* (1949). It's first chapter is appropriately called, "Descartes' Myth." First he describes what he calls "the official doctrine":

> There is a doctrine about the nature and place of minds which is so prevalent among theorists and even among laymen that it deserves to be described as the official theory. Most philosophers, psychologists and religious teachers subscribe, with minor reservations, to its main articles and, although they admit certain theoretical difficulties in it, they tend to assume that these can be overcome without serious modifications being made to the architecture of the theory. It will be argued here that the central principles of the doctrine are unsound and conflict with the whole body of what we know about minds when we are not speculating about them.
>
> The official doctrine, which hails chiefly from Descartes, is something like this. With the doubtful exceptions of idiots and infants in arms every human being has both a body and a mind. Some would prefer to say that every human being is both a body and a mind. His body and his mind are ordinarily harnessed together, but after the death of the body his mind may continue to exist and function.
>
> Human bodies are in space and are subject to the mechanical laws which govern all other bodies in space. Bodily processes and states can be inspected by external observers. So a man's bodily life is as much a public affair as are the lives of animals and reptiles and even as the careers of trees, crystals and planets.
>
> But minds are not in space, nor are their operations subject to mechanical laws. The workings of one mind are not witnessable by other observers; its career is private. Only I can take direct cognisance of the states and

[7] John Watson, *Behaviorism* (New York: Norton, 1930).

processes of my own mind. A person therefore lives through two collateral histories, one consisting of what happens in and to his body, the other consisting of what happens in and to his mind. The first is public, the second private. The events in the first history are events in the physical world, those in the second are events in the mental world.

It has been disputed whether a person does or can directly monitor all or only some of the episodes of his own private history; but, according to the official doctrine, of at least some of these episodes he has direct and unchallengeable cognisance. In consciousness, self-consciousness and introspection he is directly and authentically apprised of the present states and operations of his mind. He may have great or small uncertainties about concurrent and adjacent episodes in the physical world, but he can have none about at least part of what is momentarily occupying his mind.

It is customary to express this bifurcation of his two lives and of his two worlds by saying that the things and events which belong to the physical world, including his own body, are external, while the workings of his own mind are internal. This antithesis of outer and inner is of course meant to be construed as a metaphor, since minds, not being in space, could not be described as being spatially inside anything else, or as having things going on spatially inside themselves. But relapses from this good intention are common and theorists are found speculating how stimuli, the physical sources of which are yards or miles outside a person's skin, can generate mental responses inside his skull, or how decisions framed inside his cranium can set going movements of his extremities.

Even when 'inner' and 'outer' are construed as metaphors, the problem how a person's mind and body influence one another is notoriously charged with theoretical difficulties. What the mind wills, the legs, arms and the tongue execute; what affects the ear and the eye has something to do with what the mind perceive'; grimaces and smiles betray the mind's moods and bodily castigations lead, it is hoped, to moral improvement. But the actual transactions between the episodes of the private history and those of the public history remain mysterious, since by definition they can belong to neither series. They could not be reported among the happenings described in a person's autobiography of his inner life, but nor could they be reported among those described in someone else's biography of that person's overt career. They can be inspected neither by introspection nor by laboratory experiment. They are theoretical shuttlecocks which are forever being bandied from the physiologist back to the psychologist and from the psychologist back to the physiologist.

Underlying this partly metaphorical representation of the bifurcation of a person's two lives there is a seemingly more profound and philosophical assumption. It is assumed that there are two different kinds of existence or status. What exists or happens may have the status of physical existence, or it may have the status of mental existence. Somewhat as the faces of coins are either heads or tails, or somewhat as living creatures are either male or female, so, it is supposed, some existing is physical existing, other existing is mental existing. It is a necessary feature of what has physical existence that it is in space and time; it is a necessary feature of what has mental existence that it is in time but not in space. What has physical existence is composed of matter, or else is a function of matter; what has mental existence consists of consciousness, or else is a function of consciousness.

.   .   .   .   .

What sort of knowledge can be secured of the workings of a mind? On the one side, according to the official theory, a person has direct knowledge of the best imaginable kind of the workings of his own mind. Mental states and processes are (or are normally) conscious states and processes, and the consciousness which irradiates them can engender no illusions and leaves the door open for no doubts. A person's present thinkings, feelings and willings, his perceivings, rememberings and imaginings are intrinsically 'phosphorescent'; their existence and their nature are inevitably betrayed to their owner. The inner life is a stream of consciousness of such a sort that it would be absurd to suggest that the mind whose life is that stream might be unaware of what is passing down it.

.   .   .   .   .

On the other side, one person has no direct access of any sort to the events of the inner life of another. He cannot do better than make problematic inferences from the observed behaviour of the other person's body to the states of mind which, by analogy from his own conduct, he supposes to be signalised by that behaviour. Direct access to the workings of a mind is the privilege of that mind itself; in default of such privileged access, the workings of one mind are inevitably occult to everyone else. For the supposed arguments from bodily movements similar to their own to mental workings similar to their own would lack any possibility of observational corroboration. Not unnaturally, therefore, an adherent of the official theory finds it difficult to resist this consequence of his premises, that he has no good reason to believe that there do exist minds other than his own. Even if he prefers to believe that to other human bodies there are harnessed minds not unlike his own, he cannot claim to be able to discover their individual characteristics, or the particular things that they undergo and do. Absolute solitude is on this showing the ineluctable destiny of the soul. Only our bodies can meet.

Then, in section 2, Ryle argues that the "official doctrine" is "absurd," and is based upon what he calls, "a category mistake":

Such in outline is the official theory. I shall often speak of it, with deliberate abusiveness, as 'the dogma of the Ghost in the Machine'. I hope to prove that it is entirely false, and false not in detail but in principle. It is not merely an assemblage of particular mistakes. It is one big mistake and a mistake of a special kind. It is, namely, a category-mistake. It represents the facts of mental life as if they belonged to one logical type or category (or range of types or categories), when they actually belong to another. The dogma is therefore a philosopher's myth. In attempting to explode the myth I shall probably be taken to be denying well-known facts about the mental life of human beings, and my plea that I aim at doing nothing more than rectify the logic of mental-conduct concepts will probably be disallowed as mere subterfuge.

I must first indicate what is meant by the phrase 'Category-mistake.' This I do in a series of illustrations.

A foreigner visiting Oxford or Cambridge for the first time is shown a number of colleges, libraries, playing fields, museums, scientific departments and administrative offices. He then asks 'But where is the university? I have seen where the members of the Colleges live, where the Registrar works, where the scientists experiment and the rest. But I have not yet seen the University in which reside and work the members of your University.' It has then to be explained to him that the University is not another collateral institution, some ulterior counterpart to the colleges, laboratories and offices which he has seen. The University is just the way in which all that he has already seen is organized. When they are seen and when their co-ordination is understood, the University has been seen. His mistake lay in his innocent assumption that it was correct to speak of Christ Church, the Bodleian Library, the Ashmolean Museum *and* the University, to speak, that is, as if 'the University' stood for an extra member of the class of which these other units are members. He was mistakenly allocating the University to the same category as that to which the other institutions belong.

The same mistake would be made by a child witnessing the march-past of a division, who, having had pointed out to him such and such battalions, batteries, squadrons, etc., asked when the division was going to appear. He would be supposing that a division was a counterpart to the units already seen, partly similar to them and partly unlike them. He would be shown his mistake by being told that in watching the battalions, batteries and squadrons marching past he had been watching the division marching past. The march-past was not a parade of battalions, batteries, squadrons *and* a division; it was a parade of the battalions, batteries and squadrons *of* a division.

One more illustration. A foreigner watching his first game of cricket learns what are the functions of the bowlers, the batsmen, the fielders, the umpires and the scorers. He then says 'But there is no one left on the field to contribute the famous element of team-spirit. I see who does the bowling, the batting and the wicket-keeping; but I do not see whose role it is to exercise *esprit de corps.*' Once more, it would have to be explained that he was looking for the wrong type of thing. Team-spirit is not another cricketing-operation supplementary to all of the other special tasks. It is, roughly, the keenness with which each of the special tasks is performed, and performing a task keenly is not performing two tasks. Certainly exhibiting team-spirit is not the same thing as bowling or catching, but nor is it a third thing such that we can say that the bowler first bowls *and* then exhibits team-spirit or that a fielder is at a given moment *either* catching *or* displaying *esprit de corps.*

These illustrations of category-mistakes have a common feature which must be noticed. The mistakes were made by people who did not know how to wield the concepts *University, division* and *team-spirit.* Their puzzles arose from inability to use certain items in the English vocabulary.[8]

A *category mistake,* in other words, is mistaking one *type* of thing for another. For example, it would be a category mistake to ask, "what color is the num-

---

[8] Gilbert Ryle, *The Concept of Mind* (New York: Barnes & Noble, 1949).

ber 3?" The philosophically interesting mistakes, of course, are neither so obvious nor so silly as the above examples. They are mistakes made when we try to think abstractly. Most important are the category mistakes that philosophers make when they talk about "the mind":

> My destructive purpose is to show that a family of radical category-mistakes is the source of the double-life theory. The representation of a person as a ghost mysteriously ensconced in a machine derives from this argument. Because, as is true, a person's thinking, feeling and purposive doing cannot be described solely in the idioms of physics, chemistry and physiology, therefore they must be described in counterpart idioms. As the human body is a complex organised unit, so the human mind must be another complex organized unit, though one made of a different sort of stuff and with a different sort of structure. Or, again, as the human body, like any other parcel of matter, is a field of causes and effects, so the mind must be another field of causes and effects, though not (Heaven be praised) mechanical causes and effects.

This disastrous category mistake, which Ryle attributes primarily to Descartes, is thinking that "the mind" and its events are some strange and mysteriously private sort of *thing* behind our behavior, when, in fact, mind is the *pattern* of our behavior, and not "behind" behavior at all:

> When two terms belong to the same category, it is proper to construct conjunctive propositions embodying them. Thus a purchaser may say that he bought a left-hand glove and a right-hand glove, but not that he bought a left-hand glove, a right-hand glove and a pair of gloves. 'She came home in a flood of tears and a sedan-chair' is a well-known joke based on the absurdity of conjoining terms of different types. It would have been equally ridiculous to construct the disjunction 'She came home either in a flood of tears or else in a sedan-chair'. Now the dogma of the Ghost in the Machine does just this. It maintains that there exist both bodies and minds; that there occur physical processes and mental processes; that there are mechanical causes of corporeal movements and mental causes of corporeal movements. I shall argue that these and other analogous conjunctions are absurd; but, it must be noticed, the argument will not show that either of the illegitimately conjoined propositions is absurd in itself. I am not, for example, denying that there occur mental processes. Doing long division is a mental process and so is making a joke. But I am saying that the phrase 'there occur mental processes' does not mean the same sort of thing as 'there occur physical processes', and, therefore, that it makes no sense to conjoin or disjoin the two.[9]

The key to Ryle's analysis is what he calls a disposition. A *disposition* is a tendency for something to happen given certain conditions. For example, we say that "if the lever is disturbed, the mousetrap will snap closed." The key is the *"if . . . then"* (or "hypothetical") form of the statement. Ryle explains this in the following way:

[9] Ryle, *The Concept of Mind.*

There are at least two quite different senses in which an occurrence is said to be 'explained'; and there are correspondingly at least two quite different senses in which we ask 'why' it occurred and two quite different senses in which we say that it happened 'because' so and so was the case. The first sense is the causal sense. To ask why the glass broke is to ask what caused it to break, and we explain, in this sense, the fracture of the glass when we report that a stone hit it. The 'because' clause in the explanation reports an event, namely the event which stood to the fracture of the glass as cause to effect.

But very frequently we look for and get explanations of occurrences in another sense of 'explanation'. We ask why the glass shivered when struck by the stone and we get the answer that it was because the glass was brittle. Now 'brittle' is a dispositional adjective; that is to say, to describe the glass as brittle is to assert a general hypothetical proposition about the glass. So when we say that the glass broke when struck because it was brittle, the 'because' clause does not report a happening or a cause; it states a law-like proposition. People commonly say of explanations of this second kind that they give the 'reason' for the glass breaking when struck.

How does the law-like general hypothetical proposition work? It says, roughly, that the glass, *if* sharply struck or twisted, etc. *would* not dissolve or stretch or evaporate but fly into fragments. The matter of fact that the glass did at a particular moment fly into fragments, when struck by a particular stone, is explained, in this sense of 'explain', when the first happening, namely the impact of the stone, satisfies the protasis of the general hypothetical proposition, and when the second happening, namely the fragmentation of the glass, satisfies its apodosis.

He then applies this concept of disposition, to his analysis of "mind." (This occupies him for most of his book.) The main idea is this: every thing "mental" is really a disposition to behave in certain ways. Consider, for example, his brief analyses of motives and acting from vanity:

This can now be applied to the explanation of actions as issuing from specified motives. When we ask 'Why did someone act in a certain way?' this question might, so far as its language goes, either be an inquiry into the cause of his acting in that way, or be an inquiry into the character of the agent which accounts for his having acted in that way on that occasion. I suggest, what I shall now try to prove, that explanations by motives are explanations of the second type and not of the first type. It is perhaps more than a merely linguistic fact that a man who reports the motive from which something is done is, in common parlance, said to be giving the 'reason' for the action. It should be also noticed that there are lots of different kinds of such explanations of human actions. A twitch may be explained by a reflex, the filling of a pipe by an inveterate habit; the answering of a letter by a motive. Some of the differences between reflexes, habits and motives will have to be described at a later stage.

The present issue is this. The statement 'he boasted from vanity' ought, on one view, to be construed as saying that 'he boasted and the cause of his boasting was the occurrence in him of a particular feeling or impulse of vanity'. On the other view, it is to be construed as saying 'he boasted on meeting the stranger and his doing so satisfies the law-like proposition that whenever he finds a chance of securing the admiration and envy of others, he does whatever he thinks will produce this admiration and envy'.

And then, the general argument:

> . . . To say that a person knows something, or aspires to be something, is not to say that he is at a particular moment in process of doing or undergoing anything, but that he is able to do certain things, when the need arises, or that he is prone to do and feel certain things in situations of certain sorts.
>
> This is, in itself, hardly more than a dull fact (almost) of ordinary grammar. The verbs 'know', 'possess' and 'aspire' do not behave like the verbs 'run', 'wake up' or 'tingle'; we cannot say 'he knew so and so for two minutes, then stopped and started again after a breather', 'he gradually aspired to be a bishop', or 'he is now engaged in possessing a bicycle'. Nor is it a peculiarity of people that we describe them in dispositional terms. We use such terms just as much for describing animals, insects, crystals and atoms. We are constantly wanting to talk about what can be relied on to happen as well as to talk about what is actually happening; we are constantly wanting to give explanations of incidents as well as to report them; and we are constantly wanting to tell how things can be managed as well as to tell what is now going on in them. . . .
>
> There is, however, a special point in drawing attention to the fact that many of the cardinal concepts in terms of which we describe specifically human behaviour are dispositional concepts, since the vogue of the paramechanical legend has led many people to ignore the ways in which these concepts actually behave and to construe them instead as items in the descriptions of occult causes and effects. Sentences embodying these dispositional words have been interpreted as being categorical reports of particular but unwitnessable matters of fact instead of being testable, open hypothetical and what I shall call 'semi-hypothetical' statements.

And, in conclusion, Ryle trades a few harsh words with psychologists, but ends up approving of their behaviorist methods.

> In the course of this book I have said very little about the science of psychology. This omission will have appeared particularly perverse, since the entire book could properly be described as an essay, not indeed in scientific but in philosophical psychology.
>
> . . . . .
>
> When we think of the science or sciences of psychology, we are apt, and often encouraged, to equate the official programmes of psychology with the researches that psychologists actually carry on, their public promises with their laboratory performances. Now when the word 'psychology' was coined, two hundred years ago, it was supposed that the two-worlds legend was true. It was supposed, in consequence, that since Newtonian science explains (it was erroneously thought) everything that exists and occurs in the physical world, there could and should be just one other counterpart science explaining

what exists and occurs in the postulated non-physical world. As Newtonian scientists studied the phenomena of the one field, so there ought to be scientists studying the phenomena of the other field. 'Psychology' was supposed to be the title of the one empirical study of 'mental phenomena'.

. . . . .

Abandonment of the two-worlds legend involves the abandonment of the idea that there is a locked door and a still to be discovered key. Those human actions and reactions, those spoken and unspoken utterances, those tones of voice, facial expressions and gestures, which have always been the data of all the other students of men, have, after all, been the right and the only manifestations to study. They and they alone have merited, but fortunately not received, the grandiose title 'mental phenomena'.

But though the official programme of psychology promised that the subject matter of its investigations would consist of happenings differing in kind from, and lying 'behind', those bits of human conduct which alone were accessible to the other studies of man, the experimental psychologists in their daily practice had perforce to break this promise. A researcher's day cannot be satisfactorily occupied in observing nonentities and describing the mythical. Practising psychologists found themselves examining the actions, grimaces and utterances of lunatics and idiots, of persons under the influence of alcohol, fatigue, terror and hypnosis, and of the victims of brain injuries. They studied sense perception as ophthalmologists, for example, study sense perception, partly by making and applying physiological experiments and partly by analysing the reactions and verbal responses of the subjects of their experiments. They studied the wits of children by collecting and comparing their failures and successes in various kinds of standardised tests. They counted the blunders made by typists at different stages of their day's work, and they examined people's differing liabilities to forget different kinds of memorised syllables and phrases by recording their successes and failures in recitations after the lapse of different periods of time. They studied the behaviour of animals in mazes and of chickens in incubators. Even the spell-binding, because so promisingly 'chemical', principle of the Association of Ideas found its chief practical application in the prompt word-responses voiced aloud by subjects to whom test words were spoken by the experimenter.

BEHAVIORISM

The general trend of this book will undoubtedly, and harmlessly be stigmatised as 'behaviourist'. So it is pertinent to say something about Behaviourism. Behaviourism was, in the beginning, a theory about the proper methods of scientific psychology. It held that the example of the other progressive sciences ought to be followed, as it had not previously been followed, by psychologists; their theories should be based upon repeatable and publicly checkable observations and experiments. But the reputed deliverances of consciousness and introspection are not publicly checkable. Only people's overt behaviour can be observed by several witnesses, measured and mechanically recorded. The early adherents of this methodological programme seem to have been in two minds whether to assert that the data of consciousness and introspection were myths, or to assert merely that they were insusceptible of scientific examination. It was not clear whether they were espousing a not very sophisticated mechanistic doctrine, like that of Hobbes and Gassendi, or whether they were still cleaving to the Cartesian para-mechanical theory, but restricting their research procedures to those that we have inherited from Galileo; whether, for example, they held that thinking just consists in making certain complex noises and movements or whether they held that though these movements and noises were connected with 'inner life' processes, the movements and noises alone were laboratory phenomena.

However it does not matter whether the early Behaviourists accepted a mechanist or a para-mechanist theory. They were in error in either case. The important thing is that the practice of describing specifically human doings according to the recommended methodology quickly made it apparent to psychologists how shadowy were the supposed 'inner-life' occurrences which the Behaviourists were at first reproached for ignoring or denying. Psychological theories which made no mention of the deliverances of 'inner perception' were at first likened to 'Hamlet' without the Prince of Denmark. But the extruded hero soon came to seem so bloodless and spineless a being that even the opponents of these theories began to feel shy of imposing heavy theoretical burdens upon his spectral shoulders.

The Behaviourists' methodological programme has been of revolutionary importance to the programme of psychology. But more, it has been one of the main sources of the philosophical suspicion that the two-worlds story is a myth. It is a matter of relatively slight importance that the champions of this methodological principle have tended to espouse as well a kind of Hobbist theory, and even to imagine that the truth of mechanism is entailed by the truth of their theory of scientific research method in psychology.

It is not for me to say to what extent the concrete research procedures of practising psychologists have been affected by their long adherence to the two-worlds story, or to what extent the Behaviourist revolt has led to modifications of their methods. For all that I know, the ill effects of the myth may, on balance, have been outweighed by the good, and the Behaviourist revolt against it may have led to reforms more nominal than real. Myths are not always detrimental to the progress of theories.[10]

There is a problem with all behaviorism, however. No matter how tempting such a theory might be in our attempt to understand other people, it is pure nonsense in one's own case. My pain is certainly not the same as my behavior, no matter how complicated, and no matter how easy it is for you to infer from that behavior that I am in pain. It must be admitted that behaviorism, which Watson invented to counteract the often absurd amount of humanistic, mentalistic concepts used in the explanation of simple animal behavior, had a beneficial effect in that context. But as an account of my feelings/your feelings—ridiculous! No matter how heavily one leans towards behaviorism and other rejections of the mental, one always bangs up against that ultimate mark of the mental, Descartes' "I think." There is no way you

[10] Ryle, *The Concept of Mind.*

can think consistently that you never think. As one of Watson's early critics commented, "what behaviorism shows is that psychologists do not always think very well, not that they don't think at all."

The rejection of dualism need not be a rejection of the mental side of the duality, although that is the obvious preference of most scientists. We have seen at least one philosopher, however, who escapes the problems of Cartesian dualism by rejecting the physical side of the problem. That is Bishop Berkeley, who quite clearly, in attacking Locke and defending his own "subjective idealism," provides a radical solution to the mind-body problem as well. His theory is that there are only minds and their ideas, no physical bodies. Therefore, there is no problem of interaction. He too (like Leibniz), however, needs God to hold his system together. But idealism has not been as rare an answer to the mind-body problem as you might think, although we see little of it nowadays. The religious idealists of the past century, in America as well as in England and Europe, were so powerful that they virtually ruled philosophy for a number of decades.[11]

The most powerful and most plausible rejection of dualism, however, consists neither of denying consciousness nor of denying physical bodies. To deny dualism by denying mind or body strikes us as a bit simple-minded; there is a better way. Why not say that there are not two things at all, as there appear to be, but only one. In other words, mind and body, or, more accurately, mental events and certain bodily events (presumably brain events) are identical. This theory, accordingly, is called *the identity theory,* and it is presently one of the hottest controversies in American philosophy. You can see that it was anticipated, in a sense, by Spinoza and Russell with their dual aspect theory. But the identity theory, unlike the others, tries to tie itself as closely as possible with current scientific research, and, although it is not a scientific theory itself, it will allow no such mysterious "something" such as we found in Spinoza and Russell. Accordingly it is usually considered a form of materialism (although it does not deny the existence—only the independence—of mental events). The following critical description of the identity theory is by the American philosopher, Jerome Shaffer.

> The last version of materialism we shall consider, and currently the most seriously discussed, is known as the identity theory. It is the theory that thoughts, feelings, wishes, and the rest of so-called mental phenomena are identical with, one and the same thing as, states and processes of the *body* (and, perhaps, more specifically, states and processes of the nervous system,

---

[11] In Eastern thought too, idealism has often been an attractive thesis, but not for theoretical reasons. The following is from *The Teaching of Buddha.*

Everything originates within the mind. Just as a magician cleverly makes whatever he wishes to appear, so this world of delusion originates within the mind. People look upon it and observe its appearing and disappearing and they believe it to be real and call it life and death. That is, everything is mind-made and has no significance apart from mind. As people come to understand this fact, they are able to remove all delusions and there is an end of all mental disturbance forever.

or even of the brain alone). Thus the having of a thought is identical with having such and such bodily cells in such and such states. . . .

The sense of "identity" relevant here is that in which we say, for example, that the morning star is "identical" with the evening star. It is not that the expression "morning star" means the same as the expression "evening star"; on the contrary, these expressions mean something different. But the object referred to by the two expressions is one and the same; there is just one heavenly body, namely, Venus, which when seen in the morning is called the morning star and when seen in the evening is called the evening star. The morning star is identical with the evening star; they are one and the same object.[12]

Of course, the identity of the mental with the physical is not exactly of this sort, since it is held to be simultaneous identity rather than the identity of a thing at one time with the same thing at a later time. To take a closer example, one can say that lightning is a particularly massive electrical discharge from one cloud to another or to the earth. Not that the word "lightning" *means* "a particularly massive electrical discharge . . ."; when Benjamin Franklin discovered that lightning was electrical, he did not make a discovery about the meaning of words. Nor when it was discovered that water was H_2O was a discovery made about the meanings of words; yet water is identical with H_2O.

In a similar fashion, the identity theorist can hold that thoughts, feelings, wishes, and the like are identical with physical states. Not "identical" in the sense that mentalistic terms are synonymous in meaning with physicalistic terms but "identical" in the sense that the actual events picked out by mentalistic terms are one and the same events as those picked out by physicalistic terms.

It is important to note that the identity theory does not have a chance of being true unless a particular sort of correspondence obtains between mental events and physical events, namely, that whenever a mental event occurs, a physical event of a particular sort (or at least one of a number of particular sorts) occurs, and vice versa. If it turned out to be the case that when a particular mental event occurred it seemed a matter of chance what physical events occurred or even whether any physical event at all occurred, or vice versa, then the identity theory would not be true. So far as our state of knowledge at the present time is concerned, it is still too early to say what the empirical facts are, although it must be said that many scientists do believe that there exists the kind of correspondences needed by identity theorists. But even if these correspondences turn out to exist, that does not mean that the identity theory will be true. For identity theorists do not hold merely that mental and physical events are correlated in a particular way but that they are one and the same events, i.e., not like lightning and thunder (which are correlated in lawful ways but not identical) but like lightning and electrical discharges (which always go together because they are one and the same).

What are the advantages of the identity theory? As a form of materialism, it does not have to cope with a world which has in it both mental

---

[12] Both refer to the planet Venus, one as seen in the morning, the other at night. But it took many years for this identity to be discovered.

phenomena and physical phenomena, and it does not have to ponder how they might be related. There exist only the physical phenomena, although there do exist two different ways of talking about such phenomena: physicalistic terminology and, in at least some situations, mentalistic terminology. We have here a dualism of language, but not a dualism of entities, events, or properties.

But do we have merely a dualism of languages and no other sort of dualism? In the case of Venus, we do indeed have only one object, but the expression "morning star" picks out one phase of that object's history, where it is in the mornings, and the expression "evening star" picks out another phase of that object's history, where it is in the evenings. If that object did not have these two distinct aspects, it would not have been a *discovery* that the morning star and the evening star were indeed one and the same body, and, further, there would be no point to the different ways of referring to it.

Now it would be admitted by identity theorists that physicalistic and mentalistic terms do not refer to different phases in the history of one and the same object. What sort of identity is intended? Let us turn to an allegedly closer analogy, that of the identity of lightning and a particular sort of electrical phenomenon. Yet here again we have two distinguishable aspects, the appearance to the naked eye on the one hand and the physical composition on the other. And this is also not the kind of identity which is plausible for mental and physical events. The appearance *to the naked eye* of a neurological event is utterly different from the experience of having a thought or a pain.

It is sometimes suggested that the physical aspect results from looking at a particular event "from the outside," whereas the mental results from looking at the same event "from the inside." When the brain surgeon observes my brain he is looking at it from the outside, whereas when I experience a mental event I am "looking" at my brain "from the inside."

Such an account gives us only a misleading analogy, rather than an accurate characterization of the relationship between the mental and the physical. The analogy suggests the difference between a man who knows his own house from the inside, in that he is free to move about within, seeing objects from different perspectives, touching them, etc., but can never get outside to see how it looks from there, and a man who cannot get inside and therefore knows only the outside appearance of the house, and perhaps what he can glimpse through the windows. But what does this have to do with the brain? Am I free to roam about inside my brain, observing what the brain surgeon may never see? Is not the "inner" aspect of my brain far more accessible to the brain surgeon than to me? He has the X rays, probes, electrodes, scalpels, and scissors for getting at the inside of my brain. If it is replied that this is only an analogy, not to be taken literally, then the question still remains how the mental and the physical are related.

Usually identity theorists at this point flee to even vaguer accounts of the relationship. They talk of different "levels of analysis," or of different "perspectives," or of different "conceptual schemes," or of different "language games." The point of such suggestions is that the difference between the mental and the physical is not a basic, fundamental, or intrinsic one, but rather a difference which is merely relative to different human purposes or standpoints. The difference is supposed to exist not in the thing itself but in the eye of the beholder.

But these are only hints. They do not tell us in precise and literal terms how the mental and the physical differ and are related. They only try to assure us that the difference does not matter to the real nature of things. But until we are given a theory to consider, we cannot accept the identity theorists' assurance that some theory will do only he does not know what it is.

One of the leading identity theorists, J. J. C. Smart, holds that mentalistic discourse is simply a vaguer, more indefinite way of talking about what could be talked about more precisely by using physiological terms. If I report a red afterimage, I mean (roughly) that something is going on which is like what goes on when I really see a red patch. I do not actually *mean* that a particular sort of brain process is occurring, but when I say something is going on I refer (very vaguely, to be sure) to just that brain process. Thus the thing referred to in my report of an afterimage is a brain process. Hence there is no need to bring in any nonphysical features. Thus even the taint of dualism is avoided.

Does this ingenious attempt to evade dualistic implications stand up under philosophical scrutiny? I am inclined to think it will not. Let us return to the man reporting the red afterimage. He was aware of the occurrence of something or other, of some feature or other. Now it seems to me obvious that he was not necessarily aware of the state of his brain at that time (I doubt that most of us are ever aware of the state of our brain) nor, in general, necessarily aware of any physical features of his body at that time. He might, of course, have been incidentally aware of some physical feature but not insofar as he was aware of the red afterimage as such. Yet he was definitely aware of something, or else how could he have made that report? So he must have been aware of some nonphysical feature. That is the only way of explaining how he was aware of anything at all.

Of course, the thing that our reporter of the afterimage was aware of might well have had further features which he was *not* aware of, particularly, in this connection, physical features. I may be aware of certain features of an object without being aware of others. So it is not ruled out that the event our reporter is aware of might be an event with predominantly physical features—he just does not notice those. But he must be aware of some of its features, or else it would not be proper to say he was aware of *that* event. And if he is not aware of any physical features, he must be aware of something else. And that shows that we cannot get rid of those nonphysical features in the way that Smart suggests. . . .

Even if the identity theorist could clarify the sense of "identity" to be used in his theory, he would still face two other problems. These concern coexistence in time and space. Coexistence in time and space are conditions that must be met if there is to be identity. That is to say, for two apparently different things to turn out to be one and the same, they must exist at the same time and in the same location. If we could show that Mr. A existed at a time when Mr. B did not, or that Mr. A existed in a place where Mr. B did not, then this would show that Mr. A and Mr. B were different men. It is by virtue of these facts about identity that an alibi can exonerate a suspect: if Mr. A was not in Chicago at the time, then he could not be one and the same with the man who stole the diamonds in Chicago.

So if mental events are to be identical with physical events, then they must fulfill the conditions of coexistence in time and space. The question is, Do they?

So far as coexistence in time is concerned, very little is known. The most relevant work consists in direct stimulation of an exposed part of the brain during surgery. Since only a local anesthetic is necessary in many such cases the patient may well be fully conscious. Then, as the surgeon stimulates different parts of his brain, the patient may report the occurrence of mental events—memories, thoughts, sensations. Do the physical events in the brain and the mental events occur at precisely the same time? It is impossible to say. All that would be required is a very small time gap to prove that the physical events were not identical with the mental events. But it is very difficult to see how the existence of so small a time gap could be established. And even if it were, what would it prove? Only that the mental event was not identical with just that physical event; it would not prove it was non-identical with any physical event. So it could well be that coexistence in time is present or is not. I do not think that we shall get much decisive information from empirical work of the sort here described. The identity theorist, then, does not have to fear refutation from this quarter, at least not for a long time.

How about coexistence in space? Do mental events occur in the same place the corresponding physical events occur? This is also a very difficult question to answer, for two reasons. First our present ignorance of neurophysiology, especially concerning the brain and how it functions, allows us to say very little about the location of the relevant physical events. This much does seem likely: they are located in the brain. Much more than that we do not at present know, although as the time passes, we should learn much more. The second reason for our difficulty in telling if there is coexistence in space has to do with the location of mental events. Where do thoughts, feelings, and wishes occur? Do they occur in the brain? Suppose you suddenly have the thought that it is almost suppertime; where does that occur? The most sensible answer would be that it occurs wherever you are when you have that thought. If you are in the library when you have that thought, then the thought occurs in the library. But it would be utterly unnatural to ask where inside your body the thought occurred; in your foot, or your liver, or your heart, or your head? It is not that any one of these places is more likely than another. They are all wrong. Not because thoughts occur somewhere *else* within your body than your foot, liver, heart, or head—but because it *makes no sense at all* to locate the occurrence of a thought at some place within your body. We would not understand someone who pointed to a place in his body and claimed that it was *there* that his entertaining of a thought was located. Certainly, if one *looked* at that place, one would not *see* anything resembling a thought. If it were replied to this that pains can be located in the body without being seen there, then it should be pointed out that one *feels* the pain there but one hardly feels a thought in the body.

The fact that it makes no sense at all to speak of mental events as occuring at some point within the body has the result that the identity theory cannot be true. This is because the corresponding physical events do occur at some point within the body, and if those physical events are identical with mental events, then those mental events must occur at the same point within the body. But those mental events do not occur at any point within the body, because any statement to the effect that they occurred here, or there, would be senseless. Hence the mental events cannot meet the condition of coexistence in space, and therefore cannot be identical with physical events.

Our inability to give the location within the body of mental events is different from our inability to give the location of the corresponding physical events within the body. In the latter case, it is that we do not know enough about the body, particularly the brain. Some day, presumably, we will know enough to pin down pretty exactly the location of the relevant physical events. But in the case of mental events it is not simply that at present we are ignorant but that someday we may well know. What would it be like to discover the location of a thought in the brain? What kind of information would we need to be able to say that the thought occurred exactly *here?* If by X rays or some other means we were able to see every event which occurred in the brain, we would never get a glimpse of a thought. If, to resort to fantasy, we could so enlarge a brain or so shrink ourselves that we could wander freely through the brain, we would still never observe a thought. All we could ever observe in the brain would be the *physical* events which occur in it. If mental events had location in the brain, there should be some means of detecting them there. But of course there is none. The very idea of it is senseless.

Some identity theorists believe this objection can be met. One approach is to reply that this objection begs the question: if the identity theory is true, and mental events are identical with brain events, then, paradoxical as it may sound, mental events do indeed have location, and are located precisely where the physical events are located. Another approach is to reply that the relevant physical events should be construed as events which happen to the body as a whole, and therefore occur where the body as a whole is located; then it is not so paradoxical to give location to the mental events, for they would be located where the body is located but would not be located in any particular part of the body.[13]

Shaffer disagrees with the identity theory, but both his presentation and his criticism of it are central to the ongoing debate today. In defending the identity theory, it is most important to stress that the identity of brain processes and thoughts is an empirical identity, that is, an identity that must be discovered through experiment and experience. It is not a logical identity, as if the two terms, "brain process" and "thought," are synonymous. The latter suggestion is obviously false, and modern defenders of the identity theory are always emphasizing that it is only future neurophysiological research that will prove them right. Shaffer's criticism, however, is based on a principle that

[13] Jerome Shaffer, *The Philosophy of Mind* (Englewood Cliffs, N.J.: Prentice-Hall, 1968).

must be distinguished from the all-too-easy attack on the logical identity suggestion. The principle is that if two things are identical, then they must have all the same properties. But, Shaffer argues, no amount of research could possibly show that brain processes and thought have the same properties. Most importantly, brain processes take place in the brain, and can be traced like any other physical processes; thoughts, on the other hand, have no spacial location, and there is nothing that research can "discover" that will show that they do. Of course, research can and has shown that certain thoughts are correlated with certain brain processes, but correlation is not yet identity, and it is only identity that will fulfill the demands of the mind-body problem, according to the defenders of the identity theory.

CHANGING OUR MINDS:
ALTERNATIVE CONCEPTIONS

It is worth reminding ourselves that these problems are relatively new. The separation of mind and body—or at least soul and body—is as old as Christian theology, but it was not considered a serious problem until Descartes. More importantly, there was no such separation in ancient times. One modern philosopher has pointed out that the Greeks didn't even have a way of characterizing "experience" in our sense. And when Aristotle wrote about "the soul," he meant nothing other than "the form of the body":

> One can no more ask if the body and the soul are one than if the wax and the impression it receives are one, or speaking generally the matter of each thing and the form of which it is the matter; for admitting that the terms unity and existence are used in many senses, the paramount sense is that of actuality. We have, then, given a general definition of what the soul is: it is substance expressed as form. It is this which makes a body what it is. . . .[14]

This is not behaviorism. Aristotle is not denying the existence of anything that we normally believe in. Yet it is clearly not a dualism of the Cartesian variety, and this raises the following question: Are there ways of conceiving of ourselves without falling into the Cartesian trap of talking about minds and bodies?

We can only suggest a few possibilities here. The first, perhaps, was advanced by Ludwig Wittgenstein in his *Philosophical Investigations*. Although he is usually considered to be an unconfessed behaviorist, a more recent and perhaps more plausible interpretation is that Wittgenstein wanted to deny the very idea that human beings are a curious combination of two very different substances or kinds of entities or events. Rather, there are just people, not

[14] Aristotle, *de Anima*, trans. W. S. Hett (Cambridge, Mass.: Harvard University Press, 1936).

minds plus bodies. This Wittgensteinian view has been defended, for example, by P. F. Strawson in his essay "Persons":

Let us think of some of the ways in which we ordinarily talk of ourselves, of some of the things which we ordinarily ascribe to ourselves. They are of many kinds. We ascribe to ourselves *actions and intentions* (I am doing, did, shall do this); *sensations* (I am warm, in pain); *thoughts and feelings* (I think, wonder, want this, am angry, disappointed, contented); *perceptions and memories* (I see this, hear the other, remember that). We ascribe to ourselves, in two senses, position: *location* (I am on the sofa) and *attitude* (I am lying down). And of course we ascribe to ourselves not only temporary conditions, states, and situations, like most of these, but also enduring characteristics, including such physical characteristics as height, coloring, shape, and weight. That is to say, among the things we ascribe to ourselves are things of a kind that we also ascribe to material bodies to which we would not dream of ascribing others of the things that we ascribe to ourselves. Now there seems nothing needing explanation in the fact that the particular height, coloring, and physical position which we ascribe to ourselves, should be ascribed to *something or other;* for that which one calls one's body is, at least, a body, a material thing. It can be picked out from others, identified by ordinary physical criteria and described in ordinary physical terms. But it can seem, and has seemed, to need explanation that one's states of consciousness, one's thoughts and sensations, are ascribed *to the very same thing* as that to which these physical characteristics, this physical situation, is ascribed. Why are one's states of consciousness ascribed to the very same thing as certain corporeal characteristics, a certain physical situation, etc.? And once this question is raised, another question follows it, viz.: Why are one's states of consciousness ascribed to (said to be of, or to belong to) anything at all? It is not to be supposed that the answers to these questions will be independent of one another.

It might indeed be thought that an answer to both of them could be found in the unique role which each person's body plays in his experience, particularly his perceptual experience. All philosophers who have concerned themselves with these questions have referred to the uniqueness of this role. (Descartes was well enough aware of its uniqueness: "I am *not* lodged in my body like a pilot in a vessel.") In what does this uniqueness consist? Well, of course, in a great many facts. We may summarize some of these facts by saying that for each person there is one body which occupies a certain *causal* position in relation to that person's perceptual experience, a causal position which is in various ways unique in relation to each of the various kinds of perceptual experience he has; and—as a further consequence—that this body is also unique for him as an *object* of the various kinds of perceptual experience which he has. This complex uniqueness of the single body appears, moreover, to be a contingent matter, or rather a cluster of contingent matters; we can, or it seems that we can, imagine many peculiar combinations of dependence and independence of aspects of our perceptual experience on the physical states or situation of more than one body.

Now I must say, straightaway, that this cluster of apparently contingent facts about the unique role which each person's body plays in his experience does not seem to me to provide, *by itself,* an answer to our questions. Of course these facts explain *something.* They provide a very good reason why a subject of experience should ha•e a *very special regard* for just one body, why he should think of it as unique and perhaps more important than any other. They explain—if I may be permitted to put it so—why I feel *peculiarly attached* to what in fact I call my own body; they even might be said to explain why, granted that I am going to speak of one body as *mine,* I should speak of this body (the body that I do speak of as mine) as mine. But they do not explain why I should have the concept of *myself* at all, why I should ascribe my thoughts and experiences to *anything.* Moreover, even if we were satisfied with some other explanation of why one's states of consciousness (thoughts and feelings and perceptions) were ascribed to *something,* and satisfied that the facts in question sufficed to explain why the "possession" of a particular body should be ascribed to the *same* thing (i.e., to explain why a particular body should be spoken of as standing in some special relation, called "being possessed by" to that thing), yet the facts in question still do not explain why we should, as we do, ascribe certain corporeal characteristics not simply to the body standing in this special relation to the thing to which we ascribe thoughts, feelings, etc., but to the thing itself to which we ascribe those thoughts and feelings. (For we say "I am bald" as well as "I am cold," I am lying on the hearthrug" as well as "I see a spider on the ceiling.") Briefly, the facts in question explain why a subject of experience should pick out one body from others, give it, perhaps, an honored name and ascribe to it whatever characteristics it has; but they do not explain why the experiences should be ascribed to any subject at all; and they do not explain why, if the experiences are to be ascribed to something, they *and* the corporeal characteristics which might be truly ascribed to the favored body, should be ascribed to the same thing. So the facts in question do not explain the use that we make of the word "I," or how any word has the use that word has. They do not explain the concept we have of a person. . . . A possible reaction at this point is to say that the concept we have is wrong or confused, or, if we make it a rule not to say that the concepts we have are confused, that the usage we have, whereby we ascribe, or seem to ascribe, such different kinds of predicate to one and the same thing, is confusing, that it conceals the true nature of the concepts involved, or something of this sort. This reaction can be found in two very important types of view about these matters. The first type of view is Cartesian, the view of Descartes and of others who think like him.

When we speak of a person, we are really referring to one or both of two distinct substances (two substances of different types), each of which has its own appropriate type of states and properties; and none of the properties or states of either can be a property or state of the other. States of consciousness belong to one of these substances, and not to the other.

. . . I have in mind a very simple but, in this question, a very central, thought: viz., that it is a necessary condition of one's ascribing states of consciousness, experiences, to oneself, in the way one does, that one should also ascribe them (or be prepared to ascribe them) to others who are not oneself. This means not less than it says. It means, for example, that the ascribing phrases should be used in just the same sense when the subject is another, as when the subject is oneself. Of course the thought that this is so gives no trouble to the non-philosopher: the thought, for example, that "in pain" means the same whether one says "I am in pain" or "He is in pain." The dictionaries do not give two sets of meanings for every expression which describes a state of consciousness: a first-person meaning, and a second- and third-person meaning. But to the philosopher this thought has given trouble; indeed it has. How could the sense be the same when the method of verification was so different in the two cases—or, rather, when there *was* a method of verification in the one case (the case of others) and not, properly speaking, in the other case (the case of oneself)? Or, again, how can it be right to talk of *ascribing* in the case of oneself? For surely there can be a question of ascribing only if there is or could be a question of identifying that to which the ascription is made? And though there may be a question of identifying the one who is in pain when that one is another, how can there be such a question when that one is oneself? But this last query answers itself as soon as we remember that we speak primarily to others, for the information of others. In one sense, indeed, there is no question of my having to *tell who it is* who is in pain, when I am. In another sense I may have to *tell who it is*, i.e., to let others know who it is.

What I have just said explains, perhaps, how one may properly be said to ascribe states of consciousness to oneself, given that one ascribes them to others. But how is it that one can ascribe them to others? Well, one thing is certain: that *if* the things one ascribes states of consciousness to, in ascribing them to others, are thought of as a set of Cartesian egos to which *only* private experiences can, in correct logical grammar, be ascribed, *then* this question is unanswerable and this problem insoluble. If, in identifying the things to which states of consciousness are to be ascribed, private experiences are to be all one has to go on, then, just for the very same reason as that for which there is, from one's own point of view, no question of telling that a private experience is one's own, there is also no question of telling that a private experience is another's. All private experiences, all states of consciousness, will be mine, i.e., no one's. To put it briefly: one can ascribe states of consciousness to oneself only if one can ascribe them to others; one can ascribe them to others only if one can identify other subjects of experience; and one cannot identify others if one can identify them *only* as subjects of experience, possessors of states of consciousness.

It might be objected that this way with Cartesianism is too short. After all, there is no difficulty about distinguishing bodies from one another, no difficulty about identifying bodies. And does not this give us an indirect way of identifying subjects of experience, while preserving the Cartesian mode? Can we not identify such a subject as, for example, "the subject that stands to that body in the same special relation as I stand to this one"; or, in other words, "the subject of those experiences which stand in the same unique causal relation to body N as *my* experiences stand to body M"? But this suggestion is useless. It requires me to have noted that *my* experiences stand in a special relation to body M, when it is just the right to speak of *my* experiences at all that is in question. (It requires me to have noted that *my* experiences stand in a special relation to body M; but it requires me to have noted this as a condition of being able to identify other subjects of experi-

ence, i.e., as a condition of having the idea of myself as a subject of experience, i.e., as a condition of thinking of any experience as *mine*.) So long as
we persist in talking, in the mode of this explanation, of experiences on the
one hand, and bodies on the other, the most I may be allowed to have
noted is that experiences, *all* experiences, stand in a special relation to body
M, that body M is unique in just this way, that this is what makes body M
unique among bodies. (This "most" is, perhaps, too much—because of the
presence of the word "experiences".) The proffered explanation runs: "Another subject of experience is distinguished and identified as the subject of
those experiences which stand in the same unique causal relationship to body
N as *my* experiences stand to body M." And the objection is: "But what is
the word 'my' doing in this explanation? (It could not get on without it.)"

What we have to acknowledge, in order to begin to free ourselves from
these difficulties, is the *primitiveness* of the concept of a person. What I
mean by the concept of a person is the concept of a type of entity such that
both predicates ascribing states of consciousness *and* predicates ascribing
corporeal characteristics, a physical situation, etc. are equally applicable to a
single individual of that single type. And what I mean by saying that this
concept is primitive can be put in a number of ways. One way is to return
to those two questions I asked earlier: viz., (1) why are states of consciousness ascribed to anything at all? and (2) why are they ascribed to the very
same thing as certain corporeal characteristics, a certain physical situation,
etc.? I remarked at the beginning that it was not to be supposed that the
answers to these questions were independent of each other. And now I shall
say that they are connected in this way: that a necessary condition of states
of consciousness being ascribed at all is that they should be ascribed to the
very same things as certain corporeal characteristics, a certain physical situation, etc. That is to say, states of consciousness could not be ascribed at
all, *unless* they were ascribed to persons, in the sense I have claimed for this
word. We are tempted to think of a person as a sort of compound of two
kinds of subject—a subject of experiences (a pure consciousness, an ego), on
the one hand, and a subject of corporeal attributes on the other.

. . . it becomes impossible to see how we could come by the idea of
different, distinguishable, identifiable subjects of experiences—different con-
sciousnesses—*if this idea is thought of as logically primitive,* as a logical ingredient in the compound idea of a person, the latter being composed of two
subjects. For there could never be any question of assigning an experience,
as such, to any subject other than oneself; and therefore never any question
of assigning it to oneself either, never any question of ascribing it to a subject at all. So the concept of the pure individual consciousness—the pure
ego—is a concept that cannot exist; or, at least, cannot exist as a primary
concept in terms of which the concept of a person can be explained or analyzed. It can only exist, if at all, as a secondary, nonprimitive concept, which
itself is to be explained, analyzed, in terms of the concept of a person. It
was the entity corresponding to this illusory primary concept of the pure
consciousness, the ego-substance, for which Hume was seeking, or ironically
pretending to seek, when he looked into himself, and complained that he
could never discover himself without a perception and could never discover
anything but the perception. More seriously—and this time there was no

irony, but a confusion, a Nemesis of confusion for Hume—it was this entity of which Hume vainly sought for the principle of unity, confessing himself perplexed and defeated; sought vainly because there is no principle of unity where there is no principle of differentiation. It was this, too, to which Kant, more perspicacious here than Hume, accorded a purely formal ("analytic") unity: the unity of the "I think" that accompanies all my perceptions and therefore might just as well accompany none. And finally it is this, perhaps, of which Wittgenstein spoke when he said of the subject, first, that there is no such thing, and, second, that it is not a part of the world, but its limit.

So, then, the word "I" never refers to this, the pure subject. But this does not mean, as the no-ownership theorist must think and as Wittgenstein, at least at one period, seemed to think, that "I" in some cases does not refer at all. It refers, because I am a person among others. And the predicates which would, *per impossibile,* belong to the pure subject if it could be referred to, belong properly to the person to which "I" does refer.

The concept of a person is logically prior to that of an individual consciousness. The concept of a person is not to be analyzed as that of an animated body or of an embodied anima. This is not to say that the concept of a pure individual consciousness might not have a logically secondary existence, if one thinks, or finds, it desirable. We speak of a dead person—a body—and in the same secondary way we might at least think of a disembodied person, retaining the logical benefit of individuality from having been a person.[15]

In this selection, Strawson makes at least two radical departures from the traditional Cartesian dualism between mind and body. To begin with, he attacks the idea that each of us is first of all a mind who "has" a body. Each of us is first of all a person, and the concept of "having a body" is no less essential than the concept of "having a mind." In other words, Strawson rejects outright Descartes' claim that he is essentially "a thinking thing," which might in fact have no body at all. We are essentially, according to Strawson, "thinking things" only if by that we mean "thinking persons." Descartes worried about how the two parts of a person can come together; Strawson says that they should never have been separated in the first place. This is one of the most famous cases in which a seemingly obvious philosophical distinction gets us into impossible trouble later on.

Second, Strawson adapts an argument from Wittgenstein which completely turns topsy-turvy Descartes' main thesis. Descartes assumed that we knew for certain our own mental states, and then by inference applied the same words to the mental states of other people. What Strawson now argues, following Wittgenstein, is that we can apply such "mental" words to our own thoughts, feelings and experiences only if we can apply them at the same time to other people. In other words, there can be no self-knowledge without knowledge of others as well.

A very different kind of answer comes to us from Husserl's phenomenology.

[15] P. F. Strawson, "Persons," in *Minnesota Studies in the Philosophy of Science,* vol. 2 (Minneapolis, Minn.: University of Minnesota Press, 1958).

Although Husserl was not particularly concerned with the mind-body problem as such, he was obviously very interested in the nature of consciousness, since it is consciousness that provides the subject matter of his entire life's work. What Husserl argued began with a violent attack on the spatial metaphors we use in talking about consciousness. At the beginning of the chapter, we mentioned these, suggesting that they were "just metaphors," symptoms of a problem but not a problem themselves. Well, Husserl shows that they are a problem, that philosophers have not used them merely as metaphors, and that it is because of their taking these metaphors literally that our problems about consciousness arise in the first place.

What Husserl attacks is the very idea of consciousness as a mysterious container, "in" which one finds ideas, thoughts, feelings, desires, etc. The same objection holds of such metaphors as "the stream of consciousness," with emotions, thoughts and feelings floating by like so much flotsam and jetsam. Consciousness must rather be viewed in two parts (though Husserl insists these must not be thought of as a separate "dualism"): there are acts of consciousness, and there are the objects of those acts. Simply stated, a phenomenologist would analyze my seeing a tree into (1) my act of seeing, and (2) the tree as seen. So far, this looks innocent enough. But its consequences are not so innocent. First, just in passing, notice what this does to Berkeley's idealism. Berkeley's whole argument rested on his thesis that all we can experience are ideas. But this is a confusion, Husserl insists, of our act of experiencing with the objects experienced. The object experienced (the tree) is not merely my idea. Accordingly, Husserl concludes that Berkeley's idealism is "absurd." And in general, Husserl's phenomenological theory insists that philosophers have been neglectful of this crucial distinction. Many attributes of the act of experiencing do not hold of the object, for example, the object, unlike the act, is not "private." One and only one person, namely myself, can perform my act of seeing. But any number of people can see the object of my seeing, the tree. Moreover, there can be no such thing, Husserl argues, as a conscious act without an object. You can see how this might provide a powerful argument against many traditional forms of skepticism.

Our concern here is Husserl's conception of consciousness, which he calls intentionality. (Accordingly, the act is often called the "intentional act," and the object is called the "intentional object.") To say that consciousness is intentional means (among other things, which are irrelevant to this chapter), that our conscious acts are always directed towards objects and that we should not, therefore, talk about conscious acts as self-contained "contents" which are mysteriously coordinated with the movements of our bodies. Rather, we can simply say that, among our various acts as persons are intentional conscious acts as well as physical actions. We can look at a tree and we can kick a tree. But there is no problem of "coordination" or interaction.

This theory was never actually developed by Husserl himself, but it was worked out in great detail by one of his "existential" followers in France, Maurice Merleau-Ponty (a close friend and student of Sartre). Coming from a very different starting point, Merleau-Ponty arrives at a position which is surprisingly close to Wittgenstein. It must not be called "behaviorist," but like Wittgenstein, Merleau-Ponty does reject the traditional way of dividing up mind and body and thereby suggests a very different conception of persons in which such problematic distinctions are not allowed to arise.

Merleau-Ponty is a very difficult author. In the following selection, he attacks dualism from the side that has so far seemed least controversial—the idea that the human body is just another "bit of matter."

> . . . the body is not a self-enclosed mechanism on which the soul could act from the outside. It is defined only by its functioning, which can present all degrees of integration. To say that the soul acts on the body is wrongly to suppose a univocal notion of the body and to add to it a second force which accounts for the rational signification of certain conducts. In this case it would be better to say that bodily functioning is integrated with a level which is higher than that of life and that the body has truly become a human body. Inversely one will say that the body has acted on the soul if the behavior can be understood without residue in terms of the vital dialectic or by known psychological mechanisms.
>
> Here again one does not, properly speaking, have the right to imagine a transitive action from substance to substance, as if the soul were a constantly present force whose activity would be held in check by a more powerful force. It would be more exact to say that the behavior had become disorganized, leaving room for less integrated structures. In brief, the alleged reciprocal action is reducible to an alternation or a substitution of dialectics. Since the physical, the vital and the mental individual are distinguished only as different degrees of integration, to the extent that man is completely identified with the third dialectic, that is, to the extent that he no longer allows systems of isolated conduct to function in him, his soul and his body are no longer distinguished.
>
> . . . . .
>
> For a being who has acquired the consciousness of self and his body, who has reached the dialectic of subject and object, the body is no longer the cause of the structure of consciousness; it has become the object of consciousness. Then one can no longer speak of a psycho-physiological parallelism: only a disintegrated consciousness can be paralleled with physiological processes, that is, with a partial functioning of the organism. By acceding to true knowledge, by going beyond the dialectic of the living or the social being and its circumscribed milieu, by becoming the pure subject who knows the world objectively, man ultimately realizes that absolute consciousness with respect to which the body and individual existence are no longer anything but objects; death is deprived of meaning. Reduced to the status of object of consciousness, the body could not be conceived as an intermediary between "things" and the consciousness which knows them; and since consciousness, having left the obscurity of instinct, no longer expresses the vital properties of objects but their *true* properties, the parallelism here is between consciousness and the true world which it knows directly. All the prob-

lems seem to be eliminated: the relations of the soul and the body—obscure as long as the body is treated in abstraction as a fragment of matter—are clarified when one sees in the body the bearer of a dialectic. Since the physical world and the organism can be conceptualized only as objects of consciousness or as significations, the problem of the relations of consciousness and its physical or organic "conditions" would exist only at the level of a confused thought which adheres to abstractions; it would disappear in the domain of truth in which the relation of the epistemological subject and its object alone subsists as original. This would constitute the only legitimate theme of philosophical reflection.

. . . the living body and the nervous system, instead of being like annexes of the physical world in which the occasional causes of perception would be prepared, are "phenomena" emerging from among those which consciousness knows. Perceptual behavior, as science studies it, is not defined in terms of nerve cells and synapses; it is not in the brain or even in the body; science has not been able to construct the "central sectors" of behavior from the outside like something which is enclosed within a cranial box; it can understand it only as a dialectic, the moments of which are not stimuli and movements but phenomenal objects and actions. The illusion of a transitive operation of stimuli on the sensory apparatus and of the latter "against" consciousness comes from the fact that we actualize separately the physical body, the body of the anatomists or even the organism of the physiologists, all of which are abstractions, snapshots taken from the functional body.

Therefore, we could not accept any of the materialistic models to represent the relations of the soul and body—but neither could we accept the mentalistic models, for example, the Cartesian metaphor of the artisan and his tool. An organ cannot be compared to an instrument, as if it existed and could be conceived apart from integral function, nor the mind to an artisan who uses it: this would be to return to a wholly external relation like that of the pilot and his ship which was rightly rejected by Descartes. The mind does not use the body, but realizes itself through it while at the same time transferring the body outside of physical space. When we were describing the structures of behavior it was indeed to show that they are irreducible to the dialectic of physical stimulus and muscular contraction and that in this sense behavior, far from being a thing which exists in-itself (*en soi*), is a whole significative for a consciousness which considers it; but it was at the same time and reciprocally to make manifest in "expressive conduct" the *view of a consciousness* under our eyes, to show a mind which *comes into the world.*

·   ·   ·   ·   ·

Our body does not always have meaning, and our thoughts, on the other hand—in timidity for example—do not always find in it the plenitude of their vital expression. In these cases of disintegration, the soul and the body are apparently distinct; and this is the truth of dualism. But the soul, if it possesses no means of expression—one should say rather, no means of actualizing itself—soon ceases to be *anything whatsoever* and in particular ceases to be the soul, as the thought of the aphasic weakens and becomes dissolved; the body which loses its meaning soon ceases to be a living body and falls back into the state of a physicochemical mass; it arrives at non-meaning only by dying. The two terms can never be distinguished absolutely without ceasing to be; thus their empirical connection is based on the original operation which establishes a meaning in a fragment of matter and makes it live, appear and be in it. In returning to this *structure* as the fundamental reality, we are rendering comprehensible both the distinction and the union of the soul and the body.

There is always a duality which reappears at one level or another: hunger or thirst prevents thought or feelings; the properly sexual dialectic ordinarily reveals itself through a passion; integration is never absolute and it always fails—at a higher level in the writer, at a lower level in the aphasic. There always comes a moment when we divest ourselves of a passion because of fatigue or self-respect. This duality is not a simple fact; it is founded in principle—all integration presupposing the normal functioning of subordinated formations, which always demand their own due.

But it is not a duality of substances; or, in other words, the notions of soul and body must be relativized: there is the body as mass of chemical components in interaction, the body as dialectic of living being and its biological milieu, and the body as dialectic of social subject and his group; even all our habits are an impalpable body for the ego of each moment. Each of these degrees is soul with respect to the preceding one, body with respect to the following one. The body in general is an ensemble of paths already traced, of powers already constituted; the body is the acquired dialectical soil upon which a higher "formation" is accomplished, and the soul is the meaning which is then established. The relations of the soul and the body can indeed be compared to those of concept and word, but on the condition of perceiving, beneath the separated products, the constituting operation which joins them. . . .

We have not completely described the structure of the body proper, which also includes an affective perspective, the importance of which is evident. But the preceding is sufficient to show that there is no enigma of "my body," nothing inexpressible in its relation to myself. It is true that, by describing it, we are transforming into signification the lived perspective which by definition is not one. But this alogical essence of perceived beings can be clearly designated: one will say, for example, that to offer themselves through profiles which I do not possess as I possess an idea is included in the idea of perceived being and of the body.[16]

In very difficult "dialectical" language, Merleau-Ponty defends a thesis which is strikingly similar to that defended by Wittgenstein and Strawson: one cannot treat a person as an uneasy conglomerate of mental parts and body parts, but must begin with the whole person. But where Wittgenstein and Strawson proceed by attacking the mental side of Cartesian dualism, Merleau-Ponty attacks anyone who would treat the human body as "just another body." The body itself is not only alive but, in an important sense, conscious. This does not mean, as in Descartes, that it is connected with a consciousness.

---

[16] Maurice Merleau-Ponty, *The Structure of Behavior,* trans. Alden L. Fisher (Boston, Mass.: Beacon Press, 1963).

It is itself aware, as we often notice when we talk of "bodily awareness" or "feeling our way." The difference between the body of a living person and a corpse is not just a difference in physiology, nor is it the difference between an "inhabited" body and an "uninhabited" body. My body and myself are essentially one, and to try to separate them, as Descartes had done is to make the relationship between "me and my body" into an unnecessary mystery.

A view that is strikingly similar to the phenomenological theory was defended in this country by William James. But instead of giving consciousness the attention it receives in Husserl, he argues that there is no such thing as consciousness as an entity, only different functions of experience:

'Thoughts' and 'things' are names for two sorts of objects, which common sense will always find contrasted and will always practically oppose to each other. Philosophy, reflecting on the contrast, has varied in the past in her explanations of it, and may be expected to vary in the future. At first, 'spirit and matter,' 'soul and body,' stood for a pair of equipollent substances quite on a par in weight and interest. But one day Kant undermined the soul and brought in the transcendental ego, and ever since then the bipolar relation has been very much off its balance. The transcendental ego seems nowadays in rationalist quarters to stand for everything, in empiricist quarters for almost nothing. In the hands of . . . writers . . . the spiritual principle attenuates itself to a thoroughly ghostly condition, being only a name for the fact that the 'content' of experience *is known*. It loses personal form and activity—these passing over to the content—and becomes a bare [consciousness], of which in its own right absolutely nothing can be said.

I believe that 'consciousness,' when once it has evaporated to this estate . . . is on the point of disappearing altogether. It is the name of a nonentity, and has no right to a place among first principles. Those who still cling to it are clinging to a mere echo, the faint rumor left behind by the disappearing 'soul' upon the air of philosophy. During the past year, I have read a number of articles whose authors seemed just on the point of abandoning the notion of consciousness, and substituting for it that of an absolute experience not due to two factors. But they were not quite radical enough, not quite daring enough in their negations. For twenty years past I have mistrusted 'consciousness' as an entity; for seven or eight years past I have suggested its non-existence to my students, and tried to give them its pragmatic-equivalent in realities of experience. It seems to me that the hour is ripe for it to be openly and universally discarded.

To deny plumply that 'consciousness' exists seems so absurd on the face of it—for undeniably 'thoughts' do exist—that I fear some readers will follow me no farther. Let me then immediately explain that I mean only to deny that the word stands for an entity, but to insist most emphatically that it does stand for a function. There is, I mean, no aboriginal stuff or quality of being, contrasted with that of which material objects are made, out of which our thoughts of them are made; but there is a function in experience which thoughts perform, and for the performance of which this quality of being is invoked. That function is *knowing*. 'Consciousness' is supposed necessary to explain the fact that things not only are, but get reported, are known. Whoever blots out the notion of consciousness from his list of first principles must still provide in some way for that function's being carried on.

.   .   .   .   .

My thesis is that if we start with the supposition that there is only one primal stuff or material in the world, a stuff of which everything is composed, and if we call that stuff 'pure experience,' then knowing can easily be explained as a particular sort of relation towards one another into which portions of pure experience may enter. The relation itself is a part of pure experience; one of its 'terms' becomes the subject or bearer of the knowledge, the knower, the other becomes the object known. This will need much explanation before it can be understood. The best way to get it understood is to contrast it with the alternative view; and for that we may take the recentest alternative, that in which the evaporation of the definite soul-substance has proceeded as far as it can go without being yet complete. If neo-Kantism has expelled earlier forms of dualism, we shall have expelled all forms if we are able to expel neo-Kantism in its turn.

For the thinkers I call neo-Kantian, the word consciousness today does no more than signalize the fact that experience is indefeasibly dualistic in structure. It means that not subject, not object, but object-plus-subject is the minimum that can actually be. The subject-object distinction meanwhile is entirely different from that between mind and matter, from that between body and soul. Souls were detachable, had separate destinies; things could happen to them. To consciousness as such nothing can happen, for, timeless itself, it is only a witness of happenings in time, in which it plays no part. It is, in a word, but the logical correlative of 'content' in an Experience of which the peculiarity is that *fact comes to light* in it, that *awareness of content* takes place. Consciousness as such is entirely impersonal—'self' and its activities belong to the content. To say that I am self-conscious, or conscious of putting forth volition, means only that certain contents, for which 'self' and 'effort of will' are the names, are not without witness as they occur.

Thus, for these belated drinkers at the Kantian spring, we should have to admit consciousness as an 'epistemological' necessity, even if we had no direct evidence of its being there.

But in addition to this, we are supposed by almost every one to have an immediate consciousness of consciousness itself. When the world of outer fact ceases to be materially present, and we merely recall it in memory, or fancy it, the consciousness is believed to stand out and to be felt as a kind of impalpable inner flowing, which, once known in this sort of experience, may equally be detected in presentations of the outer world. "The moment we try to fix our attention upon consciousness and to see *what,* distinctly, it is," says a recent writer, "it seems to vanish. It seems as if we had before us a mere emptiness. When we try to introspect the sensation of blue, all we can see is the blue; the other element is as if it were diaphanous. Yet it *can* be distinguished, if we look attentively enough, and know that there is something to look for." "Consciousness," says another philosopher, "is inexplicable and hardly describable, yet all conscious experiences have this in common that what we call their content has this peculiar reference to a centre for which 'self' is the name, in virtue of which reference alone the content is subjectively given, or appears. . . . While in this way consciousness, or reference to a self, is the only thing which distinguishes a conscious content from any sort of being that might be there with no one conscious of it, yet this only ground of the distinction defies all closer explanations. The existence of consciousness, although it is the fundamental fact of psychology, can indeed be laid down as certain, can be brought out by analysis, but can neither be defined nor deduced from anything but itself."

·   ·   ·   ·   ·

Now my contention is exactly the reverse of this. *Experience, I believe, has no such inner duplicity; and the separation of it into consciousness and content comes, not by way of subtraction, but by way of addition*—the addition, to a given concrete piece of it, of other sets of experiences, in connection with which severally its use or function may be of two different kinds. The paint will also serve here as an illustration. In a pot in a paint-shop, along with other paints, it serves in its entirety as so much saleable matter. Spread on a canvas, with other paints around it, it represents, on the contrary, a feature in a picture and performs a spiritual function. Just so, I maintain, does a given undivided portion of experience, taken in one context of associates, play the part of a knower, of a state of mind, of 'consciousness'; while in a different context the same undivided bit of experience plays the part of a thing known, of an objective 'content.' In a word, in one group it figures as a thought, in another group as a thing. And, since it can figure in both groups simultaneously we have every right to speak of it as subjective and objective both at once. The dualism connoted by such double-barrelled terms as 'experience,' 'phenomenon,' 'datum'—terms which, in philosophy at any rate, tend more and more to replace the single-barrelled terms of 'thought' and 'thing'—that dualism, I say, is still preserved in this account, but reinterpreted, so that, instead of being mysterious and elusive, it becomes verifiable and concrete. It is an affair of relations, it falls outside, not inside, the single experience considered, and can always be particularized and defined.

The entering wedge for this more concrete way of understanding the dualism was fashioned by Locke when he made the word 'idea' stand indifferently for thing and thought, and by Berkeley when he said that what common sense means by realities is exactly what the philosopher means by ideas. Neither Locke nor Berkeley thought his truth out into perfect clearness, but it seems to me that the conception I am defending does little more than consistently carry out the 'pragmatic' method which they were the first to use.

If the reader will take his own experiences, he will see what I mean. Let him begin with a perceptual experience, the 'presentation,' so called, of a physical object, his actual field of vision, the room he sits in, with the book he is reading as its centre; and let him for the present treat this complex object in the common-sense way as being 'really' what it seems to be, namely, a collection of physical things cut out from an environing world of other physical things with which these physical things have actual or potential relations. Now at the same time it is just *those self-same things* which his mind, as we say, perceives; and the whole philosophy of perception from Democritus's time downwards has been just one long wrangle over the paradox that what is evidently one reality should be in two places at once, both in outer space and in a person's mind. 'Representative' theories of perception avoid the logical paradox, but on the other hand they violate the reader's sense of life, which knows no intervening mental image but seems to see the room and the book immediately just as they physically exist.

The puzzle of how the one identical room can be in two places is at bottom just the puzzle of how one identical point can be on two lines. It can, if it be situated at their intersection; and similarly, if the 'pure experience' of the room were a place of intersection of two processes, which connected it with different groups of associates respectively, it could be counted twice over, as belonging to either group, and spoken of loosely as existing in two places, although it would remain all the time a numerically single thing.

Well, the experience is a member of diverse processes that can be followed away from it along entirely different lines. The one self-identical thing has so many relations to the rest of experience that you can take it in disparate systems of association, and treat it as belonging with opposite contexts. In one of these contexts it is your 'field of consciousness'; in another it is 'the room in which you sit,' and it enters both contexts in its wholeness, giving no pretext for being said to attach itself to consciousness by one of its parts or aspects, and to outer reality by another. What are the two processes, now, into which the room-experience simultaneously enters in this way?

One of them is the reader's personal biography, the other is the history of the house of which the room is part. The presentation, the experience, the *that* in short (for until we have decided *what* it is it must be a mere *that*) is the last term of a train of sensations, emotions, decisions, movements, classifications, expectations, etc., ending in the present, and the first term of a series of similar 'inner' operations extending into the future, on the reader's part. On the other hand, the very same *that* is the *terminus ad quem* of a lot of previous physical operations, carpentering, papering, furnishing, warming, etc., and the *terminus a quo* of a lot of future ones, in which it will be concerned when undergoing the destiny of a physical room. The physical and the mental operations form curiously incompatible groups. As a room, the experience has occupied that spot and had that environment for thirty years. As your field of consciousness it may never have existed until now. As a room, attention will go on to discover endless new details in it. As your mental state merely, few new ones will emerge under attention's eye. As a room, it will take an earthquake, or a gang of men, and in any case a certain amount of time, to destroy it. As your subjective state, the closing of your eyes, or any instantaneous play of your fancy will suffice. In the real world, fire will consume it. In your mind, you can let fire play over it without effect. As an outer object, you must pay so much a month to inhabit it. As an inner content, you may occupy it for any length of time rent-free. If, in short, you follow it in the mental direction, taking it along with events of personal biography solely, all sorts of things are true of it which are false, and false of it which are true if you treat it as a real thing experienced, follow it in the physical direction, and relate it to associates in the outer world.

. . . . .

First of all, this will be asked: "If experience has not 'conscious' existence, if it be not partly made of 'consciousness,' of what then is it made? Matter we know, and thought we know, and conscious content we know, but neutral and simple 'pure experience' is something we know not at all. Say *what* it consists of—for it must consist of something—or be willing to give it up!"

To this challenge the reply is easy. Although for fluency's sake I myself spoke early in this article of a stuff of pure experience, I have now to say that there is no *general* stuff of which experience at large is made. There are as many stuffs as there are 'natures' in the things experienced. If you ask what any one bit of pure experience is made of, the answer is always the same: "It is made of *that,* of just what appears, of space, of intensity, of flatness, brownness, heaviness, or what not. . . ." Experience is only a collective name for all these sensible natures, and save for time and space (and, if you like, for 'being') there appears no universal element of which all things are made.

But a last cry of *non possumus* will probably go up from many readers. "All very pretty as a piece of ingenuity," they will say, "but our consciousness itself intuitively contradicts you. We, for our part, *know* that we are conscious. We *feel* our thought, flowing as a life within us, in absolute contrast with the objects which it so unremittingly escorts. We can not be faithless to this immediate intuition. The dualism is a fundamental *datum:* Let no man join what God has put asunder."

My reply to this is my last word, and I greatly grieve that to many it will sound materialistic. I can not help that, however, for I, too, have my intuitions and I must obey them. Let the case be what it may in others, I am as confident as I am of anything that, in myself, the stream of thinking (which I recognize emphatically as a phenomenon) is only a careless name for what, when scrutinized, reveals itself to consist chiefly of the stream of my breathing. The 'I think' which Kant said must be able to accompany all my objects, is the 'I breathe' which actually does accompany them. There are other internal facts besides breathing (intracephalic muscular adjustments, etc., of which I have said a word in my larger Psychology), and these increase the assets of 'consciousness,' so far as the latter is subject to immediate perception; but breath, which was ever the original of 'spirit,' breath moving outwards, between the glottis and the nostrils, is, I am persuaded, the essence out of which philosophers have constructed the entity known to them as consciousness. *That entity is fictitious, while thoughts in the concrete are fully real. But thoughts in the concrete are made of the same stuff as things are.*

I wish I might believe myself to have made that plausible in this article. In another article I shall try to make the general notion of a world composed of pure experiences still more clear.[17]

[17] William James, "Does Consciousness Exist?" in *Journal of Philosophy, Psychology and Scientific Methods,* vol. 1, no. 18, September 1, 1904.

Here again, but from another perspective, the traditional Cartesian dualism is rejected. James, like Wittgenstein and Strawson, attacks the idea of separate "mental" events or "consciousness" and insists that "there is no such thing." But in saying that, he is not denying that we are conscious, or that we have feeling and experiences. He is rather saying that we have to think of these as "functions" of the overall person, not as independent and possibly separable entities.

SUMMARY AND CONCLUSION

Since Descartes' discussion of mind and body as two separate and different substances, philosophers have struggled with a number of theories to explain how mind and body worked together to constitute a complete human being. Certain properties of mind—its lack of "extension" and seeming "privileged access," and the "incorrigibility" of mental claims—made the connection between mind and body extremely problematic. Therefore, philosophers suggested that mental events and bodily events are different aspects of some other event (dual aspect theory), or that they occur in parallel, like the sound and visual tracks on a film (parallelism or pre-established harmony), or that bodily events cause mental events but not the other way around (epiphenomenalism), or that mental events and bodily events are in fact identical (identity theory). Many philosophers and psychologists embraced behaviorism, arguing that "mental event" is in fact only shorthand for a complex description of patterns of behavior. More recently, many philosophers have come to reject the distinction between mind and body altogether, insisting on the primacy and indivisibility of the concept of a person.

GLOSSARY

behaviorism: in psychology, the methodological thesis that insists that only what is publicly observable can be used as subject matter or as evidence in scientific research regarding human beings. In particular, all talk of "minds" and "mental events," "desires," "purposes," "ideas," "perceptions," and "experiences" is to be given up in favor of terms which refer only to the experimental situation or the behavior of the creature (or person) in question (for example, "stimulus," "response," "reinforcements"). In philosophy and metaphysics, the thesis that there are no "covert" or "private" mental events, only patterns of behavior and psychological ways of talking about behavior as "intelligent," "deceitful," "calculating," or "inattentive." All of these must be understood, not in terms of some process ("intelligence," "deceitful thinking," "calculating," or "lack of attending") going on "in the mind" but rather as ways of interpreting, predicting, and otherwise describing and evaluating behavior.

causal interactionism: the theory that mind and body causally interact; that mental events (for example, an "act of will") can cause a bodily consequence (for example, raising one's arm), and that a bodily change (for example, a puncture of the skin) can cause a mental consequent (for example, a pain). The theory sounds plausible enough on first hearing, but there are extremely serious objections that have been raised against it.

dual aspect theory: the theory (for example, in Spinoza) that mind and body are simply different aspects (or "attributes") of one and the same substance, thus avoiding the problem of interaction between substances.

dualism: in general, the distinction between mind and body as separate substances, or very different kinds of states and events with radically different properties.

epiphenomenalism: the thesis that mental events are epiphenomena, that is, side effects of various physical processes in the brain and nervous system but of little importance themselves. The model is a one-way causal model: body states cause changes in the mind, but mental states have no effect in themselves on the body.

identity theory: the thesis that the mind and body are identical; that is, that mental states and events are identical to certain brain and nervous system processes. The theory is usually presented as a form of materialism, but it is important to emphasize that, unlike many materialistic theories, it does not deny the existence of mental events. It denies only that they have independent existence. Mental events are nothing other than certain bodily events.

immediate: for certain and without need for argument.

incorrigibility: impossible to correct; cannot be mistaken. It has long been argued that our claims about our own mental states are incorrigible—we cannot be mistaken about them.

inference-ticket: Ryle's term for referring to the proper function of a mental state: talk, as a description of a pattern of behavior and, therefore, as an "inference-ticket" that allows us to infer what a person will do in the future. (To say "George wants an olive" is to give us an inference-ticket regarding his future behavior around olives.)

intentionality: in phenomenology, the thesis that every conscious act has an object. (The act is therefore called the "intentional act" and the object "the intentional object".) The importance of this concept is that it undercuts the metaphor of mental "contents" (as in a theater, an image explicitly used by Hume, for example). The concept was used by Husserl's teacher, Franz Brentano, who borrowed it from some medieval philosophers, before Husserl used it and made it famous.

parallelism: the thesis that mental events and bodily events parallel each other and occur in perfect coordination, but do not interact.

pre-established harmony: Leibniz's view that the coordination between our ideas and the physical events of the world and our bodies was set up by God in perfect order.

privacy: the seeming inaccessibility of mental states and events to anyone other than the person who "has" them.

private language argument: Wittgenstein's argument that, even if there were such "private objects" as mental states and events, it would be impossible for us to talk about them and impossible for us to identify them, even in our own case.

privileged access: the technical term used by philosophers to refer to the curious fact that a person usually (if not always) can immediately know, simply by paying attention, what is going on in his own mind, while other people can find out what is going on—if they can at all—only by watching the person's behavior, listening to what he or she says, or asking (and hoping they get a truthful answer). It is important to distinguish privileged access from incorrigibility. The first means that a person knows directly what is "in his mind" without having to observe his behavior; the second means that he knows for certain and beyond the possibility of error.

unconscious: Freud's famous way of referring to the fact that there are ideas, desires, memories and experiences in our minds to which we do not have privileged access, which we may be wrong about (and, therefore, about which our claims are not incorrigible), and which may be more evident to other people than to oneself. He also distinguishes a *preconscious* ("the antechamber of consciousness"). Preconscious ideas can be made conscious simply by being attended to. (For example, you do know what the capital of California is, but you weren't conscious of it before I mentioned it; it was pre-conscious.) Truly unconscious ideas, however, cannot be made conscious, even when one tries to do so.

10

FREEDOM

"Two plus two equals four"—as if freedom means that!

Fyodor Dostoevsky

"The murderer had been raised in a slum. His father abandoned him when he was seven months old; he was beaten by his older siblings and constantly abused by his mother. He never had the chance to attend school; he never could get or hold a job. By the time he robbed the store, he was near starvation, addicted to hard drugs, without friends and without help of any kind. His sister said, 'I've known since he was a child that he would do this some day.' His mother complained, 'I don't understand!' The prosecutor called it a 'cold-blooded, premeditated act.' The defense accused the whole of society, claiming that it had, through its neglect as well as its negative conditioning, made this man an inevitable killer." We know the rest of the arguments, what we don't know is their resolution. Should a man be held responsible for an act for which he has been conditioned the whole of his life? Or must we not hold out that, no matter what the circumstances, he could have resisted, he could have decided not to commit the crime, and therefore he must be held responsible.

Of all the abstract problems of philosophy, the problem of freedom has the most obvious practical consequences. If we believe a person is free to choose his/her actions and destiny, we tend to load the person with moral responsibility, praise or blame; if we believe a person is simply a victim of the fates, a cog in a mechanical universe or a pawn in the abstract hands of society, then our attitude towards his/her actions can be no different than our attitudes towards the movement of glaciers and the growth of flowers. "It happens that way," that's all.

356

Are we cogs in the universe? Are we pawns of the fates? People have often thought so. Most of the ancient Greeks believed that our destinies were already decided for us; no matter what our actions, the outcome was settled. Oedipus knew long before his tragedy that he would kill his father and marry his mother. He left his home town, trying to avoid the couple who raised him and whom he believed were his parents, changed his identity, took all precautions, and nevertheless did just what the fates ordered anyway. There have been powerful movements in Christianity that have taught that God has predetermined or knows in advance every action we will perform, as well as our ultimate chances for salvation. And today, most people believe that a person's actions and character are the causal result of his genes and his upbringing, and perhaps also the result of unconscious fears and desires that he or she may never recognize. Then too, astrology and other theories of external determination have always been popular. (For instance, "*Virgo:* It's going to be a bad day; don't get out of bed and don't talk to anyone.") And we can see why they would be. The more our actions are the results of other forces and not our own doing the less we need feel responsible for them, and the less we need worry about deciding what to do. It is already decided, and not by us.

DETERMINISM:
VARYING PERSPECTIVES

The problem of freedom occurs on different levels of generality, from the most abstract thesis that the universe as a whole is a single great machine or "substance" (as in Newton or Spinoza) to very localized theories about the psychology of the human personality. At all levels, however, the problem has usually been identified with a single claim, determinism. We were briefly introduced to determinism in Chapter 2: Spinoza defended it in his metaphysical system; Newton gave it a convincing scientific interpretation with his physical theories. In a phrase, *determinism* can be characterized by a principle already familiar to us from Chapter 3, the "principle of universal causation." "Every event has its cause(s)." That is determinism. It is the thesis that everything that happens in the universe is determined according to the laws of nature. The problem is that human actions, whatever else they might be, are also events in the universe. Accordingly, by the simplest of syllogisms, they are also determined:

> Every event has its cause(s).
> Human actions are events.
> *Therefore,* every human action has its cause(s).

But if an action is caused, can it also be free? How can we hold someone responsible for doing something if he or she had no choice in the matter and couldn't have done anything else? It is as if we were to start praising people (or blaming them) for obeying the law of gravity. What else could they possibly do?

It is important to separate determinism as we have defined it from traditional conceptions of fatalism and predestination. The Greek tragedies depend upon *fatalism,* the view that, whatever a person's actions, and whatever the circumstances, the end is inevitable. But this is not determinism, for determinism requires certain actions and circumstances as antecedent conditions of the determined outcome. According to fatalism, whatever happens, the end is inevitable. According to determinism, an event will necessarily happen if its antecedent conditions are fulfilled. Thus the Oedipus tragedy is fatalistic because, whatever Oedipus decides to do, he is fated to kill his father (whether he knows that he is doing it or not) and marry his mother (whether or not he knows that it is his mother). Determinism, on the other hand, need not say that any event is inevitable; it insists only that, *if* certain conditions exist, *then* a certain kind of event will take place, (for example, if a pot of water is heated sufficiently, then it will boil; or, if a person is forced to choose between losing his life and killing an insect, then he will take the life of the insect). This "if/then" structure is essential to determinism. (There need be no such "ifs" or "thens" to fatalism.)

We similarly distinguish between determinism and predestination. *Predestination* has been the view of many Christian theologians, according to whom our every action (and every event in the universe) is known if not also caused in advance by God. Predestination, like fatalism, does not depend upon any particular antecedent conditions, unless we want to say that God is an antecedent condition. Accordingly, we might distinguish determinism and predestination by spelling out our determinist premise further: "every event has its natural cause." The theory of predestination might hold that every event has its cause, God; but it does not hold, as determinism does, that every event has its natural cause.

The theories of fatalism and predestination are no longer topics of great philosophical debate. This is not because they are not interesting or because no one believes in them, quite the contrary, many people find them very interesting (whether they believe in them or not) and you probably know at least somebody who believes in each of them. But fatalism and predestination seem to be those sorts of views that one either believes or doesn't. There isn't much room for debate: you believe in the fates or you don't.

Determinism, therefore, is the theory that every event in the universe, including every human action, has its natural causes; given certain antecedent conditions, then an event will take place necessarily, according to the laws of nature. But we must fill out the determinist's premise by at least one more step. It is not enough to say, "every event has its natural cause(s)," since this would leave open the possibility that, although every event requires certain antecedent conditions in order to take place, the event might still be a matter of chance, at least to some extent, or a matter of human choice. In other words, it might be that the antecedent conditions limit the possibilities, but do not fully determine them. We must say, therefore, that "every event has its sufficient natural cause(s)." *Sufficient* means capable of bringing the event about by itself. Then there is no room for chance and no room for choice. And this view, which we shall call "hard" determinism ("hard" as in "hard-headed" as well as a "hard" conclusion to accept), clearly leaves no room for human freedom. Without choice, there can be no freedom, and without freedom, there is no reason to hold a person responsible for his action, no matter how virtuous or how vicious it might be. According to the hard determinist thesis, we can barely be said to be "acting" at all, for our "actions" are nothing but the result of antecedent conditions and laws of nature which leave no room for our "doing something" at all.

Are we cogs in the universe? "Hard determinism"

The hard determinist premise received its greatest impetus from Newton's physics and his picture of the universe as "matter in motion," determined according to the laws of motion and gravitation that he so elegantly formulated. But his followers applied these laws not only to the movements of the planets and the stars or to the ball rolling down an inclined plane. According to them, we too are "matter in motion," physical bodies which are subject to all of the laws of nature. What we "do" is just as determined by these laws as any other event in nature.

This "hard-headed" determinism has maintained a powerful hold on philosophers ever since Isaac Newton published his theories in the seventeenth century. The philosopher Pierre Simon La Place had such confidence in the Newtonian system that he claimed that, if he knew the location and motion of every object in the universe, he could predict the location and motion of every object in the universe at any time in the future. (He could also *retrodict*, or look back to, every past state of the universe.) This means that, if he had a proper map of the universe, including the material parts of our own bodies, he could predict everything that would ever happen, and of course, everything that we would ever do. If this is so, what possible sense could we make of our vain claims to have choices of actions, to decide what to do, or to hold ourselves and others responsible for what we have done?

La Place's confidence in the hard determinist thesis was common among the immediate successors and enthusiasts of Newton. One of the philosophers of the French Enlightenment, for example, Baron Paul Henri d'Holbach, defended the hard determinist viewpoint so uncompromisingly that he shocked even his colleagues as well as the many traditionalists.

> In whatever manner man is considered, he is connected to universal nature, and submitted to the necessary and immutable laws that she imposes on all beings she contains, according to their peculiar essences or to the respective properties with which, without consulting them, she endows each particular species. Man's life is a line that nature commands him to describe

upon the surface of the earth, without his ever being able to swerve from it, even for an instant. He is born without his own consent; his organization does in nowise depend upon himself; his ideas come to him involuntarily; his habits are in the power of those who cause him to contract them; he is unceasingly modified by causes, whether visible or concealed, over which he has no control, which necessarily regulate his mode of existence, give the hue to his way of thinking, and determine his manner of acting. He is good or bad, happy or miserable, wise or foolish, reasonable or irrational, without his will being for anything in these various states. Nevertheless, in spite of the shackles by which he is bound, it is pretended he is a free agent, or that independent of the causes by which he is moved, he determines his own will, and regulates his own condition.

However slender the foundation of his opinion, of which everything ought to point out to him the error, it is current at this day and passes for an incontestable truth with a great number of people, otherwise extremely enlightened; it is the basis of religion, which supposing relations between man and the unknown being she has placed above nature, has been incapable of imagining how man could merit reward or deserve punishment from this being, if he was not a free agent. Society has been believed interested in this system; because an idea has gone abroad, that if all the actions of man were to be contemplated as necessary, the right of punishing those who injure their associates would no longer exist. At length human vanity accommodated itself to a hypothesis which, unquestionably, appears to distinguish man from all other physical beings, by assigning to him the special privilege of a total independence of all other causes, but of which a very little reflection would have shown him the impossibility.

The will, as we have elsewhere said, is a modification of the brain, by which it is disposed to action, or prepared to give play to the organs. This will is necessarily determined by the qualities, good or bad, agreeable or painful, of the object or the motive that acts upon his sense, or of which the idea remains with him, and is resuscitated by his memory. In consequence, he acts necessarily, his action is the result of the impulse he receives either from the motive, from the object, or from the idea which has modified his brain, or disposed his will. When he does not act according to this impulse, it is because there comes some new cause, some new motive, some new idea, which modified his brain in a different manner, gives him a new impulse, determines his will in another way, by which the action of the former impulse is suspended: thus, the sight of an agreeable object, or its idea, determines his will to set him in action to procure it; but if a new object or a new idea more powerfully attracts him, it gives a new direction to his will, annihilates the effect of the former, and prevents the action by which it was to be procured. This is the mode in which reflection, experience, reason, necessarily arrests or suspends the action of man's will: without this he would of necessity have followed the anterior impulse which carried him towards a then desirable object. In all this he always acts according to necessary laws from which he has no means of emancipating himself.

· · · · ·

In short, the actions of man are never free; they are always the necessary consequence of his temperament, of the received ideas, and of the notions, either true or false, which he has formed to himself of happiness; of his opinions, strengthened by example, by education, and by daily experience. So many crimes are witnessed on the earth only because every thing conspires to render man vicious and criminal; the religion he has adopted, his government, his education, the examples set before him, irresistibly drive him on to evil: under these circumstances, morality preaches virtue to him in vain. In those societies where vice is esteemed, where crime is crowned, where venality is constantly recompense, where the most dreadful disorders are punished only in those who are too weak to enjoy the privilege of committing them with impunity, the practice of virtue is considered nothing more than a painful sacrifice of happiness. Such societies chastise, in the lower orders, those excesses which they respect in the higher ranks; and frequently have the injustice to condemn those in the penalty of death, whom public prejudices, maintained by constant example, have rendered criminal.

Man, then, is not a free agent in any one instant of his life; he is necessarily guided in each step by those advantages, whether real or fictitious, that he attaches to the objects by which his passions are roused: these passions themselves are necessary in a being who unceasingly tends towards his own happiness; their energy is necessary, since that depends on his temperament; his temperament is necessary, because it depends on the physical elements which enter into his composition; the modification of this temperament is necessary, as it is the infallible and inevitable consequence of the impulse he receives from the incessant action of moral and physical beings.[1]

Is determinism true? Determinism versus indeterminism

Why should we accept the determinist's premise? Without it, determinism cannot get to first base. Well, we have already seen the arguments traditionally advanced in earlier chapters, even by philosophers who are not themselves "hard determinists": the most general argument is that only by assuming from the outset that every event has its (sufficient natural) cause(s) can we ever understand anything. Otherwise, we should have auto mechanics always giving us back our cars (and our bills) with the unhelpful statement that "there's no cause for our troubles." We could expect the same from doctors whenever a diagnosis gave them the least bit of trouble, and we would use it ourselves every time a problem began to get difficult. A much stronger argument is made by Kant, who says that the basic rule of determinism, the principle of universal causation, is one of the rules by which we must interpret every experience. But even Hume, who denies that this principle can be justified either through reason or through experience, insists that it is a "natural habit" or custom which is indispensable to us and which we could not give up even if we wanted to. The consensus, then, has been that the principle itself is inescapable. Even Leibniz, who rejected the idea of causation altogether, insisted on his "Principle of Sufficient Reason," which came to the same end, that is, "every event has its sufficient reason."

[1] Baron Paul Henri d'Holbach, *System of Nature* (London: Kearsley, 1797).

The agreement of so many philosophers indicates the strength of the hard determinist position. Without the assumption that "every event has its sufficient natural cause(s)," human knowledge would seem to be without one of its most vital presuppositions. Not only scientific research but even our most ordinary everyday beliefs would be forced to an intolerable skeptical standstill. Our every experience would be unintelligible, and our universe would appear to be nothing but a disconnected stream of incoherent happenings, from which nothing could be predicted and nothing understood. So the answer to the question, "why should we accept the determinist's premise?" seems to be, "We cannot give it up; how could we possibly do without it?" For no matter how it is rephrased or philosophically altered (for example, by Leibniz, who eliminates the concept of "cause" from it), the assumption that every event in the universe, including our own actions, can be explained and understood, if only one knows enough about it and its antecedent conditions, is a presupposition of all human thinking that we cannot imagine doing without.

But even if the hard determinist's premise seems undeniable, it is not yet clear how we are to understand that premise. The older determinists of the Newtonian period (La Place, d'Holbach) understood the idea of a cause as a literal push or compulsion, as if one were given a shove down the stairs. On this model, our actions are no different, except in complexity, from the "actions" of billiard balls on a felt covered table, the motion of each wholly determining the motion of the next. The exact movements of every ball, of course, are not always evident. In the opening break, for example, even the most expert player cannot predict with accuracy where each ball will go. But we can be sure that each one is absolutely determined by the movements of the other balls that make contact with it, just as with the simple predictable case of a single ball hitting another straight-on.

If we view human beings as nothing more than physical bodies—bones, muscles, nerve cells, and the like—then this mechanical billiard ball model might make some sense. But there is a much weaker interpretation of the hard determinist premise which does not require us to so radically reduce people to mere bodies. Instead of talking about actual physical pushes and compulsions, we can interpret the determinist premise in the following way: to say that every event has its cause(s) is to say that if certain antecedent conditions are satisfied, then we can predict that such-and-such will occur. On the stronger mechanistic determinist interpretation, causes are actual pushes and, on such an interpretation, the notion of freedom is clearly impossible. But on the weaker interpretation, of determinism as predictability, there may yet be room for us to talk about freedom of action. For example, we may be able to predict our friend's decision, but that does not seem to mean that he was forced to make it. We may be able to predict his action, but only because, knowing him, we know what he will probably do. On the second interpretation, perhaps we can have determinism and freedom.

Many philosophers would defend determinism only as predictability on the basis of probability. We might easily be wrong. To say that every event is determined, on this view, means only that it is predictable if we know enough about antecedent conditions. But it has been objected, against the determinist, that the fact of such predictability is not sufficient to defend determinism in anything like the "hard" sense. It is one thing to say that all events, including human actions, are actually caused or compelled by physical forces. It is something quite different to say that all events, including human actions, are predictable. They might be predictable, for example, only on the basis of certain statistical probabilities. "Most people in this circumstance would do that." "The odds are for it," in other words. Or, in the case of human actions, the predictability might still be due to human choices; we can predict each other's actions because we know how we would probably choose in the same circumstances. But there is no need here to talk about "causes" or compulsions. Nor, it has been argued, should we even talk any longer about "determinism," if this is all that we mean by it.

This antideterminist thesis has been called by the name, indeterminism. Indeterminism is the explicit rejection of determinism, the view that determinism is false, and that every event does not have a cause. The advantages of this theory are obvious, for it would seem that, as soon as we allow that there are some events that are uncaused, human actions might be among them. And that means that we can be held properly responsible for our actions and not simply explain them by appealing to certain antecedent conditions. But is the indeterminist thesis plausible?

The indeterminist argument has recently received a boost from physics, the very science that gave rise to the determinist threat in the first place. It was Newtonian physics that gave determinism its strongest claims. And you remember La Place boasting that if he knew the location and motion of every particle in the universe, he could predict every future state of the universe at any time. But it has been shown in recent physics that such knowledge is impossible. One of the most important discoveries of modern physics is the *Heisenberg Uncertainty Principle* (named after its discoverer, Werner Heisenberg), which says that we cannot know both the location and the momentum of a sub-atomic particle. In coming to know the one, we make it impossible for us to know the other at the same time. From this principle, the British physicist-philosopher Sir Arthur Eddington advanced the indeterminist argument that determinism is false on physical grounds. Every event in the universe is not predictable. And furthermore, many scientists now agree, on the basis of such considerations, that the concept of "cause" does not apply to certain sub-atomic particles either. Therefore, the determinist premise, that "every event in the universe has its sufficient natural cause," is false. Some events, namely those involving some sub-atomic particles, are not caused, not predictable, and therefore not determined, on any interpretation. And since all events and objects involve sub-atomic particles as their basic constituents, it can therefore be argued that no event is caused or strictly predictable, or determined. Of course, one can predict most events with a large degree of success, but only, according to these modern physical theories, with a high degree of statistical probability, not because of any causes or compulsions. But if not all events are determined, then perhaps human actions are not determined but free. And if they are predictable, it is not because they are caused.

The object of indeterminism is to deny the determinist position in order to make room for human freedom. But there are, unfortunately, two serious objections to this indeterminist argument: first, even if we suppose that the conclusions of modern physical ("quantum") theory are correct (a matter still in dispute among physicists), it is clear that determinism is of importance to us primarily as a theory of macroscopic bodies (that is, visible size—people, trees, cars) not sub-atomic particles. And no one has ever concluded that quantum theory and modern physics actually refute Newton's theories. Rather, it supplements them, puts them in their place, and qualifies them in ways which would have been unthinkable in the eighteenth century. But, as for the determinism of the gravitation of the planets or the rolling of a ball down an inclined plane, the spectacular discoveries of modern particle physics doesn't affect them in the least. And, with regard to the physical determinism of our own bodies, the case remains as before. It might be true that it is impossible to predict what a sub-atomic particle in our bodies might do. But it does not follow that it is impossible to predict what our bodies will do. Falling out of a plane, we still fall at exactly the same speed as a sack of potatoes. And that is all the determinist needs to continue his attack on our concept of freedom. Second, even if there should be such indeterminism, indeterminism is not the same as freedom. Suppose there should be a "gap" in the causal determinism of our decisions by the various neurological processes of our brains; that would mean, at most, that what we do is not determined at all—or is determined only randomly. Suppose, all of a sudden, your legs started moving and you found yourself kicking a fire hydrant; surely this is not what we mean by a "free action." Freedom means, at least, that we are free to choose what we shall do and that our decisions are effective. Indeterminism robs us of our freedom, therefore, just as much as determinism. And the argument against determinism, in any case, is not yet sufficiently persuasive to allow the indeterminist his conclusions.

The role of consciousness

Hard determinism is true of us as physical bodies. But, you might insist, we are not just physical bodies, we are also conscious. We can make decisions. We have a will of our own. (The somewhat antique notion of "will" often enters into these controversies, and so the problem of freedom is often called "the free will problem." But we shall not use this terminology here.)

Whatever we are besides physical bodies, our physical bodies are still subject to all of the laws of Newtonian physics. You can see the problem. If our bodies are just cogs in the universe, what does it matter whether we are conscious or not? If you fall out of an airplane, you fall and accelerate at exactly the same rate as a sack of potatoes. The fact that you, unlike the potatoes, are aware of your falling, scared out of your mind, and wishing or praying like crazy that some miracle will save you, makes not a bit of difference. But perhaps this is so with all of our actions as well? Our bodies are composed of bits of matter, various molecules undergoing chemical interactions and acted upon by the various laws of physics. No one can deny that they are subject to all the laws of physical nature. But once all the parts are determined in their various movements and activities, what is left for consciousness to do?

There are two possible replies to this problem, but both seem to support the hard determinist position and leave us without the freedom we are trying to find room for. Suppose one insists that consciousness, unlike our physical bodies, is not part of the scheme of determinism? Consciousness, unlike our bodies, is free, free to make decisions, free to choose what to do. But if our bodies are determined in their movements, then what can consciousness do, even if it is "free." Whatever consciousness decides, it cannot have any possible effect on the movements of our bodies, in other words, it cannot affect our actions. Our "decisions," then, would be mere vanities, like fancy switches on a machine that in fact don't do anything at all. Consciousness, on this view, is nothing but a sideshow, for whatever it "decides," what we will do and what will happen are already determined by other antecedent conditions that have nothing to do with the "decision." In crude form, this was Spinoza's ethical position, and also that of some of the early Stoic philosophers. Everything is determined by the laws of nature; it is absurd to fight against Nature, and you couldn't if you tried anyway. All that can be done is to accept the necessity of whatever happens and recognize our consciousness and our apparent freedom as a luxurious vanity. Every human action has its sufficient natural causes apart from consciousness. And so consciousness can make no difference whatsoever.

Most hard determinists, however, would probably not agree with the idea that any event, even a non-physical event such as an act of consciousness, could be "outside" the determinism of Nature. Most hard determinists would argue that our thoughts and feelings, even our decisions, are caused by the states of our brains and nervous systems. Our "decisions" are nothing but the conscious effects of complex causal antecedents, most of which we still don't understand, but definitely part of the deterministic scheme of things. How consciousness enters this deterministic scheme is open to all of the questions that we asked in the last chapter—whether, for example, there can be causal connections between consciousness and our bodies, whether consciousness is merely an "epiphenomenon" of our brain states or identical to them or whether we should no longer speak of "consciousness" at all. But, however those disputes are resolved, the hard determinist will insist that consciousness cannot be an exception to determinism.

If consciousness is part of the deterministic scheme of things, could we not say that what happens in consciousness, particularly our decisions, thereby cause movements of our bodies, and therefore control our actions? This attractive compromise, however, faces an overwhelming problem. If one accepts the determinist's premise, then our decisions cannot cause our actions unless it is also true that our decisions, as part of the deterministic scheme, are caused in turn. Our decisions, therefore, are also determined, and, no matter that it might seem as if we have a choice of actions, what we decide is already determined by those antecedent conditions that determine our decision.

Suppose, for example, you are deciding whether or not to go to the movies. Whether or not you go depends upon your decision. But your decision, in turn, depends upon its causal antecedents. Now suppose that we knew enough about your upbringing and tastes, your character and the workings of your brain such that we could see that your decision—let's say to go to the movies—is nothing more than the result of all of these conditions. What sense would it make, then, to say that you decided to go? Of course, it is true that you went through all of the motions of "making a decision." But the outcome of that decision, even if it was the causal result of the decision, was nevertheless nothing more than the result of conditions that preceded and had nothing to do with the decision. It is as if I gave you a choice of two alternatives, only one of which was possible anyway. That is hardly a choice. And so, if a decision enters into our actions, it must be a decision whose outcome is already determined in advance. The hard determinist thus wins in either case. If consciousness is not part of the deterministic scheme, it can have no possible effects on our actions. If it is part of the deterministic scheme of things, then it cannot be free. In either case, hard determinism is undeniable and freedom turns out to be an illusion.

"Soft" determinism

The philosophers of the Newtonian tradition, those "hard" determinists who believe that determinism precludes the possibility of freedom of choice and action, have always had a powerful and simple argument on their side. But, because of the urgency of our demand that we hold ourselves and each other responsible for our actions, most philosophers have not accepted "hard" determinism, even though they have accepted the determinist argument. Accordingly, many philosophers have espoused what has been called *soft determinism*. (The name comes from William James, who was not one of them.) Soft determinists, unlike the uncompromising hard determinists, believe that human freedom and determinism are compatible positions. On the one hand, they accept the determinist's argument, but, on the other, they refuse to give up the all-important demand for human freedom and responsibility. (Accordingly, they are often called *compatibilists,* and their position, *compatibilism.*)

The key to the "soft determinist" position is that an action or a decision, though fully determined, is free if it "flows from the agent's character." John Stuart Mill, for example, defends such a position in the following way:

The question, whether the law of causality applies in the same strict sense to human actions as to other phenomena, is the celebrated controversy concerning the freedom of the will; which, from at least as far back as the time of Pelagius, has divided both the philosophical and the religious world. The affirmative opinion is commonly called the doctrine of Necessity, as asserting human volitions and actions to be necessary and inevitable. The negative maintains that the will is not determined, like other phenomena, by antecedents, but determines itself; that our volitions are not, properly speaking, the effects of causes, or at least have no causes which they uniformly and implicitly obey.

I have already made it sufficiently apparent that the former of these opinions is that which I consider the true one; but the misleading terms in which it is often expressed, and the indistinct manner in which it is usually apprehended, have both obstructed its reception, and perverted its influence when received. The metaphysical theory of free-will, as held by philosophers (for the practical feeling of it, common in a greater or less degree to all mankind, is in no way inconsistent with the contrary theory), was invented because the supposed alternative of admitting human actions to be *necessary* was deemed inconsistent with every one's instinctive consciousness, as well as humiliating to the pride and even degrading to the moral nature of man. Nor do I deny that the doctrine, as sometimes held, is open to these imputations; for the misapprehension in which I shall be able to show that they originate, unfortunately is not confined to the opponents of the doctrine, but is participated in by many, perhaps we might say by most, of its supporters.

Correctly conceived, the doctrine called Philosophical Necessity is simply this: that, given the motives which are present to an individual's mind, and given likewise the character and disposition of the individual, the manner in which he will act might be unerringly inferred; that if we knew the person thoroughly, and knew all the inducements which are acting upon him, we could foretell his conduct with as much certainty as we can predict any physical event. This proposition I take to be a mere interpretation of universal experience, a statement in words of what every one is internally convinced of. No one who believed that he knew thoroughly the circumstances of any case, and the characters of the different persons concerned, would hesitate to foretell how all of them would act. Whatever degree of doubt he may in fact feel, arises from the uncertainty whether he really knows the circumstances, or the character of some one or other of the persons, with the degree of accuracy required; but by no means from thinking that if he did know these things, there could be any uncertainty what the conduct would be. Nor does this full assurance conflict in the smallest degree with what is called our feeling of freedom. We do not feel ourselves the less free, because those to whom we are intimately known are well assured how we shall will to act in a particular case. We often, on the contrary, regard the doubt what our conduct will be, as a mark of ignorance of our character, and sometimes even resent it as an imputation. The religious metaphysicians who have asserted the freedom of the will, have always maintained it to be consistent with divine foreknowledge of our actions: and if with divine, then with any other foreknowledge. We may be free, and yet another may have reason to be perfectly certain what use we shall make of our freedom.

It is not, therefore, the doctrine that our volitions and actions are invariable consequents of our antecedent states of mind, that is either contradicted by our consciousness, or felt to be degrading.

But the doctrine of causation, when considered as obtaining between our volitions and their antecedents, is almost universally conceived as involving more than this. Many do not believe, and very few practically feel, that there is nothing in causation but invariable, certain, and unconditional sequence. There are few to whom mere constancy of succession appears a sufficiently stringent bond of union for so peculiar a relation as that of cause and effect. Even if the reason repudiates, the imagination retains, the feeling of some more intimate connection, of some peculiar tie, or mysterious constraint exercised by the antecedent over the consequent. Now this it is which, considered as applying to the human will, conflicts with our consciousness, and revolts our feelings. We are certain that, in the case of our volitions, there is not this mysterious constraint. We know that we are not compelled, as by a magical spell, to obey any particular motive. We feel, that if we wished to prove that we have the power of resisting the motive, we could do so (that wish being, it needs scarcely be observed, a *new antecedent*); and it would be humiliating to our pride, and (what is of more importance) paralyzing to our desire of excellence, if we thought otherwise. But neither is any such mysterious compulsion now supposed, by the best philosophical authorities, to be exercised by any other cause over its effect. Those who think that causes draw their effects after them by a mystical tie, are right in believing that the relation between volitions and their antecedents is of another nature. But they should go farther, and admit that this is also true of all other effects and their antecedents. If such a tie is considered to be involved in the word Necessity, the doctrine is not true of human actions; but neither is it then true of inanimate objects. It would be more correct to say that matter is not bound by necessity, than that mind is so.

. . . . .

I am inclined to think that this error is almost wholly an effect of the associations with a word, and that it would be prevented, by forbearing to employ, for the expression of the simple fact of causation, so extremely inappropriate a term as Necessity. That word, in its other acceptations, involves much more than mere uniformity of sequence: it implies irresistibleness. Applied to the will, it only means that the given cause will be followed by the effect, subject to all possibilities of counter-action by other causes; but in common use it stands for the operation of those causes exclusively which are supposed too powerful to be counter-acted at all. When we say that all human actions take place of necessity, we only mean that they will certainly happen if nothing prevents; when we say that dying of want, to those who can not get food, is a necessity, we mean that it will certainly happen whatever may be done to prevent it. The application of the same term to the agencies on which human actions depend, as is used to express those agencies of nature which are really uncontrollable, can not fail, when habitual, to create a feeling of uncontrollableness in the former also. This, however, is a mere illusion. There are physical sequences which we call necessary, as death for want of food or air; there are others which, though as much cases of causation as the former, are not said to be necessary, as death from poison, which an antidote, or the use of the stomach-pump, will sometimes avert. It is apt to be forgotten by people's feelings, even if remembered by their understandings, that human actions are in this last predicament: they are never (except in some cases of mania) ruled by any one motive with such absolute sway that there is no room for the influence of any other. The causes, therefore, on which action depends, are never uncontrollable; and any given effect is only necessary provided that the causes tending to produce it are not controlled. That whatever happens, could not have happened otherwise, unless something had taken place which was capable of preventing it, no one surely needs hesitate to admit. But to call this by the name Necessity is to use the term in a sense so different from its primitive and familiar meaning, from that which it bears in the common occasions of life, as to amount almost to a play upon words. The associations derived from the ordinary sense of the term will adhere to it in spite of all we can do; and though the doctrine of Necessity, as stated by most who hold it, is very remote from fatalism, it is probable that most necessitarians are fatalists, more or less, in their feelings.

A fatalist believes, or half believes (for nobody is a consistent fatalist), not only that whatever is about to happen will be the infallible result of the causes which produce it (which is the true necessitarian doctrine), but moreover that there is no use in struggling against it; that it will happen, however we may strive to prevent it. Now, a necessitarian, believing that our actions follow from our characters, and that our characters follow from our organization, our education, and our circumstances, is apt to be, with more or less of consciousness on his part, a fatalist as to his own actions, and to believe that his nature is such, or that his education and circumstances have so moulded his character, that nothing can now prevent him from feeling and acting in a particular way, or at least that no effort of his own can hinder it. In the words of the sect which in our own day has most perseveringly inculcated and most perversely misunderstood this great doctrine, his character is formed *for* him, and not *by* him; therefore his wishing that it had been formed differently is of no use; he has no power to alter it. But this is a grand error. He has, to a certain extent, a power to alter his character. Its being, in the ultimate resort, formed for him, is not inconsistent with its being, in part, formed *by* him as one of the intermediate agents. His character is formed by his circumstances (including among these his particular organization); but his own desire to mould it in a particular way, is one of those circumstances, and by no means one of the least influential. We can not, indeed, directly will to be different from what we are. But neither did those who are supposed to have formed our characters directly will that we should be what we are. Their will had no direct power except over their own actions. They made us what they did make us, by willing, not the end, but the requisite means; and we, when our habits are not too inveterate, can, by similarly willing the requisite means, make ourselves different. If they could place us under the influence of certain circumstances, we, in like manner, can place ourselves under the influence of other circumstances. We are exactly as capable of making our own character, *if we will,* as others are of making it for us.

Yes (answers the Owenite),[2] but these words, "if we will," surrender the whole point: since the will to alter our own character is given us, not by any efforts of ours, but by circumstances which we can not help, it comes to us either from external causes, or not at all. Most true: if the Owenite stops here, he is in a position from which nothing can expel him. Our character is formed by us as well as for us; but the wish which induces us to attempt to form it is formed for us; and how? Not, in general, by our organization, nor wholly by our education, but by our experience; experience of the painful consequences of the character we previously had; or by some strong feeling of admiration or aspiration, accidentally aroused. But to think that we have no power of altering our character, and to think that we shall not use our power unless we desire to use it, are very different things, and have a very different effect on the mind. A person who does not wish to alter his character, can not be the person who is supposed to feel discouraged or paralyzed by thinking himself unable to do it. The depressing effect of the fatalist doctrine can only be felt where there *is* a wish to do what that doctrine represents as impossible. It is of no consequence what we think forms our character, when we have no desire of our own about forming it; but it is of great consequence that we should not be prevented from forming such a desire by thinking the attainment impracticable, and that if we have the desire, we should know that the work is not so irrevocably done as to be incapable of being altered.

And indeed, if we examine closely, we shall find that this feeling, of our being able to modify our own character *if we wish,* is itself the feeling of moral freedom which we are conscious of. A person feels morally free who feels that his habits or his temptations are not his masters, but he theirs; who, even in yielding to them, knows that he could resist; that were he desirous of altogether throwing them off, there would not be required for that purpose a stronger desire than he knows himself to be capable of feeling. It is of course necessary, to render our consciousness of freedom complete, that we should have succeeded in making our character all we have hitherto attempted to make it; for if we have wished and not attained, we have, to that extent, not power over our own character; we are not free. Or at least, we must feel that our wish, if not strong enough to alter our character, is strong enough to conquer our character when the two are brought into conflict in any particular case of conduct. And hence it is said with truth, that none but a person of confirmed virtue is completely free.

The application of so improper a term as Necessity to the doctrine of cause and effect in the matter of human character, seems to me one of the most signal instances in philosophy of the abuse of terms, and its practical consequences one of the most striking examples of the power of language over our associations. The subject will never be generally understood until that objectionable term is dropped. The free-will doctrine, by keeping in view precisely that portion of the truth which the word Necessity puts out of sight, namely the power of the mind to co-operate in the formation of its own character, has given to its adherents a practical feeling much nearer to the truth than has generally (I believe) existed in the minds of necessitarians.

[2] From Robert Owen (1771–1858), a political reformer.

The latter may have had a stronger sense of the importance of what human beings can do to shape the characters of one another; but the free-will doctrine has, I believe, fostered in its supporters a much stronger spirit of self-culture.[3]

In this selection, Mill slides between the harsh alternatives of "hard determinism" and indeterminism. He begins by accepting determinism and the idea that all human actions are "necessary and inevitable," given their causes. But he then goes on to say that these causes are themselves within human control, that we can alter the causes of events and even, by taking certain steps, alter our own characters. But this is not in the least to deny determinism; nor does it deny that we are in control and have "free will" in an important sense. Human actions, following from their various causes, (including "character" or personality) are as predictable as any other events. But predictability is not incompatible with freedom, for freedom means, according to Mill, nothing other than acting in accordance with one's own character, desires, and wishes. Since these are the causes of our actions, that means that Mill can defend both determinism and freedom at the same time.

David Hume is also a "soft determinist," and he too argues that the reconciliation of "liberty and necessity" is to be found in the fact that a person's actions "flow from one's character or disposition." He begins, as Mill began, by pointing out the evident uniformity of human nature, the fact that the better we know someone the more predictable his or her actions. He says that it is general knowledge that "a man who at noon leaves his purse full of gold at a major intersection of the city may as well expect that it will fly away like a feather as that he will find it untouched an hour after." Having established the general predictability of human behavior, Hume then launches into his by now familiar favorite theme, the concept of causality:

It would seem, indeed, that men begin at the wrong end of this question concerning liberty and necessity when they enter upon it by examining the faculties of the soul, the influence of the understanding, and the operations of the will. Let them first discuss a more simple question, namely, the question of body and brute unintelligent matter, and try whether they can there form any idea of causation and necessity, except that of a constant conjunction of objects and subsequent inference of the mind from one to another. If these circumstances form, in reality, the whole of that necessity which we conceive in matter, and if these circumstances be also universally acknowledged to take place in the operations of the mind, the dispute is at an end; at least, must be owned to be thenceforth merely verbal. But as long as we will rashly suppose that we have some further idea of necessity and causation in the operations of external objects, at the same time that we can find nothing further in the voluntary actions of the mind, there is no possibility of bringing the question to any determinate issue while we proceed upon so erroneous a supposition. The only method of undeceiving us is to mount up higher, to examine the narrow extent of science when applied to material causes, and to

[3] John Stuart Mill, *A System of Logic,* 8th ed. (New York: Harper & Row, 1874).

convince ourselves that all we know of them is the constant conjunction and inference above mentioned. We may, perhaps, find that it is with difficulty we are induced to fix such narrow limits to human understanding, but we can afterwards find no difficulty when we come to apply this doctrine to the actions of the will. For as it is evident that these have a regular conjunction with motives and circumstances and character, and as we always draw inferences from one to the other, we must be obliged to acknowledge in words that necessity which we have already avowed in every deliberation of our lives and in every step of our conduct and behaviour.

But to proceed in this reconciling project with regard to the question of liberty and necessity; the most contentious question of metaphysics, the most contentious science; it will not require many words to prove, that all mankind have ever agreed in the doctrine of liberty as well as in that of necessity, and that the whole dispute, in this respect also, has been hitherto merely verbal. For what is meant by liberty, when applied to voluntary actions? We cannot surely mean that actions have so little connexion with motives, inclinations, and circumstances, that one does not follow with a certain degree of uniformity from the other, and that one affords no inference by which we can conclude the existence of the other. For these are plain and acknowledged matters of fact. By liberty, then, we can only mean *a power of acting or not acting according to the determinations of the will;* that is, if we choose to remain at rest, we may; if we choose to move, we also may. Now this hypothetical liberty is universally allowed to belong to everyone who is not a prisoner and in chains. Here then is no subject of dispute.

Whatever definition we may give of liberty, we should be careful to observe two requisite circumstances: *first,* that it be consistent with plain matter of fact; *secondly,* that it be consistent with itself. If we observe these circumstances and render our definition intelligible, I am persuaded that all mankind will be found of one opinion with regard to it.

It is universally allowed that nothing exists without a cause of its existence, and that chance, when strictly examined, is a mere negative word and means not any real power which has anywhere a being in nature. But it is pretended that some causes are necessary, some not necessary. Here then is the advantage of definitions. Let anyone *define* a cause without comprehending, as a part of the definition, a *necessary connexion* with its effect, and let him show distinctly the origin of the idea expressed by the definition, and I shall readily give up the whole controversy. But if the foregoing explication of the matter be received, this must be absolutely impracticable. Had not objects a regular conjunction with each other, we should never have entertained any notion of cause and effect; and this regular conjunction produces that inference of the understanding which is the only connexion that we can have any comprehension of. Whoever attempts a definition of cause exclusive of these circumstances will be obliged either to employ unintelligible terms or such as are synonymous to the term which he endeavours to define. And if the definition above mentioned be admitted, liberty, when opposed to necessity, not to constraint, is the same thing with chance, which is universally allowed to have no existence. . . .

All laws being founded on rewards and punishments, it is supposed as a fundamental principle, that these motives have a regular and uniform influence on the mind, and both produce the good and prevent the evil actions. We may give to this influence what name we please; but, as it is usually conjoined with the action, it must be esteemed a *cause,* and be looked upon as an instance of that necessity, which we would here establish.

The only proper object of hatred or vengeance is a person or creature, endowed with thought and consciousness; and when any criminal or injurious actions excite that passion, it is only by their relation to the person, or connexion with him. Actions are, by their very nature, temporary and perishing; and where they proceed not from some *cause* in the character and disposition of the person who performed them, they can neither redound to his honour, if good; nor infamy, if evil. The actions themselves may be blameable; they may be contrary to all the rules of morality and religion: But the person is not answerable for them; and as they proceeded from nothing in him that is durable and constant, and leave nothing of that nature behind them, it is impossible he can, upon their account, become the object of punishment or vengeance. According to the principle, therefore, which denies necessity, and consequently causes, a man is as pure and untainted, after having committed the most horrid crime, as at the first moment of his birth, nor is his character anywise concerned in his actions, since they are not derived from it, and the wickedness of the one can never be used as a proof of the depravity of the other.

Men are not blamed for such actions as they perform ignorantly and casually, whatever may be the consequences. Why? but because the principles of these actions are only momentary, and terminate in them alone. Men are less blamed for such actions as they perform hastily and unpremeditately than for such as proceed from deliberation. For what reason? but because a hasty temper, though a constant cause or principle in the mind, operates only by intervals, and infects not the whole character. Again, repentance wipes off every crime, if attended with a reformation of life and manners. How is this to be accounted for? but by asserting that actions render a person criminal merely as they are proofs of criminal principles in the mind; and when, by an alteration of these principles, they cease to be just proofs, they likewise cease to be criminal. But, except upon the doctrine of necessity, they never were just proofs, and consequently never were criminal.

It will be equally easy to prove, and from the same arguments, that *liberty,* according to that definition above mentioned, in which all men agree, is also essential to morality, and that no human actions, where it is wanting, are susceptible of any moral qualities, or can be the objects either of approbation or dislike. For as actions are objects of our moral sentiment, so far only as they are indications of the internal character, passions, and affections; it is impossible that they can give rise either to praise or blame, where they proceed not from these principles, but are derived altogether from external violence.[4]

In other words, Hume too suggests that, not only is freedom of choice and action possible within the framework of determinism, but determinism is even necessary if we are to make sense out of the notion of freedom of choice

[4] David Hume, *An Enquiry Concerning Human Understanding,* 2nd ed., ed. L. A. Selby-Bigge (Oxford: Oxford University Press, 1902).

and responsibility. His language is convoluted, but his point is plain: we can make sense of the notion of voluntary action only because there is a uniform ("necessary") connection between our motives, inclinations, circumstances and characters and what we do. But now suppose we ask; can we be said to be responsible even for those acts that are caused by our character? After all, did we choose our character, as Mill suggests? Could we have done other than what we did? Even if we had wanted to? And are we free to want what we want? All this leads up to the question: is soft determinism really so "soft" after all?

Compulsion

The basis of compatibilism or "soft determinism" is that we somehow carve a space within determinism for those actions which we insist on calling "free" and for which we hold ourselves and other people responsible. But this means that "free actions" must also be actions that are determined by antecedent conditions and causes. Free as well as unfree acts (like falling down the stairs) are caused according to the determinist argument. The distinction, therefore, as we saw in both Mill and Hume, depends upon whether the determining factors are within the agent or "outside" of him. In the latter case, we say that the act was not free but *compelled* or "done under compulsion." This distinction is not a new one. Aristotle, for example, many centuries ago, defined a voluntary action as one which was (1) not done under compulsion and (2) not done from ignorance.

> . . . It is only voluntary feelings and actions for which praise and blame are given; those that are involuntary are condoned, and sometimes even pitied. Hence it seems to be necessary for the student of ethics to define the difference between the Voluntary and the Involuntary; and this will also be of service to the legislator in assigning rewards and punishments.
>
> It is then generally held that actions are involuntary when done (a) under compulsion or (b) through ignorance; and that (a) an act is compulsory when its origin is from without, being of such a nature that the agent, or person compelled, contributes nothing to it: for example, when a ship's captain is carried somewhere by stress of weather, or by people who have him in their power. But there is some doubt about actions done through fear of a worse alternative, or for some noble object—as for instance if a tyrant having a man's parents and children in his power commands him to do something base, when if he complies their lives will be spared but if he refuses they will be put to death. It is open to question whether such actions are voluntary or involuntary. A somewhat similar case is when cargo is jettisoned in a storm; apart from circumstances, no one voluntarily throws away his property, but to save his own life and that of his shipmates any sane man would do so. Acts of this kind, then, are 'mixed' or composite; but they ap-

proximate rather to the voluntary class. For at the actual time when they are done they are chosen or willed; and the end or motive of an act varies with the occasion, so that the terms 'voluntary' and 'involuntary' should be used with reference to the time of action; now the actual deed in the cases in question is done voluntarily, for the origin of the movement of the parts of the body instrumental to the act lies in the agent; and when the origin of an action is in oneself, it is in one's own power to do it or not. Such acts therefore are voluntary, though perhaps involuntary apart from circumstances— for no one would choose to do any such action in and for itself.

Sometimes indeed men are actually praised for deeds of this 'mixed' class, namely when they submit to some disgrace or pain as the price of some great and noble object; though if they do so without any such motive they are blamed, since it is contemptible to submit to a great disgrace with no advantage or only a trifling one in view. In other cases again, such submission though not praised is condoned, when a man does something wrong through fear of penalties that impose too great a strain on human nature, and that no one could endure. Yet there seem to be some acts which a man cannot be compelled to do; and rather than do them he ought to submit to the most terrible death: for instance, we think it ridiculous that Alcmaeon in Euripides' play is compelled by certain threats to murder his mother! But it is sometimes difficult to decide how far we ought to go in choosing to do a given act rather than suffer a given penalty, or in enduring a given penalty rather than commit a given action; and it is still more difficult to abide by our decision when made, since in most of such dilemmas the penalty threatened is painful and the deed forced upon us dishonourable, which is why praise and blame are bestowed according as we do or do not yield to such compulsion.

What kind of actions then are to be called 'compulsory'? Used without qualification, perhaps this term applies to any case where the cause of the action lies in things outside the agent, and when the agent contributes nothing. But when actions intrinsically involuntary are yet in given circumstances deliberately chosen in preference to a given alternative, and when their origin lies in the agent, these actions are to be pronounced intrinsically involuntary but voluntary in the circumstances, and in preference to the alternative. They approximate however rather to the voluntary class, since conduct consists of particular things done, and the particular things done in the cases in question are voluntary. But it is not easy to lay down rules for deciding which of two alternatives is to be chosen, for particular cases differ widely.

To apply the term 'compulsory' to acts done for the sake of pleasure or for noble objects, on the plea that these exercise constraint on us from without, is to make every action compulsory. For (1) pleasure and nobility between them supply the motives of all actions whatsoever. Also (2) to act under compulsion and involuntarily is painful, but actions aiming at something pleasant or noble are pleasant. And (3) it is absurd to blame external things, instead of blaming ourselves for falling an easy prey to their attractions; or to take the credit of our noble deeds to ourselves, while putting the blame for our disgraceful ones upon the temptations of pleasure. It appears therefore that an act is compulsory when its origin is from outside, the person compelled contributing nothing to it.[5]

What is compulsion? According to Aristotle, an act is compulsory "when its origin is without" such that the person who acts "contributes nothing to it." Thus a person who is literally pushed into doing something is compelled rather than free. But what are we to say of certain other cases, (which Aristotle did not know about). For example, what of the person who is neurotic, who acts compulsively or "irrationally" because of mental illness? In ancient times, it might have been said that such a person was "possessed," as if something "external" (a demon or an evil spirit) had "taken over" and compelled certain actions. But today, we are fully aware that such "compulsions" are clearly within the person and not "external" at all. In fact, it is clear that the neurotic always contributes to the neurosis as well as suffers from it, and thus, according to Aristotle's criterion, such acts are not really compelled at all. Or, to take a much more difficult kind of case, what are we to say of those celebrated "brainwashing" cases (as with Patty Hearst or during the Korean War) in which a person seemingly performs an action voluntarily, but only after she or he has been "conditioned" in a dramatic and sometimes brutal way. Sometimes, even the person's "character" itself is changed. Should we hold a person responsible for such actions? (This question was the main point in dispute in the Patty Hearst case, for example.) Similarly, should we hold a person responsible for actions performed under great stress, or as the result of a violent emotion (rage or infatuation, for example)? Should we hold a person responsible for actions performed under the influence of drugs or alcohol (assuming that we might well hold them responsible for taking the drugs or drinking in the first place)? You can see that the distinction between "free" actions and acts that are "compelled" is not nearly as clear as it first seemed. We can easily distinguish between a person who breaks into a store and a person who is pushed through the front window. But in many cases where freedom is most in question, in cases of neurosis and brainwashing, and even in cases of great passion and chemical "influences," the distinction between what is "external" to the person and what is within his character is not clear at all.

There are more serious problems with the notion of "compulsion," however. Even if we admit that there are some problematic examples of actions which are not clearly either "free" or "compelled," (neurosis and brainwashing, great passion and drugs), we would want to insist that at least some actions are clearly free and not compelled. For example, I write a check to the American Cancer society, just because I believe that it is an important organization and want to make a contribution. No one has solicited me, no one has encouraged me to do it, and no one need know that I do it. Can even this act, so seemingly performed "of my own free will," be counted as a "free action?"

[5] Aristotle, *Nichomachean Ethics,* BK. III, trans. H. Rackham (Cambridge, Mass.: Harvard University Press, 1934).

The "soft determinist" would say that the above action is "free" because it flows from my generous character. But what sense does it make to say that this kind of determinism, determinism by a person's character, makes an act any more free than an act that is determined by anything else? Even in our "freest" acts, it can be argued that the desires and decisions, in short, our "personality" is wholly determined by forces which are outside of us and beyond our control. Consider the following argument, for example, by Professor John Hospers, who uses Freud and psychoanalysis as the basis for his claim that all of our acts are compelled and not free, insofar as all of our acts are brought about by a set of psychological determinants over which we have no control:

> . . . As a preparation for developing my own views on the subject, I want to mention a factor that I think is of enormous importance and relevance: namely, unconscious motivation. There are many actions—not those of an insane person (however the term "insane" be defined), nor of a person ignorant of the effects of his action, nor ignorant of some relevant fact about the situation, nor in any obvious way mentally deranged—for which human beings in general and the courts in particular are inclined to hold the doer responsible, and for which, I would say, he should not be held responsible. The deed may be planned, it may be carried out in cold calculation, it may spring from the agent's character and be continuous with the rest of his behavior, and it may be perfectly true that he could have done differently *if* he had wanted to; nonetheless his behavior was brought about by unconscious conflicts developed in infancy, over which he had no control and of which (without training in psychiatry) he does not even have knowledge. He may even *think* he knows why he acted as he did, he may *think* he has conscious control over his actions, he may even *think* he is fully responsible for them; but he is not. Psychiatric casebooks provide hundreds of examples. The law and common sense, though puzzled sometimes by such cases, are gradually becoming aware that they exist; but at this early stage countless tragic blunders still occur because neither the law nor the public in general is aware of the genesis of criminal actions. The mother blames her daughter for choosing the wrong men as candidates for husbands; but though the daughter thinks she is choosing freely and spends a considerable amount of time "deciding" among them, the identification with her sick father, resulting from Oedipal fantasies in early childhood, prevents her from caring for any but sick men, twenty or thirty years older than herself. Blaming her is beside the point; she cannot help it, and she cannot change it. Countless criminal acts are thought out in great detail; yet the participants are (without their own knowledge) acting out fantasies, fears, and defenses from early childhood, over whose coming and going they have no conscious control.
>
> Now, I am not saying that none of these persons should be in jails or asylums. Often society must be protected against them. Nor am I saying that people should cease the practices of blaming and praising, punishing and rewarding; in general these devices are justified by the results—although very often they have practically no effect; the deeds are done from inner com-

pulsion, which is not lessened when the threat of punishment is great. I am only saying that frequently persons we think responsible are not properly to be called so; we mistakenly think them responsible because we assume they are like those in whom no unconscious drive (toward this type of behavior) is present, and that their behavior can be changed by reasoning, exhorting, or threatening.

· · · · ·

[Are we] in the final analysis, *responsible for any of our actions at all.* The issue may be put this way: How can anyone be responsible for his actions, since they grow out of his character, which is shaped and molded and made what it is by influences—some hereditary, but most of them stemming from early parental environment—that were not of his own making or choosing? This question, I believe, still troubles many people who would agree to all the distinctions we have just made but still have the feeling that "this isn't all." They have the uneasy suspicion that there is a more ultimate sense, a "deeper" sense, in which we are *not* responsible for our actions, since we are not responsible for the character out of which those actions spring. This, of course, is the sense Professor Edwards was describing.

Let us take as an example a criminal who, let us say, strangled several persons and is himself now condemned to die in the electric chair. Jury and public alike hold him fully responsible (at least they utter the words "he is responsible"), for the murders were planned down to the minutest detail, and the defendant tells the jury exactly how he planned them. But now we find out how it all came about; we learn of parents who rejected him from babyhood, of the childhood spent in one foster home after another, where it was always plain to him that he was not wanted; of the constantly frustrated early desire for affection, the hard shell of nonchalance and bitterness that he assumed to cover the painful and humiliating fact of being unwanted, and his subsequent attempts to heal these wounds to his shattered ego through defensive aggression.

> The criminal is the most passive person in this world, helpless as a baby in his motorically inexpressible fury. Not only does he try to wreak revenge on the mother of the earliest period of his babyhood; his criminality is based on the inner feeling of being incapable of making the mother even feel that the child seeks revenge on her. The situation is that of a dwarf trying to annoy a giant who superciliously refuses to see these attempts. . . . Because of his inner feeling of being a dwarf, the criminotic uses, so to speak, dynamite. Of that the giant must take cognizance. True, the "revenge" harms the avenger. He may be legally executed. However, the primary inner aim of forcing the giant to acknowledge the dwarf's fury is fulfilled.[6]

The poor victim is not conscious of the inner forces that exact from him this ghastly toll; he battles, he schemes, he revels in pseudo-aggression, he is miserable, but he does not know what works within him to produce these

[6] Edmund Bergler, *The Basic Neurosis* (New York: Grune and Stratton, 1949).

catastrophic acts of crime. His aggressive actions are the wriggling of a worm on a fisherman's hook. And if this is so, it seems difficult to say any longer, "He is responsible." Rather, we shall put him behind bars for the protection of society, but we shall no longer flatter our feeling of moral superiority by calling him personally responsible for what he did.

Let us suppose it were established that a man commits murder only if, sometime during the previous week, he has eaten a certain combination of foods—say, tuna fish salad at a meal also including peas, mushroom soup, and blueberry pie. What if we were to track down the factors common to all murders committed in this country during the last twenty years and found this factor present in all of them, and only in them? The example is of course empirically absurd; but may it not be that there is *some* combinations of factors that regularly leads to homicide, factors such as are described in general terms in the above quotation? (Indeed the situation in the quotation is less fortunate than in our hypothetical example, for it is easy to avoid certain foods once we have been warned about them, but the situation of the infant is thrust on him; something has already happened to him once and for all, before he knows it has happened.) When such specific factors are discovered, won't they make it clear that it is foolish and pointless, as well as immoral, to hold human beings responsible for crimes? Or, if one prefers biological to psychological factors, suppose a neurologist is called in to testify at a murder trial and produces X-ray pictures of the brain of the criminal; anyone can see, he argues, that the *cella turcica* was already calcified at the age of nineteen; it should be a flexible bone, growing, enabling the gland to grow. All the defendant's disorders might have resulted from this early calcification. Now, this particular explanation may be empirically false; but who can say that no such factors, far more complex, to be sure, exist?

When we know such things as these, we no longer feel so much tempted to say that the criminal is responsible for his crime; and we tend also (do we not?) to excuse him—not legally (we still confine him to prison) but morally; we no longer call him a monster or hold him personally responsible for what he did. Moreover, we do this in general, not merely in the case of crime: "You must excuse Grandmother for being irritable; she's really quite ill and is suffering some pain all the time." Or: "The dog always bites children after she's had a litter of pups; you can't blame her for it: she's not feeling well, and besides she naturally wants to defend them." Or: "She's nervous and jumpy, but do excuse her: she has a severe glandular disturbance."

Let us note that the more *thoroughly* and *in detail* we know the causal factors leading a person to behave as he does, the more we tend to exempt him from responsibility. When we know nothing of the man except what we see him do, we say he is an ungrateful cad who expects much of other people and does nothing in return, and we are usually indignant. When we learn that his parents were the same way and, having no guilt feelings about this mode of behavior themselves, brought him up to be greedy and avaricious, we see that we could hardly expect him to have developed moral feelings in this direction. When we learn, in addition, that he is not aware of being ungrateful or selfish, but unconsciously represses the memory of events unfavorable to himself, we feel that the situation is unfortunate but "not really his fault." When we know that this behavior of his, which makes others angry, occurs more constantly when he feels tense or insecure, and that he now feels tense and insecure, and that relief from pressure will diminish it, then we tend to "feel sorry for the poor guy" and say he's more to be pitied than censured. We no longer want to say that he is personally responsible; we might rather blame nature or his parents for having given him an unfortunate constitution or temperament.

But one may still object that so far we have talked only about neurotic behavior. Isn't nonneurotic or normal or not unconsciously motivated (or whatever you want to call it) behavior still within the area of responsibility? There are reasons for answering "No" even here, for the normal person no more than the neurotic one has caused his own character, which makes him what he is. Granted that neurotics are not responsible for their behavior (that part of it which we call neurotic) because it stems from undigested infantile conflicts that they had no part in bringing about, and that are external to them just as surely as if their behavior had been forced on them by a malevolent deity (which is indeed one theory on the subject); but the so-called normal person is equally the product of causes in which his volition took no part. And if, unlike the neurotic's, his behavior is changeable by rational considerations, and if he has the will power to overcome the effects of an unfortunate early environment, this again is no credit to him; he is just lucky. If energy is available to him in a form in which it can be mobilized for constructive purposes, this is no credit to him, for this too is part of his psychic legacy. Those of us who can discipline ourselves and develop habits of concentration of purpose tend to blame those who cannot, and call them lazy and weak-willed; but what we fail to see is that they literally *cannot* do what we expect; if their psyches were structured like ours, they could, but as they are burdened with a tyrannical super-ego (to use psychoanalytic jargon for the moment), and a weak defenseless ego whose energies are constantly consumed in fighting endless charges of the superego, they simply cannot do it, and it is irrational to expect it of them. We cannot with justification blame them for their inability, any more than we can congratulate ourselves for our ability. This lesson is hard to learn, for we constantly and naïvely assume that other people are constructed as we ourselves are.

For example: A child raised under slum conditions, whose parents are socially ambitious and envy families with money, but who nevertheless squander the little they have on drink, may simply be unable in later life to mobilize a drive sufficient to overcome these early conditions. Common sense would expect that he would develop the virtue of thrift; he would make quite sure that he would never again endure the grinding poverty he had experienced as a child. But in fact it is not so: the exact conditions are too complex to be specified in detail here, but when certain conditions are fulfilled (concerning the subject's early life), he will always thereafter be a spendthrift, and no rational considerations will be able to change this. He will listen to the rational considerations and see the force of these, but they will not be able to change him, even if he tries; he cannot change his wasteful habits any more than he can lift the Empire State Building with his bare hands. We moralize and plead with him to be thrifty, but we do not see how strong, how utterly overpowering, and how constantly with him, is the opposite drive, which is so easily manageable with us. But he is possessed by the all-consuming, all-encompassing urge to make the world see that he belongs, that he has arrived, that he is just as well off as anyone else, that the awful humiliations were not real, that they never actually occurred, for isn't he now able to spend and spend? The humiliation must be blotted out; and conspicuous, flashy, expensive, and wasteful buying will do this; it shows the world what the world must know! True, it is only for the moment; true, it is in the end self-defeating, for wasteful consumption is the best way to bring poverty back again; but the person with an overpowering drive to mend a lesion to his narcissism cannot resist the avalanche of that drive with his puny rational consideration. A man with his back against the wall and a gun at his throat doesn't think of what may happen ten years hence. (Consciously, of course, he knows nothing of this drive; all that appears to consciousness is its shattering effects; he knows only that he must keep on spending—not why—and that he is unable to resist.) He hasn't in him the psychic capacity, the energy to stem the tide of a drive that at the moment is all-powerful. We, seated comfortably away from this flood, sit in judgment on him and blame him and exhort him and criticize him; but he, carried along by the flood, cannot do otherwise than he does. He may fight with all the strength of which he is capable, but it is not enough. And we, who are rational enough at least to exonerate a man in a situation of "overpowering impulse" when we recognize it to be one, do not even recognize this as an example of it; and so, in addition to being swept away in the flood that childhood conditions rendered inevitable, he must also endure our lectures, our criticisms, and our moral excoriation.

But, one will say, he could have overcome his spendthrift tendencies; some people do. Quite true: some people do. They are lucky. They have it in them to overcome early deficiencies by exerting great effort, and they are capable of exerting the effort. Some of us, luckier still, can overcome them with but little effort; and a few, the luckiest, haven't the deficiencies to overcome. It's all a matter of luck. The least lucky are those who can't overcome them, even with great effort, and those who haven't the ability to exert the effort.

But, one persists, it isn't a matter simply of luck; it *is* a matter of effort. Very well then, it's a matter of effort; without exerting the effort you may not overcome the deficiency. But whether or not you are the kind of person who has it in him to exert the effort is a matter of luck.

. . . . .

The position, then, is this: if we *can* overcome the effects of early environment, the ability to do so is itself a product of the early environment. We did not give ourselves this ability; and if we lack it we cannot be blamed for not having it. Sometimes, to be sure, moral exhortation brings out an ability that is there but not being used, and in this lies its *occasional* utility; but very often its use is pointless, because the ability is not there. The only thing that can overcome a desire, as Spinoza said, is a stronger contrary desire; and many times there simply is no wherewithal for producing a stronger contrary desire. Those of us who do have the wherewithal are lucky.

There is one possible practical advantage in remembering this. It may prevent us (unless we are compulsive blamers) from indulging in righteous indignation and committing the sin of spiritual pride, thanking God that we are not as this publican here. And it will protect from our useless moralizings those who are least equipped by nature for enduring them. As with responsibility, so with deserts. Someone commits a crime and is punished by the state; "he deserved it," we say self-righteously—as if we were moral and he immoral, when in fact we are lucky and he is unlucky—forgetting that there, but for the grace of God and a fortunate early environment, go we.[7]

What emerges from the foregoing arguments is not an attractive conclusion. No matter how we try to wriggle free of total determinism, it seems as if we keep finding ourselves enmeshed back in "hard" determinism. We tried to clear a small space within determinism for those acts we want to call "free," but we found such a space hard to find. We suggested that perhaps an act is free if one of its causes is a decision, but then we saw that, if this were so, then the decision itself must be caused in turn and thus is not really a decision at all. We suggested that an action is free if it "flows from a person's character"; but then we saw that it can be argued that an act which "flows from a person's character" is no more within his control and no more his responsibility than any other act. We might want to say that a person's act is free if, in this case, he or she could have done otherwise, but what does this mean, given the previous arguments, except that the act would have been different if the circumstances had been different, or if the person had been, in effect, another person. For example, it is true that you could have changed the course of World War II—but if what? If you had been born Winston Churchill, perhaps. But that is a nonsensical "if." Does it make any more sense, however, to say that "you could have been a professional football player?" If what? If circumstances had been different? If you had been born with a different body, raised in a different environment? But isn't this to say, for each of these "ifs," that you would be (slightly but significantly) a different person than you are? It looks as if we are trapped by the tautology that each of us is whoever he or she is. It is true of the geranium that if it had been planted in better soil, it would be larger; and if the ball had been dropped from a greater height it would have landed harder; and if you were raised differently, placed in different circumstances, then you might have acted other than you did. But this has nothing to do with "freedom." Your actions were no more free than the growth of the plant or the falling of the ball. Of course, there is a difference: you think that you've made some decision. But why should what you think change the way things are determined? You might pretend to be flying after you've fallen out of the plane. But you're still falling, and what seems to be

[7] John Hospers, "What Means This Freedom?" in *Determinism and Freedom in the Age of Modern Science*, ed. Sidney Hook (New York: New York University Press, 1958).

the case doesn't matter at all. Soft determinism doesn't make determinism (or the fall from the plane) any "softer" after all.

Deterministic fantasies

Not everyone views determinism with horror. The eminent American psychologist, B. F. Skinner, for example, applauds the determinist's argument as a means of controlling human behavior and changing it for the better. In his recent best-seller, *Beyond Freedom and Dignity,* Skinner argues that we have made a fetish of freedom and that we should replace this with an acceptance of determinism. Behavioral scientists can and should be given the power to "engineer" human behavior in accordance with an agreed-upon set of ideals (social harmony, individual happiness and productivity). In an essay of a few decades ago, Skinner argued:

> Perhaps the most crucial part of our democratic philosophy to be reconsidered is our attitude toward freedom—or its reciprocal, the control of human behavior. We do not oppose all forms of control because it is "human nature" to do so. The reaction is not characteristic of all men under all conditions of life. It is an attitude which has been carefully engineered, in large part by what we call the "literature" of democracy. With respect to some methods of control (for example, the threat of force), very little engineering is needed, for the techniques or their immediate consequences are objectionable. Society has suppressed these methods by branding them "wrong," "illegal," or "sinful." But to encourage these attitudes toward objectionable forms of control, it has been necessary to disguise the real nature of certain indispensable techniques, the commonest examples of which are education, moral discourse, and persuasion. The actual procedures appear harmless enough. They consist of supplying information, presenting opportunities for action, pointing out logical relationships, appealing to reason or "enlightened understanding," and so on. Through a masterful piece of misrepresentation, the illusion is fostered that these procedures do not involve the control of behavior; at most, they are simply ways of "getting someone to change his mind." But analysis not only reveals the presence of well-defined behavioral processes, it demonstrates a kind of control no less inexorable, though in some ways more acceptable, than the bully's threat of force.
>
> Let us suppose that someone in whom we are interested is acting unwisely—he is careless in the way he deals with his friends, he drives too fast, or he holds his golf club the wrong way. We could probably help him by issuing a series of commands: don't nag, don't drive over sixty, don't hold your club that way. Much less objectionable would be "an appeal to reason." We could show him how people are affected by his treatment of them, how accident rates rise sharply at higher speeds, how a particular grip on the club alters the way the ball is struck and corrects a slice. In doing so we resort to verbal mediating devices which emphasize and support certain "contingencies of reinforcement"—that is, certain relations between behavior

and its consequences—which strengthen the behavior we wish to set up. The same consequences would possibly set up the behavior without our help, and they eventually take control no matter which form of help we give. The appeal to reason has certain advantages over the authoritative command. A threat of punishment, no matter how subtle, generates emotional reactions and tendencies to escape or revolt. Perhaps the controllee merely "feels resentment" at being made to act in a given way, but even that is to be avoided. When we "appeal to reason," he "feels freer to do as he pleases." The fact is that we have exerted *less* control than in using a threat; since other conditions may contribute to the result, the effect may be delayed or, possibly in a given instance, lacking. But if we have worked a change in his behavior at all, it is because we have altered relevant environmental conditions, and the processes we have set in motion are just as real and just as inexorable, if not as comprehensive, as in the most authoritative coercion.

"Arranging an opportunity for action" is another example of disguised control. The power of the negative form has already been exposed in the analysis of censorship. Restriction of opportunity is recognized as far from harmless. As Ralph Barton Perry said in an article which appeared in the Spring, 1953, *Pacific Spectator*, "Whoever determines what alternatives shall be made known to man controls what that man shall choose *from*. He is deprived of freedom in proportion as he is denied access to *any* ideas, or is confined to any range of ideas short of the totality of relevant possibilities." But there is a positive side as well. When we present a relevant state of affairs, we increase the likelihood that a given form of behavior will be emitted. To the extent that the probability of action has changed, we have made a definite contribution. The teacher of history controls a student's behavior (or, if the reader prefers, "deprives him of freedom") just as much in *presenting* historical facts as in suppressing them. Other conditions will no doubt affect the student, but the contribution made to his behavior by the presentation of material is fixed and, within its range, irresistible.

The methods of education, moral discourse, and persuasion are acceptable not because they recognize the freedom of the individual or his right to dissent, but because they make only *partial* contributions to the control of his behavior. The freedom they recognize is freedom from a more coercive form of control. The dissent which they tolerate is the possible effect of other determiners of action. Since these sanctioned methods are frequently ineffective, we have been able to convince ourselves that they do not represent control at all. When they show too much strength to permit disguise, we give them other names and suppress them as energetically as we suppress the use of force. Education grown too powerful is rejected as propaganda or 'brain-washing," while really effective persuasion is decried as "undue influence," "demagoguery," "seduction," and so on.

If we are not to rely solely upon accident for the innovations which give rise to cultural evolution, we must accept the fact that some kind of control of human behavior is inevitable. We cannot use good sense in human affairs unless someone engages in the design and construction of environmental conditions which affect the behavior of men. Environmental changes have always been the condition for the improvement of cultural patterns, and we can hardly use the more effective methods of science without making changes on a grander scale. We are all controlled by the world in which we live, and part of that world has been and will be constructed by men. The question is this: Are we to be controlled by accident, by tyrants, or by ourselves in effective cultural design?

The danger of the misuse of power is possibly greater than ever. It is not allayed by disguising the facts. We cannot make wise decisions if we continue to pretend that human behavior is not controlled, or if we refuse to engage in control when valuable results might be forthcoming. Such measures weaken only ourselves, leaving the strength of science to others. The first step in a defense against tyranny is the fullest possible exposure of controlling techniques. A second step has already been taken successfully in restricting the use of physical force. Slowly, and as yet imperfectly, we have worked out an ethical and governmental design in which the strong man is not allowed to use the power deriving from his strength to control his fellow men. He is restrained by a superior force created for that purpose—the ethical pressure of the group, or more explicit religious and governmental measures. We tend to distrust superior forces, as we currently hesitate to relinquish sovereignty in order to set up an international police force. But it is only through such countercontrol that we have achieved what we call peace—a condition in which men are not permitted to control each other through force. In other words, control itself must be controlled.

Science has turned up dangerous processes and materials before. To use the facts and techniques of a science of man to the fullest extent without making some monstrous mistake will be difficult and obviously perilous. It is no time for self-deception, emotional indulgence, or the assumption of attitudes which are no longer useful. Man is facing a difficult test. He must keep his head now, or he must start again—a long way back.[8]

In his novel, *Walden II,* Skinner gives us a prototype for his deterministic utopia:

"I think Mrs. Nash's puzzlement," said Frazier, as we left the building, "is proof enough that our children are seldom envious or jealous. Mrs. Nash was twelve years old when Walden Two was founded. It was a little late to undo her early training, but I think we were successful. She's a good example of the Walden Two product. She could probably recall the experience of jealousy, but it's not part of her present life."

"Surely that's going too far!" said Castle. "You can't be so godlike as all that! You must be assailed by emotions just as much as the rest of us!"

"We can discuss the question of godlikeness later, if you wish," replied Frazier. "As to emotions—we aren't free of them all, nor should we like to be. But the meaner and more annoying—the emotions which breed unhappiness—are almost unknown here, like unhappiness itself. We don't need them any longer in our struggle for existence, and it's easier on our circulatory system, and certainly pleasanter, to dispense with them."

"If you've discovered how to do that, you are indeed a genius," said Castle. He seemed almost stunned as Frazier nodded assent. "We all know that

---

[8] B. F. Skinner, "Freedom and the Control of Men," in *The American Scholar,* 1955–56.

emotions are useless and bad for our peace of mind and our blood pressure," he went on. "But how arrange things otherwise?"

"We arrange them otherwise here," said Frazier. He was showing a mildness of manner which I was coming to recognize as a sign of confidence.

"But emotions are—fun!" said Barbara. "Life wouldn't be worth living without them."

"Some of them, yes," said Frazier. "The productive and strengthening emotions—joy and love. But sorrow and hate—and the high-voltage excitements of anger, fear, and rage—are out of proportion with the needs of modern life, and they're wasteful and dangerous. Mr. Castle has mentioned jealousy—a minor form of anger, I think we may call it. Naturally we avoid it. It has served its purpose in the evolution of man; we've no further use for it. If we allowed it to persist, it would only sap the life out of us. In a cooperative society there's no jealousy because there's no need for jealousy."

"How do you make sure that jealousy isn't needed in Walden Two?" I said.

"In Walden Two problems can't be solved by attacking others," said Frazier with marked finality.

"That's not the same as eliminating jealousy, though," I said.

"Of course it's not. But when a particular emotion is no longer a useful part of a behavioral repertoire, we proceed to eliminate it."

"Yes, but how?"

"It's simply a matter of behavioral engineering," said Frazier.

"Behavioral engineering?"

"Each of us," Frazier began, "is engaged in a pitched battle with the rest of mankind."

"A curious premise for a Utopia," said Castle. "Even a pessimist like myself takes a more hopeful view than that."

"You do, you do," said Frazier. "But let's be realistic. Each of us has interests which conflict with the interests of everybody else. That's our original sin, and it can't be helped. Now, 'everybody else' we call 'society.' It's a powerful opponent, and it always wins. Oh, here and there an individual prevails for a while and gets what he wants. Sometimes he storms the culture of a society and changes it slightly to his own advantage. But society wins in the long run, for it has the advantage of numbers and of age. Many prevail against one, and men against a baby. Society attacks early, when the individual is helpless. It enslaves him almost before he has tasted freedom. The 'ologies' will tell you how it's done. Theology calls it building a conscience or developing a spirit of selflessness. Psychology calls it the growth of the super-ego.

"Considering how long society has been at it, you'd expect a better job. But the campaigns have been badly planned and the victory has never been secure. The behavior of the individual has been shaped according to revelations of 'good conduct,' never as the result of experimental study. But why not experiment? The questions are simple enough. What's the best behavior for the individual so far as the group is concerned? And how can the individual be induced to behave in that way? Why not explore these questions in a scientific spirit?

"We could do just that in Walden Two. We had already worked out a code of conduct—subject, of course, to experimental modification. The code would keep things running smoothly if everybody lived up to it. Our job was to see that everybody did. Now, you can't get people to follow a useful code by making them into so many jacks-in-the-box. You can't foresee all future circumstances, and you can't specify adequate future conduct. You don't know what will be required. Instead you have to set up certain behavioral processes which will lead the individual to design his own 'good' conduct when the time comes. We call that sort of thing 'self-control.' But don't be misled, the control always rests in the last analysis in the hands of society. . . ."[9]

But not every visionary has looked upon determinism with delight. More often, determinism has appeared in novels as a nightmare, as the philosophical basis of societies more oppressive and authoritarian than any we have ever seen. The most famous examples are George Orwell's *1984* and Aldous Huxley's *Brave New World*. In both novels, the techniques of psychology and drugs are used to manipulate the inhabitants of entire societies and force them to conform to a single set of behavioral standards, concerning which they have no choice whatsoever. A more recent and now well-known example of a similar nightmarish fantasy is Anthony Burgess' *Clockwork Orange*. A young hoodlum named Alex is released from prison on the condition that he undergo an "experiment" which will recondition him and make him "fit" into the society he formerly threatened. Burgess' unusual language makes the reading a bit difficult, but the meaning of most of his terms should be obvious after a moment's reflection.

'How about you putting me in for this thing, sir, if I may make so bold as to make the suggestion?'
You could viddy him thinking about that while he puffed away at his cancer, wondering how much to say to me about what he knew about this veshch I'd mentioned. Then he said: 'I take it you're referring to Ludovico's Technique.' He was still very wary.
'I don't know what it's called, sir,' I said. 'All I know is that it gets you out quickly and makes sure that you don't get in again.'

. . . . .

[Alex volunteers for the unknown experiment and is accepted:] '. . . Thank you very much, sir. I've done my best here, really I have. I'm very grateful to all concerned.'
'Don't be,' like sighed the Governor. 'This is not a reward. This is far from being a reward. Now, there is a form here to be signed. It says that you are willing to have the residue of your sentence commuted to submission to what is called here, ridiculious expression, Reclamation Treatment. Will you sign?'
'Most certainly I will sign,' I said, 'sir. And very many thanks.' So I was given an ink-pencil and I signed my name nice and flowy. The Governor said:
'Right. That's the lot, I think.' The Chief Chasso said:

[9] B. F. Skinner, *Walden II* (New York: Macmillan, 1965).

'The Prison Chaplain would like a word with him, sir.'

·   ·   ·   ·   ·

[The Prison Chaplain tells him:] 'Very hard ethical questions are involved,' he went on. 'You are to be made into a good boy, 6655321. Never again will you have the desire to commit acts of violence or to offend in any way whatsoever against the State's Peace. I hope you take all that in. I hope you are absolutely clear in your own mind about that.' I said:

'Oh, it will be nice to be good, sir.' But I had a real horrorshow smeck at that inside, brothers. He said:

'It may not be nice to be good, little 6655321. It may be horrible to be good. And when I say that to you I realize how self-contradictory that sounds. I know I shall have many sleepless nights about this. What does God want? Does God want goodness or the choice of goodness? Is a man who chooses the bad perhaps in some way better than a man who has the good imposed upon him? Deep and hard questions, little 6655321. But all I want to say to you now is this: if at any time in the future you look back to these times and remember me, the lowest and humblest of all God's servitors, do not, I pray, think evil of me in your heart, thinking me in any way involved in what is now about to happen to you. And now, talking of praying, I realize sadly that there will be little point in praying for you. You are passing now to a region where you will be beyond the reach of the power of prayer. A terrible terrible thing to consider. And yet, in a sense, in choosing to be deprived of the ability to make an ethical choice, you have in a sense really chosen the good. So I shall like to think. So, God help us all, 6655321, I shall like to think.' And then he began to cry.

·   ·   ·   ·   ·

[In the laboratory, Alex questions the Doctor:] 'What exactly is it, sir, that you're going to do?'

'Oh,' said Dr Branom, his cold stetho going all down my back, 'it's quite simple, really. We just show you some films.'

'Films?' I said. I could hardly believe my ookos, brothers, as you may well understand. 'You mean,' I said, 'it will be just like going to the pictures?'

'They'll be special films,' said this Dr Branom. 'Very special films. You'll be having the first session this afternoon. Yes,' he said, getting up from bending over me, 'you seem to be quite a fit young boy. A bit undernourished, perhaps. That will be the fault of the prison food. Put your pyjama top back on. After every meal,' he said, sitting on the edge of the bed, 'we shall be giving you a shot in the arm. That should help.' I felt really grateful to this very nice Dr Branom. I said:

'Vitamins, sir, will it be?'

'Something like that,' he said, smiling real horrorshow and friendly. 'Just a jab in the arm after every meal.'

And now for the treatment: 'You never know. Oh, you never know. Trust us, friend. It's better this way.' And then I found they were strapping my rookers to the chair-arms and my nogas were like stuck to a foot-rest. It seemed a bit bezoomny to me but I let them get on with what they wanted to get on with. If I was to be a free young malchick again in a fortnight's time I would put up with much in the meantime, O my brothers. One veshch I did not like, though, was when they put like clips on the skin of my forehead, so that my top glazz-lids were pulled up and up and up and I could not shut my glazzies no matter how I tried. I tried to smeck and said: 'This must be a real horrorshow film if you're so keen on my viddying it.' And one of the white-coat vecks said, smecking:

'Horrorshow is right, friend. A real show of horrors.' And then I had like a cap stuck on my gulliver and I could viddy all wires running away from it, and they stuck a like suction pad on my belly and one on the old ticktocker, and I could just about viddy wires running away from those. Then there was the shoom of a door opening and you could tell some very important chelloveck was coming in by the way the white-coated under-vecks went all stiff. And then I viddied this Dr Brodsky. He was a malenky veck, very fat, with all curly hair curling all over his gulliver, and on his spuddy nose he had very thick ochkies. I could just viddy that he had a real horrorshow suit on, absolutely the heighth of fashion, and he had a like very delicate and subtle von of operating-theatres coming from him. With him was Dr Branom, all smiling like as though to give me confidence. 'Everything ready?' said Dr Brodsky in a very breathy goloss. Then I could slooshy voices saying Right right right from like a distance, then nearer to, then there was a quiet like humming shoom as though things had been switched on. And then the lights went out and there was Your Humble Narrator And Friend sitting alone in the dark, all on his frightened oddy knocky, not able to move nor shut his glazzies nor anything. And then, O my brothers, the film-show started off with some very gromky atmosphere music coming from the speakers, very fierce and full of discord. And then on the screen the picture came on, but there was no title and no credits. What came on was a street, as it might have been any street in any town, and it was a real dark nochy and the lamps were lit. It was a very good like professional piece of sinny, and there were none of these flickers and blobs you get, say, when you viddy one of these dirty films in somebody's house in a back street. All the time the music bumped out, very like sinister. And then you could viddy an old man coming down the street, very starry, and then there leaped out on this starry veck two malchicks dressed in the heighth of fashion, as it was at this time (still thin trousers but no like cravat any more, more of a real tie), and then they started to filly with him. You could slooshy his screams and moans, very realistic, and you could even get the like heavy breathing and panting of the two tolchocking malchicks. They made a real pudding out of this starry veck, going crack crack crack at him with their fisty rookers, tearing his platties off and then finishing up by booting his nagoy plott (this lay all krovyred in the grahzny mud of the gutter) and then running off very skorry. Then there was the close-up gulliver of this beaten-up starry veck, and the krovvy flowed beautiful red. It's funny how the colours of the like real world only seem really real when you viddy them on the screen.

Now all the time I was watching this I was beginning to get very aware of a like not feeling all that well, and this I put down to the under-nourishment and my stomach not quite ready for the rich pishcha and vitamins I was getting here. But I tried to forget this, concentrating on the next film which came on at once, my brothers, without any break at all. This time the film like jumped right away on a young devotchka who was being given the old in-out by first one malchick then another then another then another, she creeching away very gromky through the speakers and like very pathetic and tragic music going on at the same time. This was real, very real, though if you thought about it properly you couldn't imagine lewdies actually agreeing to having all this done to them in a film, and if these films were made by the Good or the State you couldn't imagine them being allowed to take these films without like interfering with what was going on. So it must have been very clever what they call cutting or editing or some such veshch. For it was very real. And when it came to the sixth or seventh malchick leering and smecking and then going into it and the devotchka creeching on the sound-track like bezoomny, then I began to feel sick. I had like pains all over and felt I could sick up and at the same time not sick up, and I began to feel like in distress, O my brothers, being fixed rigid too on this chair. When this bit of film was over I could slooshy the goloss of this Dr Brodsky from over by the switchboard saying: 'Reaction about twelve point five? Promising, promising.'

. . . . .

'I want to be sick. Please let me be sick. Please bring something for me to be sick into.' But this Dr Brodsky called back:

'Imagination only. You've nothing to worry about. Next film coming up.' That was perhaps meant to be a joke, for I heard a like smeck coming from the dark.

. . . . .

'Stop the film! Please, please stop it! I can't stand any more.' And then the goloss of this Dr Brodsky said:

'Stop it? *Stop it,* did you say? Why, we've hardly started.' And he and the others smecked quite loud.

. . . . .

'Dr Brodsky is pleased with you. You had a very positive response. Tomorrow, of course, there'll be two sessions, morning and afternoon, and I should imagine that you'll be feeling a bit limp at the end of the day. But we have to be hard on you, you have to be cured.' I said:

'You mean I have to sit through—? You mean I have to look at—? Oh, no,' I said. 'It was horrible.'

'Of course it was horrible,' smiled Dr Branom. 'Violence is a very horrible thing. That's what you're learning now. Your body is learning it.'

'But,' I said, 'I don't understand. I don't understand about feeling sick like I did. I never used to feel sick before. I used to feel like very the opposite. I mean, doing it or watching it I used to feel real horrorshow. I just don't understand why or how or what—'

'Life is a very wonderful thing,' said Dr Branom in a like very holy goloss. 'The processes of life, the make-up of the human organism, who can fully understand these miracles? Dr Brodsky is, of course, a remarkable man. What is happening to you now is what should happen to any normal healthy human organism contemplating the actions of the forces of evil, the workings of the principle of destruction. You are being made sane, you are being made healthy.'

· · · · ·

'The point is,' this Minister of the Inferior was saying real gromky, 'that it works.'

'Oh,' the prison charlie said, like sighing, 'it works all right, God help the lot of us.'[10]

DEMANDING TO BE FREE

The demand for freedom and responsibility is not going to be satisfied by these different variations of determinism, no matter how "soft" they pretend to be. What we need is a breach in determinism, a conception of our actions, or at least our decisions, as truly free and not determined in any of the ways discussed previously.

The classic statement of this claim to freedom and responsibility is to be found in the philosophy of Immanuel Kant. (I am sure that you now appreciate how truly monumental Kant's philosophy has been. We shall see more of him in the next chapter as well.) We have already seen that Kant gave an unqualified endorsement of determinism, arguing that the principle (of universal causation) upon which it is based is nothing less than a necessary rule of all human experience. And this includes human actions:

> Actions of men are determined in conformity with the order of Nature, by their empirical character and other causes; if we could exhaust all the appearances, there would not be found a single human action which would not be predicted with certainty.[11]

This is surely a statement of the hardest of "hard" determinism. But Kant also appreciated, as much as any philosopher ever has, the importance of unqualified freedom for human responsibility. (He called freedom, as he had called God, a "postulate" [or presupposition] of practical reason.) But how could he defend both universal determinism and human freedom? Determinism is true of every possible event and object of human knowledge, Kant says, but it does not follow that it is also applicable to human acts of will or decisions to act. Action is a wholly different matter than knowledge. The metaphysics with which Kant defends this view is far too complicated to even summarize here. But the basic principle is simple enough: Kant says that we adopt two different standpoints towards the world, one theoretical, one practical. Insofar as we want to know something, we adopt the standpoint of science

10 Anthony Burgess, *A Clockwork Orange* (New York: Norton, 1962).
11 Immanuel Kant, *The Critique of Pure Reason,* trans. Norman Kemp Smith (New York: St. Martin's Press, 1933).

and determinism. And within that standpoint, every event, including human actions, is determined, brought about by sufficient natural causes (including the states of our brains and various psychological factors). But when we are ready to do something, we switch to the practical standpoint. And the main point is this: insofar as we are acting or deciding to act, we *must* consider our own acts or will and decisions as the sufficient causes of our actions, and we cannot continue the causal chain backwards to consider whether those acts of will are themselves caused. When we act, in other words, we cannot think of ourselves except as acting freely.

Suppose that you are about to make a decision; you are finally going to give up smoking. A friend offers you a cigarette on the second day. Yes or no? Do you smoke it? Now it might very well be that, given your personality, your weakness for past habits and any number of other psychological factors, you are clearly determined to accept, and thus break your resolution. Your friend, who knows you quite well, may even know this. But you can't think of yourself in this deterministic way, for insofar as you have to make a decision, you can't simply "find out" what you will do. In other words, you can't simply predict your own behavior, no matter how much you know about the various causes and factors which allow your friend to predict your behavior. If you were to predict, "I'm going to start smoking again anyway," you would not be simply predicting, you would be, in that very act, breaking your resolution, that is, deciding to break it. So, when your own acts and decisions are concerned, you have to act as if you were totally free. This in a way denies determinism. It says, as you are the one that has to make the decision, determinism isn't relevant. (Kant says, "and to have to think yourself free is to *be* free.")

Other philosophers, however, have taken a much stronger stance on this need to see oneself as free. Kant defends both determinism and freedom. Many philosophers who follow him do not. They take the practical side of his argument and defend it against determinism.

Advocates of human freedom have always rejected the determinist's premise, just because it seems to close off the possibility of human freedom and responsibility. A widely-read argument for this position has been formulated by the Scottish philosopher C. A. Campbell. The position he defends is called "Libertarianism" (not to be confused with the political philosophy of the same name).

The present state of philosophical opinion on free will is, for certain definitely assignable reasons, profoundly unsatisfactory. In my judgement, a thoroughly perverse attitude to the whole problem has been created by the almost universal acquiescence in the view that free will in what is often called the "vulgar" sense is too obviously nonsensical a notion to deserve serious discussion. Free will in a more "refined" sense—which is apt to mean free will purged of all elements that may cause embarrassment to a Deterministic psychology or a Deterministic metaphysics—is, it is understood, a conception which may be defended by the philosopher without loss of caste. But in its "vulgar" sense, as maintained, for example, by the plain man, who clings to a belief in genuinely open possibilities, it is (we are told) a wild and even obnoxious delusion, long ago discredited for sober thinkers.

Now, as it happens, I myself firmly believe that free will, in something extremely like the "vulgar" sense, is a fact. And I am anxious to-day to do what I can, within the limits of a single lecture, to justify that belief. I propose therefore to develop a statement of the Libertarian's position which will try to make clear why he finds himself obliged to hold what he does hold.

Let us begin by noting that the problem of free will gets its urgency for the ordinary educated man by reason of its close connection with the conception of moral responsibility. When we regard a man as morally responsible for an act, we regard him as a legitimate object of moral praise or blame in respect of it. But it seems plain that a man cannot be a legitimate object of moral praise or blame for an act unless in willing the act he is in some important sense a "free" agent. Evidently free will in some sense, therefore, is a precondition of moral responsibility. Without doubt it is the realisation that any threat to freedom is thus a threat to moral responsibility—with all that that implies—combined with the knowledge that there are a variety of considerations, philosophic, scientific, and theological, tending to place freedom in jeopardy, that gives to the problem of free will its perennial and universal appeal. And it is therefore in close connection with the question of the conditions of moral responsibility that any discussion of the problem must proceed, if it is not to be academic in the worst sense of the term.

We raise the question at once, therefore, what are the conditions, in respect of freedom, which must attach to an act in order to make it a morally responsible act? It seems to me that the fundamental conditions are two. I shall state them with all possible brevity, for we have a long road to travel.

The first condition is the universally recognised one that the act must be *self*-caused, *self*-determined. But it is important to accept this condition in its full rigour. The agent must be not merely *a* cause but the *sole* cause of that for which he is deemed morally responsible. If entities other than the self have also a causal influence upon an act, then that act is not one for which we can say without qualification that the *self* is morally responsible. If in respect of it we hold the self responsible at all, it can only be for some feature of the act—assuming the possibility of disengaging such a feature—of which the self *is* the sole cause. I do not see how this conclusion can be evaded. But it has awkward implications which have led not a few people to abandon the notion of individual moral responsibility altogether.

The first condition, however, is quite clearly not sufficient. It is possible to conceive an act of which the agent is the sole cause, but which is at the same time an act *necessitated* by the agent's nature.

. . . In the case of such an act, where the agent could not do otherwise than he did, we must all agree, I think, that it would be inept to say that he *ought* to have done otherwise and is thus morally blameworthy, or *ought not* to have done otherwise and is thus morally praiseworthy. It is perfectly true that we do sometimes hold a person morally responsible for an act, even when we believe that he, being what he now is, virtually could not do otherwise.

But underlying that judgement is always the assumption that the person has *come* to be what he now is in virtue of past acts of will in which he *was* confronted by real alternatives, by genuinely open possibilities: and, strictly speaking, it is in respect of these *past* acts of his that we praise or blame the agent *now*. For ultimate analysis, the agent's power of alternative action would seem to be an inexpugnable condition of his liability to moral praise or blame, i.e. of his moral responsibility.[12]

A person's act is free, according to Campbell, if (1) it is self-determined and (2) if the person could have done otherwise. If these two conditions are to hold, Campbell then argues, both the hard determinist and the soft determinist must be wrong. The only way for these two conditions to hold is if determinism does not apply to human actions, that is, if we determine our own actions without being determined in turn. His argument then turns on the fact that such acts seem free to us as agents:

> Let us proceed, then, by following up this clue. Let us ask, why do human beings so obstinately persist in believing that there is an indissoluble core of purely *self*-originated activity which even heredity and environment are powerless to affect? There can be little doubt, I think, of the answer in general terms. They do so, at bottom, because they feel certain of the existence of such activity from their immediate practical experience of themselves. Nor can there be in the end much doubt, I think, in what function of the self that activity is to be located. There seems to me to be one, and only one, function of the self with respect to which the agent can even pretend to have an assurance of that absolute self-origination which is here at issue. But to render precise the nature of that function is obviously of quite paramount importance: and we can do so, I think, only by way of a somewhat thorough analysis—which I now propose to attempt—of the experiential situation in which it occurs, viz. the situation of "moral temptation."
>
> It is characteristic of that situation that in it I am aware of an end *A* which I believe to be morally right, and also of an end *B*, incompatible with *A*, towards which, in virtue of that system of conative dispositions which constitutes my "character" as so far formed, I entertain a .strong desire. There may be, and perhaps must be, desiring elements in my nature which are directed to *A* also. But what gives to the situation its specific character as one of moral temptation is that the urge of our desiring nature towards the right end, *A*, is felt to be *relatively* weak. We are sure that if our desiring nature is permitted to issue directly in action, it is end *B* that we shall choose. That is what is meant by saying, as William James does, that end *B* is "in the line of least resistance" relatively to our conative dispositions. The expression is, of course, a metaphorical one, but it serves to describe, graphically enough, a situation of which we all have frequent experience, viz. where we recognise a specific end as that towards which the "set" of our desiring nature most strongly inclines us, and which we shall indubitably choose if no inhibiting factor intervenes.[13]

[12] C. A. Campbell, *In Defence of Free Will, An Inaugural Lecture* (Glasgow: Jackson, Son and Co., 1938).

[13] Campbell, *In Defence of Free Will, An Inaugural Lecture.*

In resisting moral temptation, in other words, we have the undeniable experience of resisting desires which may be very much part of our "character," and when we succeed in resisting them, we may even act "out of character." Here is Campbell's reply to the "soft determinist," who calls an act "free" only when it is "in character." To the contrary, he argues, an act is most free precisely when it is not "in character":

> . . . if my analysis is correct, in the function of moral decision in situations of moral temptation, we have an act of the self which at least *appears to the agent* to satisfy both of the conditions of freedom which we laid down at the beginning. The vital question now is, is this "appearance" true or false? Is the act of decision really what it appears to the agent to be, determined solely by the self, and capable of alternative forms of expression? If it is, then we have here a free act which serves as an adequate basis for moral responsibility. We shall be entitled to regard the agent as morally praiseworthy or morally blameworthy according as he decides to put forth effort or let his desiring nature have its way. We shall be entitled, in short, to judge the agent as he most certainly judges himself in the situation of moral temptation. If, on the other hand, there is good reason to believe that the agent is the victim of illusion in supposing his act of decision to bear this character, then in my opinion the whole conception of moral responsibility must be jettisoned altogether. For it seems to me certain that there is no other function of the self that even looks as though it satisfied the required conditions of the free act.

. . . . .

Libertarianism holds that the act of moral decision is the *self's* act, and yet insists at the same time that it is not influenced by any of those determinate features in the self's nature which go to constitute its "character." But, it is asked, do not these two propositions contradict one another? Surely a *self*-determination which is determination by something other than the self's *character* is a contradiction in terms? What meaning is there in the conception of a "self" in abstraction from its "character"? If you really wish to maintain, it is urged, that the act of decision is not determined by the self's character, you ought to admit frankly that it is not determined by the *self* at all. But in that case, of course, you will not be advocating a freedom which lends any kind of support to moral responsibility; indeed very much the reverse.

Now this criticism, and all of its kind, seem to me to be the product of a simple, but extraordinarily pervasive, error: the error of confining one's self to the categories of the external observer in dealing with the actions of human agents. Let me explain.

It is perfectly true that the stand-point of the external observer, which we are obliged to adopt in dealing with physical processes, does not furnish us with even a glimmering of a notion of what can be meant by an entity which acts causally and yet not through any of the determinate features of its character. So far as we confine ourselves to external observation, I agree that this notion must seem to us pure nonsense. But then we are *not* obliged to confine ourselves to external observation in dealing with the human agent.

Here, though here alone, we have the inestimable advantage of being able to apprehend operations from the *inside,* from the stand-point of *living experience.* But if we do adopt this internal stand-point—surely a proper stand-point, and one which we should be only too glad to adopt if we could in the case of other entities—the situation is entirely changed. We find that we not merely can, but constantly do, attach meaning to a causation which is the self's causation but is yet not exercised by the self's character. We have seen as much already in our analysis of the situation of moral temptation. When confronted by such a situation, we saw, we are certain that it lies with our *self* to decide whether we shall let our character as so far formed dictate our action or whether we shall by effort oppose its dictates and rise to duty. We are certain, in other words, that the act is *not* determined by our *character,* while we remain equally certain that the act *is* determined by our *self.*[14]

Existentialism

Kant's suggestion has been taken up in a very different way in European philosophy, particularly by the existentialists. Like Kant, they accept (or at least do not bother to reject) determinism in science. But they insist that, even if determinism is true, one must always view *him/herself as agent* as necessarily free. When you have to decide what to do, all the knowledge of the possible factors determining your decision are not sufficient to cause you to decide. For you cannot predict your own decision without at the same time making it.

Jean-Paul Sartre, the leading existentialist today, has defended the Kantian claim for human freedom as far as it can possibly be defended. In his mammoth book, *Being and Nothingness* Sartre argued that we are, always, absolutely free. This means, as Kant had insisted, that insofar as we act (and Sartre says that we are always acting) our decisions and our actions cannot be viewed as having any causes whatsoever. We must make decisions, and no amount of information and no number of causal circumstances can ever replace our need to make them. We can, of course, refuse to make decisions, acting as if they were made for us, as if circumstances already determined them, as if the fates had already established the outcome. But, even in these cases, we are making decisions, "choosing not to choose," in a classic Sartrian phrase. We are "condemned to be free," he says, in a phrase that has since become famous. Again, desires may enter into consideration, but only as "consideration." We can always act against a desire, any desire, no matter how strong, if only we are sufficiently decided that we shall do so. A starving man may yet refuse food, if, for example, he is taking part in a hunger strike for a political cause to which he is dedicated. A mother may refuse to save her own life if it would be at the expense of her children. A student may miss his favorite television show if he has resolved to study for tomorrow's test. Whether trivial or grandiose, our every act is a decision, and our every decision is free. And

[14] Campbell, *In Defence of Free Will, An Inaugural Lecture.*

even if we fail to live up to them, or find that we "cannot" make them, we are responsible nevertheless. There is no escape from freedom, or responsibility.

Although the considerations which are about to follow are of interest primarily to the ethicist, it may nevertheless be worthwhile after these descriptions and arguments to return to the freedom of the for-itself and try to understand what the fact of this freedom represents for human destiny.

The essential consequence of our earlier remarks is that man being condemned to be free carries the weight of the whole world on his shoulders; he is responsible for the world and for himself as a way of being. We are taking the word "responsibility" in its ordinary sense as "consciousness (of) being the incontestable author of an event or of an object." In this sense the responsibility of the for-itself is overwhelming since he is the one by whom it happens that *there is* a world; since he is also the one who makes himself be, then whatever may be the situation in which he finds himself, the for-itself must wholly assume this situation with its peculiar coefficient of adversity, even though it be insupportable. He must assume the situation with the proud consciousness of being the author of it, for the very worst disadvantages or the worst threats which can endanger my person have meaning only in and through my project; and it is on the ground of the engagement which I am that they appear. It is therefore senseless to think of complaining since nothing foreign has decided what we feel, what we live, or what we are.

Furthermore this absolute responsibility is not resignation; it is simply the logical requirement of the consequences of our freedom. What happens to me happens through me, and I can neither affect myself with it nor revolt against it nor resign myself to it. Moreover everything which happens to me is *mine*. By this we must understand first of all that I am always equal to what happens to me *qua* man, for what happens to a man through other men and through himself can be only human. The most terrible situations of war, the worst tortures do not create a non-human state of things; there is no non-human situation. It is only through fear, flight, and recourse to magical types of conduct that I shall decide on the non-human, but this decision is human, and I shall carry the entire responsibility for it. But in addition the situation is *mine* because it is the image of my free choice of myself, and everything which it presents to me is *mine* in that this represents me and symbolizes me. Is it not I who decide the coefficient of adversity in things and even their unpredictability by deciding myself?

Thus there are no *accidents* in a life; a community event which suddenly bursts forth and involves me in it does not come from the outside. If I am mobilized in a war, this war is *my* war; it is in my image and I deserve it. I deserve it first because I could always get out of it by suicide or by desertion; these ultimate possibles are those which must always be present for us when there is a question of envisaging a situation. For lack of getting out of it, I have *chosen* it. This can be due to inertia, to cowardice in the face of public opinion, or because I prefer certain other values to the value of the refusal to join in the war (the good opinion of my relatives, the honor of my family, *etc.*). Any way you look at it, it is a matter of a choice. This choice will be repeated later on again and again without a break until the end of the war. Therefore we must agree with the statement by J. Romains, "In war there are no innocent victims." If therefore I have preferred war to death or to dishonor, everything takes place as if I bore the entire responsibility for this war. Of course others have declared it, and one might be tempted perhaps to consider me as a simple accomplice. But this notion of complicity has only a juridical sense, and it does not hold here. For it depended on me that for me and by me this war should not exist, and I have decided that it does exist. There was no compulsion here, for the compulsion could have got no hold on a freedom. I did not have any excuse; . . . the peculiar character of human-reality is that it is without excuse. Therefore it remains for me only to lay claim to this war.

But in addition the war is *mine* because by the sole fact that it arises in a situation which I cause to be and that I can discover it there only by engaging myself for or against it, I can no longer distinguish at present the choice which I make of myself from the choice which I make of the war. To live this war is to choose myself through it and to choose it through my choice of myself. There can be no question of considering it as "four years of vacation" or as a "reprieve," as a "recess," the essential part of my responsibilities being elsewhere in my married, family, or professional life. In this war which I have chosen I choose myself from day to day, and I make it mine by making myself. If it is going to be four empty years, then it is I who bear the responsibility for this.

Finally, . . . each person is an absolute choice of self from the standpoint of a world of knowledges and of techniques which this choice both assumes and illumines; each person is an absolute upsurge at an absolute date and is perfectly unthinkable at another date. It is therefore a waste of time to ask what I should have been if this war had not broken out, for I have chosen myself as one of the possible meanings of the epoch which imperceptibly led to war. I am not distinct from this same epoch; I could not be transported to another epoch without contradiction. Thus *I am* this war which restricts and limits and makes comprehensible the period which preceded it. In this sense we may define more precisely the responsibility of the for-itself if to the earlier quoted statement, "There are no innocent victims," we add the words, "We have the war we deserve." Thus, totally free, undistinguishable from the period for which I have chosen to be the meaning, as profoundly responsible for the war as if I had myself declared it, unable to live without integrating it in *my* situation, engaging myself in it wholly and stamping it with my seal, I must be without remorse or regrets as I am without excuse; for from the instant of my upsurge into being, I carry the weight of the world by myself alone without anything or any person being able to lighten it.

Yet this responsibility is of a very particular type. Someone will say, "I did not ask to be born." This is a naïve way of throwing greater emphasis on our facticity. I am responsible for everything, in fact, except for my very responsibility, for I am not the foundation of my being. Therefore everything takes place as if I were compelled to be responsible. I am *abandoned* in the world, not in the sense that I might remain abandoned and passive in a hostile universe like a board floating on the water, but rather in the sense that I find myself suddenly alone and without help, engaged in a world for which I bear the whole responsibility without being able, whatever I do, to tear myself away from this responsibility for an instant. For I am responsible for my very desire of fleeing responsibilities. To make myself passive in the world, to refuse to act upon things and upon Others is still to choose myself, and suicide is one mode among others of being-in-the-world. Yet I find an absolute responsibility for the fact that my facticity (here the fact of my birth) is directly inapprehensible and even inconceivable, for this fact of my birth never appears as a brute fact but always across a projective reconstruction of my for-itself. I am ashamed of being born or I am astonished at it or I rejoice over it, or in attempting to get rid of my life I affirm that I live and I assume this life as bad. Thus in a certain sense I *choose* being born. This choice itself is integrally affected with facticity since I am not able not to choose, but this facticity in turn will appear only in so far as I surpass it toward my ends. Thus facticity is everywhere but inapprehensible; I never encounter anything except my responsibility. That is why I can not ask, "*Why* was I born?" or curse the day of my birth or declare that I did not ask to be born, for these various attitudes toward my birth—*i.e.,* toward the *fact* that I realize a presence in the world—are absolutely nothing else but ways of assuming this birth in full responsibility and of making it *mine.* Here again I encounter only myself and my projects so that finally my abandonment—*i.e.,* my facticity—consists simply in the fact that I am condemned to be wholly responsible for myself. I am the being which *is* in such a way that in its being its being is in question. And this "is" of my being *is* as present and inapprehensible.

Under these conditions since every event in the world can be revealed to me only as an *opportunity* (an opportunity made use of, lacked, neglected, *etc.*), or better yet since everything which happens to us can be considered as a *chance* (*i.e.,* can appear to us only as a way of realizing this being which is in question in our being) and since others as transcendences-transcended are themselves only *opportunities* and *chances,* the responsibility of the for-itself extends to the entire world as a peopled-world. It is precisely thus that the for-itself apprehends itself in anguish; that is, as a being which is neither the foundation of its own being nor of the Other's being nor of the in-itselfs which form the world, but a being which is compelled to decide the meaning of being—within it and everywhere outside of it. The one who realizes in anguish his condition as *being* thrown into a responsibility which extends to his very abandonment has no longer either remorse or regret or excuse; he is no longer anything but a freedom which perfectly reveals itself and whose being resides in this very revelation. But as we pointed out . . . , most of the time we flee anguish in bad faith.[15]

Sartre's position is the culmination of a full century of existentialist thought, beginning with Søren Kierkegaard in the 1840's. Kierkegaard too argued that one is responsible for whatever one is, and that self-conscious choice and commitment were the factors that made a person most human. Sartre's very strong sense of responsibility goes even so far as to ascribe an act of choice to those situations in which we seem clearly to be only victims, for example, in war. "There are no accidents in a life," he argues. It is always my choice as to how I shall act in and deal with a situation. One can

[15] Jean-Paul Sartre, *Being and Nothingness,* trans. Hazel E. Barnes (New York: Philosophical Library, 1956).

always complain, "I didn't ask to be born," Sartre says, but this is only one of many ways we have of trying to avoid responsibility. Given the fact that we have been born, raised in certain conditions and so forth, it is now entirely up to us as to what we shall make of all this. Instead of looking at the events of the world as problems and intrusions, Sartre ultimately says, we should learn to look at everything as an opportunity. Here is the optimistic note to his very strong defense of human freedom.

Freedom and perversity

What all of these arguments demand is the following: in one's own case, in making your decision, there can be no appeal to determinism, even if determinism is true. Whatever might be theoretically determined, in practice, you must choose. And since freedom is the key to our self-esteem and our pride in ourselves, some people will demand it at any cost.

The most brilliant if bizarre example of this existentialist demand is formulated by the strange character in Dostoevsky's short novel, *Notes from the Underground*. The argument is simple. Any prediction can be thwarted, as long as you know about it. If they say, "you'll do x"; do y. Now, suppose that determinism is true. In particular, suppose that psychological determinism is true and that its basic law is this, "people always act to their own advantage." Now, what does this have to do with the predictability of a person's actions? Absolutely nothing, if you are sufficiently determined not to be predictable. Accordingly, the character in this novel is, more than anything else, spiteful. His main concern is not being predictable, in proving his freedom, even if it means making himself miserable. Now you might say that his spite itself is the determinant of his behavior, and of course it is. But the very point of the argument is that causes and explanations of any kind are simply beside the point. Let the underground man know what you expect him to do, and he'll do precisely the opposite. And if you predict he'll act spiteful, he'll be as agreeable as can be—just out of spite!

> I am a sick man . . . I am a spiteful man. I am an unpleasant man. I think my liver is diseased. However, I don't know beans about my disease, and I am not sure what is bothering me. I don't treat it and never have, though I respect medicine and doctors. Besides, I am extremely superstitious, let's say sufficiently so to respect medicine. (I am educated enough not to be superstitious, but I am.) No, I refuse to treat it out of spite. You probably will not understand that. Well, but *I* understand it. Of course, I can't explain to you just whom I am annoying in this case by my spite. I am perfectly well aware that I cannot "get even" with the doctors by not consulting them. I know better than anyone that I thereby injure only myself and no one else. But still, if I don't treat it, it is out of spite. My liver is bad, well then—let it get even worse!

. . . . .

. . . But these are all golden dreams. Oh, tell me, who first declared, who first proclaimed, that man only does nasty things because he does not know his own real interests: and that if he were enlightened, if his eyes were opened to his real normal interests, man would at once cease to do nasty things, would at once become good and noble because, being enlightened and understanding his real advantage, he would see his own advantage in the good and nothing else, and we all know that not a single man can knowingly act to his own disadvantage. Consequently, so to say, he would begin doing good through necessity. Oh, the babe! Oh, the pure, innocent child! Why, in the first place, when in all these thousands of years has there ever been a time when man has acted only for his own advantage? What is to be done with the millions of facts that bear witness that men, *knowingly,* that is, fully understanding their real advantages, have left them in the background and have rushed headlong on another path, to risk, to chance, compelled to this course by nobody and by nothing, but, as it were, precisely because they did not want the beaten track, and stubbornly, wilfully, went off on another difficult, absurd way seeking it almost in the darkness. After all, it means that this stubbornness and wilfulness were more pleasant to them than any advantage. Advantage! What is advantage? And will you take it upon yourself to define with perfect accuracy in exactly what the advantage of man consists of? And what if it so happens that a man's advantage *sometimes* not only may, but even must, consist exactly in his desiring under certain conditions what is harmful to himself and not what is advantageous. And if so, if there can be such a condition then the whole principle becomes worthless. What do you think—are there such cases? You laugh; laugh away, gentlemen, so long as you answer me: have man's advantages been calculated with perfect certainty? Are there not some which not only have been included but cannot possibly be included under any classification? After all, you, gentlemen, so far as I know, have taken your whole register of human advantages from the average of statistical figures and scientific-economic formulas. After all, your advantages are prosperity, wealth, freedom, peace— and so on, and so on. So that a man who, for instance, would openly and knowingly oppose that whole list would, to your thinking, and indeed to mine too, of course, be an obscurantist or an absolute madman, would he not? But, after all, here is something amazing: why does it happen that all these statisticians, sages and lovers of humanity, when they calculate human advantages invariably leave one out? They don't even take it into their calculation in the form in which it should be taken, and the whole reckoning depends upon that. There would be no great harm to take it, this advantage, and to add it to the list. But the trouble is, that this strange advantage does not fall under any classification and does not figure in any list. For instance, I have a friend. Bah, gentlemen! But after all he is your friend, too; and indeed there is no one, no one, to whom he is not a friend! When he prepares for any undertaking this gentleman immediately explains to you, pompously and clearly, exactly how he must act in accordance with the laws of reason and truth. What is more, he will talk to you with excitement and passion of the real normal interests of man; with irony he will reproach the short-sighted fools who do not understand their own advantage, for the true significance of virtue; and, within a quarter of an hour, without any sudden outside provocation, but precisely through that something internal which is stronger than all his advantages, he will go off on quite a different tack—that is, act directly opposite to what he has just been saying himself, in opposition to the laws of reason, in opposition to his own advantage—in fact, in opposition to everything. I warn you that my friend is a compound personality, and therefore it is somehow difficult to blame him as an individual. The fact is, gentlemen, it seems that something that is dearer to almost every man than his greatest advantages must really exist, or (not to be illogical) there is one most advantageous advantage (the very one omitted of which we spoke just now) which is more important and more advantageous than all other advantages, for which, if necessary, a man is ready to act in opposition to all laws, that is, in opposition to reason, honor, peace, prosperity—in short, in opposition to all those wonderful and useful things if only he can attain that fundamental, most advantageous advantage which is dearer to him than all.

And what is that "advantageous advantage?" Nothing other than:

One's own free unfettered choice, one's own fancy, however wild it may be, one's own fancy worked up at times to frenzy. That is the "most advantageous advantage," which is always overlooked.[16]

Freedom, in other words, is itself what we most demand, whatever the cost, whatever the difficulties, and whatever the arguments against it. Whatever else may be true, we will refuse to see ourselves as anything but free. For it is freedom that makes us human.

SUMMARY AND CONCLUSION

To say that a person's act is free is to be able to ascribe responsibility. The defense of freedom therefore becomes extremely important to us. Our confidence in the universality of scientific explanations, however, seems to imply the thesis of determinism, which holds that every event has its sufficient natural cause. Human actions, as events, thus seem to be determined, and thus not free. In this chapter, we have attempted to explore the various ways in which philosophers have attempted to reconcile these two vital beliefs—that at least some human acts are free, and that science can ultimately (at least in principle) explain everything.

There have been philosophers who have defended determinism ("hard determinism") to the exclusion of freedom. There have been philosophers who have defended freedom to the exclusion of determinism ("libertarians" and "indeterminists"). Most philosophers, however, have tried to defend both theses (and so are often called "compatibilists"). They have argued that determinism does not preclude freedom if an act flows from a person's decision

[16] Fyodor Dostoevsky, *Notes from the Underground*, in *Notes from the Underground and The Grand Inquisitor*, trans. Ralph Matlaw (New York: E. P. Dutton, 1960).

or character ("soft determinists"), or that, even if determinism is true, we cannot help but think of ourselves as free (Kant and the existentialists).

GLOSSARY

antecedent conditions: those circumstances, states of affairs, or events which regularly precede and can be said to cause an event. The antecedent conditions of boiling water, for example, are the application of heat to water, under normal atmospheric pressure, etc. A determinist would say that the antecedent conditions of a human action would be the state of his or her nervous system, a developed character (with personality traits), certain desires and beliefs, and the circumstances (or "stimulus") in which the action takes place.

cause: that which brings something about. On the hard determinist interpretation, a cause is an antecedent condition which, together with other antecedent conditions, is sufficient to make the occurrence of some event necessary, according to the laws of nature. On a weaker interpretation, a cause may simply be an event (or condition) which regularly precedes another event, and thus can be used to predict when the latter will occur. (For example, if we say "a cause of forest fires is lightning," we mean "whenever lightning strikes a sufficiently dry forest, fire will occur.")

compatibilism: the thesis that both determinism (on some interpretation) and free action can be true. Determinism does not rule out free action and the possibility of free action does not require that determinism be false. They are compatible positions.

compulsion: "being forced to do something." One acts from compulsion (or is compelled to act) when he or she could not have done otherwise. Some philosophers distinguish between *external* compulsions (for example, being pushed) and *internal* compulsions (for example, a neurotic obsession).

determinism: the thesis that every event has its sufficient natural cause(s), that every event is caused by its antecedent conditions, or that every event is predictable on the basis of such conditions.

fatalism: the thesis that certain events (or perhaps all events) are going to happen inevitably, regardless of what efforts we take to prevent them.

free will: among philosophers, a somewhat antiquated expression (as in "he did it of his own free will"), which means that a person is capable of making decisions which are not determined by antecedent conditions. Of course there may be antecedent considerations, such as what a person wants, what a person believes, but free will means that such considerations never determine a person's decision. At most they "enter into the decision."

freedom: the idea that a human decision or action is a person's own responsibility, and that praise and blame may be appropriately ascribed. The most extreme interpretation of "freedom" is the absence of any causes or determinations. Thus an indeterminist would say that an event was free if it had no causes; a libertarian would say that a human act was free if it was only self-caused, but not determined by anything else, (including a person's character). Certain determinists, however ("soft determinists") would say that an act is free if only it is "in character" and based upon a person's desires and personality. Most generally, we say that a person's act was free, whether or not it was the result of a conscious decision and whether or not certain causes may have been involved, if we would say that he or she could have done otherwise.

Heisenberg Uncertainty Principle: an important principle of recent physics that demonstrates that we cannot know both the position and the momentum of certain sub-atomic particles, for in our attempts to know one, we make it impossible to know the other. This principle has been used to attack the very idea of "determinism" in its classical formulations, for determinism requires just the "certainty" of possible prediction that the Heisenberg Principle rejects.

indeterminism: the thesis that at least some events in the universe are not determined, are not caused by antecedent conditions, and may not be predictable.

predestination: the thesis (usually in a theological context) that every event is destined to happen (as in fatalism) whatever efforts we make to prevent it. The usual version is that God knows and perhaps causes all things to happen, and therefore everything must happen precisely as he knows (and possibly causes) it to happen.

prediction: to say that some event will happen before it happens. Determinism normally includes the thesis that, if we know enough about the antecedent conditions of an event, we can always predict that it will occur. But prediction does not require determinism. One might predict the outcome of some state of affairs on the basis of statistical probabilities, without knowing any antecedent conditions and perhaps even without assuming that there are any such conditions (in quantum physics, for example). And it is also possible that a person might predict the future on the basis of lucky guesses or E.S.P., again without necessarily accepting determinism.

responsibility: answerable or accountable for some act or event presumed to be within a person's control.

retrodiction: to say, on the basis of certain present evidence, what must have happened in the past. For example, the astronomer who looks at the present course of a comet can retrodict certain facts about its history. For the determinist, retrodiction is as important to his thesis as prediction.

soft determinism: a thesis which accepts determinism but claims that certain kinds of causes, namely, a person's character, still allow us to call his actions "free." The soft determinist is therefore a compatibilist, for he believes in both freedom and determinism.

sufficient cause: capable of bringing something about by itself (for example, four healthy people are sufficient to push a Volkswagen up a hill).

11

MORALITY
AND THE GOOD LIFE

What I really lack is to be clear in my mind what I am to do.

Søren Kierkegaard

What should we do? And what should we not do? These are questions of a different kind than those we have asked so far. Many philosophers would say that they are questions of *value,* rather than questions of knowledge and reality. They are questions whose answers point to specific actions and ways of acting. What acts should we praise? What acts should we condemn and blame? These are the questions of morality, the concern for which Socrates was willing to give up his life. *Morality* is a set of principles or rules that guide our actions: for example, they may forbid us to kill each other, encourage us to help each other, tell us not to lie, command us to keep our promises.

But morality is a piece of a much larger quest, which gives morality its importance. Why shouldn't we kill each other? Why should we help each other? What reasons can we give to defend one sexual ethic rather than another? And, in general, why should we be moral? The answer to this last question must be larger than morality itself, for it must supply us with the reasons for accepting moral principles and rules. That answer is called *the good life.* It is a phrase without precise meaning, but we all know quite well what it signifies. How should we live? What do we want? And what should we want? What do we most enjoy? What should we most enjoy? What is worth working for? And what is not worth the effort? What should we accept? And what should we try to change? These are questions for which we all have answers before we enter philosophy, but philosophy sometimes has surprising results in changing them, or at least in giving us better arguments to support them.

405

Unfortunately, many of our moral opinions and thoughts about the good life are not well developed or consistent. The result is that we move from day to day with a set of half-digested principles which don't always agree, which sometimes send us off in this direction and other times in that, and which leave us with the feeling, perhaps after one of our greatest accomplishments, "did we really want that in the first place?" The business of moral philosophy and the search for the good life is to put an end to such confusions. Its goal is to develop a set of principles and a view of our aims in life that will allow us to live with that same enviable clarity and confidence with which Socrates lived out his long life. (This general quest, which includes morality as well as the search for the good life, is usually called *ethics.*)

THE GOOD LIFE

Hedonism

In Plato's dialogues, in which Socrates is the leading character, the recurrent theme is the search for the good life. And from Socrates' discussions with his fellow Greeks, it is evident that this was not at all a new question, but one about which virtually everyone had very strong opinions. And almost all of these opinions are still defended today. Most prominent among them is the philosophy called *hedonism,* the view that says the good life is in getting as much pleasure out of life as you possibly can. In the ancient world, this was defended by one of Socrates' students, Aristippus, who argued that the only good is pleasure, and the only good life is the life of continuous pleasure: pleasures of the moment, without any regard for "long term" pleasures or "delayed gratification," without any distinction between "better" or more sophisticated pleasures and "lower" or more bestial pleasures. Pleasure is pleasure, and the good life is nothing but pleasure.

Much more famously, "pleasure as the only good," was defended by the philosopher Epicurus, whose philosophy became so well known that we still refer to a person who spends his life seeking out pleasures as an *Epicurean.*

> It should be recognized that within the category of desire certain desires are natural, certain others unnecessary and trivial; that in the case of the natural desires certain ones are necessary, certain others merely natural; and that in the case of necessary desires certain ones are necessary for happiness, others to promote freedom from bodily discomfort, others for the maintenance of life itself. A steady view of these matters shows us how to refer all moral choice and aversion to bodily health and imperturbability of mind, these being the twin goals of happy living. It is on this account that we do everything we do—to achieve freedom from pain and freedom from fear. When once we come by this, the tumult in the soul is calmed and the human being does not

have to go about looking for something that is lacking or to search for something additional with which to supplement the welfare of soul and body. Accordingly we have need of pleasure only when we feel pain because of the absence of pleasure, but whenever we do not feel pain we no longer stand in need of pleasure. And so we speak of pleasure as the starting point and the goal of the happy life because we realize that it is our primary native good, because every act of choice and aversion originates with it, and because we come back to it when we judge every good by using the pleasure feeling as our criterion.

Because of the very fact that pleasure is our primary and congenial good we do not select every pleasure; there are times when we forgo certain pleasures, particularly when they are followed by too much unpleasantness. Furthermore, we regard certain states of pain as preferable to pleasures, particularly when greater satisfaction results from our having submitted to discomforts for a long period of time. Thus every pleasure is a good by reason of its having a nature akin to our own, but not every pleasure is desirable. In like manner, every state of pain is an evil, but not all pains are uniformly to be rejected. At any rate, it is our duty to judge all such cases by measuring pleasures against pains, with a view to their respective assets and liabilities, inasmuch as we do experience the good as being bad at times and, contrariwise, the bad as being good.

In addition, we consider limitation of the appetites a major good, and we recommend this practice not for the purpose of enjoying just a few things and no more, but rather for the purpose of enjoying those few in case we do not have much. We are firmly convinced that those who need expensive fare least are the ones who relish it most keenly and that a natural way of life is easily procured, while trivialities are hard to come by. Plain foods afford pleasure equivalent to that of a sumptuous diet, provided that the pains of penury are wholly eliminated. Barley bread and water yield the peak of pleasure whenever a person who needs them sets them in front of himself. Hence becoming habituated to a simple rather than a lavish way of life provides us with the full complement of health; it makes a person ready for the necessary business of life; it puts us in a position of advantage when we happen upon sumptuous fare at intervals and prepares us to be fearless in facing fortune.

Thus when I say that pleasure is the goal of living I do not mean the pleasures of libertines or the pleasures inherent in positive enjoyment, as is supposed by certain persons who are ignorant of our doctrine or who are not in agreement with it or who interpret it perversely. I mean, on the contrary, the pleasure that consists in freedom from bodily pain and mental agitation. The pleasant life is not the product of one drinking party after another or of sexual intercourse with women and boys or of the seafood and other delicacies afforded by a luxurious table. On the contrary, it is the result of sober thinking—namely, investigation of the reasons for every act of choice and aversion, and elimination of those false ideas about the gods and death which are the chief source of mental disturbances.[1]

---

[1] Epicurus, *Letter to Menoeceus,* in *The Philosophy of Epicurus,* ed. George K. Strodach (Evanston, Ill.: Northwestern University Press, 1963).

Notice that Epicurus does not advocate simple self-indulgence (as Aristippus does); he advocates the life of pleasure, not simply "one drinking party after another or sexual intercourse." The pleasures of the mind and spirit, and fellowship with other people are much more important, because they are, ultimately, much more pleasurable.

Hedonism is an attractive candidate for the good life, but Socrates and people ever since have seen that it has certain limitations. You might notice that people talk a lot more about hedonism than they actually practice it. Students often talk about hedonism, but their ambitions and worries about school and careers show that they want something more than just pleasure—success, security, social standing, respect, power, money, freedom. This is not to deny that they also want pleasures, but more as distractions, entertainments, and mere enjoyments than as the goal of life as such. Compared with the average domesticated cat, for example, we are masters in self-denial. We put off meals when we are hungry, because we have work to do or because we are on diets. We suppress our sexual impulses because it would be awkward or embarrassing to act on them in the middle of class or at the dinner table; we want much more than "just sex" (unlike most cats). We act more or less mannerly and in a "civilized" fashion even when we pursue our pleasures directly. Very few people would be willing to give up all respect for the sake of pleasure, and most of our ambitions take priority over passing pleasures, at least most of the time. True, many people argue that the reason that they deny themselves pleasures now is in order to get more pleasure later. But, if that is so, then most people are surely fooling themselves, for we all know that work and responsibility breed more work and more responsibility. Social respect and manners constantly require more respectable behavior and more manners, and the idea that we are simply delaying our pleasure is usually disproved by our own actions. People also argue that the work itself, or the respect, or the success, is what gives them pleasure, but here philosophers have pointed out a crucial distinction, between acting for the sake of pleasure and acting for some other goal whose achievement gives pleasure. Hedonism is the first, not the second. Even Aristotle pointed out that pleasure is not an activity itself, but that which accompanies satisfying activities. Our goal is not the pleasure but the activity itself; the pleasure is more like a bonus, the "completion" of good activity. It is inseparable from the good life, but it is not the good life itself. Aristotle says:

> One might think that all men desire pleasure because they all aim at life; life is an activity, and each man is active about those things and with those faculties that he loves most; e.g. the musician is active with his hearing in reference to tunes, the student with his mind in reference to theoretical questions, and so on in each case; now pleasure completes the activities, and therefore life, which they desire. It is with good reason, then, that they aim at pleasure too, since for every one it completes life, which is desirable. But whether we choose life for the sake of pleasure or pleasure for the sake of life is a question we may dismiss for the present. For they seem to be bound

up together and not to admit of separation, since without activity pleasure does not arise, and every activity is completed by the attendant pleasure.

This may be seen, too, from the fact that each of the pleasures is bound up with the activity it completes. For an activity is intensified by its proper pleasure, since each class of things is better judged of and brought to precision by those who engage in the activity with pleasure; e.g. it is those who enjoy geometrical thinking that become geometers and grasp the various propositions better, and, similarly, those who are fond of music or of building, and so on, make progress in their proper function by enjoying it; so the pleasures intensify the activities, and what intensifies a thing is proper to it, but things different in kind have properties different in kind.

Now since activities differ in respect of goodness and badness, and some are worthy to be chosen, others to be avoided, and others neutral, so, too, are the pleasures; for to each activity there is a proper pleasure. The pleasure proper to a worthy activity is good and that proper to an unworthy activity bad; just as the appetites for noble objects are laudable, those for base objects culpable.[2]

There is a trivial sense, therefore, in which one might say that pleasure is part of the goal of every activity, just because pleasure is nothing other than the satisfaction of whatever goals we have. But this is surely not hedonism. If hedonism means anything, it must be a life in which pleasure as such is desired—the taste of delicious food, the feelings of good sex, the relaxed ease of having your back rubbed. If a businessman enjoys his success, that does not mean that he is a hedonist. His goal is success, and the good life for him is success, whether or not he gets enjoyment as well. This does not mean that people who are not hedonists can have no pleasure or should avoid it for the sake of their chosen goals. But it does mean that pleasure is not their primary goal, however often they may enjoy themselves as well.

There are actually very few hedonists among us. For several years I have told my students about a certain imaginary invention (based upon the researches of a Cornell psychologist, James Olds). It is a box, fixed with electrodes and medical equipment. A person is strapped in, the electricity is turned on, and he or she experiences continuing waves of pleasurable sensations. The box is equipped to take care of all of a person's biological needs, and a person will live in the box at least as long as he or she would outside of it. The only hitch is this: once you get into the box, you will never get out of it. Here is the life of absolute pleasure, but in return for it, you must give up your ambitions and your friends, sports, reading, sex, food, and television. Of course, after only a few months in the box you will become grotesquely out of shape, pale and not much more interesting than a soaking avocado pit, which by this time you will strongly resemble. But you won't care about any of this—you will be leading the life of total pleasure. Would you do it? In my years of teaching several thousand students, I have found only a dozen or so who would. Most of us desire other satisfactions over and above sensory pleasures.

[2] Aristotle, *Nichomachean Ethics*, BK. X, in *The Oxford Translation of Aristotle*, trans. W. D. Ross (Oxford: Oxford University Press, 1925).

Success

In our society, the good life is often equated with success. Success may mean money, but it does not mean only this. It involves social status and respectability as well (although these often go together). There are curious twists: for example, a gangster may be admired as eminently successful, no matter how he acquired his wealth and status. Some creative people and hermits may be admired and idolized as successful despite the fact that they are, by any customary measure, total failures. But once again, we must be careful not to confuse what people say they take to be the good life with the way they actually live. Many people who work very hard for success will say that they are working towards their retirement, or in order to have enough security to enjoy themselves, or in order to have enough money to buy themselves lavish pleasures. But, again, their lives often show differently, as people work themselves into exhaustion long after they have "made it," to such an extent that they are no longer capable of enjoying the simplest pleasures that are available to any bum in a public park. You might say that they are success misers, just as people became money misers, working at first in order to get something else, but ultimately working simply for the thing itself. Money misers start earning money like everyone else, to buy homes, cars, T.V. sets, but they end up liking the money itself so much that they work only for it. Success misers work hard for security, social status, or wealth, but end up working just for the success itself. Thus we have to see success as a separate conception of the good life, not simply a means to pleasure and therefore not as a form of hedonism. It is extremely powerful in our world, and many people who would not admit to accepting it obviously do.

The life of seeking success has its problems. There is always the real possibility of failure, of course, but this is equally an argument against almost every life style. In any case, the threat of failure is not a good reason to reject a life style—the problem is rather the threat of success. We all know stories of successful people in their mid-forties or fifties committing suicide, just when it would seem that they have achieved what they have been working for most of their lives. Why? Because, once earned, their success proved not to be what they wanted after all. It is here that the tragic question, "is this what I wanted in the first place?" appears. It is tragic because, it seems, we rarely ask that all-important question while we are striving for something but only after we've achieved it. And when our goal is years or decades away, the question may appear too late to do us any good at all.

It may be a well-known truism that people who live for success (or money or social standing) are often not satisfied when they have achieved it, but the reaction to that observation, which is captured in the short phrase from Ecclesiastes, "all is vanity," is not thereby justified. If a certain conception of the good life fails us, that doesn't mean that there is no good life, much less that life isn't really worth living. It does not even mean that success is not worth having, or that success is wrong. It only means that success, by itself, does not seem to give us the good life.

Asceticism

In our society, the failure of this success conception of the good life, the "success ethic," has given rise to a reaction in precisely the opposite direction. In place of success, many people demand simplicity and lack of responsibility, enforced poverty, and freedom from possessions. At the extremes, this manifests itself in our choice of folk heroes, off in the wilderness as pioneers, rebels or mountain men. More moderately, it manifests itself in the return to the country, life on the farm or in a small commune, largely by people who have been brought up in large cities and nurtured on the success ethic. It is worth noting that this is not at all a new philosophy. It was in reaction to the decadent success ethic of the Roman empire, for example, that simple Christian asceticism began. (*Asceticism* is the proper word for this life of simplicity and self-denial.) And even before Christianity, around the time of Socrates, a group of philosophers who called themselves *Cynics* defended a similar life style. (The word "cynic" comes from the Greek word for dog.) The most famous of them was Diogenes, who lived in a bathtub, owned nothing but a single lantern, with which he is said to have searched the faces of everyone, "looking for even one honest man." When Alexander the Great came to his city, he asked to see Diogenes, of whom he had heard much. On their meeting, Alexander asked Diogenes, "what can I do for you?" And Diogenes turned to the ruler of most of the world and said, "move over, you're blocking the sunlight."

Asceticism has often flourished in great societies in a state of confusion, in which the success ethic has run away with itself and its limitations have started to become apparent. As a therapeutic rebellion and a lesson in how simply one can live, it has an important significance. But it too must be considered with caution, particularly because it is a reaction. It may be an overreaction. To reject an excess of the success ethic need not mean that we reject ambition altogether or praise failure, poverty and lack of responsibility for their own sakes. As a corrective, the ascetic life may be extremely important, but as a candidate for the good life, self-denial and minimal satisfaction do not make it very attractive. It often represents a way of giving up the search for the good life, and merely "getting by."

It is important to add, however, that a great many people have accepted the ascetic life for other reasons, in other words, as the means to the good life, but not as the good life itself. A great many religious people, for example, have accepted asceticism as a way to salvation or "purification." But it is not the self-denial itself that they praise, but self-denial as a means to the holy life. Some artists adopt the ascetic life, but only because it seems to them the best way to achieve what they really consider the good life, namely, creativity. And it is important not to confuse asceticism, with its extremes of self-denial, with that familiar belief that the "simplest" pleasures in life are not only the best but the easiest to obtain. Many try to "simplify" their lives, just because society makes life so bureaucratically and socially complicated. But they do this "in order to enjoy life more," not for purely ascetic reasons. But here too, asceticism is a corrective and a means, not an end in itself.

The question then arises, "does anyone ever choose asceticism just for its own sake, as the good life itself?" Even the Cynics, for example, were after something more than mere self-denial; like many people in our own times, they were trying to avoid the hypocrisies and insatiable social demands that made most people unhappy. Similarly, the early Christians chose asceticism as a way to "purification" and salvation, not for its own sake.

Freedom

Freedom can be singled out as a separate conception of the good life. Usually, freedom is considered a means, the freedom to do what one wants: to satisfy pleasures or ambitions, create or worship, retreat from society or live as one will. But, like other means, freedom may become an end in itself. The person who throws over a promising career and takes to the open road might be said to value his freedom more than any pleasures or successes. Freedom from ties and responsibilities may be preferable to an intimate relationship or marriage, just because it is more "free." The life of freedom need not be any particular way of life, in the sense that one might, within it, be religious, hedonistic, or ambitious. The question is ultimately, which is more important—the freedom itself or these other concerns? The extreme of this conception is the peculiar and extravagant conception of freedom portrayed in Dostoevsky's "underground man." He was willing to give up everything, not only success and pleasure but even his health, just in order to realize his "most advantageous advantage," his freedom.

Power and creativity

There are many other conceptions of the good life. Indeed, there are as many possible conceptions as there are human goals (although most goals, for example, keeping one's teeth clean or keeping the roof from leaking, would be very rare as ultimate goals). Some of the other most common conceptions of the good life are very close to those we have discussed so far: for example the life in pursuit of great wealth or political power is very much like the life of the success ethic. But then there is another sense of "power" that is not political but personal. It is the power to grow as a person, to "expand one's consciousness" to develop one's talents and to create. Friedrich Nietzsche, for example, defends such a conception of the good life under the phrase of "the will to power." Arguing against those many philosophers, particularly the British moralists, who argue that man acts only for pleasure, Nietzsche sarcastically quips: "Man does not desire pleasure; only the Englishman does." What all people ultimately want, Nietzsche argues, is power:

> Not need, nor desire—no the love of power is the demon of man. One may give them everything—health, nourishment, quarters, they remain unhappy; for the demon insists on being satisfied. One may take away everything from them and satisfy this demon: they then are almost happy.[3]

All other seeming conceptions of the good life, Nietzsche adds, are in fact different ways of seeking power. Even religion, as well as the contemporary scramble for wealth:

> Long ago, power inspired people to burn Jews, heretics and good books, and destroyed entire higher cultures, as that of Peru and Mexico. The means of the craving for power have changed, but the same volcano is still glowing. What one formerly did 'for God's sake' one does for money, which *now* gives the highest feeling of power.[4]

But the highest sense of power, Nietzsche argues, is reserved for those people who live autonomously and creatively, as artists, philosophers or saints.

> Whether it be hedonism, pessimism, utilitarianism, or the search for personal happiness, all those modes of thinking which measure the worth of things according to *pleasure* and *pain*, that is, according to accompanying circumstances and secondary considerations, are plausible modes of thought and naivetés, which every one conscious of *creative* powers and an artist's conscience will look down upon with scorn, though not without sympathy.[5]

Mozart, for example, considered the good life to be the life of artistic creativity, which is not to deny that he enjoyed a great many of the pleasures of life along the way. The good life for Socrates was a life in accordance with the moral principles he had defended in his philosophizing, though he too had more than his share of pleasure and success as well. For him, the good life was the life of wisdom, the life of principles and creative thinking. And these were worth holding onto even when they meant his death.

Religion

The religious conception of the good life also deserves special consideration, not when it is simply intermingled with the other goals and ambitions of life and squeezed into Sunday mornings, but when it is truly the goal of life to which all other goals are subordinated. Nietzsche chooses the Buddha as his

[3] Friedrich Nietzsche, *Dawn,* in *Nietzsche,* trans. Walter Kaufmann (Princeton: Princeton University Press, 1950).

[4] Nietzsche, *Dawn.*

[5] Friedrich Nietzsche, *Beyond Good and Evil,* trans. Helen Zimmern, in *The Complete Works of Friedrich Nietzsche,* Oscar Levy, General Editor (1909–11) (New York: Russell & Russell, 1964).

example; Christ would be another. But it is never altogether clear how many other people have completely endorsed this conception of the good life. There are millions of people who have said that they do, but whether their lives bear out their statements is something that we must always view, particularly in our own case, with a cautious eye. The religious life is a life of devotion: in the Christian tradition, it is sometimes said to be "living with the fear of God in one's heart." The religious life, however, need not be based on "fear," but the point is that the truly religious person lives with an emotional attachment to his or her religion that permeates and dominates everything else. This is not to say that the religious person doesn't perform any but religious acts (prayer, for example) but religious behavior must have the primary place in his or her life.

Each of these conceptions of the good life is fairly specific; it singles out one goal or type of goal among the many that we desire and claims that one goal as the mark of the good life. But, once we have begun thinking about it, all of these seem one-sided. Who wants pleasure if it means giving up all friends and social ties? Who wants power or success if it makes us miserable? Who would even want to be creative if nothing but misery came from it? Wouldn't it be better to be both creative and enjoy life? or be creative and successful as well? And even the religious life can be challenged in this way. Wouldn't a religious person have a better life if he or she not only devoted him or herself to God exclusively but also enjoyed the blessings of the secular world, without diminishing religious faith? The good life, in other words, seems to be something more general than any single goal, no matter how grand that single goal may seem to many people. Yet we should not conclude that the good life is simply "the best of everything," without further qualification. Even if we reject these one-sided views, we may still find that the good life has but a single goal.

In search of happiness

In the ancient world, Aristotle examined the different one-sided conceptions of the good life and rejected them in favor of a single conception with which most of us are probably in agreement—happiness. Happiness is the good life, although happiness itself is not a single activity but the result of a great many activities. As in Nietzsche's will to power, Aristotle takes personal development or self-realization as his goals. In his *Ethics,* Aristotle examines two one-sided conceptions of the good life, pleasure and success (which meant political success for him) and rejects them; yet he also insists that one could not possibly lead the good life without them. But they themselves are not the good life, only necessary conditions for it. The good life is *happiness,* which is defined as that which is wanted "for its own sake" and not "for the sake of anything else." (Ultimately, he defends a third conception of the good life as the main ingredient in happiness, the life of philosophical contemplation.)

. . . To judge from the lives that men lead, most men, and men of the most vulgar type, seem (not without some ground) to identify the good, or happiness, with pleasure; which is the reason why they love the life of enjoyment. For there are, we may say, three prominent types of life—that just mentioned, the political, and thirdly the contemplative life. Now the mass of mankind are evidently quite slavish in their tastes, preferring a life suitable to beasts, but they get some ground for their view from the fact that many of those in high places share the tastes of Sardanapallus. A consideration of the prominent types of life shows that people of superior refinement and of active disposition identify happiness with honour; for this is, roughly speaking, the end of the political life. But it seems too superficial to be what we are looking for, since it is thought to depend on those who bestow honour rather than on him who receives it, but the good we divine to be something proper to a man and not easily taken from him. Further, men seem to pursue honour in order that they may be assured of their goodness; at least it is by men of practical wisdom that they seek to be honoured, and among those who know them, and on the ground of their virtue; clearly then, according to them, at any rate, virtue is better. And perhaps one might even suppose this to be rather than honour, the end of the political life. But even this appears somewhat incomplete; for possession of virtue seems actually compatible with being asleep, or with lifelong inactivity, and, further, with the greatest sufferings and misfortunes; but a man who was living so no one would call happy, unless he were maintaining a thesis at all costs. But enough of this; for the subject has been sufficiently treated even in the current discussions. Third comes the contemplative life, which we shall consider later.

The life of money-making is one undertaken under compulsion, and wealth is evidently not the good we are seeking; for it is merely useful and for the sake of something else. And so one might rather take the aforenamed objects to be ends; for they are loved for themselves. But it is evident that not even these are ends; yet many arguments have been thrown away in support of them. . . .

Let us again return to the good we are seeking, and ask what it can be. It seems different in different actions and arts; it is different in medicine, in strategy, and in the other arts likewise. What then is the good of each? Surely that for whose sake everything else is done. In medicine this is health, in strategy victory, in architecture a house, in any other sphere something else, and in every action and pursuit the end; for it is for the sake of this that all men do whatever else they do. Therefore, if there is an end for all that we do, this will be the good achievable by action, and if there are more than one, these will be the goods achievable by action.

So the argument has by a different course reached the same point; but we must try to state this even more clearly. Since there are evidently more than one end, and we choose some of these (e.g., wealth, flutes, and in general instruments) for the sake of something else, clearly not all ends are final ends; but the chief good is evidently something final. Therefore, if there is only one final end, this will be what we are seeking, and if there are more than one, the most final of these will be what we are seeking. Now we call that which is in itself worthy of pursuit more final than that which is worthy of pursuit for the sake of something else, and that which is never desirable for the sake of something else more final than the things that are desirable both in themselves and for the sake of that other thing, and therefore we call final without qualification that which is always desirable in itself and never for the sake of something else.

Now such a thing happiness, above all else, is held to be; for this we choose always for itself and never for the sake of something else, but honour, pleasure, reason, and every virtue we choose indeed for themselves (for if nothing resulted from them we should still choose each of them), but we choose them also for the sake of happiness, judging that by means of them we shall be happy. Happiness, on the other hand, no one chooses for the sake of these, nor, in general, for anything other than itself.

From the point of view of self-sufficiency the same result seems to follow; for the final good is thought to be self-sufficient. Now by self-sufficient we do not mean that which is sufficient for a man by himself, for one who lives a solitary life, but also for parents, children, wife, and in general for his friends and fellow citizens, since man is born for citizenship. But some limit must be set to this; for if we extend our requirements to ancestors and descendants and friends' friends we are in for an infinite series. . . . The self-sufficient we now define as that which when isolated makes life desirable and lacking in nothing; and such we think happiness to be; and further we think it most desirable of all things, without being counted as one good thing among others—if it were so counted it would clearly be made desirable by the addition of even the least of goods; for that which is added becomes an excess of goods, and of goods the greater is always more desirable. Happiness, then, is something final and self-sufficient, and is the end of action.[6]

Most people would probably agree with Aristotle, that happiness is what constitutes the good life. But Aristotle sees that this is an answer which, in itself, is of no help at all. "Happiness," as Aristotle argues in other paragraphs of this same book, is nothing other than the name that we generally agree to give to whatever makes up the good life. We need some idea what happiness is, and Aristotle here gives us his idea: happiness is living according to rationality ("a rational principle").

. . . Verbally there is very general agreement; for both the general run of men and people of superior refinement say that it is happiness, and identify living well and doing well with being happy; but with regard to what happiness is they differ, and the many do not give the same account as the wise. For the former think it is some plain and obvious thing, like pleasure, wealth, or honour; they differ, however, from one another—and often even the same man identifies it with different things, with health when he is ill, with wealth when he is poor; but, conscious of their ignorance, they admire those who proclaim some great ideal that is above their comprehension. Now some thought that apart from these many goods there is another which is self-subsistent and causes the goodness of all these as well.

．　．　．　．　．

Presumably, however, to say that happiness is the chief good seems a platitude, and a clearer account of what it is is still desired. This might per-

[6] Aristotle, *Nichomachean Ethics.*

haps be given, if we could first ascertain the function of man. For just as for a flute-player, a sculptor, or any artist, and, in general, for all things that have a function or activity, the good and the 'well' is thought to reside in the function, so would it seem to be for man, if he has a function. Have the carpenter, then, and the tanner certain functions or activities, and has man none? Is he born without a function? Or as eye, hand, foot, and in general each of the parts evidently has a function, may one lay it down that man similarly has a function apart from all these? What then can this be? Life seems to be common even to plants, but we are seeking what is peculiar to man. Let us exclude, therefore, the life of nutrition and growth. Next there would be a life of perception, but *it* also seems to be common even to the horse, the ox, and every animal. There remains, then, an active life of the element that has a rational principle; of this, one part has such a principle in the sense of being obedient to one, the other in the sense of possessing one and exercising thought. And, as 'life of the rational element' also has two meanings, we must state that life in the sense of activity is what we mean; for this seems to be the more proper sense of the term. The function of man is an activity of soul which follows or implies a rational principle. . . .[7]

It is important to notice the structure of Aristotle's argument here, for we shall see it emerge often in philosophy as well as in our own thought. The argument is an argument on the basis of what is "natural" to man. The good life for man is that which is "natural" to him. Everything in this world, according to Aristotle, has its "natural" purposes and goals, and happiness is that goal for man. At the very beginning of his *Ethics,* Aristotle tells us:

Every art and every inquiry, and similarly every action and pursuit, is thought to aim at some good; and for this reason the good has rightly been declared to be that at which all things aim. But a certain difference is found among ends; some are activities, others are products apart from the activities that produce them. Where there are ends apart from the actions, it is the nature of the products to be better than the activities. Now, as there are many actions, arts, and sciences, their ends also are many; the end of the medical art is health, that of shipbuilding a vessel, that of strategy victory, that of economics wealth. But where such arts fall under a single capacity—as bridle-making and the other arts concerned with the equipment of horses fall under the art of riding, and this and every military action under strategy, in the same way other arts fall under yet others—in all of these the ends of the master arts are to be preferred to all the subordinate ends; for it is for the sake of the former that the latter are pursued. It makes no difference whether the activities themselves are the ends of the actions, or something else apart from the activities, as in the case of the sciences just mentioned.

If, then, there is some end of the things we do, which we desire for its own sake (everything else being desired for the sake of this), and if we do not choose everything for the sake of something else (for at that rate the process would go on to infinity, so that our desire would be empty and vain), clearly this must be the good and the chief good. Will not the knowledge of

7 Aristotle, *Nichomachean Ethics.*

it, then, have a great influence on life? Shall we not, like archers who have a mark to aim at, be more likely to hit upon what is right? If so, we must try, in outline at least to determine what it is. . . .[8]

We see here the same logical strategy that Aristotle used in Chapter 1; the idea that every act is for the sake of something else (we want to earn a dollar to buy ourselves some food, and we want that to satisfy our hunger). But since there can be no "infinite regress," there must be some ultimate end, namely happiness. But what is happiness for man must be what is "natural" to him, and that means, according to Aristotle, what is special or unique to him as well. Thus mere "nutrition and growth," that is, eating and keeping physically healthy, cannot in themselves be happiness (although it is necessary for happiness) because even plants, Aristotle says, have this "goal." Yet he also insists that we cannot be happy without these things. Nor can happiness lie in simple experience, even exciting experiences (being on drugs all the time or living your life in a movie house) since even a cow has this as the "end" of its life. But again, we cannot be happy without many and varied and mostly pleasant experiences. What is unique to man, Aristotle concludes, is his rationality, his ability to act on rational principles. It is the exercise of this rational ability that is happiness.

Of the various conceptions of the good life as pleasure, success, asceticism, freedom, power, creativity, religion, and happiness, some are available to virtually everyone (for example the life of simple pleasures or of asceticism), others are available only to a lucky few (the life of creativity, Aristotle's elite conception of happiness). But it must have struck you by now that all of these conceptions of the good life have left something out! However radical the differences between hedonism and the religious life, the success ethic and the ascetic life, the life of seeking wealth and the life of freedom, creativity or happiness in general, there is something that they all share in common. They are all self-centered; they make no mention of other people. They are all, in one form or another, varieties of *egoism*. This will not be true of Aristotle's philosophy as he develops it, we shall see; nor is it true of Socrates' moral life. One might hesitate to include the religious life of an isolated monk or an ascetic as "selfish" in any sense, but this much is clear, they take little account of our relations with other people and place their emphasis upon the good life for a single person.

EGOISM VERSUS ALTRUISM

There is a general philosophy of life that seems to have always been around, *egoism,* the view that people act for their own interests. People may also be moral, religious, socially helpful, but ultimately always with an eye to their

---

[8] Aristotle, *Nichomachean Ethics.*

own benefits. One of Socrates' opponents in *The Republic* states this view with
brutal clarity:

> What people say is that to do wrong is, in itself, a desirable thing; on
> the other hand, it is not at all desirable to suffer wrong, and the harm to the
> sufferer outweighs the advantage to the doer. Consequently, when men have
> had a taste of both, those who have not the power to seize the advantage
> and escape the harm decide that they would be better off if they made a
> compact neither to do wrong nor to suffer it. Hence they began to make laws
> and covenants with one another; and whatever the law prescribed they called
> lawful and right. That is what right or justice is and how it came into
> existence; it stands half-way between the best thing of all—to do wrong
> with impunity—and the worst, which is to suffer wrong without the power
> to retaliate. So justice is accepted as a compromise, and valued, not as
> good in itself, but for lack of power to do wrong; no man worthy of the
> name, who had that power, would ever enter into such a compact with any-
> one; he would be mad if he did. That, Socrates, is the nature of justice ac-
> cording to this account, and such the circumstances in which it arose.
>
> The next point is that men practise it against the grain, for lack of
> power to do wrong. How true that is, we shall best see if we imagine two
> men, one just, the other unjust, given full license to do whatever they like,
> and then follow them to observe where each will be led by his desires. We
> shall catch the just man taking the same road as the unjust; he will be moved
> by self-interest, the end which it is natural to every creature to pursue as
> good, until forcibly turned aside by law and custom to respect the principle
> of equality.
>
> Now, the easiest way to give them that complete liberty of action would
> be to imagine them possessed of the talisman found by Gyges, the ancestor
> of the famous Lydian. The story tells how he was a shepherd in the King's
> service. One day there was a great storm, and the ground where his flock
> was feeding was rent by an earthquake. Astonished at the sight, he went
> down into the chasm and saw, among other wonders of which the story
> tells, a brazen horse, hollow, with windows in its sides. Peering in, he saw a
> dead body, which seemed to be of more than human size. It was naked save
> for a gold ring, which he took from the finger and made his way out. When
> the shepherds met, as they did every month, to send an account to the King
> of the state of his flocks, Gyges came wearing the ring. As he was sitting
> with the others, he happened to turn the bezel of the ring inside his hand.
> At once he became invisible, and his companions, to his surprise, began to
> speak of him as if he had left them. Then, as he was fingering the ring, he
> turned the bezel outwards and became visible again. With that, he set about
> testing the ring to see if it really had this power, and always with the same
> result: according as he turned the bezel inside or out he vanised and re-
> appeared. After this discovery he contrived to be one of the messengers sent
> to the court. There he seduced the Queen, and with her help murdered the
> King and seized the throne.
>
> Now suppose there were two such magic rings, and one were given to
> the just man, the other to the unjust. No one, it is commonly believed,
> would have such iron strength of mind as to stand fast in doing right or

keep his hands off other men's goods, when he could go to the market-place and fearlessly help himself to anything he wanted, enter houses and sleep with any woman he chose, set prisoners free and kill men at his pleasure, and in a word go about among men with the powers of a god. He would behave no better than the other; both would take the same course. Surely this would be strong proof that men do right only under compulsion; no individual thinks of it as good for him personally, since he does wrong whenever he finds he has the power. Every man believes that wrongdoing pays him personally much better, and, according to this theory, that is the truth. Granted full licence to do as he liked, people would think him a miserable fool if they found him refusing to wrong his neighbours or to touch their belongings, though in public they would keep up a pretence of praising his conduct, for fear of being wrong themselves. So much for that.[9]

Egoism is the thesis that everyone acts for his or her own advantage, and the only reason why people act respectfully or kindly toward each other is because that too, for one reason or another, is to their advantage. It might be fear of punishment that makes them act "correctly"; some have "ulterior motives," that is, they expect other things later on, perhaps a favor in return, or reward in heaven after they die, or they are trying to avoid guilt, or are after a feeling of self-satisfaction. In popular language, the egoist position is often called "selfishness."

One of the most widely read contemporary egoists, Ayn Rand, has written of "the virture of selfishness." According to her, we all should act for our own interests. But this indicates that we must distinguish two very different forms of egoism, although people often confuse them. First, there is the position that everyone in fact acts according to his or her own interests; our psychology is such that we cannot help but act in this way. Accordingly, this position is called *psychological egoism*. The second position must be defended or attacked independently of the first. It is the thesis that people ought to act to satisfy their own interests, and this presupposes that they have a choice whether to act that way or not. This position is *ethical egoism*.

Both egoist positions are contrasted with what is usually called *altruism*, that is, acting for the sake of other people's interests. There are degrees of altruism. One may be altruistic because one acts morally, because he or she recognizes an obligation to other people. Or one may be altruistic in actually taking another person's interests as important or even more important than one's own interests, such as one often finds between lovers or brothers and sisters. Altruism can also be divided into two distinct theses, although these are not so often distinguished. There is *psychological altruism*, which says that people "naturally" act for each other's sakes. (We shall see this thesis defended by several important philosophers in later sections.) It has rarely been argued, however, that people are compelled to act altruistically. Thus psychological egoism is usually defended for all cases, psychological altruism, in contrast, is

[9] Plato, *The Republic,* BK. II, trans. Francis M. Cornford (Oxford: Oxford University Press, 1941).

only defended for some cases. *Ethical altruism,* on the other hand, says that people ought to act with each other's interests in mind. This is, of course, a basic statement of morality, best summarized in the so-called Golden Rule: "Do unto others as you would have them do unto you." (We shall see a modern version of this ancient teaching in the philosophy of Immanuel Kant.)

The most familiar and most difficult question is about psychological egoism: is it true that people only act for their own self-interest? A famous story about Abraham Lincoln is an apt illustration of the thesis. As he was arguing the psychological egoist position with a friend, his coach was passing a mud slide, where a mother pig was squealing as her piglets were drowning. Lincoln stopped the coach, saved the piglets, then moved on. His friend asked him whether that wasn't a clear case of altruism. Lincoln replied: "Why that was the very essence of selfishness. I should have had no peace of mind all day had I gone on and left that suffering old sow worrying over those piglets. I did it to get peace of mind, don't you see?"[10]

There are many actions which are based upon self-interest and are "selfish" without any question. The question is: are there any actions which are not based on self-interest? Lincoln's response is an excellent example because it would seem as if his action is not for selfish reasons at all. Yet, according to him, there was a selfish reason behind his actions; his own sense of satisfaction and "peace of mind." Could this be true of all our actions?

The arguments that are still considered to be the most powerful and definitive against psychological egoism were formulated as sermons by an English Bishop, Joseph Butler. Bishop Butler argued that such reasoning as Lincoln's turned on a number of fallacies. Butler begins by accepting the distinction between "private good and a person's own preservation and happiness" and "respect to society and the promotion of public good and the happiness of society." But then he insists that these are not, as the egoists argue, always in conflict and fighting against each other. To the contrary, they are almost always in perfect harmony.

> From this review and comparison of the nature of man as respecting self and as respecting society, it will plainly appear that there are as real and the same kind of indications in human nature that we were made for society and to do good to our fellow creatures, as that we were intended to take care of our own life and health and private good; and that the same objections lie against one of these assertions as against the other.
>
> First, there is a natural principle of *benevolence* in man, which is in some degree to *society* what *self-love* is to the *individual.* And if there be in mankind any disposition to friendship; if there be any such thing as compassion, for compassion is momentary love; if there be any such thing as the paternal or filial affections; if there by any affection in human nature the object and end of which is the good of another—this is itself benevolence or the love of another. Be it ever so short, be it in ever so low a degree, or ever so unhappily confined, it proves the assertion and points out what we were

[10] quoted in F. Sharp, *Ethics* (New York: Appleton-Century-Crofts, 1928).

designed for, as really as though it were in a higher degree and more extensive. I must however remind you that though benevolence and self-love are different, though the former tends most directly to public good, and the latter to private, yet they are so perfectly coincident that the greatest satisfactions to ourselves depend upon our having benevolence in a due degree, and that self-love is one chief security of our right behavior toward society. It may be added that their mutual coinciding, so that we can scarce promote one without the other, is equally a proof that we were made for both.

. . . . .

Secondly, this will further appear, from observing that the *several passions and affections,* which are distinct both from benevolence and self-love, do in general contribute and lead us to *public* good as really as to *private.* It might be thought too minute and particular, and would carry us too great a length, to distinguish between and compare together the several passions or appetites distinct from benevolence, whose primary use and intention is the security and good of society; and the passions distinct from self-love, whose primary intention and design is the security and good of the individual. It is enough to the present argument that desire of esteem from others, contempt and esteem of them, love of society as distinct from affection to the good of it, indignation against successful vice—that these are public affections or passions, have an immediate respect to others, naturally lead us to regulate our behavior in such a manner as will be of service to our fellow creatures. If any or all of these may be considered likewise as private affections, as tending to private good, this does not hinder them from being public affections, too, or destroy the good influence of them upon society, and their tendency to public good. It may be added that as persons without any conviction from reason of the desirableness of life would yet of course preserve it merely from the appetite of hunger, so by acting merely from regard (suppose) to reputation, without any consideration of the good of others, men often contribute to public good. In both these instances they are plainly instruments in the hands of another, in the hands of Providence, to carry on ends, the preservation of the individual and good of society, which they themselves have not in their view or intention. The sum is, men have various appetites, passions, and particular affections, quite distinct both from self-love and from benevolence—all of these have a tendency to promote both public and private good, and may be considered as respecting others and ourselves equally and in common; but some of them seem most immediately to respect others, or tend to public good, others of them most immediately to respect self, or tend to private good; as the former are not benevolence, so the latter are not self-love; neither sort are instances of our love either to ourselves or others, but only instances of our Maker's care and love both of the individual and the species, and proofs that He intended we should be instruments of good to each other, as well as that we should be so to ourselves.

Thirdly, there is a principle of reflection in men by which they distinguish between, approve and disapprove, their own actions. We are plainly constituted such sort of creatures as to reflect upon our own nature. The mind can take a view of what passes within itself, its propensions, aversions, passions, affections, as respecting such objects and in such degrees, and of the several actions consequent thereupon. In this survey it approves of one, disapproves of another, and toward a third is affected in neither of these ways, but is quite indifferent. This principle in man by which he approves or disapproves his heart, temper, and actions, is conscience.

.   .   .   .   .

And that this faculty tends to restrain men from doing mischief to each other, and leads them to do good, is too manifest to need being insisted upon. Thus a parent has the affection of love to his children; this leads him to take care of, to educate, to make due provision for them; the natural affection leads to this, but the reflection that it is his proper business, what belongs to him, that it is right and commendable so to do—this added to the affection becomes a much more settled principle and carries him on through more labor and difficulties for the sake of his children than he would undergo from that affection alone, if he thought it, and the course of action it led to, either indifferent or criminal. This indeed is impossible, to do that which is good and not to approve of it; for which reason they are frequently not considered as distinct, though they really are, for men often approve of the actions of others which they will not imitate, and likewise do that which they approve not. It cannot possibly be denied that there is this principle of reflection or conscience in human nature. Suppose a man to relieve an innocent person in great distress, suppose the same man afterwards, in the fury of anger, to do the greatest mischief to a person who had given no just cause of offense; to aggravate the injury, add the circumstances of former friendship and obligation from the injured person, let the man who is supposed to have done these two different actions coolly reflect upon them afterwards, without regard to their consequences to himself; to assert that any common man would be affected in the same way toward these different actions, that he would make no distinction between them, but approve or disapprove them equally, is too glaring a falsity to need being confuted. There is therefore this principle of reflection or conscience in mankind. It is needless to compare the respect it has to private good with the respect it has to public, since it plainly tends as much to the latter as to the former, and is commonly thought to tend chiefly to the latter. This faculty is now mentioned merely as another part in the inward frame of man, pointing out to us in some degree what we are intended for, and as what will naturally and of course have some influence. The particular place assigned to it by nature, what authority it has, and how great influence it ought to have, shall be hereafter considered.

From this comparison of benevolence and self-love, of our public and private affections, of the courses of life they lead to, and of the principle of reflection or conscience as respecting each of them, it is as manifest that we were made for society and to promote the happiness of it, as that we were intended to take care of our own life and health and private good.

.   .   .   .   .

If it be said that there are persons in the world who are in great measure without the natural affections toward their fellow creatures, there are like-

wise instances of persons without the common natural affections to themselves; but the nature of man is not to be judged of by either of these, but by
what appears in the common world, in the bulk of mankind.[11]

In short, Butler argues that merely acting on one's own desires does not
make an action selfish, for all actions are, in some sense, based on our desires,
but at least some of those desires are desires to serve someone else's interests.
Thus the "object" of desire is what makes an act selfish or unselfish, not
merely the fact that one's own desire is acted upon. Nor can simply acting
with some benefit to oneself make an action selfish, for even if we agreed that
an act gives us some benefit (for example, peace of mind), it may still be the
case that most of the benefit is for someone else. Even if peace of mind typically
follows virtuous actions, that does not show that our motivation is selfish. The
satisfaction that accompanies good acts is itself not the motivation of the act.
Here is the answer to Lincoln. His act was, despite his philosophical claims, an
altruistic one; his satisfaction was not the motive of the act but only its consequence. (This part of the argument is identical with Aristotle's argument
against hedonism; pleasure often accompanies or follows our actions, but that
does not mean that we act in order to obtain that pleasure.) And, if psychological egoism is not always true, then altruism is at least possible.

But even if altruism is possible, it is still an open question whether it is
desirable. An ethical egoist, for example, would admit that altruism is possible,
but would attack it all the same. Ayn Rand, for example, in her popular
polemics on "the virtue of selfishness" argues, after first attacking the common
notion of selfishness, that the strict definition of this word is "concern with
one's own interest." She then launches into a diatribe against altruism.

> If it is true that what I mean by "selfishness" is not what is meant
> conventionally, then *this* is one of the worst indictments of altruism: it
> means that altruism *permits no concept* of a self-respecting, self-supporting
> man—a man who supports his life by his own effort and neither sacrifices
> himself nor others. It means that altruism permits no view of men except as
> sacrificial animals and profiteers-on-sacrifice, as victims and parasites—that
> it permits no concept of a benevolent coexistence among men—that it per-
> mits no concept of *justice*.[12]

The argument here is extreme and utilizes the same kind of fallacy that
the psychological egoist employs. The argument contrasts the notion of "acting
in one's own interest" (that is, selfishness) with self-sacrificing and lack of
self-respect. That is, if an act is for the benefit of others, then it cannot be to
one's own benefit as well. Similarly, if an act is not in one's own interests, it is
an act that denies one's self-respect. You can see how unjust this extreme
contrast is, treating all human situations as if they must be either white or
black. Our every action and intention is aimed at a large number of goals:
some are immediate, others are long range, some are means, others are ends,

---

[11] Bishop Joseph Butler, *Five Sermons* (New York: Bobbs-Merrill, 1950).
[12] Ayn Rand, *The Virtue of Selfishness* (New York: Signet, 1961).

some are central, others are virtually by-products. But to pretend that every action and intention can be simply defined by a single goal—either self-interest or other people's interest—is to treat human action as we might treat the actions of rats or bees, as inhumanly simple-minded.

It is true that people who follow the rules of morality without any exception may hurt themselves and other people as well. A person who refuses to tell a lie under any circumstances may well be self-sacrificing in just this way. But surely this is not the central source of all our modern woes. For every act of unnecessary self-sacrifice, there are a hundred acts of inconsiderate selfishness, which degrade the doer and do harm to others. But the problem is not, as Ms. Rand suggests, to choose between these. It does not follow from the fact that unnecessary self-sacrifice is undesirable that acting for the benefit of others is equally undesirable. Acting for the benefit of others is only rarely self-sacrifice, and very rarely unnecessary self-sacrifice. Even the paragon of self-sacrifice, the martyr, sees him or herself as gaining at least self-respect. And the paragon of action in one's own interest according to Ms. Rand's own ethic, the business-person who dedicates everything to personal achievement, may end up "sacrificing" him or herself and self-respect most of all.

To act strictly according to "one's own self-interest" is to rob oneself of the richness of goals for both self and others that gives human action its complex social and personal textures. This is not for a second to say that we should always—or even ever—act against our self-interests. It is rather to say that any philosophy of human life will have to begin with a far richer conception of morality and human motivation than this limited ethical egoism. This is the main thrust of Bishop Butler's arguments.

In order to make her thesis more palatable, Ms. Rand adds the insistence that what she means by "selfishness" must be both rational selfishness and enlightened egoism. What this means, however, is that what initially seems to be in our self-interest may not be, and what seems not to be in our self-interest may, on a larger view, be in our self-interest after all. Thus she argues that acting in one's own self interest, in an enlightened way, will result in the mutual benefit of us all. Now, in one sense, this is an extremely respectable philosophy, and we shall discuss it at length under the name *utilitarianism*. But it is important to distinguish the two theses, for the utilitarian is perfectly aware that the general welfare may require the sacrifice of personal self-interests in a great many cases. Ms. Rand refuses to acknowledge this. And to suppose that acting in our exclusive self-interest without sacrifice or attention to the welfare of others will in fact turn out to be to our mutual benefit is so contrary to our every experience that it cannot be made into a convincing thesis even in fiction. Not only is it unlikely that a compendium of selfish acts will add up to everybody's good, the very fact that everyone is "out for his or her own interest" will cause more conflict and harm through mutual jealousy and unnecessary competitiveness than mere selfishness will. Psychological egoism is a problem; if it is true then we have to teach people to consider other people's interests to be their own. But ethical egoism is more than a problem; as an ideology, telling us all to be even more selfish than we usually are, it may be a social disaster.

Psychological altruism in a universal sense has never had much of a following as such. The view that people always act for other people's benefit is so contrary to our experience that virtually no one, no matter how idealistic, has ever defended it. At most, it is argued that we have the psychological capacity for altruism, that we at least sometimes feel pangs of sympathy for the other person, and, if certain misunderstandings and unnecessary social pressures are corrected, then people will act altruistically. We shall later see such positions argued by David Hume and Jean-Jacques Rousseau. But again, we must distinguish the claim that we can act altruistically from the claim that we ought to do so.

Among the various possibilities of altruism, one stands out above all others—morality. Morality is not, strictly speaking, action for the sake of others, although that is typically a part of it. Morality is action for the sake of principle. And since these principles are believed to hold whatever a person's self-interests, it makes little sense to suppose that morality itself is selfish. Of course, it may still be that people are moral only because of selfish reasons, because of fear of being punished, for example, or because they believe it will bring them reward in heaven. And we all know people who use morality to further their own self-interests. But whether or not this is so, morality must be discussed in its own terms, even if there may be egoistic or selfish motivation "behind it" as well.

MORALITY

Morality gives us the rules by which we live with other people. It sets limits to our desires and our actions. It tells us what is permitted and what is not. It gives us guiding principles for making decisions. It tells us what we ought and what we ought not to do. But what is this "morality" that sounds so impersonal and "above" us? It is important to begin with an appreciation for the metaphor, which so well characterizes moral rules. Nietzsche describes it this way: "A tablet of virtues hangs over every people."

This "tablet of virtues" is morality. The prototype of morality, on this view, are those ancient codes, carved in stone, with commands that are eternal and absolute. We know best the two tablets inscribed by God, in front of Moses, which we call the Ten Commandments. And they are indeed *commandments*. "Thou shalt" and "Thou shalt not" is all they say. And this is the essence of morality. It consists of commands. These commands, unlike the conceptions of the good life that we discussed in the first section, do not appeal to individual pleasures or desires. They do not make different demands on different individuals or societies. Quite to the contrary, they are absolute rules which tell us what we must do or not do, no matter who we are, no matter what we want, and regardless of whether our interests will be served by the command or not. "Thou shalt not kill" means, even if you want to, even if you have the power to, and even if you can escape all punishment you are absolutely forbidden to kill.

The image of morality as coming "from above" is appropriate. First, because moral laws are often said, and not only in our society, to come from God. Secondly, because we learn these laws from our parents, who literally "stand over us" and indoctrinate us with them through their shouts, commands, examples, threats, and gestures. Finally, and most importantly, morality itself is "above" any given individual or individuals, whether it is canonized in the laws of society or not. Morality is not just another aid in getting us what we want, it is entirely concerned with right and wrong. And these considerations are "above" tampering by any individual, no matter how powerful, as if they have a life of their own.

This characteristic of morality as independent of individual desires and ambitions has led many people to characterize morality simply in terms of some absolute and independent agency. Most often, this absolute and independent agency is God. Saint Augustine, for example, talks about morality in this way.

> . . . Unless you turn to Him and repay the existence that He gave you, you won't be "nothing"; you will be wretched. All things owe to God, first of all, what they are insofar as they are natures. Then, those who have received a will owe to Him whatever better thing they can will to be, and whatever they ought to be. No man is ever blamed for what he has not been given, but he is justly blamed if he has not done what he should have done; and if he has received free will and sufficient power, he stands under obligation. When a man does not do what he ought, God the Creator is not at fault. It is to His glory that a man suffers justly; and by blaming a man for not doing what he should have done, you are praising what he ought to do. You are praised for seeing what you ought to do, even though you see this only through God, who is immutable Truth:[13]

And St. Thomas Aquinas: ". . . it is apparent that things prescribed by divine law are right, not only because they are put forth by law, but also because they are in accord with nature." Or ". . . Therefore by divine law precepts had to be given, so that each man would give his neighbor his due and would abstain from doing injuries to him."[14] And in the Bible: "When thou shalt harken—to the voice of the Lord thy God, to keep all his commandments, which I command thee this day, to do that which is right in the Eyes of the Lord thy God."[15]

But, whether or not one believes in God, it is clear that something further is needed to help us define morality. Even assuming that there is a God, we need a way of determining what His moral commands must be. One might say that He has given these commands to various individuals, but the fact is

[13] St. Augustine, *On Freedom* (New York: Bobbs-Merrill, 1956).
[14] St. Thomas Aquinas, *Summa Contra Gentiles,* BK. III (New York: Doubleday, 1955).
[15] Deuteronomy, 13:18

that different people seem to have very different ideas about the morality that God has given them. Some, for example, would say that it explicitly rules out abortion and infanticide. Others would argue that God does not rule these out, but makes it clear that they are, like other forms of killing (a "holy war," for example), justifiable only in certain circumstances. And in view of such disagreements, we cannot simply appeal to God but must, for reasons that we can formulate and defend, define our morality for ourselves. There is the further question, which has often been debated, whether we should follow God's laws just because they are His or rather, whether God is good because His laws are good. If the latter, then we have to decide what is good in order to know that God is good. If the former, then one has to decide whether or not to believe in God precisely on the basis of whether we can accept those laws. Either way, we have to decide for ourselves what laws of morality we are willing to accept.

Similar considerations hold true of that familiar appeal to conscience in determining what we ought to do or not do. Even if one believes that conscience is God-given, the same problems emerge again. Should we follow our consciences just because "conscience tells us to?" Or do we follow our conscience just because we know that what our conscience commands is good. And if one believes that conscience is simply the internalization of the moral teachings of one's parents and society, then the question takes an extra dimension: should we accept or reject what we have been taught? Since our consciences often disagree, we must still decide which rules of conscience one ought to obey. Conscience doesn't determine what we ought to do, it only reminds us of rules we have already accepted.

IS MORALITY RELATIVE?

Moralities, like lifestyles and conceptions of the good life, vary from culture to culture, and even from person to person. But while there is nothing surprising about the fact that lifestyles vary, there is a problem in the variation of moralities. Morality, by its very nature, is supposed to be a set of universal principles, principles which do not distinguish between cultures or peoples or lifestyles. If it is morally reprehensible to kill for fun, then it is morally reprehensible in every society, in every culture, for every lifestyle, and for every person, no matter who he or she is. And this will be true even if the society or person in question does not agree with that moral principle. Aristotle, for example, discusses at length what he calls "the wicked man," who does evil because he believes in immoral principles and therefore acts without regret, unlike the person who acts badly from momentary weakness, force of circumstances, desperation, or misinformation. But on what grounds can one society or person claim that another society's or person's principles are immoral? How could European Christians, for example, be justified in criticizing the sexual morality of Polynesians in the South Pacific? The Polynesians were a separate society, with their own mores and principles which worked quite well for them, possibly even better in certain ways than the European customs worked in Europe. Yet European missionaries felt no hesitation whatever in condemning their sexual practices as "immoral." And similarly but more seriously, what gives us the right to criticize a culture across the world that still believes in genocide as a legitimate consequence of war or in torture as a way of keeping civil order? We surely feel that we have the right to speak up in such cases, but then we too are asserting the universality of our morality, extending it even to people who might explicitly reject our principles. How can we do this? What justifies such an extension?

The problem of relativism has become extremely controversial since the nineteenth century, when anthropologists began telling us of exotic societies with moralities so different from ours. In a sense, relativism has always been a threat to established morality, for even the Greeks came into contact with societies that were much different from theirs. (Thus their tendency to immediately label anything non-Greek "barbarian," so that they didn't have to consider the possibility of relativism.) Kant was the most vigorous opponent of relativism, for his conception of morality was such that, if a human being was to count as rational at all, he or she had to agree to at least the basic principles of a universal morality. There were people and societies that did not, but that, according to Kant, only proved that they were less than rational (and therefore less than human as well). Today, we tend to be more liberal in our acceptance of different styles of life, but few people would be ready to deny that some moral principles, at least, hold of every society whatever. The principle that unnecessary cruelty is wrong, for example, would be such a principle, although people might well disagree about what was "cruel" and what was "unnecessary."

Philosophers generally distinguish two theses. First, there is the factual claim that different societies have different moralities. This is called *cultural relativism*. The difficult question is whether these different moralities are only different superficially or whether they are fundamentally different. For example, eskimos of certain tribes kill their elders by leaving them to freeze on the ice; we consider that grossly immoral (we send most of our elders to frigid "old-age homes" instead). But the question of cultural relativity is whether this difference is merely the reflection of different interpretations of some basic moral principle (such as, don't kill anyone unless it is absolutely necessary for the survival of the rest) or whether it really is a wholly different morality. This is among the most controversial anthropological questions of our time. But philosophers are interested in a somewhat different question: assuming that two moralities really are fundamentally different, is it possible that each is as correct as the other? The philosopher who says "yes" is an *ethical relativist*. And it is ethical relativism that will occupy us here.

In the following selection, the English-American philosopher Walter Stace presents the ethical relativist position and its traditional opponent, *ethical absolutism,* the view that there is only one correct morality. Stace's own answer to the problem is more of an absolutist solution: later in the same work he says that "happiness" is a universal and absolute value, and therefore cross-cultural evaluations are possible.

There is an opinion widely current nowadays in philosophical circles which passes under the name of "ethical relativity." Exactly what this phrase means or implies is certainly far from clear. But unquestionably it stands as a label for the opinions of a group of ethical philosophers whose position is roughly on the extreme left wing among the moral theorizers of the day. And perhaps one may best understand it by placing it in contrast with the opposite kind of extreme view against which, undoubtedly, it has arisen as a protest. For among moral philosophers one may clearly distinguish a left and a right wing. Those of the left wing are the ethical relativists. They are the revolutionaries, the clever young men, the up to date. Those of the right wing we may call the ethical absolutists. They are the conservatives and the old-fashioned.

According to the absolutists there is but one eternally true and valid moral code. This moral code applies with rigid impartiality to all men. What is a duty for me must likewise be a duty for you. And this will be true whether you are an Englishman, a Chinaman, or a Hottentot. If cannibalism is an abomination in England or America, it is an abomination in central Africa, notwithstanding that the African may think otherwise. The fact that he sees nothing wrong in his cannibal practices does not make them for him morally right. They are as much contrary to morality for him as they are for us. The only difference is that he is an ignorant savage who does not know this. There is not one law for one man or race of men, another for another. There is not one moral standard for Europeans, another for Indians, another for Chinese. There is but one law, one standard, one morality, for all men. And this standard, this law, is absolute and unvarying.

Moreover, as the one moral law extends its dominion over all the corners of the earth, so too it is not limited in its application by any considerations of time or period. That which is right now was right in the centuries of Greece and Rome, nay, in the very ages of the cave man. That which is evil now was evil then. If slavery is morally wicked today, it was morally wicked among the ancient Athenians, notwithstanding that their greatest men accepted it as a necessary condition of human society. Their opinion did not make slavery a moral good for them. It only showed that they were, in spite of their otherwise noble conceptions, ignorant of what is truly right and good in this matter.

The ethical absolutist recognizes as a fact that moral customs and moral ideas differ from country to country and from age to age. This indeed seems manifest and not to be disputed. We think slavery morally wrong, the Greeks thought it morally unobjectionable. The inhabitants of New Guinea certainly have very different moral ideas from ours. But the fact that the Greeks or the inhabitants of New Guinea think something right does not make it right, even for them. Nor does the fact that we think the same things wrong make them wrong. They are *in themselves* either right or wrong. What we have to do is to discover which they are. What anyone thinks makes no difference.

It is here just as it is in matters of physical science. We believe the earth to be a globe. Our ancestors may have thought it flat. This does not show that it *was* flat, and is *now* a globe. What it shows is that men having in other ages been ignorant about the shape of the earth have now learned the truth. So if the Greeks thought slavery morally legitimate, this does not indicate that it was for them and in that age morally legitimate, but rather that they were ignorant of the truth of the matter.

. . . . .

Now ethical absolutism was, in its central ideas, the product of Christian theology. The connection is not difficult to detect. For morality has been conceived, during the Christian dispensation, as issuing from the will of God. That indeed was its single and all-sufficient source. There would be no point, for the naïve believer in the faith, in the philosopher's questions regarding the foundations of morality and the basis of moral obligation. Even to ask such questions is a mark of incipient religious scepticism. For the true believer the author of the moral law is God. What pleases God, what God commands—that is the definition of right. What displeases God, what he forbids—that is the definition of wrong. Now there is, for the Christian monotheist, only one God ruling over the entire universe. And this God is rational, self-consistent. He does not act upon whims. Consequently his will and his commands must be the same everywhere. They will be unvarying for all peoples and in all ages. If the heathen have other moral ideas than ours—inferior ideas—that can only be because they live in ignorance of the true God. If they knew God and his commands, their ethical precepts would be the same as ours.

. . . . .

This explains why ethical absolutism, until very recently, was not only believed by philosophers but *taken for granted without any argument*. The ideas of philosophers, like the ideas of everyone else, are largely moulded by the civilizations in which they live. Their philosophies are largely attempts to state in abstract terms and in self-consistent language the stock of ideas which they have breathed in from the atmosphere of their social environment. This accounts for the large number of so-called "unrecognized presuppositions" with which systems of philosophy always abound. These presuppositions are simply the ideas which the authors of the systems have breathed in with the intellectual atmospheres by which they happen to be surrounded—which they have taken over therefore as a matter of course, without argument, without criticism, without even a suspicion that they might be false.

It is not therefore at all surprising to find that Immanuel Kant, writing in the latter half of the eighteenth century, not only took the tenets of ethical absolutism for granted, but evidently considered that no instructed person would dispute them. It is a noticeable feature of his ethical philosophy that he gives no reasons whatever to support his belief in the existence of a universally valid moral law. He assumes as a matter of course that his readers will accept this view. And he proceeds at once to enquire what is the metaphysical foundation of the universal moral law. That alone is what interests him. *Assuming* that there does exist such a law, how, he asks, can this be the case, and what, in the way of transcendental truth, does it imply? It never occurs to him to reflect that any philosopher who should choose to question his fundamental assumption could outflank his whole ethical position; and that if this assumption should prove false his entire moral philosophy would fall to the ground like a pack of cards.

We can now turn to the consideration of ethical relativity which is the proper subject of this chapter. The revolt of the relativists against absolutism is, I believe, part and parcel of the general revolutionary tendency of our times. In particular it is a result of the decay of belief in the dogmas of orthodox religion. Belief in absolutism was supported, as we have seen, by belief in Christian monotheism. And now that, in an age of widespread religious scepticism, that support is withdrawn, absolutism tends to collapse. Revolutionary movements are as a rule, at any rate in their first onset, purely negative. They attack and destroy. And ethical relativity is, in its essence, a purely negative creed. It is simply a denial of ethical absolutism. That is why the best way of explaining it is to begin by explaining ethical absolutism. If we understand that what the latter asserts the former denies, then we understand ethical relativity.

Any ethical position which denies that there is a single moral standard which is equally applicable to all men at all times may fairly be called a species of ethical relativity. There is not, the relativist asserts, merely one moral law, one code, one standard. There are many moral laws, codes, standards. What morality ordains in one place or age may be quite different from what morality ordains in another place or age. The moral code of Chinamen is quite different from that of Europeans, that of African savages quite different from both. Any morality, therefore, is relative to the age, the place, and the circumstances in which it is found. It is in no sense absolute.

This does not mean merely—as one might at first sight be inclined to suppose—that the very same kind of action which is *thought* right in one country and period may be *thought* wrong in another. This would be a mere platitude, the truth of which everyone would have to admit. Even the absolutist would admit this—would even wish to emphasize it—since he is well aware that different peoples have different sets of moral ideas, and his whole point is that some of these sets of ideas are false. What the relativist means to assert is, not this platitude, but that the very same kind of action which *is* right in one country and period may *be* wrong in another. And this, far from being a platitude, is a very startling assertion.

It is very important to grasp thoroughly the difference between the two ideas. For there is reason to think that many minds tend to find ethical relativity attractive because they fail to keep them clearly apart. It is so very obvious that moral ideas differ from country to country and from age to age. And it is so very easy, if you are mentally lazy, to suppose that to say this means the same as to say that no universal moral standard exists,— or in other words that it implies ethical relativity. We fail to see that the word "standard" is used in two different senses. It is perfectly true that, in one sense, there are many variable moral standards. We speak of judging a man by the standard of his time. And this implies that different times have different standards. And this, of course, is quite true. But when the word "standard" is used in this sense it means simply the set of moral ideas current during the period in question. It means what people *think* right, whether as a matter of fact it *is* right or not. On the other hand when the absolutist asserts that there exists a single universal moral "standard," he is not using the word in this sense at all. He means by "standard" what *is* right as distinct from what people merely think right. His point is that although what people think right varies in different countries and periods, yet what actually is right is everywhere and always the same. And it follows that when the ethical relativist disputes the position of the absolutist and denies that any universal moral standard exists he too means by "standard" what actually is right. But it is exceedingly easy, if we are not careful, to slip loosely from using the word in the first sense to using it in the second sense; and to suppose that the variability of moral beliefs is the same thing as the variability of what really is moral. And unless we keep the two senses of the word "standard" distinct, we are likely to think the creed of ethical relativity much more plausible than it actually is.

The genuine relativist, then, does not merely mean that Chinamen may think right what Frenchmen think wrong. He means that what *is* wrong for the Frenchman may *be* right for the Chinaman. And if one enquires how, in those circumstances, one is to know what actually is right in China or in France, the answer comes quite glibly. What is right in China is the same as what people think right in China; and what is right in France is the same as what people think right in France. So that, if you want to know what is moral in any particular country or age all you have to do is to ascertain what are the moral ideas current in that age or country. Those ideas are, *for that age or country,* right. Thus what is morally right is identified with what is thought to be morally right, and the distinction which we made above between these two is simply denied. To put the same thing in another way, it is denied that there can be or ought to be any distinction between the two senses of the word "standard." There is only one kind of standard of right and wrong, namely, the moral ideas current in any particular age or country.

· · · · ·

To sum up. The ethical relativist consistently denies, it would seem, whatever the ethical absolutist asserts. For the absolutist there is a single universal moral standard. For the relativist there is no such standard. There are only local, ephemeral, and variable standards. For the absolutist there are two senses of the word "standard." Standards in the sense of sets of current moral ideas are relative and changeable. But the standard in the sense of what is actually morally right is absolute and unchanging. For the relativist no such distinction can be made. There is only one meaning of the word standard, namely, that which refers to local and variable sets of moral ideas. Or if it is insisted that the word must be allowed two meanings, then the relativist will say that there is at any rate no actual example of a standard in the absolute sense, and that the word as thus used is an empty name to which nothing in reality corresponds; so that the distinction between the two meanings becomes empty and useless. Finally—though this is merely saying the same thing in another way—the absolutist makes a distinction between what actually is right and what is thought right. The relativist rejects this distinction and identifies what is moral with what is thought moral by certain human beings or groups of human beings.[16]

SUMMARY AND CONCLUSION

"The good life" is the traditional philosophical name for the ideal human life. While there has been general agreement about a few conditions necessary for the good life, for example general health and freedom from enduring physical pain, there have been many different views concerning the primary goals of the ideal life for men and women. Many philosophers and many ordinary people have argued that the good life is the life of pleasure, eating, drinking, sex and whatever else one most enjoys. But are these in fact the goals of our lives, or are they only welcome distractions and rewards? Other people and other philosophers have suggested that success is the key to the good life. Still others have said "wealth," or "power." There have been philosophers who have denied all of these and instead sought a life of minimal desires and expectations, the life of asceticism. Many thinkers have argued that religion is the key to the good life, while others have argued that creativity is the most important goal for people to strive for. Finally, some philosophers have held the view that happiness is the goal of the good life. But happiness, unlike these other suggestions, is not a single goal to be striven for so much as the result of successfully completing one's goals in general. Thus the question arises, "what is necessary for us to be happy?"

Those conceptions of the good life that focus solely on one's own desires and interests are called "egoism." According to the doctrine of ethical egoism, we ought to look after our own interests; according to the doctrine of psychological egoism, we cannot help but look after our own interests, even when we seem to be concerned with other people. Against this, the doctrine of psychological altruism says that true concern for other people is possible, and ethical altruism further insists that we ought to help other people, even when it goes against our own interests.

Among those conceptions of the good life that include concern for other people, one set of considerations requires special attention. When action is based on universal principles about what one ought to do, we have entered the realm of morality. Morality is a set of commandments that are binding on everyone, regardless of who they are, and regardless of the particular circumstances of the case, the particular feelings of everyone involved, and the power or status of the people involved. For example, the commandment, "do not kill!" is a moral commandment because it applies to everyone, in every society,

[16] Walter Stace, *The Concept of Morals* (New York: Macmillan, 1937).

and not just to some people and not others. If it is really immoral to kill, then it is immoral for anyone to kill, no matter what the circumstances. Of course, we qualify such principles in many ways, making certain kinds of exceptions and exclusions. (For example, that it is permissible to kill someone in self-defense.) But these qualifications too are a matter of universality; an exception that can be made for one person must be made for anyone else in similar circumstances. The key to morality is precisely this emphasis on universality.

If moral principles are universal, does that mean that they apply equally in every society and for every person, no matter whether they accept that morality or not? Many philosophers have insisted that, no matter what the differences in cultures and lifestyles, moral principles are absolute, and therefore applicable without exception. Other philosophers have insisted that a set of moral principles is relative to a particular society; that morality can be judged only within that particular society and not absolutely.

GLOSSARY

altruism: the thesis that one ought to act for the sake of the interests of others.

asceticism: a conception of the good life that preaches self-denial and simplicity. The life of a monk, for example, may be said to be ascetic in this sense.

conscience: a sense or feeling about what is right and wrong, usually without argument. (It is like intuition in matters of knowledge.) In Christian moral theory, it is a moral sense instilled in us by God. In Freudian psychology, it is the internalization of the moral lessons given us as children by our parents and teachers.

contemplation (the life of): according to Aristotle (and other philosophers), the happiest life, the life of thought and philosophy.

cultural relativism: the thesis that different societies have different moralities. It is important to stress that these moralities must be fundamentally different, not only different in details. Some societies consider an act as stealing while others do not; but a society that does not have a conception of private property might be fundamentally different from one that does.

egoism: the thesis that people act for their own interests. *Psychological egoism* is merely the thesis that they in fact act in their own interests; *ethical egoism* is the thesis that people ought to act in their own interests.

ethics: a system of moral principles and a conception of the good life. Or, the study of moral principles and the search for the good life.

ethical egoism: the thesis that people ought to act in their own interests.

ethical relativism: the thesis that different moralities may be equally correct, even if they directly contradict each other. A morality is "correct," on this thesis, merely if it is correct according to the particular society that accepts it.

good life (the): the ideal way for a person to live.

happiness: the achievement of the good life. In Aristotle, the name we all agree to give to the good life, whatever it is. Happiness, in this sense, must not be confused with pleasure, which is but one (among many) concerns and conceptions of the good life.

hedonism: the conception of the good life that takes pleasure to be the ultimate good.

morality: in general, the rules for right action and prohibitions against wrong acts. Sometimes, morality is that single set of absolute rules and prohibitions that are valid for all men at all times and all societies. More loosely, a morality can be any set of ultimate principles, and there might be any number of moralities in different societies.

pleasure: in general, simply enjoying oneself or being pleased. Narrowly, pleasure is a more-or-less distinct set of physical sensations, as in sexual touch or culinary taste. More broadly, it may mean anything that satisfies. These differences are important for those who say the good life is pleasure (hedonists). The life of physical pleasure is a very narrow life that rules out a great many activities; the life of being satisfied, however, rules nothing out, and could be used to describe even the life of a religious ascetic or a success-driven businessman. Accordingly, there is no point in talking about pleasure in this general sense as a specific philosophy.

psychological egoism: the thesis that people always act for their own self-interest, even when it seems as if they are acting for other people's benefit (for example, in giving to charity, the egoist would say, the person is simply making him/herself feel self-righteous).

relativism: the thesis that morals are relative to particular societies, particular interests, particular circumstances or particular individuals. (See, *cultural relativism, ethical relativism.*)

selfishness: acting in one's own interest to the exclusion of other's interests. The word has a nasty connotation, and so should be separated from the more neutral claims of the psychological egoist. To say that a person is acting selfishly is to condemn him or her and say that the action is blameworthy. It is possible to act for one's own interests, however, and not be selfish, for one may also act for the benefit of others. A selfish act is to the exclusion of other people's interests; an act may be both in one's own interests and in the interests of others, however.

12

PERSPECTIVES ON MORALITY

Act as if the maxim of your action were to become by your will a universal law of nature.

Immanuel Kant

Morality is generally characterized by its independence of individual interests and desires. But because of this, the question arises, why should people act contrary to their own interests and desires? In other words, why should we be moral? This question, in turn, illuminates the nature of morality. For many authors, morality is once again tied to self-interest, at least in an abstract way, and they argue that morality is the best way of satisfying everyone's interests. Other philosophers retain the rigid distinction between morality and self-interest and insist that obedience to morality is good for its own sake, or equivalent to being rational, or simply required in order to make us human. Finally, some authors have argued that morality is only one among many sets of principles, which we may but need not choose to obey.

In this chapter, we shall look at five different perspectives on morality. First, we shall discuss the ethics of Aristotle, who based his conception of morality on the concept of "virtue" and his idea that man is by nature a social and a rational animal. In this discussion, we shall also have the opportunity of examining a moral system that is significantly different, but still closely related to our own. Second, we shall discuss the moral theories of Hume and Rousseau, who take morality to be based upon certain distinctive feelings. Then, we shall examine the moral theory of Immanuel Kant, who insisted that morality is strictly a matter of practical reason, divorced from all personal interests and desires, and based solely upon universal principles or laws. We shall then discuss the moral theories of the "utilitarians," who argued

437

that moral principles were merely rules of thumb for achieving the greatest good for the greatest number of people, and who thereby tried to reconcile the interests of the individual with the interests of everyone else. Finally, we shall discuss the more radical theories of Nietzsche and the existentialists, who insist that, in an important sense we choose our moralities, and that this choice cannot be justified in any of the ways argued by other modern philosophers. For Nietzsche, at least, this view also includes a retrospective appreciation of the morality of the Greeks, and he argues that we should inject some of their conceptions into our own.

MORALITY AS VIRTUE:
ARISTOTLE

Aristotle's *Ethics* (properly called the *Nichomachean Ethics*) is the best systematic guide to ancient Greek moral thinking in our possession. The key to Greek ethics is the concept of virtue. This in turn is based upon a very special conception of man, and the key to Aristotle's ethics, as we saw in an earlier section, is to find "the natural good for man." This is, as we saw, a conception of man as rational. Virtue, accordingly, is rational activity, activity in accordance with a rational principle. Happiness, in its turn, is defined as "activity of the soul in accordance with perfect virtue." (This is the key phrase of his work.) This "perfect virtue" is also called excellence, and thus Aristotle's ethics is often called an ethics of self-realization, whose goal is to make each individual as perfect as possible in all ways:

> The function of man is a certain kind of life, and this to be an activity or actions of the soul implying a rational principle, and the function of a good man is the good and noble performance of these, and if any action is well performed when it is performed in accordance with the appropriate excellence: if this is the case, human good turns out to be activity of soul in accordance with virtue, and if there are more than one virtue, in accordance with the best and most complete.
>
> But we must add 'in a complete life.' For one swallow does not make a summer, nor does one day; and so too one day, or a short time, does not make a man blessed and happy. . . . happiness is an activity of soul in accordance with perfect virtue. . . .[1]

So far, however, it sounds as if virtue and happiness are strictly individual matters. But this is not the case. As important as these other principles is Aristotle's well-known belief that man is a social animal. Thus the principles of reason and rationality that enter into his *Ethics* will have the interests of society as well as the individual built into them. (Aristotle even says that there is no real distinction between ethics and politics, and that the proper end of

[1] Aristotle, *Nichomachean Ethics*, in *The Oxford Translation of Aristotle*, trans. W. D. Ross (Oxford: Oxford University Press, 1925).

ethics is politics.) Virtue, accordingly, is also a social conception, and most of the virtues Aristotle discusses, for example, justice and courage, have much to do with one's role in society. Happiness in general, therefore, has its social dimensions. For example, Aristotle argues that both respect and honor are ingredients in the good life. This is very different from those conceptions of the good life (for example, hedonism) that can be sought after in the absence of society or in rebellion against society. For Aristotle, the happy person, the virtuous person, is mainly a good citizen. It is necessary to add, however, that the only people who could qualify for Aristotle's good life were Greek citizens, which meant that women, children, slaves, and anyone who did not have the good fortune to be born Greek did not even have a chance at being happy, in Aristotle's sense.[2]

Not only does happiness have a social dimension and not only are the virtues socially defined, but the good life, according to Aristotle, must be taught to us by society. Accordingly, Aristotle talks a great deal about the need for "good education," and he goes so far as to say that, if a person has not been brought up "properly," then no amount of philosophy will be able to make him either virtuous or happy. He also says that young people, because they are "inexperienced in the actions of life" and are "so ruled by their passions," should not try to learn moral philosophy, which depends upon maturity and rationality. On this point, however, we will ignore Aristotle's warnings. For we have seen that growing older and more "mature" is certainly no guarantee of wisdom, and the passions of youth are sometimes more virtuous than the "rationality" of established maturity.

We have already seen Aristotle's beginning: every act has its goal (or "good"), and ultimately there is a goal (or "chief good") towards which all human acts aim, and that is generally called happiness (*eudaimonia*). But, Aristotle adds, this is not much help, for people give very different accounts of what they take to be the ingredients in happiness. Some say that it is pleasure, others say it is wealth or honor. We have seen Aristotle's arguments against these views (p. 415) and his conclusion that happiness must be "activity in accordance with rational principle." And that means, virtuous activity. The key to Aristotle's ethics, then, lies in his concept of virtue:

> Virtue being of two kinds, intellectual and moral, intellectual virtue in the main owes both its birth and its growth to teaching (for which reason it requires experience and time), while moral virtue comes about as a result of habit, whence also its name *ethike* is one that is formed by a slight variation from the word *ethos* (habit). From this it is also plain that none of the moral virtues arises in us by nature; for nothing that exists by nature

[2] Even in an introductory course, it is necessary to say something about Aristotle's special notion of *happiness*. It is not at all like our conception of "feeling happy." Aristotle's term (*eudaimonia*) means more like "living well," and it includes such matters as one's status in society and virtuous acts as well as good feelings. No matter how good you feel about yourself—even if you are in a state of ecstasy all of the time— you would not be happy in Aristotle's sense unless you had these other advantages and acted virtuously as well.

can form a habit contrary to its nature. For instance the stone which by nature moves downwards cannot be habituated to move upwards, not even if one tries to train it by throwing it up ten thousand times; nor can fire be habituated to move downwards, nor can anything else that by nature behaves in one way be trained to behave in another. Neither by nature, then, nor contrary to nature do the virtues arise in us; rather we are adapted by nature to receive them, and are made perfect by habit.

Again, of all the things that come to us by nature we first acquire the potentiality and later exhibit the activity (this is plain in the case of the senses; for it was not by often seeing or often hearing that we got these senses, but on the contrary we had them before we used them, and did not come to have them by using them); but the virtues we get by first exercising them, as also happens in the case of the arts as well. For the things we have to learn before we can do them, we learn by doing them, e.g., men become builders by building and lyre-players by playing the lyre; so too we become just by doing just acts, temperate by doing temperate acts, brave by doing brave acts. . . .

Again, it is from the same causes and by the same means that every virtue is both produced and destroyed, and similarly every art; for it is from playing the lyre that both good and bad lyre-players are produced. And the corresponding statement is true of builders and of all the rest; men will be good or bad builders as a result of building well or badly. For if this were not so, there would have been no need of a teacher, but all men would have been born good or bad at their craft. This, then, is the case with the virtues also; by doing the acts that we do in our transactions with other men we become just or unjust, and by doing the acts that we do in the presence of danger, and being habituated to feel fear or confidence, we become brave or cowardly. The same is true of appetites and feelings of anger; some men become temperate and good-tempered, others self-indulgent and irascible, by behaving in one way or the other in the appropriate circumstances. Thus, in one word, states of character arise out of like activities. This is why the activities we exhibit must be of a certain kind; it is because the states of character correspond to the differences between these. It makes no small difference, then, whether we form habits of one kind or of another from our very youth; it makes a very great difference, or rather *all* the difference. . . .[3]

Aristotle's point here is not just that the virtues are acquired by practice, he is also arguing that virtue is a state of character. The virtuous person wants to do virtuous acts and he does them "naturally." We sometimes think that we are moral just because we believe in moral principles. But believing isn't enough, virtuous action is required. But not even virtuous action by itself is enough to make us virtuous. We sometimes think a person is virtuous because he "forces himself" to do what he is supposed to. Not according to Aristotle. The virtuous person is one who does what he is supposed to do because he wants to, because it is built into his very character. It is even essential, according to Aristotle, that the virtuous man enjoys being virtuous:

vs. Kant

[3] Aristotle, *Nichomachean Ethics.*

. . . neither the virtues nor the vices are *passions,* because we are not called good or bad on the ground of our passions, but are so called on the ground of our virtues and our vices, and because we are neither praised nor blamed for our passions (for the man who feels fear or anger is not praised, nor is the man who simply feels anger blamed, but the man who feels it in a certain way), but for our virtues and our vices we are praised or blamed.

Again, we feel anger and fear without choice, but the virtues are modes of choice or involve choice. Further, in respect of the passions we are said to be moved, but in respect of the virtues and the vices we are said not to be moved but to be disposed in a particular way.

For these reasons also they are not *faculties;* for we are neither called good nor bad, nor praised nor blamed, for the simple capacity of feeling the passions; again, we have the faculties of nature, but we are not made good or bad by nature; we have spoken of this before.

If, then, the virtues are neither passions nor faculties, all that remains is that they should be *states of character.*

Aristotle then goes on to say specifically what sort of state of character a virtue is. First, of course, it is that which brings out what is most excellent in us:

. . . the excellence of the eye makes both the eye and its work good; for it is by the excellence of the eye that we see well. Similarly the excellence of the horse makes a horse both good in itself and good at running and at carrying its rider and at awaiting the attack of the enemy. Therefore, if this is true in every case, the virtue of man also will be the state of character which makes a man good and which makes him do his own work well.[4]

And here Aristotle gives us perhaps his most famous doctrine, the idea that virtues are "means between the extremes." This is often misinterpreted, however, to read, "everything in moderation." In a way, what Aristotle teaches is very different from this; he tells us that we can't do too much of a good thing, that is, if it is a virtue. One can't be too courageous (as opposed to being rash or cowardly), or too just. What he intends by "the means between the extremes" is this:

. . . By the intermediate in the object I mean that which is equidistant from each of the extremes, which is one and the same for all men; by the intermediate relatively to us that which is neither too much nor too little— and this is not one, nor the same for all. For instance, if ten is many and two is few, six is the intermediate, taken in terms of the object; for it exceeds and is exceeded by an equal amount; this is intermediate according to arithmetical proportion. But the intermediate relatively to us is not to be taken so; if ten pounds are too much for a particular person to eat and two too little, it does not follow that the trainer will order six pounds; for this also is perhaps too much for the person who is to take it, or too little—too little for Milo, too much for the beginner in athletic exercises. The same is true of running and wrestling. Thus a master of any art avoids excess and defect, but seeks the intermediate and chooses this—the intermediate not in the object but relatively to us.

[4] Aristotle, *Nichomachean Ethics.*

If it is thus, then, that every art does its work well—by looking to the intermediate and judging its works by this standard (so that we often say of good works of art that it is not possible either to take away or to add anything, implying that excess and defect destroy the goodness of works of art, while the mean preserves it; and good artists, as we say, look to this in their work), and if, further, virtue is more exact and better than any art, as nature also is, then virtue must have the quality of aiming at the intermediate. I mean moral virtue; for it is this that is concerned with passions and actions, and in these there is excess, defect, and the intermediate. For instance, both fear and confidence and appetite and anger and pity and in general pleasure and pain may be felt both too much and too little, and in both cases not well; but to feel them at the right times, with reference to the right objects, towards the right people, with the right motive, and in the right way, is what is both intermediate and best, and this is characteristic of virtue. Similarly with regard to actions also there is excess, defect, and the intermediate. Now virtue is concerned with passions and actions, in which excess is a form of failure, and so is defect, while the intermediate is praised and is a form of success; and being praised and being successful are both characteristics of virtue. Therefore virtue is a kind of mean, since, as we have seen, it aims at what is intermediate.

Again, it is possible to fail in many ways. . . ., while to succeed is possible only in one way (for which reason also one is easy and the other difficult—to miss the mark easy, to hit it difficult); for these reasons also, then, excess and defect are characteristic of vice, and the mean of virtue;

For men are good in but one way, but bad in many.

Virtue, then, is a state of character concerned with choice, lying in a mean, i.e., the mean relative to us, this being determined by a rational principle, and by that principle by which the man of practical wisdom would determine it. Now it is a mean between two vices, that which depends on excess and that which depends on defect; and again it is a mean because the vices respectively fall short of or exceed what is right in both passions and actions, while virtue both finds and chooses that which is intermediate. Hence in respect of its substance and the definition which states its essence virtue is a mean, with regard to what is best and right and extreme.

But not every action nor every passion admits of a mean; for some have names that already imply badness, e.g., spite, shamelessness, envy, and in the case of actions adultery, theft, murder; for all of these and suchlike things imply by their names that they are themselves bad, and not the excesses or deficiencies of them. It is not possible, then, ever to be right with regard to them; one must always be wrong. Nor does goodness or badness with regard to such things depend on committing adultery with the right woman, at the right time, and in the right way, but simply to do any of them is to do wrong. It would be equally absurd, then, to expect that in unjust, cowardly, and voluptuous action there should be a mean, an excess, and a deficiency; for at that rate there would be a mean of excess and of deficiency, an excess of excess, and a deficiency of deficiency. But as there is no excess and deficiency of temperance and courage because what is intermediate is in a sense an extreme, so too of the actions we have mentioned there is no mean nor any excess and deficiency, but however they are done they are wrong; for in general there is neither a mean of excess and deficiency, nor excess and deficiency of a mean.

Now, finally, Aristotle gives us his examples of virtue:

With regard to feelings of fear and confidence courage is the mean; of the people who exceed, he who exceeds in fearlessness has no name (many of the states have no name), while the man who exceeds in confidence is rash, and he who exceeds in fear and falls short in confidence is a coward. With regard to pleasures and pains—not all of them, and not so much with regard to the pains—the mean is temperance, the excess self-indulgence. Persons deficient with regard to the pleasures are not often found; hence such persons also have received no name. But let us call them 'insensible.'

With regard to giving and taking of money the mean is liberality, the excess and the defect prodigality and meanness. In these actions people exceed and fall short in contrary ways; the prodigal exceeds in spending and falls short in taking, while the mean man exceeds in taking and falls short in spending. . . . With regard to money there are also other dispositions— a mean, magnificence (for the magnificent man differs from the liberal man; the former deals with large sums, the latter with small ones), and excess, tastelessness and vulgarity, and a deficiency, niggardliness. . . .

With regard to honour and dishonour the mean is proper pride, the excess is known as a sort of 'empty vanity,' and the deficiency is undue humility; and as we said liberality was related to magnificence, differing from it by dealing with small sums, so there is a state similarly related to proper pride, being concerned with small honours while that is concerned with great. For it is possible to desire honour as one ought, and more than one ought, and less, and the man who exceeds in his desires is called ambitious, the man who falls short unambitious, while the intermediate person has no name.

. . . . .

With regard to anger also there is an excess, a deficiency, and a mean. Although they can scarcely be said to have names, yet since we call the intermediate person good-tempered let us call the mean good temper; of the persons at the extremes let the one who exceeds be called irascible, and his vice irascibility, and the man who falls short an inirascible sort of person, and the deficiency inirascibility.

There are also three other means, which have a certain likeness to one another, but differ from one another: for they are all concerned with intercourse in words and actions, but differ in that one is concerned with truth in this sphere, the other two with pleasantness; and of this one kind is exhibited in giving amusement, the other in all the circumstances of life. We must therefore speak of these two, that we may the better see that in all things the mean is praiseworthy, and the extremes neither praiseworthy nor right, but worthy of blame. Now most of these states also have no names, but we must try, as in the other cases, to invent names ourselves so that we may be clear and easy to follow. With regard to truth, then, the intermediate is a truthful sort of person and the mean may be called truthfulness, while the pretence which exaggerates is boastfulness and the person characterized by it a boaster, and that which understates is mock modesty and the person characterized by it mock-modest. With regard to pleasantness in the giving of amusement the intermediate person is ready-witted and the disposition ready wit, the excess is buffoonery and the person characterized by it a buffoon, while the man who falls short is a sort of boor and his state is boorishness. With regard to the remaining kind of pleasantness, that which is exhibited in life in general, the man who is pleasant in the right way is friendly and the mean is friendliness, while the man who exceeds is an obsequious person if he has no end in view, a flatterer if he is aiming at his own advantage, and the man who falls short and is unpleasant in all circumstances is a quarrelsome and surly sort of person.

There are also means in the passions and concerned with the passions; since shame is not a virtue, and yet praise is extended to the modest man. For even in these matters one man is said to be intermediate, and another to exceed, as for instance the bashful man who is ashamed of everything; while he who falls short or is not ashamed of anything at all is shameless, and the intermediate person is modest. Righteous indignation is a mean between envy and spite, and these states are concerned with the pain and pleasures that are felt at the fortunes of our neighbours; the man who is characterized by righteous indignation is pained at undeserved good fortune, the envious man, going beyond him, is pained at all good fortune, and the spiteful man falls so far short of being pained that he even rejoices. . . .[5]

It is worth making a short list of Aristotle's <u>moral virtues</u>. Many of them are our own virtues also, but some of them are far more appropriate to an aristocratic, warrior society than they are to our own. In order to illustrate Aristotle's idea that virtues are the means between the extremes, I have included "the extremes" in parentheses for contrast:

Courage, particularly courage in battle (extremes: cowardice; rashness). What motivates courage, Aristotle tells us, is a sense of honor, not fear of punishment nor desire for reward, nor merely a sense of duty. The courageous man is afraid, he adds, because without fear there would be no courage. The man who feels no fear in the face of danger is rather rash.
Temperance, particularly concerning bodily pleasures, such as sex, food, and drinking (extremes: self-indulgence or piggishness; insensitivity). Notice that Aristotle does not say, along with many modern moralists, that pleasures are either "bad" or unimportant; in fact, he attacks the man who does not enjoy sex, food, and drinking as much as he attacks the man who over-indulges himself. He says that such people "are not even human."
Liberality, we would say, charity (extremes: prodigality or waste; meanness or stinginess). It is worth noting that Aristotle ridicules the man who gives more than he can afford to charity as much as he chastizes the man who will not give at all.

---

[5] Aristotle, _Nichomachean Ethics._

Magnificence, in other words, how extravagantly you live (extremes: vulgarity; miserliness). Aristotle says that one ought to live "like an artist" and spend lavishly. (There is little of the ascetic in Aristotle.)

Pride (extremes; humility; vanity). It is worth noting that pride is one of the seven deadly sins in Christian morality while humility is a virtue. In Aristotle's ethics, this is reversed.

Good temper (extremes: irascibility or bad tempered; too easy-going). It is important to get angry, according to Aristotle, about the right things; but not too much (which "makes a person impossible to live with").

Friendliness (extremes: obsequious; churlish). Friendship, for Aristotle, is one of the most important ingredients in the good life, and being friendly, therefore, is an extremely important virtue. But Aristotle does not say that we should be friendly to everyone; the person who is indiscriminately friendly to everyone is not worth being a friend at all.

Truthfulness (extremes: lying; boasting). Especially, telling the truth about oneself.

Wittiness (extremes: buffoonery; boorishness). We think of wittiness as a personal asset, but rarely as a virtue. Aristotle thinks that people who are incapable of telling a joke or who tell bad jokes are actually inferior. Fun is an important ingredient in Greek virtuousness.

Shame, Aristotle calls this a "quasi-virtue" (extremes: shamelessness; ————). We all make mistakes and it is a sign of virtue, according to Aristotle, that the good man feels shame when he does them. Shamelessness is a sign of wickedness. Aristotle does not even talk of the other extreme, which he did not consider a problem. (We certainly would. We call it excessive guilt.)

Justice, the cardinal virtue of the Greeks. The need for lawful and fair (which does not mean equal) treatment of other men. (The sense in which justice is a mean between extremes is too complex to discuss here. Aristotle spends a full chapter explaining it.)

Finally, Aristotle gives us his view of the good life for man; it is the life of activity in accordance with virtue, but it is also, ideally, a life of intellectual activity, or what he calls, "the life of contemplation." In other words, the happiest person is the philosopher:

> . . . happiness does not lack anything, but is self-sufficient. Now those activities are desirable in themselves from which nothing is sought beyond the activity. And of this nature virtuous actions are thought to be; for to do noble and good deeds is a thing desirable for its own sake.
>
> Pleasant amusements also are thought to be of this nature; we choose them not for the sake of other things; for we are injured rather than benefited by them, since we are led to neglect our bodies and our property. But most of the people who are deemed happy take refuge in such pastimes, which is the reason why those who are ready-witted at them are highly esteemed at the courts of tyrants; they make themselves pleasant companions in the tyrants' favourite pursuits, and that is the sort of man they want. Now these

things are thought to be of the nature of happiness because people in despotic positions spend their leisure in them, but perhaps such people prove nothing; for virtue and reason, from which good activities flow, do not depend on despotic position; nor, if these people, who have never tasted pure and generous pleasure, take refuge in the bodily pleasures, should these for that reason be thought more desirable; for boys, too, think the things that are valued among themselves are the best. It is to be expected, then, that, as different things seem valuable to boys and to men, so they should to bad men and to good. Now . . . those things are both valuable and pleasant which are such to the good man; and to each man the activity in accordance with his own disposition is most desirable, and, therefore, to the good man that which is in accordance with virtue. Happiness, therefore, does not lie in amusement; it would, indeed, be strange if the end were amusement, and one were to take trouble and suffer hardship all one's life in order to amuse oneself. For, in a word, everything that we choose we choose for the sake of something else—except happiness, which is an end. Now to exert oneself and work for the sake of amusement seems silly and utterly childish. But to amuse oneself in order that one may exert oneself, as Anacharsis puts it, seems right; for amusement is a sort of relaxation, and we need relaxation because we cannot work continuously. Relaxation, then, is not an end; for it is taken for the sake of activity.

The happy life is thought to be virtuous; now a virtuous life requires exertion, and does not consist in amusement. And we say that serious things are better than laughable things and those connected with amusement, and that the activity of the better of any two things—whether it be two elements of our being or two men—is the more serious; but the activity of the better is *ipso facto* superior and more of the nature of happiness. And any chance person—even a slave—can enjoy the bodily pleasures no less than the best man; but no one assigns to a slave a share in happiness—unless he assigns to him also a share in human life. For happiness does not lie in such occupations, but, as we have said before, in virtuous activities.

If happiness is activity in accordance with virtue, it is reasonable that it should be in accordance with the highest virtue; and this will be that of the best thing in us. Whether it be reason or something else that is this element which is thought to be our natural ruler and guide and to take thought of things noble and divine, whether it be itself also divine or only the most divine element in us, the activity of this in accordance with its proper virtue will be perfect happiness. This activity is contemplative.

·   ·   ·   ·   ·

Now this would seem to be in agreement with what we said before and with the truth. For, firstly, this activity is the best (since not only is reason the best thing in us, but the objects of reason are the best of knowable objects); and, secondly, it is the most continuous, since we can contemplate truth more continuously than we can *do* anything. And we think happiness has pleasure mingled with it, but the activity of philosophic wisdom is admittedly the pleasantest of virtuous activities; at all events the pursuit of it is thought to offer pleasures marvellous for their purity and their enduringness, and it is to be expected that those who know will pass their time more pleasantly than those who inquire. And the self-sufficiency that is spoken of must belong most to the contemplative activity. For while a philosopher, as well as a just man or one possessing any other virtue, needs the necessaries of life, when they are sufficiently equipped with things of that sort the just man needs people towards whom and with whom he shall act justly, and the temperate man, the brave man, and each of the others is in the same case, but the philosopher, even when by himself, can contemplate truth, and the better the wiser he is; he can perhaps do so better if he has fellow-workers, but still he is the most self-sufficient. And this activity alone would seem to be loved for its own sake; for nothing arises from it apart from the contemplating, while from practical activities we gain more or less apart from the action. And happiness is thought to depend on leisure; for we are busy that we may have leisure, and make war that we may live in peace. Now the activity of the practical virtues is exhibited in political or military affairs, but the actions concerned with these seem to be unleisurely. War-like actions are completely so (for no one chooses to be at war, or provokes war, for the sake of being at war; any one would seem absolutely murderous if he were to make enemies of his friends in order to bring about battle and slaughter); but the action of the statesman is also unleisurely, and —apart from the political action itself—aims at despotic power and honours, or at all events happiness, for him and his fellow citizens—a happiness different from political action, and evidently sought as being different. So if among virtuous actions political and military actions are distinguished by nobility and greatness, and these are unleisurely and aim at an end and are not desirable for their own sake, but the activity of reason, which is contemplative, seems both to be superior in serious worth and to aim at no end beyond itself, and to have its pleasure proper to itself (and this augments the activity), and the self-sufficiency, leisureliness, unweariedness (so far as this is possible for man), and all the other attributes ascribed to the supremely happy man are evidently those connected with this activity, it follows that this will be the complete happiness of man. . . .

For man, therefore, the life according to reason is best and pleasantest, since reason more than anything else *is* man. This life therefore is also the happiest.[6]

But it must not be thought that Aristotle's ideal philosopher does nothing but contemplate. He may also enjoy pleasure, wealth, honor, success and power. As a man among men, he is also virtuous and chooses to act virtuously like all good men. But in addition, he has an understanding and an appreciation of reason that makes him "dearest to the Gods and presumably the happiest among men." This is surely a flattering portrait of the place of the philosopher! But if we ignore this final self-congratulation, we can see in Aristotle a powerful conception of morality, with its emphasis on virtue, excellence and a kind of heroism (whether intellectual or moral) which is in some ways very different from our own conception of morality and the good life.

[6] Aristotle, *Nichomachean Ethics.*

MORALITY AND SENTIMENT:
HUME AND ROUSSEAU

Morality for Aristotle depended upon rules embedded and learned in a particular society, an elite society of the privileged males of the Greek aristocracy. Modern conceptions of morality, on the other hand, are usually thought to be universal, that is, not restricted to a particular society or a particular elite. It applies to women, men, poor people, rich people, adults, and children, even if they are only a few years old. At the same time, however, most modern conceptions of morality minimize Aristotle's emphasis on society and upbringing, preferring to place morals on some individual basis. In Kant's moral philosophy, we shall see that the key to morality is *individual autonomy,* the idea that every person can find for him or herself, just through the use of reason, what acts are moral and what acts are not. Before Kant, the ruling conception of morality was based upon a conception of personal feelings of a special moral kind, a "natural desire" to help one's fellow man. (As in Aristotle, this philosophy insisted that morality had to be viewed as a part of nature.)

It should be clear how this conception of morality has a distinct advantage in reconciling personal interests and moral principles. Since strong moral feelings are a kind of personal interest, one can satisfy his personal feelings and the demands of morality at the same time. (Again, this lies at the heart of Bishop Butler's arguments.) There are, of course, other personal feelings— jealousy, greed and envy—that act against these moral feelings. But at least some of our feelings are satisfied by moral action. And according to these philosophers, such moral feelings can be found in virtually all of us.

The two most famous philosophers to argue this position are David Hume, whom you already know quite well from earlier chapters, and the French philosopher Jean-Jacques Rousseau, whose political philosophy we shall study in the final chapter. The key to both of their philosophies is the notion of *sentiment,* that is, "feeling," and the notion of *sympathy,* that is, "fellow feeling" or feeling pity for other people and taking their interests into account as well as our own. Hume says:

> The hypothesis which we embrace is plain. It maintains that morality is determined by sentiment. It defines virtue to be *whatever mental action or quality gives to a spectator the pleasing sentiment of approbation;* and vice the contrary.[7]

The central concern in Hume's moral philosophy distinguishes those who defend morality as a function of reason from those who say that it is rather a matter of sentiment and passion. Elsewhere, Hume gives us his very strong opinion, that "reason is, and ought to be, the slave of the passions." Here is his argument:

[7] David Hume, *Inquiry Concerning the Principles of Morals* (La Salle, Ill.: Open Court, 1912).

There has been a controversy started of late, much better worth examination, concerning the general foundation of *morals;* whether they be derived from *reason* or from *sentiment;* whether we attain the knowledge of them by a chain of argument and induction or by an immediate feeling and finer internal sense; whether, like all sound judgment of truth and falsehood, they should be the same to every rational, intelligent being, or whether, like the perception of beauty and deformity, they be founded entirely on the particular fabric and constitution of the human species.

The ancient philosophers, though they often affirm that virtue is nothing but conformity to reason, yet, in general, seem to consider morals as deriving their existence from taste and sentiment. On the other hand, our modern inquirers, though they also talk much of the beauty of virtue and deformity of vice, yet have commonly endeavored to account for these distinctions by metaphysical reasonings and by deductions from the most abstract principles of the understanding. Such confusion reigned in these subjects that an opposition of the greatest consequence could prevail between one system and another, and even in the parts of almost each individual system, and yet nobody, till very lately, was ever sensible of it.

. . . . .

It must be acknowledged that both sides of the question are susceptible of specious arguments. Moral distinctions, it may be said, are discernible by pure *reason;* else, whence the many disputes that reign in common life, as well as in philosophy with regard to this subject, the long chain of proofs often produced on both sides, the examples cited, the authorities appealed to, the analogies employed, the fallacies detected, the inferences drawn, and the several conclusions adjusted to their proper principles? Truth is disputable, not taste: what exists in the nature of things is the standard of our judgment: what each man feels within himself is the standard of sentiment Propositions in geometry may be proved, systems in physics may be controverted, but the harmony of verse, the tenderness of passion, the brilliancy of wit must give immediate pleasure. No man reasons concerning another's beauty, but frequently concerning the justice or injustice of his actions. In every criminal trial, the first object of the prisoner is to disprove the facts alleged and deny the actions imputed to him; the second, to prove that, even if these actions were real, they might be justified as innocent and lawful. It is confessedly by deductions of the understanding that the first point is ascertained; how can we suppose a different faculty of the mind is employed in fixing the other?

On the other hand, those who would resolve all moral determinations into *sentiments* may endeavor to show that it is impossible for reason ever to draw conclusions of this nature. To virtue, say they, it belongs to be *amiable* and vice *odious.* This forms their very nature or essence. But can reason or argumentation distribute these different epithets to any subjects and pronounce beforehand that this must produce love and that hatred? Or what other reason can we ever assign for these affections but the original fabric and formation of the human mind, which is naturally adapted to receive them?

The end of all moral speculations is to teach us our duty, and, by proper representations of the deformity of vice and beauty of virtue, beget correspondent habits and engage us to avoid the one and embrace the other. But is this ever to be expected from inferences and conclusions of the understanding, which of themselves have no hold of the affections or set in motion the active powers of men? They discover truths. But where the truths which they discover are indifferent and beget no desire or aversion, they can have no influence on conduct and behavior. What is honorable, what is fair, what is becoming, what is noble, what is generous takes possession of the heart and animates us to embrace and maintain it. What is intelligible, what is evident, what is probable, what is true procures only the cool assent of the understanding and, gratifying a speculative curiosity, puts an end to our researches.

· · · · ·

Extinguish all the warm feelings and prepossessions in favor of virtue, and all disgust or aversion to vice; render men totally indifferent toward these distinctions, and morality is no longer a practical study nor has any tendency to regulate our lives and actions.

These arguments on each side (and many more might be produced) are so plausible that I am apt to suspect they may, the one as well as the other, be solid and satisfactory and that *reason* and *sentiment* concur in almost all moral determinations and conclusions. The final sentence, it is probable, which pronounces characters and actions amiable or odious, praiseworthy or blamable; that which stamps on them the mark of honor or infamy, approbation or censure; that which renders morality an active principle and constitutes virtue our happiness, and vice our misery—it is probable, I say, that this final sentence depends on some internal sense or feeling which nature has made universal in the whole species.

It is worth noting here that Hume's moral philosophy, like his philosophy of knowledge is strictly empiricist:

. . . Men are now cured of their passion for hypotheses and systems in natural philosophy and will hearken to no arguments but those which are derived from experience. It is full time they should attempt a like reformation in all moral disquisitions and reject every system of ethics, however subtle or ingenious, which is not founded on fact and observation.

Reason, Hume argues, may be of use in deciding how we can get what we want, but it is incapable of ever telling us what we ultimately want: notice the familiar argument against an infinite regress; notice also Hume's sharp distinction between reason (which is concerned with knowledge, truth, and falsehood) and taste or sentiment (that judges values, which ultimately depend upon pleasure and pain):

. . . It appears evident that the ultimate ends of human actions can never, in any case, be accounted for by *reason,* but recommend themselves entirely to the sentiments and affections of mankind without any dependence on the intellectual faculties. Ask a man *why he uses exercise;* he will answer, *because he desires to keep his health.* If you then inquire *why he desires health,* he will readily reply, *because sickness is painful.* If you push your inquiries further and desire a reason *why he hates pain,* it is impossible he can ever give any. This is an ultimate end and is never referred to any other object.

Perhaps to your second question, *why he desires health,* he may also reply that *it is necessary for the exercise of his calling.* If you ask *why he is anxious on that head,* he will answer, *because he desires to get money.* If you demand, *why? It is the instrument of pleasure,* says he. And beyond this, it is an absurdity to ask for a reason. It is impossible there can be a progress *in infinitum* and that one thing can always be a reason why another is desired. Something must be desirable on its own account and because of its immediate accord or agreement with human sentiment and affection.

Now, as virtue is an end and is desirable on its own account, without fee or reward, merely for the immediate satisfaction which it conveys, it is requisite that there should be some sentiment which it touches—some internal taste or feeling, or whatever you please to call it, which distinguishes moral good and evil and which embraces the one and rejects the other.

Thus, the distinct boundaries and offices of *reason* and of *taste* are easily ascertained. The former conveys the knowledge of truth and falsehood; the latter gives the sentiment of beauty and deformity, vice and virtue. The one discovers objects as they really stand in nature, without addition or diminution; the other has a productive faculty; and gliding or straining all natural objects with the colors borrowed from internal sentiment, raises, in a manner, a new creation. Reason, being cool and disengaged, is no motive to action and directs only the impulse received from appetite or inclination by showing us the means of attaining happiness or avoiding misery. Taste, as it gives pleasure or pain, and thereby constitutes happiness or misery, becomes a motive to action and is the first spring or impulse to desire and volition. From circumstances and relations, known or supposed, the former leads us to the discovery of the concealed and unknown. After all circumstances and relations are laid before us, the latter makes us feel from the whole a new sentiment of blame or approbation.[8]

Elsewhere, Hume argues a razor-sharp distinction between facts and values. He argues, with characteristic conciseness, that "it is impossible to derive an 'ought' from an 'is'," that is, any notions of value or what we *ought to do* cannot be derived from any statements of fact. One can know, as a matter of fact, that pushing this button will kill a thousand innocent children, but from that fact alone, it does not follow that I ought not push the button. What I ought to do—or ought not to do—depends on something that is not a matter of fact or reason at all, my moral feelings or sentiments. Without these sentiments, no action is either moral or immoral, praiseworthy or blameworthy, or of any value whatever. Accordingly, in one of his most shocking statements, Hume says that it would not be irrational for him to prefer the death of a thousand Orientals to the pricking of his little finger. This is not to say that

---

[8] Hume, *Inquiry Concerning the Principles of Morals.*

he would prefer this, but there is *nothing in reason* to forbid it. Values are a matter of sentiment, not of reason.

A similar theory of sentiment is defended by Jean-Jacques Rousseau. Although he is often characterized as the first great "Romantic," it is worth noting that Rousseau is not nearly so antagonistic to reason as his reputation suggests. Sentiment, on his theory, is tied to a kind of "natural reason." And the key to his theory, therefore, is the concept of conscience, a powerful kind of moral feeling which has its own kind of divine reason. As in Hume, it is only detached reason that offers us no guidance. Notice that he too reconciles "self-love" and "moral goodness" as ultimately having the same goals:

> Let us lay it down as an incontrovertible rule that the first impulses of nature are always right; there is no original sin in the human heart, the how and why of the entrance of every vice can be traced. The only natural passion is self-love or selfishness taken in a wider sense. This selfishness is good in itself and in relation to ourselves; and as the child has no necessary relations to other people he is naturally indifferent to them; his self-love only becomes good or bad by the use made of it and the relations established by its means. Until the time is ripe for the appearance of reason, that guide of selfishness, the main thing is that the child shall do nothing because you are watching him or listening to him; in a word, nothing because of other people, but only what nature asks of him; then he will never do wrong.
>
> I do not mean to say that he will never do any mischief, never hurt himself, never break a costly ornament if you leave it within his reach. He might do much damage without doing wrong, since wrong-doing depends on the harmful intention which will never be his. If once he meant to do harm, his whole education would be ruined; he would be almost hopelessly bad. . . .
>
> The morality of our actions consists entirely in the judgments we ourselves form with regard to them. If good is good, it must be good in the depth of our heart as well as in our actions; and the first reward of justice is the consciousness that we are acting justly. If moral goodness is in accordance with our nature, man can only be healthy in mind and body when he is good. If it is not so, and if man is by nature evil, he cannot cease to be evil without corrupting his nature, and goodness in him is a crime against nature. If he is made to do harm to his fellow-creatures, as the wolf is made to devour his prey, a humane man would be as depraved a creature as a pitiful wolf; and virtue alone would cause remorse.
>
> My young friend, let us look within, let us set aside all personal prejudices and see whither our inclinations lead us. Do we take more pleasure in the sight of the sufferings of others or their joys? Is it pleasanter to do a kind action or an unkind action, and which leaves the more delightful memory behind it? Why do you enjoy the theatre? Do you delight in the crimes you behold? Do you weep over the punishment which overtakes the criminal? They say we are indifferent to everything but self-interest; yet we find our consolation in our sufferings in the charms of friendship and humanity, and even in our pleasures we should be too lonely and miserable if we had no one to share them with us. If there is no such thing as morality

in man's heart, what is the source of his rapturous admiration of noble
deeds, his passionate devotion to great men? What connection is there between self-interest and this enthusiasm for virtue?

.   .   .   .   .

Take from our hearts this love of what is noble and you rob us of the joy
of life. The mean-spirited man in whom these delicious feelings have been
stifled among vile passions, who by thinking of no one but himself comes at
last to love no one but himself, this man feels no raptures, his cold heart no
longer throbs with joy, and his eyes no longer fill with the sweet tears of
sympathy, he delights in nothing; the wretch has neither life nor feeling,
he is already dead.

There are many bad men in this world, but there are few of these dead
souls, alive only to self-interest, and insensible to all that is right and good.
We only delight in injustice so long as it is to our own advantage; in every
other case we wish the innocent to be protected. If we see some act of
violence or injustice in town or country, our hearts are at once stirred to
their depths by an instinctive anger and wrath, which bids us go to the help
of the oppressed; but we are restrained by a stronger duty, and the law
deprives us of our right to protect the innocent. On the other hand, if some
deed of mercy or generosity meets our eye, what reverence and love does it
inspire! Do we not say to ourselves, "I should like to have done that myself"?
What does it matter to us that two thousand years ago a man was just or
unjust? and yet we take the same interest in ancient history as if it happened
yesterday. What are the crimes of Cataline to me? I shall not be his victim.
Why then have I the same horror of his crimes as if he were living now?
We do not hate the wicked merely because of the harm they do to ourselves, but because they are wicked. Not only do we wish to be happy ourselves, we wish others to be happy too, and if this happiness does not interfere with our own happiness, it increases it. In conclusion, whether we will
or not, we pity the unfortunate; when we see their suffering we suffer too.
Even the most depraved are not wholly without this instinct, and it often
leads them to self-contradiction. The highwayman who robs the traveller,
clothes the nakedness of the poor; the fiercest murderer supports a fainting
man.

Men speak of the voice of remorse, the secret punishment of hidden
crimes, by which such are often brought to light. Alas! who does not know
its unwelcome voice? We speak from experience, and we would gladly
stifle this imperious feeling which causes us such agony. Let us obey the call
of nature; we shall see that her yoke is easy and that when we give heed to
her voice we find a joy in the answer of a good conscience. The wicked
fears and flees from her; he delights to escape from himself; his anxious eyes
look around him for some object of diversion; without bitter satire and rude
mockery he would always be sorrowful; the scornful laugh is his one
pleasure. Not so the just man, who finds his peace within himself; there is
joy not malice in his laughter, a joy which springs from his own heart; he
is as cheerful alone as in company, his satisfaction does not depend on those
who approach him; it includes them.

.   .   .   .   .

It is no part of my scheme to enter at present into metaphysical discussions which neither you nor I can understand, discussions which really lead nowhere. I have told you already that I do not wish to philosophise with you, but to help you to consult your own heart. If all the philosophers in the world should prove that I am wrong, and you feel that I am right, that is all I ask.

For this purpose it is enough to lead you to distinguish between our acquired ideas and our natural feelings; for feeling precedes knowledge; and since we do not learn to seek what is good for us and avoid what is bad for us, but get this desire from nature, in the same way the love of good and the hatred of evil are as natural to us as our self-love. The decrees of conscience are not judgments but feelings. Although all our ideas come from without, the feelings by which they are weighed are within us, and it is by these feelings alone that we perceive fitness or unfitness of things in relation to ourselves, which leads us to seek or shun these things.

To exist is to feel; our feeling is undoubtedly earlier than our intelligence, and we had feelings before we had ideas. Whatever may be the cause of our being, it has provided for our preservation by giving us feelings suited to our nature; and no one can deny that these at least are innate. These feelings, so far as the individual is concerned, are self-love, fear, pain, the dread of death, the desire for comfort. Again, if, as it is impossible to doubt, man is by nature sociable, or at least fitted to become sociable, he can only be so by means of other innate feelings, relative to his kind; for if only physical well-being were considered, men would certainly be scattered rather than brought together. But the motive power of conscience is derived from the moral system formed through this twofold relation to himself and to his fellow-men. To know good is not to love it; this knowledge is not innate in man; but as soon as his reason leads him to perceive it, his conscience impels him to love it; it is this feeling which is innate.

So I do not think, my young friend, that it is impossible to explain the immediate force of conscience as a result of our own nature, independent of reason itself. And even should it be impossible, it is unnecessary; for those who deny this principle, admitted and received by everybody else in the world, do not prove that there is no such thing; they are content to affirm, and when we affirm its existence we have quite as good grounds as they, while we have moreover the witness within us, the voice of conscience, which speaks on its own behalf. If the first beams of judgment dazzle us and confuse the objects we behold, let us wait till our feeble sight grows clear and strong, and in the light of reason we shall soon behold these very objects as nature has already showed them to us. Or rather let us be simpler and less pretentious; let us be content with the first feelings we experience in ourselves, since science always brings us back to these, unless it has led us astray.

Conscience! Conscience! Divine instinct, immortal voice from heaven; sure guide for a creature ignorant and finite indeed; yet intelligent and free; infallible judge of good and evil, making man like to God! In thee consists the excellence of man's nature and the morality of his actions; apart from thee, I find nothing in myself to raise me above the beasts—nothing but the sad privilege of wandering from one error to another, by the help of an unbridled understanding and a reason which knows no principle.[9]

But, as we pointed out before, there is a problem with this notion of conscience, and with all appeals of morality to personal feeling. What if different people disagree? Whose conscience, or whose feelings should we accept? And even if we find ourselves in agreement, how do we know that our consciences or feelings are right? It is with these questions in mind that we turn to the moral philosophy of Kant.

MORALITY AND REASON: KANT

Aristotle, Hume, and Rousseau all give feeling an important place in their conceptions of morality. For Aristotle, the virtuous man wants to act virtuously and enjoys doing so. For Hume and Rousseau, sentiment defines morality. On all such accounts, our concept of *duty*—what we ought to do—is derivative, at least in part, from such feelings and from our upbringing. But what if feelings disagree? What if people are brought up to value different things? What are we to say of a person who is brought up by criminals to value what is wicked and to enjoy cruelty? And what are we to say, most importantly of all, in those familiar cases in which a person's feelings all draw him or her towards personal interests but duty calls in the opposite direction? This is the problem that Kant considered, and because of it, he rejected all attempts to base morality on feelings of any kind. Morality, he argued must be based solely on reason and reason alone.

Hume had restricted the notion of reason to concern with knowledge, truth and falsity; Kant replies that reason also has a practical side, one which is capable of telling us what to do as well as how to do it. Rousseau had said that morality must be universal, common to all men, even in a pre-societal "state of nature"; Kant (who very much admired Rousseau) agrees, but says that the nature of this universality cannot lie in people's feelings, which may vary from person to person and society to society, but only in reason, which by its very nature must be universal. And Aristotle had insisted that morality must be taught within society, and that morals were very much a matter of public opinion and practices; but unlike most modern philosophers, Kant insisted on the independence of morality from society. What is most important, he argues, is that morality be autonomous, a function of individual reason, such that every rational person is capable of finding out what is right and what is wrong for him/herself. But where Hume and Rousseau had looked for morality in individual feeling, Kant again insists that it must be found through an examination of reason, nothing else. This is the key to Kant's moral philosophy: morality consists solely of rational principles.

[9] Jean-Jaques Rousseau, *Emile*, trans. Barbara Foxley (New York: E. P. Dutton, 1968).

Since morality is based on reason, according to Kant, it does not depend on particular societies or particular circumstances; it does not depend on individual feelings or desires (Kant summarizes all such personal feelings, desires, ambitions, impulses, and emotions as *inclinations*). The purpose of moral philosophy, therefore, is to examine our ability to reason practically, and to determine from this examination the fundamental principles which lie at the basis of every morality, for every person and in every society. In direct contrast to Aristotle, Kant begins by saying that what is ultimately good is none of those benefits and virtues that make up Greek happiness, but rather what he calls a good will. And a good will, in turn, is the will that exercises pure practical reason.

> Nothing can possibly be conceived in the world, or even out of it, which can be called good without qualification, except a *good will*. Intelligence, wit, judgment, and other *talents* of the mind, however they may be named, or courage, resolution, perseverance, as qualities of temperament, are undoubtedly good and desirable in many respects; but these gifts of nature may also become extremely bad and mischievous if the will which is to make use of them, and which, therefore, constitutes what is called *character,* is not good. It is the same with the *gifts of fortune.* Power, riches, honor, even health, and the general well-being and contentment with one's condition which is called *happiness,* inspire pride, and often presumption, if there is not a good will to correct the influence of these on the mind, and with this also to rectify the whole principle of acting, and adapt it to its end. The sight of a being who is not adorned with a single feature of a pure and good will, enjoying unbroken prosperity, can never give pleasure to an impartial rational spectator. Thus a good will appears to constitute the indispensable condition even of being worthy of happiness.[10]

The argument behind this opening move is this: it makes no sense to blame or praise a person for his or her character or abilities or the consequences of his or her actions, there are many factors that contribute to a person's control. Whether or not a person is wealthy, intelligent, courageous, witty and so on (Aristotle's virtues) is often due to his or her upbringing and heredity rather than any personal choice. But what we *will,* that is, what we try to do, is wholly within our control. Therefore, it is the only thing that is ultimately worth moral consideration. Notice that Kant is concerned with questions of morality, and not questions of the good life in general. What makes us happy is not particularly his concern. He is only concerned with what makes a person morally worthy of being happy.

> A good will is good not because of what it performs or effects, not by its aptness for the attainment of some proposed end, but simply by virtue of the volition—that is, it is good in itself, and considered by itself is to be esteemed much higher than all that can be brought about by it in favor of any inclination, nay, even of the sum-total of all inclinations. Even if it should happen

---

[10] Immanuel Kant, *Fundamental Principles of the Metaphysics of Morals,* trans. T. K. Abbot (New York: Longmans, Green, 1898).

that, owing to special disfavor of fortune, or the niggardly provision of a step-motherly nature, this will should wholly lack power to accomplish its pur-pose, if with its greatest efforts it should yet achieve nothing, and there should remain only the good will (not, to be sure, a mere wish, but the summoning of all means in our power), then, like a jewel, it would still shine by its own light, as a thing which has its whole value in itself. Its usefulness or fruitlessness can neither add to nor take away anything from this value. It would be, as it were, only the setting to enable us to handle it the more conveniently in common commerce, or to attract to it the atten-tion of those who are not yet connoisseurs, but not to recommend it to true connoisseurs, or to determine its value.

There is, however, something so strange in this idea of the absolute value of the mere will, in which no account is taken of its utility, that not-withstanding the thorough assent of even common reason to the idea, yet a suspicion must arise that it may perhaps really be the product of mere high-flown fancy, and that we may have misunderstood the purpose of nature in assigning reason as the governor of our will. Therefore we will examine this idea from this point of view.[11]

Kant's argument here is surprisingly similar to Aristotle's argument in his *Ethics.* You remember that Aristotle argues that the good for man must be found in man's nature, in that which is unique to him. The assumption is that, since man is singularly endowed with reason, then reason must have a special significance in human life. Kant's argument also begins with the observation that man, unlike other creatures, is capable of reasoning. But why should he have such a capacity? Not in order to make him happy, Kant argues, because any number of instincts would have served that end more effectively. (Remem-ber that Kant is presupposing God as Creator here, so he believes, like Leibniz, that everything exists for some sufficient reason.)

> . . . our existence has a different and far nobler end, for which, and not for happiness, reason is properly intended, and which must, therefore, be regarded as the supreme condition to which the private ends of man must, for the most part, be postponed.[12]

This "far nobler end" and "supreme condition" is what Kant calls *duty.* "The notion of duty," he tells us, "includes that of a good will," but a good will which subjects itself to rational principles. Those rational principles are moral laws, and it is action in accordance with such laws that alone makes a man good.

It is important, however, to make a distinction, which Aristotle makes too: it is one thing to do what duty requires for some personal interest, and it is something else to do one's duty just because it is one's duty. For example, a grocer might refuse to cheat his customers (which is his duty) because it would be bad for business; then he is not acting for the sake of duty, but for personal interests. But he may refuse to cheat his customers just because he

---

[11] Kant, *Fundamental Principles of the Metaphysics of Morals.*
[12] Kant, *Fundamental Principles of the Metaphysics of Morals.*

knows that he ought not to. This does count as doing his duty, and thereby makes him morally worthy.

I omit here all actions which are already recognized as inconsistent with duty, although they may be useful for this or that purpose, for with these the question whether they are done *from duty* cannot arise at all, since they even conflict with it. I also set aside those actions which really conform to duty, but to which men have *no* direct *inclination,* performing them because they are impelled thereto by some other inclination. For in this case we can readily distinguish whether the action which agrees with duty is done *from duty* or from a selfish view. It is much harder to make this distinction when the action accords with duty, and the subject has besides a *direct* inclination to it. For example, it is always a matter of duty that a dealer should not overcharge an inexperienced purchaser; and wherever there is much commerce the prudent tradesman does not overcharge, but keeps a fixed price for everyone, so that a child buys of him as well as any other. Men are thus *honestly* served; but this is not enough to make us believe that the tradesman has so acted from duty and from principles of honesty; his own advantage required it; it is out of the question in this case to suppose that he might besides have a direct inclination in favor of the buyers, so that, as it were, from love he should give no advantage to one over another. Accordingly the action was done neither from duty nor from direct inclination, but merely with a selfish view.

On the other hand, it is a duty to maintain one's life; and, in addition, everyone has also a direct inclination to do so. But on this account the often anxious care which most men take for it has no intrinsic worth, and their maxim has no moral import. They preserve their life *as duty requires,* no doubt, but not *because duty requires.* On the other hand, if adversity and hopeless sorrow have completely taken away the relish for life, if the unfortunate one, strong in mind, indignant at his fate rather than desponding or dejected, wishes for death, and yet preserves his life without loving it— not from inclination or fear, but from duty—then his maxim has a moral worth.

To be beneficent when we can is a duty; and besides this, there are many minds so sympathetically constituted that, without any other motive of vanity or self-interest, they find a pleasure in spreading joy around them, and can take delight in the satisfaction of others so far as it is their own work. But I maintain that in such a case an action of this kind, however proper, however amiable it may be, has nevertheless no true moral worth, but is on a level with other inclinations, for example, the inclination to honor, which, if it is happily directed to that which is in fact of public utility and accordant with duty, and consequently honorable, deserves praise and encouragement, but not esteem. For the maxim lacks the moral import, namely, that such actions be done *from duty,* not from inclination. Put the case that the mind of that philanthropist was clouded by sorrow of his own, extinguishing all sympathy with the lot of others, and that while he still has the power to benefit others in distress, he is not touched by their trouble because he is absorbed with his own; and now suppose that he tears himself out of this dead insensibility and performs the action without any inclination to it, but simply from duty, then first has his action its genuine moral worth. Further still, if nature has put little sympathy in the heart of this or that man, if he, supposed to be an upright man, is by temperament cold and indifferent to the sufferings of others, perhaps because in respect of his own he is provided with the special gift of patience and fortitude, and supposes, or even requires, that others should have the same—and such a man would certainly not be the meanest product of nature—but if nature had not specially framed him for a philanthropist, would he not still find in himself a source from whence to give himself a far higher worth than that of a good-natured temperament could be? Unquestionably. It is just in this that the moral worth of the character is brought out which is incomparably the highest of all, namely, that he is beneficent, not from inclination, but from duty.[13]

In a curious two short paragraphs, Kant tells us that we have a duty to make ourselves happy, not because we want to be happy (wants are never duties), but because it is necessary for us to do our other duties. Then, with reference to the Bible, Kant makes a famous (or infamous) distinction between two kinds of love, practical love, which is commanded as a duty, and pathological love, in other words, what we would call the *emotion* of love.

To secure one's own happiness is a duty, at least indirectly; for discontent with one's condition, under a pressure of many anxieties and amidst unsatisfied wants, might easily become a great *temptation to transgression of duty*. But here again, without looking to duty, all men have already the strongest and most intimate inclination to happiness, because it is just in this idea that all inclinations are combined in one total. But the precept of happiness is often of such a sort that it greatly interferes with some inclinations, and yet a man cannot form any definite and certain conception of the sum of satisfaction of all of them which is called happiness. It is not then to be wondered at that a single inclination, definite both as to what it promises and as to the time within which it can be gratified, is often able to overcome such a fluctuating idea, and that a gouty patient, for instance, can choose to enjoy what he likes, and to suffer what he may, since, according to his calculation, on this occasion at least, he has [only] not sacrificed the enjoyment of the present moment to a possibly mistaken expectation of a happiness which is supposed to be found in health. But even in this case, if the general desire for happiness did not influence his will, and supposing that in his particular case health was not a necessary element in this calculation, there yet remains in this, as in all other cases, this law—namely, that he should promote his happiness not from inclination but from duty, and by this would his conduct first acquire true moral worth.

It is in this manner, undoubtedly, that we are to understand those passages of Scripture also in which we are commanded to love our neighbor, even our enemy. For love, as an affection, cannot be commanded, but beneficence for duty's sake may, even though we are not impelled to it by any inclination—nay, are even repelled by a natural and unconquerable aversion. This is *practical* love, and not *pathological*—a love which is seated in the

13 Kant, *Fundamental Principles of the Metaphysics of Morals.*

will, and not in the propensions of sense—in principles of action and not of tender sympathy; and it is this love alone which can be commanded.[14]

Having thus defended his primary proposition that what is ultimately good is a good will acting in accordance with practical reason, in other words, from duty, Kant moves on to two corollary propositions:

The second proposition is: That an action done from duty derives its moral worth, *not from the purpose* which is to be attained by it, but from the maxim by which it is determined, and therefore does not depend on the realization of the object of the action, but merely on the *principle of volition* by which the action has taken place, without regard to any object of desire. It is clear from what precedes that the purposes which we may have in view in our actions, or their effects regarded as ends and springs of the will cannot give to actions any unconditional or moral worth. In what, then, can their worth lie if it is not to consist in the will and in reference to its expected effect? It cannot lie anywhere but in the *principle of the will* without regard to the ends which can be attained by the action. For the will stands between its *a priori* principle, which is formal, and its *a posteriori* spring which is material, as between two roads, and as it must be determined by something, it follows that it must be determined by the formal principle of volition when an action is done from duty, in which case every material principle has been withdrawn from it.

The third proposition, which is a consequence of the two preceding, I would express thus: *Duty is the necessity of acting from respect for the law.* I may have *inclination* for an object as the effect of my proposed action, but I cannot have *respect* for it just for this reason that it is an effect and not an energy of will. Similarly, I cannot have respect for inclination, whether my own or another's; I can at most, if my own, approve it; if another's, sometimes even love it, that is, look on it as favorable to my own interest. It is only what is connected with my will as a principle, by no means as an effect—what does not subserve my inclination, but overpowers it, or at least in case of choice excludes it from its calculation—in other words, simply the law of itself, which can be an object of respect, and hence a command. Now an action done from duty must wholly exclude the influence of inclination, and with it every object of the will, so that nothing remains which can determine the will except objectively the *law,* and subjectively *pure respect* for this practical law, and consequently the maxim that I should follow this law even to the thwarting of all my inclinations.

Thus the moral worth of an action does not lie in the effect expected from it, nor in any principle of action which requires to borrow its motive from this expected effect. For all these effects—agreeableness of one's condition, and even the promotion of the happiness of others—could have been also brought about by other causes, so that for this there would have been no need of the will of a rational being; whereas it is in this alone that the supreme and unconditional good can be found. The pre-eminent good which we call moral can therefore consist in nothing else than *the conception of law* in itself, *which certainly is only possible in a rational being,*

---

[14] Kant, *Fundamental Principles of the Metaphysics of Morals.*

in so far as this conception, and not the expected effect, determines the will. This is a good which is already present in the person who acts accordingly, and we have not to wait for it to appear first in the result.

But what sort of law can that be the conception of which must determine the will, even without paying any regard to the effect expected from it, in order that this will may be called good absolutely and without qualification? As I have deprived the will of every impulses which could arise to it from obedience to any law, there remains nothing but the universal conformity of its actions to law in general, which alone is to serve the will as a principle. . . .[15]

This conception of "universal conformity to law" is Kant's central notion of duty. He defines it, as we shall see, as a generalized version of the Golden Rule: "do unto others as you would have them do unto you." The point is, decide what you ought to do by asking yourself the question, "What if everyone were to do that?" The rule, as he states it, is:

. . . I am never to act otherwise than so *that I could also will that my maxim should become a universal law.* Here, now, it is the simple conformity to law in general, without assuming any particular law applicable to certain actions, that serves the will as its principle, and must so serve it if duty is not to be a vain delusion and a chimerical notion. The common reason of men in its practical judgments perfectly coincides with this, and always has in view the principle here suggested. Let the question be, for example: May I when in distress make a promise with the intention not to keep it? I readily distinguish here between the two significations which the question may have: whether it is prudent or whether it is right to make a false promise? The former may undoubtedly often be the case. I see clearly indeed that it is not enough to extricate myself from a present difficulty by means of this subterfuge, but it must be well considered whether there may not hereafter spring from this lie much greater inconvenience than that from which I now free myself, and as, with all my supposed *cunning,* the consequences cannot be so easily foreseen but that credit once lost may be much more injurious to me than any mischief which I seek to avoid at present, it should be considered whether it would not be more *prudent* to act herein according to a universal maxim, and to make it a habit to promise nothing except with the intention of keeping it. But it is soon clear to me that such a maxim will still only be based on the fear of consequences. Now it is a wholly different thing to be truthful from duty, and to be so from apprehension of injurious consequences. In the first case, the very notion of the action implies a law for me; in the second case, I must first look about elsewhere to see what results may be combined with it which would affect myself. For to deviate from the principle of duty is beyond all doubt wicked; but to be unfaithful to my maxim of prudence may often be very advantageous to me, although to abide by it is certainly safer. The shortest way, however, and an unerring one, to discover the answer to this question whether a lying promise is consistent with duty, is to ask myself, Should I be content that my maxim (to extricate myself from difficulty by a false promise) should hold good as a

[15] Kant, *Fundamental Principles of the Metaphysics of Morals.*

universal law, for myself as well as for others; and should I be able to say to myself, "Every one may make a deceitful promise when he finds himself in a difficulty from which he cannot otherwise extricate himself"? Then I presently become aware that, while I can will the lie, I can by no means will that lying should be a universal law. For with such a law there would be no promises at all, since it would be in vain to allege my intention in regard to my future actions to those who would not believe this allegation, or if they over-hastily did so, would pay me back in my own coin. Hence my maxim, as soon as it should be made a universal law, would necessarily destroy itself.[16]

The impressive name Kant gives to this general formulation of his notion of duty is, *The Categorical Imperative.* An imperative, however, is just what we called a command in our preliminary discussion of morality. It is of the form, "Do this!" or "Don't do this!" The word that distinguishes moral commands in general is the word *ought,* and this tells us something about the term *categorical.* Some imperatives tell us to "do this!," but only in order to get or do something else. Kant calls these "hypothetical imperatives." For example, "go to law school" (if you want to be a lawyer) or "don't eat very hot curry" (unless you don't mind risking an ulcer). But imperatives with a moral ought in them are not tied to any such "if" or "in order to" conditions. They are simply "do this" or "don't do this," whatever the circumstances, whatever you would like or enjoy personally. For example, "don't lie" (no matter what). This is what Kant means by "categorical."

> Now all *imperatives* command either *hypothetically* or *categorically.* The former represent the practical necessity of a possible action as means to something else that is willed (or at least which one might possibly will). The categorical imperative would be that which represented an action as necessary of itself without reference to another end, that is, as objectively necessary.
>
> Since every practical law represents a possible action as good, and on this account, for a subject who is practically determinable by reason as necessary, all imperatives are formulae determining an action which is necessary according to the principle of a will good in some respects. If now the action is good only as a means *to something else,* then the imperative is *hypothetical;* if it is conceived as good *in itself* and consequently as being necessarily the principle of a will which of itself conforms to reason, then it is *categorical.*[17]

With hypothetical imperatives, what is commanded depends upon particular circumstances. With moral or categorical imperatives, there are universal laws which tell us what to do in every circumstance. (A *maxim,* according to Kant, is a "subjective principle of action," or what we would call an *intention.* It is distinguished from an "objective principle," that is, a universal law of reason.)

---

[16] Kant, *Fundamental Principles of the Metaphysics of Morals.*
[17] Kant, *Fundamental Principles of the Metaphysics of Morals.*

There is therefore but one categorical imperative, namely, this: *Act only on that maxim whereby thou canst at the same time will that it should become a universal law.*

Now if all imperatives of duty can be deduced from this one imperative as from their principle, then, although it should remain undecided whether what is called duty is not merely a vain notion, yet at least we shall be able to show what we understand by it and what this notion means.

Since the universality of the law according to which effects are produced constitutes what is properly called *nature* in the most general sense (as to form)—that is, the existence of things so far as it is determined by general laws—the imperative of duty may be expressed thus: *Act as if the maxim of thy action were to become by thy will a universal law of nature.*

We will now enumerate a few duties, adopting the usual division of them into duties to ourselves and to others, and into perfect and imperfect duties.

1. A man reduced to despair by a series of misfortunes feels wearied of life, but is still so far in possession of his reason that he can ask himself whether it would not be contrary to his duty to himself to take his own life. Now he inquires whether the maxim of his action could become a universal law of nature. His maxim is: From self-love I adopt it as a principle to shorten my life when its longer duration is likely to bring more evil than satisfaction. It is asked then simply whether this principle founded on self-love can become a universal law of nature. Now we see at once that a system of nature of which it should be a law to destroy life by means of the very feeling whose special nature it is to impel to the improvement of life would contradict itself, and therefore could not exist as a system of nature; hence that maxim cannot possibly exist as a universal law of nature, and consequently would be wholly inconsistent with the supreme principle of all duty.

2. Another finds himself forced by necessity to borrow money. He knows that he will not be able to repay it, but sees also that nothing will be lent to him unless he promises stoutly to repay it in a definite time. He desires to make this promise, but he has still so much conscience as to ask himself: Is it not unlawful and inconsistent with duty to get out of a difficulty in this way? Suppose, however, that he resolves to do so, then the maxim of his action would be expressed thus: When I think myself in want of money, I will borrow money and promise to repay it, although I know that I never can do so. Now this principle of self-love or of one's own advantage may perhaps be consistent with my whole future welfare; but the question now is, Is it right? I change then the suggestion of self-love into a universal law, and state the question thus: How would it be if my maxim were a universal law? Then I see at once that it could never hold as a universal law of nature, but would necessarily contradict itself. For supposing it to be a universal law that everyone when he thinks himself in a difficulty should be able to promise whatever he pleases, with the purpose of not keeping his promise, the promise itself would become impossible, as well as the end that one might have in view in it, since no one would consider that anything was promised to him, but would ridicule all such statements as vain pretenses.

3. A third finds in himself a talent which with the help of some culture might make him a useful man in many respects. But he finds himself in

comfortable circumstances and prefers to indulge in pleasure rather than to take pains in enlarging and improving his happy natural capacities. He asks, however, whether his maxim of neglect of his natural gifts, besides agreeing with his inclination to indulgence, agrees also with what is called duty. He sees then that a system of nature could indeed subsist with such a universal law, although men (like the South Sea islanders) should let their talents rest and resolve to devote their lives merely to idleness, amusement, and propagation of their species—in a word, to enjoyment; but he cannot possibly *will* that this should be a universal law of nature, or be implanted in us as such by a natural instinct. For, as a rational being, he necessarily wills that his faculties be developed, since they serve him, and have been given him, for all sorts of possible purposes.

4. A fourth, who is in prosperity, while he sees that others have to contend with great wretchedness and that he could help them, thinks: What concern is it of mine? Let everyone be as happy as Heaven pleases, or as he can make himself; I will take nothing from him nor even envy him, only I do not wish to contribute anything to his welfare or to his assistance in distress! Now no doubt, if such a mode of thinking were a universal law, the human race might very well subsist, and doubtless even better than in a state in which everyone talks of sympathy and good-will, or even takes care occasionally to put it into practice, but, on the other side, also cheats when he can, betrays the rights of men, or otherwise violates them. But although it is possible that a universal law of nature might exist in accordance with that maxim, it is impossible to *will* that such a principle should have the universal validity of a law of nature. For a will which resolved this would contradict itself, inasmuch as many cases might occur in which one would have need of the love and sympathy of others, and in which, by such a law of nature, sprung from his own will, he would deprive himself of all hope of the aid he desires.

These are a few of the many actual duties, or at least what we regard as such, which obviously fall into two classes on the one principle that we have laid down. We must be *able to will* that a maxim of our action should be a universal law. This is the canon of the moral appreciation of the action generally. Some actions are of such a character that their maxim cannot without contradiction be even *conceived* as a universal law of nature, far from it being possible that we should *will* that it *should* be so. In others, this intrinsic impossibility is not found, but still it is impossible to *will* that their maxim should be raised to the universality of a law of nature, since such a will would contradict itself. It is easily seen that the former violate strict or rigorous (inflexible) duty; the latter only laxer (meritorious) duty. Thus it has been completely shown by these examples how all duties depend as regards the nature of the obligation (not the object of the action) on the same principle.[18]

Another way of describing the categorical imperative, using a term from Kant that we've already encountered, is to say that it is an *a priori* principle, in this case, independent of any particular circumstances. Moral principles are necessary for the same reason that certain principles of knowledge are

[18] Kant, *Fundamental Principles of the Metaphysics of Morals.*

necessary, according to Kant, that is, because they are essential to human nature. It is important, therefore, for Kant to insist that moral principles, as *a priori* principles of reason, hold for every human being, in fact, even more generally, for every rational creature. (There is an extremely important point hidden in this phrase; traditionally, morality has always been defended on the basis of God's will, that is, we ought to be moral because God gave us the moral laws. According to Kant, however, God does not give the laws but, as a rational creature He is bound to them just as we are. Thus, in answer to the question, "are the laws of morality good because God is good or is God good because he obeys the laws of morality?" Kant would accept the latter.)

Kant's discussion of the categorical imperative is made confusing because, after he has told us that "there is but one categorical imperative," he then goes on to give us others. He calls these "alternative formulations of the categorical imperative," but their effect on most readers is to confuse them unnecessarily. In actuality, for Kant there are a great many categorical imperatives. The first one Kant gave us is merely the most general. More specific examples are "don't lie!" and "keep your promises!" Another general categorical imperative is "never use people!" There is, however, a sense in which "using people" may be perfectly innocent. For example, I "use" you in order to play tennis, since I could not play alone. In such a case, you derive as much benefit from my "using you" as I do, and we could say that you are "using me" as well. But there are cases in which we are tempted to "use" people for our own benefit without any regard to their interests. This is what Kant forbids.

> Now I say: man and generally any rational being *exists* as an end in himself, *not merely as a means* to be arbitrarily used by this or that will, but in all his actions, whether they concern himself or other rational beings, must be always regarded at the same time as an end. All objects of the inclinations have only a conditional worth; for if the inclinations and the wants founded on them did not exist, then their object would be without value. But the inclinations themselves, being sources of want, are so far from having an absolute worth for which they should be desired that, on the contrary, it must be the universal wish of every rational being to be wholly free from them. Thus the worth of any object which is *to be acquired* by our action is always conditional. Beings whose existence depends not on our will but on nature's, have nevertheless, if they are not rational beings, only a relative value as means, and are therefore called *things;* rational beings, on the contrary, are called *persons,* because their very nature points them out as ends in themselves, that is, as something which must not be used merely as means, and so far therefore restricts freedom of action (and is an object of respect). These, therefore, are not merely subjective ends whose existence has a worth *for us* as an effect of our action, but *objective ends,* that is, things whose existence is an end in itself—an end, moreover, for which no other can be substituted, which they should subserve *merely* as means, for otherwise nothing whatever would possess *absolute worth;* but if all worth were conditioned and therefore contingent, then there would be no supreme practical principle of reason whatever.

If then there is a supreme practical principle or, in respect of the human will, a categorical imperative, it must be one which, being drawn from the conception of that which is necessarily an end for everyone because it is *an end in itself,* constitutes an *objective* principle of will, and can therefore serve as a universal practical law. The foundation of this principle is: *rational nature exists as an end in itself.* Man necessarily conceives his own existence as being so; so far then this is a *subjective* principle of human actions. But every other rational being regards its existence similarly, just on the same rational principle that holds for me; so that it is at the same time an objective principle from which as a supreme practical law all laws of the will must be capable of being deduced. Accordingly the practical imperative will be as follows: *So act as to treat humanity, whether in thine own person or in that of any other, in every case as an end withal, never as means only.* We will now inquire whether this can be practically carried out.

To abide by the previous examples:

First, under the head of necessary duty to oneself: He who contemplates suicide should ask himself whether his action can be consistent with the idea of humanity *as an end in itself.* If he destroys himself in order to escape from painful circumstances, he uses a person merely as *a mean* to maintain a tolerable condition up to the end of life. But a man is not a thing, that is to say, something which can be used merely as means, but must in all his actions be always considered as an end in himself. I cannot, therefore, dispose in any way of a man in my own person so as to mutilate him, to damage or kill him. (It belongs to ethics proper to define this principle more precisely, so as to avoid all misunderstanding, for example, as to the amputation of the limbs in order to preserve myself; as to exposing my life to danger with a view to preserve it, etc. This question is therefore omitted here.)

Secondly, as regards necessary duties, or those of strict obligation, towards others: He who is thinking of making a lying promise to others will see at once that he would be using another man *merely as a mean,* without the latter containing at the same time the end in himself. For he whom I propose by such a promise to use for my own purposes cannot possibly assent to my mode of acting towards him, and therefore cannot himself contain the end of this action. This violation of the principle of humanity in other men is more obvious if we take in examples of attacks on the freedom and property of others. For then it is clear that he who transgresses the rights of men intends to use the person of others merely as means, without considering that as rational beings they ought always to be esteemed also as ends, that is, as beings who must be capable of containing in themselves the end of the very same action.

Thirdly, as regards contingent (meritorious) duties to oneself: It is not enough that the action does not violate humanity in our own person as an end in itself, it must also *harmonize with it.* Now there are in humanity capacities of greater perfection which belong to the end that nature has in view in regard to humanity in ourselves as the subject; to neglect these might perhaps be consistent with the *maintenance* of humanity as an end in itself, but not with the *advancement* of this end.

Fourthly, as regards meritorious duties towards others: The natural end which all men have is their own happiness. Now humanity might indeed subsist although no one should contribute anything to the happiness of others, provided he did not intentionally withdraw anything from it; but after all, this would only harmonize negatively, not positively, with *humanity as an end in itself,* if everyone does not also endeavor, as far as in him lies, to forward the ends of others. For the ends of any subject which is an end in himself ought as far as possible to be *my* ends also, if that conception is to have its *full* effect with me.

This principle that humanity and generally every rational nature is *an end in itself* (which is the supreme limiting condition of every man's freedom of action), is not borrowed from experience, *first,* because it is universal, applying as it does to all rational beings whatever, and experience is not capable of determining anything about them; *secondly,* because it does not present humanity as an end to men (subjectively), that is, as an object which men do of themselves actually adopt as an end; but as an objective end which must as a law constitute the supreme limiting condition of all our subjective ends, let them be what we will; it must therefore spring from pure reason.[19]

In Kant's own terms: every human will is a will capable of acting according to universal laws of morality, not based upon any personal inclinations or interests but obeying rational principles which are categorical. Using this as a definition of morality, Kant then looks back at his predecessors:

Looking back now on all previous attempts to discover the principle of morality, we need not wonder why they all failed. It was seen that man was bound to laws by duty, but it was not observed that the laws to which he is subject are *only those of his own giving,* though at the same time they are *universal,* and that he is only bound to act in conformity with his own will —a will, however, which is designed by nature to give universal laws. For when one has conceived man only as subject to a law (no matter what), then this law required some interest, either by way of attraction or constraint, since it did not originate as a law from *his own will,* but this will was according to a law obliged by *something else* to act in a certain manner. Now by this necessary consequence all the labor spent in finding a supreme principle of *duty* was irrevocably lost. For men never elicited duty, but only a necessity of acting from a certain interest.[20]

Any morality worthy of the name, in other words, must be a product of a person's own autonomous reason yet universal at the same time, as a product of rational will and independent of personal feeling or interest. All previous philosophy, however, has insisted upon appealing to such personal feelings and interests and thus ended up with principles that were in every case hypothetical and not, according to Kant, categorical or moral. Thus morality for Aristotle depended upon a person's being a male Greek citizen, and for Hume and Rousseau it depended upon sentiment, particularly sentiments sympathetic to

[19] Kant, *Fundamental Principles of the Metaphysics of Morals.*
[20] Kant, *Fundamental Principles of the Metaphysics of Morals.*

other people. For Kant, morality and duty are completely set apart from such personal circumstances and concerns. Morality and duty have no qualifications and, ultimately, they need have nothing to do with the good life or with happiness. In a perfect world, perhaps, doing our duty might also bring us happiness. But this is not such a world, Kant observes, and so happiness and morality are two separate concerns, with the second always to be considered the most important. (It is at this point, however, that Kant introduces his "Postulates of Practical Reason," and God in particular, in order to give us some assurance that, at least in the [very] long run, doing our duty will bring us some reward.)

Kant's conception of morality is so strict that it is hard for most people to accept. What is most difficult to accept is the idea that morality and duty have nothing to do with our personal desires, ambitions and feelings, which Kant called our inclinations. We can agree that, at least sometimes, our duties and our inclinations are in conflict. But many philosophers have felt that Kant went much too far the other way in separating them entirely. Furthermore, Kant's emphasis on the categorical imperative systematically rules out all reference to particular situations and circumstances. In response to Kant, one may ask: Isn't the right thing to do often determined only within the particular context or situation? (A very recent moral philosophy called "situation ethics" has renewed this ancient demand.) Don't we have to know the particular problems and persons involved? What is right in one situation might very well be wrong in another, just because of different personalities, for example. Some people may be extremely hurt if we tell them the "truth" about themselves. On the other hand, a little "white" lie will make them feel much better. Other people are offended at any lie, however, and prefer even hurtful truths to the "ignorant bliss" of not knowing. Must not all moral rules be tempered to the particular situation?

In a more general way, it has been objected that Kant's unqualified concept of morality is much too general to help us decide what to do in any particular situation. As an example, take the categorical imperative, "don't steal!" Although the imperative itself, as a categorical one, must be unqualified, in order to apply it at all, we have to understand the kinds of circumstances to which it applies. Can't we have a right to steal in certain circumstances? Or, to put the same point differently, aren't there some circumstances in which "stealing" isn't really stealing at all? But what then of the situation in which a starving man steals a loaf of bread from an extremely wealthy baker. Surely he is stealing, but wouldn't we say that, under the circumstances, he is justified in doing so? And this indeed is the problem: How do we decide "under which circumstances" a moral law is to be applied? Kant's formulation of the categorical imperative only tells us that we must act in such a way that anyone in similar circumstances should act the same way. What defines these "similar" circumstances? Suppose I were to say that, "anyone in these circumstances, namely, being five-foot-seven and born in Detroit in 1942, having blond hair and blue eyes, and being a graduate of C. High School may steal." Anyone in the same circumstances can steal, but, of course, I have defined the circumstances in such a way that it is extremely unlikely that anyone but myself will ever qualify. How can we avoid such trickery? Not by any considerations within the categorical imperative itself, for by its very nature it is incapable of telling us under what circumstances a moral law applies. Another way of making the same objection is to complain that there is no way of deciding how detailed the imperative must be. For example, should we simply say, "don't steal!" or rather "don't steal unless you're starving and the other person is not!" or else, "don't steal unless you're blond and blue-eyed!" etc.?

There have been other objections to Kant's severe philosophy. For example, if moral principles are categorical, then what do we do when two different moral principles conflict? The rule that tells us "don't lie!" is categorical; so is the rule that tells us "keep your promises!" Suppose that I promise not to tell anyone where you will be this weekend. Then someone trying to kill you forces me to tell. I have to say something. Either I break the promise or I lie. Kant gives us no adequate way of choosing between the promise and the lie. He has ruled out any appeal to the consequences of our actions. In Kant's argument, even if your enemy is trying to kill you, it is not morally relevant. And, most importantly, Kant has ruled out any appeal to what will make people happy, not only the person who must either lie or break a promise but everyone else who is involved as well.

UTILITARIANISM

In response to the harsh Kantian view of morality, with its neglect of happiness and the good life, a number of British philosophers, chiefly Jeremy Bentham, James Mill, and his son John Stuart Mill, developed a conception of morality that is called utilitarianism. It was an attempt to bring back personal inclinations and interests into moral considerations. Utilitarians wished to reconsider the consequences as well as the "will" of an action and to consider the particular circumstances of an action in an attempt to determine what is morally right. Most importantly, it was an attempt to return morality to the search for the personally satisfying life, which Kant had neglected.

The basis of utilitarianism is a form of hedonism, the conception of the good life that says the ultimate good is pleasure and that in the final analysis we want and ought to want this pleasure. But where traditional hedonism is concerned only with one's personal pleasure, utilitarianism is concerned with pleasure in general; that is, with one's own pleasure, the pleasure of other people involved, and even the pleasure of other people who are not directly involved. In many utilitarian writings, the notions of pleasure and happiness are used interchangeably. From our earlier discussion (and especially our discussion of Aristotle), we know that we must be cautious of any such exchange. There are many short-lived pleasures that do not make us happy; and happiness is much more than mere pleasure. But this is a major concern for the utilitarians; their whole theory revolves around a single aim, to make the most people as happy as possible, sometimes sacrificing short-term pleasures for enduring ones. Their central principle is often summarized as, "the greatest good for the greatest number."

Jeremy Bentham was motivated to formulate his utilitarian theories not so much by the strict moralism of Kant's philosophy as by the absurd complexity of the British legal system. Just as Kant sought a single principle that would simplify all morality, Bentham looked for a single principle that would simplify the law. Bentham began with the fact that people seek pleasure and avoid pain, and developed the "principle of utility" on just this basis:

> I. Nature has placed mankind under the governance of two sovereign masters, *pain* and *pleasure*. It is for them alone to point out what we ought to do, as well as to determine what we shall do. On the one hand the standard of right and wrong, on the other the chain of causes and effects, are fastened to their throne. They govern us in all we do, in all we say, in all we think; every effort we can make to throw off our subjection, will serve but to demonstrate and confirm it. In words a man may pretend to abjure their empire: but in reality he will remain subject to it all the while. The *principle of utility* recognizes the subjection, and assumes it for the foundation of that system, the object of which is to rear the fabric of felicity by the hands of reason and of law. Systems which attempt to question it, deal in sounds instead of sense, in caprice instead of reason, in darkness instead of light.
>
> But enough of metaphor and declamation: it is not by such means that moral science is to be improved.
>
> II. The principle of utility is the foundation of the present work; it will be proper therefore at the outset to give an explicit and determinate account of what is meant by it. By the principle of utility is meant that principle which approves or disapproves of every action whatsoever, according to the tendency which it appears to have to augment or diminish the happiness of the party whose interest is in question; or, what is the same thing in other words, to promote or to oppose that happiness. I say of every action whatsoever; and therefore not only of every action of a private individual, but of every measure of government.
>
> III. By utility is meant that property in any object, whereby it tends to produce benefit, advantage, pleasure, good, or happiness, (all this in the present case comes to the same thing) or (what comes again to the same thing) to prevent the happening of mischief, pain, evil, or unhappiness to the party whose interest is considered: if that party be the community in general, then the happiness of the community: if a particular individual, then the happiness of that individual.
>
> IV. The interest of the community is one of the most general expressions that can occur in the phraseology of morals: no wonder that the meaning of it is often lost. When it has a meaning, it is this. The community is a fictitious *body*, composed of the individual persons who are considered as constituting as it were its *members*. The interest of the community then is, what?—the sum of the interests of the several members who compose it.

V. It is in vain to talk of the interest of the community, without understanding what is the interest of the individual. A thing is said to promote the interest, or to be *for* the interest, of an individual, when it tends to add to the sum total of his pleasures: or, what comes to the same thing, to diminish the sum total of his pains.

VI. An action then may be said to be conformable to the principle of utility, or, for shortness' sake, to utility, (meaning with respect to the community at large) when the tendency it has to augment the happiness of the community is greater than any it has to diminish it.

VII. A measure of government (which is but a particular kind of action, performed by a particular person or persons) may be said to be conformable to or dictated by the principle of utility, when in like manner the tendency which it has to augment the happiness of the community is greater than any which it has to diminish it.[21]

Morality, according to Bentham's principle of utility, means nothing other than action which tends to increase the amount of pleasure rather than diminish it.

X. Of an action that is conformable to the principle of utility, one may always say either that it is one that ought to be done, or at least that it is not one that ought not to be done. One may say also, that it is right it should be done; at least that it is not wrong it should be done: that it is a right action; at least that it is not a wrong action. When thus interpreted, the words *ought,* and *right* and *wrong,* and others of that stamp, have a meaning: when otherwise, they have none.[22]

How does one defend this principle of utility? One cannot. To try to prove the principle is "as impossible as it is needless." People quite "naturally," whether they admit to it or not, act on the basis of it. This is not to say that they always act on it, but that is only because, according to Bentham, people do not always know what is best for them. That is the reason for formulating the principle in philosophy.

The heart of Bentham's theory is the formulation of a procedure for deciding, in every possible case, the value of alternative courses of action. The procedure simply involves the determination of alternative amounts of pleasure and pain, according to what has appropriately been called *the happiness calculus.*

I. Pleasures then, and the avoidance of pains, are the *ends* which the legislator has in view: it behoves him therefore to understand their *value.* Pleasures and pains are the *instruments* he has to work with: it behoves him therefore to understand their force, which is again, in other words, their value.

II. To a person considered *by himself,* the value of a pleasure or pain considered *by itself,* will be greater or less, according to the four following circumstances.

[21] Jeremy Bentham, *An Introduction to the Principles of Morals and Legislation* (New York: Hafner, 1948).
[22] Bentham, *An Introduction to the Principles of Morals and Legislation.*

1. Its *intensity.*   3. Its *certainty* or *uncertainty.*
2. Its *duration.*   4. Its *propinquity* or *remoteness.*

III.   These are the circumstances which are to be considered in estimating a pleasure or a pain considered each of them by itself. But when the
value of any pleasure or pain is considered for the purpose of estimating
the tendency of any *act* by which it is produced, there are two other circumstances to be taken into the account; these are,

5. Its *fecundity,* or the chance it has of being followed by sensations of
the *same* kind: that is, pleasures, if it be a pleasure: pains, if it be a pain.

6. Its *purity,* or the chance it has of *not* being followed by sensations
of the *opposite* kind: that is, pains, if it be a pleasure: pleasures, if it be a
pain.

·   ·   ·   ·   ·

Then, the test itself:

V.   To take an exact account then of the general tendency of any act
by which the interests of a community are affected, proceed as follows.
Begin with any one person of those whose interests seem most immediately
to be affected by it: and take an account,

1. Of the value of each distinguishable *pleasure* which appears to be
produced by it in the *first* instance.

2. Of the value of each *pain* which appears to be produced by it in the
first instance.

3. Of the value of each pleasure which appears to be produced by it
after the first. This constitutes the *fecundity* of the first *pleasure* and the
impurity of the first *pain.*

4. Of the value of each *pain* which appears to be produced by it after
the first. This constitutes the *fecundity* of the first *pain,* and the *impurity*
of the first pleasure.

5. Sum up all the values of all the *pleasures* on the one side, and those
of all the pains on the other. The balance, if it be on the side of pleasure,
will give the *good* tendency of the act upon the whole, with respect to the
interests of that *individual* person; if on the side of pain, the *bad* tendency
of it upon the whole.

6. Take an account of the *number* of persons whose interests appear
to be concerned; and repeat the above process with respect to each. *Sum up*
the numbers expressive of the degrees of *good* tendency, which the act
has, with respect to each individual, in regard to whom the tendency of it
is *good* upon the whole: do this again with respect to each individual, in
regard to whom the tendency of it is *bad* upon the whole. Take the balance;
which, if on the side of *pleasure,* will give the general *good tendency* of the
act, with respect to the total number of community of individuals concerned; if on the side of pain the general *evil tendency,* with respect to the
same community.[23]

Let us take an example. Bentham himself discusses the problem of lust
(Prop. XXX), which he says is always bad. Why? "Because if the effects of

[23] Bentham, *An Introduction to the Principles of Morals and Legislation.*

the motive are not bad, then we do not call it lust." Lust, in other words, is sexual desire that is so excessive that it brings about more pain than pleasure. Suppose you are sexually attracted to another person. How do you decide (assuming that there is already mutual agreement) whether to follow through or not? First, you estimate the amount of pleasure each person will gain. An important question is whether the pleasure of only these two people should be estimated or the pleasure of others besides. If it is a question of adultery, then the interests of at least a third person should be considered. But assuming that no such direct complications are involved, even the indirect interests of the rest of society must be considered. (If you and your potential lover are sufficiently young, should the happiness of your parents enter into your decision?) Then, after you have considered its initial pleasure, estimate the initial pain. (In this case, we may presume it will be slight.) Then, ask about the longer term pleasures and pains for each person involved. If a sexual relationship will leave you feeling happy about yourself and the other person, then the subsequent pleasure will be considerable. If either person will feel regrets, or degraded, or embarrassed, or if sex will spoil a good friendship, or if a sexual relationship will set up expectations which one or both of you is unwilling to fulfill, then the amount of subsequent pain may be overwhelming. Then, add up the pleasures and pains for each person, match the total amount of pleasure against the total pain, and if the balance is positive, go ahead. If the balance is negative, don't do it. Suppose, for example, you each expect a great deal of initial pleasure, and one of you expects nothing but good feelings afterwards while the other expects only mild regrets. No one else need even know, and so the balance, clearly, is very positive. But suppose neither of you expects to enjoy it all that much, and the subsequent hassles will be a prolonged and troublesome bother, then, very likely the balance will be negative. We don't often make this kind of decision in this way, we simply do what we want to do at the time. And this is precisely what Bentham says we shouldn't do. He argues that it is because we so often act on the basis of impulses without rational calculations that we end up unhappy. In other words, the fact that we are usually irrational is not an argument against Bentham's principles. Their purpose is precisely to make us rational, to help us get what we really want.

There are problems with Bentham's theory. All that is considered, according to his "happiness calculus," is solely the amount of pleasure and pain. But some of you, in response to our preceding example, might well say, "it doesn't matter how much pleasure and how little pain two people will gain if they get into a sexual relationship. Under certain circumstances (if it is adultery, or simply if they are not married) such behavior is wrong! Mere happiness is not enough!" And here we see the beginning of a swing back towards Kant. To see why such a move is necessary, let us examine the following objection to Bentham. Suppose a great many people would get a great deal of pleasure out of seeing some innocent person tortured and slaughtered like a beast. Of course the victim would suffer a great deal of pain, but by increasing the size of the crowd we could eventually obtain an amount of pleasure on the part of everyone else which more than balanced the suffering of the victim. Bentham's calculus has no way of rejecting such a gruesome outcome. A less horrible example is this; if a person gets great pleasure from some activity, and no pain, there are no other considerations that apply to him or her (assuming that his/her actions do not effect others). Are we then to say that a life of sloth and self-indulgence, if it satisfies everyone and gives them a lot of pleasure and no pain, is to be preferred to any other life of any kind? Recall, for example, the "happiness box" experiment I proposed in our discussion of hedonism. Would we in fact endorse such a life for ourselves or anyone else? Does Bentham give us any reason to try for anything "better" than being happy pigs? This was the problem that bothered Bentham's godson, John Stuart Mill.

Mill's version of utilitarianism added an important qualification to Bentham's purely quantitative calculus. He said that it is not only quantity of pleasure that counts, but the quality as well. Needless to say, this makes the calculations much more complicated. In fact, it makes them impossible, for there cannot be precise calculation of quality, even though there can be precise calculations of quantity. Mill's now famous example is the following: if a pig can live a completely satisfied life, while a morally concerned and thoughtful individual like Socrates cannot ever be so satisfied, is the life of the pig therefore preferable? Mill's answer is this:

> It is better to be a human being dissatisfied than a pig satisfied; better to be Socrates dissatisfied than a fool satisfied.

On what grounds can he say this? Aren't the pig and the fool happier?

> If the fool or the pig are of a different opinion, it is only because they only know their own side of the question. The other party [Socrates] knows both sides.[24].

There are problems that emerge from this theory. How are we to evaluate different "qualities" of pleasure, even if we have tried them all? But first, let us look at Mill's revision of utilitarianism, as summarized in his popular pamphlet, appropriately called, *Utilitarianism*. (It was Mill, not Bentham, who invented this term.) It begins with a general consideration of morality, and of Kant's moral philosophy in particular.

> Our moral faculty, according to all those of its interpreters who are entitled to the name of thinkers, supplies us only with the general principles of moral judgments; it is a branch of our reason, not of our sensitive faculty; and must be looked to for the abstract doctrines of morality, not for perception of it in the concrete. The intuitive, no less than what may be termed the inductive, school of ethics insists on the necessity of general laws. They both agree that the morality of an individual action is not a question of direct perception, but of the application of a law to an individual case. They recognize also, to a great extent, the same moral laws but differ

[24] John Stuart Mill, *Utilitarianism* (New York: Bobbs-Merrill, 1957).

as to their evidence and the source from which they derive their authority. According to the one opinion, the principles of morals are evident *a priori*, requiring nothing to command assent except that the meaning of the terms be understood. According to the other doctrine, right and wrong, as well as truth and falsehood, are questions of observation and experience. But both hold equally that morality must be deduced from principles; and the intuitive school affirm as strongly as the inductive that there is a science of morals. Yet they seldom attempt to make out a list of the *a priori* principles which are to serve as the premises of the science; still more rarely do they make any effort to reduce those various principles to one first principle, or common ground of obligation. They either assume the ordinary precepts of morals as of *a priori* authority, or they lay down as the common groundwork of those maxims, some generality much less obviously authoritative than the maxims themselves, and which has never succeeded in gaining popular acceptance. Yet to support their pretensions there ought either to be some one fundamental principle or law at the root of all morality, or, if there be several, there should be a determinate order of precedence among them; and the one principle, or the rule for deciding between the various principles when they conflict, ought to be self-evident.

To inquire how far the bad effects of this deficiency have been mitigated in practice, or to what extent the moral beliefs of mankind have been vitiated or made uncertain by the absence of any distinct recognition of an ultimate standard, would imply a complete survey and criticism of past and present ethical doctrine. It would, however, be easy to show that whatever steadiness or consistency these moral beliefs have attained has been mainly due to the tacit influence of a standard not recognized. Although the non-existence of an acknowledged first principle has made ethics not so much a guide as a consecration of men's actual sentiments, still, as men's sentiments, both in favor and of aversion, are greatly influenced by what they suppose to be the effect of things upon their happiness, the principle of utility, or, as Bentham latterly called it, the greatest happiness principle, has had a large share in forming the moral doctrines even of those who most scornfully reject its authority. Nor is there any school of thought which refuses to admit that the influence of actions on happiness is a most material and even predominant consideration in many of the details, of morals, however unwilling to acknowledge it as the fundamental principle of morality and the source of moral obligation. I might go much further and say that to all those *a priori* moralists who deem it necessary to argue at all, utilitarian arguments are indispensable. It is not my present purpose to criticize these thinkers; but I cannot help referring, for illustration, to a systematic treatise by one of the most illustrious of them, the *Metaphysics of Ethics* by Kant. This remarkable man, whose system of thought will long remain one of the landmarks in the history of philosophical speculation, does, in the treatise in question, lay down a universal first principle as the origin and ground of moral obligation; it is this: "So act that the rule on which thou actest would admit of being adopted as a law by all rational beings." But when he begins to deduce from this precept any of the actual duties of morality, he fails, almost grotesquely, to show that there would be any contradiction, and logical (not to say physical) impossibility, in the adoption by all rational beings of the most outrageously immoral rules of conduct. All he knows is that the *consequences* of their universal adoption would be such as no one would choose to incur.

Then, Mill gets down to the business of redefining utilitarianism. Like Bentham, he insists that the principle of utility cannot be proven as such, for it is the ultimate end in terms of which everything else is justified. But there is, Mill tells us, a "larger sense of the word 'proof' ":

> On the present occasion, I shall, without further discussion of the other theories, attempt to contribute something towards the understanding and appreciation of the "utilitarian" or "happiness" theory, and towards such proof as it is susceptible of. It is evident that this cannot be proof in the ordinary and popular meaning of the term. Questions of ultimate ends are not amenable to direct proof. Whatever can be proved to be good must be so by being shown to be a means to something admitted to be good without proof. The medical art is proved to be good by its conducing to health; but how is it possible to prove that health is good? The art of music is good, for the reason, among others, that it produces pleasure; but what proof is it possible to give that pleasure is good? If, then, it is asserted that there is a comprehensive formula, including all things which are in themselves good, and that whatever else is good is not so as an end but as a means, the formula may be accepted or rejected, but is not a subject of what is commonly understood by proof. We are not, however, to infer that its acceptance or rejection must depend on blind impulse, or arbitrary choice. There is a larger meaning of the word "proof," in which this question is as amenable to it as any other of the disputed questions of philosophy. The subject is within the cognizance of the rational faculty; and neither does that faculty deal with it solely in the way of intuition. Considerations may be presented capable of determining the intellect either to give or withhold its assent to the doctrine; and this is equivalent to proof.

WHAT UTILITARIANISM IS

A passing remark is all that needs be given to the ignorant blunder of supposing that those who stand up for utility as the test of right and wrong use the term in that restricted and merely colloquial sense in which utility is opposed to pleasure. An apology is due to the philosophical opponents of utilitarianism, for even the momentary appearance of confounding them with anyone capable of so absurd a misconception; which is the more extraordinary, inasmuch as the contrary accusation, of referring everything to pleasure, and that, too, in its grossest form, is another of the common charges against utilitarianism: and, as has been pointedly remarked by an able writer, the same sort of persons, and often the very same persons, denounce the theory "as impracticably dry when the word 'utility' precedes the word 'pleasure,' and as too practically voluptuous when the word 'pleasure' precedes the word 'utility'." Those who know anything about the matter are aware that every writer, from Epicurus to Bentham, who maintained the theory of utility, meant by it, not something to be contradistinguished from pleasure, but pleasure itself, together with exemption from pain; and instead of opposing the useful to the agreeable or the ornamental, have always declared that the useful means these, among other things. Yet the common herd, including the herd of writers, not only in newspapers and periodicals, but in books of weight and pretension, are perpetually falling into this shallow mistake. Having caught up the word "utilitarian," while knowing nothing whatever about it but its sound, they habitually express by it the rejection or the neglect of pleasure in some of its forms: of beauty, of ornament, or of amusement. Nor is the term thus ignorantly misapplied solely in disparagement, but occasionally in compliment, as though it implied superiority to frivolity and the mere pleasures of the moment. And this perverted use is the only one in which the word is popularly known, and the one from which the new generation are acquiring their sole notion of its meaning. Those who introduced the word, but who had for many years discontinued it as a distinctive appellation, may well feel themselves called upon to resume it if by doing so they can hope to contribute anything towards rescuing it from this utter degradation.

The creed which accepts as the foundation of morals "utility" or the "greatest happiness principle" holds that actions are right in proportion as they tend to promote happiness, wrong as they tend to produce the reverse of happiness. By happiness is intended pleasure, and the absence of pain; by unhappiness, pain, and the privation of pleasure. To give a clear view of the moral standard set up by the theory, much more requires to be said; in particular, what things it includes in the ideas of pain and pleasure; and to what extent this is left an open question. But these supplementary explanations do not affect the theory of life on which this theory of morality is grounded—namely, that pleasure and freedom from pain are the only things desirable as ends, and that all desirable things (which are as numerous in the utilitarian as in any other scheme) are desirable either for the pleasure inherent in themselves, or as means to the promotion of pleasure and the prevention of pain.

Now such a theory of life excites in many minds, and among them in some of the most estimable in feeling and purpose, inveterate dislike. To suppose that life has (as they express it) no higher end than pleasure—no better and nobler object of desire and pursuit—they designate as utterly mean and groveling; as a doctrine worthy only of swine, to whom the followers of Epicurus were, at a very early period, contemptuously likened; and modern holders of the doctrine are occasionally made the subject of equally polite comparisons by its German, French, and English assailants.

When thus attacked, the Epicureans have always answered that it is not they, but their accusers, who represent human nature in a degrading light, since the accusation supposes human beings to be capable of no pleasures except those of which swine are capable. If this supposition were true, the charge could not be gainsaid, but would then be no longer an imputation; for if the sources of pleasure were precisely the same to human beings and to swine, the rule of life which is good enough for the one would be good enough for the other. The comparison of the Epicurean life to that of beasts is felt as degrading, precisely because a beast's pleasures do not satisfy a human being's conceptions of happiness. Human beings have faculties more elevated than the animal appetites and, when once made conscious of them, do not regard anything as happiness which does not include their gratification. I do not, indeed, consider the Epicureans to have been by any means faultless in drawing out their scheme of consequences from the utilitarian principle. To do this in any sufficient manner, many Stoic, as well as Christian, elements require to be included. But there is no known Epicurean theory of life which does not assign to the pleasures of the intellect, of the feelings and imagination, and of the moral sentiments, a much higher value of pleasures than to those of mere sensation. It must be admitted, however, that utilitarian writers in general have placed the superiority of mental over bodily pleasures chiefly in the greater permanency, safety, uncostliness, etc., of the former— that is, in their circumstantial advantages rather than in their intrinsic nature. And on all these points utilitarians have fully proved their case; but they might have taken the other and, as it may be called, higher ground with entire consistency. It is quite compatible with the principle of utility to recognize the fact that some kinds of pleasure are more desirable and more valuable than others. It would be absurd that, while, in estimating all other things, quality is considered as well as quantity, the estimation of pleasures should be supposed to depend on quantity alone.

If I am asked what I mean by difference of quality in pleasures, or what makes one pleasure more valuable than another, merely as a pleasure, except its being greater in amount, there is but one possible answer. Of two pleasures, if there be one to which all or almost all who have experience of both give a decided preference, irrespective of a feeling of moral obligation to prefer it, that is the more desirable pleasure. If one of the two is, by those who are competently acquainted with both, placed so far above the other that they prefer it, even though knowing it to be attended with a greater amount of discontent, and would not resign it for any quantity of the other pleasure which their nature is capable of, we are justified in ascribing to the preferred enjoyment a superiority in quality so far outweighing quantity as to render it, in comparison, of small account.

Now it is an unquestionable fact that those who are equally acquainted with and equally capable of appreciating and enjoying both, do give a most marked preference to the manner of existence which employs their higher faculties. Few human creatures would consent to be changed into any of the lower animals for a promise of the fullest allowance of a beast's pleasures; no intelligent human being would consent to be a fool, no instructed person would be an ignoramus, no person of feeling and conscience would be selfish and base, even though they should be persuaded that the fool, the dunce, or the rascal is better satisfied with his lot than they are with theirs. They would not resign what they possess more than he for the most complete satisfaction of all the desires which they have in common with him. If they ever fancy they would, it is only in cases of unhappiness so extreme that to escape from it they would exchange their lot for almost any other, however undesirable in their own eyes. A being of higher faculties requires more to make him happy, is capable probably of more acute suffering, and certainly accessible to it at more points, than one of an inferior type; but in spite of these liabilities, he can never really wish to sink into what he feels to be a lower grade of existence. We may give what explanation we please of this unwillingness; we may attribute it to pride, a name which is given indiscriminately to some of the most and to some of the least estimable feelings of which mankind are capable: we may refer it to the love of liberty and personal independence, an appeal to which was with the Stoics one of the most effective means for the inculcation of it; to the love of power or to the love of excitement, both of which do really enter into and contribute to it; but its most appropriate appellation is a sense of dignity, which all human beings possess in one form or other, and in some, though by no means in exact, proportion to their higher faculties, and which is so essential a part of the happiness of those in whom it is strong that nothing which conflicts with it could be otherwise than momentarily an object of desire to them. Whoever supposes that this preference takes place at a sacrifice of happiness—that the superior being, in anything like equal circumstances, is not happier than the inferior—confounds the two very different ideas of happiness and content. It is indisputable that the being whose capacities of enjoyment are low has the greatest chance of having them fully satisfied; and a highly endowed being will always feel that any happiness which he can look for, as the world is constituted, is imperfect. But he can learn to bear its imperfections, if they are at all bearable; and they will not make him envy the being who is indeed unconscious of the imperfections, but only because he feels not at all the good which those imperfections qualify. It is better to be a human being dissatisfied than a pig satisfied; better to be Socrates dissatisfied than a fool satisfied. And if the fool, or the pig, are of a different opinion, it is because they only know their own side of the question. The other party to the comparison knows both sides.

It may be objected that many who are capable of the higher pleasures occasionally, under the influence of temptation, postpone them to the lower. But this is quite compatible with a full appreciation of the intrinsic superiority of the higher. Men often, from infirmity of character, make their election for the nearer good, though they know it to be the less valuable; and this no less when the choice is between two bodily pleasures than when it is between bodily and mental. They pursue sensual indulgences to the injury of health, though perfectly aware that health is the greater good. It may be further objected that many who begin with youthful enthusiasm for everything noble, as they advance in years, sink into indolence and selfishness. But I do not believe that those who undergo this very common change voluntarily choose the lower description of pleasures in preference to the higher. I believe that, before they devote themselves exclusively to the one, they have already become incapable of the other. Capacity for the nobler feelings is in most natures a very tender plant, easily killed, not only by hostile influences, but by mere want of sustenance; and in the majority of young persons it speedily dies away if the occupations to which their position in life has devoted them, and the society into which it has thrown them, are not favorable to keeping that higher capacity in exercise. Men lose their high aspirations as they lose their intellectual tastes, because they have not time or opportunity for indulging them; and they addict themselves to inferior pleasures, not because they deliberately prefer them, but because they are either the only ones to which they have access, or the only ones which they are any longer capable of enjoying. It may be questioned whether any one who has remained equally susceptible to both classes of pleasures, ever knowingly and calmly preferred the lower, though many, in all ages, have broken down in an ineffectual attempt to combine both.

I have dwelt on this point, as being a necessary part of a perfectly just conception of utility or happiness considered as the directive rule of human conduct. But it is by no means an indispensable condition to the acceptance of the utilitarian standard; for that standard is not the agent's own greatest happiness, but the greatest amount of happiness altogether; and if it may possibly be doubted whether a noble character is always the happier for its nobleness, there can be no doubt that it makes other people happier, and that the world in general is immensely a gainer by it. Utilitarianism, therefore, could only attain its end by the general cultivation of nobleness of character, even if each individual were only benefited by the nobleness of others, and his own, so far as happiness is concerned, were a sheer deduction from the benefit. But the bare enunciation of such an absurdity as this last renders refutation superfluous.

According to the greatest happiness principle, as above explained, the ultimate end, with refererence to and for the sake of which all other things are desirable—whether we are considering our own good or that of other people—is an existence exempt as far as possible from pain, and as rich as possible in enjoyments, both in point of quantity and quality; the test of quality and the rule for measuring it against quantity being the preference felt by those who, in their opportunities of experience, to which must be added their habits of self-consciousness and self-observation, are best furnished with the means of comparison. This, being, according to the utilitarian opinion, the end of human action, is necessarily also the standard of morality, which may accordingly be defined "the rules and precepts for human conduct," by the observance of which an existence such as has been described might be, to the greatest extent possible, secured to all mankind; and not to them only, but, so far as the nature of things admits, to the whole sentient creation.[25]

THE CREATION OF MORALITY:
NIETZSCHE AND EXISTENTIALISM

The single term "morality" must not mislead us. We have been discussing not simply different theories of morality but different conceptions of morality, and that means, different moralities, even if they should have many principles in common. The problem of relativism, in other words, is not confined to the comparison of exotically different cultures. It faces us in a far more urgent form in our own conceptions of morality. We might agree that killing, without extreme provocation, is wrong. But why do we believe that it is wrong? One person claims that it is wrong because the Ten Commandments (and therefore God) forbids it. Another says it is wrong because it is a mark of insensitivity and therefore a flaw in character. Another says it is wrong because

[25] Mill, *Utilitarianism.*

it violates peoples' rights, while still another says it is wrong because it increases the amount of pain in the world without equally adding to happiness. They all agree that killing is wrong, but the different reasons point to different circumstances in which each would kill. The first, if God commanded him or her to. The second, if the killing could be seen as a sign of strength and heroism. The third, if he/she found a way to take away people's right to live, or found another right that was overriding. The fourth, as a utilitarian, would only have to find a circumstance in which the death of one person was more than balanced by the increased welfare of the others (as in a criminal execution).

From the four great moral philosophies we have studied, four such conceptions emerge. They all agree on many principles, but the reasons differ widely, and some of the principles do also. But most dramatic is the difference between Aristotle's ancient Greek morality and Kant's modern morality of duty. Kant's morality may be taken as a fair representation of the modern Judeo-Christian morality in its strictest form: the emphasis on moral principle and laws, the emphasis on reason and individual autonomy, the emphasis on good intentions ("a good will") and doing one's duty. There are small differences which we have already pointed out: the Greek emphasis on pride as a virtue in contrast to the Christian condemnation of pride as a "deadly sin" (or at least a personality flaw) and its emphasis on humility. One of Aristotle's first virtues was courage in battle, while most modern moralities consider that as a special case, not as a matter of being an everyday "good person" at all. This difference might well be attributed to the different political climates of the two societies. But that is not enough. As we shall see, the differences are much deeper than that.

There are crucial differences between ancient and modern moral perspectives; the most striking is the difference in the scope of their applicability. In Aristotle's moral philosophy, only a small elite is thought to be capable of true happiness (*eudaimonia*) through virtuous action and contemplation. Other people (women, slaves, non-citizens) may live comfortably enough and do their duties and chores efficiently, but they cannot be called "happy." The elite, however, are characterized by their excellence, by their individual achievements, including wealth, power, honor, intelligence, wit, and all of those rewards that come with an aristocratic upbringing, the best of education and a life that is guaranteed in basic comforts from birth. In Kant's conception of morality, by contrast, all people who are rational (that is, everyone except morons and very young children) are to be judged by the same moral standards, the standards of duty. There are no elites. And since the judgments of moral worth are made solely on the basis of good intentions, no "external" advantages are relevant to a person's goodness or badness. In fact, it is possible that a perfectly "good" person would, with only the best intentions, cause chaos and unhappiness around him wherever he goes. And the harder he tries to make amends, the more he fouls them up. Dostoevsky wrote one of his greatest novels about just this: a perfectly good man, with all the right intentions, causes suffering and even death every time he tries to do good. Yet the point is, he is, by this modern conception, still the perfectly good man. Aristotle would find this laughable. How could we call a man virtuous just because of his intentions? How can a perfect failure be an example of ideal goodness?

In Aristotle's morality, the only people who operate on the basis of duty are those who are incapable of being truly good and truly happy. Duty is a morality for women and servants. For the elite, it is rather a question of personal excellence—in battle, in games, in business, in love, in debate, and in all things, especially philosophy. And where Kant's morality mostly consists (like the Ten Commandments) of "thou shalt not . . ." Aristotle's morality appropriately consists of personal desires and ambitions, not commands to achieve, and certainly not negative commands. The key element of Kant's philosophy, duty, is treated minimally in Aristotle, where the emphasis is on personal growth and achievement. But, on the other side, the image of the well-rounded, successful man, excellent in all things and the envy of his fellow men, plays virtually no role at all in Kant's philosophy. For him, what is important is the person who does what he or she is supposed to do. For Aristotle, the ideal is to strive for personal excellence, and doing what you are supposed to do is simply taken for granted along the way.

Now notice that both moralities have many of the same results. Aristotle's morality will praise many and condemn most of the same acts as Kant's morality: killing needlessly and stealing are wrong; telling the truth and keeping promises are right. But their conceptions of morality, and consequently, their conceptions of people are wholly different. And as we appreciate the nature of this difference, we will be in a position to understand one of the most dramatic moral revolutions of modern times, initiated by Friedrich Nietzsche. Nietzsche called himself an *immoralist,* and he attacked morality as viciously as he attacked Christianity. But though he has often been interpreted as saying that we should give up morality and feel free to kill, steal, and commit crimes of all kinds, his moral philosophy does not in fact say that at all. What he did was to attack modern morality, as summarized by Kant and Christianity, and urge us to return to ancient Greek morality as summarized by Aristotle. He also attacked utilitarianism, which he considered "vulgar." Like a great many philosophers of the nineteenth century (particularly German philosophers: Fichte, Hegel, Marx) Nietzsche saw in the ancient Greeks a sense of personal harmony and a sense of excellence that had been lost in the modern world. Nietzsche, like Aristotle, saw the concept of duty as fit for servants and slaves, but such a morality was wholly inadequate to motivate us to personal excellence and achievement. And Nietzsche, like Aristotle, was an unabashed elitist. Only a few people were capable of this "higher" morality. For the rest, the "slave morality" of duty would have to suffice. But for those few, nothing was more important than to give up the "thou shalt not . . ."'s of Morality (with a capital "m") and seek out one's own virtues and abilities. This does not mean that such a person need ever violate the laws of morality;

it means only that he or she does not consider obedience to these laws as the most important thing in life. Nor does this mean that Nietzsche is (as he is often thought to be) an ethical egoist. To say that a person should develop his or her own virtues and become excellent in as many ways as possible is not at all to say that one must act only in one's own interests. As in Aristotle, the excellence of the individual is part of and contributes to the excellence of society as a whole.

Nietzsche takes his central project as a philosopher to be what he calls, "the creation of values." In this, he is rightly listed as one of the existentialist philosophers, or, at least, as one of their most important predecessors. The phrase is perhaps misleading, however. What Nietzsche is doing is not inventing new values so much as reasserting very old ones. Furthermore, Nietzsche, like Aristotle, takes ethics to be based solely upon human nature, and so it is not a question of "creating values" so much as finding them in oneself. But where such a philosophy for Aristotle was in agreement with most of the thinking of his times, Nietzsche's thought was a radical disruption of the usual Kantian-style thinking of the modern period. And since Nietzsche, unlike Aristotle, did not believe that every human "nature" was the same, he taught that different individuals would most assuredly find and follow different values, different conceptions of excellence and thus have different moralities. For this reason, students who read Nietzsche looking for concrete moral advice, a set of principles to act on, are always disappointed. His central teaching is rather "follow yourself, don't follow me." Consequently, he can't—and won't—try to tell you how to live. But he does tell you, *to live,* and to give up the servile views that we have held of ourselves for many centuries.

Nietzsche's moral philosophy is largely critical, and most of his efforts have gone into the rejection of Kant's conception of morality in order to make room for individual self-achieving as found in Aristotle. His argument, however, is not a refutation in the usual sense. Instead, he undermines morality by showing that the motivation behind it is decrepit and weak. The central categories of Nietzsche's philosophy are strength and weakness, and he considers the Greek tradition of personal excellence a source of strength, the modern conception of morality a façade for weakness. Accordingly, he calls the first a "master morality," the second, a "slave morality" or, with reference to modern mass movements a "herd morality." The excerpts that follow, therefore, are illustrative of Nietzsche's general attack on morality. But never forget that his purpose is not merely destructive, but, in his eyes, creative, and the point is to get us to look to ourselves for values and to excel each in our own ways (the phrase "will to power" refers to just this effort to excel as individuals).

What does your conscience say? "You should become him who you are."

Herd-Instinct.—Wherever we meet with a morality we find a valuation and order of rank of the human impulses and activities. These valuations and orders of rank are always the expression of the needs of a community or herd: that which is in the first place to *its* advantage—and in the second place and third place—is also the authoritative standard for the worth of every individual. By morality the individual is taught to become a function of the herd, and to ascribe to himself value only as a function. As the conditions for the maintenance of one community have been very different from those of another community, there have been very different moralities; and in respect to the future essential transformations of herds and communities, states and societies, one can prophesy that there will still be very divergent moralities. Morality is the herd-instinct in the individual.[26]

Apart from the value of such assertions as "there is a categorical imperative in us," one can always ask: What does such an assertion indicate about him who makes it? There are systems of morals which are meant to justify their author in the eyes of other people; other systems of morals are meant to tranquillise him, and make him self-satisfied; with other systems he wants to crucify and humble himself; with others he wishes to take revenge; with others to conceal himself; with others to glorify himself and gain superiority and distinction;—this system of morals helps its author to forget, that system makes him, or something of him, forgotten; many a moralist would like to exercise power and creative arbitrariness over mankind; many another, perhaps, Kant especially, gives us to understand by his morals that "what is estimable in me, is that I know how to obey—and with you it *shall* not be otherwise than with me!" In short, systems of morals are only a *sign-language of the emotions.* . . .

In a tour through the many finer and coarser moralities which have hitherto prevailed or still prevail on the earth, I found certain traits recurring regularly together, and connected with one another, until finally two primary types revealed themselves to me, and a radical distinction was brought to light. There is *master-morality* and *slave-morality;*—I would at once add, however, that in all higher and mixed civilisations, there are also attempts at the reconciliation of the two moralities; but one finds still oftener the confusion and mutual misunderstanding of them, indeed, sometimes their close juxtaposition—even in the same man, within one soul. The distinctions of moral values have either originated in a ruling caste, pleasantly conscious of being different from the ruled—or among the ruled class, the slaves and dependents of all sorts. In the first case, (when it is the rulers who determine the conception "good," it is the exalted, proud disposition which is regarded as the distinguishing feature, and that which determines the order of rank. The noble type of man separates from himself the beings in whom the opposite of this exalted, proud disposition displays itself: he despises them. Let it at once be noted that in this first kind of morality the antithesis "good" and "bad" means practically the same as "noble" and "despicable";—the antithesis "good" and "*evil*" is of a different origin. The cowardly, the timid, the insignificant, and those thinking merely of narrow utility are despised; moreover, also, the distrustful, with their constrained glances, the self-abasing, the dog-like kind of men who let themselves be abused, the mendicant flatterers, and above all the liars:—

[26] Friedrich Nietzsche, *The Joyful Wisdom,* trans. Thomas Common, in *The Complete Works of Friedrich Nietzsche,* Oscar Levy, General Editor (1909–11) (New York: Russell & Russell, 1964).

it is a fundamental belief of all aristocrats that the common people are un-truthful. "We truthful ones"—the nobility in ancient Greece called them-selves. It is obvious that everywhere the designations of moral value were at first applied to *men,* and were only derivatively and at a later period applied to *actions;* it is a gross mistake, therefore, when historians of morals start questions like, "Why have sympathetic actions been praised?" (The noble type of man regards *himself* as a determiner of values; he does not require to be approved of; he passes the judgment: "What is injurious to me is injurious in itself"; he knows that it is he himself only who confers honour on things; he is a *creator of values.* He honours whatever he recog-nises in himself: such morality is self-glorification. In the foreground there is the feeling of plenitude, of power, which seeks to overflow, the happiness of high tension, the consciousness of a wealth which would fain give and bestow:—the noble man also helps the unfortunate, but not—or scarcely—out of pity, but rather from an impulse generated by the super-abundance of power. The noble man honours in himself the powerful one, him also who has power over himself, who knows how to speak and how to keep silence, who takes pleasure in subjecting himself to severity and hardness, and has reverence for all that is severe and hard. "Wotan placed a hard heart in my breast," says an old Scandinavian Saga: it is thus rightly expressed from the soul of a proud Viking. Such a type of man is even proud of *not* being made for sympathy; the hero of the Saga therefore adds warningly: "He who has not a hard heart when young, will never have one." The noble and brave who think thus are the furthest removed from the morality which sees precisely in sympathy, or in acting for the good of others, or in *désin-téressement,* the characteristic of the moral; faith in oneself, pride in one-self, a radical enmity and irony towards "selflessness," belong as definitely to noble morality, as do a careless scorn and precaution in presence of sympa-thy and the "warm heart."—It is the powerful who *know* how to honour, it is their art, their domain for invention. The profound reverence for age and for tradition—all law rests on this double reverence,—the belief and prejudice in favour of ancestors and unfavourable to newcomers, is typical in the morality of the powerful; and if, reversely, men of "modern ideas" believe almost instinctively in "progress" and the "future," and are more and more lacking in respect for old age, the ignoble origin of these "ideas" has complacently betrayed itself thereby. A morality of the ruling class, however, is more especially foreign and irritating to present-day taste in the sternness of its principle that one has duties only to one's equals; that one may act towards beings of a lower rank, towards all that is foreign, just as seems good to one, or "as the heart desires," and in any case "beyond good and evil": it is here that sympathy and similar sentiments can have a place. The ability and obligation to exercise prolonged gratitude and prolonged revenge—both only within the circle of equals,—artfulness in retaliation, *raffinement* of the idea in friendship, a certain necessity to have enemies (as outlets for the emotions of envy, quarrelsomeness, arrogance—in fact, in order to be a good *friend*): all these are typical characteristics of the noble morality, which, as has been pointed out, is not the morality of "modern ideas," and is therefore at present difficult to realise, and also to unearth and disclose.—It is otherwise with the second type of morality, *slave-morality.* Supposing that the abused, the oppressed, the suffering, the unemancipated, the weary, and those uncertain of themselves, should moralise, what will be the common element in their moral estimates? Probably a pessimistic suspicion with regard to the entire situation of man will find expression, perhaps a condemnation of man, together with his situation. The slave has an unfavourable eye for the virtues of the powerful; he has a scepticism and distrust, a *refinement* of distrust of everything "good" that is there honoured—he would fain persuade himself that the very happiness there is not genuine. On the other hand, *those* qualities which serve to alleviate the existence of sufferers are brought into prominence and flooded with light; it is here that sympathy, the kind, helping hand, the warm heart, patience, diligence, humility, and friendliness attain to honour for here these are the most useful qualities, and almost the only means of supporting the burden of existence. Slave-morality is essentially the morality of utility. Here is the seat of the origin of the famous antithesis "good" and "evil":—power and dangerousness are assumed to reside in the evil, a certain dreadfulness, subtlety, and strength, which do not admit of being despised. According to slave-morality, therefore, the "evil" man arouses fear; according to master-morality, it is precisely the "good" man who arouses fear and seeks to arouse it, while the bad man is regarded as the despicable being. The contrast attains its maximum when, in accordance with the logical consequences of slave-morality, a shade of depreciation— it may be slight and well-intentioned—at last attaches itself to the "good" man of this morality; because, according to the servile mode of thought, the good man must in any case be the *safe* man: he is good-natured, easily deceived, perhaps a little stupid, *un bonhomme.* Everywhere that slave-morality gains the ascendency, language shows a tendency to approximate the significations of the words "good" and "stupid."—At last fundamental difference: the desire for *freedom,* the instinct for happiness and the refinements of the feeling of liberty belong as necessarily to slave-morals and morality, as artifice and enthusiasm in reverence and devotion are the regular symptoms of an aristocratic mode of thinking and estimating.— Hence we can understand without further detail why love *as a passion*— it is our European specialty—must absolutely be of noble origin; as is well known, its invention is due to the Provençal poet-cavaliers, those brilliant, ingenious men of the *"gai saber,"* to whom Europe owes so much, and almost owes itself.

· · · · ·

And on the philosopher:

> . . . The philosophical workers, after the excellent pattern of Kant and Hegel, have to fix and formalise some great existing body of valuations —that is to say, former *determinations of value,* creations of value, which have become prevalent, and are for a time called "truths"—whether in the domain of the *logical,* the *political* (moral), or the *artistic.* It is for these investigators to make whatever has happened and been esteemed hitherto, conspicuous, conceivable, intelligible, and manageable, to shorten everything long, even "time" itself, and to *subjugate* the entire past: an immense and

wonderful task, in the carrying out of which all refined pride, all tenacious will, can surely find satisfaction. *The real philosophers, however, are commanders and law-givers;* they say: "Thus *shall* it be!" They determine first the Whither and the Why of mankind, and thereby set aside the previous labour of all philosophical workers, and all subjugators of the past—they grasp at the future with a creative hand, and whatever is and was, becomes for them thereby a means, an instrument, and a hammer. Their "knowing" is *creating,* their creating is a law-giving, their will to truth is—*Will to Power.*—Are there at present such philosophers? Have there ever been such philosophers? *Must* there not be such philosophers some day? . . .[27]

Nietzsche is often viewed as the most extreme of the anti-moralists, those who attack the traditional duty-bound Kantian-Christian conception of morality. In fact, he is but one among many philosophers who have rejected that morality in exchange for a more personal and individual set of principles. And, given his emphasis on human "nature," we can say that even Nietzsche is much more traditional than is usually supposed (though it is the Aristotelean, not the Kantian tradition). In the past few decades, however, morality has become far more personalized than even Nietzsche suggested. In Anglo-American philosophy, largely in the wake of logical positivism, ethics has been reduced to a matter of emotions, prescriptions, and attitudes rather than principles and rational laws. (Ironically, Nietzsche has always been in extreme disfavor among such philosophers while Kant was considered with extreme favor.)

The attack on the absolute moral principles of reason, which are the same for everyone, has been one of the most vigorous philosophical movements of the twentieth century, so much so that many philosophers, religious leaders and moralists have become alarmed at the destruction of uniform moral codes and have attempted to reassert the old moral laws in new ways. The problem is one of relativism. Is there a single moral code? Or are there possibly as many moralities as there are people? There are intermediary suggestions, such as relativizing morals to particular groups or societies, but the question is still the same: "is there ultimately any way of defending one moral code against any other?"

The most extreme relativist position of all has emerged from Nietzsche's existentialist successors, particularly Jean-Paul Sartre. In Sartre's philosophy, not only the idea of a uniform morality but the idea of a human nature upon which this morality might be based is completely rejected. Not because different people might have different "natures," as in Nietzsche, but because, for Sartre, our values are quite literally a question of creation, of personal commitment. In answer to any question about morality, the only ultimate answer is, "because I choose to accept these values." But what is most fascinating about Sartre's conception of morality as choice is the fact that he does not

---

[27] Friedrich Nietzsche, *Beyond Good and Evil,* trans. Helen Zimmern, in *The Complete Works of Friedrich Nietzsche,* Oscar Levy, General Editor (1909–11) (Russell & Russell, 1964).

therefore abandon general principles as Nietzsche does. Quite the contrary, he adopts an almost Kantian stance about the need to choose principles for all mankind, not just oneself. The difference is that Sartre, unlike Kant, makes no claims about the singular correctness of these principles. All he can say is, "this is what I choose mankind to be." Thus Sartre's moral philosophy is a curious mixture of the most radical relativism and the most traditional moralizing.

Man is nothing else but that which he makes of himself. That is the first principle of existentialism. And this is what people call its "subjectivity," using the word as a reproach against us. But what do we mean to say by this, but that man is of a greater dignity than a stone or a table? For we mean to say that man primarily exists—that man is, before all else, something which propels itself towards a future and is aware that it is doing so. Man is, indeed, a project which possesses a subjective life, instead of being a kind of moss, or a fungus or a cauliflower. Before that projection of the self nothing exists; not even in the heaven of intelligence: man will only attain existence when he is what he purposes to be. Not, however, what he may wish to be. For what we usually understand by wishing or willing is a conscious decision taken—much more often than not—after we have made ourselves what we are. I may wish to join a party, to write a book or to marry—but in such a case what is usually called my will is probably a manifestation of a prior and more spontaneous decision. If, however, it is true that existence is prior to essence, man is responsible for what he is. Thus, the first effect of existentialism is that it puts every man in possession of himself as he is, and places the entire responsibility for his existence squarely upon his own shoulders. And, when we say that man is responsible for himself, we do not mean that he is responsible only for his own individuality, but that he is responsible for all men. The word "subjectivism" is to be understood in two senses, and our adversaries play upon only one of them. Subjectivism means, on the one hand, the freedom of the individual subject and, on the other, that man cannot pass beyond human subjectivity. It is the latter which is the deeper meaning of existentialism. When we say that man chooses himself, we do mean that every one of us must choose himself; but by that we also mean that in choosing for himself he chooses for all men. For in effect, of all the actions a man may take in order to create himself as he wills to be, there is not one which is not creative, at the same time, of an image of man such as he believes he ought to be. To choose between this or that is at the same time to affirm the value of that which is chosen; for we are unable ever to choose the worse. What we choose is always the better; and nothing can be better for us unless it is better for all. If, moreover, existence precedes essence and we will to exist at the same time as we fashion our image, that image is valid for all and for the entire epoch in which we find ourselves. Our responsibility is thus much greater than we had supposed, for it concerns mankind as a whole. If I am a worker, for instance, I may choose to join a Christian rather than a Communist trade union. And if, by that membership, I choose to signify that resignation is, after all, the attitude that best becomes a man, that man's kingdom is not upon this earth, I do not commit myself alone to that view. Resignation is my will for everyone, and my action is, in consequence, a commitment on behalf of all mankind. Or if, to take a more personal case, I decide to marry and to have children, even though this decision proceeds simply from my situation, from my passion or my desire, I am thereby committing not only myself, but humanity as a whole, to the practice of monogamy. I am thus responsible for myself and for all men, and I am creating a certain image of man as I would have him to be. In fashioning myself I fashion man.

. . . . .

. . . Who can prove that I am the proper person to impose, by my own choice, my conception of man upon mankind? I shall never find any proof whatever; there will be no sign to convince me of it.

. . . . .

If I regard a certain course of action as good, it is only I who choose to say that it is good and not bad. . . . nevertheless I also am obliged at every instant to perform actions which are examples. Everything happens to every man as though the whole human race had its eyes fixed upon what he is doing and regulated its conduct accordingly.

. . . . .

As an example by which you may the better understand this state of abandonment, I will refer to the case of a pupil of mine, who sought me out in the following circumstances. His father was quarrelling with his mother and was also inclined to be a "collaborator"; his elder brother had been killed in the German offensive of 1940 and this young man, with a sentiment somewhat primitive but generous, burned to avenge him. His mother was living alone with him, deeply afflicted by the semi-treason of his father and by the death of her eldest son, and her one consolation was in this young man. But he, at this moment, had the choice between going to England to join the Free French Forces or of staying near his mother and helping her to live. He fully realized that this woman lived only for him and that his disappearance—or perhaps his death—would plunge her into despair. He also realized that, concretely and in fact, every action he performed on his mother's behalf would be sure of effect in the sense of aiding her to live, whereas anything he did in order to go and fight would be an ambiguous action which might vanish like water into sand and serve no purpose. For instance, to set out for England he would have to wait indefinitely in a Spanish camp on the way through Spain; or, on arriving in England or in Algiers he might be put into an office to fill up forms. Consequently, he found himself confronted by two very different modes of action; the one concrete, immediate, but directed towards only one individual; and the other an action addressed to an end infinitely greater, a national collectivity, but for that very reason ambiguous—and it might be frustrated on the way. At the same time, he was hesitating between two kinds of morality; on the one side the morality of sympathy, of personal devotion and, on the other side, a morality of wider scope but of more debatable validity. He had to choose between those two. What could help him to choose? Could the Christian doctrine? No. Christian doctrine says: Act with charity, love your neighbour, deny yourself for others, choose the way which is hardest, and so forth. But which is the harder road? To whom does one owe the more brotherly love, the patriot or the mother? Which is the more useful aim, the general one of fighting in and for the whole community, or the precise aim of helping one particular person to live? Who can give an answer to that *à priori*? No one. Nor is it given in any ethical scripture. The Kantian ethic says, Never regard another as a means, but always as an end. Very well; if I remain with my mother, I shall be regarding her as the end and not as a means: but by the same token I am in danger of treating as means those who are fighting on my behalf; and the converse is also true, that if I go to the aid of the combatants I shall be treating them as the end at the risk of treating my mother as a means.

If values are uncertain, if they are still too abstract to determine the particular, concrete case under consideration, nothing remains but to trust in our instincts. That is what this young man tried to do; and when I saw him he said, "In the end, it is feeling that counts; the direction in which it is really pushing me is the one I ought to choose. If I feel that I love my mother enough to sacrifice everything else for her—my will to be avenged, all my longings for action and adventure—then I stay with her. If, on the contrary, I feel that my love for her is not enough, I go." But how does one estimate the strength of a feeling? The value of his feeling for his mother was determined precisely by the fact that he was standing by her. I may say that I love a certain friend enough to sacrifice such or such a sum of money for him, but I cannot prove that unless I have done it. I may say, "I love my mother enough to remain with her," if actually I have remained with her. I can only estimate the strength of this affection if I have performed an action by which it is defined and ratified. But if I then appeal to this affection to justify my action, I find myself drawn into a vicious circle. . . .

In other words, feeling is formed by the deeds that one does; therefore I cannot consult it as a guide to action. And that is to say that I can neither seek within myself for an authentic impulse to action, nor can I expect, from some ethic, formulae that will enable me to act. You may say that the youth did, at least, go to a professor to ask for advice. But if you seek counsel—from a priest, for example—you have selected that priest; and at bottom you already knew, more or less, what he would advise. In other words, to choose an adviser is nevertheless to commit oneself by that choice. If you are a Christian, you will say, Consult a priest; but there are collaborationists, priests who are resisters and priests who wait for the tide to turn: which will you choose? Had this young man chosen a priest of the resistance, or one of the collaboration, he would have decided beforehand the kind of advice he was to receive. Similarly, in coming to me, he knew what advice I should give him, and I had but one reply to make. You are free, therefore choose—that is to say, invent. No rule of general morality can show you what you ought to do. . . .

To say that it does not matter what you choose is not correct. In one sense choice is possible, but what is not possible is not to choose. I can always choose, but I must know that if I do not choose, that is still a choice. This although it may appear merely formal, is of great importance as a limit to fantasy and caprice. For, when I confront a real situation—for example, that I am a sexual being, able to have relations with a being of the other sex and able to have children—I am obliged to choose my attitude to it, and in every respect I bear the responsibility of the choice which, in committing myself, also commits the whole of humanity. . . . Man finds himself in an organized situation in which he is himself involved: his choice involves mankind in its entirety, and he cannot avoid choosing. Either he must remain single, or he must marry without having children, or he must marry and have children. In any case, and whichever he may choose, it is impossible for him, in respect of this situation, not to take complete responsibility. Doubtless he chooses without reference to any pre-established values, but it is unjust to tax him with caprice. Rather let us say that the moral choice in comparable to the construction of a work of art.

· · · · ·

No one can tell what the painting of tomorrow will be like; one cannot judge a painting until it is done. What has that to do with morality? We are in the same creative situation. We never speak of a work of art as irresponsible; when we are discussing a canvas by Picasso, we understand very well that the composition became what it is at the time when he was painting it, and that his works are part and parcel of his entire life.

It is the same upon the plane of morality. There is this in common between art and morality, that in both we have to do with creation and invention. We cannot decide à priori what it is that should be done. I think it was made sufficiently clear to you in the case of that student who came to see me, that to whatever ethical system he might appeal, the Kantian or any other, he could find no sort of guidance whatever; he was obliged to invent the law for himself. Certainly we cannot say that this man, in choosing to remain with his mother—that is, in taking sentiment, personal devotion and concrete charity as his moral foundations—would be making an irresponsible choice, nor could we do so if he preferred the sacrifice of going away to England. Man makes himself; he is not found ready-made; he makes himself by the choice of his morality, and he cannot but choose a morality, such is the pressure of circumstances upon him.[28]

Sartre says that "man makes himself." He believes this to be true both individually and collectively. It is through my actions that I commit myself to values, not through principles I accept a priori or rules that are imposed upon me from God or society. If you accept the voice of some authority, you have chosen to accept that authority rather than some other. If you appeal for advice or help, you have chosen to seek that kind of advice rather than some other kind. If you refuse to choose between alternatives, then you are responsible for neglecting both or all the alternatives, for "copping-out." In any case, you must do something, even if what you do is "doing nothing." (That is, not taking one of the important alternatives before you.)

[28] Jean-Paul Sartre, *Existentialism As a Humanism,* trans. Philip Mairet (New York: Philosophical Library, 1949).

Here is Sartre's reply to his predecessors. We are no longer in the position of Aristotle, in which morality appears to us as a given, as "natural," and without alternatives of the most irresolvable kind. We can no longer trust our "sentiments," like the philosophers of the Enlightenment (Hume and Rousseau), for we now find ourselves torn with conflicting sentiments of every kind. We can no longer accept the *a priori* moralizing of Kant, for we now see that the circumstances in which we must act are never so simple that they will allow for a simple "categorical" imperative. And even "the greatest good for the greatest number" no longer provides a guide for our actions, for we no longer pretend that we can calculate the consequences of our actions with any such accuracy. And besides, who is to say what "the greatest good," or, for that matter, "the greatest number" is today? Against all of this, Sartre argues that there is simply our choice of actions and values, together with their consequences, whatever they are. There is no justification for these, and no "right" or "wrong." But this does not mean that we need not choose, or that it is all "arbitrary." To the contrary, the upshot of Sartre's thesis is precisely that we are always choosing, and that morality is nothing other than our commitments, at least for the present, to those values we choose to follow through our actions.

SUMMARY AND CONCLUSION

In this chapter, we have reviewed five competing theories of morality. (1) Aristotle takes the key to morality to be the concept of "virtue," which he argues to be activity in accordance with rational principles. He bases this argument on a concept of what is "natural" for man, but his discussion is clearly limited to a small class of Greek male citizens, whom he views as the ideal specimens of humanity. (2) Hume and Rousseau both argue that morality must be based on certain kinds of feelings or "sentiments." "Reason is and ought to be the slave of the passions" Hume argues, and Rousseau similarly argues that man is "naturally" good. (3) Kant insists that morality is strictly a matter of rational principle, divorced from all personal interests and desires ("inclinations"). This includes a rejection of Hume and Rousseau, who base morality on feelings (which are inclinations in Kant's sense). It also includes a rejection of Aristotle. Although both philosophers use the notion of a "rational principle," Kant intends his notion to apply to every human being, and therefore every person has the same duties and obligations. (4) The utilitarians, Bentham and Mill, reject Kant's divorce between morality and personal interest and argue that morality is our guide to the satisfaction of the greatest number of interests of the greatest number of people. (5) Nietzsche rejects both Kant and the utilitarians, preferring a return to the elitism and "virtue" orientation of Aristotle's morality. He argues that we create our values, and live with them according to our personal needs. Following him, the existentialists, particularly Jean-Paul Sartre, argue that all values are chosen by us; there is no "true" morality, only those values to which we have voluntarily committed ourselves.

GLOSSARY

a priori: in moral philosophy, independent of particular circumstances. In Kant's philosophy, moral laws are said to be *a priori* in this sense.

autonomy: independence. Moral autonomy is the ability of every rational person to reach his or her own moral conclusions about what is right and what is wrong. (This does not mean that they will therefore come to different conclusions.)

categorical imperative: in Kant's philosophy, a moral law, a command that is unqualified and not dependent on any conditions or qualifications. In particular, that rule that tells us to act in such a way that we would want everyone else to act the same way.

commitment: to form a binding obligation voluntarily. In Sartre's moral philosophy, a commitment is a freely chosen adoption of a moral principle or project, which one thereby vows to defend and practice, even in the absence of any other reasons for doing so. And since, according to Sartre, there are never conclusive reasons for adopting any particular moral position, one must always defend his or her position through commitment, and nothing else.

duty: what one is morally bound to do.

eudaimonia: Aristotle's word for "happiness," or, more literally, "living well."

existentialism: the modern movement in philosophy that puts great emphasis on individual choice and the voluntary acceptance of all values.

Golden Rule: "Do unto others as you would have them do unto you."

happiness calculus (also, *felicity calculus*): Bentham's technique for quantifying and adding up pleasures and pains as a way of deciding what to do.

hypothetical imperative: in Kant, a command which is conditional, depending upon particular aims or inclinations. For example, "*if* you want to be a doctor, then go to medical school." According to Kant, all other philosophers (Aristotle, Hume, Rousseau) took morality to be a hypothetical imperative. He does not.

immoralist: a person who rejects the ultimate claims of morality. An immoralist need not actually break the rules of morality; he does not consider them absolute rules and claims that other considerations (even personal considerations) may override them.

imperative: a command.

inclination: Kant's term for all personal considerations: desires, feelings, emotions, attitudes, moods, etc.

law: an objective rule which is binding on individuals whether they personally accept it or not. Contrasted with *maxim*.

master morality: in Nietzsche, a morality that takes personal self-realization as primary, so-called because it was the morality of the "masters" in the slave states of the ancient world (including Greece).

maxim: in Kant, a personal rule or intention. Contrasted with *law*.

mean (between the extremes): in Aristotle, the middle course, not too much, not too little. Courage, for example, is a mean because a person with courage is neither too timid to fight nor so lacking in fear that he/she is rash or reckless in the face of danger.

obligation: bound by duty. For example, "you have an obligation to keep your promises."

ought: the verb most often used to express moral duty or obligation. Sometimes "should" is used, but this is ambiguously between "ought" and merely "preferable." Sometimes "must" or "have to" is used, but this is ambiguously between "ought to" and "forced to."

principle of utility: in Bentham, the principle that one ought to do what gives the greatest pleasure to the greatest number of people.

rationality: acting in the best possible way; according to reason. Sometimes, rationality means simply doing what is best under the circumstances, without insisting that there is only one rational way of acting. In other words, rationality is considered relative to particular interests and circumstances. In Kant's philosophy, however, rationality refers to that faculty which allows us to act in the correct way, without reference to particular interests and circumstances.

sentiment: feeling, emotion; particularly moral feelings (as in Hume, Rousseau).

slave morality: in Nietzsche's moral philosophy, a morality that takes duties and obligations as primary, so-called because it was the morality of the slaves who were not allowed to aspire any higher than mere efficiency and personal comfort.

sympathy: fellow feeling; felt concern for other people's welfare.

utilitarianism: the moral philosophy that says that we should act in such ways as to make the greatest number of people as happy as possible.

virtue: moral excellence. In Aristotle's philosophy, a state of character according to which we enjoy doing what is right. In Kant, willing what is right (whether or not we enjoy it; in fact, especially if we don't enjoy it).

will: the power of mind that allows us to choose our own actions, or, at least, what we shall try to do. In Kant, a good will is the only thing that is good "without qualification"; in other words, acting for the right reasons and good intentions.

will to power: in Nietzsche's philosophy, the thesis that every act is ultimately aimed at superiority, sometimes over other people, but, more importantly, superiority according to one's own standards. In other words, what Aristotle meant by excellence. (Nietzsche has often been interpreted, however, to mean political power.)

13

POLITICS

Man is by nature an animal designed for living in states.

Aristotle

"Man is a social animal," wrote Aristotle. Therefore, he is a political animal as well. We live with other people, not just our friends and families but thousands and millions of others, most of whom we will never meet and many of whom we come across in only the most casual way—passing them as we cross the street or buying a ticket at the movie theater. Yet we have to be concerned about them, and they about us, for there is a sense in which we are all clearly dependent upon each other. For example, we depend on them not to attack us without reason, or steal our possessions. Of course, our confidence varies, from person to person, and from city to city. But it is clear that, in general, we have duties towards people we never know, for example, the duty not to contaminate their water or air supplies, or place their lives in danger. And they have similar duties to us. We also claim certain rights for ourselves: for example, the right not to be attacked as we walk down the street, the right to speak our mind about politically controversial issues without being thrown in jail, the right to believe in this religion or that religion or no religion without having our jobs, our homes, or our freedom taken from us.

Political and social philosophy is the study of people in societies with particular attention to the abstract claims they have on each other in the form of "rights," "duties," and "privileges," and their demands for "justice," "equality," and "freedom." (It is important to distinguish this sense of *political* freedom from the causal or metaphysical freedom that we discussed in Chapter 10. These can be and are almost always discussed independently of each other.) At least ideally, politics is continuous with morality. Our political duties and obligations, for example, are often the same as our moral duties and obligations. Our claims to certain "moral rights" are often claims to political rights as well, and political rights—particularly those very general and absolute rights which we call human rights (for example, the right not to be tortured or degraded, the right not to be exploited by powerful institutions or persons)— are typically defended on the basis of moral principles. The virtues of government are ideally the virtues of individuals: government should be just, temperate, courageous, honest, humane, considerate, and reasonable. Plato and Aristotle, for example, portrayed their visions of the ideal state in precisely these terms. (Both Plato and Aristotle, unlike most modern philosophers, actually had the opportunity to set up such governments; both failed, but for reasons that were hardly their fault.) This is not to say that all politics or all politicians are moral; we know much better than that. But it is to say that our politics are constrained and determined by our sense of morality. Morality is concerned more with relations between particular people while politics is concerned more with large and impersonal groups. But the difference is one of degree. In Ancient Greece, Plato and Aristotle lived in relatively small "city-states" (each called a *"polis"*), with fewer citizens than even most American towns. It was much easier for them to treat morality and politics together. But even today, we still speak hopefully of "the human family" and "international brother-sisterhood," which is to reassert our belief that politics—even international hot-and-cold war politics—ought to be based on interpersonal moral principles.

The key to a successful society is cooperation. With few exceptions, it is in everyone's interest that society work smoothly, without vast bureaucratic confusion, without corruption, without general chaos, without exploitation of the weaker members of society and without forcing anyone to feel that he or she is justified in stealing, cheating, murdering, or "getting even" with society as a whole. But the smooth working of society as a whole, even though it generally benefits everyone, is not the only concern. Societies of ants and bees work more "smoothly" than any human society, but they are not to be envied or imitated. Even if it is agreed that the smooth working of society is generally in everyone's interest, what we may call the public interest, individual interests deserve and sometimes demand recognition even in opposition to this broader public interest. A person who is critical of the government may very well disrupt the smooth operations of that government. He or she may even, at least for a short time, interfere with the public interest. But most of us would agree that such a person has a right to speak his or her mind, and that he or she has a right to be heard as well. Or, to take a very different example, scientists or artists might feel the need to act in ways which are very unpopular or antisocial in order to do their work with the intensity they require. Despite the fact that they might annoy us, we would say that they have a right to live that way. Or, to take still a different example, people who have sexual preferences and desires which are not approved of by most people around them—perhaps they just enjoy an occasional obscene movie—can claim to have rights as well, so long as they don't force their preferences on other people or otherwise interfere with other people's lives. But you can see that, with this last set of examples, we have entered an area of continuing controversy. Do people have rights to enjoy things that are disapproved of by the rest of society? Should governments dictate morals (for example, by passing laws against the things that most people or at least some powerful people consider "immoral")? And the very existence of such controversies shows very clearly how different we are from ants and bees. In their societies, species preservation and instinct dictates all; in our societies, there must always be a balance between the public interest on the one hand and individual rights and interests on the other. Ideally, these will agree as much as possible. In fact, they often do not agree. And this disagreement political and social philosophy makes its primary concern.

If people do not cooperate, the success of society requires that some authority have the power to bring individual interests into line with the public interest. This authority is generally called the state. The state passes laws and enforces them; its purpose is to protect the public interest. But is it only this? We would probably say "no." Its purpose is also to protect individual rights, for example, against powerful corporations and against strongly mobilized pressure groups that try to interfere with individual lives. In general, we might say that the function of the state is to protect justice. But there has been disagreement ever since ancient times about what that means, and how much the primary emphasis should be placed on the public interest and how much on individual rights and interests.

Our concept of the state and the extent of its power and authority depends very much on our conception of human nature and of people's willingness to cooperate without being forced to do so. At one extreme, there are those who place such strong emphasis on the smooth workings of society that they are willing to sacrifice most individual rights and interests; they are generally called *authoritarians* and their confidence in willing individual cooperation is very slight compared to their confidence in a strong authoritarian state. ("But he did make the trains run on time" is often said of the fascist Italian dictator, Benito Mussolini.) At the other extreme, there are people with so much confidence in individual cooperation and so little confidence in the state that they argue that the state should be eliminated altogether. They are called *anarchists*. Between these extremes are those positions that are more moderate, for example, there are people who have some confidence both in individual cooperation and in the possibility of a reasonably just state, but don't have complete confidence in either. Democrats and republicans, for example, both believe in a government that is at least partially run by the people themselves, but with sufficient power to enforce its laws over individual interests whenever necessary. All these people believe in varying solutions to the same central problem: the problem of a balance between the public interest and the need for cooperation on the one hand and individual rights and interests on the other; in other words, the problem of *justice*.

THE PROBLEM OF JUSTICE

When we think of justice, we first tend to think of criminal cases and problems of punishment. Justice, in this sense, is catching the criminal and "making him pay for his crime." The oldest sense of the word "justice," therefore, is what philosophers call *retributive* justice, or simply, "getting even." Retribution for a crime is making the criminal suffer or pay an amount appropriate to the severity of the crime. In ancient traditions, the key phrase was "an eye for an eye, a tooth for a tooth." If a criminal caused a person to be blind, he was in turn blinded. We now view this as brutal and less than civilized. But is it so clear that we have in fact given up this retributive sense of justice? Do we punish our criminals (that is, demand retribution) or do we sincerely attempt to reform them? Or is the purpose of prison simply to keep them off the street? Should we ever punish people for crimes, or should we simply protect ourselves against their doing the same thing again? If a man commits an atrocious murder, is it enough that we guarantee that he won't do another one? Or does he deserve punishment even if we know that he won't do it again?

But retributive justice and the problems of punishment are really only a small piece of a much larger concern. Justice is not just "getting even" for crimes and offenses. It concerns the running of society as a whole, in day to day civil matters as well as the more dramatic criminal concerns. Given the relative scarcity of wealth and goods, how should they be distributed? Should everyone receive exactly the same amount? Should the person who works hard at an unpleasant job receive no more than the person who refuses to work at all and prefers to watch T.V. all day and just amuse him or herself? Should the person who uses his wealth to the benefit of others receive no more than the person who "throws away" his or her money on gambling, drinking, and debauchery? If a class of people have been historically deprived of their adequate share because of the color of their skin, their religious beliefs, or their sex or age, should they now be given more than their share in compensation, or is this too an injustice against other people.

It is not only wealth and goods that are at issue here, however. Distribution of privileges and power are equally important. Who will vote? Will everyone's vote count exactly the same? Should the opinions of an illiterate who does not even know the name of his political leaders have as much say in the government as the political scientist or economist who has studied these matters for years? Should everyone be allowed to drive? Or to drink? Should everyone receive exactly the same treatment before the law? Or are there concerns that would indicate that some people (for example, congressmen or foreign diplomats) should receive special privileges. Enjoyment of society's cultural gifts is also at issue. Should everyone receive the same education? What if that turns out to be "impractical" (since job training is much more efficient than "liberal arts")? But doesn't that mean that some—the workers and career persons who are trained to do a job—are deprived of the training that is necessary to enjoy great books, music, poetry, philosophy, intellectual debate, proficiency in foreign languages, which give considerable enjoyment to those who have been taught to appreciate them?

There are also questions of status. Should there be social classes? What if it could be proved that such divisions make a society run more smoothly? How minimal should distinctions in status be? And this in turn leads to the more general question, shouldn't all members of society be able to expect equal treatment and respect, not only by the law, but in every conceivable social situation? All of these are the concerns of justice. But what is just? Who decides? And how?

Theories of justice, in one sense, are as old as human society. The ancient codes of the Hebrews, the Persians, and the Babylonians were theories of justice, in the sense that they tried, in their various ways, to develop rules to cover fair dealing and distribution of goods, the punishment of criminals, and the settling of disputes. A fully developed theory of justice, however, should go beyond this and try to analyze the nature of justice itself. The first great theories of justice to try to do this were those of Plato and Aristotle. In the *Republic,* Plato argued that justice in the state is precisely the same as justice in the individual, that is, a harmony between the various parts for the good of the whole. In other words, cooperation among all for the sake of a successful society is the key to justice. But this means that the interests of the individual take a clearly secondary role to the interests of society. In ancient Greece, this may have been only rarely true for the wealthy and powerful, but for the majority of people—especially the slaves—this secondary role was the norm. Because their docile submission was seen as necessary to the overall success of society, their individual interests and rights were extremely minimal. They expected to be rewarded and satisfied only insofar as their efforts benefited their betters, and then they expected their betters to reap far more reward from their labor than they themselves. In Plato's universe, everyone has his or her "place," and justice means that they act and are treated accordingly:

> Listen, then, and judge whether I am right. You remember how, when we first began to establish our commonwealth and several times since, we have laid down, as a universal principle, that everyone ought to perform the one function in the community for which his nature best suited him. Well, I believe that that principle, or some form of it, is justice.
>
> We certainly laid that down.
>
> Yes, and surely we have often heard people say that justice means minding one's own business and not meddling with other men's concerns; and we have often said so ourselves.
>
> We have.
>
> · · · · ·
>
> Here is another thing which leads to the same conclusion. The justice of law-suits is a duty that you expect from your Rulers, isn't it?
>
> Of course.

And the chief aim of their decisions will be that neither party shall have what belongs to another or be deprived of what is his own.

Yes.

Because that is just?

Yes.

So here again justice admittedly means that a man should possess and concern himself with what properly belongs to him.

True.

Again, do you agree with me that no great harm would be done to the community by a general interchange of most forms of work, the carpenter and the cobbler exchanging their positions and their tools and taking on each other's jobs, or even the same man undertaking both?

Yes, there would not be much harm in that.

But I think you will also agree that another kind of interchange would be disastrous. Suppose, for instance, someone whom nature designed to be an artisan or tradesman should be emboldened by some advantage, such as wealth or command of votes or bodily strength, to try to enter the order of fighting men; or some member of that order should aspire, beyond his merits, to a seat in the council-chamber of the Guardians. Such interference and exchange of social positions and tools, or the attempt to combine all these forms of work in the same person, would be fatal to the commonwealth.

Most certainly.

Where there are three orders, then, any plurality of functions or shifting from one order to another is not merely utterly harmful to the community, but one might fairly call it the extreme of wrongdoing. And you will agree that to do the greatest of wrongs to one's own community is injustice.

Surely.

This, then, is injustice. And, conversely, let us repeat that when each order—tradesman, Auxiliary, Guardian—keeps to its own proper business in the commonwealth and does its own work, that is justice and what makes a just society.

I entirely agree.[1]

Plato's rigid hierarchy of social classes and insistence on the inequality of people offends our sense of universal equality, but it is important to see that equality (or, more properly, *egalitarianism*, the view that all men and women are equal just by virtue of their being human) is a position that must be argued, and is not a "natural" state of affairs or a belief that has always been accepted by everyone. The same is true of Aristotle's theory of justice. In his *Politics*, he gives an unabashed defense of slavery, not only on the grounds that slaves are efficient and good for society as a whole, but because those who are slaves are "naturally" meant to be slaves, and would be unhappy and unable to cope if they were granted freedom and made citizens. (This is not just an ancient argument, however. I am sure you have heard similar arguments about other groups of people in your own lifetimes.) For Aristotle as for Plato, differ-

[1] Plato, *The Republic*, trans. Francis M. Cornford (Oxford: Oxford University Press, 1941).

ent people have different roles, and to treat unequals equally is as unjust, according to them, as it is to treat equals unequally. They would consider the view that morons and children and foreigners deserve the same respect and treatment as citizens ridiculous. So too would they find the contemporary argument that we should treat men and women as equals. But despite these opinions, Plato and Aristotle laid the foundations of much of our own conceptions of justice. The idea that equals must be treated as equals is the foundation of our sense of justice just as much as theirs. The difference is that we are taught to believe that everybody is an equal. Similarly, the theory of what is called *distributive justice,* the fair distribution of wealth and goods among the members of society, is a current international as well as national concern which owes much to Aristotle's original formulations. The idea that individuals are due certain rewards for their labor is also Aristotle's idea. (It is worth pointing out that he held a strict supply and demand view of wages, so he would count as the fair price of an article or a fair payment for a job only what the market would bear.) But despite his aristocratic opinions and his harsh elitism, Aristotle saw quite clearly that the members of society who depended most upon an adequate theory of justice were the poorer and less powerful members. It was for them that the just society was most vital (since the powerful and wealthy had a much better chance of taking care of themselves). And it was Aristotle who made the vital distinction, with which we began this section, between that restricted concern for justice which rights certain wrongs (in crimes, in bad business deals, and in public misfortunes) and the general concern of justice for a well-balanced and reasonable society. What follows are brief excerpts from Aristotle's analysis of the virtue of justice in his *Nichomachean Ethics:*

> Let us take as a starting-point, then, the various meanings of "an unjust man." Both the lawless man and the greedy and unfair man are thought to be unjust, so that evidently both the law-abiding and the fair man will be just. The just, then, is the lawful and the fair, the unjust the unlawful and the unfair.
>
> Since the lawless man was seen to be unjust and the law-abiding man just, evidently all lawful acts are in a sense just acts; for the acts laid down by the legislative art are lawful, and each of these, we say, is just. Now the laws in their enactments on all subjects aim at the common advantage either of all or of the best or of those who hold power, or something of the sort; so that in one sense we call those acts just that tend to produce and preserve happiness and its components for the political society. And the law bids us do both the acts of a brave man (*e.g.* not to desert our post nor take to flight nor throw away our arms), and those of a temperate man (*e.g.* not to commit adultery nor to gratify one's lust), and those of a good-tempered man (*e.g.* not to strike another nor to speak evil), and similarly with regard to the other virtues and forms of wickedness, commanding some acts and forbidding others; and the rightly-framed law does this rightly, and the hastily conceived one less well.
>
> This form of justice, then, is complete virtue, but not absolutely, but in

relation to our neighbour. And therefore justice is often thought to be the greatest of virtues, and "neither evening nor morning star" is so wonderful; and proverbially "in justice is every virtue comprehended." And it is complete virtue in its fullest sense, because it is the actual exercise of complete virtue. It is complete because he who possesses it can exercise his virtue not only in himself but towards his neighbour also; for many men can exercise virtue in their own affairs, but not in their relations to their neighbour.

. . . . .

But at all events what we are investigating is the justice which is a *part* of virtue; for there is a justice of this kind, as we maintain. Similarly it is with injustice in the particular sense that we are concerned.

That there is such a thing is indicated by the fact that while the man who exhibits in action the other forms of wickedness acts wrongly indeed, but not graspingly (*e.g.* the man who throws away his shield through cowardice or speaks harshly through bad temper or fails to help a friend with money through meanness), when a man acts graspingly he often exhibits none of these vices—no, nor all together, but certainly wickedness of some kind (for we blame him) and injustice. There is, then, another kind of injustice which is a part of injustice in the wide sense, and a use of the word "unjust" which answers to a part of what is unjust in the wide sense of "contrary to the law." Again, if one man commits adultery for the sake of gain and makes money by it, while another does so at the bidding of appetite though he loses money and is penalized for it, the latter would be held to be self-indulgent rather than grasping, but the former is unjust, but not self-indulgent; evidently, therefore, he is unjust by reason of his making gain by his act. Again, all other unjust acts are ascribed invariably to some particular kind of wickedness, for example adultery to self-indulgence, the desertion of a comrade in battle to cowardice, physical violence to anger; but if a man makes gain, his action is ascribed to no form of wickedness but injustice. Evidently, therefore, there is apart from injustice in the wide sense another, "particular," injustice which shares the name and nature of the first, because its definition falls within the same genus; for the significance of both consists in a relation to one's neighbour, but the one is concerned with honour or money or safety—or that which includes all these, if we had a single name for it—and its motive is the pleasure that arises from gain; while the other is concerned with all the objects with which the good man is concerned.

It is clear, then, that there is more than one kind of justice, and that there is one which is distinct from virtue entire; we must try to grasp its genus and differentia.

. . . . .

Of particular justice and that which is just in the corresponding sense, (A) one kind is that which is manifested in distributions of honour or money or the other things that fall to be divided among those who have a share in the constitution (for in these it is possible for one man to have a share either unequal or equal to that of another), and (B) one is that which plays a rectifying part in transactions between man and man. Of this there are two divisions; of transactions (1) some are voluntary and (2) others involuntary—

voluntary such transactions as sale, purchase, loan for consumption, pledging, loan for use, depositing, letting (they are called voluntary because the origin of these transactions is voluntary), while of the involuntary (a) some are clandestine, such as theft, adultery, poisoning, procuring, enticement of slaves, assassination, false witness, and (b) others are violent, such as assault, imprisonment, murder, robbery with violence, mutilation, abuse, insult.

.   .   .   .   .

(A) We have shown that both the unjust man and the unjust act are unfair or unequal; now it is clear that there is also an intermediate between the two unequals involved in either case. And this is the equal; for in any kind of action in which there is a more and a less there is also what is equal. If, then, the unjust is unequal, the just is equal, as all men suppose it to be, even apart from argument. And since the equal is intermediate, the just will be an intermediate. Now equality implies at least two things. The just, then, must be both intermediate and equal and relative (*i.e.* for certain persons). And *qua* intermediate it must be between certain things (which are respectively greater and less); *qua* equal, it involves *two* things; *qua* just, it is for certain people. The just, therefore, involves at least four terms; for the persons for whom it is in fact just are two, and the things in which it is manifested, the objects distributed, are two. And the same equality will exist between the persons and between the things concerned; for as the latter— the things concerned—are related, so are the former; if they are not equal, they will not have what is equal, but this is the origin of quarrels and complaints—when either equals have and are awarded unequal shares, or unequals equal shares. Further, this is plain from the fact that awards should be "according to merit;" for all men agree that what is just in distribution must be according to merit in some sense, though they do not all specify the same sort of merit, but democrats identify it with the status of freeman, supporters of oligarchy with wealth (or with noble birth), and supporters of aristocracy with excellence.

The just, then, is a species of the proportionate (proportion being not a property only of the kind of number which consists of abstract units, but of number in general). For proportion is equality of ratios, and involves four terms at least (that discrete proportion involves four terms is plain, but so does continuous proportion, for it uses one term as two and mentions it twice; for example "as the line A is to the line B, so is the line B to the line C;" the line B, then, has been mentioned twice, so that if the line B be assumed twice, the proportional terms will be four); and the just, too, involves at least four terms, and the ratio between one pair is the same as that between the other pair; for there is a similar distinction between the persons and between the things. As the term A, then, is to B, so will C be to D, and therefore, *alternando,* as A is to C, B will be to D. Therefore also the whole is in the same ratio to the whole; and this coupling the distribution effects and, if the terms are so combined, effects justly. The conjunction, then, of the term A with C and of B with D is what is just in distribution and this species of the just is intermediate, and the unjust is what violates the proportion; for the proportional is intermediate, and the just is proportional. (Mathematicians call this kind of proportion geometrical; for it is in geometrical proportion that it follows that the whole is to the whole as either part is to the corresponding part.) This proportion is not continuous; for we cannot get a single term standing for a person and a thing.

This, then, is what the just is—the proportional; the unjust is what violates the proportion. Hence one term becomes too great, the other too small, as indeed happens in practice; for the man who acts unjustly has too much, and the man who is unjustly treated too little, of what is good. In the case of evil the reverse is true; for the lesser evil is reckoned a good in comparison with the greater evil, since the lesser evil is rather to be chosen than the greater, and what is worthy of choice is good, and what is worthier of choice a greater good.

This, then, is one species of the just.

(B) The remaining one is the rectificatory, which arises in connexion with transactions both voluntary and involuntary. This form of the just has a different specific character from the former. For the justice which distributes common possessions is always in accordance with the kind of proportion mentioned above (for in the case also in which the distribution is made from the common funds of a partnership it will be according to the same ratio which the funds put into the business by the partners bear to one another); and the injustice opposed to this kind of justice is that which violates the proportion. But the justice in transactions between man and man is a sort of equality indeed, and the injustice a sort of inequality; not according to that kind of proportion, however, but according to arithmetical proportion. For it makes no difference whether a good man has defrauded a bad man or a bad man a good one, nor whether it is a good or a bad man that has committed adultery; the law looks only to the distinctive character of the injury, and treats the parties as equal, if one is in the wrong and the other is being wronged, and if one inflicted injury and the other has received it. Therefore, this kind of injustice being an inequality, the judge tries to equalize it; for in the case also in which one has received and the other has inflicted a wound, or one has slain and the other been slain, the suffering and the action have been unequally distributed; but the judge tries to equalize things by means of the penalty, taking away from the gain of the assailant. For the term "gain" is applied generally to such cases, even if it be not a term appropriate to certain cases, for example to the person who inflicts a wound—and "loss" to the sufferer; at all events when the suffering has been estimated, the one is called loss and the other gain. Therefore the equal is intermediate between the greater and the less, but the gain and the loss are respectively greater and less in contrary ways; more of the good and less of the evil are gain, and the contrary is loss; intermediate between them is, as we saw, the equal, which we say is just; therefore corrective justice will be the intermediate between loss and gain. This is why, when people dispute, they take refuge in the judge; and to go to the judge is to go to justice; for the nature of the judge is to be a sort of animate justice; and they seek the judge as an intermediate, and in some states they call judges mediators, on the assumption that if they get what is intermediate they will get what is just. The just, then, is an intermediate, since the judge is so. The judge restores equality. . . .[2]

In contrast to the Greeks, the premise of most modern theories of justice

[2] Aristotle, *Nichomachean Ethics,* trans. W. D. Ross (Oxford: Oxford University Press, 1925).

has been the equality of everyone with everyone else. No one is "better" than anyone else, whatever his or her talents, achievements, wealth, family, or intelligence. This view rules out slavery on principle, whatever the benefits to society as a whole, and whatever the alleged benefits to the slaves. Slavery is inequality, and is thus to be condemned. But this egalitarian principle has its problems too. It is obvious that, as a matter of fact, all people are not equally endowed with intelligence or talent, good looks or abilities. Is it therefore to the good of all that everyone should be treated equally? One person is a doctor, capable of saving many lives; another is a chronic profligate and drunkard. If they were to commit exactly the same crime, would it be to the public interest to give them equal jail terms? Obviously not. But would it be just to give them different terms? It doesn't appear so. One problem that recent theorists have tried to answer is connected with cases in which the public interest seems at odds with the demands for equal treatment. A similar problem gives rise to one of the "paradoxes of democracy" which we mentioned before. Does it make sense to treat the opinions of an ignorant person whose only knowledge of current events comes from fifteen minutes (at best) of television news a day in the same way that we treat the opinions of a skilled political veteran? But the ballots we vote on make no such distinction. And it is obvious that our society, despite its egalitarian principles, treats people who are cleverer at business or power-brokering much better than everyone else. Is this an example of systematic injustice? Or are there cases, even for us, in which inequality can still be justified as justice?

The theory of justice has been one of the central concerns of British philosophy for several centuries. Thomas Hobbes developed a theory which began with equality as a "natural fact" and took justice to be that which "assured peace and security to all" enforced by the government. Several years later, John Locke and then David Hume argued a similar theory of justice: again, equality was the premise, and mutual agreement the basis of government authority. For both philosophers, the ultimate criterion of justice was utility, the public interest and therefore the satisfaction of the interests of at least most citizens. The most explicit statement of this modern position could be expected to be found in the most explicit "utility" theorist of all, John Stuart Mill. The selection that follows is from his pamphlet *Utilitarianism*.

> In the case of this, as of our other moral sentiments, there is no necessary connection between the question of its origin and that of its binding force. That a feeling is bestowed on us by nature does not necessarily legitimate all its promptings. The feeling of justice might be a peculiar instinct, and might yet require, like our other instincts, to be controlled and enlightened by a higher reason. If we have intellectual instincts leading us to judge in a particular way, as well as animal instincts that prompt us to act in a particular way, there is no necessity that the former should be more infallible in their sphere than the latter in theirs; it may as well happen that wrong judgments are occasionally suggested by those, as wrong actions by these.

· · · · ·

In the first place, it is mostly considered unjust to deprive anyone of his personal liberty, his property, or any other thing which belongs to him by law. Here, therefore, is one instance of the application of the terms "just" and "unjust" in a perfectly definite sense, namely, that it is just to respect, unjust to violate, the *legal rights* of anyone. But this judgment admits of several exceptions, arising from the other forms in which the notions of justice and injustice present themselves. For example, the person who suffers the deprivation may (as the phrase is) have *forfeited* the rights which he is so deprived of—a case to which we shall return presently. But also—

Secondly, the legal rights of which he is deprived may be rights which *ought* not to have belonged to him; in other words, the law which confers on him these rights may be a bad law. When it is so or when (which is the same thing for our purpose) it is supposed to be so, opinions will differ as to the justice or injustice of infringing it. Some maintain that no law, however bad, ought to be disobeyed by an individual citizen; that his opposition to it, if shown at all, should only be shown in endeavoring to get it altered by competent authority. This opinion (which condemns many of the most illustrious benefactors of mankind, and would often protect pernicious institutions against the only weapons which, in the state of things existing at the time, have any chance of succeeding against them) is defended by those who hold it on grounds of expediency, principally on that of the importance to the common interest of mankind, of maintaining inviolate the sentiment of submission to law. Other persons, again, hold the directly contrary opinion that any law, judged to be bad, may blamelessly be disobeyed, even though it be not judged to be unjust but only inexpedient, while others would confine the license of disobedience to the case of unjust laws; but, again, some say that all laws which are inexpedient are unjust, since every law imposes some restriction on the natural liberty of mankind, which restriction is an injustice unless legitimated by tending to their good. Among these diversities of opinion it seems to be universally admitted that there may be unjust laws, and that law, consequently, is not the ultimate criterion of justice, but may give to one person a benefit, or impose on another an evil, which justice condemns. When, however, a law is thought to be unjust, it seems always to be regarded as being so in the same way in which a breach of law is unjust, namely, by infringing somebody's right, which, as it cannot in this case be a legal right, receives a different appellation and is called a moral right. We may say, therefore, that a second case of injustice consists in taking or withholding from any person that to which he has a *moral right*.

Thirdly, it is universally considered just that each person should obtain that (whether good or evil) which he *deserves,* and unjust that he should obtain a good or be made to undergo an evil which he does not deserve. This is, perhaps, the clearest and most emphatic form in which the idea of justice is conceived by the general mind. As it involves the notion of desert, the question arises what constitutes desert? Speaking in a general way, a person is understood to deserve good if he does right, evil if he does wrong; and in a more particular sense, to deserve good from those to whom he does or has done good, and evil from those to whom he does or has done evil. The precept of returning good for evil has never been regarded as a case of the fulfillment of justice, but as one in which the claims of justice are waived, in obedience to other considerations.

Fourthly, it is confessedly unjust to *break faith* with anyone: to violate an engagement, either express or implied, or disappoint expectations raised by our own conduct, at least if we have raised those expectations knowingly and voluntarily. Like the other obligations of justice already spoken of, this one is not regarded as absolute, but as capable of being overruled by a stronger obligation of justice on the other side, or by such conduct on the part of the person concerned as is deemed to absolve us from our obligation to him and to constitute a *forfeiture* of the benefit which he has been led to expect.

Fifthly, it is, by universal admission, inconsistent with justice to be *partial*—to show favor or preference to one person over another in matters to which favor and preference do not properly apply. Impartiality, however, does not seem to be regarded as a duty in itself, but rather as instrumental to some other duty; for it is admitted that favor and preference are not always censurable, and, indeed, the cases in which they are condemned are rather the exception than the rule. A person would be more likely to be blamed than applauded for giving his family or friends no superiority in good offices over strangers when he could do so without violating any other duty; and no one thinks it unjust to seek one person in preference to another as a friend, connection, or companion. Impartiality where rights are concerned is of course obligatory, but this is involved in the more general obligation of giving to everyone his right. A tribunal, for example, must be impartial because it is bound to award, without regard to any other consideration, a disputed object to the one of two parties who has the right to it. There are other cases in which impartiality means being solely influenced by desert, as with those who, in the capacity of judges, preceptors, or parents, administer reward and punishment as such. There are cases, again, in which it means being solely influenced by consideration for the public interest, as in making a selection among candidates for a government employment. Impartiality, in short, as an obligation of justice, may be said to mean being exclusively influenced by the considerations which it is supposed ought to influence the particular case in hand, and resisting solicitation of any motives which prompt to conduct different from what those considerations would dictate.

Nearly allied to the idea of impartiality is that of *equality,* which often enters as a component part both into the conception of justice and into the practice of it, and, in the eyes of many persons, constitutes its essence. But in this, still more than in any other case, the notion of justice varies in different persons, and always conforms in its variations to their notion of utility. Each person maintains that equality is the dictate of justice, except where he thinks that expediency requires inequality. The justice of giving equal protection to the rights of all is maintained by those who support the most outrageous inequality in the rights themselves. Even in slave countries it is theoretically admitted that the rights of the slave, such as they are, ought to be as sacred as those of the master, and that a tribunal which fails to enforce them with equal strictness is wanting in justice; while, at the same time, institutions which leave to the slave scarcely any rights to enforce are not deemed unjust because they are not deemed inexpedient. Those who think that utility requires distinctions of rank do not consider it unjust that riches and social privileges should be unequally dispensed; but those who think this inequality inexpedient think it unjust also. Whoever thinks that government is necessary sees no injustice in as much inequality as is constituted by giving to the magistrate powers not granted to other people. Even among those who hold leveling doctrines, there are differences of opinion about expediency. Some communists consider it unjust that the produce of the labor of the community should be shared on any other principle than that of exact equality; others think it just that those should receive most whose wants are greatest; while others hold that those who work harder, or who produce more, or whose services are more valuable to the community, may justly claim a larger quota in the division of the produce. And the sense of natural justice may be plausibly appealed to in behalf of every one of these opinions.

Justice implies something which it is not only right to do, and wrong not to do, but which some individual person can claim from us as his moral right. No one has a moral right to our generosity or beneficence because we are not morally bound to practice those virtues toward any given individual. And it will be found with respect to this as to every correct definition that the instances which seem to conflict with it are those which most confirm it. For if a moralist attempts, as some have done, to make out that mankind generally, though not any given individual, have a right to all the good we can do them, he at once, by that thesis, includes generosity and beneficence within the category of justice. He is obliged to say that our utmost exertions are *due* to our fellow creatures, thus assimilating them to a debt; or that nothing less can be a sufficient *return* for what society does for us, thus classing the case as one of gratitude; both of which are acknowledged cases of justice, and not of the virtue of beneficence; and whoever does not place the distinction between justice and morality in general, where we have now placed it, will be found to make no distinction between them at all, but to merge all morality in justice.

To recapitulate: the idea of justice supposes two things—a rule of conduct and a sentiment which sanctions the rule. The first must be supposed common to all mankind and intended for their good. The other (the sentiment) is a desire that punishment may be suffered by those who infringe the rule. There is involved, in addition, the conception of some definite person who suffers by the infringement, whose rights (to use the expression appropriated to the case) are violated by it. And the sentiment of justice appears to me to be the animal desire to repel or retaliate a hurt or damage to oneself or to those with whom one sympathizes, widened so as to include all persons, by the human capacity of enlarged sympathy and the human conception of intelligent self-interest. From the latter elements the feeling derives its morality; from the former, its peculiar impressiveness and energy of self-assertion.

I have, throughout, treated the idea of a *right* residing in the injured person and violated by the injury, not as a separate element in the composition of the idea and sentiment, but as one of the forms in which the other two elements clothe themselves. These elements are a hurt to some assignable person or persons, on the one hand, and a demand for punishment, on the other. An examination of our own minds, I think, will show that these two things include all that we mean when we speak of violation of a right. When we call anything a person's right, we mean that he has a valid claim on society to protect him in the possession of it, either by the force of law or by that of education and opinion. If he has what we consider a sufficient claim, on whatever account, to have something guaranteed to him by society, we say that he has a right to it. If we desire to prove that anything does not belong to him by right, we think this done as soon as it is admitted that society ought not to take measures for securing it to him, but should leave him to chance or to his own exertions. Thus a person is said to have a right to what he can earn in fair professional competition, because society ought not to allow any other person to hinder him from endeavoring to earn in that manner as much as he can. But he has not a right to three hundred a year, though he may happen to be earning it; because society is not called on to provide that he shall earn that sum. On the contrary, if he owns ten thousand pounds three-per-cent stock, he *has* a right to three hundred a year because society has come under an obligation to provide him with an income of that amount.

To have a right, then, is, I conceive, to have something which society ought to defend me in the possession of. If the objector goes on to ask why it ought, I can give him no other reason than general utility. If that expression does not seem to convey a sufficient feeling of the strength of the obligation, nor to account for the peculiar energy of the feeling, it is because there goes to the composition of the sentiment, not a rational only but also an animal element—the thirst for retaliation; and this thirst derives its intensity, as well as its moral justification, from the extraordinarily important and impressive kind of utility which is concerned. The interest involved is that of security, to everyone's feelings the most vital of all interests. All other earthly benefits are needed by one person, not needed by another; and many of them can, if necessary, be cheerfully foregone or replaced by something else; but security no human being can possibly do without; on it we depend for all our immunity from evil and for the whole value of all and every good, beyond the passing moment, since nothing but the gratification of the instant could be of any worth to us if we could be deprived of everything the next instant by whoever was momentarily stronger than ourselves. Now this most indispensable of all necessaries, after physical nutriment, cannot be had unless the machinery for providing it is kept unintermittedly in active play. Our notion, therefore, of the claim we have on our fellow creatures to join in making safe for us the very groundwork of our existence gathers feelings around it so much more intense than those concerned in any of the more common cases of utility that the difference in degree (as is often the case in psychology) becomes a real difference in kind. The claim assumes that character of absoluteness, that apparent infinity and incommensurability with all other considerations which constitute the distinction between the feeling of right and wrong and that of ordinary expediency and inexpediency. The feelings concerned are so powerful, and we count so positively on finding a responsive feeling in others (all being alike interested) that *ought* and *should* grow into *must,* and recognized indispensability becomes a moral necessity, analogous to physical, and often not inferior to it in binding force.

If the preceding analysis, or something resembling it, be not the correct account of the notion of justice—if justice be totally independent of utility, and be a standard *per se*, which the mind can recognize by simple introspection of itself—it is hard to understand why that internal oracle is so ambiguous, and why so many things appear either just or unjust, according to the light in which they are regarded.

We are continually informed that utility is an uncertain standard, which every different person interprets differently, and that there is no safety but in the immutable, ineffaceable, and unmistakable dictates of justice, which carry their evidence in themselves and are independent of the fluctuations of opinion. One would suppose from this that on questions of justice there could be no controversy; that, if we take that for our rule, its application to any given case could leave us in as little doubt as a mathematical demonstration. So far is this from being the fact that there is as much difference of opinion, and as much discussion, about what is just as about what is useful to society. Not only have different nations and individuals different notions of justice, but in the mind of one and the same individual, justice is not some one rule, principle, or maxim, but many which do not always coincide in their dictates, and, in choosing between which, he is guided either by some extraneous standard or by his own personal predilections.

For instance, there are some who say that it is unjust to punish anyone for the sake of example to others, that punishment is just only when intended for the good of the sufferer himself. Others maintain the extreme reverse, contending that to punish persons who have attained years of discretion, for their own benefit, is despotism and injustice, since, if the matter at issue is solely their own good, no one has a right to control their own judgment of it; but that they may justly be punished to prevent evil to others, this being the exercise of the legitimate right of self-defense. Mr. Owen, again, affirms that it is unjust to punish at all, for the criminal did not make his own character; his education and the circumstances which surrounded him have made him a criminal, and for these he is not responsible. All these opinions are extremely plausible; and so long as the question is argued as one of justice simply, without going down to the principles which lie under justice and are the source of its authority, I am unable to see how any of these reasoners can be refuted. For in truth every one of the three builds upon rules of justice confessedly true. The first appeals to the acknowledged injustice of singling out an individual and making him a sacrifice, without his consent, for other people's benefit. The second relies on the acknowledged justice of self-defense and the admitted injustice of forcing one person to conform to another's notions of what constitutes his good. The Owenite invokes the admitted principle that it is unjust to punish anyone for what he cannot help. Each is triumphant so long as he is not compelled to take into consideration any other maxims of justice than the one he has selected; but as soon as their several maxims are brought face to face, each disputant seems to have exactly as much to say for himself as the others. No one of them can carry out his own notion of justice without trampling upon another equally binding. These are difficulties; they have always been felt to be such; and many devices have been invented to turn rather than to overcome them. As a refuge from the last of the three, men imagined what they called the freedom of the will—fancying that they could not justify punishing a man whose will is in a thoroughly hateful state unless it be supposed to have come into that state through no influence of anterior circumstances. To escape from the other difficulties, a favorite contrivance has been the fiction of a contract whereby at some unknown period all the members of society engaged to obey the laws and consented to be punished for any disobedience to them, thereby giving to their legislators the right, which it is assumed they would not otherwise have had, of punishing them, either for their own good or for that of society. This happy thought was considered to get rid of the whole difficulty and to legitimate the infliction of punishment, in virtue of another received maxim of justice, *volenti non fit injuria*—that is not unjust which is done with the consent of the person who is supposed to be hurt by it. I need hardly remark that, even if the consent were not a mere fiction, this maxim is not superior in authority to the others which it is brought in to supersede. It is, on the contrary, an instructive specimen of the loose and irregular manner in which supposed principles of justice grow up. This particular one evidently came into use as a help to the coarse exigencies of court of law, which are sometimes obliged to be content with very uncertain presumptions, on account of the greater evils which would often arise from any attempt on their part to cut finer. But even courts of law are not able to adhere consistently to the maxim, for they allow voluntary engagements to be set aside on the ground of fraud, and sometimes on that of mere mistake or misinformation.

Again, when the legitimacy of inflicting punishment is admitted, how many conflicting conceptions of justice come to light in discussing the proper apportionment of punishments to offenses. No rule on the subject recommends itself so strongly to the primitive and spontaneous sentiment of justice as the *lex talionis,* an eye for an eye and a tooth for a tooth. Though this principle of the Jewish and of the Mohammedan law has been generally abandoned in Europe as a practical maxim, there is, I suspect, in most minds, a secret hankering after it; and when retribution accidentally falls on an offender in that precise shape, the general feeling of satisfaction evinced bears witness how natural is the sentiment to which this repayment in kind is acceptable. With many, the test of justice in penal infliction is that the punishment should be proportioned to the offense, meaning that it should be exactly measured by the moral guilt of the culprit (whatever be their standard for measuring moral guilt), the consideration what amount of punishment is necessary to deter from the offense having nothing to do with the question of justice, in their estimation; while there are others to whom that consideration is all in all, who maintain that it is not just, at least for man, to inflict on a fellow creature, whatever may be his offenses, any amount of suffering beyond the least that will suffice to prevent him from repeating, and others from imitating, his misconduct.

To take another example from a subject already once referred to. In co-operative industrial association, is it just or not that talent or skill should give a title to superior remuneration? On the negative side of the question it is argued that whoever does the best he can deserves equally well, and ought not in justice to be put in a position of inferiority for no fault of his own; that superior abilities have already advantages more than enough, in the admiration they excite, the personal influence they command, and the internal sources of satisfaction attending them, without adding to these a superior share of the world's goods; and that society is bound in justice rather to make compensation to the less favored for this unmerited inequality of advantages than to aggravate it. On the contrary side it is contended that society receives more from the more efficient laborer; that, his services being more useful, society owes him a larger return for them; that a greater share of the joint result is actually his work, and not to allow his claim to it is a kind of robbery; that, if he is only to receive as much as others, he can only be justly required to produce as much, and to give a smaller amount of time and exertion, proportioned to his superior efficiency. Who shall decide between these appeals to conflicting principles of justice? Justice has in this case two sides to it, which it is impossible to bring into harmony, and the two disputants have chosen opposite sides; the one looks to what it is just that the individual should receive, the other to what it is just that the community should give. Each, from his own point of view, is unanswerable; and any choice between them, on grounds of justice, must be perfectly arbitrary. Social utility alone can decide the preference.

The considerations which have now been adduced resolve, I conceive, the only real difficulty in the utilitarian theory of morals. It has always been evident that all cases of justice are also cases of expediency; the difference is in the peculiar sentiment which attaches to the former, as contradistinguished from the latter. If this characteristic sentiment has been sufficiently accounted for; if there is no necessity to assume for it any peculiarity of origin; if it is simply the natural feeling of resentment, moralized by being made coextensive with the demands of social good; and if this feeling not only does but ought to exist in all the classes of cases to which the idea of justice corresponds—that idea no longer presents itself as a stumbling block to the utilitarian ethics. Justice remains the appropriate name for certain social utilities which are vastly more important, and therefore more absolute and imperative, than any others are as a class (though not more so than others may be in particular cases); and which, therefore, ought to be, as well as naturally are, guarded by a sentiment, not only different in degree, but also in kind; distinguished from the milder feeling which attaches to the mere idea of promoting human pleasure or convenience at once by the more definite nature of its commands and by the sterner character of its sanctions.[3]

Mill's utilitarian theory of justice is a logical extension of his ethical theories: what is good and desirable is what is best for the greatest number of people. But although it might at first seem as if the greatest happiness of the greatest number leaves no room for such abstract concerns as "justice," Mill argues that, to the contrary, it is only utility that can give that abstract sense of justice some concrete basis in human life.

The problem with the utilitarian theory of justice is identical to the problem we saw with the utilitarian theory of morals. Could there not be a case in which the public interest and general utility would be served only at the clearly unjust expense of a single unfortunate individual? Suppose we lived in a society that ran extremely well, such that we had few if any complaints about our government and the way it was run, when a single muckraking journalist started turning the peace upside down with his insistence that something was very wrong in the government. We might easily suppose

[3] John Stuart Mill, *Utilitarianism* (New York: Bobbs-Merrill, 1957).

that, at least in the short run, the public confusion and trauma would be much more harmful to the public interest than the slight correction that would result from public exposure. Should the government forcefully silence the journalist? We would say "no." He has a right to his inquiries and a right to speak his mind. Or, suppose that the most efficient way to solve a series of on-going crimes was to torture a recently captured suspect and hold him without evidence? Here again, public interest and justice are at odds. Or more generally, should the government have the authority to throw people in jail just because it has reason (even good reason) to believe that they will create a public disturbance or commit certain crimes? Public interest says "yes"; justice says "no."

A partial answer to this utilitarian dilemma was clearly stated by Hume, a full century before Mill. He distinguished between the utility of a single act and the utility of a system, so that an unjust act is to be challenged not as an isolated occurrence but as an example of a general set of rules and practices.

> To make this more evident, consider, that though the rules of justice are established merely by interest, their connexion with interest is somewhat singular, and is different from what may be observed on other occasions. A single act of justice is frequently contrary to *public interest;* and were it to stand alone, without being followed by other acts, may, in itself, be very prejudicial to society. When a man of merit, of a beneficent disposition, restores a great fortune to a miser, or a seditious bigot, he has acted justly and laudably, but the public is a real sufferer. Nor is every single act of justice, considered apart, more conducive to private interest, than to public; and it is easily conceived how a man may impoverish himself by a single instance of integrity, and have reason to wish that with regard to that single act, the laws of justice were for a moment suspended in the universe. But however single acts of justice may be contrary, either to public or private interest, it is certain, that the whole plan or scheme is highly conducive, or indeed absolutely requisite, both to the support of society, and the well-being of every individual.[4]

What Hume makes clear is that the utility of an act by itself cannot give us an adequate concept of justice. We need a theory of general practices as well (a theory which, still within the confines of utilitarianism, is sometimes called *rule utilitarianism,* as opposed to *act utilitarianism*). But even this qualification allows for the possibility of a practice which is unjust but which nonetheless systematically increases general utility. It is for this reason that a concern for individual rights must always come back into the picture, not just in the sense of simple utility argued by Mill and Hume, but in a more forceful way that may even go against public utility. The most powerful contemporary theory of justice attempts to do just this by placing the emphasis on the advantages of a practice to the least advantaged members of society. The American philosopher John Rawls has argued such a theory of justice. The following selection is taken from one of his early essays, "Justice as Fairness."

[4] David Hume, *Inquiry Concerning the Principles of Morals* (La Salle, Ill.: Open Court, 1912).

It might seem at first sight that the concepts of justice and fairness are the same, and that there is no reason to distinguish them, or to say that one is more fundamental than the other. I think that this impression is mistaken. In this paper I wish to show that the fundamental idea in the concept of justice is fairness; and I wish to offer an analysis of the concept of justice from this point of view. To bring out the force of this claim, and the analysis based upon it, I shall then argue that it is this aspect of justice for which utilitarianism, in its classical form, is unable to account, but which is expressed, even if misleadingly, by the idea of the social contract.

．．．．．

Throughout I consider justice only as a virtue of social institutions, or what I shall call practices.[5] The principles of justice are regarded as formulating restrictions as to how practices may define positions and offices, and assign thereto powers and liabilities, rights and duties. Justice as a virtue of particular actions or of persons I do not take up at all. It is important to distinguish these various subjects of justice, since the meaning of the concept varies according to whether it is applied to practices, particular actions, or persons. These meanings are, indeed, connected, but they are not identical. I shall confine my discussion to the sense of justice as applied to practices, since this sense is the basic one. Once it is understood, the other senses should go quite easily.

The conception of justice which I want to develop may be stated in the form of two principles as follows: first, each person participating in a practice, or affected by it, has an equal right to the most extensive liberty compatible with a like liberty for all; and second, inequalities are arbitrary unless it is reasonable to expect that they will work out for everyone's advantage, and provided the positions and offices to which they attach, or from which they may be gained, are open to all. These principles express justice as a complex of three ideas: liberty, equality, and reward for services contributing to the common good.

The term "person" is to be construed variously depending on the circumstances. On some occasions it will mean human individuals, but in others it may refer to nations, provinces, business firms, churches, teams, and so on. The principles of justice apply in all these instances, although there is a certain logical priority to the case of human individuals. As I shall use the term "person," it will be ambiguous in the manner indicated.

The first principle holds, of course, only if other things are equal: that is, while there must always be a justification for departing from the initial position of equal liberty (which is defined by the pattern of rights and duties, powers and liabilities, established by a practice), and the burden of proof is placed on him who would depart from it, nevertheless, there can be, and often there is, a justification for doing so. Now, that similar particular cases,

[5] I use the word "practice" throughout as a sort of technical term meaning any form of activity specified by a system of rules which defines offices, roles, moves, penalties, defences, and so on, and which gives the activity its structure. As examples one may think of games and rituals, trials and parliaments, markets and systems of property. I have attempted a partial analysis of the notion of a practice in a paper, "Two Concepts of Rules," *Philosophical Review*, LXIV (1955), pp. 3–32 [Rawls' note]

as defined by a practice, should be treated similarly as they arise, is part of the very concept of a practice; it is involved in the notion of an activity in accordance with rules. The first principle expresses an analogous conception, but as applied to the structure of practices themselves. It holds, for example, that there is a presumption against the distinctions and classifications made by legal systems and other practices to the extent that they infringe on the original and equal liberty of the persons participating in them. The second principle defines how this presumption may be rebutted.

It might be argued at this point that justice requires only an equal liberty. If, however, a greater liberty were possible for all without loss or conflict, then it would be irrational to settle on a lesser liberty. There is no reason for circumscribing rights unless their exercise would be incompatible, or would render the practice defining them less effective. Therefore no serious distortion of the concept of justice is likely to follow from including within it the concept of the greatest equal liberty.

The second principle defines what sorts of inequalities are permissible; it specifies how the presumption laid down by the first principle may be put aside. Now by inequalities it is best to understand not *any* differences between offices and positions, but differences in the benefits and burdens attached to them either directly or indirectly, such as prestige and wealth, or liability to taxation and compulsory services. Players in a game do not protest against there being different positions, such as batter, pitcher, catcher, and the like, nor to there being various privileges and powers as specified by the rules; nor do the citizens of a country object to there being the different offices of government such as president, senator, governor, judge, and so on, each with their special rights and duties. It is not differences of this kind that are normally thought of as inequalities, but differences in the resulting distribution established by a practice, or made possible by it, of the things men strive to attain or avoid. Thus they may complain about the pattern of honors and rewards set up by a practice (*e.g.* the privileges and salaries of government officials) or they may object to the distribution of power and wealth which results from the various ways in which men avail themselves of the opportunities allowed by it (*e.g.* the concentration of wealth which may develop in a free price system allowing large entrepreneurial or speculative gains).

It should be noted that the second principle holds that an inequality is allowed only if there is reason to believe that the practice with the inequality, or resulting in it, will work for the advantage of *every* party engaging in it. Here it is important to stress that *every* party must gain from the inequality. Since the principle applies to practices, it implies that the representative man in every office or position defined by a practice, when he views it as a going concern, must find it reasonable to prefer his condition and prospects with the inequality to what they would be under the practice without it. The principle excludes, therefore, the justification of inequalities on the grounds that the disadvantages of those in one position are outweighed by the greater advantages of those in another position. This rather simple restriction is the main modification I wish to make in the utilitarian principle as usually understood. When coupled with the notion of a practice, it is a restriction of consequence, and one which some utilitarians, for example

Hume and Mill, have used in their discussions of justice without realizing apparently its significance, or at least without calling attention to it. Why it is a significant modification of principle, changing one's conception of justice entirely, the whole of my argument will show.

Further, it is also necessary that the various offices to which special benefits or burdens attach are open to all. It may be, for example, to the common advantage, as just defined, to attach special benefits to certain offices. Perhaps by doing so the requisite talent can be attracted to them and encouraged to give its best efforts. But any offices having special benefits must be won in a fair competition in which contestants are judged on their merits. If some offices were not open, those excluded would normally be justified in feeling unjustly treated, even if they benefited from the greater efforts of those who were allowed to compete for them. Now if one can assume that offices are open, it is necessary only to consider the design of practices themselves and how they jointly, as a system, work together. It will be a mistake to focus attention on the varying relative positions of particular persons, who may be known to us by their proper names, and to require that each such change, as a once for all transaction viewed in isolation, must be in itself just. It is the system of practices which is to be judged, and judged from a general point of view: unless one is prepared to criticize it from the standpoint of a representative man holding some particular office, one has no complaint against it.[6]

Rawls, like Hume in particular, ties the concept of "justice" to the concept of "equality." The main theme of his work is an attempt to develop this connection and to state precisely the kind of "equality" that is most important for justice. Against the conservative suggestion that people are equal in legal rights and "opportunities" alone, without any right to material goods and social services, he argues that a just society will consider the welfare of the worst-off members of society as an obligation. Here he differs with Mill and the utilitarians, who would say that such help is a matter of utility; for Rawls, it is more like a Kantian duty. Moreover, Rawls clearly distinguishes himself from socialists as well, who would argue that all property should be shared; he says only that it is obligatory to help out the worst-off members of society, but nowhere does he suggest that all people therefore ought to have equal wealth and property. Justice, in other words, does not equate fair distribution with equal distribution. Equality becomes a far more complex notion, therefore, than simple egalitarianism often takes it to be.

THE IDEA OF THE STATE

If people will not cooperate willingly and act for the public interest then they may be forced to do so. The authority with the power to define the public

[6] John Rawls, "Justice as Fairness," in *The Philosophical Review*, LXVII (April 1958).

interest and to enforce its definition is what philosophers call the *state*.[7] But it must not be thought that the state or its instrument—the government—is merely a bookkeeping and organizational institution. Ideally, in a well functioning society in which most people act in the public interest, it may be not much more than this, and then as minimally as necessary. But since people do not always act in the public interest, the role of the state is necessarily that of *legislator,* making laws and rules which tell people how to act (and how not to act), and that of *enforcer,* applying enough force through threat of punishment to make sure that people obey those laws and rules. Then too, it is the state which may have to step in when the rights of an individual are threatened, and pass laws to protect those rights and punish those who violate them. Ideally, the function of the state is to keep the balance between the public interest and individual rights, in other words, to preserve justice. Some theorists would add that the function of the state is to make life for its citizens such that the public interest and individual rights and interests almost always coincide. Others would hope that the state would serve this function so well that it would no longer be needed, except perhaps as a bureau of records and an occasional enforcer of contracts. Some people think that the state is an end in itself, a matter of pride and a rallying point for its citizens, something like a football team in a small town. Still others would say that the only proper state is virtually no state at all.

The power and authority of the state is considerable. The state has the authority to force us to give up a large portion of our earnings in taxes. It has the power to require us to serve in the military and fight wars we may not believe in or may know nothing about. Accordingly, it has the power over life and death itself, and it sometimes has the power to execute us for crimes, in the name of justice and the public interest. The state has the power to keep us from seeing certain movies that it decides are "obscene," to keep us from taking certain drugs that it decides are "dangerous," and to keep us from enjoying ourselves in ways which the state considers "licentious" or "perverse."

But what is this state? Living in a democracy, we are too easily tempted to think of state, society, and public interest all at once, without distinguishing between them. But recent issues have made it very clear that, even in a democracy, the interests of state and public interest may be very different— that the state (and the government) are always something other than "the people," even when the state (or government) has been established by an overwhelming majority of the people. The state is an abstraction which must always be distinguished from the society it rules. (The exception to this might be a small group or family meeting, where there is no government as such, and all decisions are made through continuous face-to-face debate and eventual

---

[7] This is a general term for any highest authority in a society; it includes federal government as well as "states" in a more restricted sense, for example, Alabama and Massachusetts. Thus the sovereign cities of the ancient Greeks were called "city-states."

unanimous decisions. But it is clear that no large society could be run in this enviable way, probably not even a small town.)

The state might consist of a single person, such as a king, queen, prince, or dictator. But even then, it is important to remember that it is not just the person who rules, but his *office* or position. As a person, a king might be incredibly stupid, totally ignorant, and incompetent, but as king, he commands both respect and authority. The state might be ruled by a small number of people, a central committee, a consulate, a ministry, or council. The state might be ruled by a large group of people, perhaps the wisest men in society, perhaps a representative body of people, each of whom represents or speaks in the interests of hundreds or thousands of other people, as in our congress or British parliament. At least in theory, a government might strive to be a true democracy, in which every citizen has equal power. But even where the government is, in the words of Abraham Lincoln, "of the people, by the people, and for the people," the ruling government and the state are over and above the people or society that it rules.

The three terms "state," "society," and "government" stand in close relationship to one another. It would be best to distinguish them in the following way. The state is the locus of power and authority, the power to punish, the authority to demand taxes and soldiers. The government is the instrument of the state, but different governments serve the same state. For example, the state may change governments (and on occasion even change the form of government, as when France changed from a monarchy to a republic in 1792) and still remain the same state. Thus it is both convenient and historically reasonable to identify the state with various nations, each of which is independent (or sovereign) of the laws of any other states. Societies, on the other hand, are large groups of people with common cultural and historical ties (although they may have previous ties to other societies as well, particularly in an immigrant population like America or Australia for example). A society may remain the same although the state that rules it, as well as the government, has changed. For example, Poland's liberation after the First World War was not just a change of governments, it was the recreation of Poland as a separate state. Poland as a society, however, had remained more or less identical throughout these changes.

The question of legitimacy

We have been talking about the state as the center of power and authority, and many people would simply define "politics" in terms of "power." But "power" alone is not enough to characterize the state, we must add that it is legitimate power. Legitimacy means that this power must be justified. A person or organization might have tremendous power and rule a society with an iron hand. But rulers might be gangsters, who rule by force alone. Or they might be invaders from another country, who rule without popular consent (almost everyone in the society hates them). Or they might be citizens who, because of powerful positions in the government or the army, acquire this power in illegal or unacceptable ways. The idea of the state, therefore, is not simply that it is the center of power; it is the center of legitimate power or, in other words, *authority*. When philosophers and political scientists use the term "authority," they almost always mean "legitimate authority." And sometimes, when they say that "the state has the power to do such and such," they mean "that the state has the legitimate power to do such and such." Legitimate authority (or simply, authority) has the legal power to make laws. Crude military or political power is only the ability to force people to do what one wants; it is not therefore legitimate. A central question of political philosophy, accordingly, is "what makes a state's power legitimate?" In other words, "what gives a state its authority?"

It is necessary to distinguish three different levels on which the question of legitimacy and authority must be raised. First, there is the question of the legitimacy of the state itself. On what authority did the English, for example, rule over the American colonies and consider them a part of the British Empire? Conversely, what authority did the American colonists claim when they declared themselves independent of England and set themselves up as a separate state? Much recent history involves the creation, re-creation, and re-alignment of various states. If we look at maps of Europe for the past fifty years, for example, we will see that states go into and out of existence, sometimes several times. The question of the legitimacy of the state itself, therefore, is one of the main causes of the wars and political battles of our times (and earlier times as well). Second, there is the question of the legitimacy of a certain form of government. In some Asian and Latin American countries, for example, there are frequent changes between military dictatorships and republics or democracies; in the recent history of Spain, as another example, there have been changes from a monarchy to a republic to a dictatorship back to a monarchy trying to establish democratic processes. The geographical boundaries of the state in all these instances remain the same, the population also remains pretty much the same (making allowances for casualties and refugees), but the form of government changes radically. It is possible that the same people or party, however, will remain in power even though the form of government changes. (For example, the president of a democracy may become the dictator in a dictatorship.) This brings us to our third level of legitimacy: particular governments must be shown to be legitimate within the framework of the form of government in a state. It is the form of government which confers legitimacy: for example, a democracy confers legitimacy through elections, a monarchy confers legitimacy on a new king or queen through birth. In our own state, the form of government has remained constant for the past two hundred years, but the particular governments have changed quite frequently, from one party to the other, and sometimes new parties are created and succeed in getting elected. A particular government (whether Republican or Democratic, for example) is made legitimate by the election laws created by our form of government. Usually, these laws make it clear which particular government (that is, which party) is the legitimate government at a particular time. In a close election, however, this may be in hot dispute, and it is in such instances that the distinction between the form of government and particular governments is thrown into sharp contrast.

The legitimacy of a particular government, a form of government, or a state means that its power is justified. But what justifies this power? We might say that what justifies a particular government, form of government, or state is the willingness of its citizens to obey its laws, the recognition of it by other governments and states whom it in turn recognizes, and in general the wide-spread belief in its legitimacy by virtue of which the people or party in power are accepted as such. But this extremely loose definition encounters many problems, particularly in dictatorships where people are forced to accept governments, in powerful military states which can force recognition from other states, and powerful governments which are able to force their citizens to obey them, whether they really want to or not. Moreover, the crucial belief in a government, form of government or state may be based on many different kinds of justifications. It is necessary, therefore, to mention at least five different kinds of justifications for this belief, each of which might be called a theory of legitimacy.

DIVINE RIGHT TO RULE THEORY: Since ancient times, it has been argued that kings, queens, pharoahs, princes and emperors have been given their authority directly by God or gods. Until modern times, this was a difficult theory to refute, and a dangerous one to argue against. But even in ancient times, for example, in Greece, it was maintained that this divine right had to be supported by justice and a modicum of wisdom and, at least to a small extent, the acceptance of the people ruled. But since the people who were ruled were more often than not forced to accept the authority of the divinely appointed ruler, this last qualification was mostly nominal. Kings sometimes enjoyed the support of the people, but it is debatable whether they actually needed it.

MIGHT MAKES RIGHT THEORY: This theory holds that power itself makes a government legitimate. In a sense, therefore, this theory rejects the very idea of legitimacy, since, according to it, any government or state that has power has legitimate power and therefore the distinction between legitimate and il-legitimate power disappears. For obvious reasons, this theory is usually favored more by those who are already in power than by those who are not in power. But it is rare that a government or state which has power will publicly state the might makes right theory. Usually, it will invoke one of the other theories in its defense.

The classic presentation of the might makes right theory is in Plato's *Republic,* as argued by Thrasymachus (so that Socrates can refute it, of course) :

Listen then, Thrasymachus began. What I say is that 'just' or 'right' means nothing but what is to the interest of the stronger party. Well, where is your applause? You don't mean to give it me.

I will, as soon as I understand, I said [Socrates is speaking here]. I don't see yet what you mean by right being the interest of the stronger party. For instance, Polydamas, the athlete, is stronger than we are, and it is to his interest to eat beef for the sake of his muscles; but surely you don't mean that the same diet would be good for weaker men and therefore be right for us?

You are trying to be funny, Socrates. It's a low trick to take my words in the sense you think will be most damaging.

No, no, I protested; but you must explain.

Don't you know, then, that a state may be ruled by a despot, or a democracy, or an aristocracy?

Of course.

And that the ruling element is always the strongest?

Yes.

Well then, in every case the laws are made by the ruling party in its own interest; a democracy makes democratic laws, a despot autocratic ones, and so on. By making these laws they define as 'right' for their subjects whatever is for their own interest, and they call anyone who breaks them a 'wrongdoer' and punish him accordingly. That is what I mean: in all states alike 'right' has the same meaning, namely what is for the interest of the party established in power, and that is the strongest. So the sound conclusion is that what is 'right' is the same everywhere: the interest of the stronger party.

Now I see what you mean, said I; whether it is true or not, I must try to make out. When you define right in terms of interest, you are yourself giving one of those answers you forbade to me; though, to be sure, you add 'to the stronger party.'

An insignificant addition, perhaps!

Its importance is not clear yet; what is clear is that we must find out whether your definition is true. I agree myself that right is in a sense a matter of interest; but when you add 'to the stronger party,' I don't know about that. I must consider.

Go ahead, then.

I will. Tell me this. No doubt you also think it is right to obey the men in power?

I do.

Are they infallible in every type of state, or can they sometimes make a mistake?

Of course they can make a mistake.

In framing laws, then, they may do their work well or badly?

No doubt.

Well, that is to say, when the laws they make are to their own interest; badly, when they are not?

Yes.

But the subjects are to obey any law they lay down, and they will then be doing right?

Of course.

If so, by your account, it will be right to do what is not to the interest of the stronger party, as well as what is so.

What's that you are saying?

Just what you said, I believe; but let us look again. Haven't you admitted that the rulers, when they enjoin certain acts on their subjects, sometimes mistake their own best interests, and at the same time that it is right for the subjects to obey, whatever they may enjoin?

Yes, I suppose so.

Well, that amounts to admitting that it is right to do what is not to the interest of the rulers or the stronger party. They may unwittingly enjoin what is to their own disadvantage; and you say it is right for the others to do as they are told. In that case, their duty must be the opposite of what you said, because the weaker will have been ordered to do what is against the interest of the stronger. You with your intelligence must see how that follows.

Yes, Socrates, said Polemarchus, that is undeniable.

No doubt, Cleitophon broke in, if you are to be a witness on Socrates' side.

No witness is needed, replied Polemarchus; Thrasymachus himself admits that rulers sometimes ordain acts that are to their own disadvantage, and that it is the subjects' duty to do them.

That is because Thrasymachus said it was right to do what you are told by the men in power.

Yes, but he also said that what is to the interest of the stronger party is right; and, after making both these assertions, he admitted that the stronger sometimes command the weaker subjects to act against their interests. From all which it follows that what is in the stronger's interest is no more right than what is not.

No, said Cleitophon; he meant whatever the stronger *believes* to be in his own interest. That is what the subject must do, and what Thrasymachus meant to define as right.

That was not what he said, rejoined Polemarchus.

No matter, Polemarchus, said I; if Thrasymachus says so now, let us take him in that sense. Now, Thrasymachus, tell me, was that what you intended to say—that right means what the stronger thinks is to his interest, whether it really is so or not?

Most certainly not, he replied. Do you suppose I should speak of a man as 'stronger' or 'superior' at the very moment when he is making a mistake?

I did think you said as much when you admitted that rulers are not always infallible.

That is because you are a quibbler, Socrates. Would you say a man deserves to be called a physician at the moment when he makes a mistake in treating his patient and just in respect of that mistake; or a mathematician, when he does a sum wrong and just in so far as he gets a wrong result? Of course we do commonly speak of a physician or a mathematician or a scholar having made a mistake; but really none of these, I should say, is ever mistaken, in so far as he is worthy of the name we give him. So strictly speaking—and you are all for being precise—no one who practises a craft makes mistakes. A man is mistaken when his knowledge fails him; and at that moment he is no craftsman. And what is true of craftsmanship or any sort of skill is true of the ruler: he is never mistaken so long as he is acting as a ruler; though anyone might speak of a ruler making a mistake, just as he might of a physician. You must understand that I was talking in that loose way when I answered your question just now; but the precise statement is this. The ruler, in so far as he is acting as a ruler, makes no mistakes and consequently enjoins what is best for himself; and that is what the subject is to do. So, as I said at first, 'right' means doing what is to the interest of the stronger.

Very well, Thrasymachus, said I. So you think I am quibbling?

I am sure you are.

You believe my questions were maliciously designed to damage your position?

I know it. But you will gain nothing by that. You cannot outwit me by cunning, and you are not the man to crush me in the open.

Bless your soul, I answered, I should not think of trying. But, to prevent any more misunderstanding, when you speak of that ruler or stronger party whose interest the weaker ought to serve, please make it clear whether you are using the words in the ordinary way or in that strict sense you have just defined.

I mean a ruler in the strictest possible sense. Now quibble away and be as malicious as you can. I want no mercy. But you are no match for me.

Do you think me mad enough to beard a lion or try to outwit a Thrasymachus?

You did try just now, he retorted, but it wasn't a success.

Enough of this, said I. Now tell me about the physician in that strict sense you spoke of: is it his business to earn money or to treat his patients? Remember, I mean your physician who is worthy of the name.

To treat his patients.

And what of the ship's captain in the true sense? Is he a mere seaman or the commander of the crew?

The commander.

Yes, we shall not speak of him as a seaman just because he is on board a ship. That is not the point. He is called captain because of his skill and authority over the crew.

Quite true.

And each of these people has some special interest?

No doubt.

And the craft in question exists for the very purpose of discovering that interest and providing for it?

Yes.

Can it equally be said of any craft that it has an interest, other than its own greatest possible perfection?

What do you mean by that?

Here is an illustration. If you ask me whether it is sufficient for the human body just to be itself, with no need of help from without, I should say, Certainly not; it has weaknesses and defects, and its condition is not all that it might be. That is precisely why the art of medicine was invented: it was designed to help the body and provide for its interests. Would not that be true?

It would.

But now take the art of medicine itself. Has that any defects or weaknesses? Does any art stand in need of some further perfection, as the eye would be imperfect without the power of vision or the ear without hearing, so that in their case an art is required that will study their interests and provide for their carrying out those functions? Has the art itself any corresponding need of some further art to remedy its defects and look after its interests; and will that further art require yet another, and so on for ever? Or will every art look after its own interests? Or, finally, is it not true that no art needs to have its weaknesses remedied or its interests studied either by another art or by itself, because no art has in itself any weakness or fault, and the only interest it is required to serve is that of its subject-matter? In itself, an art is sound and flawless, so long as it is entirely true to its own nature as an art in the strictest sense—and it is the strict sense that I want you to keep in view. Is not that true?

So it appears.

Then, said I, the art of medicine does not study its own interest, but the needs of the body, just as a groom shows his skill by caring for horses, not for the art of grooming. And so every art seeks, not its own advantage— for it has no deficiencies—but the interest of the subject on which it is exercised.

It appears so.

But surely, Thrasymachus, every art has authority and superior power over its subject.

To this he agreed, though very reluctantly.

So far as arts are concerned, then, no art ever studies or enjoins the interest of the superior or stronger party, but always that of the weaker over which it has authority.

Thrasymachus assented to this at last, though he tried to put up a fight. I then went on:

So the physician, as such, studies only the patient's interest, not his own. For as we agreed, the business of the physician, in the strict sense, is not to make money for himself, but to exercise his power over the patient's body; and the ship's captain, again, considered strictly as no mere sailor, but in command of the crew, will study and enjoin the interest of his subordinates, not his own.

He agreed reluctantly.

And so with government of any kind: no ruler, in so far as he is acting as ruler, will study or enjoin what is for his own interest. All that he says and does will be said and done with a view to what is good and proper for the subject for whom he practises his art.

At this point, when everyone could see that Thrasymachus' definition of justice had been turned inside out, instead of making any reply, he said:

Socrates, have you a nurse?

Why do you ask such a question as that? I said. Wouldn't it be better to answer mine?

Because she lets you go about sniffling like a child whose nose wants wiping. She hasn't even taught you to know a shepherd when you see one, or his sheep either.

What makes you say that?

Why, you imagine that a herdsman studies the interests of his flocks or cattle, tending and fattening them up with some other end in view than his master's profit or his own; and so you don't see that, in politics, the genuine ruler regards his subjects exactly like sheep, and thinks of nothing else, night and day, but the good he can get out of them for himself. You are so far out in your notions of right and wrong, justice and injustice, as not to know that 'right' actually means what is good for someone else, and to be 'just' means serving the interest of the stronger who rules, at the cost of the subject who obeys; whereas injustice is just the reverse, asserting its authority over those innocents who are called just, so that they minister solely to their master's advantage and happiness, and not in the least degree to their own. Innocent as you are yourself, Socrates, you must see that a just man always has the worst of it. Take a private business: when a partnership is wound up, you will never find that the more honest of two partners comes off with the larger share; and in their relations to the state, when there are taxes to be paid, the honest man will pay more than the other on the same amount of property; or if there is money to be distributed, the dishonest will get it all. When either of them hold some public office, even if the just man loses in no other way, his private affairs at any rate will suffer from neglect, while his principles will not allow him to help himself from the public funds; not to mention the offence he will give to his friends and relations by refusing to sacrifice those principles to do them a good turn. Injustice has all the opposite advantages. I am speaking of the type I described just now, the man who can get the better of other people on a large scale: you must fix your eye on him, if you want to judge how much it is to one's own interest not to be just. You can see that best in the most consummate form of injustice, which rewards wrongdoing with supreme welfare and happiness and reduces its victims, if they won't retaliate in kind, to misery. That form is despotism, which uses force or fraud to plunder the goods of others, public or private, sacred or profane, and to do it in a wholesale way. If you are caught committing any one of these crimes on a small scale, you are punished and disgraced; they call it sacrilege, kidnapping, burglary, theft and brigandage. But if, besides taking their property, you turn all your countrymen into slaves, you will hear no more of those ugly names; your countrymen themselves will call you the happiest of men and bless your name, and so will everyone who hears of such a complete triumph of injustice; for when people denounce injustice, it is because they are afraid of suffering wrong, not of doing it. So true is it, Socrates, that injustice, on a grand enough scale, is superior to justice in strength and freedom and autocratic power; and 'right,' as I said at first, means simply what serves the interest of the stronger party; 'wrong' means what is for the interest and profit of oneself.

Having deluged our ears with this torrent of words, as the man at the baths might empty a bucket over one's head, Thrasymachus meant to take himself off; but the company obliged him to stay and defend his position. I was specially urgent in my entreaties.

My good Thrasymachus, said I, do you propose to fling a doctrine like that at our heads and then go away without explaining it properly or letting us point out to you whether it is true or not? Is it so small a matter in your eyes to determine the whole course of conduct which every one of us must follow to get the best out of life?

Don't I realize it is a serious matter? he retorted.

Apparently not, said I; or else you have no consideration for us, and do not care whether we shall lead better or worse lives for being ignorant of this truth you profess to know. Do take the trouble to let us into your secret; if you treat us handsomely, you may be sure it will be a good investment; there are so many of us to show our gratitude. I will make no secret of my own conviction, which is that injustice is not more profitable than justice, even when left free to work its will unchecked. No; let your unjust man have full power to do wrong, whether by successful violence or by escaping detection; all the same he will not convince me that he will gain more than he would by being just. There may be others here who feel as I do, and set justice above injustice. It is for you to convince us that we are not well advised.

How can I? he replied. If you are not convinced by what I have just said, what more can I do for you? Do you want to be fed with my ideas out of a spoon?

God forbid! I exclaimed; not that. But I do want you to stand by your own words; or, if you shift your ground, shift it openly and stop trying to hoodwink us as you are doing now. You see, Thrasymachus, to go back to your earlier argument, in speaking of the shepherd you did not think it necessary to keep to that strict sense you laid down when you defined the genuine physician. You represent him, in his character of shepherd, as feeding up his flock, not for their own sake but for the table or the market, as if he were out to make money as a caterer or a cattle-dealer, rather than a shepherd. Surely the sole concern of the shepherd's art is to do the best for the charges put under its care; its own best interest is sufficiently provided for, so long as it does not fall short of all that shepherding should imply. On that principle it followed, I thought, that any kind of authority, in the state or in private life, must, in its character of authority, consider solely what is best for those under its care. Now what is your opinion? Do you think that the men who govern states—I mean rulers in the strict sense—have no reluctance to hold office?

I don't think so, he replied; I know it.

Well, but haven't you noticed, Thrasymachus, that in other positions of authority no one is willing to act unless he is paid wages, which he demands on the assumption that all the benefit of his action will go to his charges? Tell me: Don't we always distinguish one form of skill from another by its power to effect some particular result? Do say what you really think, so that we may get on.

Yes, that is the distinction.

And also each brings us some benefit that is peculiar to it: medicine gives health, for example; the art of navigation, safety at sea; and so on.

Yes.

And wage-earning brings us wages; that is its distinctive product. Now, speaking with that precision which you proposed, you would not say that the art of navigation is the same as the art of medicine, merely on the ground that a ship's captain regained his health on a voyage, because the sea air was good for him. No more would you identify the practice of medicine with wage-earning because a man may keep his health while earning wages, or a physician attending a case may receive a fee.

No.

And, since we agreed that the benefit obtained by each form of skill is peculiar to it, any common benefit enjoyed alike by all these practitioners must come from some further practice common to them all?

It would seem so.

Yes, we must say that if they all earn wages, they get that benefit in so far as they are engaged in wage-earning as well as in practising their several arts.

He agreed reluctantly.

This benefit, then—the receipt of wages—does not come to a man from his special art. If we are to speak strictly, the physician, as such, produces health; the builder, a house; and then each, in his further capacity of wage-earner, gets his pay. Thus every art has its own function and benefits its proper subject. But suppose the practitioner is not paid; does he then get any benefit from his art?

Clearly not.

And is he doing no good to anyone either, when he works for nothing?

No, I suppose he does some good.

Well then, Thrasymachus, it is now clear that no form of skill or authority provides for its own benefit. As we were saying some time ago, it always studies and prescribes what is good for its subject—the interest of the weaker party, not of the stronger. And that, my friend, is why I said that no one is willing to be in a position of authority and undertake to set straight other men's troubles, without demanding to be paid; because, if he is to do his work well, he will never, in his capacity of ruler, do, or command others to do, what is best for himself, but only what is best for the subject. For that reason, if he is to consent, he must have his recompense, in the shape of money or honour, or of punishment in case of refusal.

What do you mean, Socrates? asked Glaucon. I recognize two of your three kinds of reward; but I don't understand what you mean by speaking of punishment as a recompense.

Then you don't understand the recompense required by the best type of men, or their motive for accepting authority when they do consent. You surely know that a passion for honours or for money is rightly regarded as something to be ashamed of.

Yes, I do.

For that reason, I said, good men are unwilling to rule, either for money's sake or for honour. They have no wish to be called mercenary for demanding to be paid, or thieves for making a secret profit out of their office; nor yet will honours tempt them, for they are not ambitious. So they must be forced to consent under threat of penalty; that may be why a readiness to accept power under no such constraint is thought discreditable. And the heaviest penalty for declining to rule is to be ruled by someone inferior to yourself. That is the fear, I believe, that makes decent people accept power; and when they do so, they face the prospect of authority with no idea that they are coming into the enjoyment of a comfortable berth; it is forced upon them because they can find no one better than themselves, or even as good, to be entrusted with power. If there could ever be a society of perfect men, there might well be as much competition to evade office as there now is to gain it; and it would then be clearly seen that the genuine ruler's nature is to seek only the advantage of the subject, with the consequence that any man of understanding would sooner have another to do the best for him than be at the pains to do the best for that other himself. On this point, then, I entirely disagree with Thrasymachus' doctrine that right means what is to the interest of the stronger.[8]

UTILITARIAN THEORY: Just as utilitarianism in moral theory defends that action which will promote the greatest good for the greatest number, utilitarianism in political theory defends the government or state that will promote the greatest good for the greatest number of its citizens. Jeremy Bentham's classic treatise, for example, is called *An Introduction to the Principles of Morals and Legislation*. And Mill's pamphlet, *Utilitarianism*, is partly devoted to the political problem of justice. According to the utilitarian theory, a government is legitimate just so long as it provides the most services and best protection for its citizens in general. Or, to characterize this theory slightly differently, the utilitarian theory says that a government is justified insofar as it furthers the public interest. (Thus it might also be called public interest theory.)

JUSTICE THEORY: One possible problem with the utilitarian theory, as we have seen in other contexts in this chapter, is that it may promote the best interests of most of the people at the expense of a small minority. (Mill is particularly concerned to reject this charge in his discussion of justice, p. 509.) Neither the divine right nor might makes right theories include any mention of justice at all, and so it is important that the demand that governments and states be just be made independently of these others. Plato and Aristotle, for example, used a justice theory to defend their conceptions of the state. But the fact that Plato and Aristotle's conception of the state was so different from ours (and so unjust in some respects) points to an important qualification of this kind of theory. What the theory amounts to depends wholly on the concept of justice one defends. If justice means equality, then the legitimate state will maximize equality; if justice means "everyone in his or her proper place" (as in Plato and Aristotle), then the state will be legitimate if the various parts of the state are "in harmony" and working together smoothly.

CONSENT OF THE GOVERNED THEORY: This theory is the one that most people accept today. It is assumed, however, that the consent of the governed will also insure the public interest and justice for everyone as well. Consent of the governed theory is based on the idea that the people who are ruled should

[8] Plato, *The Republic*.

have some say in how they are ruled, and perhaps even have a choice in who rules them. These two ideas are not equivalent, although they usually go together in our society. A people might have a say in government policies without being able to choose the government, as in most monarchies, for example. Even Plato accepted this theory to some degree. In *The Republic,* he argues (through Socrates), "in our state, if anywhere, the governors and the governed will share the same conviction on the question who ought to rule. Don't you think so?"[9]

The most powerful modern versions of the consent of the governed theory are summed up in the phrase, "the social contract." According to the theory of the social contract, governments and states are legitimate only because the citizens agree to be ruled by them. The justifications for this agreement, however, vary as much as concepts of justice and other beliefs, however. We shall discuss these differences, and the social contract in general, in the following section.

These five theories are often argued together, in mutual support of one another, as well as against each other. We have already mentioned that consent of the governed theory assumes that it will serve both the public interest and justice. Divine right theory, because it is "divine" and ordained by God, is usually thought to include a concern for justice also. Might makes right theory often uses the claim that a strong central government prevents anarchy and inefficiency, and thus serves the public interest as well. An excellent example of this use of several theories together can be seen in the opening passage of our *Declaration of Independence.* Even in the first sentence of the following excerpt you can see how public interest, justice, and a theory of human rights are used together to justify the overthrow of the existing colonial government so as to establish a new one:

> We hold these Truths to be self-evident, that all Men are created equal, that they are endowed by their Creator with certain unalienable Rights, that among these are Life, Liberty, and the pursuit of Happiness— That to secure these rights, Governments are instituted among Men, deriving their just Powers from the Consent of the Governed, that whenever any Form of Government becomes destructive of these Ends, it is the Right of the People to alter or to abolish it, and to institute new Government, laying its Foundation on such Principles, and organizing its Powers in such Form, as to them shall seem most likely to effect their Safety and Happiness. Prudence, indeed, will indicate that Governments long established should not be changed for light and transient causes; and accordingly all Experience hath shewn, that Mankind are more disposed to suffer, while Evils are sufferable, than to right themselves by abolishing the Forms to which they are accustomed. But when a long Train of Abuses and Usurpations, pursuing invariably the same Object, evinces a Design to reduce them under absolute Despotism, it is their Right, it is their Duty, to throw off such Government, and to provide new Guards for their future Security.

[9] Plato, *The Republic.*

The social contract

The single most influential defense of the legitimacy of the state in modern times has been a theory called "social contract theory." The *social contract* is an agreement among people to share certain interests and make certain compromises for the good of them all. It is, in other words, a "consent of the governed theory." In one form or another, it existed even in ancient times. For example, re-read Socrates' argument in the *Crito* (pp. 4–6) where he says that, by staying in Athens, he had implicitly agreed to abide by its laws, even when those laws unfairly condemned him to death. But what is most important in understanding the nature of this social contract is that, as in Socrates' argument, there need not have been any actual, physical contract or even oral agreement in order to talk about it. We are bound by a social contract, in other words, even if we never signed or saw such a contract. Moreover, it may not be the case that there was ever such a contract, even in past history. It happens, however, that Americans are among the few people in the world whose state was actually formed explicitly by such a contract, namely, our *Constitution*. But the actual existence of such a piece of paper is not necessary to a discussion about a social contract. Simply to live in a society, according to these philosophers, is to have agreed, at least implicitly, to such an agreement. (Thus, living in a society you are expected to obey its laws; "ignorance is no excuse," and you cannot get out of an arrest by saying "I don't really live here," much less "I don't recognize your right to arrest me.")

Two very different pictures of the original social contract are presented to us by the English philosopher Thomas Hobbes and the French philosopher Jean-Jacques Rousseau. Both begin by considering man in "the state of nature," without laws and without society, before men and women came together to accept the social contract. Hobbes based his conception of the social contract, however, on an extremely unfavorable conception of human nature. He attacked the idealistic political philosophies of Plato and Aristotle for being unrealistic and assuming wrongly that people were naturally capable of virtue and wisdom. Like Machiavelli, whom he followed with praise, he considered himself to be a "realist." As with most realists, this meant seeing the nasty side of things. So, according to his theory of human nature, natural man was a selfish beast, fighting for his own interests against everyone else. Human life was a "war of all against all" and a person's life, consequently, was "nasty, brutish and short." He dismissed reason and appealed to human passions, particularly the passion for self-preservation. The social contract, therefore, was mainly an agreement of equally selfish and self-seeking persons not to commit mutual murder.

OF THE NATURAL CONDITION OF MANKIND AS CONCERNING THEIR FELICITY, AND MISERY

Men by nature equal. Nature hath made men so equal, in the faculties of the body, and mind; as that though there be found one man sometimes manifestly stronger in body, or of quicker mind than another; yet when all is reckoned together, the difference between man, and man, is not so considerable, as that one man can thereupon claim to himself any benefit, to which another may not pretend, as well as he. For as to the strength of body, the weakest has strength enough to kill the strongest, either by secret machination, or by confederacy with others, that are in the same danger with himself.

. . . . .

For such is the nature of men, that howsoever they may acknowledge many others to be more witty, or more eloquent, or more learned; yet they will hardly believe there be many so wise as themselves; for they see their own wit at hand, and other men's at a distance. But this proveth rather that men are in that point equal, than unequal. For there is not ordinarily a greater sign of the equal distribution of any thing, than that every man is contented with his share.

From equality proceeds diffidence. From this equality of ability, ariseth equality of hope in the attaining of our ends. And therefore if any two men desire the same thing, which nevertheless they cannot both enjoy, they become enemies; and in the way to their end, which is principally their own conservation, and sometimes their delectation only, endeavour to destroy, or subdue one another. And from hence it comes to pass, that where an invader hath no more to fear, than another man's single power; if one plant, sow, build, or possess a convenient seat, others may probably be expected to come prepared with forces united, to dispossess, and deprive him, not only of the fruit of his labour, but also of his life, or liberty. And the invader again is in the like danger of another.

From diffidence war. And from this diffidence of one another, there is no way for any man to secure himself, so reasonable, as anticipation; that is, by force, or wiles, to master the persons of all men he can, so long, till he see no other power great enough to endanger him: and this is no more than his own conservation requireth, and is generally allowed. Also because there be some, that taking pleasure in contemplating their own power in the acts of conquest, which they pursue farther than their security requires; if others, that otherwise would be glad to be at ease within modest bounds, should not by invasion increase their power, they would not be able, long time, by standing only on their defence, to subsist. And by consequence, such augmentation of dominion over men being necessary to a man's conservation, it ought to be allowed him.

Again, men have no pleasure, but on the contrary a great deal of grief, in keeping company, where there is no power able to over-awe them all. For every man looketh that his companion should value him, at the same rate he sets upon himself: and upon all signs of contempt, or undervaluing, naturally endeavors, as far as he dares, (which amongst them that have no common power to keep them in quiet, is far enough to make them destroy each other), to extort a greater value from his contemners, by damage; and from others, by the example.

So that in the nature of man, we find three principal causes of quarrel. First, competition; secondly, diffidence; thirdly, glory.

The first, maketh men invade for gain; the second, for safety; and the third, for reputation. The first use violence, to make themselves masters of other men's persons, wives, children, and cattle; the second, to defend them; the third, for trifles, as a word, a smile, a different opinion, and any other sign of undervalue, either direct in their persons, or by reflection in their kindred, their friends, their nation, their profession, or their name.

Out of civil states, there is always war of every one against every one. Hereby it is manifest, that during the time men live without a common power to keep them all in awe, they are in that condition which is called war; and such a war, as is of every man, against every man. For war, consisteth not in battle only, or the act of fighting; but in a tract of time, wherein the will to contend by battle is sufficiently known. . . .

The incommodities of such a war. Whatsoever therefore is consequent to a time of war, where every man is enemy to every man; the same is consequent to the time, wherein men live without other security, than what their own strength, and their own invention shall furnish them withal. In such condition, there is no place for industry; because the fruit thereof is uncertain: and consequently no culture of the earth; no navigation, nor use of the commodities that may be imported by sea; no commodious building; no instruments of moving, and removing, such things as require much force; no knowledge of the face of the earth; no account of time; no arts; no letters; no society; and which is worst of all, continual fear, and danger of violent death; and the life of man, solitary, poor, nasty, brutish, and short.

It may seem strange to some man, that has not well weighed these things; that nature should thus dissociate, and render men apt to invade, and destroy one another: and he may therefore, not trusting to this inference, made from the passions, desire perhaps to have the same confirmed by experience. Let him therefore consider with himself, when taking a journey, he arms himself, and seeks to go well accompanied; when going to sleep, he locks his doors; when even in his house he locks his chests; and this when he knows there be laws, and public officers, armed, to revenge all injuries shall be done him; what opinion he has of his fellow-subjects, when he rides armed; of his fellow citizens, when he locks his doors; and of his children, and servants, when he locks his chests. Does he not there as much accuse mankind by his actions, as I do by my words? But neither of us accuse man's nature in it. The desires, and other passions of man, are in themselves no sin. No more are the actions, that proceed from those passions, till they know a law that forbids them: which till laws be made they cannot know: nor can any law be made, till they have agreed upon the person that shall make it.

It may peradventure be thought, there was never such a time, nor condition of war as this; and I believe it was never generally so, over all the world: but there are many places, where they live so now. For the savage people in many places of America, except the government of small families, the concord whereof dependeth on natural lust, have no government at all; and live at this day in that brutish manner, as I said before. Howsoever, it may be perceived what manner of life there would be, where there were no common power to fear, by the manner of life, which men that have formerly lived under a peaceful government, use to degenerate into, in a civil war.

OF THE FIRST AND SECOND NATURAL LAWS, AND OF CONTRACTS

Right of nature what. The right of nature, which writers commonly call *jus naturale,* is the liberty each man hath, to use his own power, as he will himself, for the preservation of his own nature; that is to say, of his own life; and consequently, of doing any thing, which in his own judgment, and reason, he shall conceive to be the aptest means thereunto.

Liberty what. By liberty, is understood, according to the proper signification of the word, the absence of external impediments: which impediments, may oft take away part of a man's power to do what he would; but cannot hinder him from using the power left him, according as his judgment, and reason shall dictate to him.

A law of nature what. A law of nature, *lex naturalis,* is a precept or general rule, found out by reason, by which a man is forbidden to do that, which is destructive of his life, or taketh away the means of preserving the same; and to omit that, by which he thinketh it may be best preserved.

Difference of right and law. For though they that speak of this subject, use to confound *jus,* and *lex, right* and *law:* yet they ought to be distinguished; because right, consisteth in liberty to do, or to forbear: whereas law, determineth, and bindeth to one of them: so that law, and right, differ as much, as obligation, and liberty; which in one and the same matter are inconsistent.

Naturally every man has right to every thing. And because the condition of man, as hath been declared in the precedent chapter, is a condition of war of every one against every one; in which case every one is governed by his own reason; and there is nothing he can make use of, that may not be a help unto him, in preserving his life against his enemies; it followeth, that in such a condition, every man has a right to every thing; even to one another's body. And therefore, as long as this natural right of every man to every thing endureth, there can be no security to any man, how strong or wise soever he be, of living out the time, which nature ordinarily alloweth men to live.

The fundamental law of nature. And consequently it is a precept, or general rule of reason, *that every man, ought to endeavour peace, as far as he has hope of obtaining it; and when he cannot obtain it, that he may seek, and use, all helps, and advantages of war.*

· · · · ·

The second law of nature. From this fundamental law of nature, by which men are commanded to endeavour peace, is derived this second law; *that a man be willing, when others are so too, as far-forth, as for peace, and defence of himself he shall think it necessary, to lay down this right to all things; and be contented with so much liberty against other men, as he would allow other men against himself.* For as long as every man holdeth this right, of doing any thing he liketh; so long are all men in the condition of war. But if other men will not lay down their right, as well as he; then there is no reason for any one, to divest himself of his: for that were to expose himself to prey, which no man is bound to, rather than to dispose himself to peace. This is that law of the Gospel; *whatsoever you require that others should do to you, that do ye to them.*

. . . . .

What it is to lay down a right. To *lay down* a man's *right* to any thing, is to *divest* himself of the *liberty,* of hindering another of the benefit of his own right to the same. For he that renounceth, or passeth away his right, giveth not to any other man a right which he had not before; because there is nothing to which every man had not right by nature: but only standeth out of his way, that he may enjoy his own original right, without hindrance from him; not without hindrance from another. So that the effect which redoundeth to one man, by another man's defect of right, is but so much diminution of impediments to the use of his own right original.

. . . . .

Not all rights are alienable. Whensoever a man transferreth his right, or renounceth it; it is either in consideration of some right reciprocally transferred to himself; or for some other good he hopeth for thereby. For it is a voluntary act: and of the voluntary acts of every man, the object is some *good to himself.* And therefore there be some rights, which no man can be understood by any words, or other signs, to have abandoned, or transferred. As first a man cannot lay down the right of resisting them, that assault him by force, to take away his life; because he cannot be understood to aim thereby, at any good to himself. The same may be said of wounds, and chains, and imprisonment; both because there is no benefit consequent to such patience; as there is to the patience of suffering another to be wounded, or imprisoned: as also because a man cannot tell, when he seeth men proceed against him by violence, whether they intend his death or not. And lastly the motive, and end for which this renouncing, and transferring of right is introduced, is nothing else but the security of a man's person, in his life, and in the means of so preserving life, as not to be weary of it. And therefore if a man by words, or other signs, seem to despoil himself of the end, for which those signs were intended; he is not to be understood as if he meant it, or that it was his will; but that he was ignorant of how such words and actions were to be interpreted.

Contract what. The mutual transferring of right, is that which men call CONTRACT.

. . . . .

Covenants of mutual trust, when invalid. If a covenant be made, wherein neither of the parties perform presently, but trust one another; in the condition of mere nature, which is a condition of war of every man against every man, upon any reasonable suspicion, it is void: but if there be a common power set over them both, with right and force sufficient to compel performance, it is not void. For he that performeth first, has no assurance the other will perform after; because the bonds of words are too weak to bridle men's ambition, avarice, anger, and other passions, without the fear of some coercive power; which in the condition of mere nature, where all men are equal, and judges of the justness of their own fears, cannot possibly be supposed. And therefore he which performeth first, does but betray himself to his enemy; contrary to the right, he can never abandon, of defending his life, and means of living.

But in a civil estate, where there is a power set up to constrain those that would otherwise violate their faith, that fear is no more reasonable; and for that cause, he which by the covenant is to perform first, is obliged so to do.

The cause of fear, which maketh such a covenant invalid, must be always something arising after the covenant made; as some new fact, or other sign of the will not to perform: else it cannot make the covenant void. For that which could not hinder a man from promising, ought not to be admitted as a hindrance of performing.

Right to the end, containeth right to the means. He that transferreth any right, transferreth the means of enjoying it, as far as lieth in his power. As he that selleth land, is understood to transfer the herbage, and whatsoever grows upon it: nor can he that sells a mill turn away the stream that drives it. And they that give to a man the right of government in sovereignty, are understood to give him the right of levying money to maintain soldiers; and of appointing magistrates for the administration of justice.[10]

Hobbes begins his argument with the perhaps surprising observation that people are basically equal in nature. He is not talking here about legal equality or equal rights (for there are no laws and no legal rights) but rather equality in abilities, talents and power. This seems strange because the problem of equality usually pays attention to the great differences between people. Instead, Hobbes points out our similarities. In particular, he points out that almost everyone is strong and smart enough to kill or inflict grievous injury on others. Even a puny moron can, with a knife or a handgun, kill the strongest and smartest person on earth. Accordingly, the basis of the social contract (or "covenant") according to Hobbes is our mutual protection. Everyone agrees not to kill other people, and in return is guaranteed that he or she won't be killed. Although it is a cynical view of human nature, it also continues to be one of the most powerful arguments for strong governments. (Hobbes himself was a conservative monarchist.)

Rousseau, quite to the contrary, had an extremely optimistic view of human nature, as we saw in the preceding chapter. He believed that people were "naturally good," and it was only the corruptions of society that made them selfish and destructive. Rousseau does not take the social contract, therefore, to be simply a doctrine of protection between mutually brutish individuals. The function of the state is rather to allow people to regain the "natural goodness" that they once had in the absence of any state at all. This is not to say (although Rousseau is often interpreted this way) that he was nostalgic and wanted to "go back to the state of nature." That is imposs (It is not even clear that Rousseau believed that there ever was a "state nature" as such; his example, like Hobbes' example, is a way of giving picture of "human nature," whether or not it is historically accurate.) V

10 Thomas Hobbes, *Leviathan* (New York: Hafner, 1926).

already in society, that is a given fact. So Rousseau's aim is to develop a conception of the state which will allow us to live as morally as possible. This is important, for Rousseau, unlike most social contract theorists, is not at all a utilitarian; it is not happiness that is most important but goodness. (Hobbes, by way of contrast, took utility, pleasure and well-being, in addition to self-preservation, to be the purpose of the social contract.)

Rousseau's ambition, therefore, is not to "get us back to nature" but rather to revise our conception of the state. His "revision," however, is one of the most radical documents in modern history and has rightly been said to be one of the causes of both the American and French revolutions. The main thesis is one that Rousseau inherits from Locke; the state has legitimate power only so long as it serves the people it governs. The revolutionary corollary is that, when a state ceases to serve its citizens, the citizens have a right to overthrow that government. This was a radical claim, again reminiscent of Locke. Even Rousseau was not comfortable with it. (Locke had made his statement *after* the English Revolution.) He called revolution "the most horrible alternative," to be avoided wherever possible. But subsequent French history took his theories quite literally, and demonstrated too the "horror" that may follow too radical and abrupt a change in the authority that citizens accept as legitimate.

In earlier works, Rousseau had argued his famous thesis; that "natural man" is "naturally good" and that contemporary society has corrupted him (and her). He went on to say that it was competition and the artificiality of our lust for private property which was responsible for this corruption, and he even included marriage and romantic love as forms of this "lust for private property." In the state of nature, he suggests, people mated when they felt like it, with whomever they felt like, and duels fought between jealous rivals were unheard of. Rousseau does not suggest that we return to that pre-historic custom, but he does use it as a wedge to pry open even the most sacred of our modern civil institutions. All of these, he argues, must be re-examined, and the tool for that re-examination is the social contract.

The key to his most famous book, appropriately called *The Social Contract,* is that man must regain his freedom within society. This does not mean, however, that a person can do whatever he or she would like to do. Quite the contrary, to be a citizen, according to Rousseau, is to want and do what is good for the society as well. To be free is precisely to want to do what is good for the society as well. And, in one of the most problematic statements of the social contract, Rousseau says that a person who does not so act for the good of the society may have to "be forced to be free." Here is the basis for a strange paradox. On the one hand, Rousseau has properly been regarded as the father of the most liberal and revolutionary political theories of our time. (Marx, for example, claims a great debt to Rousseau.) His political philosophy stresses individual freedom and rights above all, even above the state itself. But there is another side to Rousseau which emerges in this paradoxical phrase;

his stress on the state as an entity in itself ("the sovereign"; presumably the king, but essentially any government) and the subservice of the individual to the state has also caused him to be labeled an authoritarian and the fore-runner of totalitarian and fascist governments.

This paradox is not easily resolved, but we can at least explain how it comes about. Rousseau believes that the state is subject to and receives its legitimacy from the people it governs. But that does not mean that individual people need have any real power in determining the form or functions of government. Rousseau is not a democrat. What he says instead is that the state is subject to what he calls the general will, which is not simply a collection of individuals but something more. For example, we talk about "the spirit of the revolution" or "the discontent of the working class," but this spirit or discon-tent is not simply the product of each individual person. A poll of workers or revolutionaries would not show it either way. The revolution may have spirit even though some participants do not, indeed, they may even dislike the whole idea. And here is the source of the paradox: legitimacy is given to the state by the general will, not by every individual person. And the person who does not agree with the general will, therefore, may very well find him or herself forced into compliance with the state. (Rousseau even says, "forced to be free.") How much force, however, is a matter that Rousseau is not very clear about, nor have his many followers agreed on that crucial point either. On one ex-treme, Rousseau's authoritarian followers have insisted that all dissent from the general will must be stifled; on the other extreme, Rousseau's most libertarian and anarchist followers have insisted that the rights of the individual to be free from government intervention and to live according to his or her own "natural goodness" outweigh any claims that the state may have. What fol-lows are selections from *The Social Contract,* beginning with one of Rousseau's best known slogans.

Man is born free; and everywhere he is in chains. One thinks himself the master of others, and still remains a greater slave than they. How did this change come about? I do not know. What can make it legitimate? That question I think I can answer.

If I took into account only force, and the effects derived from it, I should say: 'As long as a people is compelled to obey, and obeys, it does well; as soon as it can shake off the yoke, and shakes it off, it does still better; for, regaining its liberty by the same right as took it away, either it is justified in resuming it, or there was no justification for those who took it away.' But the social order is a sacred right which is the basis of all other rights. Nevertheless, this right does not come from nature, and must therefore be founded on conventions. Before coming to that, I have to prove what I have just asserted.

THE FIRST SOCIETIES

The most ancient of all societies, and the only one that is natural, is the family: and even so the children remain attached to the father only so long as they need him for their preservation. As soon as this need ceases, the natural bond is dissolved. The children, released from the obedience they owed to the father, and the father, released from the care he owed his children, return equally to independence. If they remain united, they continue so no longer naturally, but voluntarily; and the family itself is then maintained only by convention.

This common liberty results from the nature of man. His first law is to provide for his own preservation, his first cares are those which he owes to himself; and, as soon as he reaches years of discretion, he is the sole judge of the proper means of preserving himself, and consequently becomes his own master.

The family then may be called the first model of political societies: the ruler corresponds to the father, and the people to the children; and all, being born free and equal, alienate their liberty only for their own advantage. The whole difference is that, in the family, the love of the father for his children repays him for the care he takes of them, while, in the State, the pleasure of commanding takes the place of the love which the chief cannot have for the peoples under him.

· · · · ·

THE RIGHT OF THE STRONGEST

The strongest is never strong enough to be always the master, unless he transforms strength into right, and obedience into duty. Hence the right of the strongest, which, though to all seeming meant ironically, is really laid down as a fundamental principle. But are we never to have an explanation of this phrase? Force is a physical power, and I fail to see what moral effect it can have. To yield to force is an act of necessity, not of will—at the most, an act of prudence. In what sense can it be a duty?

Suppose for a moment that this so-called 'right' exists. I maintain that the sole result is a mass of inexplicable nonsense. For, if force creates right, the effect changes with the cause: every force that is greater than the first succeeds to its right. As soon as it is possible to disobey with impunity, disobedience is legitimate; and, the strongest being always in the right, the only thing that matters is to act so as to become the strongest. But what kind of right is that which perishes when force fails? If we must obey perforce, there is no need to obey because we ought; and if we are not forced to obey, we are under no obligation to do so. Clearly, the word 'right' adds nothing to force: in this connection, it means absolutely nothing.

Obey the powers that be. If this means yield to force, it is a good precept, but superfluous: I can answer for its never being violated. All power comes from God, I admit; but so does all sickness: does that mean that we are forbidden to call in the doctor? A brigand surprises me at the edge of a wood: must I not merely surrender my purse on compulsion; but, even if I could withhold it, am I in conscience bound to give it up? For certainly the pistol he holds is also a power.

Let us then admit that force does not create right, and that we are obliged to obey only legitimate powers. In that case, my original question recurs.

SLAVERY

Since no man has a natural authority over his fellow, and force creates no right, we must conclude that conventions form the basis of all legitimate authority among men.

If an individual, says Grotius, can alienate his liberty and make himself the slave of a master, why could not a whole people do the same and make itself subject to a king? There are in this passage plenty of ambiguous words which would need explaining; but let us confine ourselves to the word *alienate*. To alienate is to give or to sell. Now, a man who becomes the slave of another does not give himself; he sells himself, at the least for his subsistence: but for what does a people sell itself? A king is so far from furnishing his subjects with their subsistence that he gets his own only from them; and, according to Rabelais, kings do not live on nothing. Do subjects then give their persons on condition that the king takes their goods also? I fail to see what they have left to preserve.

It will be said that the despot assures his subjects civil tranquillity. Granted; but what do they gain, if the wars his ambition brings down upon them, his insatiable avidity, and the vexatious conduct of his ministers press harder on them than their own dissensions would have done? What do they gain, if the very tranquillity they enjoy is one of their miseries? Tranquillity is found also in dungeons; but is that enough to make them desirable places to live in? The Greeks imprisoned in the cave of the Cyclops lived there very tranquilly, while they were awaiting their turn to be devoured.

To say that a man gives himself gratuitously, is to say what is absurd and inconceivable; such an act is null and illegitimate, from the mere fact that he who does it is out of his mind. To say the same of a whole people is to suppose a people of madmen; and madness creates no right.

Even if each man could alienate himself, he could not alienate his children: they are born men and free; their liberty belongs to them, and no one but they has the right to dispose of it. Before they come to years of discretion, the father can, in their name, lay down conditions for their preservation and well-being, but he cannot give them irrevocably and without conditions: such a gift is contrary to the ends of nature, and exceeds the rights of paternity. It would therefore be necessary, in order to legitimize an arbitrary government, that in every generation the people should be in a position to accept or reject it; but, were this so, the government would be no longer arbitrary.

To renounce liberty is to renounce being a man, to surrender the rights of humanity and even its duties. For him who renounces everything no indemnity is possible. Such a renunciation is incompatible with man's nature; to remove all liberty from his will is to remove all morality from his acts. Finally, it is an empty and contradictory convention that sets up, on the one side, absolute authority, and, on the other, unlimited obedience. Is it not clear that we can be under no obligation to a person from whom we have the right to exact everything? Does not this condition alone, in the absence of equivalence or exchange, in itself involve the nullity of the act? For what right can my slave have against me, when all that he has belongs to me, and, his right being mine, this right of mine against myself is a phrase devoid of meaning?

Grotius and the rest find in war another origin for the so-called right of slavery. The victor having, as they hold, the right of killing the vanquished, the latter can buy back his life at the price of his liberty; and this convention is the more legitimate because it is to the advantage of both parties.

But it is clear that this supposed right to kill the conquered is by no means deducible from the state of war. Men, from the mere fact that, while they are living in their primitive independence, they have no mutual relations stable enough to constitute either the state of peace or the state of war, cannot be naturally enemies. War is constituted by a relation between things, and not between persons; and, as the state of war cannot arise out of simple personal relations, but only out of real relations, private war, or war of man with man, can exist neither in the state of nature, where there is no constant property, nor in the social state, where everything is under the authority of the laws.

Individual combats, duels, and encounters, are acts which cannot constitute a state; while the private wars, authorized by the Establishments of Louis IX, King of France, and suspended by the Peace of God, are abuses of feudalism, in itself an absurd system if ever there was one, and contrary to the principles of natural right and to all good polity.

War then is a relation, not between man and man, but between State and State, and individuals are enemies only accidentally, not as men, nor even as citizens, but as soldiers; not as members of their country, but as its defenders. Finally, each State can have for enemies only other States, and not men. . . .

THE SOCIAL COMPACT

I suppose men to have reached the point at which the obstacles in the way of their preservation in the state of nature show their power of resistance to be greater than the resources at the disposal of each individual for his maintenance in that state. That primitive condition can then subsist no longer; and the human race would perish unless it changed its manner of existence.

But, as men cannot engender new forces, but only unite and direct existing ones, they have no other means of preserving themselves than the formation, by aggregation, of a sum of forces great enough to overcome the resistance. These they have to bring into play by means of a single motive power, and cause to act in concert.

This sum of forces can arise only where several persons come together: but, as the force and liberty of each man are the chief instruments of his self-preservation, how can he pledge them without harming his own interests, and neglecting the care he owes to himself? This difficulty, in its bearing on my present subject, may be stated in the following terms:

'The problem is to find a form of association which will defend and protect with the whole common force the person and goods of each associate, and in which each, while uniting himself with all, may still obey himself alone, and remain as free as before.' This is the fundamental problem of which the *Social Contract* provides the solution.

The clauses of this contract are so determined by the nature of the act that the slightest modification would make them vain and ineffective; so that, although they have perhaps never been formally set forth, they are everywhere the same and everywhere tacitly admitted and recognized, until, on the violation of the social compact, each regains his original rights and resumes his natural liberty, while losing the conventional liberty in favour of which he renounced it.

These clauses, properly understood, may be reduced to one—the total alienation of each associate, together with all his rights, to the whole community; for, in the first place, as each gives himself absolutely, the conditions are the same for all; and, this being so, no one has any interest in making them burdensome to others.

Moreover, the alienation being without reserve, the union is as perfect as it can be, and no associate has anything more to demand: for, if the individuals retained certain rights, as there would be no common superior to decide between them and the public, each, being on one point his own judge, would ask to be so on all; the state of nature would thus continue, and the association would necessarily become inoperative or tyrannical.

Finally, each man, in giving himself to all, gives himself to nobody; and as there is no associate over which he does not acquire the same right as he yields others over himself, he gains an equivalent for everything he loses, and an increase of force for the preservation of what he has.

If then we discard from the social compact what is not of its essence, we shall find that it reduces itself to the following terms:

'*Each of us puts his person and all his power in common under the supreme direction of the general will, and, in our corporate capacity, we receive each member as an indivisible part of the whole.*'

At once, in place of the individual personality of each contracting party, this act of association creates a moral and collective body, composed of as many members as the assembly contains voters, and receiving from this act its unity, its common identity, its life, and its will. This public person, so formed by the union of all other persons, formerly took the name of *city,* and now takes that of *Republic* or *body politic;* it is called by its members *State* when passive, *Sovereign* when active, and *Power* when compared with others like itself. Those who are associated in it take collectively the name of *people,* and severally are called *citizens,* as sharing in the sovereign power, and *subjects,* as being under the laws of the State. But these terms are often confused and taken one for another: it is enough to know how to distinguish them when they are being used with precision.

THE SOVEREIGN

This formula shows us that the act of association comprises a mutual undertaking between the public and the individuals, and that each individual, in making a contract, as we may say, with himself, is bound in a double capacity; as a member of the Sovereign he is bound to the individuals, and as a member of the State to the Sovereign. But the maxim of civil right, that no one is bound by undertakings made to himself, does not apply in this case; for there is a great difference between incurring an obligation to yourself and incurring one to a whole of which you form a part.

Attention must further be called to the fact that public deliberation, while competent to bind all the subjects to the Sovereign, because of the two different capacities in which each of them may be regarded, cannot, for the opposite reason, bind the Sovereign to itself; and that it is consequently against the nature of the body politic for the Sovereign to impose on itself a law which it cannot infringe. Being able to regard itself in only one capacity, it is in the position of an individual who makes a contract with himself; and this makes it clear that there neither is nor can be any kind of fundamental law binding on the body of the people—not even the social contract itself. This does not mean that the body politic cannot enter into undertakings with others, provided the contract is not infringed by them; for in relation to what is external to it, it becomes a simple being, an individual.

But the body politic or the Sovereign, drawing its being wholly from the sanctity of the contract, can never bind itself, even to an outsider, to do anything derogatory to the original act, for instance, to alienate any part of itself, or to submit to another Sovereign. Violation of the act by which it exists would be self-annihilation; and that which is itself nothing can create nothing.

As soon as this multitude is so united in one body, it is impossible to offend against one of the members without attacking the body, and still more to offend against the body without the members resenting it. Duty and interest therefore equally oblige the two contracting parties to give each other help; and the same men should seek to combine, in their double capacity, all the advantages dependent upon that capacity.

Again, the Sovereign, being formed wholly of the individuals who compose it, neither has nor can have any interest contrary to theirs; and consequently the sovereign power need give no guarantee to its subjects, because it is impossible for the body to wish to hurt all its members. We shall also see later on that it cannot hurt any in particular. The Sovereign, merely by virtue of what it is, is always what it should be.

This, however, is not the case with the relation of the subjects to the Sovereign, which, despite the common interest, would have no security that they would fulfil their undertakings, unless it found means to assure itself of their fidelity.

In fact, each individual, as a man, may have a particular will contrary or dissimilar to the general will which he has as a citizen. His particular interest may speak to him quite differently from the common interest: his absolute and naturally independent existence may make him look upon what he owes to the common cause as a gratuitous contribution, the loss of which will do less harm to others than the payment of it is burdensome to himself; and, regarding the moral person which constitutes the State as a *persona ficta*, because not a man, he may wish to enjoy the rights of citizenship without being ready to fulfil the duties of a subject. The continuance of such an injustice could not but prove the undoing of the body politic.

In order then that the social compact may not be an empty formula, it tacitly includes the undertaking, which alone can give force to the rest, that whoever refuses to obey the general will shall be compelled to do so by the whole body. This means nothing less than that he will be forced to be free; for this is the condition which, by giving each citizen to his country, secures him against all personal dependence. In this lies the key to the working of the political machine; this alone legitimizes civil undertakings, which, without it, would be absurd, tyrannical, and liable to the most frightful abuses.

THE CIVIL STATE

The passage from the state of nature to the civil state produces a very remarkable change in man, by substituting justice for instinct in his conduct, and giving his actions the morality they had formerly lacked. Then only, when the voice of duty takes the place of physical impulses and right of appetite, does man, who so far had considered only himself, find that he is forced to act on different principles, and to consult his reason before listening to his inclinations. Although, in this state, he deprives himself of some advantages which he got from nature, he gains in return others so great, his faculties are so stimulated and developed, his ideas so extended, his feelings so ennobled, and his whole soul so uplifted, that, did not the abuses of this new condition often degrade him below that which he left, he would be bound to bless continually the happy moment which took him from it for ever, and, instead of a stupid and unimaginative animal, made him an intelligent being and a man.

Let us draw up the whole account in terms easily commensurable. What man loses by the social contract is his natural liberty and an unlimited right to everything he tries to get and succeeds in getting; what he gains is civil liberty and the proprietorship of all he possesses. If we are to avoid mistake in weighing one against the other, we must clearly distinguish natural liberty, which is bounded only by the strength of the individual, from civil liberty, which is limited by the general will; and possession, which is merely the effect of force or the right of the first occupier, from property, which can be founded only on a positive title.

We might, over and above all this, add, to what man acquires in the civil state, moral liberty, which alone makes him truly master of himself; for the mere impulse of appetite is slavery, while obedience to a law which we prescribe to ourselves is liberty.

THAT SOVEREIGNTY IS INALIENABLE

The first and most important deduction from the principles we have so far laid down is that the general will alone can direct the State according to the object for which it was instituted, i.e. the common good: for if the clashing of particular interests made the establishment of societies necessary, the agreement of these very interests made it possible. The common element in these different interests is what forms the social tie; and, were there no point of agreement between them all, no society could exist. It is solely on the basis of this common interest that every society should be governed.

I hold then that Sovereignty, being nothing less than the exercise of the general will, can never be alienated, and that the Sovereign, who is no less than a collective being, cannot be represented except by himself: the power indeed may be transmitted, but not the will.

In reality, if it is not impossible for a particular will to agree on some point with the general will, it is at least impossible for the agreement to be lasting and constant; for the particular will tends, by its very nature, to partiality, while the general will tends to equality. It is even more impossible to have any guarantee of this agreement; for even if it should always exist, it would be the effect not of art, but of chance. The Sovereign may indeed say: 'I now will actually what this man wills, or at least what he says he wills'; but it cannot say: 'What he wills to-morrow, I too shall will' because it is absurd for the will to bind itself for the future, nor is it incumbent on any will to consent to anything that is not for the good of the being who wills. If then the people promises simply to obey, by that very act it dissolves itself and loses what makes it a people; the moment a master exists, there is no longer a Sovereign, and from that moment the body politic has ceased to exist.

This does not mean that the commands of the rulers cannot pass for general wills, so long as the Sovereign, being free to oppose them, offers no opposition. In such a case, universal silence is taken to imply the consent of the people.

· · · · ·

Sovereignty, for the same reason as makes it inalienable, is indivisible; for will either is, or is not, general;[11] it is the will either of the body of the people, or only of a part of it. In the first case, the will, when declared, is an act of Sovereignty and constitutes law: in the second, it is merely a particular will, or act of magistracy—at the most a decree.

· · · · ·

WHETHER THE GENERAL WILL IS FALLIBLE

It follows from what has gone before that the general will is always right and tends to the public advantage; but it does not follow that the deliberations of the people are always equally correct. Our will is always for our own good, but we do not always see what that is; the people is never corrupted, but it is often deceived, and on such occasions only does it seem to will what is bad.

There is often a great deal of difference between the will of all and the general will; the latter considers only the common interest, while the former takes private interest into account, and is no more than a sum of particular wills: but take away from these same wills the pluses and minuses that cancel one another, and the general will remains as the sum of the differences.

If, when the people, being furnished with adequate information, held its deliberations, the citizens had no communication one with another, the grand total of the small differences would always give the general will, and the decision would always be good. But when factions arise, and partial associations are formed at the expense of the great association, the will of each of these associations becomes general in relation to its members, while it remains particular in relation to the State: it may then be said that there

[11] To be general, a will need not always be unanimous; but every vote must be counted: any exclusion is a breach of generality [Rousseau's note].

are no longer as many votes as there are men, but only as many as there are associations. The differences become less numerous and give a less general result. Lastly, when one of these associations is so great as to prevail over all the rest, the result is no longer a sum of small differences, but a single difference; in this case there is no longer a general will, and the opinion which prevails is purely particular.

It is therefore essential, if the general will is to be able to express itself, that there should be no partial society within the State, and that each citizen should think only his own thoughts. . . . But if there are partial societies, it is best to have as many as possible and to prevent them from being unequal. . . . These precautions are the only ones that can guarantee that the general will shall be always enlightened, and that the people shall in no way deceive itself.[12]

Although Rousseau shares with Hobbes a belief in the social contract theory, the differences between them could not be more striking. Where Hobbes begins with a brutal view of human nature forced into agreement by fear of mutual violence, Rousseau begins by saying that "man is born free." For Rousseau, the social contract is not an instrument of mutual protection but a means of improving people and bringing out what is best in them. His central theme is not antagonism but humanity's "natural goodness." With unmistakable clarity, Rousseau rejects all might makes right theories and insists that legitimacy must always be a matter of the consent of the governed. "The general will" is not a general compromise but the creation of a new power, the power of the people, which, for Rousseau, is the ultimate voice of authority.

INDIVIDUAL RIGHTS
AND FREEDOM

If our concern were only the smooth workings of society, almost any government would do—the stronger the better, the more authoritarian, the more efficient. But efficiency is only one of several concerns, and probably not the most important. You might argue that the public interest could be served by such a government, but it is clear that justice and individual rights could not. The importance of the social contract theory (and consent of the governed theories in general) is precisely its clear emphasis on justice and rights, even when these go against the general public interest. However, social contract theory by itself is not entirely clear about the status of individual rights. Those rights concerning freedom are of particular concern here. How much personal freedom does the social contract guarantee us? Thus, any discussion of justice and the state must include some special concern for the status of basic free-

---

[12] Jean Jacques Rousseau, *The Social Contract and Discourses,* trans. G. D. H. Cole (New York: Everyman's Library Edition, E. P. Dutton, 1947).

doms and "inalienable rights" (that is, rights that no one and no government may take away), as freedom to speak one's political opinions without harassment, freedom to worship (or not worship) without being penalized or punished, freedom to defend oneself against attack ("the right to bear arms" is a controversial case), and the freedom to pursue one's own interests (where these do not interfere with the rights of others). In addition, we can add the right not to be imprisoned without reason, or accused without a fair trial, or punished unduly for a crime committed. Our best known list of such freedoms and rights is the American "Bill of Rights," appended to the main body of the Constitution as a kind of contractual guarantee of personal rights.

But even if the importance of such rights is indisputable, the precise formulation and extent of those rights are highly debatable. We speak of "inalienable rights," but should such rights be left unrestricted, for example, even in wartime? It is clear, to mention the most common example, that freedom of speech does not extend so far as the right to falsely yell "fire" in a crowded theater. Freedom of speech, therefore, like other rights, is limited by considerations of public welfare and utility. But how limited? Is mere annoyance to the government sufficient? Or general boredom among the populace? Similarly, we can go back to the difficult examples we raised in earlier sections. Are the rights against imprisonment and harsh punishment always valid against overwhelming public interest? For example, are they valid in the case of a criminal who has committed crimes repeatedly? Or, to take a very difficult example, is "free enterprise" an "inalienable" right in our society? Or is free enterprise rather a theory (and a debatable one) which suggests that the public interest and justice will best be served by open competition and a free market? But that theory was before the concept of modern monopolies was developed, and before it was obvious that "free" markets could be so manipulated so as not to be either free or in the public interest at all. Is that "freedom" still a right? Or is it too to be tempered by other concerns?

One of the most important basic rights is the presumed right to own private property. John Locke, writing just after the English ("Glorious") Revolution of 1688, listed three basic rights that would become the main ingredients of both the American Declaration of Independence and a still-prominent political philosophy called liberalism. Foremost among them were "life, liberty and the right to own private property." (The original draft of the American Declaration included just these three, but Jefferson replaced the last with the less commital "pursuit of happiness.") For Locke, private property is the bulwark of freedom and the basis of other human rights. One's own body is private property in the most basic sense; no one else has the authority to violate or use it without permission. Most contemporary societies recognize this right to one's own body as fundamental. But then Locke adds, the right to own property which one has helped cultivate with his or her body ("hath mixed his labour with it") is also basic to freedom and human dignity. The Protestant work ethic emerges very powerfully in this view, in which work and rights are treated together, the first being our way of earning the second:

Though the earth and all inferior creatures be common to all men, yet every man has a *property* in his own *person*. This nobody has any right to but himself. The *labour* of his body and the *work* of his hands, we may say, are properly his. Whatsoever, then, he removes out of the state that nature hath provided and left it in, he hath mixed his labour with it, and joined to it something that is his own, and thereby makes it his property. It being by him removed from the common state nature placed it in, it hath by this labour something annexed to it that excludes the common right of other men. For this labour being the unquestionable property of the labourer, no man but he can have a right to what that is once joined to, at least where there is enough, and as good left in common for others.

He that is nourished by the acorns he picked up under an oak, or the apples he gathered from the trees in the wood, has certainly appropriated them to himself. Nobody can deny but the nourishment is his. I ask, then, when did they begin to be his? when he digested? or when he ate? or when he boiled? or when he brought them home? or when he picked them up? And 'tis plain, if the first gathering made them not his, nothing else could. That labour put a distinction between them and common. That added something to them more than Nature, the common mother of all, had done, and so they became his private right. And will any one say he had no right to those acorns or apples he thus appropriated because he had not the consent of all mankind to make them his? Was it a robbery thus to assume to himself what belonged to all in common? If such a consent as that was necessary, man had starved, notwithstanding the plenty God had given him. We see in commons, which remain so by compact, that 'tis the taking any part of what is common, and removing it out of the state Nature leaves it in, which begins the property, without which the common is of no use. And the taking of this or that part does not depend on the express consent of all the commoners. Thus, the grass my horse has bit, the turfs my servant has cut, and the ore I have digged in any place, where I have a right to them in common with others, become my property without the assignation or consent of any body. The labour that was mine, removing them out of that common state they were in, hath fixed my property in them.

And thus, I think, it is very easy to conceive, without any difficulty, how labour could at first begin a title of property in the common things of nature, and how the spending it upon our uses bounded it; so that there could then be no reason of quarrelling about title, nor any doubt about the largeness of possession it gave. Right and conveniency went together. For as a man had a right to all he could employ his labour upon, so he had no temptation to labour for more than he could make use of. This left no room for controversy about the title, nor for encroachment on the right of others. What portion a man carved to himself was easily seen; and it was useless as well as dishonest to carve himself too much, or take more than he needed.[13]

It is important to point out that discussions of rights should never be set apart from discussions of political duties and obligations. As the several versions of the social contract make clear, these are always part of one and the same

[13] John Locke, *The Second Treatise of Government* (New York: Hafner, 1956).

agreement—certain rights in return for certain obligations. To discuss freedom of speech, for example, without also discussing the obligation to be well-informed and logically coherent, is to provide a dangerously one-sided view of the problem. One way of developing this idea of an exchange of rights and obligations has been to distinguish two different senses of "freedom": a *negative* freedom from interference and a *positive* freedom to perform certain obligations. The nature of the distinction has not always been clear, but it has provided the foundation for some of the most important political theories of the last century or so.

The idea that one is "free to perform obligations" may sound odd to us because we are so used to talking exclusively about freedom from constraints and the demands made by authority. But one of the themes which has recurred since the ancient Greeks is that all rights and "freedoms from" must be coupled with duties and obligations and the freedom to perform them. In Rousseau, for example, the citizen's obligations to the state are just as important as the state's obligations to its citizens. Many philosophers are concerned that simple freedom from constraint leaves people without direction or morality and can easily degenerate into chaos and anarchy. Thus, these philosophers stress the necessity of laws and guidelines as an essential part of freedom. This is why they call it "positive" freedom, which is the type of freedom that has a direction and a built-in set of laws and constraints. This notion can be abused easily, however, for "positive freedom" can be made compatible with the most authoritarian state. (The Italian and German fascists, for example, often used the term "freedom" in this "positive" sense.) But despite possible abuses, it is important to see that there is more to freedom than simple freedom from interference. Whenever someone demands freedom, it is important to ask not only "from what?" but also "for what?"

It is also worth distinguishing several different kinds of rights and freedoms. Many rights are clearly localized to a particular state or a particular community, as for example, the right of university regents to free football game tickets and lunches at taxpayers' expense. These rights exist by convention only, and cannot be generalized from one community to another. Then, more generally, there are *civil* rights, rights which are guaranteed in a particular state. One example can be the right to equal treatment despite differences in skin color or sex or religion, as required by various state and federal laws. These are clearly much more important than the conventional rights, and they have a clearly moral basis. For that reason, even though they are defined by reference to a particular state and society, they are often generalized to other societies as well. Insofar as they are generalized in this way, they become *moral* rights or *human rights,* extendable to all people, in any society, regardless of the laws and customs of the society in which they live. Some apparent human rights have been hotly debated; for example, whether the American government has the moral authority to interfere with the infringements of certain human rights of citizens in the Soviet Union. If the right in question is harsh punishment for a seemingly minor crime, it might be argued that their system of punishment is simply more severe than ours, and we should not apply our values to their people. If the right in question is the ability of citizens to speak out against the government without threat of imprisonment or worse, a strong argument has been made that the American government does indeed have that moral authority (whether or not it wishes to risk the consequences is another matter). But if the right in question is one of those basic human rights, against torture or debasement or pointless murder, then it can be argued that everyone has a moral obligation to defend such rights. Human rights are those which transcend all social and national boundaries; they demand that people deserve certain treatment just because they are human, regardless of all else.

A right is a kind of demand, the demand that one is owed something by society and the state, usually a certain sort of consideration or treatment. But most of the rights we have been discussing are in fact rights to freedom or to liberty, that is, the right to be left alone and not interfered with. It is a belief in individual freedom that forms the basis of the liberal political philosophy, which is defined most of all by a commitment to the right of each individual to be free to do whatever he or she wishes, as long as it doesn't interfere with similar rights of others. The classic statement of this position is another pamphlet by John Stuart Mill, *On Liberty* (1859). In it, he defends the rights of individuals and minorities against the tyranny of democratic majorities, for Mill sees that liberty can be as endangered in a democracy as it can be in an authoritarian state.

> The subject of this Essay is not the so-called Liberty of the Will, so unfortunately opposed to the misnamed doctrine of Philosophical Necessity; but Civil, or Social Liberty: the nature and limits of the power which can be legitimately exercised by society over the individual. A question seldom stated, and hardly ever discussed, in general terms, but which profoundly influences the practical controversies of the age by its latent presence, and is likely soon to make itself recognised as the vital question of the future. It is so far from being new, that, in a certain sense, it has divided mankind, almost from the remotest ages; but in the stage of progress into which the more civilised portions of the species have now entered, it presents itself under new conditions, and requires a different and more fundamental treatment.
>
> The struggle between Liberty and Authority is the most conspicuous feature in the portions of history with which we are earliest familiar, particularly in that of Greece, Rome, and England. But in old times this contest was between subjects, or some classes of subjects, and the Government. By liberty, was meant protection against the tyranny of the political rulers. The rulers were conceived (except in some of the popular governments of Greece) as in a necessarily antagonistic position to the people whom they ruled. They consisted of a governing One, or a governing tribe or caste, who derived their authority from inheritance or conquest, who, at all events, did not hold it at the pleasure of the governed, and whose supremacy men did not venture, perhaps did not desire, to contest, whatever precautions might be taken against its oppressive exercise. Their power was regarded as neces-

sary, but also as highly dangerous; as a weapon which they would attempt to use against their subjects, no less than against external enemies. To prevent the weaker members of the community from being preyed upon by innumerable vultures, it was needful that there should be an animal of prey stronger than the rest, commissioned to keep them down. But as the king of the vultures would be no less bent upon preying on the flock than any of the minor harpies, it was indispensable to be in a perpetual attitude of defence against his beak and claws. The aim, therefore, of patriots was to set limits to the power which the ruler should be suffered to exercise over the community; and this limitation was what they meant by liberty. It was attempted in two ways. First, by obtaining a recognition of certain immunities, called political liberties or rights, which was to be regarded as a breach of duty in the ruler to infringe, and which if he did infringe, specific resistance, or general rebellion, was held to be justifiable. A second, and generally a later expedient, was the establishment of constitutional checks, by which the consent of the community, or of a body of some sort, supposed to represent its interests, was made a necessary condition to some of the more important acts of the governing power. To the first of these modes of limitation, the ruling power, in most European countries, was compelled, more or less, to submit. It was not so with the second; and, to attain this, or when already in some degree possessed, to attain it more completely, became everywhere the principal object of the lovers of liberty. And so long as mankind were content to combat one enemy by another, and to be ruled by a master, on condition of being guaranteed more or less efficaciously against his tyranny, they did not carry their aspirations beyond this point.

A time, however, came, in the progress of human affairs, when men ceased to think it a necessity of nature that their governors should be an independent power, opposed in interest to themselves. It appeared to them much better that the various magistrates of the State should be their tenants or delegates, revocable at their pleasure. In that way alone, it seemed, could they have complete security that the powers of government would never be abused to their disadvantage. By degrees this new demand for elective and temporary rulers became the prominent object of the exertions of the popular party, wherever any such party existed; and superseded, to a considerable extent, the previous efforts to limit the power of rulers. As the struggle proceeded for making the ruling power emanate from the periodical choice of the ruled, some persons began to think that too much importance had been attached to the limitation of the power itself. *That* (it might seem) was a resource against rulers whose interests were habitually opposed to those of the people. What was now wanted was, that the rulers should be identified with the people; that their interest and will should be the interest and will of the nation. The nation did not need to be protected against its own will. There was no fear of its tyrannising over itself. Let the rulers be effectually responsible to it, promptly removable by it, and it could afford to trust them with power of which it could itself dictate the use to be made. Their power was but the nation's own power, concentrated, and in a form convenient for exercise. This mode of thought, or rather perhaps of feeling, was common among the last generation of European liberalism, in the Continental section of which it still apparently predominates. Those who admit any limit to what a government may do, except in the case of such governments as they think ought not to exist, stand out as brilliant exceptions among the political thinkers of the Continent. A similar tone of sentiment might by this time have been prevalent in our own country, if the circumstances which for a time encouraged it had continued unaltered.

But, in political and philosophical theories, as well as in persons, success discloses faults and infirmities which failure might have concealed from observation. The notion, that the people have no need to limit their power over themselves, might seem axiomatic, when popular government was a thing only dreamed about, or read of as having existed at some distant period of the past. Neither was that notion necessarily disturbed by such temporary aberrations as those of the French Revolution, the worst of which were the work of a usurping few, and which, in any case, belonged, not to the permanent working of popular institutions, but to a sudden and convulsive outbreak against monarchical and aristocratic despotism. In time, however, a democratic republic came to occupy a large portion of the earth's surface, and made itself felt as one of the most powerful members of the community of nations; and elective and responsible government became subject to the observations and criticisms which wait upon a great existing fact. It was now perceived that such phrases as "self-government," and "the power of the people over themselves," do not express the true state of the case. The "people" who exercise the power are not always the same people with those over whom it is exercised; and the "self-government" spoken of is not the government of each by himself, but of each by all the rest. The will of the people, moreover, practically means the will of the most numerous or the most active *part* of the people; the majority, or those who succeed in making themselves accepted as the majority; the people, consequently *may* desire to oppress a part of their number; and precautions are as much needed against this as against any other abuse of power. The limitation, therefore, of the power of government over individuals loses none of its importance when the holders of power are regularly accountable to the community, that is, to the strongest party therein. This view of things, recommending itself equally to the intelligence of thinkers and to the inclination of those important classes in European society to whose real or supposed interests democracy is adverse, has had no difficulty in establishing itself; and in political speculations "the tyranny of the majority" is now generally included among the evils against which society requires to be on its guard.

Like other tyrannies, the tyranny of the majority was at first, and is still vulgarly, held in dread, chiefly as operating through the acts of the public authorities. But reflecting persons perceived that when society is itself the tyrant—society collectively over the separate individuals who compose it— its means of tyrannising are not restricted to the acts which it may do by the hands of its political functionaries. Society can and does execute its own mandates: and if it issues wrong mandates instead of right, or any mandates at all in things with which it ought not to meddle, it practises a social tyranny more formidable than many kinds of political oppression, since, though not usually upheld by such extreme penalties, it leaves fewer means of escape, penetrating much more deeply into the details of life, and enslaving the soul itself. Protection, therefore, against the tyranny of the magistrate is not enough: there needs protection also against the tyranny of the prevailing opinion and feeling; against the tendency of society to impose, by other means than civil penalties, its own ideas and practices as rules of conduct on those who dissent from them; to fetter the development, and, if possible, prevent the formation, of any individuality not in harmony with its ways, and compels all characters to fashion themselves upon the model of its own. There is a limit to the legitimate interference of collective opinion with individual independence: and to find that limit, and maintain it against encroachment, is as indispensable to a good condition of human affairs, as protection against political despotism.

. . . . .

The likings and dislikings of society, or of some powerful portion of it, are thus the main thing which has practically determined the rules laid down for general observance, under the penalties of law or opinion. And in general, those who have been in advance of society in thought and feeling, have left this condition of things unassailed in principle, however they may have come into conflict with it in some of its details. They have occupied themselves rather in inquiring what things society ought to like or dislike, than in questioning whether its likings or dislikings should be a law to individuals. They preferred endeavouring to alter the feelings of mankind on the particular points on which they were themselves heretical, rather than make common cause in defence of freedom, with heretics generally. The only case in which the higher ground has been taken on principle and maintained with consistency, by any but an individual here and there, is that of religious belief: a case instructive in many ways, and not least so as forming a most striking instance of the fallibility of what is called the moral sense: for the *odium theologicum,* in a sincere bigot, is one of the most unequivocal cases of moral feeling. Those who first broke the yoke of what called itself the Universal Church, were in general as little willing to permit difference of religious opinion as that church itself. But when the heat of the conflict was over, without giving a complete victory to any party, and each church or sect was reduced to limit its hopes to retaining possession of the ground it already occupied; minorities, seeing that they had no chance of becoming majorities, were under the necessity of pleading to those whom they could not convert, for permission to differ. It is accordingly on this battle field almost solely, that the rights of the individual against society have been asserted on broad grounds of principle, and the claim of society to exercise authority over dissentients openly controverted. The great writers to whom the world owes what religious liberty it possesses, have mostly asserted freedom of conscience as an indefeasible right, and denied absolutely that a human being is accountable to others for his religious belief. Yet so natural to mankind is intolerance in whatever they really care about, that religious freedom has hardly anywhere been practically realised, except where religious indifference, which dislikes to have its peace disturbed by theological quarrels, has added its weight to the scale. In the minds of almost all religious persons, even in the most tolerant countries, the duty of toleration is admitted with tacit reserves. One person will bear with dissent in matters of church government, but not of dogma; another can tolerate everybody, short of a

Papist or a Unitarian; another every one who believes in revealed religion; a few extend their charity a little further, but stop at the belief in a God and in a future state. Wherever the sentiment of the majority is still genuine and intense, it is found to have abated little of its claim to be obeyed.

In England, from the peculiar circumstances of our political history, though the yoke of opinion is perhaps heavier, that of law is lighter, than in most other countries of Europe; and there is considerable jealousy of direct interference, by the legislative or the executive power, with private conduct; not so much from any just regard for the independence of the individual, as from the still subsisting habit of looking on the government as representing an opposite interest to the public. The majority have not yet learnt to feel the power of the government their power, or its opinions their opinions. When they do so, individual liberty will probably be as much exposed to invasion from the government, as it already is from public opinion. But, as yet, there is a considerable amount of feeling ready to be called forth against any attempt of the law to control individuals in things in which they have not hitherto been accustomed to be controlled by it; and this with very little discrimination as to whether the matter is, or is not, within the legitimate sphere of legal control; insomuch that the feeling, highly salutary on the whole, is perhaps quite as often misplaced as well grounded in the particular instances of its application. There is, in fact, no recognised principle by which the propriety or impropriety of government interference is customarily tested. People decide according to their personal preferences. Some, whenever they see any good to be done, or evil to be remedied, would willingly instigate the government to undertake the business; while others prefer to bear almost any amount of social evil, rather than add one to the departments of human interests amenable to governmental control. And men range themselves on one or the other side in any particular case, according to this general direction of their sentiments; or according to the degree of interest which they feel in the particular thing which it is proposed that the government should do, or according to the belief they entertain that the government would, or would not, do it in the manner they prefer; but very rarely on account of any opinion to which they consistently adhere, as to what things are fit to be done by a government. And it seems to me that in consequence of this absence of rule or principle, one side is at present as often wrong as the other; the interference of government is, with about equal frequency, improperly invoked and improperly condemned.

Mill then goes on to offer a "very simple principle," that individual liberty is to be considered inviolable, except when other people are threatened with harm.

The object of this Essay is to assert one very simple principle, as entitled to govern absolutely the dealings of society with the individual in the way of compulsion and control, whether the means used be physical force in the form of legal penalties, or the moral coercion of public opinion. That principle is, that the sole end for which mankind are warranted, individually or collectively, in interfering with the liberty of action of any of their number, is self-protection. That the only purpose for which power can be rightfully exercised over any member of a civilised community, against his will, is to prevent harm to others. His own good, either physical or moral, is not a sufficient warrant. He cannot rightfully be compelled to do or forbear because it will be better for him to do so, because it will make him happier, because, in the opinions of others, to do so would be wise, or even right. These are good reasons for remonstrating with him, or reasoning with him, or persuading him, or entreating him, but not for compelling him, or visiting him with any evil in case he do otherwise. To justify that, the conduct from which it is desired to deter him must be calculated to produce evil to some one else. The only part of the conduct of any one, for which he is amenable to society, is that which concerns others. In the part which merely concerns himself, his independence is, of right, absolute. Over himself, over his own body and mind, the individual is sovereign.

It is, perhaps, hardly necessary to say that this doctrine is meant to apply only to human beings in the maturity of their faculties. We are not speaking of children, or of young persons below the age which the law may fix as that of manhood or womanhood. Those who are still in a state to require being taken care of by others, must be protected against their own actions as well as against external injury. For the same reason, we may leave out of consideration those backward states of society in which the race itself may be considered as in its nonage. The early difficulties in the way of spontaneous progress are so great, that there is seldom any choice of means for overcoming them; and a ruler full of the spirit of improvement is warranted in the use of any expedients that will attain an end, perhaps otherwise unattainable. Despotism is a legitimate mode of government in dealing with barbarians, provided the end be their improvement,[14] and the means justified by actually affecting that end. Liberty, as a principle, has no application to any state of things anterior to the time when mankind have become capable of being improved by free and equal discussion.

It is proper to state that I forego any advantage which could be derived to my argument from the idea of abstract right, as a thing independent of utility. I regard utility as the ultimate appeal on all ethical questions; but it must be utility in the largest sense, grounded on the permanent interests of a man as a progressive being. Those interests, I contend, authorise the subjection of individual spontaneity to external control, only in respect to those actions of each, which concern the interest of other people. If any one does an act hurtful to others, there is a *prima facie* case for punishing him, by law, or, where legal penalties are not safely applicable, by general disapprobation. There are also many positive acts for the benefit of others, which he may rightfully be compelled to perform; such as to give evidence in a court of justice; to bear his fair share in the common defence, or in any other joint work necessary to the interest of the society of which he enjoys the protection; and to perform certain acts of individual beneficence, such as saving a fellow creature's life, or interposing to protect the defenceless against ill-usage, things which whenever it is obviously a man's duty to do,

---

[14] Notice the political implications for this qualification, however, in "underdeveloped" countries and colonies. The principle of *paternalism*—that one ought to take care of those who cannot take care of themselves—is easily abused, and therefore always dangerous.

he may rightfully be made responsible to society for not doing. A person may cause evil to others not only by his actions but by his inaction, and in either case he is justly accountable to them for the injury. The latter case, it is true, requires a much more cautious exercise of compulsion than the former. To make any one answerable for doing evil to others is the rule; to make him answerable for not preventing evil is, comparatively speaking, the exception. Yet there are many cases clear enough and grave enough to justify that exception. In all things which regard the external relations of the individual, he is *de jure* amenable to those whose interests are concerned, and, if need be, to society as their protector. There are often good reasons for not holding him to the responsibility; but these reasons must arise from the special expediencies of the case: either because it is a kind of case in which he is on the whole likely to act better, when left to his own discretion, than when controlled in any way in which society have it in their power to control him; or because the attempt to exercise control would produce other evils, greater than those which it would prevent. When such reasons as these preclude the enforcement of responsibility, the conscience of the agent himself should step into the vacant judgment seat, and protect those interests of others which have no external protection; judging himself all the more rigidly, because the case does not admit of his being made accountable to the judgment of his fellow creatures.

But there is a sphere of action in which society, as distinguished from the individual, has, if any, only an indirect interest; comprehending all that portion of a person's life and conduct which affects only himself, or if it also affects others, only with their free, voluntary, and undeceived consent and participation. When I say only himself, I mean directly, and in the first instance; for whatever affects himself, may affect others through himself; and the objection which may be grounded on this contingency, will receive consideration in the sequel. This, then, is the appropriate region of human liberty. It comprises, first, the inward domain of consciousness; demanding liberty of conscience in the most comprehensive sense; liberty of thought and feeling; absolute freedom of opinion and sentiment on all subjects, practical or speculative, scientific, moral, or theological. The liberty of expressing and publishing opinions may seem to fall under a different principle, since it belongs to that part of the conduct of an individual which concerns other people; but, being almost of as much importance as the liberty of thought itself, and resting in great part on the same reasons, is practically inseparable from it. Secondly, the principle requires liberty of tastes and pursuits; of framing the plan of our life to suit our own character; of doing as we like, subject to such consequences as may follow: without impediment from our fellow creatures, so long as what we do does not harm them, even though they should think our conduct foolish, perverse, or wrong. Thirdly, from this liberty of each individual, follows the liberty, within the same limits, of combination among individuals; freedom to unite, for any purpose not involving harm to others: the persons combining being supposed to be of full age, and not forced or deceived.

No society in which these liberties are not, on the whole, respected, is free, whatever may be its form of government; and none is completely free in which they do not exist absolute and unqualified. The only freedom which deserves the name, is that of pursuing our own good in our own way, so long as we do not attempt to deprive others of theirs, or impede their efforts to obtain it. Each is the proper guardian of his own health, whether bodily, *or* mental and spiritual. Mankind are greater gainers by suffering each other to live as seems good to themselves, than by compelling each to live as seems good to the rest.[15]

Mill's main concern in this essay is the extent to which government and public interest have authority over individuals and individual actions. If an action harms other people or presents a public menace, then government does have the authority to prevent it or punish a person for doing it. But if an action is not harmful to others, the government has no such authority. In the question of freedom of speech, for example, this means that governments have no authority to censor some comment or publication unless it clearly harms other people, not merely annoys or personally offends them. Mill is particularly concerned with protecting individuals against "the tyranny of the majority." The public interest is authoritative to "a limit," but that limit does not include interfering with personal affairs or opinions.

A DIFFERENT SENSE
OF FREEDOM: MARX

From a liberal perspective, this English emphasis on rights and liberty seems indisputable. But what happens when the "natural right" to private property is abused, when people take more than they can use personally and use their excess possession merely as a means to manipulate other people? And it is all well and good to defend such rights as freedom of speech and religion, but what if many people in the society find themselves far more concerned just with the exigencies of existence—putting food on the table, surviving a dangerous job, and not having enough protection under the law to prevent them from being grossly exploited and underpaid for unrewarding and painful labor? There is an obvious sense in which people in such conditions are not at all "free," even if they are guaranteed freedom of speech and religion. Freedom from government persecution is not necessarily freedom from economic exploitation. And it is the latter freedom that concerns Karl Marx and his frequent co-author Friedrich Engels.

It is worth mentioning that Locke wrote his two treatises on government before the industrial revolution; Marx wrote when that revolution was at its peak, transforming cities like Manchester England into virtual slave-farms of underpaid, overworked laborers. With this in mind, the freedoms of speech and religion protected by well-to-do and comfortable liberals seemed not nearly so important as the basic freedom to a decent life. So Marx turned

[15] John Stuart Mill, *On Liberty* (London: Longmans, 1859).

from political liberties to economic necessities, and turned his attention from the supposed right to private property to the abuse of private property.

Although Marx insists on "the abolition of private property" as the central theme of communism, he still retains the idea that a man or woman has the right to the products of his or her own labor. What he rejects is the ownership of property that one has not personally produced and that serves only as a means for getting richer at the expense of other people, who are thereby forced to work without enjoying the products of their labor. This is what Marx means by his very important notion of *alienation*. A person is alienated if he or she is no longer working for him or herself, but only for the benefit of another person. Even though a person might get paid for this labor, that does not make it less alienated. A factory worker may be well-paid, but he is alienated insofar as his work is meaningless to him, and the profits of his work do not go to him but to someone else. Thus, despite their obvious differences, Marx and Locke agree to this extent: a person has a right to something "if he has mixed his labour with it." Both philosophers agree on the importance of human productivity and creativity to the good life, and the person's right to his or her own creation is therefore essential to any adequate society.

Marx was a *historical materialist*, by which is meant that he placed new emphasis on the economic modes of production of goods and saw history and politics (and all other human enterprises) as conditioned by economic relations. Accordingly, the key to human freedom and the lack of freedom was also economic. In the following passage from his early writings (of 1844), Marx summarizes his notion of alienation as the unnatural separation of a person from the object he or she creates, resulting in separation ("alienation") from other people and, ultimately, from oneself. Quite the contrary of the "natural" identity the worker should feel with what he or she has made, the object produced is "set against him [or her] as an alien and hostile force." Instead of pride or enjoyment, the worker feels only resentment against those who have made the labor meaningless, and the pay received for this only makes it clearer how personally irrelevant it is:

> We shall begin from a *contemporary* economic fact. The worker becomes poorer the more wealth he produces and the more his production increases in power and extent. The worker becomes an ever cheaper commodity the more goods he creates. The *devaluation* of the human world increases in direct relation with the *increase in value* of the world of things. Labor does not only create goods; it also produces itself and the worker as a *commodity*, and indeed in the same proportion as it produces goods.
>
> This fact simply implies that the object produced by labor, its product, now stands opposed to it as an *alien being*, as a *power independent* of the producer. The product of labor is labor which has been embodied in an object and turned into a physical thing; this product is an *objectification* of labor. The performance of work is at the same time its objectification. The performance of work appears in the sphere of political economy as a *vitiation* of the worker, objectification as a *loss* and as *servitude to the object*, and appropriation as *alienation*.

So much does the performance of work appear as vitiation that the worker is vitiated to the point of starvation. So much does objectification appear as loss of the object that the worker is deprived of the most essential things not only of life but also of work. Labor itself becomes an object which he can acquire only by the greatest effort and with unpredictable interruptions. So much does the appropriation of the object appear as alienation that the more objects the worker produces the fewer he can possess and the more he falls under the domination of his product, of capital.

All these consequences follow from the fact that the worker is related to the *product of his labor* as to an *alien* object. For it is clear on this presupposition that the more the worker expends himself in work the more powerful becomes the world of objects which he creates in face of himself, the poorer he becomes in his inner life, and the less he belongs to himself. The life which he has given to the object sets itself against him as an alien and hostile force.[16]

Marx introduces the new concept of freedom from alienation, which requires a return to the "natural" state in which people and their labor are one. (In this notion of return to the natural state, Marx is heavily influenced by Rousseau.) It is important to emphasize that nowhere does Marx suggest or desire that people should someday be free of work. According to him, work makes us human. Instead, he argues that we should make ourselves free of alienated work. This does not mean that he denies other freedoms—freedom of speech, for example—but he does argue that such freedoms are meaningless in the face of the cruel economic necessities that rule most people's lives. Men and women, desperate for a job and forced to undertake meaningless tasks for forty hours a week, need more than just the freedom to speak out. They require freedom from the economic exploitation that keeps them in such desperate circumstances. They must have, in general, freedom from material need. Marx makes a great deal of what he considers humanity's crucial difference from the animals, their ability to work and produce, thereby freeing themselves from the needs of nature.

Marx is a very modern theorist. He no longer argues on the basis of endless human requirements for food and shelter but sees that in the modern world the means of producing enough food and shelter for everyone are already at hand. What is needed is simply a more equitable form of distribution. This means, no private property, except for those products a person makes directly. There can be factories, but no "owners," as opposed to the laborers. There might be "corporations," but only if they are nothing more than a coalition of the workers, who share in the benefits of their own work.

But this Marxist vision, in which there are no owners except the workers, and in which everyone is a worker and no one is alienated from his or her work, is not going to come about without enormous upheaval. Marx's "classless society" requires a thorough-going revolution—not so much a political revolution as an economic one. This is the key to Marx's concept of freedom. It proposes freedom from want and freedom from economic exploitation, not

[16] Karl Marx, *Early Writings*, trans. T. Bottomore (New York: McGraw-Hill, 1964).

political freedom in terms of rights and the freedom from government interference that we have mainly discussed so far. The revolution he envisions, in which the various economic classes of society will continue to war against each other until all such classes disappear, may therefore be called a battle for freedom just as much as the traditional liberal battles for freedom of speech and self-government. It is a revolution which he sees as inevitable, which has been in the making since ancient times, and in which the theme "workers of the world unite; you have nothing to lose but your chains" will become the rallying cry around which the human world will experience its greatest upheaval ever.

The excerpt that follows, the *Communist Manifesto* of 1848, is the most popular statement of Marx's theory. Marx wrote it with his friend and long-time collaborator, Friedrich Engels. In it, they explain human history in terms of historical materialism, define the two social classes they see at war with each other, the *bourgeoisie* or ownership class and the *proletariat* or working class, and suggest the course that history now has to take. They are not just predicting and theorizing, however, but are also advocating the revolution they describe in no uncertain terms.

BOURGEOIS AND PROLETARIANS

The history of all hitherto existing society is the history of class struggles.

Freeman and slave, patrician and plebeian, lord and serf, guild-master and journeyman, in a word, oppressor and oppressed, stood in constant opposition to one another, carried on an uninterrupted, now hidden, now open fight, a fight that each time ended, either in a revolutionary re-constitution of society at large, or in the common ruin of the contending classes.

In the earlier epochs of history, we find almost everywhere a complicated arrangement of society into various orders, a manifold gradation of social rank. In ancient Rome we have patricians, knights, plebeians, slaves; in the middle ages, feudal lords, vassals, guild-masters, journeymen, apprentices, serfs; in almost all of these classes, again, subordinate gradations.

The modern bourgeois society that has sprouted from the ruins of feudal society, has not done away with class antagonisms. It has but established new classes, new conditions of oppression, new forms of struggle in place of the old ones.

Our epoch, the epoch of the bourgeoisie, possesses, however, this distinctive feature; it has simplified the class antagonisms. Society as a whole is more and more splitting up into two great hostile camps, into two great classes directly facing each other: Bourgeoisie and Proletariat.

THE RISE OF THE BOURGEOISIE

From the serfs of the middle ages sprang the chartered burghers of the earliest towns. From these burgesses the first elements of the bourgeoisie were developed.

The discovery of America, the rounding of the Cape, opened up fresh ground for the rising bourgeoisie. The East-Indian and Chinese markets, the colonization of America, trade with the colonies, the increase in the means of exchange and in commodities generally, gave to commerce, to navigation, to industry, an impulse never before known, and thereby, to the revolutionary element in the tottering feudal society, a rapid development.

The feudal system of industry, under which industrial production was monopolized by closed guilds, now no longer sufficed for the growing wants of the new markets. The manufacturing system took its place. The guild-masters were pushed on one side by the manufacturing middle-class; division of labor between the different corporate guilds vanished in the face of division of labor in each single workshop.

Meantime the markets kept ever growing, the demand, ever rising. Even manufacture no longer sufficed. Thereupon, steam and machinery revolutionized industrial production. The place of manufacture was taken by the giant, Modern Industry, the place of the industrial middle-class, by industrial millionaires, the leaders of whole industrial armies, the modern bourgeois.

Modern industry has established the world-market, for which the discovery of America paved the way. This market has given an immense development to commerce, to navigation, to communication by land. This development has, in its turn, reacted on the extension of industry; and in proportion as industry, commerce, navigation, railways extended, in the same proportion the bourgeoisie developed, increased its capital, and pushed into the background every class handed down from the Middle Ages.

We see, therefore, how the modern bourgeoisie is itself the product of a long course of development, of a series of revolutions in the modes of production and of exchange.

Each step in the development of the bourgeoisie was accompanied by a corresponding political advance of that class. An oppressed class under the sway of the feudal nobility, an armed and self-governing association in the mediaeval commune, here independent urban republic (as in Italy and Germany), there taxable "third estate" of the monarchy (as in France), afterwards, in the period of manufacture proper, serving either the semifeudal or the absolute monarchy as a counterpoise against the nobility, and, in fact, cornerstone of the great monarchies in general, the bourgeoisie has at last, since the establishment of Modern Industry and of the world-market, conquered for itself, in the modern representative State, exclusive political sway. *The executive of the modern State is but a committee for managing the common affairs of the whole bourgeoisie.*

REVOLUTIONARY ROLE OF THE BOURGEOISIE

The bourgeoisie, historically, has played a most revolutionary part.

The bourgeoisie, wherever it has got the upper hand, has put an end to all feudal, patriarchal, idyllic relations. It has pitilessly torn asunder the motley feudal ties that bound man to his "natural superiors," and has left remaining no other nexus between man and man than naked self-interest, callous "cash payment." It has drowned the most heavenly ecstasies of religious fervor, of chivalrous enthusiasm, of philistine sentimentalism, in the icy water of egotistical calculation. It has resolved personal worth into exchange value, and in place of the numberless indefeasible chartered freedoms, has set up that single, unconscionable freedom—Free Trade. In one word, for exploitation, veiled by religious and political illusions, it has substituted naked, shameless, direct, brutal exploitation.

The bourgeoisie has stripped of its halo every occupation hitherto honored and looked up to with reverent awe. It has converted the physician, the lawyer, the priest, the poet, the man of science, into its paid wage-laborers.

The bourgeoisie has torn away from the family its sentimental veil, and has reduced the family relation to a mere money relation.

The bourgeoisie has disclosed how it came to pass that the brutal display of vigor in the Middle Ages, which Reactionists so much admire, found its fitting complement in the most slothful indolence. It has been the first to show what man's activity can bring about. It has accomplished wonders far surpassing Egyptian pyramids, Roman aqueducts, and Gothic cathedrals; it has conducted expeditions that put in the shade all former Exoduses of nations and crusades.

The bourgeoisie cannot exist without constantly revolutionizing the instruments of production, and thereby the relations of production, and with them the whole relations of society. Conservation of the old modes of production in unaltered form, was, on the contrary, the first condition of existence for all earlier industrial classes. Constant revolutionizing of production, uninterrupted disturbance of all social conditions, everlasting uncertainty and agitation distinguish the bourgeois epoch from all earlier ones. All fixed, fast-frozen relations, with their train of ancient and venerable prejudices and opinions, are swept away, all new-formed ones become antiquated before they can ossify. All that is solid melts into air, all that is holy is profaned, and man is at last compelled to face, with sober senses, his real conditions of life, and his relations with his kind.

The need of a constantly expanding market for its products chases the bourgeoisie over the whole surface of the globe. It must nestle everywhere, settle everywhere, establish connections everywhere.

The bourgeoisie has through its exploitation of the world-market given a cosmopolitan character to production and consumption in every country. To the great chagrin of Reactionists, it has drawn from under the feet of industry the national ground on which it stood. All old-established national industries have been destroyed or are daily being destroyed. They are dislodged by new industries, whose introduction becomes a life and death question for all civilized nations, by industries that no longer work up indigenous raw material, but raw material drawn from the remotest zones; industries whose products are consumed, not only at home, but in every quarter of the globe. In place of the old wants, satisfied by the productions of the country, we find new wants, requiring for their satisfaction the products of distant lands and climes. In place of the old local and national seclusion and self-sufficiency, we have intercourse in every direction, universal inter-dependence of nations. And as in material, so also in intellectual production. The intellectual creations of individual nations become common property. National one-sidedness and narrow-mindedness become more and more impossible, and from the numerous national and local literatures there arises a world-literature.

The bourgeoisie, by the rapid improvement of all instruments of production, by the immensely facilitated means of communication, draws all, even the most barbarian, nations into civilization. The cheap prices of its commodities are the heavy artillery with which it batters down all Chinese walls, with which it forces the barbarians' intensely obstinate hatred of foreigners to capitulate. It compels all nations, on pain of extinction, to adopt the bourgeois mode of production; it compels them to introduce what it calls civilization into their midst, i.e., to become bourgeois themselves. In a word, it creates a world after its own image.

The bourgeoisie has subjected the country to the rule of the towns. It has created enormous cities, has greatly increased the urban population as compared with the rural, and has thus rescued a considerable part of the population from the idiocy of rural life. Just as it has made the country dependent on the towns, so it has made barbarian and semi-barbarian countries dependent on the civilized ones, nations of peasants on nations of bourgeois, the East on the West.

The bourgeoisie keeps more and more doing away with the scattered state of the population, of the means of production, and of property. It has agglomerated population, centralized means of production, and has concentrated property in a few hands. The necessary consequence of this was political centralization. Independent, or but loosely connected provinces, with separate interests, laws, governments and systems of taxation, became lumped together in one nation, with one government, one code of laws, one national class-interest, one frontier and one customs-tariff.

The bourgeoisie, during its rule of scarce one hundred years, has created more massive and more colossal productive forces than have all preceding generations together. Subjection of Nature's forces to man, machinery, application of chemistry to industry and agriculture, steam-navigation, railways, electric telegraphs, clearing of whole continents for cultivation, canalization of rivers, whole populations conjured out of the ground—what earlier century had even a presentiment that such productive forces slumbered in the lap of social labor?

THE REVOLT OF PRODUCTIVE FORCES
AGAINST PROPERTY RELATIONS

We see then: the means of production and of exchange on whose foundation the bourgeoisie built itself up, were generated in feudal society. At a certain stage in the development of these means of production and of exchange, the conditions under which feudal society produced and exchanged, the feudal organization of agriculture and manufacturing industry, in one word, the feudal relations of property became no longer compatible with the already developed productive forces; they became so many fetters. They had to burst asunder; they were burst asunder.

Into their places stepped free competition, accompanied by a social and political constitution adapted to it, and by the economical and political sway of the bourgeois class.

A similar movement is going on before our own eyes. *Modern bourgeois* society with its relations of production, of exchange and of property, a society that has conjured up such gigantic means of production and of exchange, *is like the sorcerer, who is no longer able to control the powers of the nether world whom he has called up by his spells.* For many a decade past the history of industry and commerce is but the history of the revolt of modern productive forces against modern conditions of production, against the property relations that are the conditions for the existence of the bourgeoisie and of its rule. It is enough to mention the commercial crises that by their periodical return put on its trial, each time more threateningly, the existence of the entire bourgeois society. In these crises a great part not only of the existing products, but also of the previously created productive forces, are periodically destroyed. In these crises there breaks out an epidemic that, in all earlier epochs, would have seemed an absurdity—the epidemic of over-production. Society suddenly finds itself put back into a state of momentary barbarism; it appears as if a famine, a universal war of devastation had cut off the supply of every means of subsistence; industry and commerce seem to be destroyed; and why? Because there is too much civilization, too much means of subsistence, too much industry, too much commerce. The productive forces at the disposal of society no longer tend to further the development of the conditions of bourgeois property; on the contrary, they have become too powerful for these conditions, by which they are fettered, and so soon as they overcome these fetters, they bring disorder into the whole of bourgeois society, endanger the existence of bourgeois property. The conditions of bourgeois society are too narrow to comprise the wealth created by them. And how does the bourgeoisie get over these crises? On the one hand by enforced destruction of a mass of productive forces; on the other, by the conquest of new markets, and by the more thorough exploitation of the old ones. That is to say, by paving the way for more extensive and more destructive crises, and by diminishing the means whereby crises are prevented. The weapons with which the bourgeoisie felled feudalism to the ground are now turned against the bourgeoisie itself.

But not only has the bourgeoisie forged the weapons that bring death to itself; it has also called into existence the men who are to wield those weapons—the modern working-class—the proletarians.

THE STRUGGLE AND VICTORY OF THE PROLETARIAT

The proletariat goes through various stages of development. With its birth begins its struggle with the bourgeoisie. At first the contest is carried on by individual laborers, then by the workpeople of a factory, then by the operatives of one trade, in one locality, against the individual bourgeois who directly exploits them. They direct their attacks not against the bourgeois conditions of production, but against the instruments of production themselves; they destroy imported wares that compete with their labor, they smash to pieces machinery, they set factories ablaze, they seek to restore by force the vanished status of the workman of the Middle Ages.

At this stage the laborers still form an incoherent mass scattered over the whole country, and broken up by their mutual competition. If anywhere they unite to form more compact bodies, this is not yet the consequence of their own active union, but of the union of the bourgeoisie, which class, in order to attain its own political ends, is compelled to set the whole proletariat in motion, and is moreover, yet, for a time, able to do so. At this stage, therefore, the proletarians do not fight their enemies, but the enemies of their enemies, the remnants of absolute monarchy, the landowners, the non-industrial bourgeois, the petty bourgeoisie. Thus the whole historical movement is concentrated in the hands of the bourgeoisie; every victory so obtained is a victory for the bourgeoisie.

But with the development of industry the proletariat not only increases in number, it becomes concentrated in greater masses, its strength grows, and it feels that strength more. The various interests and conditions of life within the ranks of the proletariat are more and more equalized, in proportion as machinery obliterates all distinctions of labor, and nearly everywhere reduces wages to the same low level. The growing competition among the bourgeois, and the resulting commercial crises, make the wages of the workers ever more fluctuating. The unceasing improvement of machinery, ever more rapidly developing, makes their livelihood more and more precarious; the collisions between individual workmen and individual bourgeois take more and more the character of collisions between two classes. Thereupon the workers begin to form combinations (Trades' Unions) against the bourgeois; they club together in order to keep up the rate of wages; they found permanent associations in order to make provision beforehand for these occasional revolts. Here and there the contest breaks out into riots.

Now and then the workers are victorious, but only for a time. The real fruit of their battle lies, not in the immediate result, but in the ever-expanding union of the workers. This union is helped on by the improved means of communication that are created by modern industry, and that place the workers of different localities in contact with one another. It was just this contact that was needed to centralize the numerous local struggles, all of the same character, into one national struggle between classes. But every class struggle is a political struggle. And that union, to attain which the burghers of the Middle Ages, with their miserable highways, required centuries, the modern proletarians, thanks to railways, achieve in a few years.

This organization of the proletarians into a class, and consequently into a political party, is continually being upset again by the competition between the workers themselves. But it ever rises up again, stronger, firmer, mightier. It compels legislative recognition of particular interest of the workers, by taking advantage of the divisions among the bourgeoisie itself. Thus the ten-hour bill in England was carried.

Altogether collisions between the classes of the old society further, in many ways, the course of development of the proletariat. The bourgeoisie finds itself involved in a constant battle. At first with the aristocracy; later on, with those portions of the bourgeoisie itself, whose interests have become antagonistic to the progress of industry; at all times, with the bourgeoisie of foreign countries. In all these battles it sees itself compelled to appeal to the proletariat, to ask for its help, and thus, to drag it into the political arena. The bourgeoisie itself, therefore, supplies the proletariat with its own elements of political and general education, in other words, it furnishes the proletariat with weapons for fighting the bourgeoisie.

Further, as we have already seen, entire sections of the ruling classes are, by the advance of industry, precipitated into the proletariat, or are at least threatened in their conditions of existence. These also supply the proletariat with fresh elements of enlightenment and progress.

Finally, in times when the class-struggle nears the decisive hour, the process of dissolution going on within the ruling class, in fact, within the whole range of old society, assumes such a violent, glaring character, that a small section of the ruling class cuts itself adrift, and joins the revolutionary class, the class that holds the future in its hands. Just as, therefore, at an earlier period, a section of the nobility went over to the bourgeoisie, so now a portion of the bourgeoisie goes over to the proletariat, and in particular, a portion of the bourgeois ideologists, who have raised themselves to the level of comprehending theoretically the historical movements as a whole.

PROPERTY AND FREEDOM

All property relations in the past have continually been subject to historical change consequent upon the change in historical conditions.

The French Revolution, for example, abolished feudal property in favor of bourgeois property.

The distinguishing feature of Communism is not the abolition of property generally, but the abolition of bourgeois property. But modern bourgeois private property is the final and most complete expression of the system of producing and appropriating products, that is based on class antagonism, on the exploitation of the many by the few.

In this sense, the theory of the Communists may be summed up in the single sentence: Abolition of private property. . . .

You are horrified at our intending to do away with private property. But in your existing society, private property is already done away with for nine-tenths of the population; its existence for the few is solely due to its non-existence in the hands of those nine-tenths. You reproach us, therefore, with intending to do away with a form of property, the necessary condition for whose existence is the nonexistence of any property for the immense majority of society.

In a word, you reproach us with intending to do away with your property. Precisely so; that is just what we intend.

From the moment when labor can no longer be converted into capital, money, or rent, into a social power capable of being monopolized, *i.e.,* from the moment when individual property can no longer be transformed into bourgeois property, into capital, from that moment, you say, individuality vanishes.

You must, therefore, confess that by "individual" you mean no other person than the bourgeois, than the middle-class owner of property. This person must, indeed, be swept out of the way, and made impossible.

Communism deprives no man of the power to appropriate the products of society; all that it does is to deprive him of the power to subjugate the labor of others by means of such appropriation. . . .

And then, Marx's final optimism:

When, in the course of development, class distinctions have disappeared, and all production has been concentrated in the hands of a vast association of the whole nation, the public power will lose its political character. Political power, properly so called, is merely the organized power of one class for oppressing another. If the proletariat during its contest with the bourgeoisie is compelled, by the force of circumstances, to organize itself as a class; if, by means of a revolution, it makes itself the ruling class, and, as such sweeps away by force the old conditions of production, then it will, along with these conditions, have swept away the conditions for the existence of class antagonisms, and of classes generally, and will thereby have abolished its own supremacy as a class.

In place of the old bourgeois society, with its classes and class antagonisms, we shall have an association, in which the free development of each is the condition for the free development of all.[17]

THE ABSOLUTE STATE:
FASCISM

We think of "fascism" as a nasty word. People of very different political persuasions accuse their opponents of "fascism" if they consider their policies oppressive. But this is a new meaning of the word. "Fascism" once was the proud name of a political theory, the theory of the absolute state. In the 1920's, Benito Mussolini swept into power in Italy with enormous popularity, a popularity he retained until his disastrous alliance with Adolf Hitler (also a fascist), in the Second World War. For Mussolini, and for most of his followers, "fascism" had an almost religious significance: the state was raised to an almost divine status. The state was like a god, the source of laws and duties not unlike those discussed in the Bible. The individual existed only to serve and identify with the state. According to fascism, if some people were brutally repressed, it was only for the good of the general will and the state. (Rousseau's notion of "the general will" often enters into fascist theory.) If fascism had to use force to protect the government, that force, so it was argued, was ultimately for the good of its people. And if fascism so often meant war, what better way to bring the citizens together into a virtual family? This identification of the state with the family plays a central part in the almost religious language of fascism. What follows is an extract from one of Mussolini's most often-quoted speeches:

Fascism is a religious conception in which man is seen in his immanent relationship with a superior law and with an objective Will that transcends the particular individual and raises him to conscious membership of a spiritual society. Whoever has seen in the religious politics of the Fascist regime nothing but mere opportunism has not understood that Fascism besides being a system of government is also, and above all, a system of thought.

Fascism is a historical conception, in which man is what he is only in so far as he works with the spiritual process in which he finds himself, in the family or social group, in the nation and in the history in which all nations collaborate. From this follows the great value of tradition, in memories, in language, in customs, in the standards of social life. Outside history

[17] Karl Marx and Friedrich Engels, *Communist Manifesto,* trans. Samuel Moore (Chicago: Regnery, 1969).

man is nothing. Consequently, Fascism is opposed to all the individualistic abstractions of a materalistic nature like those of the eighteenth century; and it is opposed to all Jacobin utopias and innovations. It does not consider that "happiness" is possible upon earth, as it appeared to be in the desire of the economic literature of the eighteenth century, and hence it rejects all teleological theories according to which mankind would reach a definitive stabilized condition at a certain period in history. This implies putting oneself outside history and life, which is a continual change and coming to be. Politically, Fascism wishes to be a realistic doctrine; practically, it aspires to solve only the problems which arise historically of themselves and that of themselves find or suggest their own solution. To act among men, as to act in the natural world, it is necessary to enter into the process of reality and to master the already operating forces.

Against individualism, the Fascist conception is for the State; and it is for the individual in so far as he coincides with the State, which is the conscience and universal will of man in his historical existence. It is opposed to classical Liberalism, which arose from the necessity of reacting against absolutism, and which brought its historical purpose to an end when the State was transformed into the conscience and will of the people. Liberalism denied the State in the interests of the particular individual; Fascism reaffirms the State as the true reality of the individual. And if liberty is to be the attribute of the real man, and not of that abstract puppet envisaged by individualistic Liberalism, Fascism is for liberty. And for the only liberty which can be a real thing, the liberty of the State and of the individual within the State. Therefore, for the Fascist, everything is in the State, and nothing human or spiritual exists, much less has value, outside the State. In this sense Fascism is totalitarian, and the Fascist State, the synthesis and unity of all values, interprets, develops and gives strength to the whole life of the people.

. . . . .

This higher personality is truly the nation in so far as it is the State. It is not the nation that generates the State, as according to the old naturalistic concept which served as the basis of the political theories of the national States of the nineteenth century. Rather the nation is created by the State, which gives to the people, conscious of its own moral unity, a will and therefore an effective existence. The right of a nation to independence derives not from a literary and ideal consciousness of its own being, still less from a more or less unconscious and inert acceptance of a *de facto* situation, but from an active consciousness, from a political will in action and ready to demonstrate its own rights: that is to say, from a state already coming into being. The State, in fact, as the universal ethical will, is the creator of right.[18]

In the other political theories we have discussed, the state and its interests are always balanced against the interests of the public and the individual

[18] Benito Mussolini, "The Doctrine of Fascism," trans. I. S. Munro (Rome: Encyclopedie Italiano, 1934).

citizen. This is the main point of most social contract theories, of consent of the governed theories, of utilitarian and justice theories, and the main goal of Marx's theory as well (although Marx is more concerned with economic power than just political power). In fascism, by contrast, the balance tips towards the interests of the state. This is not to say that the purpose of fascism is not also to serve the public interest and the individual citizen, but, in terms of priorities, the state comes first. In social contract theories (including democratic theories), a state which does not serve the public interest can be legitimately overthrown; in fascist theory, the state has absolute legitimacy whether or not it succeeds in satisfying its citizens, and this is part of its religious significance.

In view of the fascist doctrine of the absolute state, it is in the interest of the state, but not its obligation, to have its citizens support it as enthusiastically as possible. This means that the fascist state will try to get the approval of its people perhaps just as fervently as a democratic state, but primarily in order to enhance its own power. About 400 years before the advent of modern fascism, one of Mussolini's countrymen, Niccolo Machiavelli, wrote a short treatise designed to instruct the leaders of absolute states on the art of keeping their power, including the art of winning and keeping public support. In *The Prince* (1513), Machiavelli writes a "how to" book for rulers, telling them the best ways of winning wars, tricking their enemies, and, in general, keeping power. (Machiavelli himself was not a fascist, he also wrote the *Discourses,* which deals in part with how to establish a republic. But *The Prince* has always served as the classic book for fascist theories.) The following is a representative excerpt from *The Prince.* Notice that its concern throughout is "how to stay in power," not how to be just, or fair, or even good. Justice or compassion are but means of keeping power, and that is the key to modern fascism as well.

OF CRUELTY AND CLEMENCY, AND WHETHER IT IS
BETTER TO BE LOVED THAN FEARED

Coming down now to the other aforementioned qualities, I say that every prince ought to desire the reputation of being merciful, and not cruel; at the same time, he should be careful not to misuse that mercy. Cesare Borgia was reputed cruel, yet by his cruelty he reunited the Romagna to his states, and restored that province to order, peace, and loyalty; and if we carefully examine his course, we shall find it to have been really much more merciful than the course of the people of Florence, who, to escape the reputation of cruelty, allowed Pistoia to be destroyed. A prince, therefore, should not mind the ill repute of cruelty, when he can thereby keep his subjects united and loyal; for a few displays of severity will really be more merciful than to allow, by an excess of clemency, disorders to occur, which are apt to result in rapine and murder; for these injure a whole community, while the executions ordered by the prince fall only upon a few individuals. And, above all others, the new prince will find it almost impossible to avoid the reputation of cruelty because new states are generally exposed to many dangers. It was on this account that Virgil made Dido to excuse the severity of her government, because it was still new, saying,—

'My cruel fate,
And doubts attending an unsettled state,
Force me to guard my coasts from foreign foes.'[19]

A prince, however, should be slow to believe and to act; nor should he
be too easily alarmed by his own fears, and should proceed moderately and
with prudence and humanity, so that an excess of confidence may not make
him incautious, nor too much mistrust make him intolerant. This, then,
gives rise to the question "whether it be better to be beloved than feared,
or to be feared than beloved." It will naturally be answered that it would
be desirable to be both the one and the other; but as it is difficult to be both
at the same time, it is much more safe to be feared than to be loved, when
you have to choose between the two. For it may be said of men in general
that they are ungrateful and fickle, dissemblers, avoiders of danger, and
greedy of gain. So long as you shower benefits upon them, they are all
yours; they offer you their blood, their substance, their lives, and their children, provided the necessity for it is far off; but when it is near at hand,
then they revolt. And the prince who relies upon their words, without having
otherwise provided for his security, is ruined; for friendships that are won
by rewards, and not by greatness and nobility of soul, although deserved,
yet are not real, and cannot be depended upon in time of adversity.

Besides, men have less hesitation in offending one who makes himself
beloved than one who makes himself feared; for love holds by a bond of obligation which, as mankind is bad, is broken on every occasion whenever it
is for the interest of the obliged party to break it. But fear holds by the apprehension of punishment, which never leaves men. A prince, however,
should make himself feared in such a manner that, if he has not won the
affections of his people, he shall at least not incur their hatred; for the being
feared, and not hated, can go very well together, if the prince abstains from
taking the substance of his subjects, and leaves them their women. And if
you should be obliged to inflict capital punishment upon any one, then be
sure to do so only when there is manifest cause and proper justification for
it; and, above all things, abstain from taking people's property, for men will
sooner forget the death of their fathers than the loss of their patrimony.
Besides, there will never be any lack of reasons for taking people's property;
and a prince who once begins to live by rapine will ever find excuses for
seizing other people's property. On the other hand, reasons for taking life
are not so easily found, and are more readily exhausted. But when a prince is
at the head of his army, with a multitude of soldiers under his command,
then it is above all things necessary for him to disregard the reputation of
cruelty; for without such severity an army cannot be kept together, nor
disposed for any successful feat of arms.

Among the many admirable qualities of Hannibal, it is related of him
that, having an immense army composed of a very great variety of races of
men, which he led to war in foreign countries, no quarrels ever occurred
among them, nor were there ever any dissensions between them and their
chief, either in his good or in his adverse fortunes; which can only be accounted for by his extreme cruelty. This, together with his boundless cour-

---

[19] Translated from Latin by John Dryden.

age, made him ever venerated and terrible in the eyes of his soldiers; and without that extreme severity all his other virtues would not have sufficed to produce that result.

Inconsiderate writers have, on the one hand, admired his great deeds, and, on the other, condemned the principal cause of the same. And the proof that his other virtues would not have sufficed him may be seen from the case of Scipio, who was one of the most remarkable men, not only of his own time, but in all history. His armies revolted in Spain solely in consequence of his extreme clemency, which allowed his soldiers more license than comports with proper military discipline. This fact was censured in the Roman Senate by Fabius Maximus, who called Scipio the corrupter of the Roman soldiers. The tribe of the Locrians having been wantonly destroyed by one of the lieutenants of Scipio, he neither punished him for that nor for his insolence,—simply because of his own easy nature; so that, when somebody wished to excuse Scipio in the Senate, he said, "that there were many men who knew better how to avoid errors themselves than to punish them in others." This easy nature of Scipio's would in time have dimmed his fame and glory if he had persevered in it under the Empire; but living as he did under the government of the Senate, this dangerous quality of his was not only covered up, but actually redounded to his honor.

To come back now to the question whether it be better to be beloved than feared, I conclude that, as men love of their own free will, but are inspired with fear by the will of the prince, a wise prince should always rely upon himself, and not upon the will of others; but, above all, should he always strive to avoid being hated, as I have already said above.[20]

THE ALTERNATIVE
TO GOVERNMENT: ANARCHISM

We have all known and heard about bad governments. Sometimes it is a single corrupt politician that is bad, other times it is the political system itself. But those political (or perhaps "antipolitical") philosophers who call themselves "anarchists" would say that it is the very nature of government that is "bad," insofar as every government has and exercises unjustified power over its citizens. No one and no institution, including governments, have the right to interfere with our lives, according to the anarchist. Of course, we must agree not to kill each other (as the social contract insists), but we don't need a government in order to enforce such agreements. Proper upbringing and mutual respect alone will be sufficient. Sometimes anarchists are also tied to theories of revolution, insofar as they believe that it is economic inequality and desperation that force most people to commit crimes and destroy social harmony. But in a society where people had no unsatisfied needs, they argue, there would be no need for violence or robbery either. It is essential to anarchism to have an

[20] Niccolo Machiavelli, *The Prince,* trans. Christian E. Detmold (New York: Airmont, 1965).

optimistic Rousseauian view of human nature as "naturally good." It is impossible to accept a Hobbesian "mutual-murder" view and still have faith in people's ability to live together without governments. Anarchists often suggest breaking mass societies into smaller units, such as communes and local communities, in which mutual personal relationships make the need for impersonal government unnecessary. In such communities, there may be those who are in charge of certain tasks, but this is a matter of efficiency and administration, not a matter of power. There may be rules but not laws, for the very idea of enforcement of laws presupposes a government in power and is antithetical to the anarchist ideal.

"Anarchism" has often been used as a nasty word pointing to total chaos. Politicians in power often refer to the alternative to their rule as "anarchy and chaos," as if anarchy must always be sheer confusion. Although the word originally meant simply "without a leader," it perhaps has taken on the meaning of chaos because of those anarchists in history who have attacked their governments in a wild and destructive fashion. The word now conjures up images of "bomb-throwing anarchists" and widespread rape and murder. But this is not essential to anarchism as a political theory. (Sometimes the word "anarchism" is used to refer to the theory; "anarchy" is used to point to political confusion and chaos.) Many anarchists would argue that it is only because governments treat us like children that we can no longer conceive what it would be like without them. But if we are to take the notion of individual freedom and rights seriously, according to the anarchist, then we will have to conclude that the only good government is no government, for any government is by its very existence a threat to individual freedom and an infringement of individual rights.

The anarchist position is forcefully argued by the Russian revolutionary, Mikhail Bakunin. In the following selection, he attacks all "man-made laws" and governments and urges us to obey only "natural laws," the laws of "human nature":

Natural and Man-Made Laws. Man can never be altogether free in relation to natural and social laws.

What is freedom? What is slavery? Does man's freedom consist in revolting against all laws? We say *No*, in so far as laws are natural, economic, and social laws, not authoritatively imposed but inherent in things, in relations, in situations, the natural development of which is expressed by those laws. We say *Yes* if they are political and juridical laws, imposed by men upon men: whether violently by the right of force; whether by deceit and hypocrisy—in the name of religion or any doctrine whatever; or finally, by dint of the fiction, the democratic falsehood called *universal suffrage*.

Man Cannot Revolt Against Nor Escape from Nature. Against the laws of Nature no revolt is possible on the part of man, the simple reason being that he himself is a product of Nature and that he exists only by virtue of those laws. A rebellion on his part would be . . . a ridiculous attempt, it would be a revolt against himself, a veritable suicide. And when man has a determination to destroy himself, or even when he carries out such a design, he again acts in accordance with those same natural laws, from which nothing can exempt him: neither thought, nor will, nor despair, nor any other passion, nor life, nor death.

Man himself is nothing but Nature. His most sublime or most monstrous sentiments, the most perverted, the most egoistic, or the most heroic resolves or manifestations of his will, his most abstract, most theological, or most insane thoughts—all that is nothing else but Nature. Nature envelops, permeates, constitutes his whole existence. How can he ever escape this Nature?

The Sources of Escapism. It is really to be wondered at how man could ever conceive this idea of escaping from Nature. Separation from Nature being utterly impossible, how could man ever dream of such a thing? Whence this monstrous dream? Whence does it come if not from *theology,* the science of Non-Being, and later from *metaphysics,* which is the impossible reconciliation of Non-Existence with reality?

We must distinguish well between natural laws and authoritarian, arbitrary, political, religious, criminal, and civil laws which the privileged classes have established in the course of history, always in the interest of exploitation of the labor of the toiling masses—laws which, under the pretense of a fictitious morality were ever the source of the deepest immorality: consequently, involuntary and inescapable obedience to all laws which, independently of human will, constitute the very life of Nature and society; and at the same time independence as complete as possible for everyone in relation to all pretensions to command, coming from any human will whatever, individual as well as collective, and tending to assert themselves not by way of natural influence, but by imposing their law, their despotism.

. . . . .

In Nature as in human society, which in itself is nothing but Nature, everything that lives does so only under the supreme condition of intervening in the most positive manner in the life of others—intervening in as powerful a manner as the particular nature of a given individual permits it to do so. To do away with this reciprocal influence would spell death in the full sense of the word. And when we demand liberty for the masses, we do not pretend to have abolished any of the natural influences exerted upon the masses by any individual or group of individuals. What we want is the abolition of fictitious, privileged, legal, and official influences.

Liberty in Conformity with Natural Laws. Man's freedom consists solely in this: that he obeys natural laws because he has *himself* recognized them as such, and not because they have been imposed upon him by any extrinsic will whatever, divine or human, collective or individual.

As against natural laws there is only one kind of liberty possible for man—and that is to recognize and apply them on an ever-extending scale in conformity with the goal of emancipation, or humanization—individual or collective—which he pursues. These laws, once recognized, exercise an authority which has never been disputed by the great mass of mankind.

One must, for instance, be a madman or a theologian, or at least a meta-physician, a jurist, or a bourgeois economist to revolt against the law according to which twice two makes four. One must have faith to imagine that one will not burn in fire or that he will not drown in water unless he has recourse to some subterfuge, which, in its turn, is founded on some other natural law. But these revolts, or rather these attempts at or wild fancies of impossible revolts, constitute only very rare exceptions; for in general it may be said that the mass of mankind, in their daily lives, let themselves be governed, in an almost absolute fashion, by common sense, that is, by the sum of generally recognized natural laws.

．　．　．　．　．

Freedom Is Valid Only When Shared by Everyone. The materialist, realist, and collectivist definition of liberty is altogether opposed to that of the idealists. The materialist definition runs like this: Man becomes man and arrives at awareness as well as realization of his humanity only in society and only through the collective action of the whole society. He frees himself from the yoke of external Nature only by collective and social labor, which alone is capable of transforming the surface of the earth into an abode favorable to the development of humanity. And without this material emancipation there can be no intellectual or moral emancipation for anyone.

Man cannot free himself from the yoke of his own nature, that is, he can subordinate his instincts and his bodily movements to the direction of his ever-developing mind only with the aid of education and upbringing. Both, however, are pre-eminently and exclusively social phenomena. For outside of society man would always remain a wild beast or a saint, which is about the same. Finally, an isolated man cannot have awareness of his liberty. To be free signifies that man shall be recognized and treated as such by another man, by all men who surround him. Liberty then is not a fact springing from isolation but from reciprocal action, a fact not of exclusion, but, on the contrary, of social interaction—for the freedom of every individual is simply the reflection of his humanity or his human right in the consciousness of all free men, his brothers, his equals.

I can call myself and feel myself a free man only in the presence of and in relation to other men. In the presence of an animal of inferior species, I am neither free nor am I a man, for that animal is incapable of conceiving, and consequently incapable of recognizing my humanity. I myself am human and free only inasmuch as I recognize the freedom and humanity of all people surrounding me. It is only when I respect their human character that I respect my own humanity.

A cannibal who eats his captives, treating them as savage animals, is not a man but a beast. The master of slaves is not a man but a master. In ignoring the humanity of his slaves, he ignores his own humanity. Every ancient society furnishes good proofs thereof: the Greeks, the Romans, did not feel free as men, they did not consider themselves as such from the point of view of human right. They believed themselves privileged as Greeks, as Romans, only in their own fatherland, and only so long as the latter remained unconquered and on the contrary conquering other countries because of the special protection of their national gods. And they did not wonder and did not hold it their right or duty to revolt when, having been vanquished, they themselves fell into slavery.

. . . . .

Freedom of Individual Increased and Not Limited by Freedom of All. I am free only when all human beings surrounding me—men and women alike—are equally free. The freedom of others, far from limiting or negating my liberty, is on the contrary its necessary condition and confirmation. I become free in the true sense only by virtue of the liberty of others, so much so that the greater the number of free people surrounding me and the deeper and greater and more extensive their liberty, the deeper and larger becomes my liberty.

On the contrary, it is the slavery of men that sets up a barrier to my liberty, or (which practically amounts to the same) it is their bestiality which constitutes a negation of my humanity because, I repeat again, I can call myself a truly free person only when my freedom or, (which is the same) my human dignity, my human right, the essence of which is to obey no one and to follow only the guidance of my own ideas—when this freedom, reflected by the equally free consciousness of all men, comes back to me confirmed by everybody's assent. My personal freedom, thus confirmed by the freedom of everyone else, extends to infinity.

The Constituent Elements of Freedom. We can see then that freedom, as understood by materialists, is something very positive, very complex, and above all eminently social, since it can be realized only by society and only under conditions of strict equality and solidarity of each person with all his fellows. One can distinguish in it three phases of development, three elements, the first of which is highly positive and social. It is the full development and the full enjoyment by everyone of all the faculties and human powers through the means of education, scientific upbringing, and material prosperity, and all that can be given to everyone only by collective labor, and by the material and mental, muscular, and nervous labor of society as a whole.

Rebellion the Second Element of Liberty. The second element or phase of liberty is negative in character. It is the element of *revolt* on the part of the human individual against all divine and human authority, collective and individual. It is first of all a revolt against the tyranny of the supreme phantom of theology, against God. . . .

. . . Following that and coming as a consequence of the revolt against God, there is the revolt against the tyranny of man, against authority, individual as well as collective, represented and legalized by the State.

The Implication of the Theory of the Pre-Social Existence of Individual Freedom. But if the metaphysicians affirm that men, especially those who believe in the immortality of the soul, stand outside of the society of free beings, we inevitably arrive at the conclusion that men can unite in a society only at the cost of their own liberty, their natural independence, and by sacrificing first their personal and their local interests. Such self-renunciation and self-sacrifice are thus all the more imperative the more numerous society is in point of membership and the greater the complexity of its organization. In this sense the State is the expression of all the individual sacrifices. Given this abstract and at the same time violent origin, the State has to restrict liberty to an ever greater extent, doing it in the name of a falsehood called "the good of the people," which in reality represents exclusively the interests of the dominant class. Thus the State appears as an inevitable negation and annihilation of all liberty, of all individual and collective interests.

Freedom the Ultimate Aim of Human Development. But we who believe neither in God nor in the immortality of the soul, nor in the freedom of will, we maintain that liberty should be understood in its larger connotation as the goal of the historic progress of humanity. By a strange, although logical contrast, our adversaries, the idealists of theology and metaphysics, take the principle of liberty as the foundation and the starting point of their theories, to deduce from it the indispensability of slavery for all men. We, materialists in theory, aim in practice to create and consolidate a rational and noble idealism. Our enemies, the divine and transcendental idealists, sink into a practical bloody, and vile materialism, impelled by the same logic according to which every development is the negation of the basic principle.

We are convinced that all the wealth and all the intellectual, moral, and material development of man, as well as the degree of independence he already has attained—that all this is the product of life in society. Outside of society, man would not only fail to be free; he would not even grow to the stature of a true man, that is, a being aware of himself and who feels and has the power of speech. It was only the intercourse of minds and collective labor that forced man out of the stage of being a savage and a brute, which consituted his original nature, or the starting point of his ultimate development.

Freedom and Socialism Are Mutually Complementary. *The serious realization of liberty, justice, and peace will be impossible so long as the vast majority of the population remains dispossessed in point of elementary needs, so long as it is deprived of education and is condemned to political and social insignificance and slavery—in fact if not by law—by the poverty as well as the necessity of working without rest or leisure, producing all the wealth, upon which the world now prides itself, and receiving in return only such a small part thereof that it hardly suffices to assure [the worker's] bread for the next day; . . . we are convinced that freedom without Socialism is privilege and injustice, and that Socialism without freedom is slavery and brutality.*

It is characteristic of privilege and of every privileged position to kill the minds and hearts of men. The privileged man, whether politically or economically, is a mentally and morally depraved man. That is a social law which admits of no exception and which holds good in relation to whole nations as well as to classes, groups, and individuals. It is the law of equality, the supreme condition of freedom and humanity.

Socialism and Equality. Much as one may resort to all kinds of subterfuges, much as one may try to obscure the issue, and to falsify social science for the benefit of bourgeois exploitation, all sensible people who have no interest in deceiving themselves, now understand that so long as a certain number of people possessing economic privileges have the means to lead a life which is beyond the reach of the workers; that so long as a more or less considerable number inherit, in various proportions, capital and land which is not the product of their own labor, while on the other hand the vast majority of workers do not inherit anything at all; so long as land rent and interest on capital enable those privileged people to live without working—so long as such a state of things exists, equality is inconceivable.

Even assuming that everyone in society works—whether by compulsion or by free choice—but that one class in society, thanks to its economic situation and enjoying as a result thereof special political and social privileges, can devote itself exclusively to mental work, while the vast majority of people struggle hard for a bare living; in a word, so long as individuals on coming into life do not find in society the same means of livelihood, the same education, upbringing, work, and enjoyment—political, economic, and social equality will be impossible.

It was in the name of equality that the bourgeoisie overthrew and massacred the nobility. And it is in the name of equality that we now demand either the violent death or the voluntary suicide of the bourgeoisie, only with this difference—that being less bloodthirsty than the bourgeoisie of the revolutionary period, we do not want the death of men but the abolition of positions and things. If the bourgeoisie resigns itself to the inevitable changes, not a hair on its head will be touched. But so much the worse for it, if, forgetting prudence and sacrificing its individual interests to the collective interests of its class, a class doomed to extinction, it places itself athwart the course of the historic justice of the people, in order to save a position which will soon become utterly untenable.

The Nature of True Freedom. I am a fanatical lover of freedom, viewing it as the only milieu in the midst of which the intelligence, dignity, and happiness of men can grow; but not of that formal liberty, vouchsafed, measured, and regulated by the State, which is an eternal falsehood and which in reality represents only the privilege of the select few based upon the slavery of the rest; and not of that individualist, egoistic, jejune, and fictitious liberty proclaimed by Jean Jacques Rousseau as well as by all the other schools of bourgeois liberalism, which regard the so-called public right represented by the State as being the limit of the right of everyone, which necessarily and always results in the whittling down of the right of everyone to the zero point.

No, I have in mind the only liberty worthy of that name, liberty consisting in the full development of all the material, intellectual, and moral powers latent in every man; a liberty which does not recognize any other restrictions but those which are traced by the laws of our own nature, which, properly speaking, is tantamount to saying that there are no restrictions at all, since these laws are not imposed upon us by some outside legislator standing above us or alongside us. Those laws are imminent, inherent in us; they constitute the very basis of our being, material as well as intellectual and moral; and instead of finding in them a limit to our liberty we should regard them as its real conditions and as its effective reason.

I have in mind this liberty of everyone which, far from finding itself checked by the freedom of others, is, on the contrary, confirmed by it and extended to infinity. And I have in mind the freedom of every individual unlimited by the freedom of all, freedom in solidarity, freedom in equality, freedom triumphing over brute force and the principle of authority (which was ever the ideal expression of this force); a freedom which, having overthrown all the heavenly and earthly idols, will have founded and organized a new world, the world of human solidarity, upon the ruins of all the churches and states.

I am a convinced partisan *of economic and social equality* because I know that outside of this equality, freedom, justice, human dignity, morality, and the well-being of individuals as well as the flourishing of nations, are a lie.

We already have said that by freedom we understand on one hand the development, as complete as possible, of all the natural faculties of every individual, and on the other hand his independence not in relation to natural and social laws, but in relation to all laws imposed by other human wills, whether collective or isolated.

We understand by freedom, from the positive point of view, the development, as complete as possible, of all faculties which man has within himself, and, from the negative point of view, the independence of the will of everyone from the will of others.

We are convinced—and modern history fully confirms our conviction—that so long as humanity is divided into an exploiting minority and an exploited majority, freedom is impossible, becoming instead a falsehood. If you want freedom for all, you must strive together with us to attain universal equality.

How Can Freedom and Equality Be Assured? Do you want to make it impossible for anyone to oppress his fellow-man? Then make sure that no one shall possess power. Do you want men to respect the liberty, rights, and personality of their fellows? Make sure that they shall be compelled to respect them, *forced not by the will nor by the oppressive action of other men, and not by the repression of the State and its laws, necessarily represented and applied by men,* which in turn makes slaves of them, but by the very organization of social environment—an organization so constituted that by affording everyone the fullest enjoyment of his liberty, it does not permit anyone to rise above others nor dominate them in any way but through the natural influence of the intellectual and moral qualities which he possesses, *without this influence ever being imposed as a right and without leaning upon any political institution whatever.*[21]

SUMMARY AND CONCLUSION

In some areas of philosophy, the question arises, "what does this have to do with everyday life?" In political philosophy, as in moral philosophy, the con-

[21] Mikhail Bakunin, *The Political Philosophy of Bakunin,* ed. G. P. Maximoff (New York: Free Press, 1953).

nection between philosophy and "everyday life" is obvious. It is no coincidence that the major revolutions of the eighteenth and nineteenth centuries came soon after a flurry of philosophical radicalism. And we know that much of the world is divided and ruled according to rival political philosophies at the present time.

What is always at issue is the concept of justice. The idea that people are equal and should be treated equally, the idea that people have natural or human rights which no one and no government can take away from them, and the idea that people should equally share the material goods of society have all been the subject of constant debate—and sometimes wars and revolutions—for most of modern times. Then too, the nature of the state itself has been part of that debate as well as the stage on which the debate has been carried out. How much should the state serve the people and how much the people serve the state? What constitutes a good state? And when, if ever, do people have the right to overthrow the state, or a particular government, or a particular law? There is no way we can even begin to give adequate answers to these complex questions in the context of a general introduction to philosophy; but neither is there any way in which we can avoid asking them in the world as it is today.

GLOSSARY

alienation: in Marx, the unnatural separation of a person from the products he or she makes, from other people, or from oneself.

anarchism: the view that no government has the legitimate authority to coerce people and that the public interest and individual rights can only be served without a state of any kind.

authority: that which controls, usually, that which has the right to control. (For example, the government has the authority to tax your income.)

civil rights: those rights which are determined by a particular state and its laws; constitutional rights, for example, are civil rights in this sense, guaranteed by the law of the land.

democracy: that form of government in which policies or at least the makers of policy are chosen by popular mandate.

distributive justice: the ideal of everyone receiving his or her fair share. For example, concerns over ownership of land, just wages, and fair prices are all matters of distributive justice.

egalitarianism: the view that all people are equal in rights and respect.

equality: in political philosophy, the nondiscriminatory treatment of every person, regardless of sex, race, religion, physical or mental abilities, wealth, social status, etc.

fascism: the view that the best government is the strongest, and that the government has the right—and perhaps the duty—to control the lives of every citizen for the sake of the most efficient society.

freedom: see liberty

general will: in Rousseau, the collective voice of the people, which has ultimate sovereignty, even above the king.

government: the instrument of authority; that body which rules, passes and enforces laws, etc.

human rights: those rights which are considered to be universal, "inalienable," and common to every person, regardless of where or when he or she lives. For example, freedom from torture and degradation would be a human right.

inalienable rights: those rights which no one and no government can take away, for example, the right of a person to protect his or her own life. In other words, *human rights.*

justice: in the general sense, the virtues of an ideal society. In the more particular sense, the balance of public interest and individual rights, the fair sharing of the available goods of society, the proper punishment of criminals, and the fair restitution of victims of crime and misfortune within society.

legitimacy: the right to have authority; sanctioned power (for example, through the grace of god, or by means of legal succession, or by appeal to justice, or to the general consent of the people governed).

liberty: (political freedom) the ability to act without restraint or threat of punishment. For example, the ability to travel between states without a passport, the ability to speak one's opinions without prosecution, the ability to work for or choose one's own profession or career. This ability, however, is not mere physical or mental ability; one might have the liberty to travel or to try to become a doctor without having the means to do so. It is also important to distinguish this political sense of liberty or freedom from the metaphysical or causal sense discussed in Chapter 10: whether our acts are really free in that sense must be distinguished from the question whether we are constrained or free to act in this political sense. The first refers to the causes of human behavior; the second refers only to the existence of legislation and political forces constraining our behavior.

retributive justice: "getting even," "an eye for an eye. . . ."

rights: demands which a member of society is entitled to make upon his society. Everyone, for example, has a right to police protection. Some people, by virtue of their position, have special rights; for example, congressmen have the right to send mail to their constituents without paying postage.

social contract: an agreement, tacit or explicit that all members of society shall abide by the laws of the state in order to maximize the public interest and insure cooperation among themselves. It is important that such a contract need never have actually been signed in history; what is important is that every member of a society, by choosing to remain in that society, implicitly makes such an agreement.

society: a group of people with common historical and cultural ties, usually but not always members of the same state and ruled by the same government.

sovereign: independent. A sovereign state is one which is subject to the laws of no other state. A sovereign is a person (for example, a king) who is not subject or answerable to the commands of anyone else. A people are sovereign when their wishes are ultimate in the same way, and not subject to commands by anyone else or any government. (To say that a people is sovereign is not to say that the will of any individual or group is sovereign within it.)

state: the center of authority in a society, for example, the largest political unit in a society. Usually, a state is a nation, for example, America, West Germany, etc. Usually, but not always, coextensive with a society, and usually, but not always, distinguished by a single form of government and a single government (for example, the American federal government).

BRIEF BIOGRAPHIES

Anaximander (611–547? B.C.): Pre-Socratic philosopher who taught that reality is ultimately composed of an indeterminate something that we can never know directly through experience.

Anaximenes (6th century B.C.): Pre-Socratic philosopher who taught that the basic element of reality was air and that all things in the universe are different forms of air.

Anselm, Saint (1033–1109): Archbishop of Canterbury and author of the ontological argument for God's existence. He was one of the main defenders of the intellect and "understanding" against the then current anti-intellectualism of the church. He is best known for his *Monologion* and *Proslogion,* in which the ontological argument is developed.

Aquinas, Saint Thomas (1225–74): Architect of the most comprehensive theological structure of the Roman Catholic Church, the *Summa Theologica,* which has long been recognized as the "official" statement of orthodox Christian beliefs by many theologians. Aquinas borrowed many of his arguments from Aristotle, as can be seen in his "five ways" of demonstrating the existence of God.

Aristippus (435?–356? B.C.): One of the Cynics and a student of Socrates, who taught that the good life consists solely of immediate pleasures.

Aristotle (384–322 B.C.): One of the greatest Western philosophers. Aristotle was born in northern Greece (Stagira); his father was the physician to Philip, king of Macedonia, and he himself was to become the tutor to Philip's son, Alexander the Great. For eighteen years, Aristotle was a student in Plato's academy in Athens. After Plato's death, he turned to the study of biology, and many of his most lasting contributions that ruled Western science until the Renaissance were in this subject. He was with Alexander until 335 B.C., when he returned to Athens to set up his own school, the Lyceum. After Alexander's death, the anti-Macedonian sentiment in Athens forced Aristotle to flee (commenting that the Athenians would not sin twice against philosophy). In addition to his biological studies, Aristotle virtually created the sciences of logic and linguistics, developed extravagant theories in physics and astronomy, and made significant contributions to metaphysics, ethics, politics, and aesthetics. His *Metaphysics* is still a basic text on the subject, and his *Nichomachean Ethics* codified ancient Greek morality. This latter work stresses individual virtue and excellence for a small elite of Greek citizens. The best life of all, according to Aristotle, is the life of contemplation, that is, the life of a philosopher, for it is the most self-contained and the "closest to the gods." But such contemplation must be in addition to the pleasures of life, honor, wealth, and virtuous action.

Augustine, Saint (354–430): The main figure in the development of medieval Christian thought from its roots in classical Greece and Rome. Augustine was born in North Africa and lived during the "decline" of the Roman Empire. After exploring various pagan beliefs, he was converted to Christianity and became Bishop of Hippo in North Africa. He is best known for his theological treatise, *The City of God,* and for his very personal *Confessions.*

Austin, John Langshaw (1911–60): Oxford "ordinary language" philosopher who had enormous influence on the development of "therapeutic" philosophy through attention to the details and nuances of everyday speech.

Ayer, Alfred J. (1910–): Oxford philosopher who became the major British defender of the powerful philosophical movement called logical positivism (logical empiricism). His *Language, Truth and Logic* (1936) was England's (and soon

America's) first introduction to the very important work that had been developed in Austria by Rudolf Carnap, Hans Reichenbach, Moritz Schlick, C. G. Hempel, and Otto Neurath (the "Vienna Circle"). The main thesis of *Language, Truth and Logic,* and of logical positivism in general, is, in an updated version of Hume, that all knowledge can only be divided into matters of empirical fact and matters of language and logic, and that all other claims are "meaningless," including the concepts of metaphysics, religion, ethics, and aesthetics.

Bakunin, Mikhail (1814–76): Russian anarchist, born into a noble family but who preferred the life of a Bohemian intellectual rather than the military career prepared for him. He traveled in western Europe and met Marxist and other socialist revolutionaries, returned to Russia, spent fifteen years in prison and Siberia for his political activities, and finally sought refuge in the United States. He summarized his own philosophy by the phrase, "The urge to destruction is also a creative urge."

Bentham, Jeremy (1748–1832): A leader in the legal reform movement in England and the founding father of that ethical position called Utilitarianism. His *principle of utility,* which says that one should act to produce the greatest good for the greatest number of people, was the central theme of Utilitarianism and slowly worked its way into the confusion of rules and statutes that constituted the English legal system of his day. His best known work is his *Introduction to the Principles of Morals and Legislation* (1789).

Berkeley, Bishop George (1685–1753): Wrote virtually all the works that made him famous before he turned twenty-eight. He was born, raised, and educated in Ireland, and as a student he immersed himself in the writings of the important philosophers of the time, particularly Locke, Newton, and some of the French metaphysicians. In later life, Berkeley became an educational missionary, visiting America and Bermuda, and then a bishop, eventually moving to Oxford. Unlike Locke and Hume, whose interests spread across the whole of philosophy, science, and human affairs, Berkeley restricted himself to a single problem—perception—and his entire philosophy is aptly summarized in his famous phrase, "to be is to be perceived" (*esse est percipi*). His arguments for this position are most thoroughly outlined in his *Treatise Concerning the Principles of Human Knowledge* (1710).

Blandshard, Brand (1892–): Contemporary idealist and main American defender of the coherence theory of truth, still working at Yale University.

Bradley, Francis Herbert (1846–1924): The best known and perhaps the most brilliant of the "British idealists" working at the turn of this century. He is best known for his work, *Appearance and Reality* (1893), in which he argues a very strong version of the coherence theory of truth.

Butler, Bishop Joseph (1692–1752): Powerful English clergyman who formulated what are still recognized as the standard arguments against psychological egoism in his *Fifteen Sermons* (1726).

Cynics (4th century B.C.): Group of post-Socratic philosophers who taught that the good life was a life of complete autonomy. Therefore they minimized the social values of success, wealth, and honor and focused their attention on what makes a person wholly self-sufficient. For Diogenes, this consisted of the simplest life possible, based upon simple pleasures and simple virtues. For Aristippus, this consisted of a life of immediate pleasure.

Davidson, Donald (1917–): Contemporary American philosopher who has become one of the leading philosophers of language in the world. One of his continuous efforts is to generalize Alfred Tarski's semantic theory of truth for natural languages.

Democritus (5th century B.C.): Pre-Socratic philosopher who taught that reality is divisible into small "atoms," which combine to make up all things but which themselves are eternal and indivisible.

Descartes, René (1596–1650): French philosopher who is usually considered the "father of modern philosophy." He was raised in the French aristocracy and educated at the excellent Jesuit College of La Flèche. He became skilled in the classics, law, and medicine; however, he decided that they fell far short of proper knowledge, and so he turned to modern science and mathematics. His first book was a defense of Copernicus, which he prudently did not publish. He discovered, while still a young man, the connections between algebra and geometry (which we now call "analytic geometry") and used this discovery as a model for the rest of his career. Basing the principles of philosophy and theology on a similar mathematical basis, he was able to develop a method in philosophy that could be carried through according to individual reason and no longer depended upon appeal to authorities whose insights and methods were questionable. In *Discourse on Method* (1637), he set out these basic principles, which he had already used in *Meditations on First Philosophy* (not published until 1641), to reexamine the foundations of philosophy. He sought a basic premise from which, as in a geometrical proof, he could deduce all those principles that could be known with certainty.

Diogenes (412?–323? B.C.): Cynic philosopher who lived an extremely simple life. Offered anything he wanted by Alexander the Great, he replied, "Get out of my light."

Epicurus (342?–270 B.C.): Greek philosopher who argued that the good life was pleasure but not just the immediate pleasure talked about by Aristippus. Some pleasures last longer than others; some have a lower price than others. Accordingly, he taught self-control and avoidance of violent pleasures, which often caused more pain than ultimate pleasure. Ultimately, what was most pleasurable, according to Epicurus, was a life of peace and quiet. Today, we use the word "Epicurean" to describe someone who often indulges in pleasures, particularly sophisticated pleasures (gourmet food, for example).

Fichte, Johann Gottlieb (1762–1814): German philosopher, student of Immanuel Kant, who turned Kant's "transcendental" philosophy into a practically oriented and relativistic "ethical idealism." He taught that "the philosophy a man chooses depends upon the kind of man he is." One of the first German nationalists.

Frege, Gottlob (1848–1925): Brilliant logician whose work on the foundations of arithmetic inspired Bertrand Russell and Alfred North Whitehead and turned the current of logical thinking from the Mill-like empiricism that was then reigning (in Germany as well as England) to a hardheaded mathematical discipline. He is often said to have been the pioneer and innovator of modern mathematical logic. Most important, perhaps, is his *Foundations of Arithmetic* (1884).

Goodman, Nelson (1906–   ): Contemporary American pragmatist who, together with W. V. O. Quine, has made pragmatism once again a dominant force in philosophy.

Hegel, Georg Wilhelm Friedrich (1770–1831): German philosopher who, during the age of Napoleon, wrote his *Phenomenology of Spirit* (1807), which was the single most powerful influence in European philosophy—after Kant's works—for the next hundred years. He argued that there were many different views of the world, that none of them should be thought to be wholly correct or incorrect in exclusion of the others, but that these various views could still be compared and evaluated according to a "dialectic," in which some views are shown to be more developed, more inclusive, and more adequate than others.

Heidegger, Martin (1889–1976): German phenomenologist and student of Edmund Husserl, whose rebellion against his teacher began the "existential" movement in phenomenology. His best known work is *Being and Time* (1927). Although focusing on metaphysics and phenomenology, this work is also one of the first existentialist studies of "human nature."

Hempel, Carl Gustav (1905–   ): Contemporary American philosopher of science and mathematics, member of the "Vienna Circle," and one of the continuing most powerful voices of the empiricist tradition. A good collection of his essays is *Aspects of Scientific Explanation* (1965).

Heraclitus (5th century B.C.): Pre-Socratic philosopher who taught that the basic element of reality was fire and that all things are in constant flux but yet are unified by an underlying logic or *logos*.

Hobbes, Thomas (1588–1679): The author of *Leviathan* (1651) and one of England's first great modern philosophers. He is generally credited with the formulation of the theory of the "social contract" for the establishment of governments and society, and he was one of the first philosophers to base his theory of government on a conception of man prior to his "civilization," in what he called "the state of nature." This was, according to Hobbes, "selfish, nasty, brutish and short." Therefore, people were motivated to become part of society for their mutual protection. Hobbes also defended a materialist conception of the universe. Even the human mind, he argued, was nothing more than "matter in motion."

d'Holbach, Baron Paul Henri (1723–89): French philosopher and one of the leaders of the Enlightenment. An ardent materialist and atheist, he represented the most radical fringe of the brilliant free-thinkers of prerevolutionary France.

Hospers, John (1918–   ): Professor of philosophy at the University of Southern California, articulate follower of Ayn Rand, and one-time Libertarian candidate for President of the United States.

Hume, David (1711–76): Often admired as the outstanding genius of British philosophy. Born in Scotland (Edinburgh), where he spent much of his life, he took trips to London and Paris. After a vacation in France, he wrote the *Treatise of Human Nature* (1739). He achieved notoriety as well as literary fame in his lifetime, being involved in scandals, proscribed by the Church, and refused professorships at the leading universities for his "heresies." Yet he was, by all accounts, an utterly delightful man who never lost his sense of humor. He was "the life of the party" in London, Edinburgh, and Paris, and he has long set the standard of the ideal thinker for British philosophers. Hume's *Inquiry Concerning the Principles of Morals* (1751) created as much of a stir in the intellectual world as his *Inquiry Concerning Human Understanding* (1748). Like the latter book, the book on morality was a rewriting of his youthful *Treatise*, which never received the attention it deserved. Hume's thesis in moral philosophy was as skeptical and shocking as his thesis in epistemology: there is no knowledge of right and wrong and no rational defense of moral principles. These are based upon sentiment or feeling and, as such, cannot be defended by argument.

Husserl, Edmund (1859–1938): German-Czech philosopher and mathematician who was the founder of phenomenology, a modern form of rationalist intuitionism. With Gottlob Frege, he fought against the empiricist view of necessary truth defended by John Stuart Mill and developed an alternative view in which matters of necessity were not matters of ordinary experience but rather of a special kind of intuition. His best known works in English are *Ideas* (Vol. 1) (1913) and *Cartesian Meditations* (1913).

James, William (1842–1910): Perhaps the greatest American philosopher (and psychologist) until this day. He developed the particularly American philosophy of pragmatism from the brilliant but obscure formulations of his colleague at Harvard, Charles Sanders Pierce, into a popular and still very powerful intellectual force. James was born in New York City and graduated from Harvard with a medical degree, but he decided to teach (at Harvard) rather than to practice medicine. His best known work in philosophy, besides his work called *Pragmatism: A New Name for Some Old Ways of Thinking* (1907), is *The Varieties of Religious Experience* (1902). He also established himself as one of the fathers of modern psychology with his *Principles of Psychology* (1890).

Kant, Immanuel (1724–1804): German philosopher, probably the greatest philosopher since Plato and Aristotle, who lived his entire life in a small town in East

Prussia (Königsburg). He was a professor at the university there for over thirty years; he never married, and his neighbors said that his habits were so regular that they could set their watches by him. (A later German poet said, "It is hard to write about Kant's life, for he had no life.") Yet, from a safe distance, he was one of the most persistent defenders of the French Revolution and, in philosophy, created no less a revolution himself. His philosophical system, embodied in three huge volumes called *Critique of Pure Reason* (1781), *Critique of Practical Reason* (1788), and *Critique of Judgment* (1790), changed the thinking of philosophers as much as the revolution changed France. His central thesis was the defense of what he called "synthetic *a priori*" judgments (and their moral and religious equivalents) by showing their necessity for all human experience. In this way, he escaped from Hume's skepticism and avoided the dead-end intuitionism of his rationalist predecessors.

Kierkegaard, Søren (1813–1855): Danish philosopher and theologian who is generally recognized as the father of existentialism and the founder of many varieties of contemporary religious irrationalism. Kierkegaard dedicated himself to religious writing after a short and not altogether successful attempt at the wild life and a brief engagement, which he broke off in order to devote himself to his work. The basic tenet of Kierkegaard's philosophy was the need for each individual to choose his own way of life. Christianity, as one of the possible choices, could not be considered anything other than just such a choice, a passionate choice, which had nothing to do with doctrines, churches, social groups, and ceremonies.

Leibniz, Gottfried Wilhelm von (1646–1716): Leibniz has been called "the last of the universal geniuses." He was one of the inventors of the calculus, the father of modern formal linguistics, the inventor of a primitive computer, a military strategist (who may have influenced Napoleon), a physicist who in his own time was thought to be the rival of Newton, and, most of all, a great philosopher. He grew up in Leipzig, but traveled considerably (to Paris and Amsterdam and all over Germany). He spoke personally with most of the great philosophers of his time and debated with them constantly. His metaphysics is a curious combination of traditional theology and a radical alternative to the physical theories of Newton, to whose philosophy he had once been attracted, but which he had given up as "absurd." His short *Monadology* (1714) is a summary of his mature metaphysical theories.

Locke, John (1632–1704): Spent his early life in the English countryside, including many years at Oxford, where he taught philosophy and the classics until he earned a medical degree and turned to medicine. Much of Locke's mature life, however, was spent in politics, and he joined a more or less revolutionary group that was fighting for the overthrow of the government. He was forced to flee England in 1683, and he lived in Holland until the Glorious Revolution of 1688. For his part in the struggle, he received a government position, although he spent most of his time writing his two *Treatises on Government* (1689) to justify the revolution and its political principles and defending his *Essay Concerning Human Understanding* (1690), which he had written while in exile. He is generally credited not only as the founder of British empiricism but as the father of modern political liberalism as well.

logical positivism (roughly, from 1929 until the Nazis proscribed it in 1938): A powerful school of philosophy that originated in Vienna with a group of scientists and philosophers of anti-Nazi, liberal, antimetaphysical, and scientific persuasion— the "Vienna Circle." Against the horrendous mythologies and superstitions propagandized by the Nazis, using the old metaphysics as a tool, these philosophers used the clarity of science to dispel nonsense and to defend common sense. Accordingly, the group was broken by the Nazis, and most of its members, except for Moritz Schlick, who was shot by an insane student, left for America, England, and Holland. The main thrust of logical positivism is its total rejection of metaphysics in favor of a strong emphasis on science and verifiability through experience. The method of the logical positivists, accordingly, is strongly empiricist (they actually called themselves "logical empiricists") and has much in common with the method of Hume, according to which all knowledge is to be defended either as a matter of empirical fact to be verified (that is, confirmed) through experience or as a matter of logic and language to be demonstrated through analysis. Arithmetic and geometry, for the logical positivists, consist of analytic truths.

Marx, Karl (1818–83): German philosopher and social theorist who formulated the philosophical basis for one of the most powerful political ideologies of this century. He received a doctorate in philosophy but could not teach in Germany because of his radical views. He spent most of his life abroad, in Paris, Brussels, and London, developing his theories and writing for various journals and newspapers (including the *New York Herald Tribune*). His attacks on established beliefs and advocacy of revolution were constant throughout his life and forced him into exile. The quotation in the text is taken from Marx's critique of G. W. F. Hegel, whom he had studied and followed as a young student, and whose concept of "dialectic" he used in developing a powerful social-political philosophy of class conflict and economic determination.

Merleau-Ponty, Maurice (1908–61): French "existentialist," the most serious of the existential phenomenologists who followed Husserl in France. His most important work is generally considered the *Phenomenology of Perception* (1945). He is also well known for his political writings and his art criticism. In his early *Structure of Behavior* (1942), he argued that the human body cannot be considered merely another "fragment of matter," in other words, merely a body, but must be viewed as the center of our experience.

Mill, John Stuart (1806–73): Son of James Mill, also a philosopher, and one of the documented supergeniuses of modern history. His intellectual feats by the age of ten would have been to the credit of most scholars at the age of sixty. He pushed himself so hard, however, that he suffered a nervous breakdown in 1826, at the age of twenty, and turned his attention from the "hard" sciences to poetry and political reform. He is best known for his moral and political writings, particularly *On Liberty* (1859) and *Utilitarianism* (1861). His logic and epistemology are the best to be found in the British empiricist tradition of the nineteenth century. His views on mathematics, for example, became one of those positions that every writer on the subject had either to accept or to fight forcefully.

Nietzsche, Friedrich (1844–1900): German philosopher who declared himself the archenemy of traditional morality and Christianity and spent much of his life writing polemics against them. His most sustained and vicious attack (partly included in the text) is in one of his last books, *Antichrist* (1888). Although generally known as an immoralist (a name he chose for himself), Nietzsche's moral philosophy is actually an attack on one conception of morality in order to replace it with another. The morality he attacked was the morality of traditional Christianity as defined by Kant. The morality he sought to defend was the ancient morality of personal excellence, as defined by Aristotle. He referred to the first as "slave morality," suggesting that it was suitable only for the weak and servile, and to the latter as "master morality," suggesting that it was the morality of the strong and independent few.

Parmenides (5th century B.C.): Pre-Socratic philosopher who taught that reality was eternal and unchanging and that, therefore, we could not know it as such.

Pascal, Blaise (1623–62): French scientist and philosopher with mildly mystical tendencies. He stressed confidence in the "heart" rather than in reason, and many of his best known writings are concerned with the problems of religious faith. However, he was also one of the inventors of the computer and a famous mathematician. His best known work is *Pensées* ("Thoughts") (1669).

Plato (427–347 B.C.): Plato was born into a family of wealth and political power. But in Athens, he fell under the influence of Socrates and turned his talents to philosophy. He combined his heritage with his interests in his famous conception of the "philosopher-king," the ideal wise ruler, who certainly did not exist in Athens. He was disillusioned by Socrates' death and devoted his life to continuing his work. Plato set up the Academy for this purpose and spent the rest of his life teaching there. He first set down his reminiscences of Socrates' life and death, and, using the dialogue form, with Socrates as his mouthpiece, he extended Socrates' thought into entirely new areas, notably, metaphysics and the theory of knowledge. Plato incorporated a theory of morality into his metaphysics and politics, particularly in *The Republic*. Like all Greeks, he saw ethics as a part of politics and the good life for the individual in terms of the strength and harmony of the society. In *The Republic*, accordingly, Socrates argues against the various views of selfishness and hedonism that would interfere with such a conception. Virtue, he argues, is the harmony of the individual soul as well as the harmony of the individual within the society. It is still difficult, since we have nothing from Socrates himself, to know how much is original Plato and how much is transcribed Socrates.

Pythagoras (6th–5th century B.C.): The religious mystic who believed that numbers were the essence of all things. One of the Pre-Socratics.

Quine, Willard Van Orman (1908–): Contemporary American pragmatist whose early attacks on logical positivism and its basic tenets have been responsible for several of the dominant concerns of recent American philosophy. His attack on Immanuel Kant's distinction between "analytic" and "synthetic" sentences, for example, along with the more traditional distinctions between necessity and contingency, have thrown the entire philosophical enterprise into considerable turmoil. According to Quine, there are no indubitably "necessary" statements or beliefs, just those that happen, at a particular point in our knowledge and interests, to hold a relatively protected place in the overall system of our beliefs for ostensibly practical reasons. He is the author of *Word and Object* (1960) and many other works in logic and the philosophy of language.

Rawls, John (1921–): Author of *A Theory of Justice* (1971) and professor of philosophy at Harvard University.

Rousseau, Jean Jacques (1712–78): Stormy Enlightenment philosopher who fought with most of his peers (including David Hume) and developed a dramatic conception of "natural morality," which he opposed to what he saw as the fraud and hypocrisy of contemporary civilized man. He formulated a picture of man in "the state of nature," before civilization, in which his "natural goodness" was not yet "corrupted" by society. The key to this idea was his conception of moral sentiment, which was innate in all people and not learned from society. His writings were condemned, and he spent much of his life running from the police. He died in total poverty, but only a few years after his death, his political ideas became the central ideology of the French Revolution.

Russell, Bertrand (1872–1970): One of the greatest philosophers of our century. As a young man, he wrote, with Alfred North Whitehead, a book called *Principia Mathematica* (1903), which set the stage for modern logic and foundations of mathematics and gave logic a central role as a philosophical tool. He wrote an enormous number of philosophical books on virtually every topic, including several notorious polemics in favor of what was branded "free love" and atheism. He was a persistent and harsh critic of religion in general and Christianity in particular, as a source of superstition and legitimized murder. Russell was a committed pacifist and wrote at least one of his most famous books while sitting in prison for his antiwar activities. Like his famous predecessor, David Hume (with whom he has much in common), Russell was too controversial for most universities, and a famous court case prevented him from teaching in the United States. But as a wealthy aristocrat, he was not seriously inconvenienced by such problems. He won the Nobel prize in 1950.

Ryle, Gilbert (1900–): Oxford "ordinary language" philosopher whose book, *The Concept of Mind* (1949), set the stage for several decades of debate over his quasi-behavioristic resolution of the mind-body problem. His main thesis is that the distinction between mind and body rests on what he calls a "category mistake," that is, wrongly believing something to be one kind of thing when it is really another. In particular, it has been thought that mental events were events on a par with, but wholly different from, bodily events. Instead, Ryle argues, to talk about mind is to talk about behavioral dispositions and abilities (To say that a person *wants* to do something is to say that he *would* do that if given the opportunity.).

Sartre, Jean-Paul (1905–): Contemporary French philosopher who began as a literary writer and a phenomenologist, in the style of Edmund Husserl, but who converted that austere philosophy to his own radical ends. He is generally regarded as the main proponent of the philosophy of "existentialism." Sartre's existentialism is a moral philosophy as well as a philosophy of freedom. It denies that there is any such thing as "human nature" and therefore insists that "man makes himself." That is, through our various choices and moral commitments, we define what we want humanity to be. According to Sartre, we do not simply find moral principles upon which we should act, but rather we *choose* those moral principles *through our acting*. Thus, Sartre's moral philosophy places most of its emphasis on action and minimizes the importance of moral deliberation and all that sort of moralizing in which we simply talk about what is good rather than actually doing it. For Sartre, it is action that is ultimately good, rather than simply a "good will," as in Kant. In his novels and plays, Sartre's characters are always torn by alternative identities, suffering just because they cannot make up their minds. In his greatest work, *Being and Nothingness* (1943), Sartre argues that everyone "is who he is not, and is not who he is," by which he means (in a paradoxical phrase) that our identity is never simply the totality of facts ("facticity") that are true of us, but we always identify ourselves with our plans and intentions for the future (our "transcendence") as well. And this means that, so long as we are alive, we have no fixed "identity" at all.

Shaffer, Jerome (1929–): American philosopher, presently teaching at the University of Connecticut. One of the best known critics of the now-influential "identity theory" of mind and body.

Socrates (470–399 B.C.): Athenian philosopher with a gift for rhetoric and debating. He had a notoriously poor marriage, several children, and lived in poverty most of his life. Socrates began his studies in the physical sciences but soon turned to the study of human nature, morality, and politics. He became famous debating with the many "sophists" who wandered about giving practical training in argument and persuasion (the ancient equivalent of law school). Socrates found their general skepticism intolerable and urged a return to the absolute ideals of wisdom, virtue, justice, and the good life. In his philosophy, he approached these questions as matters of finding the exact definitions of these concepts in order to clarify our pursuit of them. In doing so, he developed a brilliant technique of dialogue or "dialectic" in which he would discover these definitions by constant debating, forcing his opponents or students to advance varying theories, which he in turn would knock down. In the process, the correct definition would slowly emerge. In his not always tactful search for truth, however, Socrates made many enemies, who eventually had him condemned to death, a cruel and unfair verdict he accepted with dignity.

Spinoza, Benedictus de (1632–77): Spinoza was born Baruch ben Michael, the son of Jewish refugees from the Spanish Inquisition. He was born and grew up in Amsterdam, a relative haven of toleration in a world still dangerous because of religious hatreds. He studied to be a rabbi, making himself familiar with Christian theology as well. He was always a recluse and was later ostracized by his fellow Jews for his heretical beliefs, wandering about the country making a living by grinding lenses. His philosophy, almost entirely contained in a single book, *Ethics* (1677), is a ?ical reinterpretation of God as identical to the universe (pantheism) and a pro- argument concerning the uselessness of human struggle in the face of a ly determined universe.

Stoics (4th century B.C., with revisions until the 1st century A.D.): An ancient movement in philosophy that taught self-control and minimized passion, with a willingness to endure whatever fate has in store. Some believers were Zeno of Citium in Greece (not the same as Zeno of the paradoxes) and Marcus Aurelius in Rome.

Strawson, Peter Frederick (1919–): Contemporary Oxford philosopher whose book, *Individuals* (1959), was responsible for reintroducing systematic metaphysics into current British philosophy. He called his metaphysics "descriptive," however, by which he meant to insist that it was only to be construed as an analysis and description of "our conceptual framework," not of "reality-in-itself." In the third chapter of that book, Strawson argues the thesis that the distinction between mind and body can be made only after we have recognized the primary category of "persons." Persons are not conglomerates of minds and bodies, and we can talk of minds and bodies only because we first have a way of specifying the different attributes of a person.

Tarski, Alfred (1902–): American logician who formulated the still controversial "semantic theory of truth" in 1944.

Thales (6th century B.C.): The first known Greek philosopher, who taught that all things were ultimately composed of water.

Tillich, Paul (1886–1965): German-born philosopher who spent many of his later years teaching in the United States. He is among the best known of those modern theologians who, like the Romantics of the last century, place the emphasis on emotion and "concern" rather than on reason in religion. In Tillich's theology, God is no longer the transcendent judge of the scriptures but simply the symbol of our "ultimate concern." He is the author of *Systematic Theology* (1953–63), *The Dynamics of Faith* (1957), and *The Courage to Be* (1952).

Watson, John (1878–1958): American psychologist generally recognized as the founder of behaviorism. He attacked the notion of "consciousness" as a remnant of the age-old religious belief in the "soul" and urged that we give up such "magical" nonsense in favor of a purely scientific view, which allows us to talk sensibly only about observables; in other words, human behavior rather than the human "mind." He is the author of *Behaviorism* (1924).

Whitehead, Alfred North (1861–1947): Famous logician who, together with Bertrand Russell, established the basis of modern logic and, late in life, turned to metaphysics. In place of the concept of substance, however, he argued for a concept of process, a universe in constant evolutionary change.

Wittgenstein, Ludwig (1899–1951): Austrian-born philosopher who became the single most powerful influence on twentieth-century "analytic" philosophy. He entered philosophy as an engineer, studied with Bertrand Russell, and wrote the book, *Tractatus Logico-Philosophicus* (1922), which inspired logical positivism. Giving up philosophy for a number of years and changing his mind about his arguments in the *Tractatus*, he returned to philosophy at Cambridge and developed that "therapeutic" brand of philosophy that became known as "ordinary language" philosophy. In his later works, culminating in his *Philosophical Investigations*, (1953, published posthumously), Wittgenstein initiated a devastating attack on Cartesian dualism and the problems it carried with it. His so-called "private language argument," in fact culled from a series of aphorisms, argues that even if there were such "private" occurrences as mental events, we should have no way of talking about them and no way of knowing about them, even in our own case. But although he is often described as a "behaviorist," Wittgenstein is better described as one of those philosophers who was groping for an entirely new conception of a "person" or, at least, attempting to wholly reject all the old ones.

Zeno of Elea (5th century B.C.): Pre-Socratic philosopher and student of Parmenides who taught that motion was unreal and developed a series of brilliant paradoxes in order to prove it.

BIBLIOGRAPHY

INTRODUCTION—PHILOSOPHY

A large number of alternative views of philosophy are available in Charles I. Bontempo and S. Jack Odell, eds., *The Owl of Minerva* (New York: McGraw-Hill, 1975). The trial, imprisonment, and death of Socrates are recounted by Plato in the dialogues *Apology, Crito,* and *Phaedo* in *The Last Days of Socrates,* trans. Hugh Tredennick (London: Penguin, 1954). An excellent account of Socrates' life is A. E. Taylor, *Socrates* (New York: Doubleday, Anchor, 1959). The best single book on the Enlightenment is Peter Gay, *The Enlightenment: An Interpretation* (New York: Vintage, 1966); a simpler discussion is Robert Anchor, *The Enlightenment Tradition* (New York: Harper & Row, 1967); and a philosophical anthology of the period is Isaiah Berlin, *The Age of Enlightenment* (New York: Mentor, 1955). A valuable supplement to René Descartes' first "Meditation" is his *Discourse on Method,* in *The Philosophical Works of Descartes,* 2 vols., trans. Elizabeth S. Haldane and G. R. T. Ross (Cambridge: Cambridge University Press, 1911, 1931). Two standard introductions to logic are W. Salmon, *Logic* (Englewood Cliffs, N.J.: Prentice-Hall, 1963) and I. Copi, *Introduction to Logic* (New York: Macmillan, 1961).

CHAPTER 1—REALITY: ANCIENT VIEWS

General surveys of ancient Greek philosophy can be found in J. Burnet, *Early Greek Philosophy* (London: Black, 1958) and W. K. C. Guthrie, *The Greek Philosophers: From Thales to Aristotle* (New York: Harper & Row, 1960). The most important texts from the Pre-Socratics are in G. S. Kirk and J. E. Raven, *The Presocratic Philosophers* (Cambridge: Cambridge University Press, 1957). Plato's dialogues are collected in *Plato, Dialogues,* 4th ed., trans. Benjamin Jowett (Oxford: Oxford University Press, 1953); a helpful survey of his work is A. E. Taylor, *Plato, The Man and His Work* (New York: Dial, 1936). Aristotle's works are collected in R. McKeon, ed., *The Basic Works of Aristotle* (New York: Random House, 1941). An excellent survey of all Aristotle's works is W. D. Ross, *Aristotle* (New York: Meridian, 1959). Brief surveys of the Pre-Socratics, Socrates, Plato, and Aristotle are D. J. O'Connor, ed., *A Critical History of Western Philosophy* (New York: Free Press, 1964) and P. Edwards, ed., *The Encyclopedia of Philosophy* (New York: Macmillan, 1967). General introductions to metaphysics are Richard Taylor, *Metaphysics* (Englewood Cliffs, N.J.: Prentice-Hall, 1963) and D. F. Pears, ed., *The Nature of Metaphysics* (London: Macmillan, 1957). An exciting history of metaphysics is A. Lovejoy, *The Great Chain of Being* (Cambridge, Mass.: Harvard University Press, 1936).

CHAPTER 2—REALITY: MODERN VIEWS

Benedictus de Spinoza's *Ethics* is in *The Rationalists* (New York: Doubleday, 1960); an excellent account of Spinoza's philosophy is S. Hampshire, *Spinoza* (London: Penguin, 1951). A convenient collection of Gottfried W. von Leibniz's major works is Philip Wiener, ed., *Leibniz, Selections* (New York: Charles Scribner's Sons, 1951).

Two recent studies of Leibniz are Ruth Saw, *Leibniz* (London: Penguin, 1954) and Hidé Ishiguro, *Leibniz's Philosophy of Logic and Language* (Ithaca, N.Y.: Cornell University Press, 1972). An important but biased study is Bertrand Russell, *A Critical Exposition of the Philosophy of Leibniz* (London: George Allen and Unwin, 1937). To study more recent metaphysical systems, see A. Lovejoy, *The Great Chain of Being* (Cambridge, Mass.: Harvard University Press, 1936); Jacques Maritain, *A Preface to Metaphysics* (London: Sheed, 1948); Henri Bergson, *An Introduction to Metaphysics,* trans. T. E. Hulme (New York: Bobbs-Merrill, 1949); Martin Heidegger, *An Introduction to Metaphysics,* trans. Ralph Manheim (New Haven, Conn.: Yale University Press, 1959); and R. G. Collingwood, *An Essay on Metaphysics* (Oxford: Clarendon Press, 1940).

CHAPTER 3—KNOWLEDGE

Several studies of the various problems in René Descartes' epistemology are in Willis Doney, ed., *Descartes* (New York: Doubleday, Anchor, 1967). Gottfried W. von Leibniz's reply to John Locke is spelled out at length in Leibniz's *New Essays on Human Understanding,* trans. A. G. Langley (La Salle, Ill.: Open Court, 1949). Locke's *Essay Concerning Human Understanding* is published by Dover Publications (New York, 1959). Bishop Berkeley's *Treatise* is printed in full in T. E. Jessop, ed., *Berkeley: Philosophical Writings* (Austin, Texas: University of Texas Press, 1953). Of special interest is Berkeley's *Three Dialogues Between Hylas and Philonous* (La Salle, Ill.: Open Court, 1935), in which the arguments of his *Treatise* are worked out in entertaining dialogue form. David Hume's *Treatise of Human Nature* is available edited by L. A. Selby-Bigge (Oxford: Oxford University Press, 1888), but most beginners will find Hume's *Enquiry Concerning Human Understanding* (Oxford: Oxford University Press, 1902) much easier reading. Bertrand Russell, *Problems of Philosophy* (London: Oxford University Press, 1912) is an excellent introduction to the problems of epistemology and some of the problems of metaphysics. Two more modern epistemological studies are A. J. Ayer, *The Problem of Knowledge* (New York: St. Martin's Press, 1956) and Roderick Chisholm, *Theory of Knowledge* (Englewood Cliffs, N.J.: Prentice-Hall, 1956). A modern series of studies is R. J. Swartz, ed., *Perceiving, Sensing, Knowing* (New York: Doubleday, Anchor, 1965). For a comprehensive anthology on epistemology, see E. Nagel and R. Brandt, eds., *Meaning and Knowledge* (New York: Harcourt Brace Jovanovich, 1965).

CHAPTER 4—NECESSITY

Two recent anthologies are Robert Sleigh, ed., *Necessary Truth* (Englewood Cliffs, N.J.: Prentice-Hall, 1972) and L. W. Sumner and John Woods, *Necessary Truth: A Book of Readings* (New York: Random House, 1970). For a comprehensive anthology on the foundations of mathematics, see P. Benacerraf and H. Putnam, eds., *Philosophy of Mathematics* (Englewood Cliffs, N.J.: Prentice-Hall, 1964). W. V. O. Quine's now-classic attack on the notion of "analytic truth" is in "Two Dogmas of Empiricism," in *From a Logical Point of View* (Cambridge, Mass.: Harvard University Press, 1953). An attempted rebuttal is by H. P. Grice and P. F. Strawson, "In Defense of a Dogma," in *Philosophical Review,* 65 (1956). Selections in the chapter are developed at length in A. J. Ayer, *Language, Truth and Logic* (New York: Dover Publications, 1946); John Stuart Mill, *A System of Logic,* 8th ed. (New

York: Harper, 1874); Edmund Husserl, *Ideas,* trans. W. R. Boyce-Gibson (New York: Macmillan, 1962); Immanuel Kant, *The Critique of Pure Reason,* trans. Norman Kemp-Smith (London: St. Martin's Press, 1933). Reasonably straightforward expositions of Husserl and Kant can be found in R. Schmitt, "Phenomenology," in *The Encyclopedia of Philosophy,* ed. P. Edwards (New York: Macmillan, 1967) and S. Körner, *Kant* (London: Penguin, 1955).

CHAPTER 5—TRUTH AND RATIONALITY

Discussion and criticism of the various theories of truth can be found in Alan R. White, *Truth* (New York: Doubleday, Anchor, 1970). A discussion of Alfred Tarski's theory is in W. V. O. Quine, *Philosophy of Logic* (Englewood Cliffs, N.J.: Prentice-Hall, 1970). Brand Blandshard's argument is developed in his *Nature of Thought* (New York: Macmillan, 1941). William James develops his pragmatic theory in his *Pragmatism: A New Name for Some Old Ways of Thinking* (New York: Longmans Green, 1907). Two brief but helpful introductions to Immanuel Kant's philosophy are J. Kemp, *The Philosophy of Kant* (London: Oxford University Press, 1968) and G. J. Warnock, "Kant," in *A Critical History of Western Philosophy,* ed. D. J. O'Connor (New York: Free Press, 1964).

CHAPTER 6—IS IT ALL RELATIVE?

An excellent history of the past century of philosophy is J. Passmore, *A Hundred Years of Philosophy* (London: Penguin, 1957). A good but difficult study of the development of philosophy in Europe after Immanuel Kant is K. Lowith, *From Hegel to Nietzsche,* trans. D. Green (New York: Doubleday, 1964). Easier to read is Richard Schacht, *Hegel and After* (Pittsburgh, Penn.: University of Pittsburgh Press, 1975). A good survey of G. W. F. Hegel's philosophy is J. N. Findlay, *Hegel: A Re-Examination* (New York: Collier, 1962). Good reviews of Karl Marx are D. McClellan, *The Thought of Karl Marx* (New York: Harper & Row, 1971); Herbert Marcuse, *Reason and Revolution,* 2nd ed. (New York: Humanities Press, 1968); Sidney Hook, *From Hegel to Marx* (Ann Arbor, Mich.: University of Michigan Press, 1962); and S. Avineri, *The Social and Political Thought of Karl Marx* (Cambridge: Cambridge University Press, 1968). A good study of Friedrich Nietzsche is Walter Kaufmann, *Nietzsche* (Princeton, N.J.: Princeton University Press, 1950). A good complete history of phenomenology is H. Spiegelberg, *The Phenomenological Movement,* 2nd ed., 2 vols. (New York: Humanities Press, 1969). Good surveys of English philosophy from G. E. Moore and Bertrand Russell to the present day are J. O. Urmson, *Philosophical Analysis* (Oxford: Clarendon Press, 1956) and G. J. Warnock, *English Philosophy Since 1900,* 2nd ed. (Oxford: Oxford University Press, 1969). An examination of logical positivism by an insider is A. J. Ayer, ed., *Logical Positivism* (New York: Free Press, 1959). A harsher critic is J. Weinberg, *An Examination of Logical Positivism* (London: Littlefield, 1960). For a good brief survey, see also Anthony Quinton, "Contemporary British Philosophy," in *A Critical History of Western Philosophy,* ed. D. J. O'Connor (New York: Free Press, 1964). Two short but good surveys of existentialism are M. Warnock, *Existentialism* (London: Oxford University Press, 1970) and M. Grene, *Introduction to Existentialism* (Chicago: University of Chicago Press, 1959). See also William Barrett, *Irrational Man* (New York: Doubleday, Anchor, 1958). An excellent selection of American pragmatists is presented in

Amelie Rorty, ed., *Pragmatic Philosophy* (New York: Doubleday, Anchor, 1966). More modern studies in pragmatism include W. V. O. Quine, *Ontological Relativity and Other Essays* (New York: Columbia University Press, 1969) and Nelson Goodman, *Problems and Projects* (New York: Bobbs-Merrill, 1971). For a contemporary debate on relativism in science, see Thomas S. Kuhn, *The Structure of Scientific Revolutions* (Chicago: University of Chicago Press, 1962) and Israel Scheffler, *Science and Subjectivity* (Indianapolis, Ind.: Bobbs-Merrill, 1967).

CHAPTER 7—RELIGION

Several good anthologies on the philosophy of religion are S. Cahn, ed., *Philosophy of Religion* (New York: Harper & Row, 1970); J. Hick, ed., *Faith and the Philosophers* (New York: St. Martin's Press, 1964); and N. Smart, ed., *Historical Selections in the Philosophy of Religion* (New York: Harper & Row, 1962). A general discussion of religious issues is J. Hick, *Faith and Knowledge,* 2nd ed. (Ithaca, N.Y.: Cornell University Press, 1966). A good series of studies on the problem of evil is N. Pike, ed., *God and Evil* (Englewood Cliffs, N.J.: Prentice-Hall, 1964). David Hume's *Dialogues on Natural Religion* (New York: Bobbs-Merrill, 1963) makes excellent and provocative reading. A convenient collection of Søren Kierkegaard's writings is W. H. Auden, *The Living Thoughts of Kierkegaard* (Bloomington, Ind.: Indiana University Press, 1963). Two good studies of Kierkegaard are J. Collins, *The Mind of Kierkegaard* (Chicago: Regnery, 1953) and Louis Mackey, *Kierkegaard: A Kind of Poet* (Philadelphia: University of Pennsylvania Press, 1972). The selections from Karl Marx, Friedrich Nietzsche, and Sigmund Freud are developed in Karl Marx, *Early Writings,* trans. T. Bottomore (New York: McGraw-Hill, 1963); Friedrich Nietzsche, *The Antichrist,* in *The Viking Portable Nietzsche,* trans. Walter Kaufman (New York: Viking, 1959); and Sigmund Freud, *The Future of an Illusion,* trans. W. D. Robson-Scott (New York: Doubleday, Anchor, 1953).

CHAPTER 8—SELF-IDENTITY

A recent anthology on the question of self-identity is J. Perry, *Personal Identity* (New York: Lieber-Atherton, 1975). An extended study of this traditional problem is Sidney Shoemaker, *Self-Knowledge and Self-Identity* (Ithaca, N.Y.: Cornell University Press, 1963). Jean-Paul Sartre's existentialist view of the self is developed in his essay, "Transcendence of the Ego" (New York: Noonday, 1957). Hermann Hesse's complex theory of the self is best developed in *Steppenwolf,* rev. ed., trans. Basil Creighton (New York: Holt, Rinehart and Winston, 1970), but it is most simply portrayed in *Siddhartha,* trans. H. Rosner (New York: New Directions, 1951). Further reading in Eastern conceptions of the self may begin with D. Suzuki, *Zen Buddhism,* ed. W. Barrett (New York: Doubleday, 1956) or C. Moore, ed., *The Individual in East and West* (Honolulu: East-West Center Press, 1967). A good introduction to G. W. F. Hegel's very difficult philosophy is the introduction to his lectures on the philosophy of history, in his *Reason in History,* trans. R. Hartman (New York: Bobbs-Merrill, 1953).

CHAPTER 9—MIND AND BODY

A good short survey of the "mind-body problem" is Keith Campbell, *Body and Mind* (New York: Doubleday, Anchor, 1970); a helpful introduction to the problem and the various alternatives is J. Shaffer, *The Philosophy of Mind* (Englewood Cliffs, N.J.: Prentice-Hall, 1968). A good historical discussion of the reactions against Cartesian dualism is A. Lovejoy, *The Revolt Against Dualism* (La Salle, Ill.: Open Court, 1955). Two more recent anthologies, with special attention to the "identity theory," are David Rosenthal, ed., *Materialism and the Mind-Body Problem* (Englewood Cliffs, N.J.: Prentice-Hall, 1971) and C. V. Borst, ed., *The Mind-Brain Identity Theory* (New York: St. Martin's Press, 1970).

CHAPTER 10—FREEDOM

General anthologies are Sidney Hook, ed., *Determinism and Freedom in the Age of Modern Science* (New York: Macmillan, Collier, 1961); B. Berofsky, ed., *Free Will and Determinism* (New York: Harper & Row, 1966); and H. Morris, ed., *Freedom and Responsibility* (Stanford, Calif.: Stanford University Press, 1961). See also D. F. Pears, ed., *Freedom and the Will* (New York: St. Martin's Press, 1963).

CHAPTER 11—MORALITY AND THE GOOD LIFE

A comprehensive but brief history of ethics is A. MacIntyre, *A Short History of Ethics* (New York: Macmillan, 1966). A general schematic discussion of the problems of ethics is W. Frankena, *Ethics* (Englewood Cliffs, N.J.: Prentice-Hall, 1963). A much more detailed survey of the problems and the recent history of ethics is Richard R. Brandt, *Ethical Theory* (Englewood Cliffs, N.J.: Prentice-Hall, 1959). Also available is a companion anthology, Richard R. Brandt, *Value and Obligation* (New York: Harcourt Brace Jovanovich, 1961). The classic arguments against egoism are in J. Butler, *Fifteen Sermons Upon Human Nature* (London: Macmillan, 1900). A more modern and technical set of arguments are in T. Nagel, *The Possibility of Altruism* (New York: Oxford University Press, 1970). Textbooks that include various discussions of ethical options are R. N. Beck and J. B. Orr, *Ethical Choice* (New York: Free Press, 1970) and John Hospers, *Human Conduct* (New York: Harcourt Brace Jovanovich, 1962). Several articles on ethical relativism are collected in J. Ladd, ed., *Ethical Relativism* (Belmont, Calif.: Wadsworth, 1973). See also W. Stace, *The Concept of Morals* (New York: Macmillan, 1962).

CHAPTER 12—PERSPECTIVES ON MORALITY

Aristotle's *Nichomachean Ethics* is translated by W. D. Ross (Oxford: Oxford University Press, 1925). Ross also has a good summary of the arguments in his *Aristotle* (New York: Meridian, 1959). Some excellent articles on Aristotle's ethics are collected in J. Walsh and H. Shapiro, eds., *Aristotle's Ethics* (Belmont, Calif.: Wadsworth, 1967) and J. Moravscik, ed., *Aristotle* (New York: Doubleday, Anchor, 1966). David Hume's moral philosophy is most accessible in his *Enquiry Concerning the Principles of Morals* (La Salle, Ill.: Open Court, 1912). Jean Jacques Rousseau's moral theories are to be found in his second discourse, "On the Origins of Inequality," in *The Social Contract* (New York: Dutton, 1950) and in *Emile* (New York: Dutton, 1970). The best summary of Immanuel Kant's moral philosophy is his own *Foundations of the Metaphysics of Morals,* available in various translations, the most helpful, because of the commentary, being *Groundwork of the Metaphysics of Morals,* trans. H. J. Paton (New York: Harper & Row, 1957). See also Immanuel Kant, *Lectures on*

Ethics, trans. L. Infield (New York: Harper & Row, 1963). John Stuart Mill's utilitarianism is well summarized in his pamphlet, *Utilitarianism* (New York: Dutton, 1910). A good summary of Friedrich Nietzsche's ethics is in Walter Kaufmann, *Nietzsche* (Princeton, N.J.: Princeton University Press, 1950). A good summary of existentialist ethics is M. Warnock, *Existentialist Ethics* (New York: St. Martin's Press, 1967).

CHAPTER 13—POLITICS

Plato, *The Republic,* trans. Francis M. Cornford (Oxford: Oxford University Press, 1941) is still standard reading for the basics and some thought-provoking alternatives in political philosophy. See also Aristotle, *Politics,* in *The Basic Works of Aristotle,* ed. R. McKeon (New York: Random House, 1941). Our own national documents, the Declaration of Independence and the Constitution, are always important reading. John Stuart Mill, *On Liberty,* ed. C. Shields (New York: Bobbs-Merrill, 1956) has long been the classic defense of liberalism. Michael Oakeshott, *Rationalism in Politics* (New York: Basic Books, 1962) is an important challenge to liberal philosophy. Karl Marx's *Communist Manifesto,* trans. S. Moore (Chicago: Regnery, 1969) and his early political writings, *Early Writings,* trans. T. Bottomore (New York: McGraw-Hill, 1963) are essential reading for beginning students in political philosophy. Niccolò Machiavelli, *The Prince,* trans. C. Detmold (New York: Airmont, 1965) and Jean Jacques Rousseau, *The Social Contract* (New York: Dutton, 1950) are both important and rewarding reading. For more general discussions of the philosophy of politics, see F. Olafson, ed., *Justice and Social Policy* (Englewood Cliffs, N.J.: Prentice-Hall, 1961); G. Sabine, *A History of Political Theory,* 3rd ed. (New York: Holt, Rinehart and Winston, 1961); and P. Laslett and W. G. Runciman, eds., *Philosophy, Politics and Society* (Oxford: Blackwell, 1964).

INDEX OF GLOSSARY TERMS

SUBJECT INDEX

absolutes, of knowledge, 192, 194–95; of
   morals, 426–28, 430–35; of space and
   time, 76, 80; of truth, 140, 191–92,
   194–95; *see also* relativism
absolutism, 192, 206, 430–34
abstract, 19
accidental property, 48
action-at-a-distance, 75, 80
Adam, 210, 231
agnostic, 212
agnosticism, 260
alienation, 304–05, 557–58, 578
altruism, 418–26, 435
analytic philosophy, 196–202, 206
analytic truths, *see* truth
anarchism, 570–77
anarchists, 497, 570, 571
anarchy, 10, 571, 578
Anaximander, 27, 28
Anaximenes, 28
animism, 30, 52, 80, 193
Anselm, St., 213–15
antecedent conditions, 358–59, 403
anthropomorphic, 211, 260
Apology (Plato), 2–4
a posteriori, 147, 152, 153, 163, 460
appearance, *see* reality
a priori, 73, 117, 118, 119, 120, 131–32,
   138, 140, 144–45, 147, 151–57, 162,
   163, 186, 249, 251, 252, 460, 493;
   see also empirical knowledge
Aquinas, St. Thomas, 49, 219–21
argument, 8, 9, 10, 11, 17–18, 19, 50, 51
argument from design, *see* teleological
   argument
Aristippus, 406
Aristophanes, 1, 2
Aristotle, 7, 25, 32, 33–34, 46–52, 59, 65,
   68, 91, 160, 168, 169, 181, 193, 219,
   275, 302, 338, 374, 376, 499; on
   cause, 49–50; on ethics, 415–18, 438–
   47; on metaphysics, 33–34, 47–50; on
   Plato, 33, 47, 48, 51; on politics, 501–
   04; on substance, 47, 52; on voluntary
   action, 374
asceticism, 411–12, 435
association of ideas, 127
assumption, 8, 10, 19, 50, 51
atheism, 233, 242, 253, 260
atheist, 2, 8, 57, 58, 212, 226, 232, 242,
   249–50, 253
atoms, 29
attribute, 58, 59, 60, 64, 80, 221, 225, 231,
   249, 250
Augustine, St., 427
Austin, J. L., 180, 201, 202

authority, 11, 26, 518–45, 578
autonomy, 19, 445–68, 493
axiom, 12, 19, 59, 60, 66, 143, 147–49,
   151, 160
Ayer, A. J., 137–38, 143–45, 151, 242,
   249–53

bad faith, 285–86, 306
Bakunin, Mikhail, 571–77
Becoming, 30, 33, 46, 52, 168
begging the question, 19
behaviorism, 320–32, 338, 353
Being, 29, 30, 33, 34, 38, 44–45, 47, 51,
   52, 158, 168, 210–11, 215, 301
Being and Nothingness (Sartre), 285–87,
   396
Bentham, Jeremy, 469, 470–74
Berkeley, Bishop George, 84, 104–11, 115,
   127, 169, 314, 332, 344, 350
best of all possible worlds, 77–78, 80
Beyond Freedom and Dignity (Skinner),
   383
Beyond Good and Evil (Nietzsche), 255,
   413, 483–87
Blandshard, Brand, 173–75
bourgeoisie, 559–66
Bradley, F. H., 197
Brave New World (Huxley), 387
British empiricists, 84, 91–126
British philosophy, 84, 196–202
Brothers Karamazov, The (Dostoevsky),
   242–49
Buddha, 292–93
Buddhist, 292–94
Burgess, Anthony, 387
Butler, Bishop Joseph, 421–24

calculus, 136, 163
Campbell, C. A., 392–96
Candide (Voltaire), 77, 223
Carroll, Lewis, 265
Cartesian dualism, 309, 323, 332, 338, 340,
   341, 343, 347, 353
Cartesianism, 19
categorical imperative, 462–69, 493
category, 185, 206
category mistake, 325–27
Catholic Church, 11, 301
causal interactionism, 318–19, 354
causal theory of perception, 97–99, 104,
   116, 127
cause, 49, 53, 59, 60, 62, 65, 67, 75, 97,
   115, 116–24, 126, 127, 220, 318–19,
   357–74, 403, 404; Aristotle on, 49,
   374–76; efficient, 220; first, 49, 67,
   221; Hume on, 115–26, 361, 371–74;

BENZIGER BRUCE & GLENCOE, INC.   For the excerpts from *Summa Theologica* by St. Thomas Aquinas, translated by the Fathers of the English Dominican Province. Published in 1948 by Benziger Bruce & Glencoe, Inc. Reprinted by permission.

THE BOBBS-MERRILL COMPANY, INC.   For the excerpts from *Treatise Concerning the Principles of Human Knowledge* by George Berkeley, © 1957 by The Liberal Arts Press, published by The Bobbs-Merrill Company, Inc. For the excerpt from *Five Sermons* by Joseph Butler, copyright 1950, The Liberal Arts Press, Inc., reprinted by permission of The Bobbs-Merrill Company, Inc. For the excerpt from *Reason in History* by G. W. F. Hegel, translated by Robert S. Hartman, copyright © 1953 by The Liberal Arts Press, Inc., reprinted by permission of The Bobbs-Merrill Company, Inc. For the excerpt from *Critique of Practical Reason and Other Writings on Moral Philosophy* by Immanuel Kant, translated by Lewis White Beck, copyright © 1949 by University of Chicago Press, reprinted by permission of The Bobbs-Merrill Company, Inc. For the excerpt from *Prolegomena to Any Future Metaphysics* by Immanuel Kant, edited by Lewis White Beck, copyright © 1950 by The Liberal Arts Press, Inc., reprinted by permission of The Bobbs-Merrill Company, Inc.

BUKKYO DENDO KYOKAI   For the excerpts from *The Teaching of Buddha.* Copyright © 1966 by Bukkyo Dendo Kyokai, Tokyo.

CAMBRIDGE UNIVERSITY PRESS   For the excerpts from *The Philosophical Works of Descartes* by René Descartes, translated by Elizabeth S. Haldane and G. R. T. Ross. For the excerpt from *Plato's Phaedo,* translated by R. Hackforth. Reprinted by permission of the publisher, Cambridge University Press.

J. M. DENT & SONS LTD.   For the excerpt from *Emile* by Jean-Jacques Rousseau, translated by Barbara Foxley. For the excerpt from *The Social Contract* by Jean-Jacques Rousseau, translated by G. D. H. Cole. Both published by Everyman's Library, and reprinted by permission of J. M. Dent & Sons Ltd.

DOMINICAN PROVINCIAL   For the excerpts from *Summa Theologica* by St. Thomas Aquinas, translated by the Fathers of the English Dominican Province. Reprinted by permission.

DOUBLEDAY & COMPANY, INC.   For the excerpts from "Ethics" by Benedictus de Spinoza, translated by R. H. M. Elwes, from *The Rationalists.* For the excerpts from "Monadology" by Gottfried Wilhelm Freiherr von Leibniz, translated by George Montgomery, from *The Rationalists.* Published by Anchor Books.

E. P. DUTTON & COMPANY, INC.   For the excerpt from *Notes from Underground and The Grand Inquisitor* by Fyodor Dostoevsky. Translated by Ralph E. Matlaw. Copyright © 1960 by E. P. Dutton & Co., Inc., and reprinted with their permission. For the excerpt from *The Social Contract and Discourses* by Jean-Jacques Rousseau. Translated by G. D. H. Cole. An Everyman's Library Edition. Published in the United States by E. P. Dutton & Co., Inc., and reprinted with their permission. For the excerpt from *Emile* by Jean-Jacques Rousseau. Translated by Barbara Foxley. An Everyman's Library Edition. Published in the United States by E. P. Dutton & Co., Inc., and reprinted with their permission.

ÉDITIONS GALLIMARD   For the excerpts from *Being and Nothingness* by Jean-Paul Sartre, translated by H. Barnes. © Editions Gallimard 1943. Reprinted by permission.

ÉDITIONS NAGEL   For the excerpts from *Existentialism As a Humanism* by Jean-Paul Sartre, translated by P. Mairet. Reprinted by permission.

BURT FRANKLIN AND COMPANY, INC.   For the excerpt from *System of Nature* by Baron Paul Henri d'Holbach, translated by H. D. Robinson.

VICTOR GOLLANCZ LTD.   For the excerpts from *Language, Truth and Logic* by A. J. Ayer. Reprinted by permission.

SANFORD J. GREENBURGER ASSOCIATES, INC.   For the excerpts from *Being and Nothingness* by Jean-Paul Sartre. Copyright © 1956 by Philosophical Library, Inc. Reprinted by permission of Philosophical Library.

GROVE PRESS, INC. For the excerpt from *The Dwarfs* by Harold Pinter. Reprinted by permission of Grove Press, Inc. Copyright © 1961 by Harold Pinter.

HAMISH HAMILTON LTD. For the excerpts from *No Exit* in *No Exit and Other Plays* by Jean-Paul Sartre, translated by Stuart Gilbert. Copyright 1946 by Stuart Gilbert. Reprinted by permission of Hamish Hamilton, Ltd.

HARPER & ROW, PUBLISHERS, INC. For the excerpt from *Being and Time* by Martin Heidegger, translated by MacQuarrie and Robinson. For the excerpt from *Phenomenology and the Crisis of Philosophy* by Edmund Husserl, translated by J. B. Baillie. For the excerpts from *A System of Logic* by J. S. Mill. Abridged from pp. 11–17, 18, 22, 88–89, 116–117, 319 and 320–321 in *The Concept of Mind* by Gilbert Ryle. Copyright, 1949, by Gilbert Ryle. By permission of Harper & Row (Barnes & Noble Books). From pp. 44–48 in *Dynamics of Faith* by Paul Tillich. Volume 10 of World Perspectives, Planned and Edited by Ruth Nanda Anshen. Copyright © 1957 by Paul Tillich. By permission of Harper & Row, Publishers, Inc.

HARVARD UNIVERSITY PRESS For the excerpts from *Metaphysics,* Books VI and IV by Aristotle, translated by Hugh Tredennick. Copyright 1935 and 1933, Harvard University Press. For the excerpt from *De Anima* by Aristotle, translated by Hett. Copyright 1936, Harvard University Press. For the excerpt from *From A Logical Point of View* by Willard V. Quine. Copyright 1921, Harvard University Press. Reprinted by permission.

WILLIAM HEINEMANN LTD. For the excerpt from *A Clockwork Orange* by Anthony Burgess. Published in Great Britain by William Heinemann Ltd. Reprinted by permission.

THE HOGARTH PRESS LTD. For the excerpts from *The Standard Edition of the Complete Psychological Works of Sigmund Freud,* Volume 21 (*The Future of An Illusion*) and Volume 22 (*New Introductory Lectures on Psycho-Analysis*), revised and edited by James Strachey. Reprinted by permission of Sigmund Freud Copyrights Ltd., The Institute of Psycho-Analysis, and The Hogarth Press Ltd.

HOLMES MCDOUGALL LTD. For the excerpts from *In Defense of Free Will* by C. A. Campbell. Reprinted by permission of the publisher, Holmes McDougall Ltd.

HOLT, RINEHART AND WINSTON For the excerpt from *Steppenwolf* by Hermann Hesse. Translated by Basil Creighton. Copyright 1929, © 1957 by Holt, Rinehart and Winston. Reprinted by permission of Holt, Rinehart and Winston, Publishers.

HUMANITIES PRESS, INC. For the excerpt from *Tractatus Logico-Philosophicus* by Ludwig Wittgenstein, translated by D. F. Pears and B. F. McGuinness. Reprinted by permission of Humanities Press, Inc., New Jersey.

HUTCHINSON PUBLISHING GROUP LTD. For the excerpts from *The Concept of Mind* by Gilbert Ryle. Reprinted by permission of the publisher, Hutchinson Publishing Group Ltd.

ALEXANDER R. JAMES For the excerpt from *Pragmatism: A New Name for Some Old Ways of Thinking* by William James. For the excerpt from *The Will to Believe and Other Essays in Popular Philosophy* by William James.

MACMILLIAN PUBLISHING CO., INC. For the excerpt from *The Political Philosophy of Bakunin* by Michael Bakunin, edited by G. P. Maximoff. Copyright The Free Press, a Division of Macmillan Publishing Co., Inc., 1953. For the excerpt from *Ideas* by Edmund Husserl, translated by W. R. Boyce-Gibson. First Collier Books Edition 1962. First published in 1931. For the excerpt from *Walden Two* by B. F. Skinner. Copyright 1948, 1976 by B. F. Skinner. For the excerpts from *The Concept of Morals* by Walter Stace. Copyright 1937 by Macmillan Publishing Co., Inc., renewed 1965 by Walter Stace. All reprinted with permission of Macmillan Publishing Co., Inc.

MACMILLAN ADMINISTRATION (BASINGSTOKE) LTD. For the excerpts from *The Critique of Pure Reason* by Immanuel Kant, translated by Norman Kemp-Smith. Reprinted by permission of Macmillan London and Basingstoke.

THE MATHEMATICAL ASSOCIATION OF AMERICA For the excerpt from "On the Nature of Mathematical Truth" by C. G. Hempel (*American Mathematical Monthly*, LII, 1945).

McGRAW-HILL BOOK COMPANY For the excerpts from *Karl Marx: Early Writings* by Karl Marx, translated by T. B. Bottomore. Copyright 1963, McGraw-Hill Book Company. Used with permission of McGraw-Hill Book Company.

NEW YORK UNIVERSITY PRESS For the excerpts from "What Means This Freedom" by John Hospers. From *Determinism and Freedom in the Age of Modern Science*, edited by Sidney Hook. © 1958 by New York University. Reprinted by permission of New York University Press.

NORTHWESTERN UNIVERSITY PRESS For the excerpt from *The Philosophy of Epicurus*, edited by George K. Strodach (Evanston, Illinois: Northwestern University Press, 1962). Reprinted by permission.

W. W. NORTON & COMPANY, INC. Reprinted from *A Clockwork Orange* by Anthony Burgess. Copyright © 1963 by W. W. Norton & Company, Inc. Copyright © 1962 by Anthony Burgess. Reprinted from *The Future of An Illusion* by Sigmund Freud. Newly Translated from the German and Edited by James Strachey. Copyright © 1961 by James Strachey. Reprinted from *New Introductory Lectures on Psychoanalysis* by Sigmund Freud. Newly Translated and Edited by James Strachey. Copyright © 1964, 1964 by James Strachey. Reprinted from *Behaviorism* by John B. Watson. Copyright 1924, 1925 by The People's Institute Publishing Company, Inc. Copyright 1930 by W. W. Norton & Company, Inc. Copyright renewed 1952, 1953, 1958 by John B. Watson. All by permission of W. W. Norton & Company, Inc.

OPEN COURT PUBLISHING COMPANY For permission to quote from *New Essays Concerning Human Understanding* by Gottfried Leibniz, translated by A. G. Langley. Reprinted by permission.

OXFORD UNIVERSITY PRESS For the excerpts from *Enquiry Concerning Human Understanding*, Second Edition, by David Hume, edited by L. A. Selby-Bigge. For the excerpts from *Treatise of Human Nature*, by David Hume, edited by L. A. Selby-Bigge. For the excerpt from *Dialogues on Natural Religion* by David Hume, edited by Norman Kemp-Smith. For the excerpt from *The Dialogues of Plato*, Fourth Edition, translated by Benjamin Jowett. For the excerpts from *The Republic of Plato*, translated by F. M. Cornford. For the excerpts from "Nichomachean Ethics," translated by W. D. Ross, from *The Oxford Translation of Aristotle*, Volume 9, edited by W. D. Ross. For the excerpt from *The Problems of Philosophy* by Bertrand Russell. All reprinted by permission of the Oxford University Press.

PENGUIN BOOKS LTD. For the excerpt from *Steppenwolf* by Hermann Hesse, translated by Basil Creighton, revised by Joseph Mileck. Copyright 1929, © 1957 by Holt, Rinehart and Winston. For the excerpts from *Plato: Protagoras and Meno*, translated by W. K. C. Guthrie (1956), pp. 128–39, © W. K. C. Guthrie, 1956. For the excerpt from *Crito* by Plato, in *The Last Days of Socrates*, translated by Hugh Tredennick (1959), pp. 81–96, © Hugh Tredennick, 1954, 1959. All reprinted by permission of Penguin Books Ltd.

PITMAN PUBLISHING LTD. For the excerpts from *Karl Marx: Early Writings* translated by T. B. Bottomore. Reprinted by permission of the publisher, Pitman Publishing Ltd.

THE PHILOSOPHICAL REVIEW For the excerpt from "Justice to Fairness" by John Rawls (*The Philosophical Review*, LXVII, April 1958). Reprinted by permission of the author and the publisher.

PHILOSOPHY AND PHENOMENOLOGICAL RESEARCH For the excerpt from "The Semantic Theory of Truth" by Alfred Tarski (*Philosophy and Phenomenological Research*, Volume IV, No. 3, March 1944). Reprinted by permission.

PRENTICE-HALL, INC. For the excerpts from *Philosophy of Mind* by Jerome A. Shaffer, © 1968, pp. 42, 43–46, 47–49. Reprinted by permission of Prentice-Hall, Inc., Englewood Cliffs, New Jersey.

PRINCETON UNIVERSITY PRESS For the excerpts from *Concluding Unscientific Postscript* by Søren Kierkegaard, translated by David F. Swenson and Walter Lowrie (copyright 1941, © 1969 by Princeton University Press; Princeton Paperback, 1968): pp. 189–356. Reprinted by permission of Princeton University Press and the American Scandinavian Foundation. For the excerpts from *Philosophical Fragments* by Søren Kierkegaard. Translated and Introduced by David Swenson. New introduction and commentary by Niels Thulstrup. Translation revised and commentary translated by Howard V. Hong. (copyright © 1936, 1962 by Princeton University Press; Princeton Paperback, 1967): pp. 49–53. Omission of footnotes on pp. 51 and 52. Reprinted by permission of Princeton University Press.

RANDOM HOUSE, INC. For the excerpts from *The Divided Self* by R. D. Laing. Copyright © 1960 by Tavistock Publishers, Ltd. Reprinted by permission of Pantheon Books, a Division of Random House, Inc. For the excerpts from *No Exit and The Flies* by Jean-Paul Sartre, translated by Stuart Gilbert. Copyright 1946 by Stuart Gilbert. Reprinted by permission of Alfred A. Knopf, Inc. For the excerpts from *Beyond Good and Evil* by Friedrich Nietzsche, translated with commentary, by Walter Kaufmann. Copyright © 1966 by Random House, Inc. Reprinted by permission of the publisher.

ROUTLEDGE & KEGAN PAUL LTD. For the excerpt from *Tractatus Logico-Philosophicus* by Ludwig Wittgenstein, translated by D. F. Pears and B. F. McGuinness (London: Routledge & Kegan Paul Ltd.). Reprinted by permission.

RUSSELL & RUSSELL, PUBLISHERS For the excerpts from *Beyond Good and Evil* by Friedrich Nietzsche, translated by Helen Zimmern. For the excerpts from *The Joyful Wisdom* by Friedrich Nietzsche, translated by Thomas Common. Both from *The Complete Works of Friedrich Nietzsche,* Oscar Levy, General Editor [1909–1911] New York: Russell & Russell, 1964. Reprinted by permission.

ST. MARTIN'S PRESS, INC. For the excerpts from *The Critique of Pure Reason* by Immanuel Kant, translated by Norman Kemp-Smith. Reprinted by permission of St. Martin's Press, Inc.

B. F. SKINNER For the excerpt from "Freedom and the Control of Men" by B. F. Skinner (*The American Scholar,* Winter 1955–56). Reprinted by permission.

UNIVERSITY OF MINNESOTA PRESS For the excerpts from "Persons" by P. F. Strawson in *Minnesota Studies in the Philosophy of Science,* Vol. II (Minneapolis: University of Minnesota Press), pp. 330–353. © Copyright 1958 by the University of Minnesota. Reprinted by permission of the publisher.

THE VIKING PRESS, INC. For the excerpts from *The Portable Nietzsche* translated and edited by Walter Kaufmann. Copyright 1954 by The Viking Press, Inc. Reprinted by permission of The Viking Press.

THE WESTMINSTER PRESS For the excerpt from *A Scholastic Miscellany,* Vol. X, The Library of Christian Classics, edited and translated by Eugene R. Fairweather. Published simultaneously in Great Britain and the United States of America by SCM Press, Ltd., London, and The Westminster Press, Philadelphia. First published in 1956. Used by permission.

A
B 7
C 8
D 9
E 0
F 1
G 2
H 3
I 4
J 5